CP/3409

e.encyclopedia

 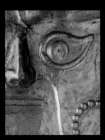  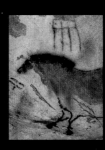 

DK

LONDON, NEW YORK, MELBOURNE,
MUNICH and DELHI

Project Editors Sue Nicholson, Fran Baines, Clare Lister, Sarah Goulding, Jane Yorke, Karen O'Brien, Katherine Pearce, Jayne Miller, Mariza O'Keeffe

Project Designers Owen Peyton Jones, Smiljka Surla, Yumiko Tahata, Ann Cannings, Alex Menday

Editors Jo Bourne, Janet Sacks, Catherine Bradley

Designers Philip Lord, Peter Bailey, Rebecca Johns, Jim Green, Adrienne Hutchinson, Joanne Little, Bob Gordon, Becky Painter

Managing Editor Camilla Hallinan

Managing Art Editor Sophia M Tampakopoulos Turner

Digital Content Manager Fergus Day
DTP Co-ordinators Toby Beedell, Andy Hilliard, Eric Shapland
Cartography Simon Mumford

Picture Research Sarah Pownall, Alison Prior, Fran Vargo
Picture Librarian Sarah Mills
Production Linda Dare, Seyhan Esen
Jacket Natalie Godwin, Neal Cobourne

Category Publisher Sue Grabham

Art Director Mark Richards

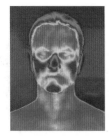  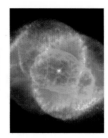  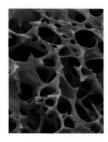 

Contributors and Consultants Simon Adams, Andy Catling, Ian Chilvers, Dr Sue Davidson, Dr Roger Few, David Glover, David Goldblatt, Dr Jen Green, Dr John Haywood, Adam Hibbert, Elaine Jackson, Robin Kerrod, Claire Llewellyn, Dr Jacqueline Mitton, Ben Morgan, Peggy Morgan, Alison Porter, Janet Sacks, Keith Shadwick, Dr Tim Shakesby, Professor Robert Spicer, Philip Steele, Dr Richard Walker, Jude Welton

First published in Great Britain in 2003
This edition published in Great Britain in 2006
by Dorling Kindersley Limited, 80 Strand, London WC2R 0RL
A Penguin Company

Copyright © 2003, 2006 Dorling Kindersley Limited
Reprinted with revisions 2004, 2006
2 4 6 8 10 9 7 5 3

Google™ is a trademark of Google Technology Inc.

A CIP catalogue for this book is available from the British Library.

ISBN-13: 978-1-40531-552-4

Colour reproduction by Colourscan, Singapore
Printed and bound in Hong Kong by Toppan.

Discover more at
www.dk.com

e.encyclopedia

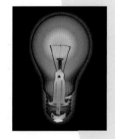

Google

CONTENTS

MEASUREMENTS AND ABBREVIATIONS

METRIC		IMPERIAL		DATES	
mm	millimetre	in	inches	c.	circa (about)
cm	centimetre	ft	feet	BC	before Christ
m	metre	yd	yards	AD	Anno Domini (in the year of Our Lord), after the birth of Christ
km	kilometre				
sq km	square kilometre	sq miles	square miles		
km²	square kilometre	miles²	square miles	b.	born
km/h	kilometres per hour	mph	miles per hour	d.	died
°C	degrees Celsius	°F	degrees Fahrenheit	r.	reigned
g	grams	oz	ounces		
kg	kilograms	lb	pounds	billion = thousand million	

FROM THE BOOK TO THE NET AND BACK AGAIN

The e.encyclopedia has its own website, created by DK and Google™. When you look up a subject in the book, the article gives you key facts and displays a keyword that links you to a wealth of extra information online. Just follow these easy steps.

1 **Enter this website address**

Address : http://www.dke-encyc.com

2 **Find the keyword in the book**

astronauts

You can use only the keywords from the book to search on our website for the specially selected DK/Google links. The keywords are displayed in grey circles.

3 **Enter the keyword, eg astronauts**

astronauts

Be safe while you are online:

• Always get permission from an adult before connecting to the Internet.

• Never give out personal information about yourself.

• Never arrange to meet someone you have talked to online.

• If a site asks you to log in with your name or email address, ask permission from an adult first.

• Do not reply to emails from strangers – tell an adult.

Parents: Dorling Kindersley actively and regularly reviews and updates the links. However, content may change. Dorling Kindersley is not responsible for any site but its own. We recommend that children are supervised while online, that they do not use chat rooms, and that filtering software is used to block unsuitable material.

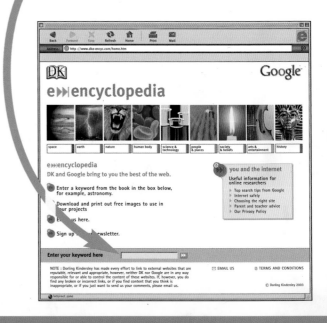

4 Click on your chosen link...

▶▶ Take a tour of a space station

Links include:

Let Google direct you to more great sites about your subject

Download fantastic pictures!

Links include:

- ▶▶ animations
- ▶▶ videos
- ▶▶ sound buttons
- ▶▶ virtual tours
- ▶▶ interactive quizzes
- ▶▶ databases
- ▶▶ timelines
- ▶▶ realtime reports

Shuttle orbiter

The pictures are free of charge, but can be used for personal non-commercial use only.

5 Go back to the book for your next subject...

Headword identifies main entry

Opening paragraph clearly defines the headword

Photographs are clearly explained with annotations and captions

Questions and answers give you in-depth information about the topic

Key concepts highlighted in grey direct you to sub-entries below

Sub-entry with its own definition, questions, and answers

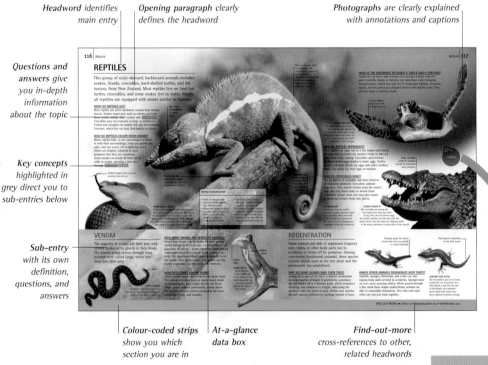

Colour-coded strips show you which section you are in

At-a-glance data box

Find-out-more cross-references to other, related headwords

You will find:

- ■ e-links
- ■ data boxes
- ■ biographies
- ■ timelines
- ■ cross-references
- ■ full index

...and enter a new keyword online

reptiles

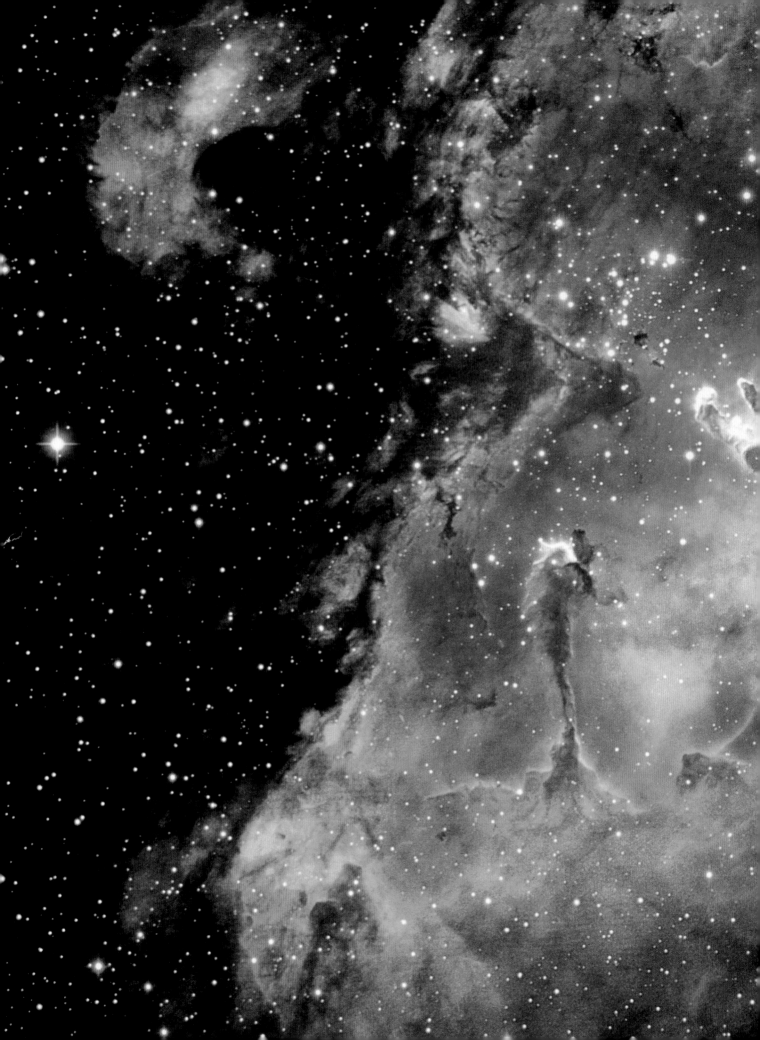

SPACE

SPACE

When you look up at the night sky, the blackness you see is space. It is the great void, or emptiness, in which Earth, the Moon, the Sun, and the stars travel. Space is totally silent and most of it is incredibly cold – around –270°C (–454°F). It is also called outer space.

WHERE DOES SPACE BEGIN?

From Earth, space begins at the outer edge of our planet's atmosphere. There is no clear line between the atmosphere and space – the atmosphere gradually fades away until it merges into space about 500 km (300 miles) above Earth. However, there are tiny traces of atmosphere even farther out than this.

WHERE IS EARTH IN SPACE?

Earth is a tiny speck of matter in space. It is one of nine planets which circle round the Sun. In turn, the Sun is one of several hundred billion stars, which together form a great star island in space called the Milky Way Galaxy. There are billions of galaxies in space. Together, all the galaxies and the enormous voids between them make up the Universe.

HOW MUCH SPACE IS THERE?

Astronomers believe that space is infinite – it has no edge or boundary. Earth's nearest neighbour in space, the Moon, is 384,400 km (238,900 miles) away on average. The Sun is 150 million km (93 million miles) away. Most other stars in the Milky Way are between a million and a billion times more distant than the Sun. Other galaxies are millions of times farther still.

WHAT IS A LIGHT YEAR?

A light year is a unit for measuring distances in space. It is the distance that light travels in a year – about 9.5 million million km (5.9 million million miles). Proxima Centauri is the nearest star to the Sun. It lies about 4.2 light years away from Earth, which means that its light takes 4.2 years to reach us.

WHAT CAN WE SEE WHEN WE LOOK INTO SPACE?

Without a telescope, we can see about 2,500 stars on a really dark night. We often see the Moon, and sometimes the planets Mercury, Venus, Mars, Jupiter, and Saturn, as well as comets. The farthest thing we can see just with our eyes is the Andromeda Galaxy.

space

THE MILKY WAY ▶
This pale band of light in the night sky is the Milky Way. Its light comes from hundreds of billions of stars in our galaxy. Billions more stars are hidden behind giant, dark clouds of dust and gas.

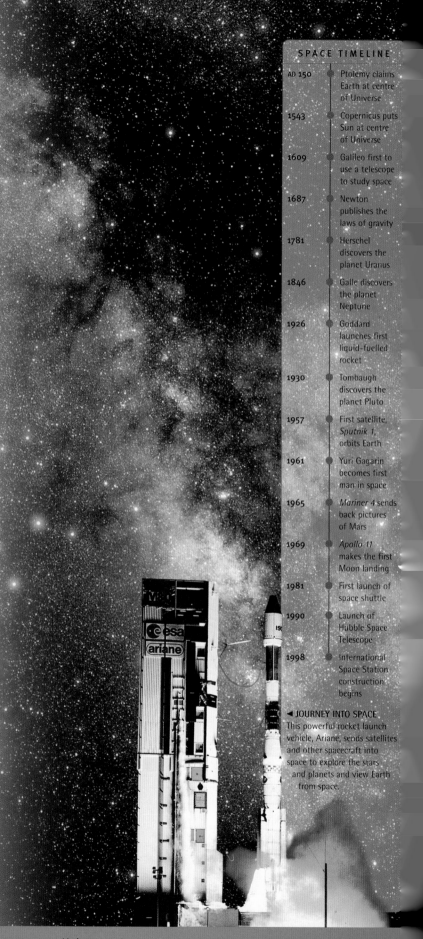

SPACE TIMELINE	
AD 150	Ptolemy claims Earth at centre of Universe
1543	Copernicus puts Sun at centre of Universe
1609	Galileo first to use a telescope to study space
1687	Newton publishes the laws of gravity
1781	Herschel discovers the planet Uranus
1846	Galle discovers the planet Neptune
1926	Goddard launches first liquid-fuelled rocket
1930	Tombaugh discovers the planet Pluto
1957	First satellite, *Sputnik 1*, orbits Earth
1961	Yuri Gagarin becomes first man in space
1965	*Mariner 4* sends back pictures of Mars
1969	*Apollo 11* makes the first Moon landing
1981	First launch of space shuttle
1990	Launch of Hubble Space Telescope
1998	International Space Station construction begins

◄ JOURNEY INTO SPACE
This powerful rocket launch vehicle, Ariane, sends satellites and other spacecraft into space to explore the stars and planets and view Earth from space.

ASTRONOMY

Astronomy is the science that studies the stars and all the other bodies (objects) in space. The ▶▶TELESCOPE is an astronomer's most useful tool – it makes faint and far-distant objects visible.

WHEN DID PEOPLE FIRST STUDY THE SKY?
Records from the earliest civilizations show that people studied the Sun, Moon, and stars more than 5,000 years ago. The priests of Babylon and Ancient Egypt recorded the movements of the Moon and the stars and used them to create a calendar for farming and religious events – but people probably studied the sky long before that.

WHAT DO ASTRONOMERS STUDY TODAY?
Modern astronomers are trying to answer big questions about the Universe. By studying stars at different stages of life, they work out how stars are born, live, and die. By studying galaxies, they are finding out how and when the Universe began and how it might end. They also explore the planets and other bodies in the Solar System.

▲ SIGHTING THE STARS
Early Indian astronomers watched the stars with an astrolabe, an instrument for measuring star positions and movements.

astronomy

POWERFUL TELESCOPE ▶
The William Herschel Telescope is at the Roque de los Muchachos Observatory on La Palma, in the Canary Islands. It is a large reflector telescope – its primary (main) mirror is 4.2 m (13 ft 9 in) wide.

Telescope can be pointed to any part of the sky, locked on to a star or other body, and moved to follow it across the sky

Open frame makes the telescope lighter and easier to move

TELESCOPES

An astronomical telescope uses lenses or mirrors to gather and focus the light from distant objects. This makes it easier to study them in detail. The first person to observe the heavens using a telescope was the Italian scientist Galileo Galilei, in 1609.

WHAT TYPES OF TELESCOPE ARE THERE?
Galileo's telescope used glass lenses to gather and bend light to a focus. This kind of telescope is called a refractor, because the lenses refract (bend) light. A telescope that uses mirrors is called a reflector – the mirrors reflect light to bring it to a focus. Some telescopes are launched into space for a clearer view. Space telescopes gather light and invisible rays, such as gamma, ultraviolet, infrared, and X-rays.

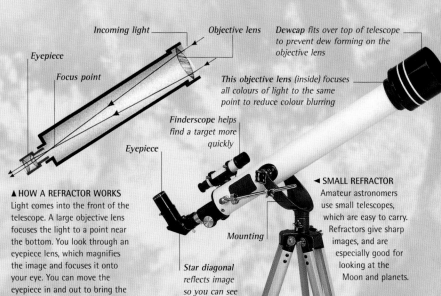

Incoming light

Eyepiece

Focus point

Objective lens

Dewcap fits over top of telescope to prevent dew forming on the objective lens

This objective lens (inside) focuses all colours of light to the same point to reduce colour blurring

Finderscope helps find a target more quickly

Eyepiece

▲ HOW A REFRACTOR WORKS
Light comes into the front of the telescope. A large objective lens focuses the light to a point near the bottom. You look through an eyepiece lens, which magnifies the image and focuses it onto your eye. You can move the eyepiece in and out to bring the image into sharp focus.

Mounting

Star diagonal reflects image so you can see it from above

◀ SMALL REFRACTOR
Amateur astronomers use small telescopes, which are easy to carry. Refractors give sharp images, and are especially good for looking at the Moon and planets.

Tripod

FIND OUT MORE ▶▶ Lenses 181 • Light 178–179 • Observatories 12

OBSERVATORIES

Astronomers gather information about space in buildings called observatories. Most astronomers use an optical telescope to look at light from space. Radio astronomers use a radio telescope or an ▶▶ ARRAY .

e ▶▶
observatory

WHY ARE MOST OBSERVATORIES ON TOP OF MOUNTAINS?

Optical telescope observatories are built on high ground above the thickest layers of Earth's atmosphere. Astronomers can see into space more clearly from there because there are fewer air currents, and the air is cleaner and contains less moisture.

HOW DO RADIO TELESCOPES WORK?

Huge, dish-shaped radio telescopes pick up radio waves from space. The dish gathers the signals and reflects them onto an aerial. The aerial sends electrical signals to a receiver, then to a computer, which converts them into a false-colour radio picture.

Dome opens at night to reveal sky to telescope

Main building houses a 3.6 m (11 ft 10 in) telescope

The New Technology Telescope has a mirror 3.5 m (11 ft 6 in) wide and sits in a rotating room, so that the astronomer can turn with the telescope

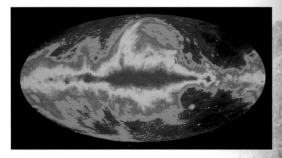

▲ RADIO MAP OF SKY
If our eyes could detect radio waves, this is how we would see the sky from Earth. The red band shows the strongest signals.

LA SILLA OBSERVATORY ▶
The telescope domes at La Silla Observatory, in Chile, are 2,400 m (7,900 ft) above sea level and remote from artificial light and pollution.

ARRAYS

Astronomers often use several radio telescopes working together as an array. An array creates a large total area for collecting signals, and can reveal far more detail than one dish on its own. The signals from each dish are combined using a technique called interferometry.

WHAT DO ASTRONOMERS USE ARRAYS FOR?

Using arrays, radio astronomers can make detailed radio maps of many different kinds of objects in space. The objects they study include quasars and radio galaxies with immense plumes of radio-emitting gas stretching for millions of light years, the remains of supernovas (exploded stars), gas bubbles blown off dying stars, and the planets Jupiter and Saturn.

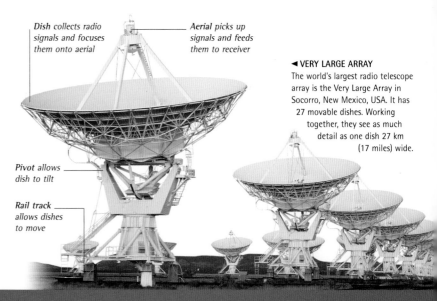

Dish collects radio signals and focuses them onto aerial

Aerial picks up signals and feeds them to receiver

◀ VERY LARGE ARRAY
The world's largest radio telescope array is the Very Large Array in Socorro, New Mexico, USA. It has 27 movable dishes. Working together, they see as much detail as one dish 27 km (17 miles) wide.

Pivot allows dish to tilt

Rail track allows dishes to move

FIND OUT MORE ▶▶ Astronomy 11 • Space Observatories 29 • Stars 24–25 • Telecommunications 192–193

CONSTELLATIONS

Groups of bright stars that appear close together in the sky are called constellations. They form patterns that never seem to change over hundreds, even thousands, of years. The sky is divided up into 88 constellations.

Vega will be the pole star in about AD 14,000

Betelgeuse is 400 times wider than the Sun

The edge of the map marks the celestial equator, the division between the northern and southern hemispheres

Stars appear to circle around the centre star, Polaris

▲ CONSTELLATIONS OF THE NORTHERN CELESTIAL HEMISPHERE
1 Pisces, 2 Pegasus, 3 Delphinus, 4 Aquila, 5 Sagitta, 6 Cygnus, 7 Andromeda, 8 Triangulum, 9 Aries, 10 Cetus, 11 Taurus, 12 Perseus, 13 Cassiopeia, 14 Cepheus, 15 Lyra, 16 Ophiuchus, 17 Serpens Caput, 18 Corona Borealis, 19 Hercules, 20 Draco, 21 Ursa Minor, 22 Polaris (current Pole Star or North Star), 23 Auriga, 24 Orion, 25 Gemini, 26 Monoceros, 27 Canis Minor, 28 Hydra, 29 Cancer, 30 Ursa Major, 31 Leo Minor, 32 Leo, 33 Canes Venatici, 34 Virgo, 35 Boötes

HOW DID CONSTELLATIONS GET THEIR NAMES?
Many of the constellations were named by ancient astronomers after things they thought the star patterns looked like – for example, a lion (Leo) or a swan (Cygnus), or a character who featured in their myths, such as the hero Hercules.

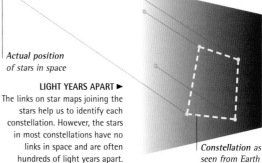

Actual position of stars in space

LIGHT YEARS APART ▶
The links on star maps joining the stars help us to identify each constellation. However, the stars in most constellations have no links in space and are often hundreds of light years apart.

Constellation as seen from Earth

ARE THE STARS IN CONSTELLATIONS REALLY GROUPED TOGETHER IN SPACE?
The stars seem to be close together because they are in the same direction in space from Earth, but each star may lie 10 or 1,000 light years away from us.

Constellation Dorado includes the nearest galaxy to us – the Large Magellanic Cloud

Stars near the edge become visible month by month throughout the year

Sirius is the brightest star in the night sky

The Milky Way is a faint belt of stars that circles the whole sky

▲ CONSTELLATIONS OF THE SOUTHERN CELESTIAL HEMISPHERE
1 Cetus, 2 Eridanus, 3 Orion, 4 Monoceros, 5 Canis Major, 6 Lepus, 7 Columba, 8 Caelum, 9 Horologium, 10 Fornax, 11 Phoenix, 12 Sculptor, 13 Aquarius, 14 Piscis Austrinus, 15 Capricornus, 16 Microscopium, 17 Grus, 18 Indus, 19 Tucana, 20 Pavo, 21 Apus, 22 Hydrus, 23 Reticulum, 24 Mensa, 25 Chameleon, 26 Dorado, 27 Pictor, 28 Volans, 29 Carina, 30 Puppis, 31 Vela, 32 Musca, 33 Crux, 34 Antlia, 35 Hydra, 36 Sextans, 37 Crater, 38 Corvus, 39 Virgo, 40 Libra, 41 Centaurus, 42 Lupus, 43 Norma, 44 Triangulum Australe, 45 Ara, 46 Sagittarius, 47 Aquila, 48 Corona Australis, 49 Ophiuchus, 50 Scorpius

e ▶▶ constellation

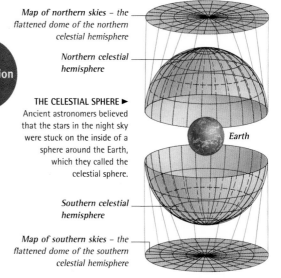

Map of northern skies – the flattened dome of the northern celestial hemisphere

Northern celestial hemisphere

THE CELESTIAL SPHERE ▶
Ancient astronomers believed that the stars in the night sky were stuck on the inside of a sphere around the Earth, which they called the celestial sphere.

Earth

Southern celestial hemisphere

Map of southern skies – the flattened dome of the southern celestial hemisphere

CAN EVERYONE SEE ALL OF THE CONSTELLATIONS?
If you live on the Equator, you will be able to see all the constellations at some time during the year. If you live north or south of the Equator, there are some stars around the opposite pole you will never be able to see – they will always be below your horizon.

FIND OUT MORE ▶▶ Astronomy 11 • Space 10 • Stars 24–25

SOLAR SYSTEM

Our local star, the Sun, and everything that circles around it, is known as the Solar System. The Sun's gravity holds planets, asteroids, comets, dust, and other bodies in oval paths, or orbits, around it. This gravity is so powerful that some objects are in orbits trillions (thousands of billions) of kilometres out from the Sun.

▼ CIRCLING THE SUN
The planets travel round the Sun in huge elliptical (oval) orbits. The four inner planets (nearest the Sun) are much hotter, faster, and closer together than the five outer planets. Apart from Pluto's, the orbits all lie in roughly the same plane, or level, in space.

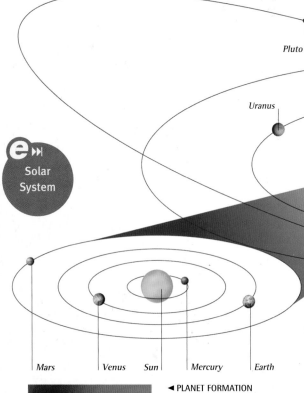

Pluto
Saturn
Uranus
Neptune
Jupiter

e ▸▸ Solar System

Mars | *Venus* | *Sun* | *Mercury* | *Earth*

◀ PLANET FORMATION
Gas giant planets such as Jupiter formed in the outer reaches of the Solar System, where the Sun's gravity is weaker, space is colder, and there were large amounts of ice and gas. This picture shows a gas giant just beginning to form (at the right).

WHAT ARE THE MAIN BODIES IN THE SOLAR SYSTEM?

The Earth is one of nine ▸▸ PLANETS in the Solar System. Most planets have natural satellites (moons) circling them. Swarms of mini-planets, called asteroids, also travel in the Solar System, and much farther out are icy lumps that become glowing comets when they near the Sun.

HOW DID THE SOLAR SYSTEM FORM?

The Sun and planets were born in a huge cloud of cold, swirling gas, called the solar nebula. The cloud collapsed under its own gravity into a fast-spinning, ball-shaped mass. The centre part became denser and hotter and eventually began shining brightly as the Sun. Rocks, dust, and gases circling in a disc around the Sun began lumping together, eventually forming the planets.

PLANETS

A planet is a world that orbits a star. There are nine planets going around the Sun – Mercury, Venus, Earth, Mars, Jupiter, Saturn, Uranus, Neptune, and Pluto. They take different amounts of time to orbit the Sun, from only 88 days for Mercury to nearly 250 years for Pluto.

WHAT ARE PLANETS MADE OF?

The four planets closest to the Sun are largely made up of rock, like the Earth, and are called the terrestrial (Earth-like) planets. The next four planets are much larger and made mainly from hydrogen and helium. They are often called gas giants. Pluto is different again, a deep-frozen world of rock and ice.

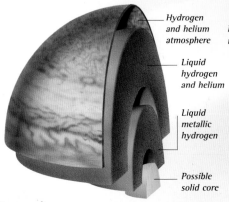

Hydrogen and helium atmosphere
Liquid hydrogen and helium
Liquid metallic hydrogen
Possible solid core

▲ GIANT PLANET
Jupiter is mainly hydrogen and helium. Below the cloudy atmosphere, the pressure is so great that these gases turn into a great liquid ocean.

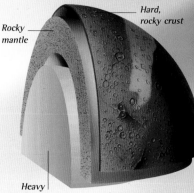

Hard, rocky crust
Rocky mantle
Heavy iron core

▲ ROCKY PLANET
A rocky planet, such as Mars, has a thin crust made up of hard rock. Underneath is another rocky layer called the mantle. A huge mass of iron makes up the centre, or core.

FIND OUT MORE ▸▸ Earth 16 • Jupiter 19 • Mars 19 • Mercury 18 • Neptune 21 • Pluto 21 • Saturn 20 • Uranus 20 • Venus 18

SUN

At the centre of the Solar System is the Sun, a vast globe of glowing gas that pours energy into space as light and heat. From Earth, it looks the same size as the Moon, which covers it during a ▶▶ SOLAR ECLIPSE.

SUN DATA	
Diameter (distance across)	1.4 million km (865,000 miles)
Average distance from Earth	150 million km (93 million miles)
Time to spin around own axis	25.4 days (at equator)
Mass	330,000 x Earth's mass
Density	1.4 x density of water
Average surface temperature	5,500°C (9,900°F)
Core temperature	15 million°C (27 million°F)
Age	4,600 million years

WHAT IS THE SUN MADE OF?

The Sun is made up mainly of hydrogen (about 73 per cent) and helium (about 25 per cent). There are also traces of around 60 other elements (about 2 per cent). Hydrogen is the fuel in the nuclear reactions that produce the Sun's energy.

WHAT IS THE SURFACE OF THE SUN LIKE?

The surface of the Sun heaves and boils as pockets of hot gas well up and sink back down. This gives the surface a grainy look, which is known as granulation. Violent explosions called solar flares rip through the surface, and giant fountain-like eruptions called prominences shoot superhot gas far into space. Darker areas called sunspots often appear. They are about 1,500°C (2,700°F) cooler than the gas around them.

Solar flare, a violent explosion on the surface

▲ MAGNETIC LOOPS
Magnetized loops of gas at a million°C (1.8 million°F) arch for thousands of kilometres above the Sun's visible surface.

Convective zone, where rising currents of hot gas carry energy to the surface

Core, where massive nuclear reactions create enormous amounts of energy

Radiative zone, where energy from the core travels outwards by radiation

Prominence, a huge fountain of hot gas leaping thousands of kilometres above the Sun's surface

INSIDE THE SUN ▶
Nuclear reactions produce the Sun's energy in the central core, where temperatures reach 15 million°C (27 million°F). The energy is carried to the surface first by radiation, then by convection.

SOLAR ECLIPSES

A solar eclipse happens when the Moon passes between the Earth and the Sun. It is a partial eclipse if the Moon only covers part of the Sun, and a total eclipse if the Sun is covered completely. Two to five solar eclipses can be seen from somewhere on Earth each year.

Moon covers up more and more of Sun

Totality

Sun uncovered more and more as Moon moves on

WHAT HAPPENS DURING A TOTAL SOLAR ECLIPSE?

When the Sun is completely covered, day suddenly turns into night, the air chills, and birds start to roost. Totality (the period of darkness) can last up to 7½ minutes, but is usually much shorter. During totality, the pink inner atmosphere of the Sun, the chromosphere, shows up. The pearly white outer atmosphere, the corona, is also visible, and prominences can sometimes be seen around the Moon's dark edge.

Sun

▲ ECLIPSE SEQUENCE
The whole of a total solar eclipse takes about two hours. Light gradually fades as the Moon covers more and more of the Sun. During totality, when the Sun is completely covered, its faint outer atmosphere shows up as a white haze around the Moon's disc.

EARTH

The planet we live on is the third closest planet to the Sun. It takes one year to orbit the Sun, and one day to spin around on its ▶▶AXIS. From space, Earth looks mainly blue because that is the colour of its oceans, which cover more than 70 per cent of its surface.

WHAT IS THE EARTH MADE OF?

Earth is one of four rocky planets in the Solar System. Underneath an atmosphere, which contains mainly oxygen and nitrogen gases, there is a hard rock crust. Beneath the crust is a layer of heavier rock called the mantle. At the Earth's centre is a huge mass of iron, which is molten (liquid) on the outside but solid inside. This is called the core.

WHAT MAKES EARTH DIFFERENT FROM ALL THE OTHER PLANETS?

Earth is the only planet that provides the right conditions for life. Temperatures are not too hot and not too cold, there is liquid water, and there is oxygen in the atmosphere. With warmth, water, and oxygen, Earth is home for millions of different living species, from tiny bacteria to giant blue whales.

EARTH DATA

Diameter (width) at equator	12,756 km (7,926 miles)
Average distance from Sun	149.6 million km (93 million miles)
Time to orbit Sun	365.25 days
Time to spin around own axis	23.93 hours
Mass	6,000 million million million tonnes (5,900 million million million tons)
Surface temperature	–70°C to +55°C (–94°F to +131°F)
Number of moons	1 (the Moon)

AXIS

As Earth travels in slow orbit around the Sun, it also spins around an imaginary line called its axis. This straight line passes through the North and South Poles, and turning around it gives us our day and night – one half of Earth faces the Sun while the other side is dark.

e▶▶
Earth

IS THE AXIS TILTED?

Earth's axis is not at right angles to its orbit – it tilts over at an angle of 23.5 degrees. This tilted axis causes our seasons. As Earth travels on its year-long orbit of the Sun, its North Pole leans first towards the Sun, then, six months later, leans away from it. This makes northern parts of our planet warmer, then cooler, giving us summer and winter. As the North Pole leans one way, the South Pole leans in the opposite direction, so the north and south of the planet have opposite seasons.

Earth's axis slowly traces an imaginary circle in space

EARTH'S WOBBLING AXIS ▶
As Earth spins on its axis and orbits the Sun, it also wobbles very, very slowly. In our lifetimes, the axis will always seem to point in the same direction in space, but over 26,000 years, it creeps around an imaginary circle. At present, the axis points almost at the star Polaris in the north, so Polaris is called the Pole Star.

Axis stays tilted at 23.5° as Earth wobbles

23.5°

FIND OUT MORE ▶▶ Life on Earth 70–71 • Planet Earth 36–37

MOON

In space, the closest object to Earth is the Moon. It orbits Earth and appears to change shape as it moves – the different shapes are called ▶▶ PHASES . The Moon has no light of its own but shines by reflecting sunlight. It is the only other world that humans have set foot on.

WHAT IS THE MOON MADE OF?

The Moon is rocky. It has no atmosphere to protect it, so anything heading towards the Moon will crash into its surface, which is covered with craters from meteorites. The Moon has a hard outer crust of granite-like rock. The typical rock of the mare (plains) regions is similar to volcanic basalt on Earth. The Moon's core, or centre, may be partly molten (liquid).

HOW DOES THE MOON AFFECT THE EARTH?

The Moon's gravity pulls on Earth's oceans and distorts them, causing tides. The water on the side of Earth nearest the Moon experiences the biggest pull, and bulges outwards. The water on the opposite side also bulges, and the two bulges follow the Moon's motion and the Earth's rotation.

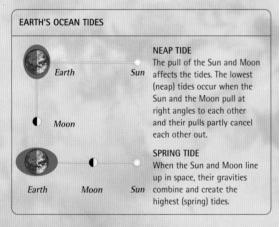

EARTH'S OCEAN TIDES

Earth   *Sun*

Moon

NEAP TIDE
The pull of the Sun and Moon affects the tides. The lowest (neap) tides occur when the Sun and the Moon pull at right angles to each other and their pulls partly cancel each other out.

Earth   *Moon*   *Sun*

SPRING TIDE
When the Sun and Moon line up in space, their gravities combine and create the highest (spring) tides.

▲ CRATERED SURFACE
Craters are found everywhere on the Moon. Most of them are billions of years old. Some measure more than 250 km (152 miles) across.

Mare, a flat dusty plain   *Crater, a pit gouged out by a meteorite*

▲ THE MOON FROM SPACE
This view of the Moon can be seen only from space. The picture was taken during the Apollo 16 Moon mission.

MOON DATA

Diameter (width) at equator	3,476 km (2,160 miles)
Average distance from Earth	384,400 km (238,900 miles)
Time to orbit Earth	27.3 days
Time to spin around own axis	27.3 days
Time to go through phases	29.5 days (1 month)
Mass	0.01 x Earth's mass
Gravity	0.17 x Earth's gravity
Average temperature	-20°C (-4°F)

PHASES

Our changing views of light on the Moon are called phases. As on Earth, one half of the Moon is lit up by the Sun while the other half is dark. As the Moon orbits us, we see it from different angles, with its light side pointing towards us or away from us.

HOW DOES THE MOON GO THROUGH ITS PHASES?

The phases begin when the Moon comes between the Sun and the Earth. The bright side of the Moon is facing away from us, and we see the dark near side. We call this the New Moon. As the Moon moves along its orbit, we see more and more of the near side lit up, until we see it all lit up at Full Moon. Then we see less and less of the Moon lit up, until it shrinks to a crescent and then disappears at the next New Moon.

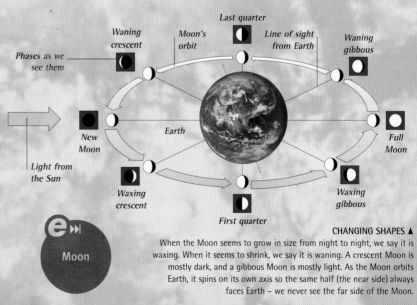

Waning crescent   *Moon's orbit*   *Last quarter*   *Line of sight from Earth*   *Waning gibbous*

Phases as we see them

New Moon   *Earth*   *Full Moon*

Light from the Sun

Waxing crescent   *First quarter*   *Waxing gibbous*

e ▶▶ Moon

CHANGING SHAPES ▲
When the Moon seems to grow in size from night to night, we say it is waxing. When it seems to shrink, we say it is waning. A crescent Moon is mostly dark, and a gibbous Moon is mostly light. As the Moon orbits Earth, it spins on its own axis so the same half (the near side) always faces Earth – we never see the far side of the Moon.

FIND OUT MORE ▶▶ Coasts 59 • Forces 164 • Meteors 23 • Space Travel 30

MERCURY

A rocky sphere, with a huge iron core, Mercury is the closest planet to the Sun. It can sometimes be glimpsed from Earth near the horizon, in the east at dawn or in the west at sunset.

Mercury's atmosphere is so thin that it barely exists

Magnetic-field sensor

◄ MARINER 10
The only spacecraft that has photographed Mercury, *Mariner 10* made three fly-bys of Mercury in 1974 and 1975.

Cameras

Rocky crust and mantle cover an iron core that is 3,600 km (2,200 miles) thick

Antenna

Solar panel

WHAT IS THE TEMPERATURE ON MERCURY?
By day, temperatures on Mercury soar as high as 450°C (840°F). This is because Mercury spins round so slowly on its axis that one place is exposed to the hot Sun for 88 days at a time. At night, with little atmosphere, the planet cools rapidly, and temperatures drop to –180°C (–290°F).

WHAT IS MERCURY'S SURFACE LIKE?
The *Mariner 10* spacecraft found Mercury's surface covered in bowl-shaped craters, made mostly by meteorite impacts billions of years ago. One huge impact created the Caloris Basin, which is 1,300 km (800 miles) wide and ringed by mountain ranges.

e ►►
Mercury

MERCURY DATA	
Diameter (width) at equator	4,880 km (3,032 miles)
Average distance from Sun	57.9 million km (36 million miles)
Time to orbit Sun	88 days
Time to spin around own axis	58.7 days
Mass	0.06 x Earth's mass
Surface gravity	0.38 x Earth's gravity
Average surface temperature	167°C (333°F)
Number of moons	0

◄ SCARRED SURFACE
Craters large and small cover 60 per cent of Mercury's dark surface. The rocky ground is also crossed by cracks and ridges, and smooth plains created by ancient lava flows.

FIND OUT MORE ►► Interplanetary Spacecraft 29 • Meteors 23 • Volcanoes 44

VENUS

Seen from Earth shining brightly in the west at sunset, Venus is called the evening star. It is a rocky planet, and the second closest planet to the Sun.

WHY CAN'T WE SEE VENUS'S SURFACE?
Thick clouds in Venus's atmosphere stop us seeing its surface. Radar-carrying spacecraft, such as *Magellan*, have scanned the surface, showing that it is dotted with volcanoes and covered with rolling lava plains.

HOW HOT IS VENUS?
Temperatures on Venus soar to over 460°C (860°F), making it hotter than any other planet. Its carbon dioxide atmosphere, which is 100 times heavier than Earth's, traps heat like a greenhouse.

Thick sulphuric acid clouds hide Venus's surface

e ►►
Venus

VENUS DATA	
Diameter (width) at equator	12,104 km (7,521 miles)
Average distance from Sun	108.2 million km (67.2 million miles)
Time to orbit Sun	224.7 days
Time to spin around own axis	243 days
Mass	0.82 x Earth's mass
Gravity	0.9 x Earth's gravity
Average surface temperature	464°C (867°F)
Number of moons	0

◄ TOWERING VOLCANOES
Maat Mons, one of Venus's many volcanoes, is about 9 km (5.6 miles) high. Radar images show that it is surrounded by lava flows from repeated eruptions.

FIND OUT MORE ►► Earth 16 • Solar System 14 • Volcanoes 44

MARS

MARS DATA	
Diameter (width) at equator	6,794 km (4,222 miles)
Average distance from Sun	227.9 million km (141.6 million miles)
Time to orbit Sun	687 days
Time to spin around own axis	24.63 hours
Mass	0.11 x Earth's mass
Gravity	0.38 x Earth's gravity
Average surface temperature	-63°C (-81°F)
Number of moons	2 (Phobos and Deimos)

This rocky planet has a thin atmosphere and ice caps at its poles. Strong winds can whip up dust storms that cover the whole planet. All the water on Mars is frozen into rocks – primitive life may once have formed there.

WHY IS MARS CALLED THE RED PLANET?

Mars appears reddish in Earth's night sky. The planet was named after the Roman god of war because its colour symbolizes fire, blood, and war. Close-up photographs show that the Martian surface is a rusty red colour. This is because there are iron compounds in the rocks and soil.

◄ ROCK-STREWN SURFACE
NASA's Mars Pathfinder sent back this view of the Martian surface in 1997. It shows a variety of small rocks scattered in a kind of sandy soil.

Ice caps made from frozen carbon dioxide, water, and dust cover the poles

e ►► Mars

WHAT IS MARS'S SURFACE LIKE?

Mars has polar ice caps, vast sandy deserts, heavily cratered regions, and high volcanic ridges. It boasts the biggest volcano in the Solar System, Olympus Mons, and the biggest canyon system, Valles Marineris.

FIND OUT MORE ►► Extraterrestrial Life 22 • Volcanoes 44

JUPITER

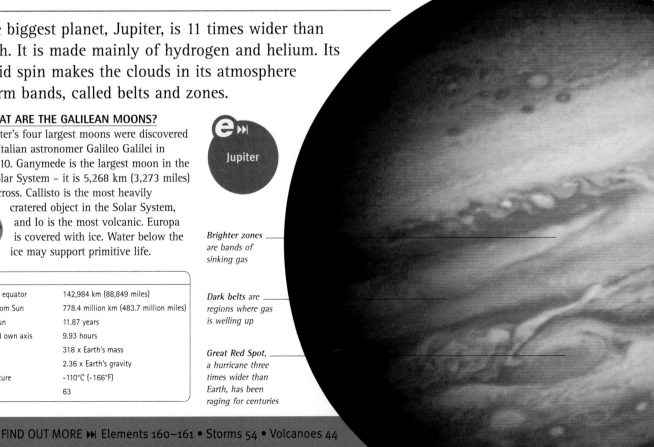

The biggest planet, Jupiter, is 11 times wider than Earth. It is made mainly of hydrogen and helium. Its rapid spin makes the clouds in its atmosphere form bands, called belts and zones.

WHAT ARE THE GALILEAN MOONS?

GANYMEDE

CALLISTO

IO

EUROPA

Jupiter's four largest moons were discovered by Italian astronomer Galileo Galilei in 1610. Ganymede is the largest moon in the Solar System – it is 5,268 km (3,273 miles) across. Callisto is the most heavily cratered object in the Solar System, and Io is the most volcanic. Europa is covered with ice. Water below the ice may support primitive life.

e ►► Jupiter

Brighter zones are bands of sinking gas

Dark belts are regions where gas is welling up

Great Red Spot, a hurricane three times wider than Earth, has been raging for centuries

JUPITER DATA	
Diameter (width) at equator	142,984 km (88,849 miles)
Average distance from Sun	778.4 million km (483.7 million miles)
Time to orbit the Sun	11.87 years
Time to spin around own axis	9.93 hours
Mass	318 x Earth's mass
Gravity	2.36 x Earth's gravity
Cloud-top temperature	-110°C (-166°F)
Number of moons	63

FIND OUT MORE ►► Elements 160–161 • Storms 54 • Volcanoes 44

SATURN

This giant planet has a magnificent system of shining rings circling its equator. Saturn is the second largest planet in the Solar System, and is made mainly of hydrogen and helium.

e ▸▸
Saturn

WHAT ARE SATURN'S RINGS?

Saturn's seven rings may look solid, but in reality they are scattered chunks of rock and ice. The largest lumps are hundreds of metres across and the smallest are specks of dust. The rings may be the broken remains of one or more comets.

WHAT IS TITAN LIKE?

Bigger than the planet Mercury, Titan is Saturn's largest moon. Measuring 5,150 km (3,200 miles) across, it is the second largest moon in the Solar System. Titan's temperature is about –180°C (–292°F), and it is the only moon with a thick atmosphere.

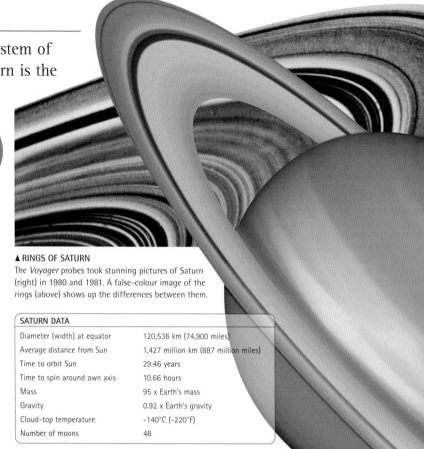

▲ RINGS OF SATURN
The *Voyager* probes took stunning pictures of Saturn (right) in 1980 and 1981. A false-colour image of the rings (above) shows up the differences between them.

◄ TITAN
Although Titan's icy surface is hidden under an orange haze, infrared telescopes, radar, and a probe that landed on its surface, have revealed what look like lakes and rivers of liquid methane.

SATURN DATA	
Diameter (width) at equator	120,536 km (74,900 miles)
Average distance from Sun	1,427 million km (887 million miles)
Time to orbit Sun	29.46 years
Time to spin around own axis	10.66 hours
Mass	95 x Earth's mass
Gravity	0.92 x Earth's gravity
Cloud-top temperature	–140°C (–220°F)
Number of moons	48

FIND OUT MORE ▸▸ Interplanetary Spacecraft 29 • Mercury 18 • Solar System 14

URANUS

Tilted at 98°, Uranus seems to be spinning on its side. As it moves in its orbit, first one pole and then the other points straight at the Sun. Uranus is the third largest planet, a ringed gas giant with 11 narrow rings.

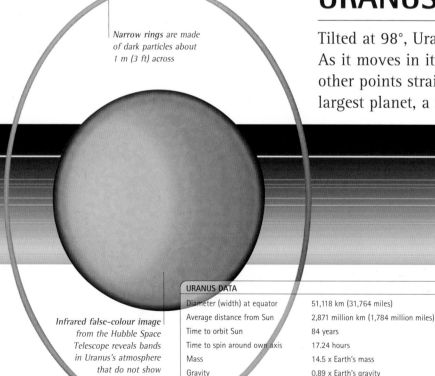

Narrow rings are made of dark particles about 1 m (3 ft) across

Infrared false-colour image from the Hubble Space Telescope reveals bands in Uranus's atmosphere that do not show up in ordinary light

◄ RING SYSTEM
Uranus's 11 rings appear almost upright because of the planet's tilt. The outer Epsilon ring is the thickest, 100 km (62 miles) across.

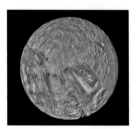

AMAZING MOON MIRANDA ▸
Miranda's surface is a patchwork of geological features, including strange grooves, cliffs, and valleys.

WHO DISCOVERED URANUS?

In 1781, English astronomer William Herschel spied Uranus through his home-made telescope. It was the first planet to be discovered with a telescope.

e ▸▸
Uranus

WHAT ARE URANUS'S MOONS LIKE?

Uranus has at least 27 moons, and most are tiny. Titania, 1,578 km (981 miles) across, is the biggest. The smallest, including Trinculo and Margaret, are about 10 km (6 miles) wide. Many of the moons are named after Shakespeare characters.

URANUS DATA	
Diameter (width) at equator	51,118 km (31,764 miles)
Average distance from Sun	2,871 million km (1,784 million miles)
Time to orbit Sun	84 years
Time to spin around own axis	17.24 hours
Mass	14.5 x Earth's mass
Gravity	0.89 x Earth's gravity
Cloud-top temperature	–197°C (–322°F)
Number of moons	27

FIND OUT MORE ▸▸ Astronomy 11 • Earth 16 • Solar System 14

NEPTUNE

Neptune is 30 times farther from the Sun than Earth, and has the most powerful hurricanes of any planet in the Solar System. It is a gas giant with faint rings. **▶▶ TRITON** is the largest of its 13 known moons.

e ▶▶
Neptune

Dark spots, circled by white methane clouds, sometimes form where there is a great storm

Fierce winds blow at speeds up to 1,200 km/h (750 mph)

WHAT IS NEPTUNE MADE OF?
Neptune's atmosphere is made of hydrogen, helium, and methane, flecked with wisps of white clouds. The methane gas makes the planet appear deep blue. Underneath, there is a vast liquid mantle and a small core of silicate rock at the centre.

TRITON

Bigger than the planet Pluto, Triton is Neptune's largest moon. It has the coldest surface in the Solar System, -235°C (-391°F).

WHAT IS TRITON'S SURFACE LIKE?
Triton's beautiful frozen surface is covered with icy craters and pinkish snow. In some regions, jets of nitrogen gas erupt like geysers and carry fine dust in the wind. This dust then falls and settles on the ground in dark streaks.

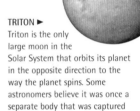

TRITON ▶
Triton is the only large moon in the Solar System that orbits its planet in the opposite direction to the way the planet spins. Some astronomers believe it was once a separate body that was captured by Neptune's gravity.

NEPTUNE DATA	
Diameter (width) at equator	49,532 km (30,779 miles)
Average distance from Sun	4,498 million km (2,795 million miles)
Time to orbit Sun	164.8 years
Time to spin around own axis	16.11 hours
Mass	17.2 x Earth's mass
Gravity	1.13 x Earth's gravity
Cloud-top temperature	-200°C (-328°F)
Number of moons	13

FIND OUT MORE ▶▶ Earth 16 • Elements 160 • Solar System 14 • Storms 54

PLUTO

This deep-frozen world of rock and ice was the last planet to be discovered – US astronomer Clyde Tombaugh spotted it in 1930. It is the smallest planet and usually the farthest from the Sun. It travels in a highly elliptical (oval) orbit that sometimes brings it closer to the Sun than Neptune.

IS PLUTO REALLY A PLANET?
Pluto is very small and unlike any other planet. Its surface is covered with frozen nitrogen and methane, which evaporate to form a slight atmosphere when Pluto is nearest the Sun. Astronomers now think that Pluto is not a true planet but one of the larger bodies in the Kuiper belt, and probably not the biggest.

WHAT IS THE KUIPER BELT?
The ring of icy bodies found in the outer Solar System beyond Neptune is called the Kuiper Belt. Dozens of Kuiper Belt Objects (KBOs) have been detected using the world's most powerful telescopes. Many KBOs end up circling closer to the Sun and become comets.

e ▶▶
Pluto

Charon, discovered in 1978

Pluto

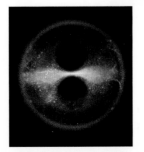

ICY EXTREMITIES ▶
A computer simulation shows icy lumps at the edge of the Solar System. The large circle is the Oort Cloud, nearly a light year out from the Sun, and the horizontal band in the middle is the Kuiper Belt.

PLUTO DATA	
Diameter (width) at equator	2,274 km (1,413 miles)
Average distance from Sun	5,900 million km (3,666 million miles)
Time to orbit Sun	247.7 years
Time to spin around own axis	6.39 days
Mass	0.002 x Earth's mass
Gravity	0.067 x Earth's gravity
Average surface temperature	-223°C (-369°F)
Number of moons	3 (of which Charon is the largest)

EXTRATERRESTRIAL LIFE

Extraterrestrial life means life outside the Earth, or alien life. No life has been found on other planets in the Solar System, but it might exist on planets around other stars.

HOW CAN LIFE EXIST ON OTHER PLANETS?
Life could be widespread on distant planets because life elements, such as carbon, hydrogen, and oxygen, are common in space. A living planet also needs energy (warmth and light) and water. In ▶▶ SETI projects, astronomers are searching for intelligent life.

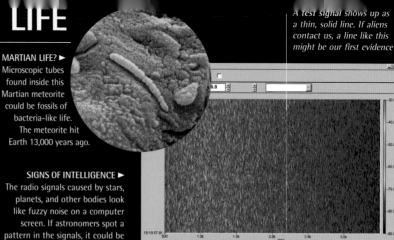

A test signal shows up as a thin, solid line. If aliens contact us, a line like this might be our first evidence

MARTIAN LIFE? ▶
Microscopic tubes found inside this Martian meteorite could be fossils of bacteria-like life. The meteorite hit Earth 13,000 years ago.

SIGNS OF INTELLIGENCE ▶
The radio signals caused by stars, planets, and other bodies look like fuzzy noise on a computer screen. If astronomers spot a pattern in the signals, it could be proof of extraterrestrial life.

e ▶▶
ET life

◀ ARECIBO DISH
The giant radio telescope at Arecibo in Puerto Rico scans distant star systems for signs of intelligent life. The main reflector dish is 305 m (1,000 ft) across and is set in a natural bowl in the mountains.

SETI

SETI stands for the Search for Extraterrestrial Intelligence. Astronomers tune into radio waves from outer space, looking for coded signals that might come from other intelligent beings.

ARE WE SENDING ANY MESSAGES INTO SPACE?
In 1974, the Arecibo radio telescope beamed a radio message to the stars in digital code, describing life on Earth. Pictures and sound recordings have also been carried into space by the probes *Pioneer 10* and *11*, and *Voyager 1* and *2*.

FIND OUT MORE ▶▶ Astronomy 11 • Life on Earth 70 • Observatories 12 • Space Travel 30

COMETS

A comet is a small, icy lump that travels in towards the Sun from the outer reaches of the Solar System. As it warms up, it develops a shining head and two tails.

WHERE DO COMETS COME FROM?
Comets seem to be bits left over from the formation of the Solar System. Some are in a belt beyond Neptune. Millions more form a giant spherical swarm, called the Oort Cloud, nearly a light year from the Sun. When a comet travels in from the edge of the Solar System and is warmed by the Sun, the gas and dust it gives off make it look much brighter.

HOW OFTEN HAS HALLEY'S COMET BEEN SEEN?
English astronomer Edmond Halley was the first to realize that the comet he saw in 1682 was a regular visitor to Earth's skies, returning every 76 years or so. Historical records show that Halley's Comet was spotted as long ago as 240 BC. It made its last visit in 1986 and is due to return in 2061.

Nucleus and coma make up the comet's head

Gas and dust streaming from the comet form two separate tails that can stretch for hundreds of millions of kilometres

Coma thins out behind head

▲ HEAD AND TAILS
Inside the gas cloud that makes up a comet's coma is a tiny, solid nucleus of snow and dust, a few kilometres across.

e ▶▶
comets

▲ HALLEY'S COMET IN 1066 ...
The return of Halley's Comet in 1066 is recorded on the Bayeux Tapestry, which shows the Norman conquest of Britain.

▲ ... AND IN 1986
From Earth, Halley's Comet was faint but visible with binoculars. Space probe *Giotto* flew close to the comet to take measurements.

FIND OUT MORE ▶▶ Interplanetary Spacecraft 29 • Pluto 21 • Solar System 14

ASTEROIDS

An asteroid is a lump of rock that circles the Sun. Asteroids are also called minor planets. The biggest one, Ceres, is 930 km (578 miles) across.

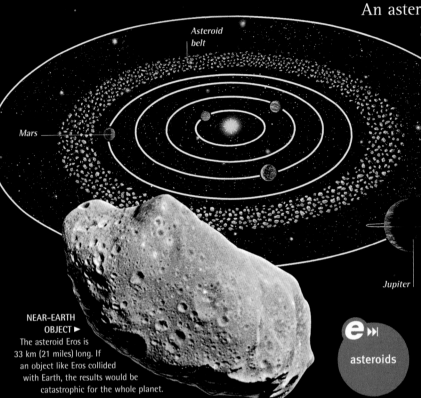

Asteroid belt

Mars

Jupiter

WHAT ARE ASTEROIDS MADE OF?
There are three main kinds of asteroids, made up of rock, or metal, or a mixture of the two. The rocky ones, known as carbonaceous (C-types), are usually dark and difficult to spot. The lighter-coloured ones, known as silicaceous (S-types), contain some metal. The pure metal M-types are the brightest and rarest.

WHAT IS THE ASTEROID BELT?
Most asteroids circle the Sun in a broad band between Mars and Jupiter called the asteroid belt, which is about 345 million km (214 million miles) wide. The asteroids are pieces left over from when the major planets formed from small chunks of rock. Some of the asteroids travel outside the belt, moving out towards Saturn or in towards Earth. Asteroids that come close to Earth are called Near-Earth Objects.

NEAR-EARTH OBJECT ▶
The asteroid Eros is 33 km (21 miles) long. If an object like Eros collided with Earth, the results would be catastrophic for the whole planet.

e ⏩ asteroids

FIND OUT MORE ⏩ Jupiter 19 • Solar System 14

METEORS

A meteor, or shooting star, is a streak of light in the sky caused by a piece of dust or rock from space burning up in Earth's atmosphere. Space rocks that hit Earth are called ⏩ METEORITES .

e ⏩ meteors

WHAT IS A METEOR SHOWER?
In a meteor shower, we see more meteors than usual coming from one patch of sky. Most showers take place on the same date every year – the Orionids, for example, are in October, when Earth passes through the dusty trail of Halley's Comet.

SHOOTING STARS ▶
During a meteor shower, you might spot dozens of meteors. They seem to come from the same spot in the sky, which is called the radiant.

METEORITES

A meteorite is a lump of space rock or metal, usually from an asteroid, that hits the surface of Earth, often leaving a crater.

WHAT ARE METEORITES MADE OF?
Most of the 3,000 meteorites that hit Earth each year are lumps of stone. The rest are mainly metal, made of iron-nickel and small amounts of other minerals.

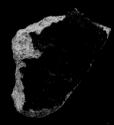

▲ STONY METEORITE
This stony meteorite has a dark crust, showing where it melted as it fell through the atmosphere.

▲ IRON METEORITE
This cut and polished iron-nickel meteorite collided with Earth about 50,000 years ago.

▲ METEOR CRATER
A meteorite 30 m (100 ft) wide made the 1.2-km- (0.7-mile-) wide Meteor Crater in Arizona, USA.

FIND OUT MORE ⏩ Comets 22 • Rocks 46–47

STARS

Great globes of intensely hot gas called stars pour light and heat into space. A star is born in a vast ▶◀ NEBULA of gas and dust and may shine steadily for billions of years. All the stars except the Sun lie so far away that their light takes years to reach us.

ARE ALL THE STARS THE SAME?
Stars can be very different from each other – in colour, brightness, temperature, size, and mass. For example, hot blue-white stars can reach 30,000°C (54,000°F) at their surface, ten times hotter than the coolest stars. A supergiant star can be a billion km (600 million miles) across, but a neutron star is only the size of a city.

HOW DO STARS PRODUCE THEIR ENERGY?
Energy is produced in a star's centre, or core, where pressures are enormous and temperatures reach 15 million °C (27 million °F). This causes nuclear fusion – the nuclei of hydrogen atoms collide and fuse (join) together to form helium. These reactions release vast amounts of energy, which makes the star shine.

◀ STAR CLUSTER
In the constellation Hercules is this cluster of hundreds of thousands of stars packed close together. Known as M13, it is a globular cluster. Globular clusters are found orbiting the centre of our galaxy. Looser, open clusters of hundreds of stars are found in the galaxy's spiral arms.

DO OTHER STARS HAVE PLANETS AROUND THEM?
Since 1995, astronomers have found many planets circling other stars. These extrasolar planets are too far away to see, but we can detect them because their gravity pulls at the stars, making them wobble.

▼ SUPERNOVA 1987A
In 1987, astronomers witnessed the brightest supernova (star explosion) of the century. It was the death of a blue supergiant star in a nearby galaxy. This picture is a computer simulation of what happened to the core about three minutes after it collapsed. Matter is rippling through the core's outer shell (pale orange), creating violent turbulence.

Outer layers of the star are blasted out into space

Exploding star originally had a mass 20 times the mass of the Sun

Collapsing iron core sends out massive shockwaves

NEBULAS

A nebula is a huge cloud of gas and dust found in the space between the stars. Some nebulas glow. Others are dark – we can see them only when they are silhouetted against stars or bright clouds. New stars are born inside dark nebulas.

WHAT ARE NEBULAS MADE OF?
Nebulas contain all the ingredients needed to form stars and planets, including atoms of hydrogen, oxygen, and nitrogen, and graphite, a form of carbon. They also contain water and many other molecules.

HOW DO NEBULAS GLOW?
Many nebulas shine. Some shine by reflecting the light from nearby stars. Others create their own light – their gas particles glow when they are energized (given energy) by radiation from nearby stars.

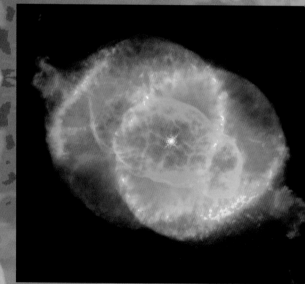

THE CAT'S-EYE NEBULA ▶
This mass of glowing gas is a planetary nebula. It is made up of layers of gas given off by the star at the centre, which is dying. The star is tiny and very hot, and is known as a white dwarf. A typical white dwarf has the mass of the Sun squeezed into a body the size of Earth, and a temperature of over 10,000°C (18,000°F).

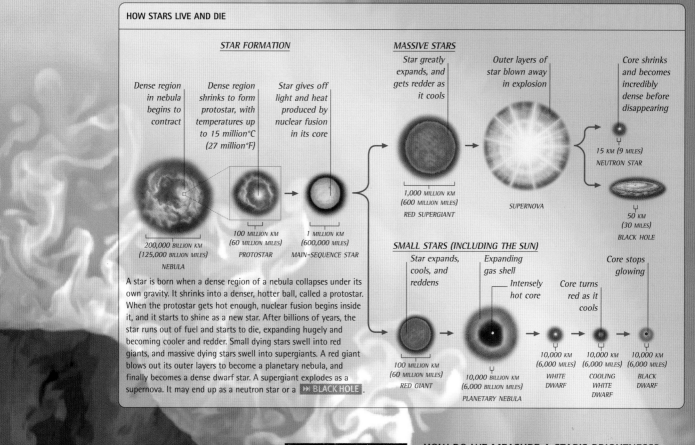

HOW STARS LIVE AND DIE

STAR FORMATION

Dense region in nebula begins to contract

Dense region shrinks to form protostar, with temperatures up to 15 million°C (27 million°F)

Star gives off light and heat produced by nuclear fusion in its core

200,000 BILLION KM (125,000 BILLION MILES)
NEBULA

100 MILLION KM (60 MILLION MILES)
PROTOSTAR

1 MILLION KM (600,000 MILES)
MAIN-SEQUENCE STAR

MASSIVE STARS

Star greatly expands, and gets redder as it cools

Outer layers of star blown away in explosion

Core shrinks and becomes incredibly dense before disappearing

1,000 MILLION KM (600 MILLION MILES)
RED SUPERGIANT

SUPERNOVA

15 KM (9 MILES)
NEUTRON STAR

50 KM (30 MILES)
BLACK HOLE

SMALL STARS (INCLUDING THE SUN)

Star expands, cools, and reddens

Expanding gas shell

Intensely hot core

Core turns red as it cools

Core stops glowing

100 MILLION KM (60 MILLION MILES)
RED GIANT

10,000 BILLION KM (6,000 BILLION MILES)
PLANETARY NEBULA

10,000 KM (6,000 MILES)
WHITE DWARF

10,000 KM (6,000 MILES)
COOLING WHITE DWARF

10,000 KM (6,000 MILES)
BLACK DWARF

A star is born when a dense region of a nebula collapses under its own gravity. It shrinks into a denser, hotter ball, called a protostar. When the protostar gets hot enough, nuclear fusion begins inside it, and it starts to shine as a new star. After billions of years, the star runs out of fuel and starts to die, expanding hugely and becoming cooler and redder. Small dying stars swell into red giants, and massive dying stars swell into supergiants. A red giant blows out its outer layers to become a planetary nebula, and finally becomes a dense dwarf star. A supergiant explodes as a supernova. It may end up as a neutron star or a ▶▶ BLACK HOLE .

HOW DO WE MEASURE A STAR'S BRIGHTNESS?

Astronomers measure star brightness in magnitudes. The lower the magnitude, the brighter the star. Most stars we can see with our eyes are magnitude 1–6, but the faintest stars visible with telescopes are magnitude 29. Exceptionally bright stars have negative magnitudes, such as –1.44 for Sirius.

◀ DOUBLE STAR
The large glowing light at the centre of this X-ray image is not a single star – it is actually made up of two stars circling around each other. It is a double-star system called a binary.

🔴 e ▶▶ stars

BLACK HOLES

A black hole is a region of space with such strong gravity that it swallows up everything that comes near it, even light. A black hole may form when a very massive star blasts itself apart as a supernova. The core of the star collapses so violently that all its matter is crushed into almost no space at all, leaving behind a region of intense gravity – a black hole.

WHAT ARE SUPERMASSIVE BLACK HOLES?

Ordinary black holes are formed when massive stars die, and they typically have the mass of about 5–10 Suns. A supermassive black hole, however, has a mass millions of times greater, and is formed when huge gas clouds collapse. Supermassive black holes seem to be the power source of high-energy active galaxies, such as quasars. Astronomers believe that a supermassive black hole lurks at the centre of our own galaxy.

BLACK HOLE RADIATION ▶
A computer simulation shows the radiation in space around a black hole. As matter spirals into the hole, it is accelerated and heated to temperatures up to 100 million°C (180 million°F). It gives off high-energy radiation, such as X-rays, in pathways that are distorted by the intense gravity.

FIND OUT MORE ▶▶ Galaxies 27 • Matter 156 • Solar System 14 • Sun 15 • Telecommunications 192 • Universe 26

UNIVERSE

The Universe is everything that exists –
space and all the stars, planets, and
other matter it contains. Astronomers
believe that a huge explosion called
the ▸▸ BIG BANG created the Universe.

e▸▸
Universe

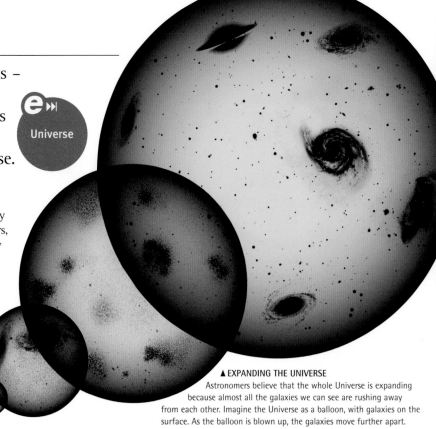

WHAT IS THE UNIVERSE MADE OF?
Between groups of galaxies, most of the Universe
seems empty, but it is full of a mysterious dark energy
and radiation, such as light and radio waves. The stars,
nebulas, and planets in galaxies are made of ordinary
matter, but galaxies are also surrounded by vast
amounts of invisible ▸▸ DARK MATTER. Four basic
forces control the Universe – electromagnetism, the
weak force, the strong force, and gravity.

HOW BIG IS THE UNIVERSE?
The Universe is bigger than we can ever see
or imagine. Astronomers can now spot objects
more than 12 billion (12 thousand million)
light years away from Earth. They lie an
incredible 115,000,000,000,000,000,000,00 km
(70 billion trillion miles) away.

▲ EXPANDING THE UNIVERSE
Astronomers believe that the whole Universe is expanding
because almost all the galaxies we can see are rushing away
from each other. Imagine the Universe as a balloon, with galaxies on the
surface. As the balloon is blown up, the galaxies move further apart.

BIG BANG

Astronomers believe that a giant explosion,
the Big Bang, created the Universe about
14 billion years ago. Before that, there was
nothing – no matter, no space, and no
time. The Universe began expanding at
the Big Bang, and it is expanding still.

WHAT HAPPENED AFTER THE BIG BANG?
In a fraction of a second, the newborn Universe grew
from the size of an atom to a searingly hot fireball
bigger than a galaxy. As it spread out and cooled, it
formed a thick soup of tiny particles of matter. It took
another 300,000 years for the first atoms to appear.

HOW DO WE KNOW ABOUT THE BIG BANG?
The Universe is expanding, so it was smaller in the
past, and there must have been a moment when it
began as something tiny. Scientists have also found
that the background temperature of space matches
their calculations for the dying heat of the Big Bang.

▲ BIG BANG RIPPLES
Minute ripples in the background
temperature of space (above)
show how stars and galaxies could
have begun to form from matter
created in the Big Bang (top).

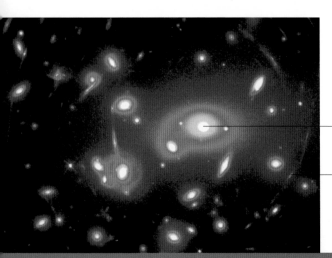

◄ GRAVITATIONAL LENSING
The gravity of this galaxy cluster
acts like a lens. It bends light
from distant galaxies, stretching
it into curved shapes and broken
rings. Most of the gravity comes
from invisible dark matter.

*This galaxy cluster's gravity
is distorting the image of the
galaxies behind it*

*Light from a galaxy
10 billion light years away is
bent into a curve by gravity*

DARK MATTER

We only know dark matter exists because
its gravity pulls on stars and galaxies, and
bends light rays. No-one has discovered
what it is made of. There is ten times more
dark matter than ordinary matter.

CAN DARK MATTER SLOW THE UNIVERSE DOWN?
Until recently, some scientists believed that the gravity
of dark and ordinary matter was slowing down the
expansion of the Universe. New evidence shows that a
mysterious dark energy is working against gravity,
and in fact making the Universe expand even faster.

FIND OUT MORE ▸▸ Energy 166 • Forces 164 • Light 178–179 • Matter 156 • Space 10 • Stars 24–25 • Time 158

GALAXIES

A galaxy is a vast collection of stars, gas, and dust spinning in space and held together by gravity. All the stars in the sky belong to our own galaxy, the ▶▶ MILKY WAY .

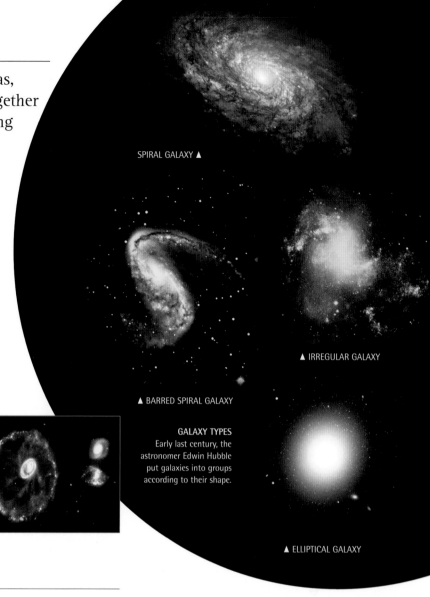

SPIRAL GALAXY ▲

▲ IRREGULAR GALAXY

▲ BARRED SPIRAL GALAXY

GALAXY TYPES
Early last century, the astronomer Edwin Hubble put galaxies into groups according to their shape.

▲ ELLIPTICAL GALAXY

HOW MANY DIFFERENT GALAXIES ARE THERE?
The Universe contains a hundred billion galaxies, and there are four main types. Spiral galaxies have a central bulge of stars, with other stars in a pattern of curved arms. Barred spirals have arms coming from a bar through their centre. Ellipticals are round or oval, with no spiral arms. An irregular is a galaxy with no special shape. Galaxies in a ▶◀ GALAXY CLUSTER are mostly spirals and ellipticals.

WHAT ARE ACTIVE GALAXIES?
A few galaxies, called active galaxies, create huge amounts of energy. At their centre, they have a massive black hole that generates a trillion times more power than our Sun, and spits out jets of electrically charged particles. Quasars and radio galaxies are both types of active galaxy.

galaxies

WHEN GALAXIES COLLIDE ▶
Galaxies sometimes collide with one another. The larger Cartwheel Galaxy shown here was once an ordinary spiral galaxy. But some 300 million years ago, a smaller galaxy passed through it, breaking up its spiral arms and producing a ring of new stars.

MILKY WAY

Our home in the Universe is the Milky Way Galaxy. It is a spiral galaxy that contains our Sun and 200 billion other stars, among vast clouds of dust and gas. The Milky Way measures about 100,000 light years across.

◀ ABOVE THE SPIRAL
Viewed from above, the Milky Way Galaxy would look like a slowly spinning Catherine-wheel firework, with spectacular spiral arms.

HOW DOES THE MILKY WAY LOOK FROM EARTH?
Earth sits out near the end of one of the Milky Way's spiral arms, so we have an excellent view of the rest of our galaxy. From Earth, the Milky Way appears as a pale band of light across the night sky. It is a flat spiral, and we see it from the side, so it seems long and thin to us. The dark rifts in the Milky Way are huge dust clouds that hide the stars behind them.

GALAXY CLUSTERS

A galaxy cluster is a large number of galaxies that are grouped together in space. The Virgo Cluster, for example, contains at least 2,000 galaxies.

MAPPING THE UNIVERSE ▶
A supercluster is a group of clusters. This computer-generated map shows the superclusters of galaxies that make up our part of the Universe. They are separated by vast empty spaces called voids.

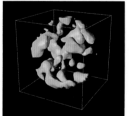

WHAT IS THE LOCAL GROUP?
Our Milky Way Galaxy belongs to a galaxy cluster called the Local Group. It contains about 30 galaxies, including our near neighbours, the Andromeda Galaxy and the Magellanic Clouds, which we can see with the naked eye. Most of the galaxies are ellipticals or irregulars.

COMA CLUSTER ▶
A view of the Coma Cluster, which contains up to 3,000 galaxies. It lies about 300 million light years away, in the constellation Coma Berenices. Most of the objects in this picture are galaxies.

FIND OUT MORE ▶▶ Earth 16 • Solar System 14 • Space 10 • Stars 24–25 • Sun 15

ROCKETS

Spacecraft are launched into space by rockets – the only engines powerful enough to overcome Earth's gravity and lift objects into space. Most spacecraft use launch vehicles with several linked rocket units, or stages.

HOW DO ROCKETS WORK?
Rockets burn fuel mixtures called ▶▶ PROPELLANTS . The burning fuel creates a stream of hot gases that shoots out of the rocket's exhaust nozzle. The backward force of the gas jet gives the rocket a forward force called thrust. The rocket's forward thrust propels the spacecraft into space.

PROPELLANTS

Rocket propellants contain fuel and oxidant. The fuel needs oxygen to burn, and the oxidant provides the oxygen. Most engines can take the oxygen they need from the Earth's atmosphere, but in airless space a rocket has to carry its own oxygen supply.

WHAT KINDS OF PROPELLANTS DO ROCKETS USE?
Most rockets burn liquid propellants, and some burn solid propellants. The Space Shuttle main engines burn liquid hydrogen and liquid oxygen. Its booster rockets burn solid propellants. When a shuttle lifts off, almost 90 per cent of its weight is propellant.

rockets

Upper stage burns for about 4 minutes after ignition

Core stage burns for about 5 minutes after ignition

Four boosters burn for about 2 minutes after ignition

SOYUZ LIFT-OFF ▶
The Russians have used the same kind of Soyuz rocket to launch spacecraft since 1967.

FIND OUT MORE ▶▶ Elements 160–161 • Engines 198–199 • Forces 164 • Space Travel 30

SATELLITES

A spacecraft that travels in a steady path, or orbit, around the Earth is called a satellite. Satellites receive and send on communication and navigation signals, watch the weather, survey the land, and study space.

HOW DO SATELLITES STAY UP IN SPACE?
Satellites stay up in orbit because of their speed. A satellite in orbit about 300 km (190 miles) above Earth must travel at a speed of 28,000 km/h (17,400 mph) to stay in space. This speed is called its orbital velocity. There are several types of ▶▶ SATELLITE ORBIT .

SATELLITE ORBITS

Satellites travel around Earth in elliptical (oval) orbits, over the equator, the poles, or on paths in between.

DO SATELLITES EVER RETURN TO EARTH?
Low-flying satellites may fall back to Earth after only a few months because they pass through traces of air in the upper atmosphere, which slow them down. High-flying satellites can stay in space forever.

◀ INTEGRAL SATELLITE
Launched into orbit in 2002, Integral is an astronomy satellite that studies sources of gamma rays in space. Its elliptical orbit takes it as far as 150,000 km (93,000 miles) above Earth.

Payload module contains scientific instruments

Service module contains spacecraft electronics

Solar panels provide electrical power

satellites

Highly elliptical orbit

Geostationary orbit

Equatorial orbit

Polar orbit

◀ ORBITS
Satellites fly around Earth in different orbits. In a geostationary orbit, a satellite hovers over one fixed place as the Earth rotates.

FIND OUT MORE ▶▶ Mass Media 298–299 • Telecommunications 192–193 • Weather 50

SPACE OBSERVATORIES

A spacecraft launched to observe the Sun, stars, and remote galaxies is called a space observatory. The ▸▸ HUBBLE SPACE TELESCOPE was the first really important space observatory.

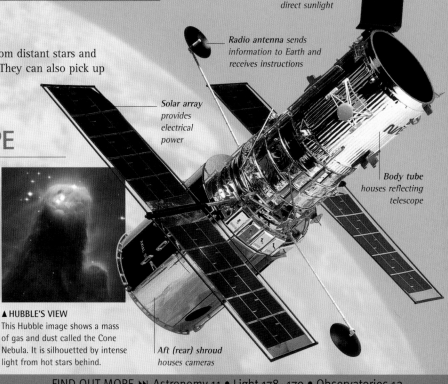

Sunshade protects the telescope from direct sunlight

Radio antenna sends information to Earth and receives instructions

Solar array provides electrical power

Body tube houses reflecting telescope

Aft (rear) shroud houses cameras

WHY ARE OBSERVATORIES LAUNCHED INTO SPACE?

Earth's moving atmosphere bends and distorts the light from distant stars and galaxies. In space, observatories can see far more clearly. They can also pick up radiation (such as X-rays) that we can't detect on Earth because it is absorbed by molecules in the atmosphere.

HUBBLE SPACE TELESCOPE

Launched from the Space Shuttle *Discovery* in 1990, the Hubble Space Telescope (HST) orbits about 600 km (370 miles) above Earth. It sends back some of the most detailed images of the Universe ever seen.

e ▸▸ space observatory

▲ HUBBLE'S VIEW
This Hubble image shows a mass of gas and dust called the Cone Nebula. It is silhouetted by intense light from hot stars behind.

HOW DOES THE HST WORK?

The HST is a reflecting telescope – it uses mirrors to gather and focus light. The focused light is fed to electronic cameras and infrared detectors to create images. The main light sensors are CCDs (charge-coupled devices), like the ones used in digital cameras.

FIND OUT MORE ▸▸ Astronomy 11 • Light 178–179 • Observatories 12

INTERPLANETARY SPACECRAFT

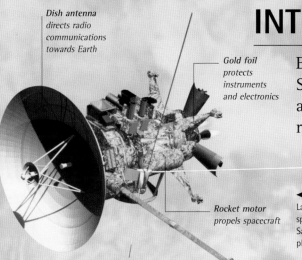

Dish antenna directs radio communications towards Earth

Gold foil protects instruments and electronics

Rocket motor propels spacecraft

◄ CASSINI SPACECRAFT
Launched in 1997, the *Cassini* spacecraft went into orbit around Saturn in 2004 to explore the planet and its moons.

Exploring the planets and other bodies in the Solar System are interplanetary spacecraft. They carry advanced cameras and other instruments to detect radiation, magnetism, and tiny particles of matter.

e ▸▸ spacecraft

WHERE HAVE INTERPLANETARY SPACECRAFT BEEN?

The first spacecraft were sent to explore the Moon, then the nearest planets, Venus and Mars. By now, all the planets except Pluto have been visited. Most spacecraft fly by their targets, but some release a ▸▸ PROBE to explore the surface. Interplanetary spacecraft have also explored comets and asteroids.

PROBES

A probe is a part of a larger spacecraft that is released to drop into the atmosphere or to the surface of a planet or a moon.

WHAT IS THE HUYGENS PROBE?

The *Cassini* orbiter carried a probe called *Huygens*. In 2005, *Huygens* parachuted down through the atmosphere of Titan, Saturn's largest moon, sending back information as it fell to the surface.

▲ VIKING LANDER ON MARS
Two landers touched down on Mars in 1976, taking photos and monitoring the weather.

KEY INTERPLANETARY MISSIONS

DATE	MISSION	TARGET
1959	Luna 2	First to photograph far side of Moon
1965	Mariner 4	First close-up images of another planet (Mars)
1973	Pioneer 10	First close-up of Jupiter
1976	Viking 1, 2	First to land on Mars
1986	Voyager 2	First to explore Uranus
1986	Giotto	First close encounter with a comet (Halley's)
2000	NEAR	First to land on an asteroid (Eros)

FIND OUT MORE ▸▸ Mars 19 • Saturn 20 • Solar System 14

SPACE TRAVEL

People began travelling in space in 1961 in tiny spacecraft called capsules, which were launched from Earth by powerful rockets. Russian crews still travel in this kind of craft, in *Soyuz* capsules. From 1981, Americans started travelling into space in rocket-planes called space shuttles.

Apollo *spacecraft* carried astronauts

Third-stage *engine propelled spacecraft to the Moon*

Second-stage *engines lifted rocket 185 km (115 miles) above ground*

First-stage *engines lifted rocket 65 km (40 miles) off the ground*

HOW DO HUMANS SURVIVE IN SPACE?
There is no oxygen in space, so all manned spacecraft carry a life-support system. This supplies air for people to breathe. The system also includes equipment to keep the air at a comfortable temperature and pressure, and to remove carbon dioxide and odours.

HOW DOES SPACE TRAVEL AFFECT PEOPLE?
When people travel in space, they seem to become weightless. This often makes them feel sick. Their bodies do not have to work as hard, because they are not fighting gravity to sit or stand up. If they stay in space for a long time, the weightlessness makes their muscles start to waste away. Exercise and a special diet help to combat these effects.

WHAT IS THE FARTHEST ANYONE HAS TRAVELLED IN SPACE?
Astronauts on the ▶▶ APOLLO PROJECT travelled as far as the Moon, about 385,000 km (239,000 miles) away. Russian cosmonaut Valeri Poliakov travelled a distance of about 280 million km (174 million miles) around the Earth while in the Mir space station.

◀ SATURN V LAUNCH
The Saturn V rocket was used for all the Moon landing missions in the 1960s and 1970s. At lift-off, the thrust was more than the combined thrust of 30 jumbo jets taking off.

MISSION CONTROL ▶
All US manned space missions are under the control of Mission Control at the Johnson Space Center in Texas.

APOLLO PROJECT

In the space race of the 1960s, the US Apollo Project beat the Soviet Union by landing the first astronauts on the Moon. The first Moon landing, by *Apollo 11*, took place on 20 July 1969, when Neil Armstrong and Buzz Aldrin became the first humans to set foot on another world.

WHAT WAS THE APOLLO SPACECRAFT LIKE?
The *Apollo* spacecraft was launched from Earth by the *Saturn V* rocket. On the launch pad, the whole assembly stood 111 m (365 ft) tall. The spacecraft itself weighed 45 tonnes (44 tons). It was made from three main modules (sections). The command module for flight control housed the three-man crew. The service module carried equipment, fuel, and a rocket motor. The lunar module detached from the craft and landed two astronauts on the Moon's surface.

▲ LUNAR MODULE
Apollo 11's lunar module, *Eagle*, orbited the Moon during the first Moon landing mission.

▲ MAN ON THE MOON
Buzz Aldrin walked on the Sea of Tranquillity during the two hours he spent on the Moon's surface.

▲ SPLASHDOWN
Three giant parachutes slowed the falling Apollo command module for a gentle splashdown in the Pacific Ocean.

HOW MANY APOLLO LANDINGS WERE THERE?
There were six Moon landings, beginning with Apollo 11 in July 1969 and ending with Apollo 17 in December 1972. During the missions, 12 astronauts explored the lunar surface for a total of over 80 hours and brought back nearly 400 kg (880 lb) of Moon rock and dust for examination on Earth.

e ▶▶
space travel

ASTRONAUTS

Anyone who travels in space is called an astronaut. The Russians call their space travellers cosmonauts. Most astronauts stay in space for only a few days, but some remain there for months in the International Space Station (ISS).

Helmet with gold-coated visor to reflect light and heat

Portable life-support system in backpack, provides oxygen, water (to cool the suit), and electricity. It will keep an astronaut alive for up to 8 hours

WHAT KINDS OF TASKS DO ASTRONAUTS PERFORM?
On missions into orbit, a commander and pilot fly the spacecraft. On past missions, specialists have made observations, carried out experiments and, if necessary, performed ▶▶ EXTRAVEHICULAR ACTIVITIES (EVAs).

HOW DO ASTRONAUTS TRAIN FOR THEIR MISSIONS?
Pilots and commanders have flight training in jet planes and flight simulators. Mission specialists rehearse mission procedures and experiments. They may train for EVA submerged in water tanks, where conditions are similar to the weightlessness of space.

Space gloves are heated to keep astronaut's fingers flexible in extreme cold

Tool clips for attaching drills, screwdrivers, and wrenches

e ▶▶
astronauts

Backpack control box

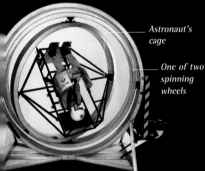

Astronaut's cage

One of two spinning wheels

▲ MULTI-AXIS WHEEL
Astronauts are whirled round to prepare their bodies for the strange sensations of space flight.

▲ FIRST PERSON IN SPACE
Cosmonaut Yuri Gagarin made one orbit of Earth in a *Vostok* capsule on 12 April 1961.

▲ SUITED FOR SPACEWALKING
A spacesuit is a multilayer garment that provides an astronaut with pressurized oxygen and protection from the hazards of space – extreme heat and cold, radiation, and meteorite particles.

EXTRAVEHICULAR ACTIVITIES

Any work that astronauts perform outside a spacecraft is called extravehicular activity (EVA) or spacewalking. On EVA, astronauts wear protective spacesuits and are attached to the spacecraft by a safety tether. In 1982, astronauts tried out a jet-propelled backpack called a manned manoeuvring unit (MMU).

WORKING IN SPACE ▶
An astronaut is at work on the ISS, high above the Earth. The tools he uses are tethered to his suit so they don't float away – he, in turn, is tethered to the craft.

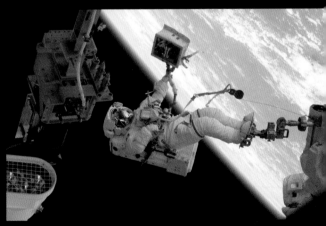

WHY DO ASTRONAUTS NEED TO LEAVE A SPACECRAFT?
One major job for spacewalking astronauts has been to help rescue and repair satellites. On some missions, shuttle astronauts have carried out in-orbit servicing on the Hubble Space Telescope, replacing faulty or outdated equipment. Astronauts may also carry out space construction work. Lengthy EVAs are helping to assemble the International Space Station (ISS) from parts ferried into orbit by other vehicles.

NASA PROJECT BADGE

LANDMARK EVAs			
DATE	MISSION	ASTRONAUT	EVA
1965	Voskhod 2	Alexei Leonov	1st spacewalk (10 mins)
1969	Apollo 11	Neil Armstrong	1st Moonwalk (2 hours 30 mins)
2001	ISS	Jim Voss	Longest spacewalk (8 hours 56 mins)

FIND OUT MORE ▶▶ Forces 164 • Space Observatories 29 • Space Stations 33

SPACE SHUTTLE

The USA created the Space Shuttle as a re-usable launch vehicle to carry astronauts and cargo into space and back again. It is made from three parts – a winged **ORBITER** , an external fuel tank, and two solid rocket boosters (SRBs).

HOW DOES THE SHUTTLE OPERATE?
At lift-off, the orbiter's main engines and the SRBs all fire together. Two minutes later, the SRBs separate and parachute back to Earth to be used again. About six minutes later, the external fuel tank separates and breaks up in the Earth's atmosphere. The winged orbiter uses its orbital manouevring system (OMS) to reach the correct orbit.

Crew compartment provides two levels of living space – the flight deck and mid-deck

Payload (cargo)

Delta wing is aerodynamically shaped so orbiter can glide through Earth's atmosphere

Pods house OMS engines and fuel tanks

Three Shuttle main engines (SMEs) used for lift-off, burning liquid hydrogen and liquid oxygen

Payload bay

Payload-bay doors open to release the payload

◀ SPACE SHUTTLE ORBITER
The orbiter is about 37 m (121 ft) long and has a wingspan of nearly 24 m (79 ft).

▲ SHUTTLE FLIGHT PATTERN
The Space Shuttle lifts off (top). The external tank and boosters are jettisoned, or cast off, before the orbiter reaches orbit (middle). After its mission, the orbiter returns to Earth unpowered, like a glider. It lands on a runway, and uses a parachute as a brake (bottom).

WHAT DOES THE SHUTTLE CARRY?
The Shuttle has carried parts of the International Space Station (ISS) into orbit. It has also carried some new satellites into orbit, and equipment to repair existing satellites. Other payloads (cargoes) have included space laboratories, telescopes, and smaller spacecraft that went on to explore the Solar System.

◀ AFT (REAR) FLIGHT DECK
On the left of the aft flight deck is the instrument console. The astronaut on the right is the flight engineer at his computer. Another astronaut is entering from the forward flight deck, or cockpit, where the commander and the pilot fly the shuttle.

Space Shuttle

ORBITER

This is the main part of the Space Shuttle that carries the crew and payload. It is thrust into space by rockets, operates as a spacecraft in space, re-enters Earth's atmosphere, and lands as a glider.

WHAT IS THE ORBITER MADE OF?
The orbiter is designed to withstand harsh conditions in space. The main structure is built from strong aluminium. For protection against heat, it is covered in insulating materials, such as thick ceramic tiles. Fuel cells combine hydrogen and oxygen to provide electrical power and water for drinking and washing.

LANDMARK SHUTTLE MISSIONS			
DATE	*MISSION*	*ORBITER*	*EVENT*
1981	STS-1	Columbia	First Shuttle mission
1995	STS-71	Atlantis	First link-up with Russia's space station Mir
1998	STS-88	Endeavour	First International Space Station mission

FIND OUT MORE ▸▸ Rockets 28 • Satellites 28 • Space Stations 33 • Space Travel 30

SPACE STATIONS

In a space station, a large manned spacecraft orbiting Earth, astronauts can live and work in space for long periods. The ▶▶ INTERNATIONAL SPACE STATION (ISS) is the biggest structure ever to be built in space.

WHAT ARE SPACE STATIONS USED FOR?

Space stations are used to carry out research. Astronauts have examined the behaviour of materials and living things in a microgravity (near-weightless) environment, and how space flight affects the human body.

Solar panels power ISS

Thermal panels control temperature

▲ MIR
Russia's Mir space station is shown docked (linked up) with a US Space Shuttle. Launched in 1986, Mir was permanently manned by a crew of two or three cosmonauts, plus guests from dozens of nations. Mir fell back to Earth in 2001.

Truss acts as framework for ISS

Research laboratories

Re-supply orbiter docks with ISS

External equipment platform

◀ THE ISS
When completed, the International Space Station will be the biggest, most complex space station ever. With a length of 80 m (260 ft) and a wingspan of 110 m (360 ft), it will have a mass of nearly 500 tonnes (492 tons).

▲ SKYLAB
Skylab was a US space station launched in 1973. Three three-man crews worked in Skylab for 28, 59, and 84 days. It was allowed to fall back to Earth in 1979.

HOW ARE SPACE STATIONS BUILT?

Early space stations such as Russia's Salyuts and the US Skylab were built on Earth and launched into orbit as complete units. Larger stations, such as Mir, were assembled in orbit from modules (sections) ferried up from Earth when ready. The ISS is also being built like this.

INTERNATIONAL SPACE STATION

The ISS is currently the only space station in orbit around the Earth. It is being built from more than 100 separate main parts, The US National Aeronautics and Space Administration (NASA), provides most of the station hardware and is in charge of construction. Russia, Europe (through the European Space Agency), Japan, and Canada also supply major units.

WHAT IS IT LIKE INSIDE THE ISS?

The living and work space on the ISS is the same size as the passenger space on a 747 aircraft. There are four laboratory modules where astronauts carry out scientific research. The main living accommodation, for a crew of seven, is in the US habitation module. It has two decks and contains sleep stations, a galley (kitchen), medical facility, gym, toilet, and shower in a space about 8m (26 ft) long and 4m (13 ft) wide.

▲ EVA ON THE ISS
Robot arms on the shuttle and the ISS connect new sections of the station, but spacewalking astronauts are needed to complete the job. More than 850 hours of extravehicular activity (EVA) will be required before assembly of the station is complete. Afterwards, astronauts will have to make regular EVAs to carry out maintenance and repairs.

space stations

FIND OUT MORE ▶▶ Astronauts 31 • Forces 164 • Space Travel 30

EARTH

PLANET EARTH

Planet Earth is a dense, rocky ball about 12,750 km (7,920 miles) across. It is one of nine planets circling our local star, the Sun. The Earth is the only planet we know of that can support life. From space, its surface looks blue and cool, but inside it is so hot that rock can melt.

YOUNG PLANET

Around 4,500 million years ago, the young Earth was bombarded from space by huge rocky meteorites and asteroids. Molten (liquid) rock from the Earth's fiery centre erupted from thousands of volcanoes. As the Earth slowly began to cool, clouds of gas and water vapour escaped from cracks in the crust (the planet's thinner, outer layer) and formed the first atmosphere. The water vapour eventually formed the oceans.

HOW WAS THE EARTH FORMED?

The Sun began to form around 5,000 million years ago out of a cloud of whirling dust and gas in space. As it formed, the Sun's gravity gradually pulled the dust and gas into lumps, which became the planets. At first, the Earth was a ball of molten rock. Its surface rock slowly began to cool and harden around 4,200 million years ago.

IS THE EARTH THE SAME ALL THE WAY THROUGH?

Our planet is made of four main layers. The outer layer is called the crust. Below is the mantle, which is solid near the top and molten below. Temperatures become hotter near the Earth's centre. The outer core is a mass of molten rock. The temperature of the inner core is over 5,000°C (9,000°F).

e ▸▸
Planet Earth

EARTH'S ATMOSPHERE

The Earth's atmosphere is a layer of gases about 700 km (430 miles) thick. Without the atmosphere there could be no life on the Earth. It protects us from harmful rays in sunlight, and prevents the Earth from becoming too hot or too cold.

Crust

Atmosphere

Mantle

Molten outer core

Solid inner core of white-hot nickel and iron

▲ EARTH'S STRUCTURE

The crust is made up of oceanic crust, below the oceans, and continental crust, which carries the Earth's land. It is the Earth's thinnest layer, at only 6–70 km (4–43 miles) thick. The mantle, at 2,900 km (1,800 miles) deep, is the thickest layer. The outer core is around 2,000 km (1,240 miles) thick. The inner core at the centre of the Earth is about 2,740 km (1,702 miles) across.

HOW DOES THE EARTH SUPPORT LIFE?

The Earth is just the right distance from the Sun so that temperatures are bearable – neither too hot, nor too cold. The Earth's atmosphere and oceans also help to control temperatures. Earth also has air we breathe and water – both vital for life.

HOW DOES EARTH MOVE THROUGH SPACE?

The Earth takes one year, or 365.242 days, to orbit, or travel, around the Sun. At the same time, it spins on its axis (an imaginary line joining the North and South poles). As it spins, the Earth is tilted on its axis at an angle of 23.5˚. This tilt produces the ▶▶ SEASONS .

Continent (large area of land)

Ocean

◀ EARTH'S OCEANS
The Earth's oceans cover almost two-thirds of its surface, making the planet look blue from space. The oceans formed 4,500 million years ago, as the Earth's surface cooled.

EARTH'S FORMATION	
5,000 million years ago	The solar system begins to form from gas and dust swirling in space.
4,600 million years ago	Earth begins to form as a ball of molten rock.
4,500 million years ago	Volcanoes erupt gas and steam to form the oceans, and molten rock.
4,200 million years ago	Earth's surface cools and the hard outer crust forms.
3,600 million years ago	The first continents form; life begins on Earth.

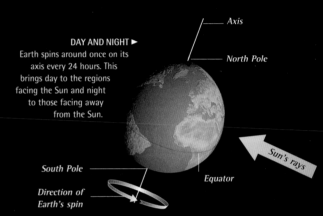

DAY AND NIGHT ▶
Earth spins around once on its axis every 24 hours. This brings day to the regions facing the Sun and night to those facing away from the Sun.

Axis

North Pole

South Pole

Equator

Sun's rays

Direction of Earth's spin

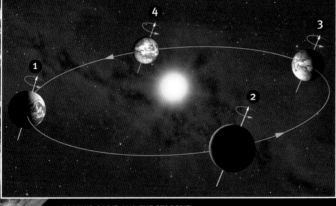

▲ EARTH'S ORBIT AND THE SEASONS
When the North Pole tilts towards the Sun, regions in the northern hemisphere have summer while the southern hemisphere has winter (1). As the Earth continues on its orbit, the seasons change to autumn in the northern hemisphere and spring in the southern hemisphere (2). When the South Pole tilts towards the Sun, the southern hemisphere has summer and it is winter in the north (3). This gradually gives way to autumn in the southern hemisphere and spring in the northern hemisphere (4) as the Earth continues around the Sun.

SEASONS

Seasons are regular weather patterns in different places on the Earth's surface caused by the Earth's tilt. At any time, one hemisphere (half of Earth above or below the Equator) leans towards the Sun, exposing it closer to the Sun's light and heat, and bringing warm summer days. The other half tilts away and has winter.

DO ALL PARTS OF THE EARTH HAVE SEASONS?

Most regions experience seasonal change throughout the year. However, the seasons are least noticeable in tropical regions near the Equator (an imaginary line around the Earth's middle) because the Equator does not tilt away from the Sun for part of the year.

▲ THE CHANGING SEASONS
Temperate lands lying between tropics and poles have four distinct seasons. In spring, days become warmer and longer and new leaves sprout on trees. Summer is the warmest season. In autumn, the days grow cooler and shorter. Winter is the coldest season.

▲ SEASONS IN THE TROPICS
Regions on or near the Equator are hot and wet all year round. Farther north and south of the Equator are tropical grasslands (above). These are always hot but have distinct wet and dry seasons.

FIND OUT MORE ▶▶ Asteroids 23 • Atmosphere 49 • Climate Zones 63 • Life on Earth 70–71 • Solar System 14

EARTH SCIENCES

Earth science is the study of our planet's physical characteristics, from earthquakes to raindrops, and floods to fossils. It contains many branches, such as ▶▌ GEOLOGY and oceanography (the study of the world's oceans).

WHY IS EARTH SCIENCE USEFUL?

Earth science affects our everyday lives. For example, meteorologists study the weather and watch for dangerous storms. Hydrologists study water and warn of floods. Seismologists study earthquakes and try to predict where they will strike. Geologists study rocks and help to locate useful minerals.

HOW DO EARTH SCIENTISTS WORK?

Earth scientists mainly work "in the field" – climbing mountains, exploring the sea bed, crawling through caves, or wading in swamps. They measure and collect samples (such as rocks or river water), then they record their findings on charts and maps.

e ▶▌
Earth sciences

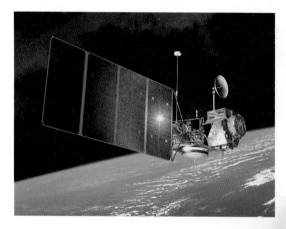

EXTREME CONDITIONS ▶
Volcanologists study volcanic eruptions at close quarters, wearing tough suits and helmets to protect them from the heat and deadly fumes.

◀ EARTH SCIENCE FROM SPACE
The TOPEX/Poseidon satellite circles the Earth 1,300 km (800 miles) above the Earth's surface. It uses special sensing equipment to collect information about the oceans, which it then sends back to scientists on Earth.

GEOLOGY

Geology is the study of the rocks that form the planet's surface. Geologists examine rocks to find out about the history of the Earth and how the Earth was formed.

HOW DO GEOLOGISTS DATE ROCKS?

Rocks are dated using several methods. Geologists called stratigraphers study the distribution and order of rock layers, or strata. The youngest rocks are usually found in layers near the surface; older rocks lie deeper below. Some rocks contain radioactive elements that can be dated because they decay, or change, at a particular rate.

HOW DO FOSSILS HELP TO DATE ROCKS?

Fossils (remains or prints of living things preserved in certain types of rock) tell scientists the relative age of that rock – that is, whether it is older or younger than other rocks. This helps scientists to work out the history of rock formation in different areas. The first fossils were formed around 3,600 million years ago.

▲ DRAGONFLY FOSSIL
Most fossils are of small, shelled sea creatures. Fossils of mammals and insects, such as this dragonfly, are much rarer.

FIND OUT MORE ▶▌ Earthquakes 43 • Fossils 76 • Nuclear Energy 167 • Rocks 46–47

CONTINENTS

Dry land covers just under one-third of the Earth's surface. It is made up mostly of seven huge landmasses called continents, plus many smaller islands. The largest continent, Asia, is 43,608,000 sq km (16,838,365 sq miles). The smallest, Australia, is 7,686,850 sq km (2,967,892 sq miles).

ALFRED LOTHAR WEGENER
German, 1880-1930
Scientist Alfred Wegener put forward the idea of drifting continents in 1919. He noticed that the shapes of continents fitted together like a giant jigsaw puzzle, which suggested they had once been joined. His ideas were not generally accepted until the 1960s.

HAVE THE EARTH'S CONTINENTS ALWAYS LOOKED THE SAME?

The world looked very different millions of years ago, when all the continents were joined in one huge block of land, or supercontinent, called Pangaea. This was surrounded by a vast ocean, called Panthalassa. Over millions of years, Pangaea split into smaller continents, which drifted across the Earth's surface.

WHY DO THE EARTH'S CONTINENTS MOVE?

The continents (and oceans) rest on top of giant slabs called ▶▶ TECTONIC PLATES which make up the Earth's outer crust. These plates float like rafts on the hot, semi-liquid mantle below the crust. Slow-moving currents deep inside the Earth send the plates (and the land or ocean that rests on them) slowly moving across the surface of the planet.

220 MILLION YEARS AGO   180 MILLION YEARS AGO   65 MILLION YEARS AGO

◀ MOVING CONTINENTS
Pangaea slowly split into two huge landmasses – Laurasia and Gondwanaland. Later, as the Atlantic Ocean was formed, these broke up into separate, smaller continents. Over millions of years, the continents slowly drifted to their present positions and are still moving today.

TECTONIC PLATES

The Earth's outer crust is split into seven large tectonic plates and about twelve smaller ones. Studying plate tectonics (plate movement) helps scientists to work out why earthquakes strike and volcanoes erupt and how mountains form.

WHAT DO TECTONIC PLATES DO?

As the plates slowly drift across the planet's surface, they may slide past each other, grind against one another, pull apart, or do all three. The boundary between two tectonic plates is called a plate margin. Mountains, earthquakes, and volcanoes usually occur at plate margins where the Earth's crust is thinner than in the centre of the plates.

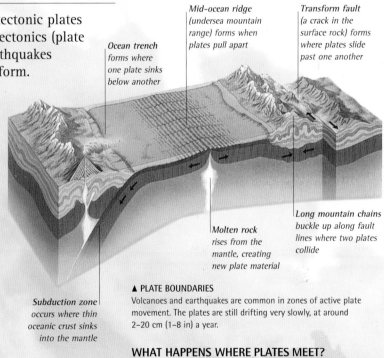

Ocean trench forms where one plate sinks below another

Mid-ocean ridge (undersea mountain range) forms when plates pull apart

Transform fault (a crack in the surface rock) forms where plates slide past one another

Molten rock rises from the mantle, creating new plate material

Long mountain chains buckle up along fault lines where two plates collide

Subduction zone occurs where thin oceanic crust sinks into the mantle

▲ PLATE BOUNDARIES
Volcanoes and earthquakes are common in zones of active plate movement. The plates are still drifting very slowly, at around 2–20 cm (1–8 in) a year.

WHAT HAPPENS WHERE PLATES MEET?

When plates carrying continents collide, the land may crumple up and form a massive mountain range. If one plate is forced under the other, oceanic crust sinks into the mantle and melts. Where plates pull apart, molten rock rises up from inside the Earth. This cools and adds new material to the plates.

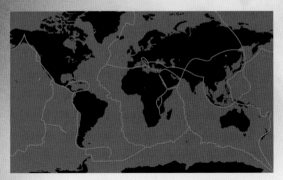

▲ WORLD-SIZED JIGSAW
The Earth's tectonic plates fit together like the pieces of a giant jigsaw. Oceanic plates make up most of the sea floor. The Earth's continents are embedded in continental plates. Some plates carry both land and sea.

continents

FIND OUT MORE ▶▶ Earthquakes 43 • Mountains 45 • Rocks 46–47 • Volcanoes 44

OCEANS

The Earth's five oceans (the Pacific, Atlantic, Indian, Southern, and Arctic) are constantly moving as tides rise and fall and winds whip up ⏩ **WAVES** and help to drive ocean currents. The oceans are major sources of minerals and food.

OCEAN LIFE ►
The oceans are home to a huge variety of plant and animal life. Microscopic plants drift in the sunlit surface waters, forming the basis of most of the ocean food chain. They provide food for tiny animal plankton, which are eaten by fish, which, in turn, are eaten by larger predators, such as sharks).

◄ SUNLIT ZONE
0–200 m (0–650 ft)
The oceans' sunlit waters, just below the surface, are home to most plant and animal life, including plankton, jellyfish, flying fish, shoaling fish, tuna, swordfish, and sharks.

◄ TWILIGHT ZONE
200–2,000 m (650–6,500 ft)
Below the sunlit waters, the light begins to fade until, by 1,000 m (3,280 ft), it is completely dark. Marine life includes lantern fish, squid, prawns, and deep-diving sperm whales.

◄ DEEPSEA ZONE
2,000–10,000 m (6,500–33,000 ft)
The deepest parts of the ocean are near freezing and pitch black. Marine life includes gulper eels, anglerfish, and rattail fish.

WHY IS THE SEA SALTY?

Sea water contains traces of minerals washed from the land by rivers. These dissolved minerals are mainly chloride and sodium, which together make salt. Most oceans contain about one part salt for every 35 parts water. The world's saltiest sea, the Dead Sea, contains around one part salt for every five parts water, making it seven times saltier than the rest of the oceans.

WHAT CAUSES THE OCEAN CURRENTS?

Water in the oceans is constantly moving in huge, slow circles called gyres. Prevailing (regular) winds blowing across the oceans start currents near the water's surface, which may flow for thousands of kilometres. Warm surface currents are heated by the Sun. Some warm currents affect the climate of the land that they flow past. For example, the Gulf Stream keeps northern ports ice-free in winter. There are also cold currents deep in the oceans that flow from the poles and across the ⏩ **OCEAN FLOOR** towards the Equator.

▼ OCEAN SURFACE CURRENTS
The world's oceans are interlinked in one continuous expanse of water. Winds disturb this water, forming currents. On this map, warm surface currents are shown in red. Cold currents are in blue.

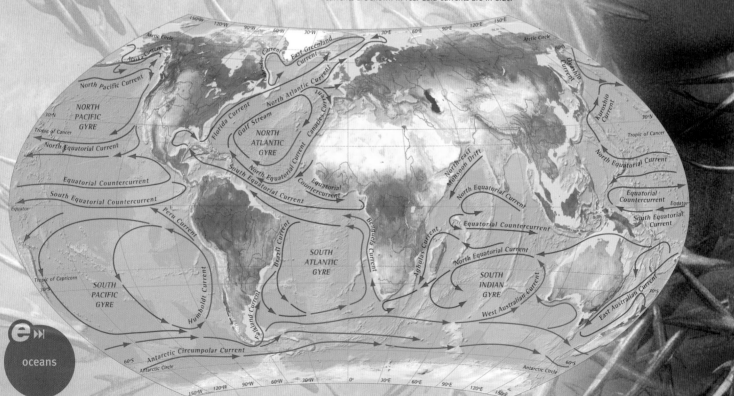

OCEAN FLOOR

The ocean floor has landscapes as dramatic and varied as those of the Earth's continents. Some parts have deep chasms, or towering cliffs, or volcanoes. Other places are vast, featureless plains. Many features of the ocean floor are caused by movements of the tectonic plates that form the Earth's crust.

ARE THE OCEANS EXPANDING?

Some of the oceans are expanding, as molten rock wells up at the edges of tectonic plates to make new crust. In the Atlantic Ocean, new crust is forming along the Mid-Atlantic Ridge, which runs down the ocean's centre. The Atlantic is growing about 2.5 cm (1 in) wider each year.

▼ FEATURES OF THE OCEAN FLOOR
The vast, flat plain at the bottom of the oceans is dotted with isolated mountains called seamounts, which were probably once volcanic islands. Ridges form where magma (hot, molten rock) rises from below the crust, then cools and hardens.

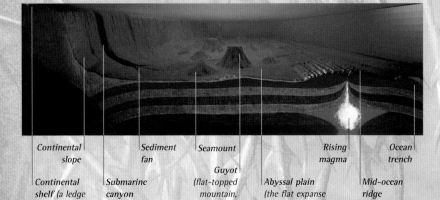

Continental slope

Continental shelf (a ledge of land around each continent)

Sediment fan

Submarine canyon

Seamount

Guyot (flat-topped mountain, eroded by waves)

Abyssal plain (the flat expanse of ocean floor)

Rising magma

Mid-ocean ridge

Ocean trench

WAVES

The surface of the sea is never completely still, even in calm weather. Winds ruffle the surface to form ripples. If the wind keeps blowing strongly, the ripples grow into waves. As the waves approach land, their size and strength increases until they break onto the shore, to build up beaches or wear away coasts.

WHAT IS A TSUNAMI?

Tsunamis are giant waves usually caused by undersea earthquakes or volcanic eruptions. Far out to sea, tsunamis are not so noticeable. However, as they reach land, they can tower up to 75 m (250 ft) high. Giant tsunamis have smashed ports and even drowned whole islands. Tsunamis are sometimes wrongly called "tidal waves", but they are not caused by tides.

▼ BREAKING WAVES
Waves may travel great distances across the ocean, but the water in each wave stays in the same place, moving round in circles. As a wave reaches the shore, the circulation of water at the bottom of the wave is blocked by the seabed and the top spills over.

Spilling breaker – a type of tall, tumbling wave that breaks on a shallow beach

Crest (top of a wave)

Spray thrown up as crest tumbles over and breaks onto the shore

ISLANDS

An island is an area of land smaller than a continent and entirely surrounded by water. Islands range from single rocks to huge landmasses, such as the island of Greenland. There are two main types of island – continental islands and oceanic islands. Islands are also found in rivers and lakes.

▲ OCEANIC ISLAND

Oceanic islands are often far from the mainland. From above, they look like tiny specks in a vast glittering ocean. Many tropical oceanic islands have coral reefs fringing their bases, or barrier reefs separated from the main island by a lagoon.

WHAT IS A CONTINENTAL ISLAND?

Continental islands are found in shallow seas off large landmasses. They were formed when rising seas (for example, at the end of an ice age) cut off part of the land from a continent. Great Britain is an example of a continental island.

HOW ARE VOLCANIC ISLANDS FORMED?

Volcanic islands are formed by volcanic activity on the sea bed, often near the boundaries of the tectonic plates that form the Earth's crust. Where two plates pull apart, lava erupts to form an undersea ridge. Layers of lava build up until a ridge breaks the sea's surface to form an island. Sometimes a whole chain of volcanic islands called an island arc is formed in this way. Some island arcs contain thousands of islands.

HOW DO CORAL REEFS FORM?

A coral reef is formed from the hard shelly remains of coral polyps. These tiny creatures live in large colonies on rocks in shallow, sunlit water, such as the top of a seamount. When they die, their chalky, tube-shaped skeletons remain and new, young coral grows on top. The coral skeletons build up over many years until they reach the sea's surface, forming a reef.

▼ AN ISLAND IS BORN

In November 1963, sailors saw a plume of smoke and ash rising from the sea off Iceland from an undersea volcanic eruption. A day later, as the eruption continued, lava broke the surface to form land. The new island was named Surtsey after the Norse god of fire.

FORMATION OF A CORAL ATOLL

A fringing coral reef forms in the shallows around the base of a seamount, or volcanic island, in warm tropical waters.

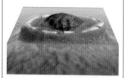

A barrier, or offshore reef, is formed as the coral slowly builds up, while the cone is worn away or covered by rising sea levels.

A ring-shaped coral atoll with a central lagoon is all that remains after a seamount is submerged.

WORLD'S LARGEST ISLAND ▼

Greenland, in the Arctic Ocean, is the world's largest island, at 2.2 million sq km (0.85 million sq miles). Although huge, few people live there because it is almost permanently covered in snow and ice.

EARTHQUAKES

Earthquakes are vibrations triggered by sudden rock movements deep underground, which cause the Earth's surface to shake. Major earthquakes can shatter whole cities, killing people and bringing buildings and bridges crashing down.

WHAT CAUSES EARTHQUAKES?

Earthquakes are caused by the movements of the huge tectonic plates that make up the Earth's outer crust. Driven by currents in the semi-molten layer below the crust, the plates slowly drift over the Earth's surface and collide, grind together, or pull apart. Most earthquakes occur on fault lines – cracks in the Earth's crust where two plates meet and grind together.

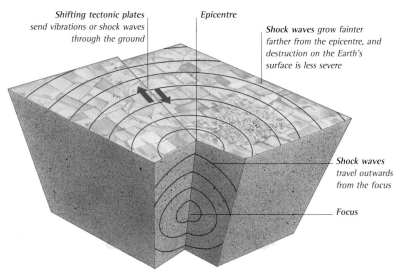

Shifting tectonic plates send vibrations or shock waves through the ground

Epicentre

Shock waves grow fainter farther from the epicentre, and destruction on the Earth's surface is less severe

Shock waves travel outwards from the focus

Focus

▲ SEISMIC WAVES
Most earthquakes begin deep underground at a point called the focus. As the rocks shatter at the focus, shock waves called seismic waves radiate outwards in all directions. The point on the Earth's surface directly above the focus is called the epicentre. This is where most damage occurs.

▲ EARTHQUAKE DAMAGE
Most earthquakes last only a few seconds, but the destruction they cause can take years to clear up. The shaking can cause certain types of soil to liquefy (turn to mud), making buildings sink or fall. An earthquake in Kobe, Japan, in 1995 (above), damaged many of the city's roads.

WHAT HAPPENS DURING AN EARTHQUAKE?

As tectonic plates grind together at a fault line, the rocks on either side stretch to absorb a certain amount of pressure. If the pressure becomes too great, the rocks shatter, releasing shock waves that shake the surface. Buildings then sway and topple, and fires may start as gas and electricity lines are ripped apart.

WHERE DO MOST EARTHQUAKES STRIKE?

Most earthquakes and also volcanic eruptions occur on or near to the edges of the Earth's tectonic plates. They are most common on the "Ring of Fire", the name given to the edge of the vast Pacific Plate that lies beneath the Pacific Ocean. Japan, the Philippines, New Zealand, and the western coastline of North and South America all lie in this major fault zone.

HOW ARE EARTHQUAKES MEASURED?

The study of earthquakes is called seismology. Scientists measure and record earthquakes using devices called seismometers. The size of an earthquake is measured according to its magnitude (the size of the shock waves and the energy produced) or its effects.

◄ THE SAN ANDREAS FAULT
The San Andreas region on the western coast of North America lies on the "Ring of Fire." Rocks along a fault line where two plates meet are cracked and buckled.

earthquakes

FIND OUT MORE ▶▶ Continents 39 • Earth Sciences 38 • Planet Earth 36–37 • Volcanoes 44

VOLCANOES

A volcano is a vent or weak spot in the Earth's crust through which magma (hot, melted rock) escapes as ▸▸ **LAVA**. In some places, lava oozes slowly out of the ground. In others, there's a violent eruption.

A cloud of gas, steam, and rock fragments bursts out of the volcano

Magma is forced up the main vent and through narrower side vents called branch pipes

Magma chamber forms deep underground beneath the Earth's crust

Red-hot lava flows down the side of the volcano

Layers of ash and lava build up to form a volcanic mountain

HOW DOES A VOLCANO ERUPT?
A volcano erupts when magma wells up from deep inside the Earth. In violent eruptions, the magma fills a hollow chamber below a vent blocked by cooled and hardened rock. Gas and water mingle with the magma, forming an explosive mixture. The pressure builds up in the chamber until the magma, gas, and steam are forced upwards and blast through the vent.

ARE ALL VOLCANOES DANGEROUS?
There are around 25 major volcanic eruptions on land every year and thousands of minor ones, many of which take place under the sea. Active volcanoes are those that may erupt at any time. Dormant (sleeping) volcanoes have not erupted for centuries but may still do so. Extinct volcanoes are no longer likely to erupt.

◀ **A VIOLENT ERUPTION**
Violent eruptions fling out red-hot lumps of rock and scorching ash, which cool to form a distinctive cone-shaped mountain.

e ▸▸
volcanoes

▲ **CLOUD OF ASH**
The eruption of Mount St Helens in Washington State, USA, sent a cloud of fine ash 20 km (13 miles) into the sky.

▲ **FOUNTAIN OF FIRE**
Some volcanoes with narrow vents shoot jets of magma up to 200 m (660 ft) into the sky, splattering the surrounding land.

▲ **AFTERMATH**
A huge flow of lava can destroy everything in its path, like this village near Mount Kilauea Volcano in Hawaii, USA.

LAVA

Lava is the name given to magma once it has reached the Earth's surface. Lava may be thick and sticky or thin and runny, depending on the minerals the lava contains and the temperature and pressure when it was formed.

ARE VOLCANOES ALL THE SAME SHAPE?
Volcanoes are different shapes depending on the type of lava and shape of their vents. Shield volcanoes have broad, shallow cones and are made of runny, flowing lava. Fissure volcanoes are long cracks in the crust. Violent eruptions usually produce steep-sided conical mountains. Composite cones are built up from alternate layers of lava and ash.

Vent
Magma
SHIELD VOLCANO

Fissure
Magma
FISSURE VOLCANO

Ash
Lava
Vent
Branch pipe
Magma
COMPOSITE CONE VOLCANO

FIND OUT MORE ▸▸ Earthquakes 43 • Islands 42 • Rocks 46–47

MOUNTAINS

A mountain is a steep-sided mass of rock, rising at least 600 m (2,000 ft) above sea level. Mountains are found on land and under the sea. Some are isolated peaks, but most are found in a ▶▶ RANGE .

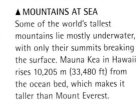

Mauna Kea

HOW ARE MOUNTAINS FORMED?
Mountains are formed by movements of the huge tectonic plates that make up Earth's crust. Fold mountains are formed when plates collide. Block mountains occur when a slab of land is forced upwards. Volcanic mountains are built up from layers of cooled and hardened lava and ash.

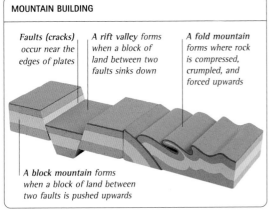

MOUNTAIN BUILDING

Faults (cracks) occur near the edges of plates

A rift valley forms when a block of land between two faults sinks down

A fold mountain forms where rock is compressed, crumpled, and forced upwards

A block mountain forms when a block of land between two faults is pushed upwards

THE HIMALAYAS ▶
The Himalayas are fold mountains that formed as the plate carrying India collided with that carrying southern Asia. These mountains are still rising, by about 1 m (3.3 ft) every 1,000 years.

ARE MOUNTAINS STILL GROWING?
Some relatively young mountains are still rising, as colliding plates continue to force the land at their edges upward. At the same time, mountains are constantly eroded by ice, rain, and the wind.

WHY ARE MANY MOUNTAINS SNOW-CAPPED?
Mountaintops are cold because the thin air high up does not hold the Sun's heat well, and the temperature falls 1°C (1.8°F) for every 150 m (500 ft) of height. It is therefore cold enough to snow over high peaks (even on the Equator) and, as the temperature rarely rises above freezing, the snow never melts.

▲ MOUNTAINS AT SEA
Some of the world's tallest mountains lie mostly underwater, with only their summits breaking the surface. Mauna Kea in Hawaii rises 10,205 m (33,480 ft) from the ocean bed, which makes it taller than Mount Everest.

Mount Everest is the world's highest mountain, at 8,850 m (29,035 ft) above sea level

Cornice are overhanging masses of snow that build up on ridges, blown by the wind

e ▶▶
mountains

▲ ANDEAN PEAKS
The Andes Mountains were formed when one of the Earth's tectonic plates, the Nazca plate, collided into the plate carrying South America, slowly pushing up the rocks into a series of high, jagged peaks.

RANGES

Most mountains are found in groups called ranges, such as the Jura Mountains in Europe and the Sierra Nevada Mountains of California, the United States. Often, a series of ranges is connected in a larger chain of mountains called a cordillera.

WHERE IS THE WORLD'S LONGEST MOUNTAIN CHAIN?
The longest mountain chain on land is the Andes, which runs for 7,200 km (4,470 miles) down the western edge of South America. An undersea mountain chain called the Mid-Atlantic Ridge is even longer. It stretches 11,300 km (7,000 miles) down the centre of the Atlantic Ocean.

FIND OUT MORE ▶▶ Continents 39 • Erosion 55 • Ice 58 • Rocks 46–47 • South America 232–233

ROCKS

The Earth's crust is made of rocks, and rocks are made of natural substances called ▶▶ **MINERALS**. There are three main types of rock – sedimentary, igneous, and metamorphic rock. Each type is formed in different ways. The oldest rocks on Earth were formed about 3.8 billion years ago.

WHAT ARE IGNEOUS ROCKS?

Igneous rocks form when magma (molten rock) rises from deep underground and cools and solidifies at or near the Earth's surface. Igneous rock that forms under the ground may later reach the surface because of geological upheaval. It may also be exposed as the rocks above are worn away.

Basalt, an igneous rock, is the most common rock on the Earth's surface

Hexagonal columns formed when the molten basalt lava flow cooled, contracted, and split

Glaciers erode rock and carry fragments downhill

Igneous rocks are formed when magma emerges as lava, cools, and solidifies

Rivers wear away rock and carry rock fragments and sediment to the sea

Metamorphic rock melts and may rise to the Earth's surface as magma

Heat and pressure change sedimentary rock into metamorphic rock

Sedimentary rocks form from layers of sediment on lake and ocean beds

▲ THE ROCK CYCLE
The rocks that form Earth's crust are continually destroyed and remade in an endless process called the rock cycle. Rock is formed by melting; by cooling and solidifying; by changing through heat and pressure; by weathering and erosion; and by compression and cementation.

WHAT ARE SEDIMENTARY ROCKS MADE OF?

Sedimentary rocks are made of fine rock particles that have been worn away and then carried by rivers, glaciers, or the wind and collect in lakes and oceans. The tiny fragments are then compressed (squashed) and cemented together to form sedimentary rock in a process called lithification.

HOW ARE METAMORPHIC ROCKS CREATED?

Metamorphic rocks are formed when existing rocks are changed underground by great heat or pressure, or both. When volcanoes erupt and when mountains are formed by the movement of the Earth's tectonic plates, rocks are heated and squeezed. The minerals in the rocks are then changed, forming metamorphic rocks.

IGNEOUS ROCK
Igneous or volcanic rock includes granite (above) and basalt.

SEDIMENTARY ROCK
This rock includes sandstone (above), limestone, and chalk.

METAMORPHIC ROCK
Metamorphic rock includes marble (above), slate, and schist.

◀ THE GIANT'S CAUSEWAY
Made up of hexagonal (six-sided) columns of the igneous rock basalt, this famous rock formation is found in Northern Ireland.

MINERALS

Rocks are made of natural, non-living chemical substances called minerals. Some rocks contain only one mineral. For example, marble is made of the white mineral calcite. Most rocks, however, contain ▶▶ CRYSTALS of several different minerals.

WHAT ARE THE MOST VALUABLE MINERALS?

Some of the most valuable minerals are ores – minerals that contain metals such as gold, iron, and aluminium. Of these, gold is the most precious because it is soft and easy to work and does not tarnish. Other minerals are prized as ▶▶ GEMSTONES. Fossil fuels, such as coal, produce energy. Minerals such as sulphur and mica are used in industry. Granite and sandstone are used as building stones.

e ▶▶
rocks

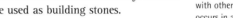
Gold

Quartz

▲ GOLD ORE
In most ores, metals are found mixed with other substances. However, gold occurs in a pure form in rocks such as quartz (shown above).

CRYSTALS

Crystals are solid, regular, geometric shapes formed by most minerals. They have smooth surfaces (called faces), straight edges, and symmetrical corners because they are built up from a regular framework of atoms (tiny particles) called a lattice.

HOW DO CRYSTALS FORM?

Crystals form as a molten solid (such as molten rock) cools, or as liquid evaporates (turns into water vapour) from a solution that contains a dissolved mineral. A crystal grows as more and more atoms join onto the basic lattice. Slow-growing crystals are larger than those that form quickly.

Pyramid-shaped amethyst crystals

AMETHYST CRYSTALS ▶
These purple crystals are a type of quartz. They formed in hot water, rich in the mineral silica.

GEMSTONES

About 50 of the 3,000 minerals found on Earth are prized as gemstones. Although they may not shine in their natural state, they can be cut and polished to form sparkling stones. Diamonds, the hardest minerals on Earth, are made of pure, crystallized carbon and are among the world's most prized gemstones.

WHERE ARE GEMSTONES FOUND?

Many gemstones are found in mountainous regions, usually in rocks that have been subjected to great heat or pressure. They are also found in the sediment on lake and river beds. Diamonds are often mined from rocks found deep underground.

▲ RUBY RED
Rubies are made of a mineral called corundum. Rare, deep-red rubies are precious stones, as are diamonds and emeralds.

FIND OUT MORE ▶▶ Atoms 157 • Chemistry 162 • Erosion 55 • Ice 58 • Volcanoes 44

SOIL

Soil is one of Earth's most precious resources. It provides the support and nourishment that plants need in order to grow. In turn, plants provide food for animals and people. As well as rock fragments, ▶▶ SOIL LAYERS contain air and water, and plant and animal remains.

▲ CLAY
Clay soils are usually sticky and waterlogged.

HOW IS SOIL FORMED?

Soil is formed as rock is broken up by ice, frost, wind, and water. Plants take root among the rock fragments and bind them together. When plants die, they fertilize the soil. Soil takes many years to form but it can be destroyed very quickly by bad farming methods, such as deforestation (clearing the land of trees).

ARE THERE DIFFERENT TYPES OF SOIL?

There are three main types of soil – clay, sandy, and loamy. There are also other types of soil, depending on the type of underlying rock, and the climate and vegetation. Loams are a mixture of clay, sand, and silt, and are more fertile than other soils.

◀ SAND
Sandy soils are loose and dry.

Grass   Wildflowers   Roots   Humus   *Decomposing leaf*

◀ BUSY BURROWERS
Earthworms and other burrowing animals such as moles, mice, and rabbits make their homes underground, in the topsoil. Their tunnels allow air and water to enter the soil, which helps to enrich it. Up to one million earthworms live in just 1 sq km (0.4 sq miles) of soil.

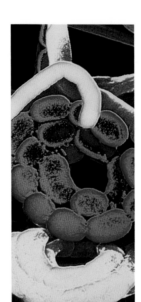

◀ BORDER ZONE
Soil forms a vital zone above rock in which living things can grow.

▲ PEAT
Acidic peaty soils are made up of rotting plants.

▲ CHALK
Chalky soils are thin and dry.

soil

◀ LIFE IN THE SOIL
A small patch of soil just 1 sq m (1 sq yd) holds up to a billion living things. These include insects, spiders, worms, centipedes, mites, fungi, and tens of thousands of bacteria (shown magnified).

HOW DO LIVING THINGS HELP THE SOIL?

Living things play an important role in helping to recycle nutrients (nourishing minerals) that enrich the soil. When plants and animals die, their remains are broken down by scavenging creatures, such as beetles, microscopic bacteria, and fungi. This releases minerals into the soil. The minerals fertilize plants so they can grow, and so the cycle of life begins again.

SOIL LAYERS

Soil scientists divide the soil into layers from the surface down to the underlying bedrock. This is called a soil profile. The layers in a soil profile are known as horizons. The depth of each horizon varies among different types of soil.

HOW MANY SOIL LAYERS ARE THERE?

A layer of dark, fertile humus made of rotting plants lies at the soil's surface. Underneath, the topsoil contains plant roots, and plant and animal remains that bacteria and fungi are helping to rot down. The subsoil contains fewer plant and animal remains but has plenty of minerals washed down from the layers above. Below are rock fragments, then solid bedrock.

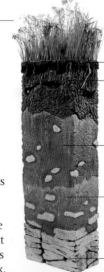

◀ SOIL PROFILE
This slice of soil from surface to bedrock shows its five layers.

Humus

Topsoil (A horizon) often rich in humus and minerals

Subsoil (B horizon) poor in humus, rich in minerals

Weathered rock fragments (C horizon) little or no plant or animal life

Bedrock (D horizon)

FIND OUT MORE ▶▶ Erosion 55 • Micro-organisms 85 • Plants 88–89 • Rocks 46–47

ATMOSPHERE

Most life on Earth depends on the atmosphere, a layer of gases around our planet. This layer, extending about 700 km (430 miles) into space, protects us from meteorites and warms the Earth's surface. It includes the ▶▶ OZONE LAYER , which shields us from the Sun's harmful rays.

DOES THE ATMOSPHERE REMAIN THE SAME FROM EARTH TO SPACE?
The Earth's atmosphere contains five main layers – the troposphere, stratosphere, mesosphere, thermosphere, and exosphere. The main gases in the atmosphere are nitrogen (78 per cent) and oxygen (21 per cent). There are also small amounts of argon, carbon dioxide, and water vapour.

WHAT IS ATMOSPHERIC PRESSURE?
Atmospheric (air) pressure is the force produced by air as it pushes against its surroundings. This force is over 1 kg per sq cm (14 lb per sq in). We cannot feel it, however, because the air presses evenly from all directions, and our body fluids press outwards. Air pressure is greatest at sea level and decreases with altitude.

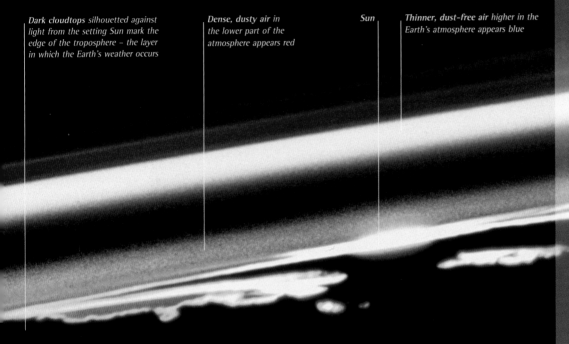

Dark cloudtops silhouetted against light from the setting Sun mark the edge of the troposphere – the layer in which the Earth's weather occurs

Dense, dusty air in the lower part of the atmosphere appears red

Sun

Thinner, dust-free air higher in the Earth's atmosphere appears blue

FIVE ATMOSPHERE LAYERS

5. EXOSPHERE
Situated 450–900 km (280–560 miles) above the Earth's surface, the exosphere is the atmosphere's outer layer, on the edge of space.

4. THERMOSPHERE
The thermosphere extends 80–450 km (50–280 miles) into space and contains the ionosphere, a layer of electrically charged particles from which radio waves for communications can be bounced back to the Earth.

3. MESOSPHERE
The mesosphere lies 50–80 km (30–50 miles) above the Earth's surface. Meteors (fragments of rock and dust from space) mostly burn up here, creating shooting stars.

2. STRATOSPHERE
Lying 12–50 km (7–30 miles) above the Earth's surface, the stratosphere is a calm layer above the winds and weather. The lower stratosphere contains the ozone layer.

1. TROPOSPHERE
Extending to about 12 km (7 miles) into space, the troposphere contains 75 per cent of the air and water in the atmosphere.

OZONE LAYER

A layer of ozone gas in the stratosphere protects us from harmful ultraviolet (UV) rays in sunlight. UV rays can cause skin cancer, eye damage, and other health problems in humans and animals. In the 1980s, scientists discovered that the ozone layer is getting thinner and that so-called "holes" (areas containing less ozone) were appearing over Antarctica and the Arctic each spring.

WHAT IS CAUSING HOLES IN THE OZONE LAYER?
Chemicals called CFCs (chlorofluorocarbons), used in the manufacture of fridges and aerosol sprays, are causing the holes in the ozone layer. CFCs collect in the upper atmosphere, where they destroy ozone. During the 1990s, the holes steadily got bigger. Most countries have now stopped using CFCs, which should prevent the damage getting worse.

atmosphere

The ozone hole as recorded in September 2000, measured 28 million sq km (11 million sq miles)

Antarctica shown here in dark yellow beneath the ozone hole in pale yellow

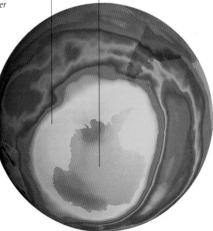

OZONE LOSS ▶
The hole over Antarctica is shown in this false-colour image of Earth taken by satellite. Yellow indicates the thinnest ozone covering, blue indicates the thickest.

FIND OUT MORE ▶▶ Human Impact 64–65 • Space 10 • Weather 50

WEATHER

Weather is what is happening in the atmosphere now, at any place on the Earth's surface. It includes the temperature and whether it is wet and windy or dry and calm.

WHAT CAUSES THE WEATHER?

The Sun provides the energy that drives the Earth's weather. The Sun heats the air in various parts of the Earth's atmosphere by different amounts. Masses of warm and cold air then move from place to place, creating winds. Winds bring sunny, wet, or stormy conditions. People find out the type of weather to expect in a ▶▶ FORECAST.

weather

▲ MORNING MIST
Fog over the Golden Gate Bridge in San Francisco, USA, usually burns away quickly in the heat of the morning Sun. Weather conditions can change daily, hourly, or even from minute to minute.

FORECASTS

A weather forecast is a prediction of weather conditions over a particular area, either for a few days (called a short-range forecast), or for several weeks (called a long-range forecast). The people who study the weather and make weather forecasts are called meteorologists.

WHY DO WE NEED WEATHER FORECASTS?

Weather forecasts help people to plan – from what to wear, when to travel, and which products to stock in supermarkets. Forecasts are especially important for farmers, builders, sailors, and anyone else who works outdoors. Sometimes, an accurate forecast may mean the difference between life and death.

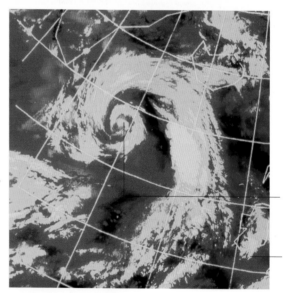

◀ MAPPING THE WEATHER
Weather experts monitor the movements of air masses and clouds using satellite images. The images are coloured by computer to pick out the movement of clouds. This false-colour satellite image shows winds spiralling over the Atlantic Ocean, indicating unsettled, stormy weather.

Winds swirl around an area of low pressure, created when a mass of warm air is forced upwards by a mass of cold air

Low-level clouds are shown in yellow; high-level clouds appear white

STORM TRACKING ▶
A meteorologist tracks a storm using images taken by satellite. Weather centres issue weather warnings to all regions in the storm's path.

Image of spiralling winds photographed by a weather satellite is displayed on a computer screen

Supercomputers condense the huge amount of data from satellites

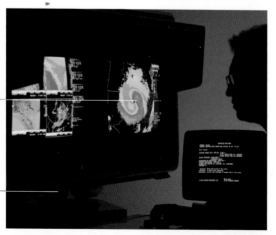

HOW DO EXPERTS PREDICT THE WEATHER?

Meteorologists receive information about air temperature, wind speeds, clouds, and rainfall from over 50,000 weather stations worldwide – on land and on ships and buoys at sea. The data is fed into huge computers, which produce charts and forecasts. These are used, with satellite images, to predict the weather.

HOW DO WEATHER SATELLITES WORK?

Weather satellites carry two types of sensor. An imager takes photographs of movements in the Earth's atmosphere. A sounder reads the temperature of the air and clouds.

FIND OUT MORE ▶▶ Atmosphere 49 • Climate 62 • Rain 52–53 • Winds 51

WINDS

Winds are moving currents of air, which can blow over a small local area or over a much larger region. Global winds help to moderate temperatures worldwide by carrying warm air away from the tropics and cold air from the poles. Winds bring changing weather conditions, such as clear, sunny skies or torrential  **MONSOON** rain. Strong winds can bring storms and hurricanes.

WHY DO WINDS BLOW?

Winds are caused by the Sun heating air masses in different parts of the world unevenly. Air warmed by the Sun becomes less dense, or lighter, and rises. This creates an area of low pressure where there is less air pressing down on the Earth. Because air always flows from a region of high pressure to one of low pressure, cooler air flows in to fill the space left by the rising air. This is a wind.

WHAT FORCES AFFECT THE WORLD'S WINDS?

Regular wind patterns across the Earth's surface are affected by the planet's spin. This is called the Coriolis Effect. In the northern hemisphere, the Coriolis Effect causes winds to swirl clockwise. In the southern hemisphere, it causes winds to spin anticlockwise. The speed and direction of the wind is also affected by air currents blowing over natural features, such as mountains.

winds

GLOBAL WINDS
Three main belts, or bands, of prevailing winds blow on either side of the Equator. In the Tropics, trade winds blow from the northeast or southeast towards the Equator. In temperate zones, the prevailing winds are westerlies (blowing from the west). Cold, easterly winds (from the east) blow in the polar regions.

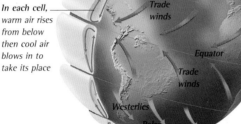

Winds blow around the globe in six main circular movements, called cells

In each cell, warm air rises from below then cool air blows in to take its place

Earth's spin

Polar easterlies

Westerlies

Trade winds

Equator

Trade winds

Westerlies

Polar easterlies

◄ **WINDY WEATHER**
Light breezes rustle leaves and twigs. In stronger gusts, whole branches sway. Strong, powerful winds may snap or uproot trees and cause widespread damage. A wind that blows most often in a particular area is called a prevailing wind.

MONSOONS

Monsoon winds are massive winds that bring heavy, seasonal rain to subtropical regions, such as southeast Asia and India, in summer. In winter, they bring dry, cooler weather. Monsoon winds are the strongest in Asia, but they also blow in West Africa, northern Australia, and parts of North and South America.

WHY DO MONSOONS CHANGE DIRECTION?

Monsoon winds change course because of seasonal temperature differences between the land and the sea. Water absorbs heat more slowly than dry land but holds the heat for longer. This makes the sea cooler than the land during the summer, and warmer during the winter. The difference in temperature causes monsoon winds to blow onshore (from sea to land) in summer, and offshore (from land to sea) in winter.

▲ **MONSOON RAIN**
The monsoon brings much-needed water to regions such as Bangladesh, in Asia, after a long, dry season. Sometimes, the rains are too heavy, washing away crops and homes and causing widespread flooding.

FIND OUT MORE ▶▶ Asia 260–261 • Atmosphere 49 • Rain 52–53 • Storms 54

RAIN

The Earth is unusual among the planets in our Solar System in having an atmosphere that contains moisture. Moisture in the air gathers in ▶▶ CLOUDS, and eventually falls as ▶▶ SNOW, ▶▶ HAIL, sleet, or rain. Any kind of falling moisture is called precipitation.

Storm clouds contain billions of tiny water droplets, which make them dark and grey

WHY DOES IT RAIN?

The Sun's heat causes moisture from oceans and lakes to evaporate into the air, forming water vapour. The vapour rises, cools, and condenses (turns into a liquid) into tiny water droplets, which form clouds. If the clouds continue to absorb moisture, they become saturated. The water droplets in the clouds collide and become bigger and heavier until the air can no longer support them. Then they fall as rain.

DO SOME PARTS OF THE WORLD RECEIVE MORE RAIN THAN OTHERS?

Around the world, rainfall patterns vary widely. In some regions rain falls almost daily. In deserts, it may not rain for years. The tropics are generally wet, while the polar regions are dry because moisture there is locked up in the form of ice.

Water droplets too heavy to float in the air fall to the ground as rain

◀ RAINBOW

A rainbow forms when sunlight passes through falling raindrops. The light is refracted (bent and split) into the seven colours that make it up – red, orange, yellow, green, blue, indigo, and violet.

RAINSTORM ▶

Dark storm clouds release lashing rain in hilly country. The water collects in lakes in the lowlands below. Raindrops falling from storm clouds can be 5 mm (³⁄₁₆ in) wide.

Rays of sunlight gleam through a gap in the clouds

THE WATER CYCLE

The water on Earth is constantly recycled between the oceans, land, and atmosphere. The water cycle, or hydrological cycle, is driven by the Sun's heat.

Life-giving rain feeds streams, rivers, and lakes. It waters plants so they can grow, and gives animals and people vital moisture.

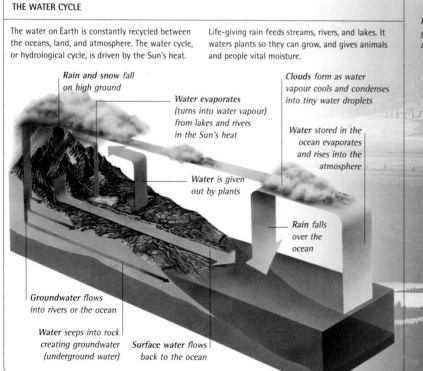

Rain and snow fall on high ground

Water evaporates (turns into water vapour) from lakes and rivers in the Sun's heat

Clouds form as water vapour cools and condenses into tiny water droplets

Water stored in the ocean evaporates and rises into the atmosphere

Water is given out by plants

Rain falls over the ocean

Groundwater flows into rivers or the ocean

Water seeps into rock creating groundwater (underground water)

Surface water flows back to the ocean

CLOUDS

Clouds are visible masses of moisture, made up of tiny ice crystals or water droplets, which are so light that they float. Clouds form in the troposphere (the lowest layer of the Earth's atmosphere) when water vapour rising high into the sky cools and condenses.

▼ CLOUDS
There are three main types of cloud: cirrus (meaning curl or wisp of hair), cumulus (meaning heap), and stratus (meaning layer). Other clouds are mixtures of these three types. Clouds are made of ice or water depending on their height above the ground.

CIRRUS **CUMULUS**

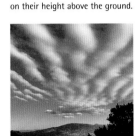

STRATUS **STRATOCUMULUS**

HOW DO CLOUDS FORM?

When the Sun shines on seas and lakes, some of the water in them evaporates into the warm air. If air currents blow the warm air over land and it rises over mountains, or if cold air pushes beneath the warm air and forces it upwards, then the warm air cools. Cold air cannot hold as much moisture as warm air, so the water vapour condenses to form clouds.

WHY ARE CLOUDS DIFFERENT SHAPES?

The way clouds form depends on their height above the ground and on the movement of air. Wispy cirrus clouds form high in the troposphere. They are made of ice crystals drawn into strands by the wind. Rapidly rising pockets of warm air cause fluffy, mid-level cumulus clouds to form. Low-lying stratus clouds are formed by air that rises slowly over a large area.

◄ SNOWFLAKES
Every snowflake has a different hexagonal (six-sided) structure. Different-shaped snowflakes form at various temperatures and heights in the atmosphere.

Stellar (star) snowflake with six sides

Some stellar snowflakes can grow as large as 5–7 cm (2–3 in) wide

SNOW

Snow falls in cold weather when ice crystals formed high in clouds join together and drop to the ground as millions of tiny snowflakes. Sleet is a mixture of rain and snow, or partly melted snow.

WHY DOES IT SNOW?

Snow forms in clouds high in the atmosphere, where it is so cold, water droplets freeze into ice crystals. The ice crystals collide and join together to make bigger crystals. When the crystals get too heavy to float, they fall to the ground as snowflakes. When snow falls, the air is just cold enough to let the flakes drift to the ground before they melt.

HAIL

Hailstones are ice pellets that grow from ice crystals formed in freezing stormclouds and then plummet to the ground. Large hailstones can shatter glass, dent car roofs, and ruin crops.

HOW DOES HAIL FORM?

Hail forms in cumulonimbus (storm) clouds that contain powerful, vertical air currents. Water droplets in the clouds freeze and are whirled up and down. Each time a hailstone is tossed upwards to the frozen cloud top, a new layer of ice forms around it. The ice builds up, layer by layer, until the hailstone becomes too heavy to remain airborne and falls to earth.

LAYERS OF ICE ►
Layers of ice are clearly visible inside this grapefruit-sized hailstone. Hailstones this size are uncommon, but many are as big as marbles.

FIND OUT MORE ►► Atmosphere 49 • Climate 62 • Ice 58 • Rivers 56–57 • Weather 50 • Winds 51

STORMS

A storm is a bout of severe weather, with strong winds roaring at more than 88 km/h (55 mph), lightning flashes, thunder, and heavy rain. ►► HURRICANES and tornadoes are whirling storms that can wreck whole towns.

e ►► storms

WHAT CAUSES LIGHTNING?

Inside black thunderclouds, ice crystals and water droplets are whirled about and clash together, producing tiny electric charges. Positive charges build up at the top of the cloud, negative charges at the base. The ground below the thundercloud is also positively charged. When the difference between the charges gets big enough, the charge is unleashed inside the cloud as sheet lightning, or to the ground as forked lightning.

WHAT CAUSES THUNDER?

When lightning surges through the air, it instantly heats the air to around 25,000°C (45,000°F). The heated air expands and sends a shock wave through the air, which we hear as a clap of thunder.

▲ **TORNADOES**
Tornadoes are dark, whirling columns of air that form beneath thunderclouds. Some produce winds of up to 450 km/h (280 mph), which can demolish houses and lift whole trains into the air.

HURRICANES

Also called a typhoon or cyclone, a hurricane is a powerful, revolving storm that strikes in the tropics. It can cause great damage when it sweeps inland.

HOW DO HURRICANES FORM?

Hurricanes form over tropical oceans in humid weather, usually in the summer and autumn months. Warm air charged with moisture from the sea starts to spiral upwards around a calm area called the eye. Cool air is then sucked into the centre, taking the place of the warm air, and fuelling the storm.

◄ **HURRICANE FRAN**
Hurricanes are so huge, they can easily be seen from space. This coloured satellite image shows Hurricane Fran approaching the North American mainland from the Caribbean Sea in 1996.

Spiral bands of rain surround the eye

The eye of the hurricane is a calm area in the middle, up to 50 km (30 miles) across

Whirling winds around the eye may reach speeds of up to 360 km/h (200 mph)

LIGHTNING STRIKES ►
Forked lightning takes the quickest path to the ground, often running down trees and tall buildings.

FIND OUT MORE ►► Climate 62 • Rain 52 • Weather 50 • Winds 51

EROSION

Erosion is the wearing down and the carrying away of the Earth's rock by the action of wind and moving water. Erosion happens fastest on steep hillsides after heavy rain, when ▸▸ LANDSLIDES sometimes strike.

HOW DOES EROSION HAPPEN?

Rocks are gradually broken down into smaller pieces by the wind, rain, snow, and frost. For example, when water freezes in rock cracks, the water expands, slowly widening the cracks and fracturing the rock. The fragments of weathered rock are then blown away by the wind or carried away by water in the form of streams and rivers, ice in glaciers, or waves pounding coasts.

erosion

WIND EROSION ▶
Top-heavy pinnacles called hoodoos are created in deserts where sand-filled winds scour rocks. Wind is the main cause of erosion in dry, desert areas. Extreme desert temperatures, with scorching days and freezing nights, also cause rocks to crack. If heavy rain falls after a long drought, flash floods then sweep away loose soil and rock.

▲ GLACIAL EROSION
Wide U-shaped valleys were formed by glaciers during past ice ages, when ice covered much of Northern Europe. Glaciers are huge, slow-moving rivers of ice, which carry boulders and stones on their sides and bases. This load scrapes away at the rock below, shaping the landscape.

▲ WATER EROSION
The Colorado River, in the United States, has worn away the rock, creating narrow gorges and steep-sided canyons. Erosion is greatest after heavy rain. The eroded rock, gravel, and silt are carried along in the river water then deposited in lakes, at deltas, or in the sea.

LANDSLIDES

Weathering and erosion usually wear away landscapes fairly slowly. A landslide occurs when a huge mass of rock and soil suddenly breaks off a hillside, engulfing everything in its path. Landslides can cause great destruction, and can even wipe out whole towns.

WHAT CAUSES LANDSLIDES?

Landslides often strike after heavy rain or snow has fallen. Loose soil and rocks begin to trickle downhill, then gravity takes over, and the whole hillside slips away. Landslides are common on slopes where the vegetation has been removed by tree-felling or farming. Without tree or plant roots to anchor the soil, heavy rain easily washes it away. Landslides, mudflows, and avalanches are called mass wasting. Mass wasting is sometimes triggered by a volcanic eruption or by an earthquake.

Forested hillside was swept away as the landslide gathered force

Trickling earth and pebbles may dislodge large boulders, causing further destruction

Rocks and earth finally come to rest on flatter ground

◀ DESTRUCTIVE SLIDE
The landslide shown here caused a roaring tide of earth and rocks to bury several streets in the town of Santa Tecla, El Salvador, in Central America. The landslide was set off by a minor earthquake. In 1970, a landslide set off by a major earthquake buried the town of Yungay in Peru, killing 18,000 people.

FIND OUT MORE ▸▸ Coasts 59 • Ice 58 • Rivers 56 • Rocks 46–47

RIVERS

A river is a natural channel down which water flows to the sea or a ⏵ **LAKE**. Throughout history, rivers have provided water for drinking, farming, and industry, and are a means of transport, food, and recreation. Some of the world's largest cities have grown up on river banks.

HOW DO RIVERS BEGIN?

Rivers usually begin as a trickle of water high in hills or mountains. Some come from rainwater or melting snow. Most emerge from underground streams, formed after rain or snow seeps into the ground then bubbles back to the surface. As the water flows downhill, the trickle swells into a stream and then, as side streams called tributaries join it, into a wider river.

WHAT IS A RIVER'S LOAD?

As a river flows, it carries along material, or debris, called its load. A river's load includes rocks, stones, and other large particles, which are washed along the river bed. Finer particles float in the water.

HOW DO RIVERS SHAPE THE LANDSCAPE?

A river's load scours the river bed, deepening its channel. The speed of the flowing water erodes the river's banks, making it wider. As the river winds through the landscape, it gradually carves out deep valleys in solid rock and deposits huge amounts of debris to form a fertile plain. In places where the river flows over soft limestone, water seeps into the rock, slowly dissolving it and forming tunnels and caves.

RIVER FEATURES ▶
In its upper level, a river is small and rushes along its course. Further downstream, as the land becomes less steep, the river's flow is less turbulent. Tributaries join it, increasing its volume of water. Lower down, the river flows more slowly over flatter ground, carving wide valleys and forming loops called meanders.

◀ RAPIDS AND WATERFALLS
Rapids are formed on a river's upper course on steeply sloping ground, where the river water tumbles over hard rocks and boulders, which are not easily worn away. A waterfall is created when a river wears away soft rock on its bed but leaves a shelf of hard rock above.

River bank is eroded on the outer side of each bend, making the channel deeper and wider

River branches into separate braids or channels on flatter ground

Islands may form if higher ground is cut off when a river flows around it

Sediment is deposited where the river slows and drops its load

Wide looping meanders form on gentle slopes in broad valleys

WHAT IS AN ESTUARY?

As a river flows into the sea, it often widens and forms a broad inlet called an estuary. The sea's tides carry salty sea water upriver to mix with the fresh river water. The salt makes tiny particles of clay in the fresh water clump together and sink, often causing sediment to build up at the river's mouth.

HOW ARE DELTAS FORMED?

A delta is an area of flat, fertile land at a river mouth. Deltas form when a slow-moving river deposits its load of sediment as it reaches the ocean. The sediment slowly builds up and dries out, forcing the river to split into separate channels.

▲ RIVER MOUTH
Marshes and swamps often form at river mouths, where the river flows over low-lying land. These wetland habitats provide a haven for wildlife, especially birds.

rivers

MISSISSIPPI DELTA ▶
A false-colour satellite image of the Mississippi Delta in the USA shows land in light blue, water in dark blue, and sediment in green. The delta has a ragged coastline shaped like a bird's foot. Other deltas have curved, fan-shaped coastlines.

LAKES

A lake is an expanse of water that forms inland where water collects in a hollow in the ground and cannot drain away through the rock below. Most lakes are fed by rivers and, to a lesser extent, rainfall.

HOW DO LAKES FORM?

Small lakes called tarns form in mountains where glaciers gouge out bowl-shaped hollows. Water collects in the craters of inactive volcanoes to form volcanic lakes. The world's largest lake, the Caspian Sea, lies in a hollow created by geological upheaval. Artificial lakes called reservoirs are created by dams.

LIFE OF A LAKE ▶
This lake lies in a lush, green valley and is topped up by river water from the surrounding hills. Lakes like this do not last forever and eventually dry out. They are slowly filled in by sediment dumped by a river, or disappear when there is less rainfall. What is left of the lake then forms a swamp, marsh, or bog.

FIND OUT MORE ▶▶ Early Farming 364–365 • Erosion 55 • Oceans 40–41 • Rocks 46–47

CAVES

Caves are hollow spaces carved into hillsides or underground by the action of water and the wind. On coasts, pounding waves sometimes hollow out caves in the bases of cliffs.

caves

Point bar built up by sediment deposited on an inside bend, where the river flows more slowly and drops its load

HOW ARE CAVES FORMED?

Caves are most common in limestone rock. Rainwater, which contains a weak acid, dissolves the soft limestone and seeps into cracks, eventually carving out channels that widen into tunnels and caves. Caves are also found in glaciers and in cooled volcanic lava.

◀ STALACTITES AND STALAGMITES
Water dripping from the ceiling of limestone caves contains dissolved minerals, such as calcite. Over thousands of years, tiny deposits of calcite build up on cave roofs to form hanging spiky columns called stalactites, and on the ground below to form stalagmites.

FIND OUT MORE ▶▶ Ice 58 • Rocks 46–47 • Volcanoes 44

ICE

At the poles and on high mountains, vast areas are covered in ice – in rivers of ice called glaciers and in layers of ice called ice sheets or ice caps. Ice is a major force of erosion on land, where glaciers gouge deep valleys in the landscape.

HOW DO GLACIERS FORM?

Glaciers form when more snow falls each winter than melts each summer. As the snow builds up, the top layers press down on the layers below and turn them to ice. When enough ice has formed, the glacier's great weight and gravity set it moving slowly downhill, at a rate of about 1 m (3.3 ft) a day. The glacier continues to advance as long as more snow is falling at its top than ice is melting at its tip.

WHAT ARE ICE CAPS?

Ice caps are vast, domed sheets of ice that cover the land in the polar regions. They are formed as snow builds up year after year, creating a thick layer of ice. Three-quarters of the world's fresh water is locked up in the polar ice caps. The ice cap covering Antarctica at the South Pole is over 4 km (2.5 miles) deep.

GLACIAL EROSION ►
Over thousands of years, as the base of the glacier scrapes over rock, it gouges out a wide, U-shaped valley. It may also carve sharp peaks called horns on mountains, and scoop rounded hollows called cirques or corries out of rock. Small lakes or tarns are often left in cirques when the glacial ice has melted.

Glacial ice can be more than 1 km (0.6 miles) deep

A lateral moraine, or heap of rock and debris, is pushed along at the glacier's sides

Deep crevices, or fissures, form where the ice cracks as it moves

Meltwater trickles from the tip, or snout, of the glacier

◄ ICEBERG
Icebergs form where glaciers and the ice caps meet the ocean. Huge chunks of ice calve, or break off, and fall into the water. Ocean currents may then carry the floating ice to warmer waters, where it can endanger shipping. In 1912, the luxury liner *Titanic* was sunk by an iceberg, and over 1,500 people drowned.

The sea's surface may freeze if the water temperature drops to −2.2°C (28°F), forming pack ice

The largest icebergs are the size of small countries and can tower up to 160 m (525 ft) above sea level

Waves and ocean currents sculpt the iceberg into pinnacles and crags above sea level and into deep caves below

Around one-ninth of an iceberg shows above the sea's surface; the rest lies underwater

FIND OUT MORE ►► Antarctica 276 • Erosion 55 • Mountains 45 • Prehistoric Life 77

COASTS

Coasts are border zones where the land meets the ocean. There is about 502,000 km (312,000 miles) of coastline worldwide. **▶▶ TIDES**, waves, and currents endlessly wear away at the land to form a variety of coastal landscapes, from sheer cliffs and rugged headlands to sandy coves and wide, lonely mudflats.

HOW DO WAVES CHANGE COASTAL LANDSCAPES?

Pounding waves continually hurl sand, pebbles, and boulders against rocky coastlines, scouring away the land. As waves wear away coastal cliffs, the coastline gradually moves inland. Elsewhere, however, tides and rivers deposit sand, mud, and pebbles to build new land in the form of river deltas, beaches, and spits.

coasts

TIDES

Once or twice daily, coastlines are washed by the tide – a regular rise and fall in the sea level. Some coastlines experience powerful tides, with rises and falls of 15 m (50 ft) or more a day. On other shores, the water level changes only by a few centimetres, so the tide is barely noticeable.

WHAT CAUSES TIDES?

Tides are caused mainly by the pull of the Moon's gravity on the Earth. This gravitational pull creates a bulge of water, or a high tide, on the sea's surface. As the Earth spins round eastwards on its axis, the bulge moves westwards, causing a high tide in different parts of the world.

WHY ARE SOME TIDES STRONGER THAN OTHERS?

Extra-strong tides called spring tides occur twice a month, when the Sun and Moon line up so that their combined gravitational pull produces an even bigger bulge on the ocean's surface. Weak tides called neap tides also occur twice every month, when the Sun and Moon are at right angles to the Earth and their pulls largely cancel each other out.

▲ SALT MARSH
Formed on flat land at river mouths, salt marshes are regularly covered by tides.

▲ FJORD
Fjords form where glaciers gouge out valleys that are later flooded by the sea.

▲ SPIT AND LAGOON
A sandy spit may form where waves deposit sediment, with a calm lagoon behind.

▲ LOW TIDE
Boats lie stranded on the shore at low tide, when the harbour at Polperro in Cornwall, Great Britain, empties of water. The tides follow a 28-day cycle, linked to the Moon's orbit around the Earth.

▲ HIGH TIDE
At high tide, boats bob on the waves as water fills the harbour. Tides rise and fall once or twice every 24 hours and 50 minutes, so high and low tides occur 50 minutes later each day.

▲ SEA STACKS
The Twelve Apostles rock formation in Victoria, Australia, was created by waves scouring away the bases of cliffs to form caves. In time, the cave roofs collapsed, forming arches of rock. Eventually, the tops of the arches crumbled, leaving behind a series of isolated pillars called stacks.

FIND OUT MORE ▶▶ Forces 164 • Moon 17 • Oceans 40–41 • Sun 15

ENERGY RESOURCES

Energy is the force that makes things work. Over many years, people have learned to produce energy from various sources, including burning ▶ **FOSSIL FUELS** and using ▶ **NUCLEAR** and ▶ **RENEWABLE ENERGY** technology.

WHAT IS FUEL?

Fuel is something that can be burned to produce energy in the form of heat or power. Fuels include coal, oil, natural gas, and wood. Humans have been burning wood for warmth, and to light homes and cook food since civilization began. However, in some parts of the world, so many trees have been cut down for fuel that firewood is now scarce.

◄ USING ENERGY
A city blazes with light. In developed countries, people consume vast amounts of energy in their daily lives.

FROM WOOD TO FIRE ►
Wood provides fuel for cooking in a remote part of China. Firewood is the main source of fuel for half the world's population.

FOSSIL FUELS

Fossil fuels are made of the fossilized remains of living things that died millions of years ago. Coal, oil, and gas are the most important fossil fuels. Today, they provide most of the world's energy.

HOW DID OIL AND NATURAL GAS FORM?

Oil is formed from the remains of tiny plants and animals that were buried and squashed on the seabed. Natural gas forms in a similar way to oil and is found trapped in underground reservoirs.

HOW ARE FOSSIL FUELS USED TO PRODUCE ENERGY?

Power stations burn fossil fuels to heat water and produce steam. The steam pushes around turbines in a generator, which then spin a magnet, creating an electric current. Oil refineries process oil to make fuel to run cars, trains, ships, and aircraft.

Coal is formed over millions of years from rotting plant material that accumulated in warm, muddy swamps

Moist, fibrous peat formed as rotting plant remains were buried and squashed. Peat gives off heat when burned

Lignite, or brown coal, is found nearest the Earth's surface. This low-grade fuel contains up to 60 per cent carbon, along with plant remains and moisture

Bituminous coal is found deeper underground. This better-quality solid fuel contains more than 80 per cent carbon and is most commonly used in industry

Hard, black anthracite is found the deepest underground. Made from more than 90 per cent carbon, it burns the best and is used in industry and to heat homes

HOW OIL FORMS

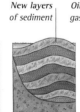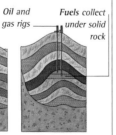

Plants and animal remains | *New layers of sediment* | *Oil and gas rigs* | *Fuels collect under solid rock*

1. Decaying plants and animals sink to the sea floor, and are buried by layers of sediment.

2. Heat and pressure increase as the sediments sink. The organic remains become oil and gas.

3. Gas and oil rise through porous (holey) rock and collect below a layer of solid rock.

energy resources

▲ COAL FORMATION
Plant remains decay to make brown, crumbly peat when they are buried and squashed. Over many thousands of years, more layers build up on top, and heat and pressure convert the remains first to lignite, then to bituminous coal, and finally to anthracite, the highest grade of coal.

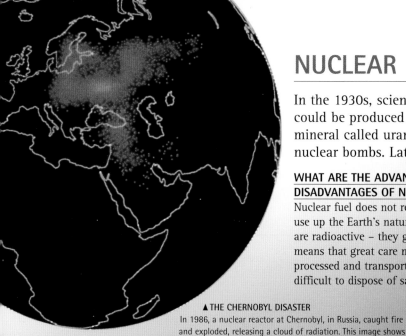

NUCLEAR ENERGY

In the 1930s, scientists discovered that huge amounts of energy could be produced by splitting atoms (tiny particles) of a rare mineral called uranium. The technology was first used to make nuclear bombs. Later, it was used to generate electricity.

WHAT ARE THE ADVANTAGES AND DISADVANTAGES OF NUCLEAR ENERGY?

Nuclear fuel does not release the same polluting gases as fossil fuels, and does not use up the Earth's natural resources. However, uranium and other nuclear materials are radioactive – they give off radiation that can harm living things. This means that great care must be taken when they are processed and transported. Nuclear fuel is also difficult to dispose of safely once used.

▲ THE CHERNOBYL DISASTER
In 1986, a nuclear reactor at Chernobyl, in Russia, caught fire and exploded, releasing a cloud of radiation. This image shows the extent of the contamination six days after the accident.

RENEWABLE ENERGY

Renewable energy is generated using the power of natural forces such as sunlight. Fossil fuels release harmful waste gases when burned, and they cannot be replaced when their limited supplies are used up. Renewable energy, however, will not run out and produces little pollution.

WHAT ARE THE SOURCES OF RENEWABLE ENERGY?

Most of the energy on Earth comes from the Sun. Solar power uses the energy in sunlight directly. Moving water (in the form of waves, tides, and flowing rivers), and the wind also contain energy that can be used to spin turbines to generate electricity. Geothermal energy taps heat from inside the Earth.

WHAT ARE THE ADVANTAGES AND DISADVANTAGES OF RENEWABLE ENERGY?

Renewable energy will last as long as the Sun shines, winds blow, waves crash, and rivers flow. These technologies are safe to use and do not pollute the environment. However, renewable energy plants can be expensive to build and may not produce enough energy to meet local requirements.

SOLAR POWER ▶
Each curved dish at a solar power station focuses radiation from the Sun onto a thermoelectric generator. A computer steers the dishes so they always turn to face the Sun during the day.

▲ WIND POWER
Windmills have been used to power machines for centuries. The spinning blades of modern wind turbines turn a shaft, which generates electricity.

▲ HYDROELECTRIC POWER
Fast-flowing river water can be used to spin turbines that work electricity generators. A dam above the hydroelectric plant controls the flow of water.

▲ GEOTHERMAL POWER
Geothermal power plants, such as this one near natural hot springs in Iceland, pipe heat from the Earth's hot interior and use it to generate electricity.

FIND OUT MORE ▶▶ Atoms 157 • Engines 198 • Fossils 76 • Industry 204 • Nuclear Energy 167

CLIMATE

Every part of the world has its own climate – a characteristic pattern of weather over a long period of time. A region's climate affects the types of plants and animals found there, and also how people live – for example, the type of houses they build and the clothes they wear.

WHAT AFFECTS AN AREA'S CLIMATE?

An area's climate is affected by three main factors – its latitude (distance north or south of the Equator), its height above sea level, and its distance from the sea. Tropical regions around the Equator have a hot climate. Temperatures cool towards the poles. The climate is also cooler on high mountains. Seas and oceans generally make coastal climates mild and wet.

WHY DO TROPICAL REGIONS HAVE HOT CLIMATES?

Because the Earth is a globe with a curved surface, the Sun's rays strike parts of its surface at different angles. Regions on or near the Equator have a hot climate because the Sun's rays beat down on them more directly and the rays are more concentrated than at regions near the poles.

WHAT IS A CONTINENTAL CLIMATE?

Regions in the centre of continents usually have more extreme weather than regions near the coast, with hot summers and cold winters. Land surfaces heat up and cool down more quickly than large areas of water, such as oceans. Areas farther inland therefore experience extreme temperature variations between summer and winter.

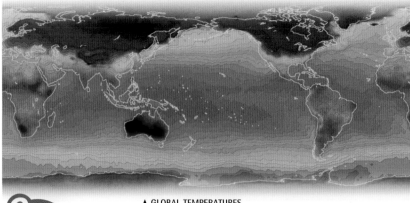

climate

▲ GLOBAL TEMPERATURES
This map of air temperatures shows the world's three main climate zones. The warmest tropical regions on and near the Equator are shown in deep red and orange. Temperate regions farther from the Equator are shown in yellow. These areas are usually mild, with warm summers and cool winters. The coldest areas, near the poles, are shown in blue.

Snow and ice cover regions above the snow line, which is at sea level at the poles and up to 5,000 m (16,400 ft) near the Equator

Hardy alpine plants, mosses, and lichens grow up to the snowline, above the treeline

Conifer forests cover high slopes up to the tree line – above that it is too cold and windy for them to survive

▲ MOUNTAIN CLIMATE
Mountain regions have a cooler climate than lowland areas because the thin air at high altitudes absorbs less of the Sun's heat. High peaks in the path of moist winds are also wetter than lowland regions.

Rain-bearing clouds blowing from the ocean make coastal regions generally wetter than areas farther inland

Growing cumulus clouds indicate changeable weather, characteristic of coastal, or maritime, climates

Trees bend towards the land, battered by strong winds blowing in off the sea

Vegetation flourishes in the mild, wet climate

◄ COASTAL CLIMATE
The ocean heats up more slowly than the land, but retains its warmth for longer. Moist sea breezes rising over the ocean and blowing inshore bring rain, cooling the land in summer, but warming it in winter, so coastal climates are generally wet and mild.

FIND OUT MORE ▶▶ Mountains 45 • Planet Earth 36–37 • Soil 48 • Winds 51

CLIMATE ZONES

The Earth has three main climate zones – tropical, temperate, and polar. These zones can be divided further into smaller zones, each with its own typical climate. A region's climate, together with its physical characteristics, determines its plant and animal life.

WHAT IS A MICROCLIMATE?
A small area with a different climate to its surroundings is said to have its own microclimate. Examples include a city or a rooftop garden. The air temperature in cities may be 6°C (11°F) warmer than the surrounding countryside because buildings and paved streets hold the Sun's heat longer than vegetation. Artificial heating in buildings also contributes to higher city temperatures.

climate zones

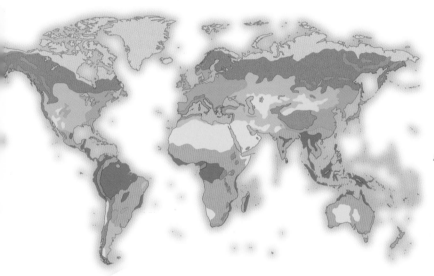

 POLAR AND TUNDRA
BOREAL FOREST
MOUNTAIN

 TEMPERATE FOREST
MEDITERRANEAN
DESERT

DRY GRASSLAND
TROPICAL GRASSLAND
TROPICAL RAINFOREST

▲ EARTH'S MAJOR CLIMATE ZONES
These are many ways to classify climate. Most methods (including the one shown here, which divides the Earth's surface into nine different climate zones) use a combination of temperature and rainfall.

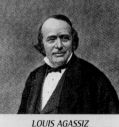

LOUIS AGASSIZ
Swiss, 1807–1873
Naturalist Louis Agassiz studied glaciers and the effects of ice erosion in areas where glaciers no longer existed. He put forward the theory that much of Europe and North America was once covered by ice sheets. Through his work, the idea of "ice ages" became generally accepted.

HAS THE EARTH'S CLIMATE CHANGED OVER TIME?
Over the past two million years, the Earth's climate has slowly changed. Long, cold periods called ice ages, or glacials, have been interspersed with warmer periods. The last glacial ended about 10,000 years ago. At its height, all of northern Europe and parts of North America, Siberia, New Zealand, Tasmania, and the southernmost tip of South America were covered by ice sheets up to 1,000 m (3,280 ft) thick.

WILL THE EARTH'S CLIMATE CHANGE IN FUTURE?
Some scientists believe that the Earth will enter another ice age in thousands of years. However, all scientists believe that pollution caused by human activities is slowly causing the planet to grow warmer – a phenomenon called global warming.

CLIMATE ZONE CLASSIFICATION

POLAR AND TUNDRA
Polar climates are cold and dry, with long, dark winters. In the tundra (a treeless region bordering the Arctic), temperatures only rise above freezing for a few months each year.

BOREAL FOREST
Boreal (cold coniferous) forests lie south of the tundra, stretching across much of northern Canada, Scandinavia, and Russia. Temperatures fall below freezing for 4–6 months a year.

MOUNTAIN
On mountains, the temperature decreases with altitude (height) and many high peaks are always covered in snow. Mountain climates are usually wetter and windier than lowland regions.

TEMPERATE FOREST
Temperate climates have warm summers and cool winters with rain all year round. Temperate forests are characterized by deciduous trees, which lose their leaves during the winter.

MEDITERRANEAN
A Mediterranean climate is found in regions bordering the Mediterranean Sea, and in Australia and California, USA. It is characterized by hot, dry summers and cool, wet winters.

DESERT
The Earth's deserts are hot and dry all year round, and usually receive less than 250 mm (10 in) of rainfall a year. Deserts are often found in the centre of continents, far from the sea.

DRY GRASSLAND
Dry grasslands are found in the centre of continents where temperate variations are extreme. They have hot summers, cold winters, and little rainfall, so very few trees can grow there.

TROPICAL GRASSLAND
Tropical grasslands, such as the African savannah, lie between desert areas and tropical rainforests. The climate is hot all year round, but with a distinct wet season and dry season.

TROPICAL RAINFOREST
Rainforests are found in tropical regions near the Equator. Here, the climate is hot and wet all year round, with temperatures remaining at around 27–28°C (80–82°F).

FIND OUT MORE ▶▶ Habitats 82–84 • Human Impact 64–65 • Winds 51

HUMAN IMPACT

Over six billion people live on planet Earth. As the population grows, we are taking more and more land to live, and using more of the world's natural resources. Many human activities also produce ▶▶ POLLUTION , which is damaging the Earth's environment.

HOW DOES FARMING CHANGE THE LANDSCAPE?

Since farming began, 10,000 years ago, many wild landscapes have been transformed to create fields for crops and raising animals. Swamps and coastal marshes have been drained. Forests have been felled and grasslands have been ploughed. However, removing tree and plant roots that help to bind the soil can make the soil loose and crumbly. High winds may then blow it away, or heavy rain may wash it into rivers. In some areas, soil erosion has turned fertile farmland into barren wastes.

WORKING FACTORIES ▶
During the manufacturing process and when they burn fossil fuels, factories such as this chemical plant release gases that harm the environment. Although they are expensive to install and run, "clean" technologies that reduce air pollution are now available and should become more common in the future.

HOW DOES INDUSTRY AFFECT THE LANDSCAPE?

In the 1700s, the dawn of the industrial age revolutionized methods of manufacturing and made them more efficient. Since then, factories have been built all over the world. Factories consume huge amounts of natural resources and energy, and many give off chemical waste, which creates problems such as air and water pollution, and ▶▶ GLOBAL WARMING .

◀ TAMING THE LAND
Crop fields stretch to the horizon on the North American prairies, where wild grasslands were once home to thousands of plant and animal species. All over the world, wild land is brought under cultivation to grow food, or bulldozed to build houses, factories, roads, and railways.

WHAT CHALLENGES FACE THE HUMAN POPULATION?

One of our main challenges is to find a balance between using and conserving the Earth's natural resources. The human species dominates the Earth in a way that no species has done before. Our demands for fuel, water, land, and food are beginning to place a strain on the planet's limited resources. What makes us different from other species, however, is our ability to recognize these global problems and our inventiveness to do something about them.

▼ GROWING CITIES
In 1900, only 10 per cent of the world's population lived in cities. Today that figure is around 50 per cent. All over the world, cities have mushroomed as more and more people have moved there to find work.

POLLUTION

All over the world, factories, power plants, farms, businesses, and homes produce huge amounts of pollution by releasing chemicals and other substances that pollute, or dirty, the natural environment. As people's use of energy and other resources grows, the Earth is becoming more polluted.

human impact

WHAT ARE THE MAIN CAUSES OF POLLUTION?
Industrial waste, sewage, and chemical pesticides from farms seep into streams and rivers. Cars, factories, and power stations burning fossil fuels give off fumes that pollute the air. Chemicals called CFCs (short for chlorofluorocarbons), used to make fridges and aerosol sprays, destroy the ozone layer, which protects us from harmful sunlight. Household and other waste buried underground pollutes the land.

HOW LONG DOES POLLUTION LAST?
Some kinds of pollution quickly disperse on the wind or are diluted by water. Other types, such as radioactive waste, stay poisonous for thousands of years. Plastics and other domestic rubbish that are buried underground in landfill sites may take many years to rot away completely.

WHAT CAN BE DONE TO REDUCE POLLUTION?
Around the world, scientists are investigating the damage caused by pollution. Governments have introduced controls that curb the pollution produced by industry and farms and restrict the development of land, especially in rural areas. Everyone can help to reduce pollution by using energy carefully and by recycling glass bottles, tin cans, plastic, and paper so that they can be reused. This helps to save precious natural resources and cuts down on waste and litter.

▲ OIL SPILLS
Accidental oil spills from damaged tankers can kill thousands of seabirds, fish, and other marine life. The world's oceans are also polluted by industrial waste and sewage dumped at sea.

▲ CITY SMOG
Car exhausts are a major source of pollution. They belch fumes into the air that sometimes form a dense, choking smog.

▲ ACID RAIN
Acid rain harms trees, poisons wildlife, and can even erode stone. It is formed when poisonous gases released from vehicles and power stations mix with moisture in the air, forming a weak damaging acid.

GLOBAL WARMING

Global warming is the slow and steady rise in the Earth's temperature caused by a build-up of "greenhouse gases" in the air due to pollution. Some experts predict temperatures will rise by 1.4–4.5°C (2.5–8.1°F) this century.

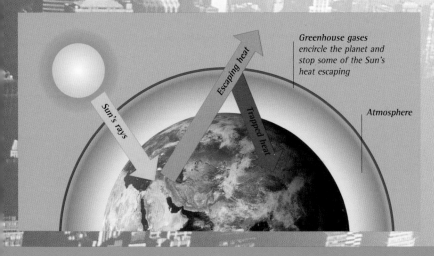

Greenhouse gases encircle the planet and stop some of the Sun's heat escaping

Atmosphere

Escaping heat

Sun's rays

Trapped heat

WHAT IS CAUSING GLOBAL WARMING?
Global warming is caused by the increased level of carbon dioxide and other greenhouse gases in the atmosphere. These gases are released from car exhausts, and when fossil fuels are burned in factories and power stations. Greenhouse gases also include CFCs from aerosols and old refrigerators, and methane from swamps, gas pipes, and rotting refuse.

HOW WILL GLOBAL WARMING AFFECT EVERYDAY LIFE?
Global warming will melt some of the polar ice caps, bringing greater risk of floods to low-lying and coastal regions worldwide. Heatwaves, droughts, hurricanes, and torrential rain will become more common. To prevent global warming, many countries are now trying to reduce their output of carbon dioxide and use renewable energy sources.

◄ THE GREENHOUSE EFFECT
Greenhouse gases occur naturally in the atmosphere. In a normal greenhouse effect, the gases trap some of the Sun's heat, making the Earth's surface warm enough for life to flourish.

FIND OUT MORE ▶▶ Energy Resources 60–61 • Industrial Revolution 418–419 • Population 218–219 • Transport 200–201

FARMING

Thousands of years ago, people began farming the land to grow cereal crops, such as wheat, and rearing animals for their meat, milk, and other products. Today, many farmers use modern techniques and equipment to produce bumper crops.

WHICH KINDS OF ANIMALS ARE DOMESTICATED?

Middle Eastern farmers began rearing herds of sheep and goats around 10,000 years ago. The most common domesticated animals today are cattle, sheep, and pigs. However, a wide range of animals including deer, rabbits, ducks, turkeys, and even ostriches are now reared for their meat, milk, or eggs.

CATTLE RANCHING ▶
The world's largest herds of beef cattle are found in North and South America, where there are plenty of wide, open grasslands for the cattle to graze. On these South American grasslands, cowboys called gauchos still round up cattle on horseback.

◀ MECHANIZED FARMING
Modern combine harvesters perform two jobs – harvesting cereal crops and threshing the grain to separate the husks containing the seeds from the stems. Farmers use different machines to plough, sow, reap, and to spray fields with fertilizers and chemicals to control weeds and pests.

e ▶▶
farming

HOW HAVE MODERN CROPS BEEN DEVELOPED?

Today's crops are descended from wild plants that produced seeds or fruits that could be eaten. Early cereal crops had small grains and therefore produced low yields. However, centuries of selective breeding (saving and sowing the best seeds) have produced large-grained varieties that give much higher yields.

WHAT ARE STAPLE FOOD CROPS?

Staple foods form the main part of people's daily diet. They include the cereal crops wheat, maize (sweetcorn), and rice. Wheat is eaten by around 35 per cent of the world's population every day. The grain is eaten whole or ground into flour, which is then used to make bread or pasta. Maize is mainly grown in tropical and subtropical countries. It is eaten as a vegetable, ground into flour or cornmeal, or used to make cooking oil.

WHERE IS RICE GROWN?

Over 90 per cent of the world's rice is grown in Asia and eaten by the people living there. Rice is also grown in the United States, mainly for export. In the United States, growing rice is highly mechanized. In Asia, the work of sowing, planting out the seedlings, and harvesting is usually done by hand.

RICE FARMING ▶
Rice is the main food for over half the world's population. It is grown in flooded fields called paddies in countries such as Thailand, China, Japan, and Indonesia.

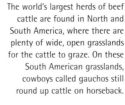

Terraces are cut into hillsides so farmers can cultivate more land

WHAT IS ORGANIC FARMING?

Many farmers spray fields with chemical pesticides and use chemical fertilizers to protect and enrich their crops. Organic farmers prefer to use natural farming methods. They enrich the soil with manure, compost, or seaweed, and use pest-eating insects or companion planting (for example, planting onions with carrots to reduce such pests as carrot-fly). Organic farmers also allow pigs and chickens to roam in fields or yards instead of keeping them in crowded pens or cages.

Paddy fields are flooded for most of the growing season because rice, a swamp plant, grows with its roots in water

FIND OUT MORE ▶▶ Agricultural Revolution 412 • Early Farming 364–365 • Genetic Engineering 210–211 • Southeast Asia 270–271

FISHING

Fish are an important food, so fishing is a major industry in many countries. However, overfishing has resulted in dwindling fish stocks in the world's oceans.

▲ TUNA FISHING
Frozen tuna are piled up on a harbour side in Tokyo, Japan. Other commercially fished species include herring, mackerel, and anchovies. An incredible 100 million tonnes (98 million tons) of fish are caught annually, along with other aquatic life, such as squid, crabs, and prawns.

WHAT IS OVERFISHING?
Overfishing is the removal of so many fish from the oceans that there are not enough fish left to breed. Many overfished species, such as cod, may eventually die out. Overfishing is happening because of the demand for fish to feed the world's population, and the efficiency of the modern fishing industry.

WHAT METHODS ARE USED BY THE FISHING INDUSTRY?
Modern fishing fleets work both in coastal waters and far out to sea, using sonar devices to locate shoals of fish, and a variety of lines, traps, and nets. Different kinds of floating nets are used to catch fish at the surface and in mid-waters. Bag-shaped trawl nets, dragged along the seabed, capture bottom-dwellers.

▲ THAI FISH FARM
Fish farms, where salmon, trout, catfish, crayfish, and prawns are reared in pens, ponds, and cages, are becoming more important as the world's seas are fished out.

fishing

FIND OUT MORE ▶▶ Endangered Species 124 • Fish 112–113 • Oceans 40–41

FORESTRY

Forestry is the management of forests with the aim of harvesting their produce, which includes timber, fuelwood, charcoal, resin, rubber, and pulp for paper. Trees also yield food in the form of fruits, nuts, and oils.

WHAT ARE THE MAIN USES OF TIMBER?
Wood is an amazingly versatile material, which can be put to thousands of different uses. As well as being burned for fuel, timber is also used in buildings and to make furniture and tools. Hardwoods, such as teak and mahogany, are prized for their beautiful grain and toughness. Fast-growing softwoods, such as pine, are mainly used for making wood pulp for paper.

RUBBER PLANTATION ▶
A sticky sap called latex lies below the bark of rubber trees. Latex becomes stretchy as it dries and, when treated, turns into rubber. Rubber trees are farmed on large rubber plantations in countries such as Malaysia (right).

Sticky sap, or latex oozes out when the bark is cut

Collecting cup is sometimes made out of a halved coconut

Slit is made at an angle in the bark of the tree

Small boats keep the floating logs on course

Logs are bundled into rafts to keep them together

◀ LOGGING INDUSTRY
Mature trees are felled with chainsaws or giant shearing blades. The logs are then trucked or floated downriver to a mill, where they are sawn into timber of different lengths. Lumber-producing countries include Canada, Russia, and Finland.

forestry

WHAT IS DEFORESTATION?
In well-managed forests, trees are cut down singly or in strips so that the forest has time to grow back. However, many of the world's forests are now being destroyed by large-scale logging, or deforestation. In particular, the tropical rainforests are disappearing rapidly – a disaster, since they are home to over half the plant and animal species on Earth.

FIND OUT MORE ▶▶ Habitats 82–84 • Industry 204 • Trees 94–95

NATURE

LIFE ON EARTH

Planet Earth is home to trillions of organisms (living things), including animals and plants. They are found on land, in lakes, rivers, and oceans, as well as in the air. Scientists use ▸▸ CLASSIFICATION to show how different species, or types, of organisms are related.

WHAT DO ALL LIVING THINGS HAVE IN COMMON?

All organisms need food for the energy required to live and grow. They all excrete (get rid of) waste products, and detect changes in their surroundings and respond to them. All living organisms follow a ▸▸ LIFE CYCLE of growth and development, reproduction, and death.

CAN LIFE EXIST WITHOUT SUNLIGHT?

Sunlight is essential for life on Earth to exist. Plants use energy from sunlight to convert water and carbon dioxide gas into food. This releases essential, life-giving oxygen into the atmosphere. Virtually all other organisms rely on plants for energy to keep them alive. Even meat-eaters indirectly absorb vegetation from their plant-eating prey.

HOW DOES THE MOVEMENT OF THE EARTH AFFECT LIFE ON OUR PLANET?

The Earth's rotation every 24 hours produces day and night. Some animals are active in the daytime, others at night. Without sunlight, plants cease making food and releasing oxygen. The annual movement of the Earth around the Sun creates the seasons. Living things are more active in spring and summer.

◀ DOLPHIN FISH
These ocean-living dolphin fish, or mahi mahi, swim in large groups called shoals. They feed on smaller fish and shrimps. Fish are well adapted to life in water. They have gills for absorbing oxygen from water, and their streamlined bodies dart easily through rivers, lakes, and oceans.

AFRICAN ELEPHANTS ▶
The largest of all land animals is the African elephant. Its massive body is supported by four pillar-like legs. Elephants have long, bendy trunks that raise water and food to the mouth and spray water over their bodies. Long, curved tusks are used for defence.

LIFE CYCLES

Every living thing goes through a sequence of changes called its life cycle. Initially it grows and develops, gradually changing shape and getting larger. Once it is fully mature, it reproduces. Finally, it dies, and is replaced by its offspring.

WHICH ORGANISMS LIVE LONGEST?

Elephants can live to the age of 70, and humans can live for more than 100 years. Some giant tortoises live for more than 150 years, but certain plants live for much, much longer. The Californian bristlecone pine tree is thought to live to 4,900 years old, and the Californian creosote bush may be 12,000 years old.

DO ALL PLANTS HAVE A ONE-YEAR LIFE CYCLE?

Annual plants, such as sunflowers, live and die within one year, but their seeds survive the winter. Biennial plants, such as carrots, flower and produce seeds in their second year and then die. Perennial plants, including oak trees, live for several years – some flower yearly, some only once in their life cycle.

5. Seeds
are scattered as the flower withers

2. Leaves
form and a stem grows

1. Seed
germinates and a root and shoot appear

4. Reproduction
occurs and the flower produces seeds

3. Flower
begins to form and upward growth slows

▲ PLANT LIFE CYCLE
The life cycle of this sunflower is completed in one growing season. Each seed contains an embryo plant and its food store, and germinates (sprouts) in the spring. The young plant grows rapidly, developing first a stem and leaves and then flowers. In summer, the flowers produce seeds, which fall to the ground ready to sprout next year.

e ▸▸ life on Earth

CLASSIFICATION

Scientists use classification to name living organisms. They sort them into groups by looking for any similarities or differences that indicate how closely related they are.

HOW DOES CLASSIFICATION WORK?

Organisms are sorted into groups ordered by size. The smallest, the species, contains organisms that breed together. Related species form a genus; several genera make a family. Linked families form an order; several orders make a class. A phylum contains a few classes. Phyla make up the largest group, the kingdom.

WHAT ARE THE FIVE KINGDOMS OF LIVING THINGS?

Organisms are divided into five kingdoms. Monerans include simple, single-celled organisms such as bacteria. Protists are mostly single-celled and include protozoa and algae. Fungi include mushrooms and moulds. Plants include flowers, trees, and ferns. Animals include lions, lizards, and lice.

CLASSIFYING A TIGER

KINGDOM	Animalia (animals) – organisms made of many cells that obtain energy from food.
PHYLUM	Chordata (chordates) – mostly vertebrates, such as birds and mammals.
CLASS	Mammalia (mammals) – vertebrates that have hair and feed their young with milk.
ORDER	Carnivora (carnivores) – hunting mammals that have gripping, cutting teeth.
FAMILY	Felidae (cats) – carnivores with sharp claws that can be retracted (drawn in).
GENUS	Panthera (big cats) – large cats that roar, including lions, leopards, and tigers.
SPECIES	*Panthera tigris* (tiger) – big cat with a striped coat, found in Asia.

PANTHERA TIGRIS ▼
A species name has two parts – generic (*Panthera*) and specific (*tigris*).

▼ THE FIVE KINGDOMS
The photographs below illustrate one species from each of the five kingdoms.

ANIMAL (LION)

PLANT (RHODODENDRON)

FUNGUS (MUSHROOM)

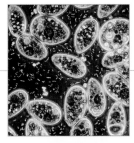

PROTIST (PROTOZOA)

MONERAN (BACTERIA)

FIND OUT MORE ▸▸ Algae 87 • Animals 96–97 • Planet Earth 36–37 • Fungi 86 • Micro-organisms 85 • Plants 88–89

BIOLOGY

The study of life and living things is called biology. Scientists who study biology are known as biologists. The main branches of biology are zoology (the study of animals), botany (the study of plants), and ▶▶ MICROBIOLOGY (the study of tiny organisms).

WHAT EXACTLY DO BIOLOGISTS STUDY?
Biologists study even more specialized branches within zoology, botany, and microbiology. Cell biology, for example, involves studying one of the smallest units of a living thing. Anatomy, on the other hand, looks at the complete structure of organisms. Whereas physiology is the study of how organisms work.

DO BIOLOGISTS ONLY STUDY STRUCTURE?
As well as learning about an organism's structure, biologists discover how an organism reproduces and grows, how it behaves, where it lives, and how it interacts with other organisms. In this way, today's biologists build up a complete picture of the biology of an organism. At one time scientists knew little more about living things than what they looked like.

Tube-like stamen is the male reproductive structure that produces pollen grains

▲ RED HIBISCUS
This tropical flowering plant has a trumpet-shaped flower and yellow brush-like anthers (male sex organs) that surround red plate-like stigmas (female sex organs). Biologists have discovered that as hummingbirds feed on hibiscus nectar (sugary liquid), they transfer dusty pollen from the anthers to the stigmas. If fertilization occurs, the plant makes seeds and reproduces.

biology

▲ STUDYING ANIMAL BEHAVIOUR
Zoologist Dr. Jane Goodall takes notes as she watches one member of a group of chimpanzees in Gombe Stream National Park, Tanzania, Africa. Goodall has spent many years studying chimpanzee behaviour.

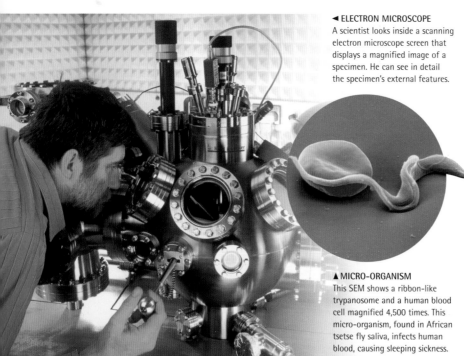

◀ ELECTRON MICROSCOPE
A scientist looks inside a scanning electron microscope screen that displays a magnified image of a specimen. He can see in detail the specimen's external features.

▲ MICRO-ORGANISM
This SEM shows a ribbon-like trypanosome and a human blood cell magnified 4,500 times. This micro-organism, found in African tsetse fly saliva, infects human blood, causing sleeping sickness.

MICROBIOLOGY

Micro-organisms are living things that are too small to be seen with the naked eye. Microbiology is the study of these micro-organisms, which include bacteria, viruses, and some fungi.

WHAT DO MICROBIOLOGISTS DO?
Some microbiologists are interested in the micro-organisms that cause diseases in animals and plants. Some specialize in those micro-organisms that may be useful for the manufacture of drugs, or food, such as bread. Others study micro-organisms that recycle essential nutrients in the Earth and its atmosphere.

HOW DO ELECTRON MICROSCOPES WORK?
Electron microscopes work by passing a beam of tiny particles called electrons through, or across the surface of, a specimen, and onto a screen. This produces a greatly magnified image. Scanning electron microscopes produce a three-dimensional image that can be captured in a photograph called an SEM.

FIND OUT MORE ▶▶ Animals 96–97 • Flowering Plants 92–93 • Micro-organisms 85

CELLS

The tiniest living unit that exists is a cell. Cells are the building blocks of all organisms. Each cell has a nucleus containing a set of building instructions called GENES .

ARE THERE DIFFERENT TYPES OF CELLS IN THE SAME ORGANISM?
Most organisms consist of many different types of cells, each with a specific role to play. Cells with a similar task, such as muscle cells in an animal, are organized into a group. This group, called a tissue, carries out a particular function, such as bending a leg.

HOW DO PLANT AND ANIMAL CELLS DIFFER?
Both plant and animal cells have a nucleus and a plasma membrane and contain cytoplasm. Plant cells, however, have a fluid-filled vacuole and green structures called chloroplasts. Chloroplasts make food using sunlight energy in a process called photosynthesis. Animal cells must absorb food to survive.

cells

Vacuole
stores watery cell sap that gives cell its shape

Cytoplasm is
the jelly-like liquid inside cell

Chloroplast (green)
captures sunlight needed to make food

Nucleus is the cell's control centre

Cell wall

Plasma membrane
is pushed up against the cell wall

Nucleus is surrounded by a double membrane

Cytoplasm is the area of a living cell, outside the nucleus, enclosed by the cell membrane. It contains materials that help the cell to function

Plasma membrane
is the thin barrier that surrounds a cell

ANIMAL CELL ▶
Unlike plant cells, which have a rigid outer wall, animal cells are more fluid in shape.

▲ PLANT CELL
This cross-section of a leaf cell shows how the vacuole (blue) sap pushes cytoplasm (yellow-green) against the cell wall (brown). This gives the cell its shape.

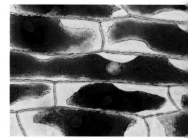

▲ ONION BULB CELLS
These magnified cells from an onion bulb have been stained red. Box-like cell walls have formed around the mature cells.

GENES

The features of living things are controlled by their genes. The genes inside an organism's cells contain the instructions to make proteins, which build that cell and control the way it works. Genes are inherited by offspring from their parents.

WHAT IS DNA?
Genes are made of a chemical substance called deoxyribonucleic acid (DNA). It is stored in the nucleus of all cells. DNA holds instructions for making the proteins needed for the growth and development of new organisms. It also passes on genetic information to the next generation.

WHAT IS A CHROMOSOME?
Inside a cell's nucleus, DNA is packaged into long, thread-like structures called chromosomes. They are visible only under a microscope when the cells divide. During cell division, chromosomes shorten and thicken, then split into identical halves, one for each new cell. Chromosome numbers vary between species.

▲ GENE DIFFERENCES
These two hamsters differ because each has different versions of the genes that control fur pattern and colour. Otherwise they look very similar because most of their genes are identical.

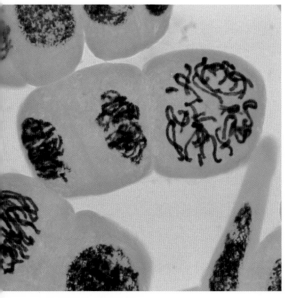

▲ CELL DIVISION IN AN ONION'S ROOT TIP
These onion cells (blue) are dividing in a process called mitosis. The cells' 16 chromosomes (black) also divide and separate, so that each new cell gains a complete set. Mitosis allows an organism to grow or repair itself.

FIND OUT MORE ▶▶ Evolution 74–75 • Micro-organisms 85

Living things gradually change over many generations in a process called evolution. Evolution ensures that organisms are fully adapted to their surroundings, and gives rise to new species, as well as making others extinct. The driving force for evolution is ▸▸ NATURAL SELECTION.

WHAT IS THE EVIDENCE FOR EVOLUTION?
Evolutionary clues are found in fossils, the ancient remains of organisms. Creatures alive today share some characteristics with fossil ancestors but have evolved new ones as well. Fossils also show that millions of living and extinct species evolved from a few simple organisms that lived billions of years ago.

HOW DO NEW SPECIES EVOLVE?
A species is a group of similar living things, such as lions, that can breed together. If a group of individuals within a species becomes separated from all the other groups of that species, they can no longer breed with them. In time, the group evolves separately and becomes increasingly different. Eventually, it is so different that it becomes a new species.

HOW LONG DOES EVOLUTION TAKE?
Evolution is a continuous process of change. Change can be very rapid in small organisms, such as bacteria, but in most living things it takes thousands of years. ▸▸ HUMAN EVOLUTION from an ape-like ancestor took millions of years and gave rise to several different species, not just our own.

SPURGE   CACTUS

▲ CONVERGENT EVOLUTION
This is the evolution of similar features in unrelated species living in similar conditions. Spurge and cactus are unrelated plants with thick, spiny water-holding stems to help them survive in dry places.

Phiomia was as big as a modern horse and had pillar-like legs and a short trunk. Sharp tusks were used for fighting and gathering food

Moeritherium, an early elephant, had a bulky body, short legs, and a long upper lip. It lived in Africa, and is thought to have bathed in lakes and rivers and fed on water plants

MOERITHERIUM
50 MILLION YEARS AGO

PHIOMIA
35 MILLION YEARS AGO

NATURAL SELECTION

Living things produce more offspring than they need to replace themselves. Only the few that are well adapted to their particular environment will survive. Thanks to this natural selection, the features needed to survive are passed on to their offspring and become more widespread, so a species gradually evolves.

HOW DOES A WELL-ADAPTED INDIVIDUAL SURVIVE?
Certain individuals have features that let them compete better for food, water, shelter, or mates. These fitter individuals are more likely to survive, breed, and pass on their advantageous features to their offspring. In this way, natural selection ensures the survival of the fittest. Naturalist Charles Darwin believed that this is how species evolve over time.

e ▸▸
evolution

CHARLES DARWIN
English, 1809–1882

Between 1831 and 1836 naturalist Charles Darwin sailed around the world, describing the animals and plants he saw. This trip convinced him that living things evolved, even though most scientists believed that they remained the same. In 1859, he published his theories in On the Origin of Species.

▲ RED CRAB SURVIVAL RACE
This forest-dweller releases many tiny offspring into the sea. After a month in the water, they race to the forest. Many die en route.

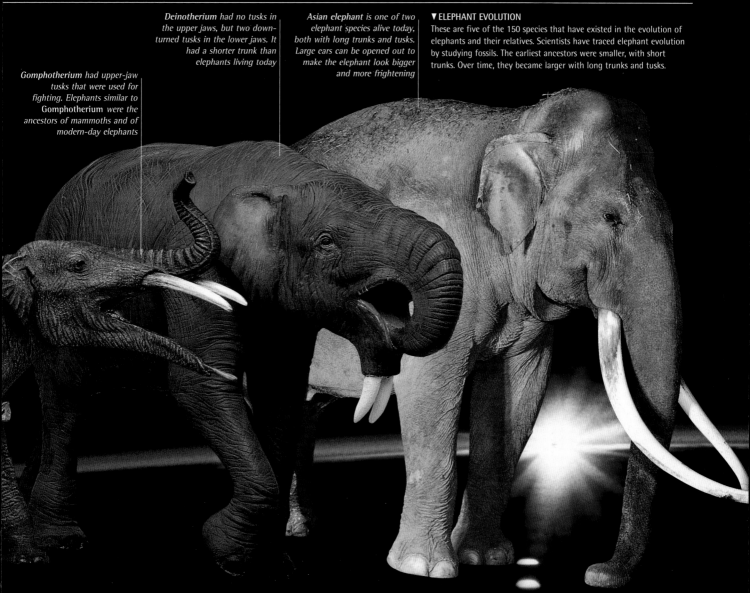

Gomphotherium had upper-jaw tusks that were used for fighting. Elephants similar to Gomphotherium were the ancestors of mammoths and of modern-day elephants

Deinotherium had no tusks in the upper jaws, but two down-turned tusks in the lower jaws. It had a shorter trunk than elephants living today

Asian elephant is one of two elephant species alive today, both with long trunks and tusks. Large ears can be opened out to make the elephant look bigger and more frightening

▼ ELEPHANT EVOLUTION
These are five of the 150 species that have existed in the evolution of elephants and their relatives. Scientists have traced elephant evolution by studying fossils. The earliest ancestors were smaller, with short trunks. Over time, they became larger with long trunks and tusks.

GOMPHOTHERIUM
20 MILLION YEARS AGO

DEINOTHERIUM
2 MILLION YEARS AGO

ASIAN ELEPHANT
PRESENT DAY

HUMAN EVOLUTION

Early humans evolved in Africa about five million years ago, from ape-like ancestors. As these ancestors moved from dense forests to open woodlands, they evolved new features, such as the ability to walk upright.

WHY WAS LEARNING TO WALK UPRIGHT IMPORTANT TO HUMAN EVOLUTION?
Walking on two legs enabled early humans to use their hands to pick up, carry, and use objects. Standing upright also allowed them to survey their surroundings and look out for prey or enemies. These new abilities led to the evolution of larger brains, which allowed them to think, plan, and communicate.

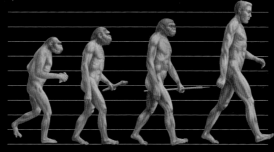

HOMO HABILIS
2.5 MYA

HOMO ERECTUS
1.75 MYA

HOMO NEANDERTHALENSIS
200,000 YA

HOMO SAPIENS
160,000 YA

▲ GENUS HOMO
Homo is the group of species, or the genus, to which modern humans (*Homo sapiens*) belong. Their earlier relatives, some of which are shown here, also belonged to this group. With time, as brain size and intelligence increased, the ability to stand upright and make effective tools developed.

Sharp cutting edge

▲ FLINT HAND-AXE
Over 200,000 years old, this flint hand-axe shows that early humans had evolved the skills to make and use tools. Its sharp edge may have been used to skin animals.

FIND OUT MORE ▶▶ Fossils 76 • Prehistoric Life 77

FOSSILS

Fossils are the ancient remains of living things preserved in rocks. They are usually formed from hard animal or plant parts, such as bone, shell, or wood. Studying fossils is a part of ▶▶ PALAEONTOLOGY .

HOW ARE FOSSILS FORMED?

When an animal dies it is rapidly covered by sediment, such as mud or sand. Its soft parts decompose (rot), but its hard parts are gradually replaced by minerals, or fossilized. At the same time, surrounding sediments turn to rock. Millions of years later, the rocks are uncovered, and the organism's imprint is exposed in its fossil.

WHAT DO FOSSILS SHOW US?

Fossils prove that ancient life forms were different from those alive today. They are laid down in layers of rocks, each layer older than the one above. Since evolution is the gradual change in living things over time, fossil layers provide an historical record of the different stages in the evolution of life.

PALAEONTOLOGY

This science studies the evolution, the way of life, and the extinction of organisms that existed in time periods before the present. Palaeontologists are scientists who study the fossil remains of species that lived a long time ago.

FOSSIL AMMONITES ▲
These are the fossilized shells of ammonites (molluscs related to present-day squids). Ammonites were marine predators that lived between 500 and 65 million years ago (mya), when they became extinct.

Coiled shell is divided into gas-filled chambers that keep the animal buoyant (afloat)

e ▶▶
fossils

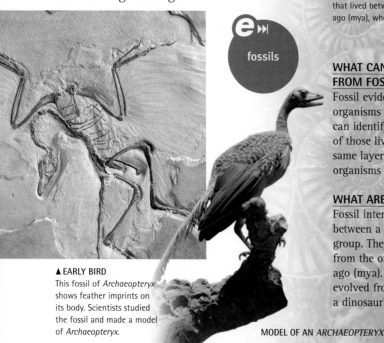

▲ EARLY BIRD
This fossil of *Archaeopteryx* shows feather imprints on its body. Scientists studied the fossil and made a model of *Archaeopteryx*.

MODEL OF AN *ARCHAEOPTERYX*

WHAT CAN PALAEONTOLOGISTS LEARN FROM FOSSILS?

Fossil evidence shows how features of today's organisms have evolved over time. Palaeontologists can identify organisms that may be ancient relatives of those living today. By looking at fossils from the same layer of rocks, they can also suggest how these organisms lived together in their ancient habitat.

WHAT ARE FOSSIL INTERMEDIATES?

Fossil intermediates are species that provide a link between a new group of organisms and an older group. They also indicate how one group evolved from the other. *Archaeopteryx* lived 150 million years ago (mya). Its fossils show how birds could have evolved from dinosaurs because its skeleton was like a dinosaur's, but it had feathers similar to a bird.

FOSSIL RECORD	
4.5 BYA	Earth forms
3.8 BYA	First living things
500 MYA	First vertebrates (fish)
440 MYA	First land plants
360 MYA	First land vertebrates (amphibians)
248 MYA	First mammals appear
150 MYA	Earliest birds
65 MYA	Dinosaurs extinct
60 MYA	Mammals become diverse
2 MYA	Ice ages
160,000 YA	Modern humans appear

FIND OUT MORE ▶▶ Dinosaurs 78–79 • Evolution 74–75

PREHISTORIC LIFE

The period between the appearance of the first organisms, 3.8 billion years ago (bya), and the first written record of history, several thousand years ago, is called prehistoric. It included sudden increases in life, and mass extinctions, for example during an ▸▸ ICE AGE.

WHAT WERE THE FIRST FORMS OF LIFE?

Bacteria and other single-celled organisms lived in the sea and remained the only life forms for billions of years. Some of these released oxygen into the air, allowing the evolution of organisms that could use oxygen. The first animals probably appeared 600 million years ago (mya), those with hard shells and body cases about 550 mya, and vertebrates (animals with backbones), such as fish, 500 mya.

WHAT WERE THE FIRST LIFE FORMS ON LAND?

The first land plants evolved from green algae found at the edge of the sea and rivers 440 mya. In time they gave rise to horsetails and clubmosses. Forests then evolved and were the home to the first land animals. Scorpions and centipedes, as well as earthworms and leeches, first appeared about 400 mya. They were followed by the first land vertebrates, which evolved from fish and were the four-legged ancestors of amphibians.

EARLY MARINE LIFE ▸
Based on Canadian fossil findings from Burgess Shale rock, this illustration shows what marine life may have looked like over 500 mya. This period, known as the Cambrian period, saw an explosion in animal species and populations.

Anomalocaris was a predator that at 60 cm (2 ft) long was one of the largest Burgess Shale animals – it had a circular mouth and grasping appendages

Hallucigenia moved on its spiny legs across the ocean floor

ICE AGES

An ice age is a period in the Earth's history when the climate is far colder than usual, and large areas of the Earth's surface are covered by ice sheets. There have been 20 ice ages in the past two and a half million years, each lasting about 100,000 years.

HOW DID ICE AGES OCCUR?

Changes in the Earth's orbit around the Sun produced cooler summers, so winter snows did not melt. As ice sheets formed, they reflected sunlight back into space so it did not warm the Earth. These changes also affected the oceans, increasing numbers of plant-like plankton, which took in carbon dioxide from the atmosphere. Since this gas helps to retain heat around the Earth, a drop in its levels accelerated cooling.

◂ WOOLLY MAMMOTH
With its thick, insulating coat, the huge woolly mammoth was well adapted to living in an ice age. It lived between two million and 10,000 years ago.

prehistoric
life

DINOSAURS

This group of land-living reptiles appeared around 230 million years ago. Like reptiles today, dinosaurs had a scaly, waterproof skin, and young that hatched from eggs. For 165 million years, a period called the Mesozoic era, they dominated life on Earth. They suddenly became extinct 65 million years ago (mya).

WHY WERE MANY DINOSAURS SO BIG?

The large size of many plant-eating dinosaurs helped protect them from fearsome meat-eaters. This led to the evolution of larger predators, big enough to tackle their prey, which in turn resulted in an increase in the size of plant-eaters. Over millions of years, both prey and predator grew bigger and bigger.

HOW MANY DIFFERENT TYPES OF DINOSAUR WERE THERE?

Dinosaurs fall into two groups. The ornithischian dinosaurs were all plant-eaters, but the saurischian dinosaurs included plant-eaters and meat-eaters. Other reptiles that lived at this time, but were not actually dinosaurs, included flying reptiles called ▶▶ PTEROSAURS, and marine reptiles such as ▶▶ ICHTHYOSAURS and plesiosaurs.

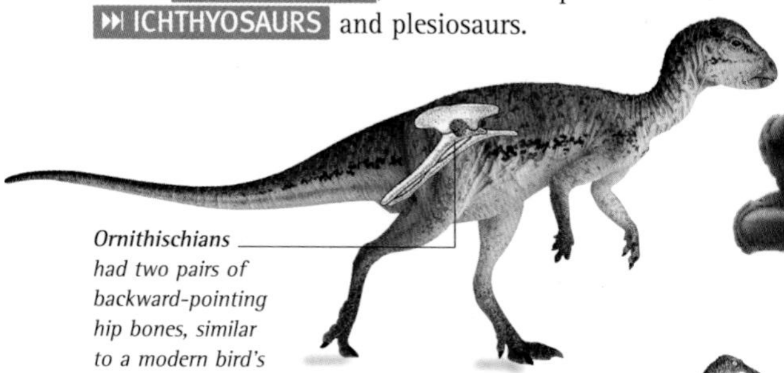

Ornithischians had two pairs of backward-pointing hip bones, similar to a modern bird's

HYPSILOPHODON

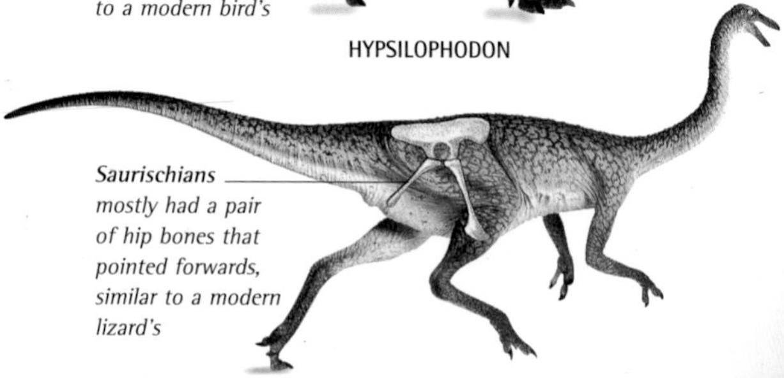

Saurischians mostly had a pair of hip bones that pointed forwards, similar to a modern lizard's

GALLIMIMUS

e ▶▶
dinosaurs

GIGANOTOSAURUS ▶
A pair of *Giganotosaurus* dinosaurs charge through a South American forest 95 mya. Weighing as much as 125 people, or about 7 tonnes (6.9 tons), and bigger than *Tyrannosaurus rex*, *Giganotosaurus* was probably the largest predator ever to walk the Earth.

Tail is stiffened with rod-like bones

Wings of leathery skin, reinforced with fine, tough fibres

◀ DIMORPHODON
This pterosaur grew up to 1 m (3 ft 3 in) long, from the tip of its tooth-lined beak to the end of its tail.

Long fourth finger
forms the edge of the wing

PTEROSAURS

Pterosaurs belong to the same group of reptiles as dinosaurs and are closely related. The largest, *Pteranodon*, had a wingspan of up to 9 m (30 ft).

WERE PTEROSAURS THE ANCESTORS OF BIRDS?
Birds and pterosaurs evolved separately. Similarities in skeletons show that birds evolved from saurischian dinosaurs. But birds and pterosaurs have similar features, including a streamlined shape, wings, hollow bones, and a lightweight beak. A furry body suggests that, like birds, pterosaurs were warm-blooded. Unrelated living things sometimes develop similar features to suit similar lifestyles.

ICHTHYOSAURS

These reptiles spent their lives in the sea, surfacing to breathe. Ichthyosaurs, which means fish lizards, gave birth to live young and fed on fish, squid, and ammonites. The largest was up to 15 m (49 ft) long.

WAS OCEAN LIFE VERY DIFFERENT IN THE AGE OF THE DINOSAURS?
Life beneath the ocean looked much as it does today. It teemed with animals such as sharks, starfish, corals, whelks, jellyfish, and lobsters. However, swimming alongside them were huge and now-extinct marine reptiles, such as plesiosaurs and ichthyosaurs.

Long, heavy tail
helped Giganotosaurus to balance as it ran

Powerful jaws
lined with saw-edged teeth tore chunks of flesh out of prey

Sharp claws
on three fingers gripped prey while Giganotosaurus took deep bites

Large feet with four claws supported the dinosaur as it moved on two legs

DINOSAUR STANCE

LIZARD STANCE

HOW WERE DINOSAURS DIFFERENT FROM REPTILES TODAY?
Dinosaurs stood upright on straight legs. Their legs were directly under them, so their bodies were always raised off the ground. This allowed them to grow bigger and let them move faster. Reptiles today have a sprawling stance, with legs held out to the sides. Their bodies are close to or resting on the ground. This limits their size and their ability to move.

▲ ICHTHYOSAURUS
The dolphin-like *Ichthyosaurus* had a streamlined body, with flippers, fins, and a long, narrow jaw with spiky teeth. It swam by beating its tail from side to side, reaching speeds of up to 40 km/h (25 mph).

FIND OUT MORE ▶▶ Birds 118–119 • Evolution 74–75 • Reptiles 116–117

ECOLOGY

All living things have complex relationships with other species and with their environment. The study of these interactions is called ecology. Ecology looks at the ▸▸ FOOD CHAIN that links the eater to the eaten. It also shows how vital chemicals are recycled by ▸▸ NUTRIENT CYCLES.

WHAT IS AN ECOSYSTEM?

From a tiny puddle to a vast forest, an ecosystem consists of a living community, its environment, and all their interactions. A community is a group of animals, plants, and micro-organisms that live together in the same area, or habitat. Its environment includes sunlight, rainfall, and shelter.

Crevices provide shelter for eels, crabs, and octopuses

Anthias fish feeding on plankton

Fish of many different species feed and breed on the reef

Coral grows slowly and is easily destroyed

CORAL REEF IN THE RED SEA, EGYPT▲
Found in shallow tropical seas, coral reefs teem with life. Corals are tiny animals whose chalky skeletons form the rocky reef. This ecosystem provides food and shelter for fish and other species.

Fish provides heron with the energy to survive

▲ WETLAND ECOSYSTEM
A great blue heron devours a fish, and the sunlight stimulates plant growth. These are just two of the many complex interactions that make up this wetland ecosystem in Florida, USA.

WHAT IS BIODIVERSITY?

Coral reefs have high biodiversity because they contain large numbers of different species. Deserts have low biodiversity because they have far fewer species. Humans have reduced biodiversity in many ecosystems by harmful activities, such as overfishing.

◀ LAVA FIELD
A volcanic eruption dramatically changed this ecosystem in Hawaii. The cooled, hard lava field is a hostile environment for living things, yet one pioneer plant has managed to grow on a tiny patch of soil blown in by the wind.

Lava flow from volcano destroyed the old ecosystem

ecology

Pioneer plant probably grew from a spore blown in the wind

WHY DO ECOSYSTEMS CHANGE?

Ecosystems are continually changing, often very slowly, sometimes very fast. A forest fire, for example, can wipe out an ecosystem without warning. Even so, a new community slowly begins to form. First, short-lived pioneer plants arrive, along with the animals that eat them. These are gradually replaced by larger plants, such as trees, and their associated animals. Eventually, a stable mix of species is established.

FOOD CHAIN

In any ecosystem, species eat and are eaten by other species. A food chain is a simple pathway that connects up to six species by what they eat. It describes the route followed by energy and nutrients as they are passed from organism to organism.

WHAT IS A FOOD WEB?

The community within an ecosystem can contain thousands of species. Each species may be part of two or more food chains. The interconnected network of food chains in an ecosystem is called a food web. It includes producers that make their own food by photosynthesis, consumers that eat plants or animals, and decomposers that break down dead organisms.

Plants are food for many animals, and for decomposers such as fungi

Fungi and bacteria feed on plant matter

Badgers eat plants and small animals, such as worms, beetles, and moles

Garden snails feed on plants

Worms feed on dead plant and animal matter

Moles feed on beetles and other insects

Beetles eat worms

▲ FOOD WEB
This simplified woodland food web includes producers (plants), consumers (animals), and decomposers (fungi).

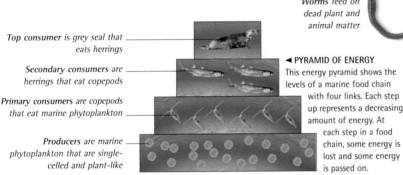

Top consumer is grey seal that eats herrings

Secondary consumers are herrings that eat copepods

Primary consumers are copepods that eat marine phytoplankton

Producers are marine phytoplankton that are single-celled and plant-like

◄ PYRAMID OF ENERGY
This energy pyramid shows the levels of a marine food chain with four links. Each step up represents a decreasing amount of energy. At each step in a food chain, some energy is lost and some energy is passed on.

WHY ARE THERE FEWER PREDATORS THAN PREY?

Predators are fewer in number than prey because they are higher up the food chain. In a food chain, an organism passes on only part of the energy it receives from food. With less energy, each level in a food chain supports fewer individuals than the one below it.

NUTRIENT CYCLES

Organisms take chemical nutrients, such as carbon, nitrogen, and water, from their surroundings. They then return or recycle them when they respire (breathe) or die.

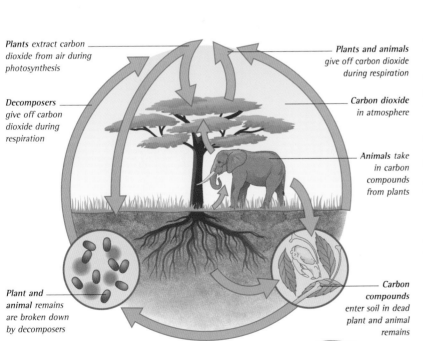

Plants extract carbon dioxide from air during photosynthesis

Decomposers give off carbon dioxide during respiration

Plant and animal remains are broken down by decomposers

Plants and animals give off carbon dioxide during respiration

Carbon dioxide in atmosphere

Animals take in carbon compounds from plants

Carbon compounds enter soil in dead plant and animal remains

CARBON CYCLE ▲
All organisms, including these African savanna species, need carbon to build their bodies. The carbon cycle ensures that carbon is recycled and never runs out.

DECOMPOSING PEACH ►
A peach rots as it is broken down by fungi and bacteria. Organisms like these that break down other organisms are called decomposers.

WHAT PART DO BACTERIA AND FUNGI PLAY IN THE CARBON CYCLE?

Certain fungi and bacteria, called decomposers, play a key role. They break down, or decompose, the remains of dead organisms. This releases carbon dioxide back into the air, where it can be re-used by plants.

WHAT IS THE NITROGEN CYCLE?

Plants take up nitrogen-containing chemicals, called nitrates, from the soil. Animals obtain nitrogen by eating plants, or animals that eat plants. Bacteria release the nitrogen in dead plant and animal matter, allowing it to be returned to the soil. Nitrogen is an important part of proteins that cells need to survive.

HOW ARE PLANTS INVOLVED IN THE WATER CYCLE?

Most rainwater flows to the sea along rivers, but some is taken up by plant roots. Water evaporates from plant leaves back into the air. Like water evaporated from the sea, it rises into the air, and falls as rain.

FIND OUT MORE ►► Animals 96–97 • Feeding 98 • Fungi 86 • Human Impact 64–65 • Micro-organisms 85 • Plants 88–89

HABITATS

Organisms are adapted to live in particular surroundings with distinctive conditions, such as rainfall and temperature. This is their habitat. The largest habitats include ▸▸ OCEANS, ▸▸ WETLANDS, ▸▸ FORESTS, ▸▸ GRASSLANDS, ▸▸ DESERTS, ▸▸ MOUNTAINS, and ▸▸ POLAR HABITATS.

WHAT IS THE DIFFERENCE BETWEEN A HOME AND A HABITAT?

A habitat is an area occupied by many species. A home is a place within a habitat where a particular animal species can protect itself and its young from the weather and predators. Homes include nests built by birds and wasps, and burrows dug by moles.

WHAT IS A MICROHABITAT?

A small part of a habitat that has its own conditions of, for example, temperature and light, and its own characteristic species, is called a microhabitat. Microhabitats include the shady area under a tree and the underside of a rock in a stream.

▲ RACCOONS
North American raccoons are successful because they can live in many habitats and eat anything. They even live in towns and cities, where they survive by raiding rubbish bins.

OCEANS

The oceans cover about 70 per cent of the Earth's surface and form the largest of the world's habitats. Life is found at all depths, from shallow surface waters to trenches over 11 km (7 miles) down.

WHY ARE PHYTOPLANKTON IMPORTANT?

All ocean life depends on microscopic plant-like organisms called phytoplankton. Floating near the ocean's surface, phytoplankton trap sunlight energy to make food. Zooplankton (tiny animals and protists) feed on phytoplankton. They in turn provide food for fish, crabs, squid, and other animals.

IS THERE LIGHT AT THE BOTTOM OF THE OCEAN?

Light penetrates the ocean's surface waters to a depth of only about 200 m (656 ft). Below this, in the twilight zone, it is much dimmer. In the deep zone, it is pitch black, and very cold. Each zone, down to the seabed, has its own community of living things.

habitats

Bromeliads grow on tree branches, high up in rainforest canopies – they thrive in the moist air

Frogs lay their eggs in bromeliad waterpools. The tadpoles then feed and grow in the pools

▲ BROMELIAD MICROHABITAT
The red leaves of this tropical forest bromeliad hold a small pool of water. The pool is a microhabitat in which frogs, mosquito larvae, and other organisms can live.

▲ CHEVRONED BARRACUDA
A school of chevroned barracuda swim in surface waters off Borneo, Malaysia. These fierce hunters round up other fish and kill them with a snapping bite of their powerful jaws.

WETLANDS

Wherever salt or fresh water cannot easily drain, a wetland forms. Wetlands cover over 6 per cent of the Earth's surface. They include marshes, swamps, waterlogged forests, peat bogs, and river deltas.

WHY ARE WETLANDS IMPORTANT?

Many wetlands contain a large diversity of species, including birds, mammals, reptiles, insects, amphibians, and plants. Wetlands also serve as nurseries where young fish and other aquatic animals grow and develop.

WHAT ARE MANGROVE SWAMPS?

These are the salt-water wetlands, populated by mangrove trees, found along tropical coastlines. Mangrove swamps teem with life, and they also help to protect the coastline from tropical storm damage.

HOW DOES A PEAT BOG DIFFER FROM A SWAMP?

Peat bogs form in cool, wet places where a lake fills with soil and vegetation. Swamps are found in places, such as river deltas, where water moves slowly enough to create permanent flooding. Plentiful vegetation provides food and homes for swamp animals.

▲ FLAMINGOS
These tropical wetland birds live on salty lakes and lagoons. They pump water through their beaks, filtering out shrimps and other small aquatic animals for food.

FORESTS

Habitats dominated by trees and shrubs are called forests. They include tropical rainforests, cool-climate coniferous forests, and temperate broad-leaved forests. These habitats all teem with life.

▲ THREE-TOED SLOTH
This South American mammal spends most of its days hanging upside down from the branches of rainforest trees.

WHY ARE RAINFORESTS SO FULL OF LIFE?

Evergreen trees continuously grow and provide food in the constant warm and wet climate of tropical rainforests. A huge variety of animals feed and shelter at all levels, from the forest floor to its canopy. Tropical rainforests contain half of all animal and plant species. Yet they cover only about 10 per cent of the Earth's surface.

Stag beetles use their massive jaws to fight over mates and territory

▲ STAG BEETLES
These fighting stag beetles live in broad-leaved forests. As young larvae they feed on rotting wood. As adults they feed upon the sap of tree trunks.

GRASSLANDS

Wherever it is too dry for forests to grow, or too wet for deserts to form, grasslands appear. The two main types are the tropical African savannah and temperate grasslands, such as the South American pampas.

HOW DO GRASSES SURVIVE GRAZING?

Grasses can withstand constant grazing because they sprout from the bottom, not from the tips. The more they are eaten, the more they grow. Grasslands support a wide variety of animals that eat grasses, as well as those that prey on grass-eaters.

HOW CAN SO MANY PLANT-EATING SPECIES LIVE IN THE SAVANNAH?

The African savannah supports many species of plant-eaters, some of which eat different parts of grasses, while others eat different savannah plants. Zebras, for example, eat the coarse, tough tops of grasses, while wildebeest prefer their leafy, middle parts.

WHY DO MANY SMALLER GRASSLAND ANIMALS LIVE UNDERGROUND?

There are few trees in the grasslands to provide shelter, so burrowing protects the animals from enemies. Burrows also protect against extreme weather conditions.

▲ AFRICAN SAVANNAH
The hot African savannah is home to vast herds of grazing animals, including these wildebeest and zebra. They in turn are hunted by predators such as lions and leopards.

FIND OUT MORE ▶▶ Deserts 84 • Mountains 84 • Polar Habitats 84

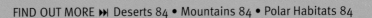

DESERTS

This dry and hostile habitat often receives less than 10 cm (4 in) of rain each year. Deserts are very hot by day, but cooler at night. Few animals and plants have adapted to survive these difficult conditions.

HOW DO DESERT PLANTS SURVIVE?

Some plants, such as cacti, have deep, wide-spreading roots to reach available water, and small leaves and waterproof skins that limit evaporation. Others spend most of their life cycle as seeds. When rare rains arrive, they sprout, flower, and produce seeds within two weeks. This event is called a desert bloom.

Strap-like leaves absorb water vapour

▲ WELWITSCHIA
This plant grows in the extremely dry Namib Desert. It survives by using its large leaves to absorb condensation from fog that rolls off the nearby ocean at night.

Sting at the end of jointed flexible tail is used for self-defence and to kill prey

▲ SCORPION
Like many desert animals, this scorpion is active at night, when temperatures are lower. Once a scorpion has detected its prey, it grips and then stings it.

MOUNTAINS

Land that is 600 m (1,970 ft) or more above the sea is a mountain. The higher you climb, the thinner the air, the lower the temperature, and the faster the wind speed are. Only the toughest species survive.

WHAT ARE MOUNTAIN ZONES?

Mountains have various zones of vegetation. Deciduous woodlands cover the foothills. These rise up to coniferous forests, which can survive the colder, windier conditions. Above the tree line (where trees can no longer grow) is an alpine meadow of hardy plants. Next is bare rock, capped by a snow field.

WHICH ANIMALS LIVE ON MOUNTAINS?

Each vegetation zone has its typical species. Woodlands and forests provide habitats for grazers, such as deer and birds. Meadows are home to rodents and rabbits and, in summer, insects and the birds that eat them. Goats and sheep live on the rocky crags, and birds of prey circle above, in search of food.

Snow field at the top of a mountain is too cold and windy for most living things

▲ EDELWEISS
Short, tough plant species, such as this Swiss edelweiss, can survive in the alpine meadow. Here above the tree line, winds are fierce and biting, and soils are thin and rocky.

POLAR HABITATS

Cold, icy polar habitats exist at the Earth's North and South poles. Polar regions have short summers, and long, harsh winters. Only animals that have adapted, with thick fur, for example, survive there.

▲ WALRUSES
These marine mammals live in herds in Arctic coastal waters. Walruses are tough-skinned, with a thick layer of blubber (fat) to protect them from the cold.

DO THE ARCTIC AND ANTARCTICA DIFFER?

The Arctic surrounds the North Pole and is a frozen ocean. Animals such as polar bears and arctic foxes live on the ice sheet. Antarctica surrounds the South Pole, is a frozen continent, and has few animals. The ocean around it is rich in nutrients and supports fish, seabirds, seals, and whales.

Chinstrap penguins gather on an iceberg in Antarctica

▲ PENGUINS
Several species of penguins live, feed, and breed in and around Antarctica. Their thick waterproof feathers and layers of fat help to keep them warm.

FIND OUT MORE ▶▶ Coasts 59 • Ice 58 • Mountains 45

MICRO-ORGANISMS

Any living thing that is invisible to the naked eye and can be seen only under a microscope is called a micro-organism. They include ▸▸ BACTERIA, protists, and some fungi, such as yeasts. ▸▸ VIRUSES are usually included, but they are not really living organisms.

WHAT IS A PROTIST?

This is a single-celled organism found in the sea, fresh water, soil, and in or on other living things. Animal-like protists, called protozoa, get their energy by eating food. They include ciliates – protists that move by beating hair-like fibres called cilia. Some protozoa cause diseases such as malaria. Plant-like protists, called algae, make their food by photosynthesis, and include ocean phytoplankton and green pond algae.

Mouth of Didinium opens wide to swallow prey whole

Paramecium *is covered with cilia that beat rhythmically to make it move*

Didinium *moves by beating two rows of cilia*

▲ DIDINIUM
Fresh water ciliate protist *Didinium* can kill and eat other protists bigger than itself. Here, it attacks *Paramecium*, another ciliate, immobilizing it with an explosive dart.

Needle-like mouthpart sucks up blood into this yellow fever mosquito

microbes

◀ YELLOW FEVER MOSQUITO
This tropical mosquito pierces human skin to feed on warm blood. It carries a virus that causes yellow fever, which is sometimes passed on as a mosquito feeds and can be fatal.

VIRUSES

Only a very powerful microscope can show the minute chemical package known as a virus. Many viruses cause disease. Viruses are active only once they have infected a living animal, plant, or bacterial cell.

HOW DO VIRUSES REPRODUCE?

A virus invades a living cell, hijacks its genes, and forces it to produce many new virus particles. These new particles then break out of the cell. Viruses are not regarded as living things because they cannot reproduce alone.

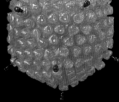

▲ COMMON COLD VIRUS
This is an adenovirus, one of the viruses that cause the common cold. Like all viruses, it consists of a thread, DNA or RNA, which carries the infection instructions. This is surrounded by a protective protein coat that can be seen here.

BACTERIA

LOUIS PASTEUR (1822–1895)
French scientist Louis Pasteur founded the science of microbiology. He proved that micro-organisms cause infectious diseases, developed vaccines, and discovered pasteurization (the heat-killing of bacteria in food).

The most abundant organisms on Earth, bacteria are found on land, in water, and in the air. Bacteria consist of one tiny cell. They have a protective cell wall, but, unlike other cells, lack a nucleus.

ARE ALL BACTERIA HARMFUL?

While some bacteria are harmful, such as those that cause diseases, others are useful. These include bacteria in our intestines that supply us with vitamins, those that are used to make foods, and soil bacteria that recycle nutrients from dead animals and plants.

Bacteria grouped together at the tip of a needle

BACTERIA ON NEEDLE ▶
This scanning electron micrograph (SEM) shows the tiny size of these rod-shaped bacteria (orange). They are clustered on the tip of a syringe needle, normally used for giving injections.

FIND OUT MORE ▸▸ Biology 72 • Cells 73 • Life on Earth 70–71

FUNGI

Neither plants nor animals, the fungi kingdom includes toadstools, puffballs, and ▶▶ MOULDS . Fungi feed on living or dead organisms by making them rot. Fungi are visible only when spore-bearing fruiting bodies form.

HOW DO FUNGI FEED?

Fungi absorb nutrients from plant or animal matter around them, which may be living or dead. They produce long, slender threads called hyphae that spread through their food. The hyphae release enzymes that break down the food into substances that the fungi can easily absorb.

HOW DO FUNGI REPRODUCE?

Most fungi reproduce by releasing tiny spores that then germinate (sprout) and grow into a new fungus. The spores are produced by, and released from, a fruiting body that is visible above the ground. Some fungi drop spores, which are blown away by the wind. Others shoot them out in an explosive burst.

ARE MUSHROOMS AND TOADSTOOLS THE SAME?

Toadstools are brightly coloured and poisonous to eat, but mushrooms are usually edible and dull in colour. Both toadstools and mushrooms are fruiting bodies (spore-bearing structures) produced by fungi. They belong to the same group, the Basidiomycetes, so scientists make no distinction between the two.

e ▶▶
fungi

DON'T EAT! ▶
The bright red colour of these fly agaric toadstool caps warns animals that they are poisonous. The caps, which are supported by stalks, produce spores. These spores are released from downward-hanging plates, or gills.

▲ PUFFBALL
When the puffball is mature, a hole forms in the top. The slightest knock then causes the puffball to shoot clouds of spores into the air.

FUNGI CLASSIFICATION

Scientists are continually revising the classification of the fungi kingdom (with more than 100,000 species), but currently they divide it into three groups:
• Pin moulds (Zygomycota);

• Yeasts, moulds, morels, and truffles (Ascomycota, or spore shooters);
• Smuts, rusts, jellies, mushrooms, and brackets (Basidiomycota, or spore droppers).

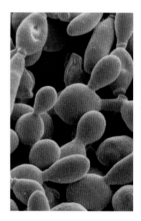

▲ BUDDING YEAST CELLS
Yeasts reproduce by budding. New cells grow out like bubbles from parent cells, then separate.

MOULDS

Fungi called moulds produce the woolly or furry growths found on rotting foods, such as bread and fruit. The growths are formed by thread-like hyphae that grow upwards and release spores from their tips. These spores then sprout on other foods.

IS MOULD USEFUL?

Some moulds are useful. *Penicillium*, for example, is a common blue mould that grows on fruit. It produces an antibiotic called penicillin, which is used to kill bacteria that cause harmful diseases. *Penicillium* moulds are also used to flavour some cheeses.

PENICILLIN TABLETS ▶
This dish shows bacteria growing on agar jelly. The white tablets contain penicillin. Clear areas around the tablets show where penicillin has killed some of the bacteria.

◀ BREAD MOULD
Pin moulds grow on starchy foods, such as bread, in a mass of grey hyphae with black tips that release spores. The spores float to other pieces of bread. Unseen here are hyphae growing into the bread and absorbing its nutrients.

FIND OUT MORE ▶▶ Micro-organisms 85 • Reproduction 101

ALGAE

Algae are plant-like organisms that make food by photosynthesis. All algae contain chlorophyll, which is green, but many are coloured brown or red by other pigments. Most algae live in water.

ARE ALGAE AND SEAWEED THE SAME THING?
All seaweeds are algae, but not all algae are seaweeds. Seaweeds are easily visible, made of many cells, and grow in the sea. There are red, brown, and green forms. Many algae, such as diatoms, are microscopic and consist of a single cell.

DIATOMS ►
These single-celled algae float in the surface waters of oceans and lakes. Each species has its own distinctively patterned, glass-like outer casing.

Air bladders keep fronds floating near sea's surface

DO ALGAE LIVE ONLY IN WATER?
Most species of algae live in the sea, in lakes, or in ponds. Some single-celled green algae live in moist conditions on land, such as on tree trunks, the surface of the soil, or on damp brickwork. Others live inside lichens.

◄ BLADDER WRACK
This seaweed, like many others, grows close to the seashore. Its leaf-like fronds are anchored to rocks by a root-like structure, or holdfast. Slimy mucus stops the fronds from drying out when they are exposed at low tide.

▲ RED SEAWEED
Smaller than other seaweeds, red seaweeds contain a pigment that lets them photosynthesize in the dim light of deeper waters.

BLADDER WRACK

algae

ALGAE CLASSIFICATION

40,000 species of plant-like organisms. Single-celled types:
• Golden algae • Yellow-green algae • Diatoms • Dinoflagellates.

Multicellular types:
• Brown seaweeds • Red seaweeds and green algae (both seaweeds and single-celled forms).

FIND OUT MORE ►► Life on Earth 70–71 • Micro-organisms 85

LICHENS

A lichen is not a single organism, but a combination of a fungus and a green alga. Lichens exist in extreme climates, from dry deserts to the icy Arctic. They grow on surfaces, such as rocks, bark, and soil.

lichens

FOLIOSE LICHEN

HOW DO FUNGI AND ALGAE LIVE IN LICHENS?
The fungus forms an outer layer that protects the alga beneath from drying out and from harmful amounts of light. The alga makes its own food by photosynthesis, and shares it with the fungus. In return, the fungus supplies the alga with essential minerals, such as nitrogen. This beneficial relationship between two different species is called symbiosis.

▲ REINDEER EATING LICHEN
In the cold, harsh conditions of the Arctic tundra, lichens are an important source of food for grazing reindeer. In winter, they reach lichens by scraping away snow with their hooves.

▲ LICHENS
Two of the three main types of lichen – fruticose (shrubby) and foliose (leafy) – are seen here growing on tree barks. The third type is crustose (flat and crusty).

FRUTICOSE LICHEN

FIND OUT MORE ►► Life on Earth 70–71

PLANTS

Plants are one of the five kingdoms of living things. They are made up of many cells and are usually rooted in soil. Their green leaves capture sunlight to make food by ▶▶ PHOTOSYNTHESIS , providing food either directly or indirectly for most other living things on Earth, as well as life-giving oxygen.

Leaf uses sunlight to make food for the seedling

GROWING PLANT ▶
An underground woodland scene reveals an oak seedling growing from a split acorn (oak seed). Although small, the seedling already shows the main features of a plant, including roots, a stem, buds, and leaves. Most species of plants, including flowering plants, grow from seeds. Each seed contains an embryo plant with its own food supply.

CAN PLANTS MOVE?

Plants cannot move around like animals, but they still show movements. Shoots grow, leaves turn towards the Sun. If a plant has flowers, they open and close. Climbing plants have fine tendrils, or stems, that reach out until they find something firm to grip onto.

WHICH ARE THE BIGGEST PLANTS?

Trees are the biggest of all plants. They grow so large because they are supported by a woody trunk that increases in width as the tree grows taller. The tallest tree, and the biggest living thing, is the Californian coast redwood, which reaches over 110 m (361 ft).

Leaf litter (dead leaves) rots on woodland floor and releases nutrients for plants

Stem supports the leaves, buds, and other parts above ground

Roots take in water and minerals for the growing oak seedling from the soil

Oak seed splits open as the embryo plant grows

PLANT CLASSIFICATION

So far, scientists have identified over 300,000 species of plants. These are divided into two groups:
• Plants that reproduce using spores, including mosses, ferns, horsetails, and four other phyla.
• Plants that reproduce using seeds, including flowering plants and conifers.

PHOTOSYNTHESIS

Animals have to find and eat food, but plants are able to make their own by using sunlight energy. This process, called photosynthesis, provides plants with the energy and raw materials for growth.

WHAT HAPPENS IN PHOTOSYNTHESIS?

The leaves of plants trap sunlight energy, which changes carbon dioxide gas and water into an energy-rich food called glucose. Glucose provides the plant with energy, and is also used to make substances such as cellulose, which builds the plant's cell walls.

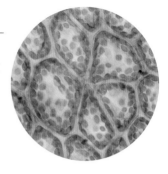

▲ CHLOROPLASTS
The green structures seen in this microscopic view of leaf cells are chloroplasts. They contain chlorophyll, a green pigment that traps sunlight energy.

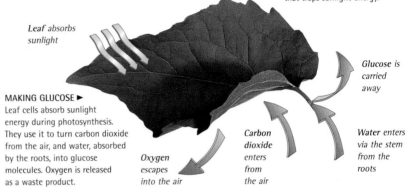

Leaf absorbs sunlight

MAKING GLUCOSE ▶
Leaf cells absorb sunlight energy during photosynthesis. They use it to turn carbon dioxide from the air, and water, absorbed by the roots, into glucose molecules. Oxygen is released as a waste product.

Glucose is carried away

Oxygen escapes into the air

Carbon dioxide enters from the air

Water enters via the stem from the roots

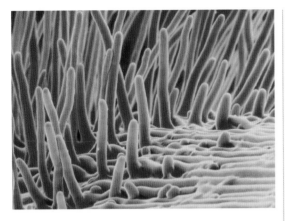

▲ ROOT HAIRS
Magnified 200 times here, root hairs are tiny projections from a plant's root. They provide a massive surface area through which the root can quickly and efficiently absorb essential water and minerals.

WHY DO PLANTS HAVE ROOTS?

Plants have roots for two main reasons. Roots anchor the plant in the soil, and prevent it being blown away by strong winds. They also take up water and minerals, such as nitrogen and sulphur, from the soil. Plants need water to replace that lost by ▶▶ TRANSPIRATION , and minerals to make substances essential for life.

HOW DO PLANTS DEFEND THEMSELVES?

Plants cannot escape from hungry plant-eaters, but they have evolved a wide range of defences. Some have thorns or spines that cut into an animal's skin, and will pierce its mouth if eaten. Others produce chemicals that taste terrible and may be very poisonous. Some have tiny hairs on their leaves that stop leaf-eating insects reaching the leaf's surface.

TRANSPIRATION

Leaves constantly lose water by evaporation through tiny pores, or stomata, that also let carbon dioxide into, and oxygen out of, the leaf. This water loss, called transpiration, creates a force that helps draw up more water from the roots.

WHAT IS THE VASCULAR SYSTEM?

Water and nutrients are moved through a plant by its vascular system. This consists of two types of microscopic tubes – xylem and phloem. Xylem carries water and minerals from the roots to the rest of the plant. Phloem carries nutrients, such as glucose, from where they are made to other parts of the plant.

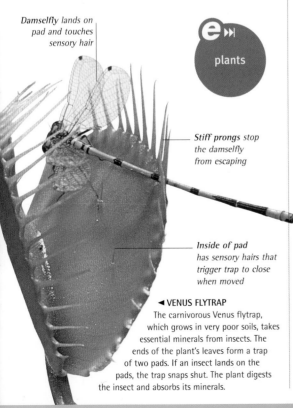

Damselfly lands on pad and touches sensory hair

e ▶▶ plants

Stiff prongs stop the damselfly from escaping

Inside of pad has sensory hairs that trigger trap to close when moved

◀ VENUS FLYTRAP
The carnivorous Venus flytrap, which grows in very poor soils, takes essential minerals from insects. The ends of the plant's leaves form a trap of two pads. If an insect lands on the pads, the trap snaps shut. The plant digests the insect and absorbs its minerals.

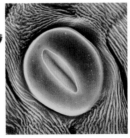

▲ STOMA AT NIGHT
Seen in microscopic view, this stoma (pore) in the leaf's surface is surrounded by two guard cells. At night, these guard cells close the stoma.

▲ STOMA IN DAYLIGHT
During the day, the guard cells open the stoma. This lets carbon dioxide enter the leaf and water vapour escape during transpiration.

PINEAPPLE SAGE

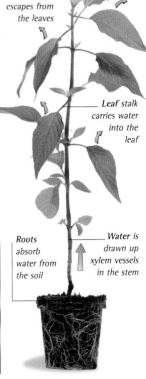

Water escapes from the leaves

Leaf stalk carries water into the leaf

Roots absorb water from the soil

Water is drawn up xylem vessels in the stem

▲ TRANSPIRATION STREAM
Water lost from leaves by transpiration is replaced by water from the roots. An unbroken column of water flows from the roots up to the leaves.

FIND OUT MORE ▶▶ Flowering Plants 92–93 • Non-Flowering Plants 90–91 • Trees 94–95

NON-FLOWERING PLANTS

Mosses, ferns, and their relatives are plants that do not produce flowers but reproduce by means of ▸▸ SPORES . Most live in shady or damp habitats. ▸▸ CONIFERS are non-flowering plants that reproduce by making seeds.

Sporophyte releases spores that grow into a new moss

HOW DO FERNS GROW?

The stem, or rhizome, of a fern grows horizontally through the soil. Tiny curled-up fronds (leaves) grow from small buds on the rhizome. The buds unroll and the frond expands. The fronds of some ferns grow 6 m (20 ft) long – others reach only 13 mm ($\frac{1}{2}$ in).

HOW DOES MOSS LIVE WITHOUT ROOTS?

Most mosses grow in short clumps or cushions. They do not have true roots, but short, slender growths, called rhizoids. Root-like rhizoids anchor moss to soil, rock, or bark, but do not draw up water. Instead, leaves absorb moisture in the air.

TREE FERN ▶
Dicksonia antarctica is a large tree fern that grows on cool, shady forest floors in Australia. Tree ferns have a large, fibrous trunk, topped with a crown of fronds (leaves). This species can grow 1–3 m (3–10 ft) tall.

Young bud unfurls into a frond, or branched leaf

e ▸▸
nonflowering plants

◀ LIVERWORT
This plant is closely related to mosses, and is found only in moist habitats. It grows on soil, trees, and wet rocks. The leaves of some species have a waxy coating to reduce water loss.

▲ **MOSS REPRODUCTION**
The leafy tips of mosses produce male and female sex cells. Male sex cells swim through water on the surface of the plant to reach and fertilize female cells. Fertilization produces a stalked sporophyte, or spore capsule, that scatters spores into the air.

Tree fern fronds can grow 1.5–2.5 m (5–8 ft) long

CLASSIFICATION OF NON-FLOWERING PLANTS

There are 11 main phyla of non-flowering plants:
• Liverworts • Mosses
• Hornworts • Whisk ferns
• Clubmosses • Horsetails

• Ferns • Conifers • Cycads
• Ginkgo • Gnetophytes.
The last four form a group called gymnosperms – they produce seeds instead of spores.

SPORES

Non-flowering plants reproduce by releasing large numbers of tiny spores. These minute organisms consist of one or a few cells inside a tough coat.

WHY IS SPORE DISPERSAL IMPORTANT?

Many non-flowering plants rely on wind to carry their reproductive spores as far away as possible. This reduces competition with the parent plant for light, water, and important nutrients. If a spore lands in a damp place, it germinates (sprouts) and grows into a new plant.

FERN SPORES ▶
Fern spores develop in protective caps called sori (singular sorus). Sori are attached to the underside of fronds. Large ferns make and release millions of spores each year.

Sorus

INSIDE A SORUS ▶
Each sorus contains a cluster of spore-producing sporangia. In dry conditions, sporangia open and scatter their spores.

Sporangium

CONIFERS

Trees and shrubs whose seeds develop in woody cones are called conifers. The 550 species include pines, firs, and cedars. Conifers form dense forests in colder, northern regions. Most keep their leaves all year long.

▲ PINE FOREST
The branches of pines and many other conifers slope downwards. This helps winter snows to slide off, preventing damage to the tree.

▲ STONE PINE CONE
Seeds mature inside the female cone, protected by its scales. In warm, dry conditions, the cone opens to release its seeds.

PINE SEEDS

HOW DO CONIFERS PRODUCE SEEDS?
Conifers have male and female cones. The male cones release pollen grains (male sex cells), which are blown by the wind. If pollen lands on the female cones, it fertilizes the female egg cells. The fertilized eggs develop into seeds. After one or two years, when the seeds have matured, the female cone opens up. It drops winged seeds, which germinate wherever they land.

WHY DO SOME CONIFERS HAVE NEEDLE-SHAPED LEAVES?
Leaves shaped like needles help conifers survive in cold, harsh climates. The leaves are tough and coated with a waxy outer coat, or cuticle. The narrow shape, toughness, and cuticles all help the leaves withstand high winds and extreme temperatures. They also reduce water loss.

DO OTHER PLANTS HAVE CONES?
A group of plants called cycads have large seed-producing cones that can grow to more than 55 cm (22 in) long. They have stout trunks topped by long, divided leaves, and look more like palm trees than conifers. Cycads grow in tropical and subtropical regions. They are descended from a group of plants that flourished 250 million years ago. Today, there are 140 species of cycads.

Male cones are soft, and drop off after shedding pollen

SCOTS PINE ►
Pine trees, like most conifers, are evergreen and keep their leaves throughout the year. The long, spiky needles stay on the tree for at least two years.

Female cones are woody, and open to release their seeds

FIND OUT MORE ▶▶ Climate 62–63 • Habitats 82–84 • Plants 88–89 • Trees 94–95

FLOWERING PLANTS

This is the most abundant and widespread group of plants on Earth. Flowering plants are found in most habitats from deserts to polar regions, and include species of trees, shrubs, and herbs. The flowers are the reproductive structures that produce new plants.

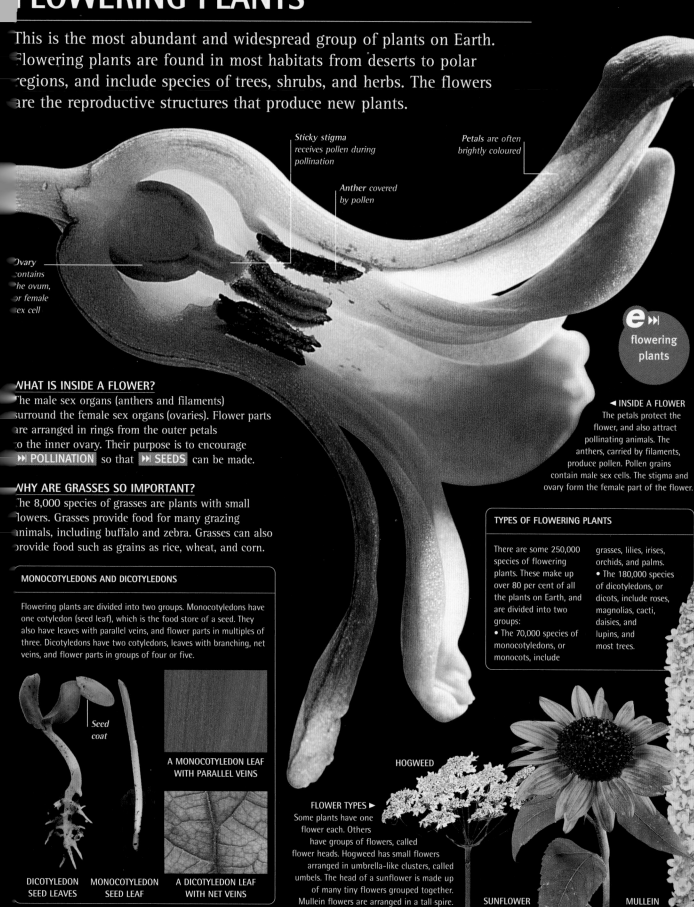

Sticky stigma receives pollen during pollination

Anther covered by pollen

Petals are often brightly coloured

Ovary contains the ovum, or female sex cell

flowering plants

WHAT IS INSIDE A FLOWER?

The male sex organs (anthers and filaments) surround the female sex organs (ovaries). Flower parts are arranged in rings from the outer petals to the inner ovary. Their purpose is to encourage ▶▶ POLLINATION so that ▶▶ SEEDS can be made.

WHY ARE GRASSES SO IMPORTANT?

The 8,000 species of grasses are plants with small flowers. Grasses provide food for many grazing animals, including buffalo and zebra. Grasses can also provide food such as grains as rice, wheat, and corn.

◄ INSIDE A FLOWER
The petals protect the flower, and also attract pollinating animals. The anthers, carried by filaments, produce pollen. Pollen grains contain male sex cells. The stigma and ovary form the female part of the flower.

TYPES OF FLOWERING PLANTS

There are some 250,000 species of flowering plants. These make up over 80 per cent of all the plants on Earth, and are divided into two groups:
• The 70,000 species of monocotyledons, or monocots, include grasses, lilies, irises, orchids, and palms.
• The 180,000 species of dicotyledons, or dicots, include roses, magnolias, cacti, daisies, and lupins, and most trees.

MONOCOTYLEDONS AND DICOTYLEDONS

Flowering plants are divided into two groups. Monocotyledons have one cotyledon (seed leaf), which is the food store of a seed. They also have leaves with parallel veins, and flower parts in multiples of three. Dicotyledons have two cotyledons, leaves with branching, net veins, and flower parts in groups of four or five.

Seed coat

A MONOCOTYLEDON LEAF WITH PARALLEL VEINS

DICOTYLEDON SEED LEAVES

MONOCOTYLEDON SEED LEAF

A DICOTYLEDON LEAF WITH NET VEINS

HOGWEED

FLOWER TYPES ▶
Some plants have one flower each. Others have groups of flowers, called flower heads. Hogweed has small flowers arranged in umbrella-like clusters, called umbels. The head of a sunflower is made up of many tiny flowers grouped together. Mullein flowers are arranged in a tall spire.

SUNFLOWER

MULLEIN

The transfer of pollen from a male anther to a female stigma is called pollination. If male and female sex cells from the same species come together, fertilization takes place and seeds are made. Pollination occurs in various ways, such as by wind or by animals.

◄ INSECT POLLINATION
Yellow pollen sticks to this bee's legs as it feeds on nectar. It will be passed to the next flower it visits.

WHAT IS NECTAR?
Many flowers attract pollinating animals with a sweet, sugary liquid called nectar. If an animal feeds on the nectar, it picks up pollen and carries it to other flowers that it lands on.

WHAT IS WIND POLLINATION?
Pollination in some flowers occurs when pollen is blown from other flowers by the wind. Animal-pollinated flowers, are strongly scented and brightly coloured, but the flowers of wind-pollinated plants, such as grasses, are often small, with no petals.

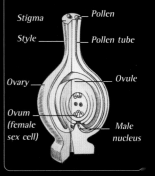

FERTILIZATION

When a pollen grain lands on a stigma of the same species, it grows a tube into the ovule (seed-forming structure). A male sex cell travels down the pollen tube and fertilizes the ovum (female sex cell) to produce an embryo plant.

Stigma — Pollen

Style — Pollen tube

Ovary — Ovule

Ovum (female sex cell) — Male nucleus

◄ POLLEN GRAIN
The spikes on this pollen grain help it stick to animals. Each grain contains the male sex cell, which fertilizes the female ovum.

SEEDS

If fertilization occurs in a flowering plant, a seed forms inside the flower's ovary. The seed consists of a tiny embryo plant, a food store for the embryo, and a protective coat.

WHAT IS A FRUIT?
As the seeds of plants develop, the ovary surrounding the seed develops into a fruit, such as an apple or a peapod. Fruits protect seeds, and help disperse them away from the parent plant so that new plants have enough water and light to grow.

First leaves make food using sunlight energy

◄ WIND DISPERSAL
Dandelion seeds hang from parachute-like fruit. When blown by the wind, the parachutes float off into the air and carry the seeds far from the parent plant.

BEAN SEEDLING ►
Just a few days after germination, the bean seedling's roots have grown down into the soil, and its shoot has grown upwards towards the Sun.

Seed

Roots take in water and minerals from the soil

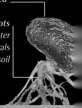

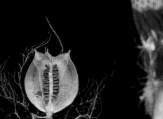

RASPBERRY   LOVE-IN-A-MIST

◄ SEED DISPERSAL IN FRUIT
The seeds of juicy fruits, such as raspberries, are dispersed in droppings of fruit-eating animals. The seeds of dry fruits, such as love-in-the-mist, are spread by wind, by sticking to animal coats, or by the fruit bursting open.

WHAT IS GERMINATION?
The first growth stage of an embryo plant from a seed is called germination. When there is enough sunlight and water, the seed germinates (sprouts), and the embryo plant starts to grow. Until it develops leaves, the seedling depends on the seed's food store.

FIND OUT MORE ▶▶ Life on Earth 70–71 • Non-Flowering Plants 90–91• Plants 88–89 • Trees 94–95

TREES

These tall, seed-producing plants have a single woody stem, called a trunk, that supports their great weight. They live for many years and do not die in winter. The largest group of trees is broad-leaved trees.

WHY ARE TREES SO IMPORTANT?

Trees release oxygen into the atmosphere for other organisms to breathe in. The roots of trees bind soil together, preventing it from being washed away. Trees also provide food and habitats for many animals, and wood for fuel, timber, and many other products.

HOW DO TREES GROW?

Trees grow in two ways. Special cells at the tips of twigs divide, making the twigs grow. Also, a layer of cells under the bark, the cambium, divides, widening the trunk and branches. The new cells that the cambium makes form a visible ring inside the trunk.

WHAT ARE BROAD-LEAVED TREES?

Unlike conifers, with their needle-shaped leaves, these trees have wide, flat leaves. Many are **▸▸ DECIDUOUS TREES** that lose their leaves in autumn, but the broad-leaved trees of a tropical rainforest are evergreen. The mass of leaves of adjacent trees form a **▸▸ CANOPY**.

▲ EVERGREEN RAINFOREST
The Amazon rainforest is the largest in the world. It contains about one-fifth of all flowering plant species.

Heartwood contains mostly dead cells

Sapwood is made up of living cells and carries water and minerals

Growth ring indicates one year's growth

Cambium

Phloem carries food up or down the trunk

Fibrous bark consists of dead cells and protects the trunk

e ▸▸ trees

INDIAN BEAN TREE (SIMPLE LEAF)

HERCULES CLUB (COMPOUND LEAF)

▲ TYPES OF LEAF
Broad-leaved trees have one of two types of leaves. A simple leaf is undivided and has its own leaf stalk. A compound leaf is divided up into several smaller leaflets that are attached to the main leaf stalk.

◄ TREE TRUNK CROSS-SECTION
The inside of a tree trunk has rings of outer sapwood and inner heartwood. Both consist of strength-giving cells called xylem. Sapwood xylem also carries water and minerals up the tree. Outside the sapwood are phloem cells, which carry food, surrounded by bark.

TREE CLASSIFICATION

Trees are divided into three groups: broad-leaved trees, palms, and conifers.
• Broad-leaved trees are the largest group, with over 10,000 species. They are dicotyledon flowering plants, and the veins in their leaves branch out like a net.
• Palm trees, with about 2,800 species, are monocotyledon flowering plants. The veins in their leaves are always parallel.
• Conifers, with 550 species, have cones instead of flowers.

DECIDUOUS TREES

Trees that lose their leaves in the autumn are called deciduous. They grow in temperate places that have warm summers and cool or cold winters.

WHY DO THESE TREES SHED THEIR LEAVES?
When trees shed their leaves they stop growing. This helps them conserve energy during winter, when there is not enough sunlight to make food. Shedding leaves also helps trees conserve water as it stops water evaporating from them.

WHY DO DECIDUOUS LEAVES CHANGE COLOUR?
In summer, these leaves are packed with the green pigment (colouring) chlorophyll, which captures sunlight energy. In autumn, chlorophyll breaks down and is reabsorbed by the tree, revealing previously hidden pigments, such as reds, yellows, and oranges.

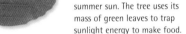

CHANGING LEAF COLOUR ▶
The leaves of deciduous trees turn from green to orange, yellow, or red with the coming of autumn, or in very dry weather conditions.

PERSIAN IRONWOOD LEAVES

Sunlight filters through to reach the forest floor

Palm tree has broad, branched leaves

▲ DECIDUOUS TREE IN SUMMER
This lime tree is bathed in summer sun. The tree uses its mass of green leaves to trap sunlight energy to make food.

DECIDUOUS TREE IN AUTUMN ▲
In autumn, temperatures are lower and there is less daylight. The lime tree's leaves turn orange or brown and start to fall.

CANOPY

The upper part of the trees in any forest or woodland is called the canopy. It is made up of their branches, twigs, and leaves. Tropical rainforest trees form a dense canopy that is home to many animals.

WHY ARE RAINFOREST TREES SO TALL?
In hot, steamy rainforests, the tightly packed trees grow rapidly and to great heights. This is because they are all competing for sunlight. The taller the tree, the more light its leaves will receive. Some trees can reach heights of up to 60 m (197 ft).

WHAT IS AN EPIPHYTE?
An epiphyte is a plant that grows on a larger one without harming it. Many epiphytes live high up in the rainforest canopy, firmly anchored by their roots to tree trunks and branches. In the canopy, epiphytes receive much more light than the plants on the forest floor, and more rain water.

◀ REACH FOR THE SUN
This is the view that someone standing on the rainforest floor would see when looking upwards. A palm tree in the shrub layer uses its large leaves to trap sparse sunlight filtering down through the canopy above.

LAYERS OF A RAINFOREST

Rainforests are made up of distinct layers. In the emergent layer, the very tallest trees stick out from the canopy. Beneath the canopy is an understorey of smaller trees and a shrub layer of big-leaved plants that can live in low-light conditions. Below this is the dark forest floor, where there are fewer, smaller plants.

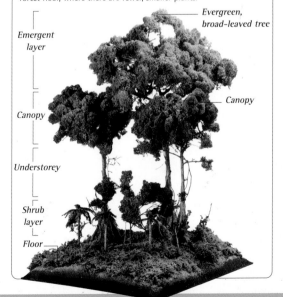

Emergent layer

Canopy

Understorey

Shrub layer

Floor

Evergreen, broad-leaved tree

Canopy

FIND OUT MORE ▶▶ Flowering Plants 92–93 • Non-Flowering Plants 90–91 • Plants 88–89

ANIMALS

Animals are grouped into two main types – vertebrates with an inner skeleton, including a backbone, and invertebrates, without a backbone. As many as ten million species (different kinds) of animals – all with their own modes of ▶ BEHAVIOUR – live on Earth.

WHICH FEATURES DO ALL ANIMALS HAVE IN COMMON?
All animals have bodies made up of many different cells and eat other organisms to survive. Unlike plants or fungi, which are rooted in one place, animals move about to find food, escape from enemies, and find a mate. Almost all animals breathe oxygen, either from the air or from water.

WHAT IS THE WORLD'S FASTEST ANIMAL?
The world's fastest animal is the peregrine falcon, which can exceed 200 km/h (124 mph) when diving through the air after prey. The fastest-powered flight is that of the spine-tailed swift. It travels at up to 170 km/h (106 mph). The quickest animal in water is the sailfish, which can swim at up to 109 km/h (68 mph).

WHAT ARE WARM-BLOODED ANIMALS?
Warm-blooded animals are those that generate their own body heat from food. Birds and mammals are warm-blooded. All other animals, including fish, reptiles, amphibians, and insects, are cold-blooded. Their body temperatures rise and fall with the temperature of their surroundings. These animals are less active in cold weather but require less food.

HOW BIG DO ANIMALS GROW?
Some animals grow to enormous sizes. The world's biggest animal, the blue whale, may reach 28 m (92 ft) long and weigh almost 150 tonnes (147 tons). On the other hand, some animals are too small to be seen with the naked eye. The world's tiniest animals are creatures called mesozoans. They consist of fewer than 50 cells and measure just 0.5 mm ($\frac{1}{50}$ in) in length.

▲ CHAMELEON
A chameleon is camouflaged to blend in with its surroundings and moves around slowly to avoid detection by its predators and prey. To feed, the chameleon shoots out its tongue at a lightning-fast speed to hit insects before they have time to react.

e ▶▶ animals

CHEETAHS ▶
The cheetah is the world's fastest land animal, capable of speeds of up to 96 km/h (60 mph) in short bursts. It hunts by ambush, creeping as close as it can to its prey before rushing in for the kill.

Muscles drive the animal forward after prey

Long legs increase stride and speed

▲ COLD SHOWER
The Asian elephant is the world's second-largest land animal (the African elephant is the largest). Like all mammals, it is warm-blooded. Due to their size, elephants can have trouble keeping cool. One solution is to seek water. Elephants also flap their ears to cool the blood flowing through them.

◀ WORKING TOGETHER
Leaf-cutter ants live in colonies of closely related individuals, all hatched from eggs laid by a single queen. Most become worker ants.

BEHAVIOUR

In order to survive, all animals must eat and avoid being eaten. They are also driven to reproduce so their species does not die out. Most animal behaviour is geared to these basic goals. Some behaviour is learned, the rest is controlled by instinct.

HOW DO ANIMALS DEFEND THEMSELVES?
Animals behave in many different ways to escape danger. Some are camouflaged to blend in with their surroundings. Behaviour such as keeping still completes their disguise. Some species defend themselves with more complex behaviour, such as pretending to be injured or dead. Hedgehogs and armadillos roll into a ball to ward off predators.

HOW IMPORTANT IS INSTINCT?
Instinct plays a major part in the behaviour of animals, especially animals that are not reared by their parents. For example, when danger threatens, snails instinctively withdraw inside their shells. Animals also learn by trial and error, repeating actions that are productive and abandoning ones that are not.

▼ IMPRINTING
Baby birds such as goslings (young geese) instinctively follow the first animal they see after hatching. This is usually their own mother, but goslings have also been known to waddle around after humans and dogs.

▲ PUFFERFISH
Pufferfish defend themselves by inflating their bodies with water. Along with their spines, this makes them harder for bigger fish to swallow. Many other species are also covered with spines to protect them from even the largest of predators.

WHY DO ANIMALS FOLLOW REGULAR CYCLES?
All animals follow regular cycles to help them survive. Many creatures are active by day, when their senses work best. Others come out at night to avoid predators, or take advantage of feeding opportunities. Most animals also follow yearly cycles, usually bearing young when food is abundant.

CLOWNFISH ▶
Clownfish hide from their enemies among the stinging tentacles of sea anemones. The fish's skin releases chemicals that stop the anemone's cells from firing. Clownfish are found in tropical seas around the world.

FIND OUT MORE ▶▶ Biology 72 • Life on Earth 70–71

FEEDING

All animals must eat other organisms to survive. Animals can be divided into two main groups, according to their feeding habits: ▶ **CARNIVORES** (meat-eaters) and ▶ **HERBIVORES** (plant-eaters).

WHAT IS AN OMNIVORE?

Most animals eat either meat or plants, but omnivores eat both. The word omnivore means "everything-eater". Bears and pigs are omnivores – so are humans. In our diet we carry on the traditions of our early ancestors, who killed game and also gathered berries and nuts.

GRIZZLY BEAR ▶
Bears eat many foods, including fruit, nuts, roots, honey, carrion (dead animals), small mammals, and salmon swimming upriver, as shown here.

WHAT IS FILTER-FEEDING?

This feeding method works by sifting large amounts of small organisms from water. It is a bit like using a sieve to catch prey. Filter-feeders come in a variety of shapes and sizes – barnacles, flamingos, and baleen whales (including the blue whale) all feed in this way.

◀ SCAVENGERS
Hyenas and vultures are scavengers – meat-eaters that get their food from the abandoned kills of others. This zebra was killed by lions, which have already eaten their fill and left.

e ▶▶
feeding

CARNIVORES

Most carnivores are predators – animals that hunt other animals for food. Predators usually have sharp teeth, claws, or beaks to tear apart their prey. Animal flesh is nourishing, so predators do not have to kill very often. It is also easy to digest.

HOW DO PREDATORS KILL THEIR PREY?

Top predators such as lions, sharks, and eagles rely on strength and speed to overcome their victims. Smaller or weaker hunters may rely on stealth or special techniques to capture prey. Some predators, such as wolves, hunt in packs. Spiders spin webs to tangle up victims. Rattlesnakes kill their prey with venom.

TOOTHY GRIN ▶
A shark's teeth are sharp and pointed to rip prey to pieces. They grow in rows and are continually shed and replaced. Some species may get through as many as 30,000 teeth in a lifetime. Not all sharks are predators – the largest, the whale shark, is a filter-feeder.

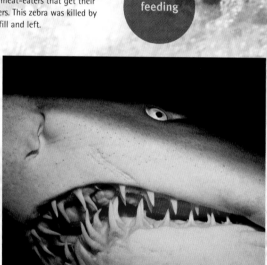

HERBIVORES

The jaws, teeth, and stomachs of herbivores are designed to tackle tough plant food. Compared with meat, plants are not very nourishing, so many herbivores spend long hours feeding.

Toucan's bill is extra-large for probing through vegetation

◀ TOUCAN
Some birds, such as the toucan, specialize in eating fruit. Packed with sugars, fruit is much more nourishing than leaves and far easier to digest. However, it is also more scattered and harder to find. Many fruit-eating birds sometimes have to eat insects. It is only in tropical rainforests that birds can find fruit all year round.

HOW DO HERBIVORES DIGEST THEIR FOOD?

Plants contain tough cellulose, which is hard to digest. Many herbivores' stomachs are filled with microbes, which break down cellulose. Some plant-eaters, such as cattle, have stomachs with several chambers. After passing through some chambers, food is returned to the mouth for more chewing to help break it down.

HOW DO HERBIVORES AVOID CARNIVORES?

Herbivores do not need quick wits to capture their food, but they must be swift or have some means of defence to avoid being eaten by predators. Many are camouflaged to blend in with their surroundings, so that hunters do not notice them. Others have tough skin, spines, or even poison to put off enemies.

FIND OUT MORE ▶▶ Digestion 144–145 • Plants 88–89 • Teeth 143

SENSES

Animals use their senses to find out about the world around them. Most have the same five senses as humans, but some have extra senses, such as ▸ ECHOLOCATION.

DO ANIMALS HAVE BETTER SENSES THAN US?
Many animals have far keener senses than humans. Sight is our most important sense, but birds such as falcons have much sharper vision. Some insects can detect ultraviolet light, which we cannot see. A bloodhound's nose is many times more sensitive than a human's. Bats, whales, and elephants can detect very high or low sounds that we cannot hear.

Nostrils pick up scent to lead cat to prey

Whiskers enable the cat to feel movement even in total darkness

NIGHT PROWLER ▲
Many nocturnal predators, including cats, have a reflective layer at the back of their eyes, which helps to gather light.

CAN ANIMALS SEE AT NIGHT?
Some animals can see quite clearly at night even when there is no moon. The large eyes of nocturnal hunters, such as owls, are designed to make the most of very dim light. Many animals active at night also have extremely good senses of hearing and smell.

Lens focuses light on to sensitive cells to help form a clear image

Antenna detects scent particles floating in the air

◀ COMPOUND EYES
Insects such as flies have huge compound eyes made up of many lenses. Each lens may be used to build up a larger picture.

WHICH ANIMALS HAVE EXTRA SENSES?
Some aquatic animals, including sharks, can pick up tiny electrical signals given off by their prey. It is believed that many migratory animals can detect the Earth's magnetic field to help find their way.

e ▸▸
senses

Hair-like projections increase the sense of touch

Forked tongue picks up scent particles

TASTING THE AIR ▶
Snakes pick up scent particles in the air with their flickering tongues. These reptiles do not have ears, but their sensitive skin can detect vibrations passing through the ground.

Heat-sensitive pits work like extra eyes

SEEING WITH SOUND ▶
Insect-eating bats have very sensitive hearing that allows them to hunt and navigate in darkness using echolocation. They make high-pitched sounds then swivel their ears to pinpoint the source of echoes, which lead them to their prey.

ECHOLOCATION

Bats, whales, and dolphins, which hunt in darkness or murky water, make sounds then listen for echoes to track their prey. The same technique helps them to navigate and avoid collisions with objects.

HOW DOLPHINS USE ECHOLOCATION TO FIND FOOD

Sounds bounce back off fish

Dolphin sends out click sounds to locate prey

Dolphin picks up returning echoes from prey ahead

HOW DOES ECHOLOCATION HELP WITH HUNTING?
Hunting bats and dolphins make streams of clicking sounds, which spread out through the air or water. The sound vibrations bounce back off objects such as flying insects or shoaling fish. The hunter uses its keen hearing to listen out for the returning echoes. These allow it to pinpoint the whereabouts of its victims, so that it can home in on its prey.

Moths and other insects make up most bat prey

FIND OUT MORE ▸▸ Ear 141 • Eye 140 • Mouth 142 • Nose 143

COMMUNICATION

Animals communicate with their own kind or other species to coordinate the search for food, attract mates, bring up young, or escape from danger. Various species send signals using sight, sounds, body language, touch, scent, complex chemicals, or a combination of all of these.

WHEN DO ANIMALS USE VISUAL SIGNALS?

Close-range visual signals are used to send a variety of messages, such as "Food is near" or "Keep away!" Birds from peacocks to robins attract mates using bright colours. Fireflies do the same with light. The white flash of a fleeing rabbit's tail warns others of danger.

WHY DO ANIMALS COMMUNICATE WITH SOUND?

Sound signals carry over considerable distances and give information immediately. Songbirds and howler monkeys call to establish territories. Whales, frogs, and crickets sing to attract a mate. Vervet monkeys warn others of different enemies by using different sounds.

▲ **SNAKE MIMIC**
Visual signals can be used for defence. This hawkmoth caterpillar has evolved a tail that looks like a snake's head. Predators are scared off by the disguise, even though the caterpillar is harmless.

communication

DO ANIMALS ALWAYS TELL THE TRUTH?

When animals communicate with their enemies, their messages are not always truthful. Dogs, cats, and other animals raise their hackles, arch their backs, or puff themselves up to look bigger. Opossums play dead to fool their enemies. Some animals mimic (copy) the appearance of dangerous creatures.

WHY DO ANIMALS USE PHEROMONES?

Animals use scent signals called pheromones to affect the behaviour of others. These complex chemicals, which include hormones, are most often transferred by air. Female moths release pheromones to attract males. In ant, bee, and termite colonies, the queen releases pheromones to convey all sorts of messages to the rest of the colony.

▲ **BODY LANGUAGE**
A wolf can give over 20 different messages by raising or flattening its ears, back, tail, and neck hairs, or by baring or hiding its teeth.

◀ **COMPLEX COMMUNICATION**
Intelligent mammals such as chimpanzees communicate with others using sounds, scent, touch, body language, and facial expressions. Chimps can even be taught to communicate with humans using sign language.

▲ **CHEMICAL CONTROL**
Pheromones released by a queen bee prevent other fertile females from developing. If the queen goes missing and the pheromones are no longer released, new queens are reared. One of these will eventually take over the hive.

FIND OUT MORE ▸▸ Senses 99 • Sound 176–177

REPRODUCTION

All animals produce offspring so their species can continue. Some animals reproduce sexually, by mating with a partner; others reproduce asexually, without mating. Animals grow up in different ways, including by ▸▸ **METAMORPHOSIS** . Care of offspring varies – some young fend for themselves.

Snake egg has leathery, waterproof shell

Baby snake looks like tiny version of the adult

PUMA FAMILY ▼

BORN INDEPENDENT ▲
Young snakes are on their own from the moment they hatch. Snakes lay large numbers of eggs so that at least some of their offspring make it to adulthood.

reproduction

HOW DO ANIMALS ATTRACT MATES?
During the breeding season, animals advertise their readiness to mate by using special calls, scents, and other signals. Some animals use elaborate displays or courtship rituals to woo a wary mate. A few creatures, such as earthworms, are hermaphrodite (both male and female), which makes it easier to find a mate.

Female mammals look after their young and feed them on a rich, nutritious food – milk. Some mammal babies take only a few weeks to grow up. Puma cubs stay with their mother for two years, learning how to hunt for themselves.

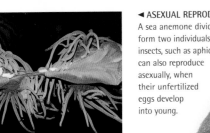

◄ ASEXUAL REPRODUCTION
A sea anemone divides to form two individuals. Some insects, such as aphids, can also reproduce asexually, when their unfertilized eggs develop into young.

WHY DO SOME ANIMALS GIVE BIRTH RATHER THAN LAY EGGS?
Animals born live are more likely to survive than those that hatch out of eggs. While developing inside their mother, babies are at less risk of being eaten than eggs.

WHY LOOK AFTER YOUNG?
Animals care for offspring to improve their chances of survival. More of these babies survive to adulthood than those whose parents leave them to fend for themselves.

4. New adult emerges after one week

1. Adult 7-spot ladybird lays groups of eggs on leaves

▲ LADYBIRD LIFE CYCLE
Like all beetles, ladybirds go through complete metamorphosis, changing directly from their larval to their adult form.

3. Dormant (sleeping) pupa formed by each larva a month after hatching

2. Larva hatches after a week

METAMORPHOSIS

Some baby animals are miniature copies of their adult relatives, but some look nothing like their parents. They go through an amazing transformation, known as a metamorphosis, before they reach adulthood.

WHAT IS COMPLETE METAMORPHOSIS?
Complete metamorphosis is the change in one step from larva to adult. Moths and butterflies undergo complete metamorphosis. Their caterpillars feed and grow, then enter a resting stage as pupae. Inside the pupal case, the caterpillar transforms into a winged adult. The way tadpoles become frogs is also complete metamorphosis.

Emerging dragonfly breaking out of its old skin

Empty case left behind on plant stem

EMERGING DRAGONFLY ►
Young dragonflies shed their skin several times as they grow, emerging from their last moult as adults. Gradual change like this is called incomplete metamorphosis.

FIND OUT MORE ▸▸ Amphibians 114–115 • Insects 110–111 • Mammals 120–123

INVERTEBRATES

About 95 per cent of all animals are invertebrates – animals without bones – and many are tiny or even microscopic.

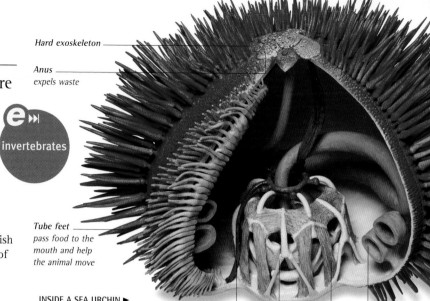

Hard exoskeleton

Anus
expels waste

e ▸▸
invertebrates

HOW DO ANIMALS SURVIVE WITHOUT BONES?

Insects, crustaceans, and many other invertebrates have a hard outer case called an exoskeleton. This protects them against knocks and predators, and prevents them drying out. Slugs, leeches, and jellyfish have soft bodies and no exoskeleton. The pressure of fluids inside their bodies maintains their shape.

Tube feet
pass food to the mouth and help the animal move

DO INVERTEBRATES' EXOSKELETONS GROW?

The hard exoskeletons of insects and creatures such as crabs do not grow with the rest of the body. As the animal grows, its exoskeleton gets too tight – so it sheds it from time to time. Underneath is a new, slightly bigger, and looser case. The animal pumps itself up with fluid before the case has time to harden.

INSIDE A SEA URCHIN ▶
Like most invertebrates, sea urchins have relatively complex internal organs. Food is broken down using five teeth contained in a central structure known as Aristotle's lantern, before passing into the intestine.

Haemal system
transports blood around the body

Tooth

Muscles
operate the movement of the teeth

Intestine
digests food

▼ INVERTEBRATE GROUPS
Invertebrates include more than 30 different phyla (major groups) of animals. Some of the most important ones are shown here.

ECHINODERMS
6,000 species include starfish, sea urchins, and sea cucumbers.

CNIDARIANS
10,000 species include corals, sea anemones, and jellyfish.

SPONGES
10,000 species include tube sponges and glass sponges.

INSECTS
800,000 species include beetles, flies, and ants.

MOLLUSCS
70,000 species include slugs, snails, mussels, and squid.

ANNELID WORMS
9,000 species include earthworms and leeches.

FIND OUT MORE ▸▸ Crustaceans 109 • Insects 110–111 • Molluscs 106

VERTEBRATES

All vertebrates have an inner skeleton, including a skull, backbone, and ribs. These complex animals vary in size from less than 1 cm (²/₅ in) to over 30 m (100 ft) long.

e ▸▸
vertebrates

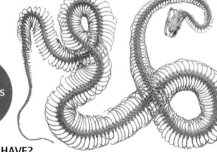

WHAT DOES THE SKELETON DO?

The skeleton is a strong frame that supports the body and anchors the muscles. Bones such as ribs protect the heart and other delicate parts, and the skull shields the brain. Most vertebrates have bony skeletons, but shark skeletons are rubbery cartilage.

HOW MANY LIMBS DO VERTEBRATES HAVE?

Most vertebrates apart from fish have four limbs. In birds and bats, the front limbs evolved (developed) into wings for flying. A fish's limbs are its fins, which vary in number between species. Snakes evolved from four-legged ancestors millions of years ago.

▲ PYTHON SKELETON
Like all vertebrates, snakes have a skull, backbone, and ribs. The backbone is made of many individual bones called vertebrae.

▼ VERTEBRATE GROUPS
Fish are the largest vertebrate group, with more species than all the other groups put together.

REPTILES
6,000 species include crocodiles, lizards, snakes, and turtles.

BIRDS
9,000 species include eagles, gulls, parrots, ducks, and perching birds.

MAMMALS
4,500 species include rodents, bats, whales, and primates.

AMPHIBIANS
4,000 species include frogs, toads, newts, and salamanders.

FISH
26,000 species include bony fish, sharks, rays, hagfish, and lampreys.

FIND OUT MORE ▸▸ Animals 96–97 • Skeleton 130–131

CNIDARIANS

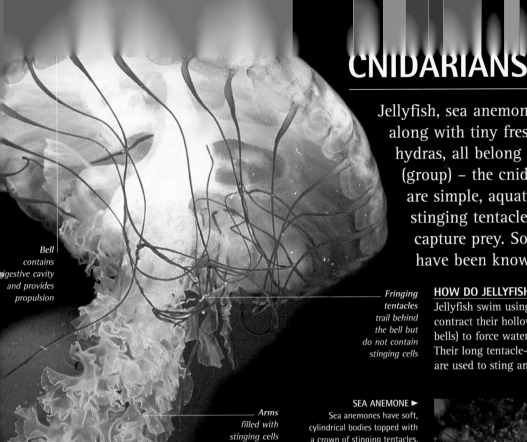

Jellyfish, sea anemones, and ►►**CORALS**, along with tiny freshwater animals called hydras, all belong to the same phylum (group) – the cnidarians. All cnidarians are simple, aquatic invertebrates with stinging tentacles, which they use to capture prey. Some are venomous and have been known to kill people.

Bell contains digestive cavity and provides propulsion

Fringing tentacles trail behind the bell but do not contain stinging cells

Arms filled with stinging cells that paralyse or kill prey

HOW DO JELLYFISH MOVE THROUGH THE WATER?
Jellyfish swim using a kind of jet propulsion. They contract their hollow, saucer-shaped bodies (called bells) to force water out, which propels them forward. Their long tentacle-like arms, which trail out behind, are used to sting and capture prey.

SEA ANEMONE ►
Sea anemones have soft, cylindrical bodies topped with a crown of stinging tentacles. Most sea anemones are no bigger than a man's hand, although the largest may grow up to 90 cm (3 ft) across.

e ►► cnidarians

HOW DO SEA ANEMONES FEED?
Sea anemones capture food with their tentacles, then pass it to the mouth in the middle of the tentacle crown. Sea anemones spend their adult lives attached to rocks on the seabed or in pools on the shore. Some sea anemones have a muscular collar, which they can pull over their tentacles if threatened.

▲ SEA NETTLE
Jellyfish tentacles are armed with stinging cells known as nematocysts. The stings of most jellyfish produce nothing more than a painful welt in humans.

CNIDARIAN CLASSIFICATION

The phylum (major group) Cnidaria contains about 10,000 species, divided into three classes:
• Hydrozoans (including hydras, the Portuguese man-of-war, and fire corals)
• Anthozoans (including all other corals and sea anemones)
• Scyphozoans (jellyfish)

CORAL

Tropical coral reefs are the ocean's richest habitats, but the creatures that create them are surprisingly small. They look like tiny sea anemones but have chalky skeletons.

WHAT IS A POLYP?
A polyp is an individual coral animal. It looks like a miniature sea anemone, and feeds on the tiny plants and animals, known as plankton, that float in seawater. Most coral polyps live in communities that slowly build up to form reefs. These reefs provide homes for all sorts of other sea-living creatures.

STAGHORN CORAL ►
Hard coral polyps emerge to feed at night, when most of the fish and other creatures that might eat them are inactive or asleep. If they are threatened, the polyps quickly withdraw into their stony shells. They re-emerge once the danger has passed.

HOW DO CORAL REEFS FORM?
Coral reefs are made from the skeletons of coral polyps. Most coral polyps have a hard, chalky body case that protects the soft parts inside. When they die, the chalky skeletons remain. Over thousands of years, they build up on top of one another to form a reef that may stretch for hundreds of kilometres.

FIND OUT MORE ►► Australasia and Oceania 272–273 • Islands 42

ECHINODERMS

Starfish, brittle stars, sea urchins, and sea cucumbers all belong to the family of echinoderms. These slow-moving, headless invertebrates are the only animals with bodies based on a five-fold structure. All echinoderms live in salt water.

Skeleton
made of tiny
chalky fragments
called ossicles

Tiny tube feet
cover the arms –
up to 2,000 in
some species

Mouth
on the underside
of the body

HOW DO STARFISH FEED?

Starfish feed by turning their stomachs inside out over their victims. They then ooze digestive juices, which dissolve their prey. Most starfish eat shellfish such as mussels. They move in search of food using the tiny, flexible tube feet that protrude from their underside.

WHAT HAPPENS WHEN A STARFISH LOSES A LIMB?

Starfish that lose limbs can grow new ones in their place. If a severed limb contains certain cells, it too can survive and will eventually grow into a whole new starfish. Losing a limb may help a starfish escape from a predator's clutches. Brittle stars are so called because their limbs break off easily.

▲ SPINY STARFISH
Starfish have a central body with limbs that radiate outwards like spokes on a wheel. Most starfish have five limbs, although some have more.

e ⏵⏵ echinoderms

◀ SEA URCHIN
Sea urchins live on the seabed or buried in sand. Like starfish, they have many tiny tube feet, which they use for crawling and feeding. Sea urchins are well protected by their many sharp spines.

Tube feet
pass algae
and animals
to mouth

Tentacles
have evolved
from tube feet

Anus
discharges
waste

Spines
of some species
are poisonous

◀ SEA CUCUMBER
These echinoderms can measure up to 1 m (3 ft 3 in) long. They live on the sea floor and feed on decaying matter. After a meal, a sea cucumber pulls its tentacles into its mouth to clean them.

ECHINODERM CLASSIFICATION

The phylum of Echinodermata includes about 6,000 species, divided into six classes:
• Sea lilies and feather stars • Starfish • Brittle stars and basket stars • Sea cucumbers • Sea urchins • Sea daisies

FIND OUT MORE ⏵⏵ Invertebrates 102

SPONGES

These animals look like plants or fungi, but they are actually simple invertebrates. Most sponges dwell in salt water, spending their lives attached to rocks or reefs.

HOW DO SPONGES FEED?

Sponges feed by drawing seawater in through pores in their surface and removing tiny plants and animals. Sponges lack the obvious body parts most animals have. They have no heart or other organs of any description. Sponges' bodies are stiffened by tiny grains of limestone, silica, or a fibre called spongin.

YELLOW TUBE SPONGES ▶
Sponges exist in a wide variety of colours and may be shaped like fingers, chimneys, or vases. They range in size from less than 10 cm (4 in) to more than 1 m (3 ft 3 in) long.

SPONGE CLASSIFICATION

This phylum includes about 5,000 species, divided into four classes:
• Calcareous sponges • Glass sponges • Demosponges (including the familiar bath sponge and tube sponges) • Scelerosponges

e ⏵⏵ sponges

FIND OUT MORE ⏵⏵ Invertebrates 102

WORMS

Earthworms are the most familiar worms, but there are thousands of other types of these soft, legless creatures. Some are microscopic, others grow to several metres long. Earthworms and roundworms are tube-shaped. Flatworms are shaped like leaves or ribbons.

WHERE DO WORMS LIVE?

Worms live on land and in water and can be found in virtually every habitat on Earth. Earthworms live in the soil. Leeches and bloodworms inhabit ponds and rivers. Most ribbon worms and some flatworms live in the oceans. Ragworms and lugworms are found on the seashore. Some worms are ▶▶ PARASITES that live on or inside other animals.

HOW DO WORMS SENSE THEIR SURROUNDINGS?

Some flatworms have simple eyes that can detect light, but most worms are blind. Their most important sense is touch. The earthworm's skin picks up vibrations caused by sounds or movements. Some predatory worms have sensitive tentacles on their heads that help them to capture their food.

POLYCLAD FLATWORM ▲
Most non-parasitic flatworms hunt or scavenge for food. Flatworms are a major group of worms that includes tapeworms and flukes.

◀ EARTHWORM
Earthworms aerate and enrich the soil as they burrow through it. They feed on plants and animals, or their rotting remains.

Saddle holds fertilized eggs after mating

Mucus keeps the body moist

Segments expand and contract to help the worm move

Tail is always longer than head end

WORM CLASSIFICATION

There are over 100,000 species of worm in three main phyla:
• Flatworms (includes turbellarians, tapeworms, and flukes)
• Segmented worms, or annelids (includes earthworms, lugworms, ragworms, and leeches)
• Roundworms (includes threadworms and pinworms)

Horny cuticle protects the body from damage

Mouth sometimes contains teeth to grind food

Anus expels solid waste

◀ CLOSE UP
Tiny bristles on the front part of an earthworm help it to grip the soil as it moves. The worm propels itself forward by elongating and contracting its body segments.

ROUNDWORM ▶
These worms are also known as nematodes. Some species contain more than 27 million eggs at any time, and more than 200,000 in a single day.

PARASITES

Parasites live on or inside other animals or plants, called their hosts. They feed on the blood or tissues of their host, or steal its food. Some parasitic worms in people survive without their host even noticing. Others can cause serious diseases.

HOW DO LEECHES FEED?

Leeches use suckers on their head and tail to latch on to animals, including humans, in order to suck their blood. They inject a chemical that keeps the host's blood flowing freely. This lets them feed until they are bloated, then they drop off. Leeches lurk in ponds, streams, and other wet places.

Hooks fix on to the host's gut

WHERE DO TAPEWORMS LIVE?

Tapeworms live in the guts of animals such as pigs, cats, and humans. The host becomes infected when it eats food containing tapeworm eggs or young. Inside the gut, the worm feeds on the host's half-digested food. As it matures, the worm produces small packages of eggs, which pass out of the victim's body.

e ▶▶
worms

Suckers create a strong grip

◀ CAT TAPEWORM
Tapeworms attach themselves to their host's intestines using hooks and suckers on their heads. This species reaches 60 cm (2 ft) long. Some tapeworms can grow up to 30 m (100 ft) long.

FIND OUT MORE ▶▶ Ecology 80 • Invertebrates 102 • Soil 48

MOLLUSCS

Soft-bodied invertebrates, molluscs include slugs, snails, octopuses, squid, clams, and mussels. Most molluscs have ▶▶ SHELLS to protect them.

▲ GIANT AFRICAN SNAIL
Gastropods such as snails glide along on a trail of slime oozing from an area by their broad, muscular foot. The distinct head often carries two pairs of tentacles. The longer set may bear eyes on the tips. Gastropods live mainly in water, but also in a variety of land habitats.

▼ OCTOPUS IN ACTION
Cephalopods such as octopuses and cuttlefish are stealthy hunters. Octopuses creep along the seabed or lie in wait for fish and crabs. They pounce on their prey, seize it with their suckered arms, and paralyse it with poisonous saliva.

MOLLUSC CLASSIFICATION
There are over 70,000 mollusc species split into several major classes:
• Gastropods (the largest class) include slugs, snails, winkles, whelks, and limpets • Bivalves include scallops, clams, and oysters • Squid, octopuses, cuttlefish, and nautilus are cephalopods • Smaller groups include tusk shells and chitons (oval molluscs with jointed plates)

WHAT FEATURES DO MOLLUSCS HAVE IN COMMON?
As well as a shell, most molluscs have a muscular foot for creeping or burrowing. Some also have a head with sense organs. The soft body includes lungs or gills for breathing, and digestive and reproductive parts, all enclosed by a skin-like organ called the mantle.

HOW DO MOLLUSCS FEED?
Most molluscs have a rasping tongue called a radula, armed with tiny teeth. This scrapes tiny plants and animals off rocks or tears food into chunks. Bivalves, such as oysters and mussels, filter food particles from the water with their gills.

HOW DO MOLLUSCS REPRODUCE?
Molluscs reproduce sexually. Slugs and snails are hermaphrodite (possessing both male and female organs), but they must still mate to fertilize their eggs. Most aquatic molluscs lay eggs that hatch into small, free-swimming larvae called veliger.

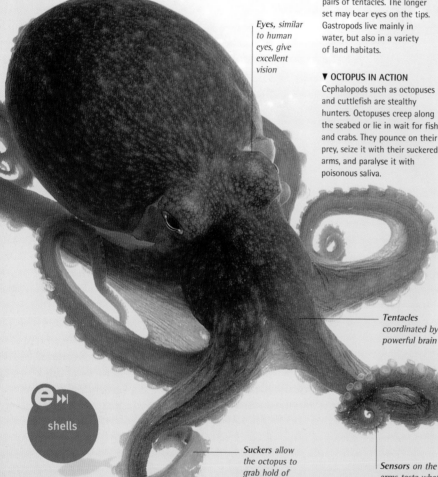

Eyes, similar to human eyes, give excellent vision

Tentacles coordinated by a powerful brain

Suckers allow the octopus to grab hold of slippery prey

Sensors on the arms taste what they touch

e ▶▶ shells

Shell can snap shut at the first sign of danger

Muscles hold shell open for feeding

Eyes along the edge of the shell look out for predators

QUEEN SCALLOP ▲
Like all bivalves, the queen scallop has a two-part shell. Most bivalves live attached to rocks or in burrows on the seabed. They take in water using a muscular tube called a syphon, and remove food particles with their gills.

SHELLS

Mollusc shells come in many shapes and sizes, but most have the same, simple function – providing somewhere to hide in times of danger. In land molluscs, the shell also helps to prevent the moist, soft-bodied creature from drying out.

NAUTILUS SHELL ▶
The nautilus is a cephalopod (a relative of squid and octopuses) with a many-chambered shell. The mollusc lives only in the shell's largest outer chamber. The smaller inner chambers are used to control the animal's buoyancy. The spiralling form can be seen clearly in this cut-away shell.

Buoyancy chamber

Outer chamber contains the living animal

WHAT ARE MOLLUSC SHELLS MADE OF?
Mollusc shells are made of a chalky material called calcium carbonate. The shell has three layers for extra strength: a tough outer layer, a chalky middle layer, and a shiny inner layer, next to the animal's skin. The shiny layer in some bivalve molluscs is known as mother-of-pearl.

HOW DO MOLLUSCS MAKE SHELLS?
A mollusc's mantle (skin) releases liquid shell materials, which harden on contact with water or air. Gastropod and nautilus shells grow from their outermost edge. As the mollusc grows, its shell develops more whorls (single turns in a spiral shell) or chambers. In bivalves, new shell material is deposited on the edge that is farthest from the hinge.

FIND OUT MORE ▶▶ Invertebrates 102

ARTHROPODS

Centipedes, millipedes, insects, crustaceans, and arachnids, including spiders, all belong to a super-group of invertebrates called arthropods. Arthropods are more numerous and varied than any other animal group.

WHAT FEATURES DO ARTHROPODS SHARE?
All arthropods have bodies divided into segments and covered with a hard ▶▶ EXOSKELETON . This tough casing is made of a protein called chitin, which is also found in human fingernails. The armour is flexible at joints on the legs, which makes arthropods nimble.

WHAT IS THE DIFFERENCE BETWEEN A CENTIPEDE AND A MILLIPEDE?
Centipedes are active hunters, while most millipedes eat plant matter. Also, centipedes have two legs per body segment. Millipedes have four. Centipedes and millipedes are collectively known as myriapods.

DO ALL CENTIPEDES HAVE ONE HUNDRED LEGS?
The word centipede means "100 legs", but some centipedes have fewer than 100 legs, and others have more. Similarly, the word millipede means "1,000 legs", but in fact no millipede has more than 750 legs.

ARTHROPOD CLASSIFICATION

Arthropods make up the largest phylum (group) in the animal kingdom. There are more than 900,000 named species divided into 13 classes:
• Crustaceans • Insects • Arachnids • Centipedes • Millipedes
• Sea spiders • Pauropods • Symphylans • Springtails • Proturans
• Two-pronged bristletails • Three-pronged bristletails • King crabs

---

◀ PILL MILLIPEDE
With their tough, rounded bodies, millipedes make difficult prey. The pill millipede has an extra trick to deter predators – it rolls into a ball when attacked. Some millipedes defend themselves with poisons, such as quinone and cyanide, produced by glands between their segments.

GIANT CENTIPEDE ▲
Centipedes paralyse or kill their prey with poison, injected by fang-like claws just behind the mouth. There are over 3,000 species of centipedes. The largest live in the tropics and may grow up to 30 cm (12 in) long – large enough to kill a mouse.

EXOSKELETON

An arthropod's exoskeleton is a protective case and an anchor point for muscles. As well as being tough, it is waterproof, helping these creatures to survive in even the harshest habitats.

Long antenna helps the lobster navigate on the sea bed

First leg, or cheliped, is modified to carry a pincer

Short antenna feels objects close to the mouthparts

Pincers, used to grab food and for defence

Carapace protects most of the vital organs

Walking legs are jointed in several places

Tailpiece moves to propel the lobster

▲ LOBSTER
The lobster's hard exoskeleton supports and protects its body. Even delicate parts, such as the legs and antennae, are completely encased. The North Atlantic lobster is the world's heaviest arthropod, weighing up to 20 kg (44 lb).

HOW DO ARTHROPODS GROW?
In order to grow, arthropods have to moult (shed their exoskeletons) every so often. They then expand their bodies before their new casing hardens. Arthropods are vulnerable while moulting, so try to find a safe place to hide before they begin.

e ▶▶ arthropods

WHERE DO ARTHROPODS LIVE?
Arthropods occur in virtually every habitat, from the cold ocean depths to the hottest deserts. They can live through extremes that would kill most vertebrates. Scorpions, for example, can survive being frozen solid.

ARACHNIDS

A large group of eight-legged arthropods, arachnids include spiders, scorpions, ticks, and mites. All scorpions and spiders are meat-eating hunters. Ticks and mites are tiny creatures with sucking or biting mouthparts. Most ticks live as parasites on animals or plants.

HOW DO SPIDERS SPIN SILK?
Spiders produce liquid silk from glands inside their abdomens. Structures called spinnerets squeeze out the silk, which the spider then pulls into long threads with its legs. Most spiders use silk to spin webs and catch flying prey. Some spiders hunt without using webs.

HOW DO SCORPIONS KILL THEIR PREY?
Scorpions use their pincers to catch and kill prey. They pounce on insects, spiders, and even mice and lizards, then use their pincers to tear them to pieces. The poisonous sting is used to kill only powerful victims that put up a fight. Scorpions hunt at night and use mainly touch and smell to sense their prey.

◄ PROTECTIVE MOTHER
The female scorpion carries her babies on her back for two to three weeks to protect them from predators. After their first moult (shedding of skin), the young leave their mother to hunt on their own. Male and female scorpions court by performing a synchronized dance. After mating, the eggs develop inside the mother's body, so she gives birth to living young.

▲ MEAL MITE
Some mites are so small that they cannot be seen with the naked eye. This photograph of a meal mite was taken with an electron microscope and magnified many thousands of times. Meal mites feed on cereals and are often found in kitchens. The long hairs help the mite to sense its surroundings.

arachnids

ARACHNID CLASSIFICATION

Almost all arachnids live on land. The class Arachnida includes about 17,000 species, divided into 10 orders:
• Scorpions • Pseudoscorpions • Spiders • Mites and ticks
• Harvestmen (daddy long legs) • Whip scorpions • Micro-whip scorpions • Solifugids (sun spiders) • Ricinuleids • Amblypygids

Forward-facing eyes make it easier to judge distances

◄ TARANTULA
Spiders kill or paralyse their prey by biting it with poisoned fangs. Then they inject digestive juices into it. Tarantulas are active hunters, pouncing on prey rather than catching it in a web. Most tarantulas live in South and Central America.

Jointed legs enable spider to move quickly

Mouthparts suck up juices of half-digested prey

Grasshopper immobilized by spider's venom

Pedipalps, used as feelers

CRUSTACEANS

These invertebrates include crabs, barnacles, ▶KRILL, and woodlice. They are sometimes called the insects of the sea, because they are the most numerous ocean arthropods. All crustaceans have hard skin, gills, and two pairs of antennae.

WHERE DO CRUSTACEANS LIVE?
Most crustaceans live in the ocean – although some species live in fresh water, and woodlice and a few crabs live on land. Prawns and shrimp swim freely in open water. Barnacles live attached to rocks, harbour walls, or the sides of ships.

WHAT DO CRUSTACEANS EAT?
Many crustaceans are scavengers, feeding on scraps and dead creatures. Crabs, shrimp, and prawns search for food mainly at night and hide in crevices by day. Some crabs and lobsters are active predators, seizing prey in their powerful claws. Barnacles filter tiny creatures from the water using their hairy legs. Woodlice munch on plant remains.

ARE BABY CRUSTACEANS LIKE THE ADULTS?
Most crustaceans hatch from eggs into nauplius larvae, which do not resemble their adult form at all. These tiny creatures float near the ocean surface, where they feed and grow. They shed their hard skin several times before becoming adults.

Legs
drawn inside shell at the first sign of danger

◀ **HERMIT CRABS**
These creatures wear empty mollusc shells for protection from predators. When they outgrow one shell, they simply move into another.

Antenna
helps feel the way in murky water

e ▶▶
crustaceans

▲ **GOOSE BARNACLES**
These crustaceans extend their slender legs to trap tiny floating creatures for food. As adults, they live fixed to one spot.

▼ **NAUPLIUS LARVAE**
Most young crustaceans float freely near the ocean's surface. Creatures that live in this way are known as plankton. The word plankton means "wanderer".

SHRIMP

CRAB

COPEPOD

CRAB LARVAE

CRUSTACEAN CLASSIFICATION

Crustaceans make up the second largest class in the animal kingdom. They include about 38,000 species, split into eight sub-classes:
• Lobsters, crabs, prawns, shrimp, and woodlice • Barnacles
• Seed shrimp • Fish lice • Copepods • Branchiopods
• Cephalocarids • Mystacocarids

KRILL

Krill are small, pinkish, shrimp-like creatures found in the oceans in huge numbers. They form an important part of the marine food chain and are the main diet of many larger sea creatures.

WHAT DO KRILL EAT?
Krill feed on plankton – tiny plants and animal larvae (young) that float with the ocean currents. They, in turn, are eaten by everything from penguins to whales. Some whales migrate thousands of kilometres from warmer waters just to feed on seasonal swarms of krill.

ARE KRILL UNDER THREAT?
Krill are extremely numerous and there is no threat of their dying out. However, they are being taken from the ocean in increasing amounts by fishermen. As krill disappear, the animals that feed on them suffer. Krill trawling in the Antarctic has had a major effect on penguin numbers.

Baleen plates
keep krill in but let water out

◀ **KRILL NUMBERS**
Krill sometimes occur in such huge numbers near the ocean's surface that their rosy colour appears to turn the water red.

HUMPBACK WHALE ▶
Baleen whales sieve up to 2 tonnes of krill from the water in a single feeding session, using fringed baleen plates in their mouths.

FIND OUT MORE ▶▶ Arthropods 107 • Invertebrates 102 • Oceans 40–41

INSECTS

The most numerous animals on Earth, insects form about 75 per cent of the animal kingdom. Around 800,000 species have been identified, but there could be up to 10 million. Insects are six-legged invertebrates with keen sense organs, including ▸▸ ANTENNAE . Some live in ▸▸ COLONIES .

Head

Large compound eyes give wide field of vision

Thorax (middle section of the body)

Wings held together at rest – unlike dragonflies' wings, which are held open

Long, delicate legs have several joints

Abdomen is long and slender to balance insect when flying

Claspers are used by male to hold female during mating

▲ DAMSELFLY
Like all adult insects, damselflies have three-part bodies, with a head, thorax, and abdomen. Damselflies and dragonflies form a very ancient group of insects. Giant dragonflies flew in swampy forests 350 million years ago, before dinosaurs existed.

WHY ARE INSECTS SO SUCCESSFUL?
The main reason for insects' success is their variety. There are so many species that there is almost nowhere on land they cannot live, and almost nothing they cannot eat. Their small size enables them to go almost anywhere in search of food. Many insects can fly, which makes it easy for them to colonize new places.

▲ BED BUG
Various insects feed on blood, including head lice, mosquitoes, and fleas. The bed bug lives in mattresses and emerges when it feels the heat of a body. Its mouthparts are adapted to pierce skin and suck up blood.

INSECT CLASSIFICATION

- Insects have thrived on Earth for over 400 million years. The insect world is divided into 29 groups, called orders.
- The largest order, the beetles (Coleoptera), contains more than 370,000 species.

- Other major orders are moths and butterflies (Lepidoptera, 150,000 species), bees, wasps, and ants (Hymenoptera, 120,000 species), flies (Diptera, 100,000 species), and bugs (Hemiptera, 80,000 species).

ANTENNAE

The main sense organs of most insects are the antennae (feelers) on their heads. These often long and slender projections are covered with tiny sensitive hairs. As well as feeling, the antennae are also used for smelling, and sometimes for taste and hearing, too.

Club-shaped antenna, different from the feathery antenna of a moth

BUTTERFLY SENSES ▶
Long antennae and large compound eyes help butterflies to sense the world around them.

WHAT DO INSECTS USE THEIR ANTENNAE FOR?
Insects use antennae to find food and detect enemies. Lice, fleas, and other insects that feed on other animals use their antennae to sense the body heat or moisture of their victims. Some male insects have especially sensitive antennae, which can pick up scents called pheromones given off by females (their mates).

WHAT OTHER SENSES DO INSECTS HAVE?
Many insects have compound eyes, with dozens of lenses that work together to form a detailed picture. Some also have sensitive bristles on their abdomens, which detect air currents caused by moving predators or prey. Insects' eardrums may be on their legs or body. Some insects, such as flies, have taste organs on their feet.

HOW DO INSECTS DEFEND THEMSELVES?

Many insects are camouflaged (naturally disguised), so that predators do not see them. Some species are armed with stings or foul-tasting poison. Many of these have bright colours, such as black-and-yellow stripes, to warn enemies away.

WHAT DO INSECTS EAT?

Insects eat a huge range of foods. Around half are plant-eaters, feeding on leaves, roots, seeds, nectar, or wood. Praying mantises are predators, hunting other small creatures. Fleas and lice are parasites, eating the flesh or blood of larger animals without killing them.

Compound eye *made of dozens of six-sided lenses*

Antenna

Wing *covered with thousands of tiny, overlapping scales*

Pupal case *in which the butterfly pupated (changed) from a caterpillar*

insects

MONARCH CATERPILLAR ▶

Many insect larvae (young) look very different from the adults. Moth and butterfly larvae are known as caterpillars. These feed on leaves, building up a lot of weight in a relatively short time. They then stop feeding and develop a solid body case in which they pupate (change) into their adult body shape.

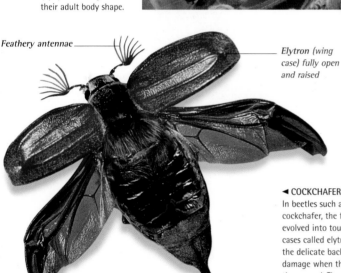

Feathery antennae

Elytron *(wing case) fully open and raised*

Back wings *unfold*

◀ COCKCHAFER BEETLE

In beetles such as this cockchafer, the front wings have evolved into tough, rounded cases called elytra. These protect the delicate back wings from damage when the beetle is on the ground. The elytra are lifted out of the way as the beetle takes off and flies.

◀ MONARCH BUTTERFLY

After metamorphosis (the change from larva to adult), an adult monarch butterfly emerges from its pupal case and slowly pumps up its wings. Like all butterflies, the monarch butterfly feeds on nectar produced by flowers.

WHERE DO INSECTS GO IN WINTER?

Many adult insects die off in winter. Their eggs or young survive in sheltered places and emerge in spring. Some insects survive the cold by hibernating. Others, such as monarch butterflies, migrate long distances to avoid the winter chill.

HOW DO INSECTS AFFECT HUMANS?

Plant-eating insects can harm crops and fruit trees. Wood-munching termites destroy homes and furniture, while biting insects can spread disease. However, many insects are helpful to humans – for example, honeybees make honey, ladybirds eat aphids (which damage garden plants), and silkworms produce silk.

COLONIES

Most insects live solitary lives, but termites, ants, and some wasps and bees live together in large colonies. Members cooperate in building the nest and finding food.

HOW DO SOCIAL INSECTS RAISE THEIR YOUNG?

Most insects take little or no care of their young, but social insects are an exception. Workers carefully guard the young and bring them food. Worker wasps bring chewed-up insects for their grubs (larvae). Honeybee grubs are fed on honey. These young insects grow up in a nursery at the heart of the nest.

TERMITE QUEEN WITH SOLDIERS AND WORKERS ▶

Each insect colony contains several different castes, or ranks. The queen's job is to lay eggs – queen termites are so full of eggs they cannot move. Large numbers of non-breeding female workers tend to the eggs and maintain the nest. Many insect colonies also have a defensive caste of soldiers, armed with huge jaws or poison.

FIND OUT MORE ▶▶ Arthropods 107 • Reproduction 101 • Senses 99

FISH

Fish are aquatic animals with an inner skeleton, including skull, ribs, and backbone. Most fish have bony skeletons, but shark and ray skeletons are made of rubbery cartilage. Fish extract oxygen from the water using ▸▸GILLS, and swim using their tail and fins. A fish's skin is covered with tough scales.

WHERE DO FISH LIVE?

Superbly adapted to life in water, fish are found throughout the world's oceans, from warm tropical seas to icy polar waters. Some fish dwell near the surface. Others live in the depths, where some use ▸▸BIOLUMINESCENCE. Fish are also found in freshwater habitats such as rivers, lakes, and swamps.

FISH CLASSIFICATION

- There are over 26,000 species of fish – more than half of all the world's vertebrates. Fish divide into three major groups.
- The first group, and by far the largest, contains the bony fish. There are more than 25,000 species alive today.

- The second group contains the 600 species of cartilaginous fish – sharks and rays.
- The smallest group, with about 60 species, is also the most primitive. Its members, the hagfish and lampreys, have skeletons but no jaws.

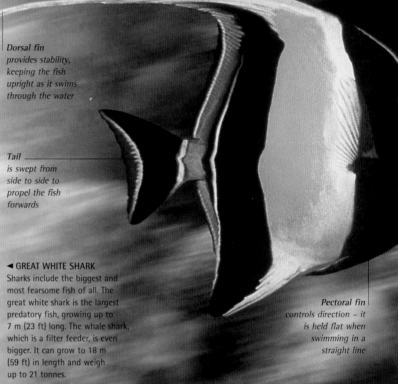

Dorsal fin provides stability, keeping the fish upright as it swims through the water

Tail is swept from side to side to propel the fish forwards

◀ GREAT WHITE SHARK
Sharks include the biggest and most fearsome fish of all. The great white shark is the largest predatory fish, growing up to 7 m (23 ft) long. The whale shark, which is a filter feeder, is even bigger. It can grow to 18 m (59 ft) in length and weigh up to 21 tonnes.

Pectoral fin controls direction – it is held flat when swimming in a straight line

GILLS

Like all animals, fish need a constant supply of oxygen to survive. They do not breathe air but extract dissolved oxygen from the water using their gills – feathery organs located behind the eyes and supplied with many tiny blood vessels.

HOW DO FISH BREATHE UNDER WATER?

Water containing dissolved oxygen is drawn in through the fish's mouth, to pass over four or five sets of gills on either side of the head. The gill arches hold delicate, flap-like membranes with very thin walls. Oxygen passes through these membranes into the fish's bloodstream, to be distributed around the body.

HOW GILLS WORK

Water enters through the mouth

Water exits body through gill slits

Oxygen is absorbed from the water, through the gill membranes

DO ANY FISH LIVE ON LAND?

No fish live on land but some can survive out of water for years. For example, when the pool or lake where they live dries up, lungfish can survive while buried in the mud, extracting oxygen from the air.

▲ MUDSKIPPER
Mudskippers come out on to muddy shores to graze algae. They keep their gills puffed out with water, returning every so often for a refill. Mudskippers wriggle over the mud using their pectoral fins.

Long snout allows the moorish idol to reach morsels of food in crevices

Anal fin provides stability, like the dorsal fin

▲ YELLOWHEAD JAWFISH
Some species of fish protect their eggs by incubating them in their mouths. Before setting off to feed, this male yellowhead jawfish will spit his mate's eggs out into his burrow, to keep them safe.

HOW DO SHARKS HUNT?

Predatory sharks detect prey with the aid of keen sensors, which can pick up tiny traces of blood from several kilometres away. They home in on victims using electrosensors that detect tiny charges given off by the prey's muscles. At close range, sharks use their eyesight to target their quarry.

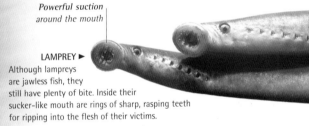

Powerful suction around the mouth

LAMPREY ▶
Although lampreys are jawless fish, they still have plenty of bite. Inside their sucker-like mouth are rings of sharp, rasping teeth for ripping into the flesh of their victims.

◀ MOORISH IDOLS
Most fish that live on tropical coral reefs are colourful and have striking markings. Coral reefs are very crowded places. Scientists think that the bright colours and patterns may help fish to recognize others of their own kind.

ARE THERE ANY PARASITIC FISH?

Lampreys are parasites. They attach themselves to larger creatures using their sucker-like mouth and drink their blood. Lamprey saliva contains a natural anticoagulant, which prevents a victim's blood from clotting, so that the lamprey can continue to feed.

BIOLUMINESCENCE

Little light from the surface reaches the twilight zone in the ocean depths below 200 m (660 ft). However, over 1,000 species of fish that live there are bioluminescent – able to produce their own natural light.

fish

WHAT IS THE PURPOSE OF BIOLUMINESCENCE?

Bioluminescence has several uses. Deep-sea anglerfish dangle a glowing lure in front of their jaws to attract prey. Other species use light to identify mates. A few even use it for camouflage – lights on the underside of the body help fish blend in with the small amount of light filtering down. Many fish nearer the surface have light-coloured bellies for the same reason.

DEEP-SEA ANGLERFISH ▶
A deep-sea anglerfish glows like an underwater light bulb. In some species, bioluminescence is caused by a chemical reaction in which energy is released as light. Other species are illuminated by glowing bacteria in their skin, and some have glands called photophores which can be switched on and off like miniature flashlights.

FIND OUT MORE ▶▶ Cnidarians 103 • Fishing 67 • Oceans 40–41

Large, bulging eyes help tree frog spot approaching predators

Eardrum hidden beneath skin

Sticky fingers give tree frogs greater grip

▲ RED-EYED TREE FROG
Frogs and toads are tail-less and have long hind legs. The most widespread amphibians, they are found in many habitats, including rainforests, woodlands, mountains, and deserts.

AMPHIBIANS

Frogs, toads, salamanders, newts, and the strange, worm-like caecilians are all amphibians – a group of smallish, generally moist-skinned vertebrates. The word amphibian, meaning "living two lives", refers to the fact that most amphibians spend part of their lives in water and part on land.

CAN AMPHIBIANS BREATHE THROUGH THEIR SKIN?
Yes, they can. Oxygen from the air or water can pass through the moist skin of amphibians to enter the blood. Many young amphibians also have feathery gills to extract oxygen from water, but later lose these and develop lungs. Some "axolotl" salamanders keep their gills throughout life.

Contrasting colours stand out like a warning flag

▲ SALAMANDER
Newts and salamanders have long tails and lizard-like bodies. They feed on slugs, insects, and other small animals. Some species, such as this fire salamander, have poison glands on their heads.

HOW DO AMPHIBIANS DEFEND THEMSELVES AGAINST PREDATORS?
Most amphibians hop or crawl to the safety of the nearest water when danger threatens. Some also have glands in their skin which ooze poisonous or foul-tasting fluids when they are attacked. The common toad and a few other species confuse predators by puffing themselves up to look bigger.

WHAT IS A CAECILIAN?
Caecilians are long, slender amphibians found in hot countries. Almost all live underground, where they burrow through the soil using their wedge-shaped heads. Like other amphibians, caecilians are predators that hunt worms, insects, and other small soil-dwellers. Most caecilians are legless, but some have tiny limbs.

▲ CAECILIAN
Most caecilians live in leaf litter or soil. Because of their secretive habits, they are rarely seen and hard to study. Caecilians have poorly developed eyes and are also known as blindworms.

Moist skin glistens in the light

COMMON FROG

Dry skin with bumps that resemble warts

GREEN TOAD

Bright colour warns other animals that frog is poisonous

WHAT DO AMPHIBIANS EAT?

All adult amphibians are meat-eating predators. Their prey include insects, slugs, worms, and even small mammals, such as mice. Aquatic amphibians eat water snails, insects, and small fish. Many amphibians hunt at night, using their keen sight, smell, and hearing to track victims.

▲ FROG AND TOAD

Adult frogs and toads have four legs and no tail. Although there is no real scientific difference between them, frogs are generally considered to be moist-skinned, hopping animals and toads dry-skinned amphibians that walk.

BLUE POISON-DART FROG ►

Poison-dart frogs are so named because South American Indians used their poison to tip blowpipe darts. One species, the golden poison-dart frog, carries enough poison to kill almost 1,000 people.

▲ COMMON TOADS SPAWNING

In the breeding season, amphibians gather to spawn (lay jelly-coated eggs in ponds, ditches, and creeks). They attract their mates using bright colours, special scents, or loud croaks.

WHY DO MOST AMPHIBIANS LIVE NEAR WATER?

The moist skin of most amphibians is not waterproof, so they live in damp places to prevent them drying out. Many amphibians lay their soft, jelly-covered eggs in water, which is known as spawning. Their young, called ▶▶ TADPOLES , grow up in the water and come on to land only when they mature.

HOW IS COLOUR IMPORTANT TO AMPHIBIANS?

Colour helps amphibians find mates and hide from predators and prey. Some species are brightly coloured to tell predators that they are poisonous. Others are camouflaged to merge in with their surroundings.

AMPHIBIAN CLASSIFICATION

- Amphibians are the most ancient class of land-living vertebrates. They are split into three orders.
- Caecilians make up the order Apoda. There are around 170 living species.

- The order Urodela contains all newts and salamanders. There are about 360 species.
- The largest order, Anura, contains the frogs and toads. Altogether, there are around 3,500 different species.

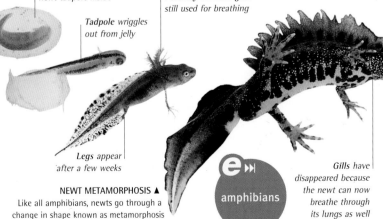

Egg with developing newt tadpole inside

Tadpole wriggles out from jelly

Feathery external gills still used for breathing

Legs appear after a few weeks

NEWT METAMORPHOSIS ▲

Like all amphibians, newts go through a change in shape known as metamorphosis as they grow from tadpoles to adults.

e ▶▶ amphibians

Gills have disappeared because the newt can now breathe through its lungs as well as its skin

TADPOLES

Most amphibians hatch as water-dwelling larvae called tadpoles. With big heads, long tails, and no limbs, they look more like fish than amphibians. As they grow older, the tail shortens and limbs develop. Finally, they start to resemble miniature adults.

HOW DO TADPOLES BREATHE?

Most tadpoles extract oxygen from fresh water using internal gills and feathery external gills on their necks. As they mature, they develop lungs and their gills normally shrivel up. Unlike their adult forms, many tadpoles are herbivorous, feeding on plants which they scrape off pond rocks using rasping teeth.

FIND OUT MORE ▶▶ Reproduction 101 • Vertebrates 102

REPTILES

This group of scaly-skinned, backboned animals includes snakes, lizards, crocodiles, hard-shelled turtles, and the tuatara, from New Zealand. Most reptiles live on land but turtles, crocodiles, and some snakes live in water. Nearly all reptiles are equipped with senses similar to humans.

WHAT DO REPTILES EAT?

Most reptiles are active predators. Lizards hunt mainly insects. Snakes target prey such as rodents and birds. Some snakes subdue their victims with ▶▶ VENOM. Crocodiles prey on creatures as large as wildebeest. Turtles and terrapins eat mainly fish and invertebrates. Tortoises, which live on land, feed mostly on plants.

HOW DO REPTILES ESCAPE FROM DANGER?

Many reptiles hide, or are camouflaged to blend in with their surroundings. Some are speedy and agile, and can scurry off at lightning speed. Others are brightly coloured to warn predators that they are venomous. Some lizards can break off their tail in order to escape, growing a new one through ▶▶ REGENERATION.

Eyes move independently of each other

Forked tongue picks up scent particles from the air

Mitten-like feet, formed from joined, opposing toes, give the chameleon a firm grip

◄ RED-TAILED RACER
Snakes gather molecules with their tongues, then transfer them to a gland on the roof of the mouth called the Jacobson's organ. This gland is very sensitive and can detect distant prey. Some vipers can detect the body heat of prey using special pits near to their eyes.

REPTILE CLASSIFICATION

- There are around 6,000 species of reptile split into four different orders.
- Snakes and lizards belong to the same order – Squamata. There are around 3,000 species of lizard and 2,500 species of snake.
- The second-largest order, Chelonia, includes all turtles, tortoises, and terrapins.
- Crocodiles and their relatives make up the order Crocodilia.
- The tuatara is the last living member of its order. The rest died out 100 million years ago.

VENOM

The majority of snakes kill their prey with venom produced by glands in their heads. The glands pump poison through long, pointed teeth called fangs, which bite deep into their prey.

HOW MANY SNAKES ARE DEADLY TO HUMANS?

Fewer than 10 per cent of snakes produce venom strong enough to kill a person. Vipers produce large quantities of venom – people bitten by diamondback rattlesnakes have been known to die in under an hour. The Australian inland taipan is thought to be the world's most deadly snake. Sea snakes are also highly poisonous, but they rarely bite humans.

HOW DOES SNAKE VENOM WORK?

Snake venom works on victims in two main ways. The venom of snakes such as vipers causes death by damaging the prey's body tissues and blood. Other snakes produce neurotoxins, which attack the victim's nervous system, paralysing the heart, breathing system, and muscles.

Rattle

◄ RATTLESNAKE
Venomous rattlesnakes send out a warning to large animals by shaking the rattle of loose scales on their tail.

Venom gland

Hollow fangs

FANGS OUT ►
Vipers lift their fangs forward just before biting, as this model shows. At rest, the fangs are held against the roof of the mouth.

Skin can change colour to camouflage the chameleon or express its mood to other chameleons. Coloured cells called chromatophores expand or contract to make this happen.

Prehensile tail can be wrapped around twigs or branches for extra stability and support

WHAT IS THE DIFFERENCE BETWEEN A TURTLE AND A TORTOISE?

Turtles live in water and tortoises live on land. Turtles from the same scientific family as tortoises are sometimes called terrapins. Terrapins have clawed feet and live in freshwater habitats. Tortoises, turtles, and terrapins have changed little in 200 million years. They all have bony or leathery shells.

Strong flippers propel the turtle through the water

GREEN TURTLE ▶
The green turtle is one of just six sea-living turtle species. Its bony shell is covered with a layer of horn. The largest sea turtle, the leatherback, may reach 2.5 m (8 ft 2 in) in length.

HOW DO REPTILES REPRODUCE?

Most reptiles lay eggs, but in a few snakes and lizards, the eggs develop inside the mother's body so that she gives birth to live young. Crocodiles and tortoises lay hard-shelled eggs similar to birds' eggs. Turtles, snakes, and most lizards lay eggs with softer leathery shells. Sea turtles lay their eggs on beaches.

Baby crocodile carried in mother's mouth for protection from predators

reptiles

HOW DO CROCODILES HUNT?

The 22 species of crocodile and their relatives are fearsome predators. Crocodiles ambush large prey. They snatch victims from the water's edge and drag them under to drown them. Crocodiles cannot chew, but may spin round to break the victim's body into pieces.

◀ CHAMELEON
Chameleons hunt by stealth, creeping forwards until their insect prey is in reach. More than half of the 85 species of chameleon live on the island of Madagascar, including this Nosy Be chameleon.

CARING PARENT ▶
Nile crocodiles are among the few reptiles that look after their young. Once she has laid her eggs, the mother watches over the nest until the babies hatch. Then she helps her offspring down to the water, sometimes carrying them in her mouth.

REGENERATION

Some animals are able to regenerate (regrow) tails, limbs, or other body parts lost in accidents or bitten off by predators. Among vertebrates (backboned animals), these species include lizards such as the tree skink and the salamander (an amphibian).

Fracture point has blood vessels that close up quickly to reduce bleeding

Tail regrows completely in less than a year

WHY DO SOME LIZARDS SHED THEIR TAILS?

Losing all or part of the tail is a defence mechanism for some species of lizard. If grabbed by a predator, the tail breaks off at a fracture point, which minimizes bleeding, and continues to wriggle, distracting the predator while the lizard escapes. Within nine months the tail regrows, stiffened by cartilage instead of bone.

WHICH OTHER ANIMALS REGENERATE BODY PARTS?

Starfish, sponges, flatworms, and crabs can also regrow body parts severed in accidents. Sponges have an even more amazing ability. When passed through a fine mesh these simple multicellular animals are able to reassemble themselves. The cells seek each other out and join back together.

▲ BEFORE AND AFTER
The tree skink is just one of many lizards that can regenerate their tails. Before it was lost, the end of this lizard's tail contained bones. Now those bones have been replaced by gristly cartilage.

FIND OUT MORE ▶▶ Cells 73 • Reproduction 101 • Vertebrates 102

BIRDS

Birds have wings covered with feathers, which allow most of them to fly. Most birds also have extremely good eyesight and hearing. They reproduce by laying eggs, and many build ▸▸ NESTS to rear their young. Some birds fly on long journeys called ▸▸ MIGRATIONS to breed or find food.

Bones are hidden beneath feathers and muscle on the leading edge of the wing

Wing feathers are long and broad to enable soaring flight

Tail feathers are used for braking and as a rudder, letting the eagle slow down or turn suddenly

Hooked beak for tearing flesh

GOLDEN EAGLE IN FLIGHT ▲
Birds of prey are powerful fliers and have superb eyesight, allowing them to spot prey on the ground even when they are hundreds of metres up in the air.

Sharp talons grab prey firmly

HOW ARE BIRDS' BODIES DESIGNED FOR FLIGHT?
Birds have evolved many features to make flight possible. The skeleton is strong but light, with a large breastbone to support powerful muscles for flapping wings up and down. The wings themselves are curved on top, flatter beneath – air travels faster over the upper surface, producing lift. The long tail helps with direction and balance, while strong legs assist take-off.

▲ BONE STRUCTURE
Birds' bones are honeycombed with holes which reduce weight but not strength. Beaks are also lighter than jaws with teeth.

BIRD CLASSIFICATION

- With around 9,000 species, birds make up the second largest vertebrate class after fish. They are also the most widespread, occurring from the polar ice caps to the most isolated islands.

- Birds are classified into 27 different orders.
- The largest order, Passeriformes or perching birds, includes well over half of all bird species.
- The smallest order has just one species – the ostrich.

NESTS

Nests are safe places where birds lay their eggs and rear their young. Adult birds do not normally sleep in nests, but roost in trees or other sheltered spots. Different species of bird build different types of nest. Some are simple, others extremely complex.

WHY DO BIRDS NEST IN TREES?
Many birds nest in trees because eggs laid there will be out of reach of many predators. Some birds nest in other inaccessible places. For example, swallows and martins nest under the eaves of houses, and storks on rooftops. Many sea birds, such as gulls, nest on cliff ledges, while kingfishers dig burrows in riverbanks.

◀ SKILLED NEST-BUILDER
African weaver birds construct elaborate nests by knotting stems of grass together. Some weaver birds nest together in huge hanging structures that are occupied all year round.

GUILLEMOT EGG ▶
Guillemots lay their eggs on narrow cliff ledges. The pointed shape enables the egg to roll safely round in a circle if knocked.

CAN ANY YOUNG BIRDS LOOK AFTER THEMSELVES?
The young of ground-nesting birds, such as ducks and geese, hatch out as fluffy chicks, which are soon able to stand and fend for themselves. Most birds, however, hatch out blind, bald, and helpless. Their parents bring them food for several weeks while their feathers sprout and they grow strong enough to leave the nest.

HOW DO FEATHERS HELP BIRDS FLY?

Feathers on a bird's wings provide a lightweight but solid surface to push against the air. As the wing flaps downward, they mesh together, then part to allow air through as it sweeps upward again. As well as allowing it to fly, a bird's feathers keep it warm and dry.

birds

◄ **FEATHER STRUCTURE**
Strands called barbs branch from the central shaft. These bear even thinner barbules, with toothed edges that zip together.

CAN ALL BIRDS FLY?

Some island birds, such as New Zealand's kiwis, lost the ability to fly because their islands had few predators. Large flightless birds such as ostriches, emus, and rheas are strong runners. Penguins cannot fly, but are expert at swimming and diving.

Serrated beak for slicing through fruit

DOWN FEATHER

CONTOUR FEATHER

▲ **FEATHER TYPES**
Birds have three types of feathers. Contour feathers cover the body, while down feathers are fluffy to provide warmth.

FLIGHT FEATHER

CHESTNUT-MANDIBLED TOUCAN ►
Many birds have extremely bright feathers. These are often grown by males to attract mates but sometimes, as with toucans, both sexes have them.

FOOT SHAPES

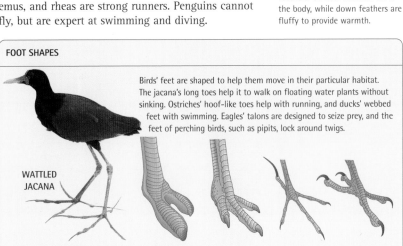

Birds' feet are shaped to help them move in their particular habitat. The jacana's long toes help it to walk on floating water plants without sinking. Ostriches' hoof-like toes help with running, and ducks' webbed feet with swimming. Eagles' talons are designed to seize prey, and the feet of perching birds, such as pipits, lock around twigs.

WATTLED JACANA

OSTRICH **RHEA** **PIPIT** **WOODPECKER**

WHAT DO BIRDS EAT?

Birds eat a wide range of plant and animal foods. Some feed on specific parts of plants, such as fruit, seeds, or nectar. Others are predators. Hawks, owls, and eagles catch smaller creatures such as rodents. Many sea birds feed on fish. Some shore birds have long beaks to probe the mud for worms.

MIGRATION

Many birds fly long distances on yearly migrations to find food, avoid drought or winter chill, or reach sheltered spots to rear their young. In spring, many fly to cooler regions where food is abundant in summer. They return to warmer lands for winter.

HOW DO BIRDS KNOW WHEN TO MIGRATE?

Changing temperatures and daylight are thought to trigger bird migrations. In some species, the young follow their parents and learn the way from them. Others set off alone, guided by instinct. Birds navigate by the position of the Sun, Moon, stars, and physical landmarks. Some can sense the Earth's magnetic field.

A LONG JOURNEY ►
The ruby-throated hummingbird migrates thousands of kilometres every year. As well as nectar, this bird feeds on insects. In the North American winter, both of these foods dry up, so the bird flies south to Central America, to find food. In spring, it flies back north to breed.

Autumn route southwards to Central America

Hummingbird is little bigger than a thumb

DO OTHER ANIMALS MIGRATE?

Many kinds of animals migrate, from mammals, reptiles, and amphibians to crustaceans, fish, and insects. Reindeer move across the Arctic tundra and wildebeest cross the African plains to find fresh grazing. In the oceans, blue and grey whales swim from polar seas to mate in the tropics.

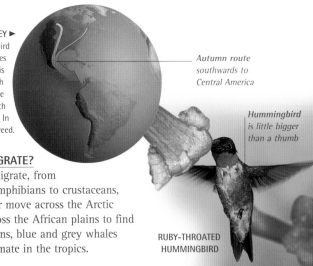

RUBY-THROATED HUMMINGBIRD

FIND OUT MORE ▸▸ Reproduction 101 • Vertebrates 102

MAMMALS

A group of warm-blooded animals with a bony skeleton, mammals include mice and other **▶▶ RODENTS**, **▶▶ PRIMATES**, such as monkeys and humans, and animals as various as hippos, deer, and cats. The 4,500 or so species include elephants, the largest creatures on land, and whales, the largest of all animals on Earth.

WHAT FEATURES DO ALL MAMMALS SHARE?
In almost all mammals, the babies develop inside the mother before they are born. This process is called **▶▶ GESTATION**. Once born, baby mammals suckle, or feed, on their mother's milk. Most mammals have hair, and all land mammals have four limbs. However, in whales, the rear limbs have disappeared.

WHAT DO MAMMALS EAT?
Mammals have become very successful because of the wide range of foods they eat. Meat-eaters include cats, hyenas, and dogs. Shrews and hedgehogs eat insects. Plant-eaters include hoofed animals such as horses and deer, and also rabbits and rodents. Some mammals are omnivores, eating both plants and meat.

▲ DOLPHIN
Dolphins and whales form a group of mammals called cetaceans. Cetaceans spend their whole lives in water and even give birth there. They resemble fish but have lungs not gills, and so must come to the surface to breathe air.

LIONS HUNTING ▶
Predators such as lions and tigers have sharp claws and long canine teeth to seize and kill their victims. Lions hunt in groups to bring down large prey such as zebras and buffalo.

GESTATION

Gestation is the time young mammals spend growing in their mother's womb. Most mammals develop in this way, so the mother gives birth to fully formed young. Many **▶▶ MARSUPIAL** babies, such as kangaroos, complete their development in their mother's pouch.

WHAT HAPPENS DURING GESTATION?
In most mammals, the fertilized egg implants itself in the mother's womb. There it develops into an embryo, which is nourished by the placenta. Marsupials have no placenta and give birth to tiny, helpless young. **▶▶ MONOTREMES**, such as the platypus, lay eggs.

HOW LONG DOES GESTATION TAKE?
Gestation takes longer in some mammals than in others. In rodents, such as hamsters, it takes just two to three weeks. Larger mammals produce fewer offspring, which usually take much longer to gestate. Elephants take the longest time of all – 20 months.

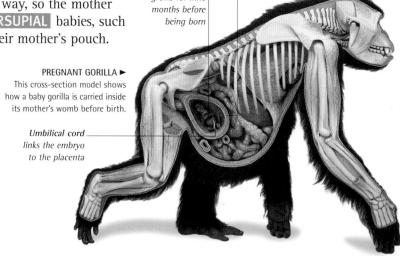

Placenta nourishes and maintains the embryo through the umbilical cord, and is expelled after birth

Gorilla embryo grows for nine months before being born

PREGNANT GORILLA ▶
This cross-section model shows how a baby gorilla is carried inside its mother's womb before birth.

Umbilical cord links the embryo to the placenta

▲ POLAR BEAR CUBS SUCKLING
At birth, young mammals are fairly weak and defenceless. One or both of the parents, and sometimes other adults, looks after the young until they are weaned and able to find food for themselves. The babies learn survival skills from the adults and often by playing with others of their own age.

HOW DO MAMMALS REPRODUCE?

All mammals reproduce sexually – sperm from the male fertilizes the female's egg. In some mammal species, males establish breeding territories, where they display to the females, showing that they are fit and strong. In others, the males fight for the right to mate. Many male hoofed mammals have horns or antlers which they crash or lock together in tests of strength.

WHY IS BEING WARM-BLOODED USEFUL?

Mammals maintain a constant body temperature, which lets them stay active in all weathers. Maintaining body temperature takes up a lot of energy, so mammals need large quantities of food. To help reduce the amount of food they must find, mammals in cold environments have thick fur or fatty blubber to retain body heat. Some go into ▸▸ HIBERNATION to survive winter.

HIBERNATION

Many mammals, such as bats, bears, and dormice, survive winter in cool and polar lands by entering a deep sleep called hibernation. This strategy helps to conserve energy that would otherwise be lost in the struggle to keep warm and find scarce food.

mammals

WHAT CHANGES HAPPEN DURING HIBERNATION?

Heartbeat, breathing, and other body processes slow right down, and the animal's temperature drops so that it feels cold to the touch. When the weather warms again in spring, these processes are reversed, and the mammal wakes up to resume active life.

◀ SURVIVING THROUGH SLEEP
A dormouse passes the winter in a snug ball of grass and bark in its underground nest. Not dead but simply saving energy, it lives on stored fat and wakes when temperatures rise again in spring.

WHAT OTHER TYPES OF ANIMAL HIBERNATE?

Hibernation is very common among cold-blooded animals, such as amphibians, reptiles, and insects, that live in cold or temperate regions. In deserts and other barren places, some animals enter a similar state, called aestivation, to survive drought.

FIND OUT MORE ▸▸ Marsupials 123 • Monotremes 123 • Primates 122 • Rodents 122

PRIMATES

These mostly tree-living mammals are divided into two groups. Prosimians, or primitive primates, include lemurs, lorises, and tarsiers. Anthropoids, or higher primates, include marmosets, apes, monkeys, and humans. Primates range in size from mouse lemurs weighing 100 g (3½ oz) to gorillas, which are 2,000 times heavier.

WHAT FEATURES DO ALL PRIMATES SHARE?

Primates are intelligent mammals. As well as hairy bodies, most have long arms and opposable thumbs and big toes, which enable them to grasp branches. Primates' eyes face forwards, giving them binocular vision, which helps them judge distances as they swing through the trees. Their main senses are sight and touch; hearing and scent are less important.

WHY DO MANY PRIMATES LIVE IN GROUPS?

By living in groups, primates can defend large feeding territories and are more likely to spot predators than they would on their own. Group living also helps with raising young. Primate babies take a long time to grow up – three to five years in apes such as chimpanzees. Having other adults around helps take the burden off mothers and gives the babies added protection.

◄ CHIMP CRACKING NUTS
Apes are the largest and most intelligent primates. Some apes use tools. Chimpanzees, for example, use stones as weapons or to crack nuts, moss to soak up water, and sticks to probe for insect food.

▲ PREHENSILE TAIL
Many South American monkeys, such as this red howler, have a grasping tail. African and Asian monkeys' tails are not prehensile.

RODENTS

With around 1,800 species, rodents make up the largest group of mammals. The smallest rodents weigh just a few grams. The largest, South America's capybara, is the size of a large dog. All rodents have chisel-like incisor teeth at the front of their jaws to gnaw food.

WHERE ARE RODENTS FOUND?

Rodents can survive almost anywhere except the sea. Marmots and lemmings inhabit snowy mountains and Arctic wastes, while jerboas and gerbils live in deserts. Rats and mice have colonized our towns and cities. Different rodents are adapted for climbing, swimming, burrowing, or gliding through the air.

WHAT DO RODENTS EAT?

Most rodents are plant-eaters, searching out food with their sensitive noses and long whiskers. Razor-sharp incisor teeth make short work of nuts and seeds. Some rodents carry food in cheek pouches.

▲ BABY HOUSE MICE
Rodents breed very quickly. Mice can produce up to 50 offspring in a year, which grow up so fast that they themselves are ready to breed in six weeks. Rodent populations multiply quickly when food is plentiful.

◄ BUSY BEAVER
Beavers fell trees with their teeth to dam rivers and form lakes. They build a home called a lodge in the middle of the lakes, where they can rear their young in safety. The lodge's entrance is under water.

MARSUPIALS

The group of marsupials includes kangaroos, wallabies, possums, gliders, and wombats. All marsupials are born early and complete their development in their mother's pouch or clinging to her fur.

▼ NEWBORN JOEY
A young kangaroo, or joey, is born after just 4–5 weeks. Blind and hairless, the tiny baby crawls up its mother's fur to her pouch and clamps onto her nipple.

◄ JOEY IN THE POUCH
The fully developed joey begins to leave its mother's pouch at six months old, but hops back in at the first hint of danger. It becomes independent when one year old.

WHERE DO MARSUPIALS LIVE?
Most marsupials live in Australia and surrounding islands, but some are found in South America, and one, the Virginia opossum, lives in North America. Marsupials multiplied and evolved into all sorts of species in Australia because there were no placental mammals there to compete with them.

WHAT DO MARSUPIALS EAT?
Many marsupials are plant-eaters. Kangaroos and wombats feed mostly on grasses, while koalas eat leaves. Some gliders feed on nectar from flowers. Tasmanian devils are solitary and nocturnal, preying on rabbits, chickens, and other small animals. Virginia opossums are omnivorous, eating fruit, eggs, insects, and other small creatures.

CLAMBERING KOALA ►
Many marsupials are expert climbers. Koalas feed exclusively on tough eucalyptus leaves. The leaves contain little nourishment, so koalas save energy by sleeping for up to 18 hours per day.

MONOTREMES

e ⏭ mammals

The small group of egg-laying mammals contains just three species – the duck-billed platypus and two types of echidna. Monotremes are found only in Australia and on the island of New Guinea. These secretive, burrowing creatures are rarely seen.

WHAT DO MONOTREMES FEED ON?
Monotremes eat invertebrates, which they search for at night. Echidnas, also known as spiny anteaters, feed on termites and other insects. They slurp them up with their long, sticky tongues. Platypuses hunt under water, searching out worms, crustaceans, and insects with their soft, sensitive beaks.

HOW MANY EGGS DO MONOTREMES LAY?
Platypuses and echidnas lay between one and three soft-shelled eggs. Female echidnas incubate their eggs in pouches on their abdomens. The platypus curls around her eggs in her burrow. When the eggs hatch, after about ten days, the babies feed on milk seeping from patches on the mother's abdomen. The young become independent after four or five months.

Long snout used for probing into termites' nests

STRANGE COMBINATION ►
The platypus has a duck-like beak, a mole-like body, webbed feet, and a beaver-like tail. When the first, stuffed specimens reached Europe in the late 1700s, people thought they were fakes.

▼ SPINY ARMOUR
The echidna bristles with defences against its enemies. Male echidnas and platypuses also have spurs on their legs.

FIND OUT MORE ⏭ Feeding 98 • Reproduction 101 • Vertebrates 102

ENDANGERED SPECIES

All over the world, plant and animal species are now at risk of ▶▶ **EXTINCTION** because of changes humans are causing to the environment. Experts estimate that up to 30,000 of these endangered species may now be dying out each year – including many that have not yet been identified.

EXTINCTION

Extinction occurs when all the members of a species die out. Extinction is a natural process that has happened throughout the 3.5 billion years that life has existed on our planet – but now many creatures are dying out at once because of humans.

WHAT IS THE WORST PROBLEM FACING WILDLIFE?
The greatest single threat to the world's wildlife is habitat loss – destruction of the wild places where animals live. In many regions, forests are felled, marshes drained, and grasslands cleared to build roads, towns, mines, and dams. Pollution from towns, farms, and factories also poisons wildlife on land and at sea.

WHY ARE ISLAND SPECIES ESPECIALLY AT RISK?
Island species are at greater risk than most because many are found nowhere else. Their populations are often very small, so they are more easily affected by new threats. Many island animals are not used to predators. When new creatures such as cats or rats are brought to islands, they can devastate wildlife.

WHAT ARE MASS EXTINCTIONS?
Mass extinctions occur when large numbers of species die out at once due to rapid changes in the environment. Around 65 million years ago, a mass extinction wiped out the dinosaurs. Now experts fear that humans are causing a new wave of extinctions.

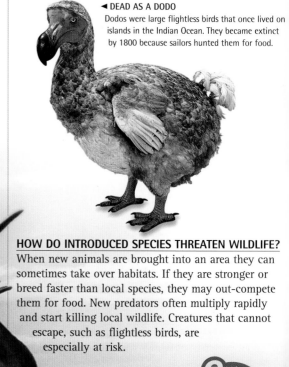

◀ DEAD AS A DODO
Dodos were large flightless birds that once lived on islands in the Indian Ocean. They became extinct by 1800 because sailors hunted them for food.

▲ SPOTTED OWL
Spotted owls are at risk because the North American forests where they live are being cut down. Tropical rainforests hold a huge variety of plants and animals, but these are also disappearing fast.

Each tusk is made of ivory worth thousands of dollars on the black market

BURNING IVORY ▶
These elephant tusks were confiscated from poachers and are being destroyed so they cannot be sold. Although elephants are protected by law, there is a large illegal market for ivory, so elephants remain in constant danger.

HOW DO INTRODUCED SPECIES THREATEN WILDLIFE?
When new animals are brought into an area they can sometimes take over habitats. If they are stronger or breed faster than local species, they may out-compete them for food. New predators often multiply rapidly and start killing local wildlife. Creatures that cannot escape, such as flightless birds, are especially at risk.

e ▶▶
endangered species

FIND OUT MORE ▶▶ Dinosaurs 78–79 • Evolution 74–75 • Habitats 82–84 • Human Impact 64–65

CONSERVATION

Governments, scientists, wildlife organizations, and volunteers undertake a range of conservation work to protect wild places and the species living there. We need plants and animals for food, clothing, and medicines. In addition, plants provide life-giving oxygen. It makes sense to protect the natural world.

WHAT IS THE BEST WAY TO SAVE WILDLIFE?
Preserving natural habitats protects all of the animals and plants that live in them. All over the world, large areas of wilderness are now protected as national parks and reserves, where harming wildlife is illegal. Types of forestry and farming that harvest resources without damaging the environment are also important. So is legislation against pollution.

▲ BACK TO THE WILD
The Arabian oryx had been hunted to the brink of extinction by the 1970s. The last few individuals were taken to zoos and bred. In the 1980s, a small number were reintroduced to Oman – where 300 live today.

HOW DO CAPTIVE BREEDING PROGRAMMES WORK?
As a first step, scientists find out about the needs of the endangered species, so that suitable conditions can be provided. Next, zoos lend each other animals for breeding. If the programme is successful, some of the offspring may be reintroduced to the wild.

HOW CAN ORDINARY PEOPLE HELP CONSERVATION?
One way to help is to join a large organization such as the World Wildlife Fund (WWF) or Greenpeace. Membership fees are used to pay for conservation work or save areas of natural habitat. You can also join local wildlife groups to conserve habitats near your home.

▲ SAFE FROM POACHERS
An endangered black rhino suckles her calf in the Ngorongoro Reserve in Tanzania, Africa. Tourist fees help pay the park's costs. Around 10 per cent of the Earth's land area is now protected by reserves.

Calf stays with mother until more than a year old

HAS CONSERVATION SAVED WILDLIFE IN THE PAST?
Without conservation, there would be a lot less wildlife around. In the second half of the 20th century, conservationists helped stop large-scale hunting of whales, allowing their populations to recover. Huge areas of rainforest and other habitats have also been protected, saving many species from extinction.

WHAT ACTION CAN BE TAKEN TO SAVE SPECIES ON THE BRINK OF EXTINCTION?
The Convention for International Trade in Endangered Species (CITES) restricts trade in threatened wildlife. In addition, many zoos run captive breeding programmes to save rare animals. In most countries, it is illegal to harm or disturb rare species.

conservation

Herdsman guards his cattle from lions and other predators

MASAI HERDSMAN WITH CATTLE HERD ▶
Farm animals, such as cattle, compete with wild animals for food. As the number of people on the planet grows, so more and more land is taken over by farming. This leaves less space for wildlife to live in.

FIND OUT MORE ▶▶ Farming 66 • Fishing 67 • Forestry 67 • Habitats 82–84 • Human Impact 64–65 • Plants 88–89

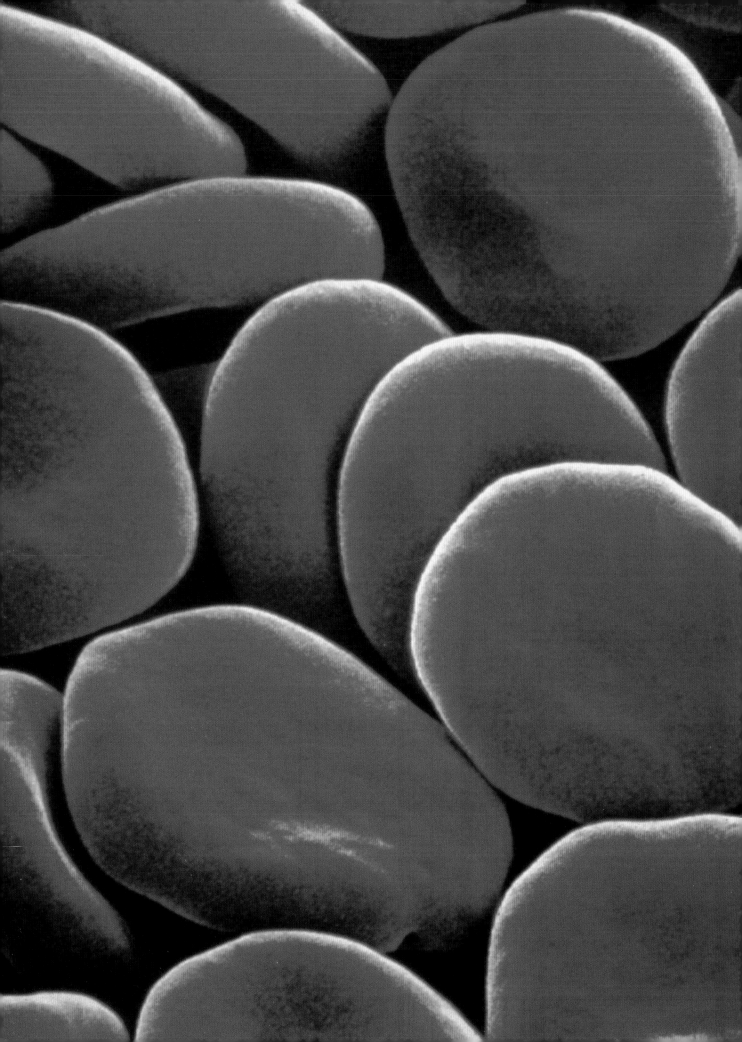

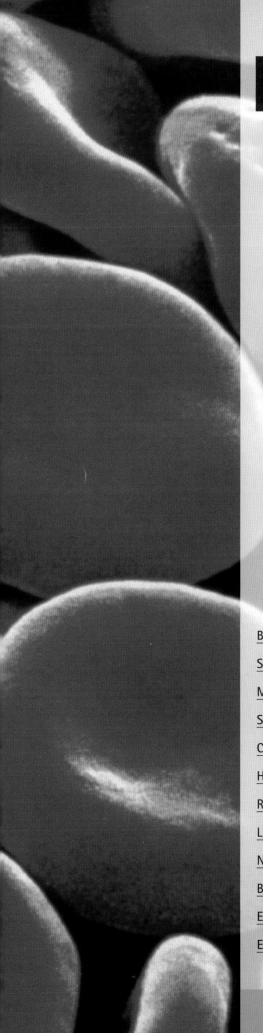

HUMAN BODY

BODY

A human body is made up of 100 trillion ▶CELLS of different types. Similar cells are grouped to form tissue, and tissues form ▶ORGANS. Using modern ▶IMAGING technology, we can look into the body and see it work.

WHAT MAKES HUMANS SPECIAL?

Humans are unique in the animal world. We are the only mammals to walk on two legs, our brains are unusually large, and our skin is almost hairless. Yet in most ways we are just like other mammals, with two pairs of limbs, two eyes and ears, and the usual mammalian internal organs.

WHY ARE WE ALL DIFFERENT?

Apart from identical twins, no two people in the world are exactly alike. We differ in many subtle ways because we each have a unique set of genes, inherited from our mother and father. Our genes control the way we grow and develop from embryos into adults.

CELLS

The microscopic units that make up all living things are called cells. In the body, there are hundreds of different types of cell, each designed to perform a specific task.

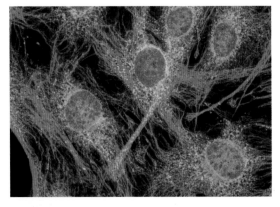

WHAT CONTROLS CELLS?

Most cells have a control centre called a nucleus. The nucleus holds the DNA which makes up the genes. Depending on the type of cell, certain genes are switched on or off. The active genes send instructions out of the nucleus, controlling all the chemical reactions that happen in the rest of the cell.

WHAT IS TISSUE?

Cells of the same type are often grouped together in a pattern, to form tissue. Muscle is made up of rows of muscle cells. Skin consists of sheets of skin cells. Blood is a liquid tissue of cells suspended in a watery fluid. There are four main types: epithelial tissue, connective tissue, muscular tissue, and nervous tissue.

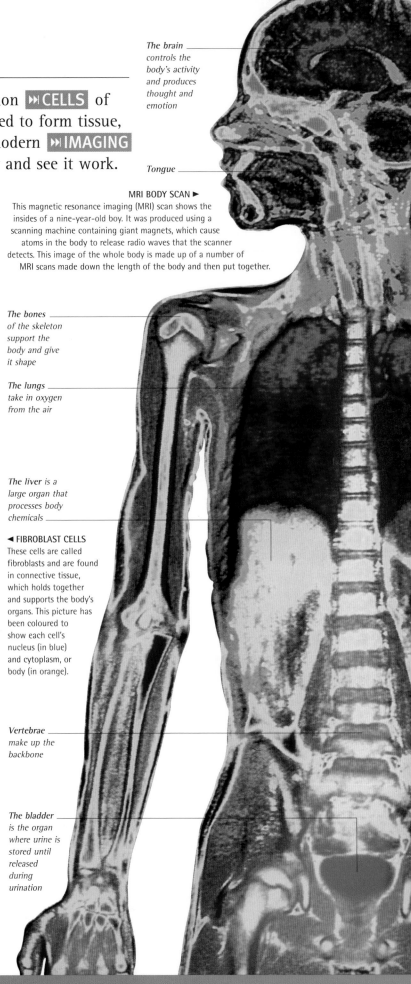

The brain controls the body's activity and produces thought and emotion

Tongue

MRI BODY SCAN ▶
This magnetic resonance imaging (MRI) scan shows the insides of a nine-year-old boy. It was produced using a scanning machine containing giant magnets, which cause atoms in the body to release radio waves that the scanner detects. This image of the whole body is made up of a number of MRI scans made down the length of the body and then put together.

The bones of the skeleton support the body and give it shape

The lungs take in oxygen from the air

The liver is a large organ that processes body chemicals

◀ FIBROBLAST CELLS
These cells are called fibroblasts and are found in connective tissue, which holds together and supports the body's organs. This picture has been coloured to show each cell's nucleus (in blue) and cytoplasm, or body (in orange).

Vertebrae make up the backbone

The bladder is the organ where urine is stored until released during urination

ORGANS

Tissues are grouped together into larger structures called organs, which carry out specific tasks. The heart, for instance, is an organ designed to pump blood.

Muscles (in blue) enable the body to move

WHAT ARE ORGANS MADE OF?

Every organ contains several different tissues. The stomach, for example, consists mostly of muscle cells, which contract to churn food around. The inner lining of the stomach is made of epithelial tissue, which is continually worn away and replaced. There are also glands that secrete digestive juices, blood vessels, nerves, and connective tissue to hold it all together.

HOW DO ORGANS WORK TOGETHER?

Organs work together in teams, called systems, to carry out tasks. For instance, the stomach, intestines, and pancreas are part of the digestive system, breaking down food into molecules that the body can absorb. Some systems work together – the skeletal and muscular systems combine to enable us to move.

BODY SYSTEMS	
Integumentary system	Hair, skin, and nails protect the body from germs, injury, heat loss, and drying out.
Skeletal system	A framework of bones and connective tissues that supports the body and, with muscles, enables it to move.
Muscular system	The system of muscles (involuntary and voluntary) that contract to make the body move.
Nervous system	The brain, nerves, sense organs, and related tissues enable the body to detect and respond to changes.
Endocrine system	A system of glands that regulates body processes by secreting chemicals, called hormones, into the blood.
Circulatory system	The heart and blood vessels transport blood to the body's cells to deliver nutrients and remove waste.
Lymphatic system	A system that returns body fluids to the bloodstream via nodes, where the fluids are screened for germs.
Immune system	An internal defence mechanism, consisting of cells and tissues that destroy invading germs and abnormal cells.
Respiratory system	The lungs and airways leading to the lungs, which take oxygen into the body and expel carbon dioxide.
Digestive system	The mouth and most of the abdominal organs work to break down food into molecules the blood can absorb.
Urinary system	The kidneys remove unwanted chemicals from the blood and expel them via the bladder and urethra.
Reproductive system	The organs involved in sexual reproduction – the penis and testes in men; ovaries, uterus, and vagina in women.

IMAGING

Modern imaging techniques enable doctors to see inside the body without cutting it open. There are many different techniques, each suited to looking at particular tissues or processes.

▲ PET SCAN OF THE BRAIN
Positron emission tomography (PET) uses injected radioactive substances to reveal activity in organs and tissues. The coloured areas above show the parts of the brain used during speech.

DO X-RAYS SHOW ONLY BONES?

No, X-rays can also be used to look at soft tissues, such as the breast or blood vessels, to check if they are healthy. For blood vessels, a harmless dye that absorbs X-rays is first injected into the vessels – X-rays will then show their outline. This type of image is called an angiogram.

WHAT IS A CT SCAN?

A computed tomography (CT) scan is a computer-generated image built from X-ray beams. A machine slowly moves over the area of the body examined, taking X-ray pictures from many angles. A computer then analyses the X-rays to build up a detailed cross-section of the body, including its soft tissues.

HOW IS ULTRASOUND USED?

Ultrasound scanning is one of the most common imaging techniques. High-frequency sound waves are bounced off internal organs and the pattern of echoes is displayed on a TV screen. Ultrasound scanners are good for studying moving liquids, such as blood or fluid in the uterus (womb).

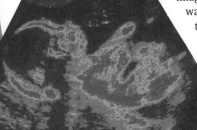

◄ ULTRASOUND OF A FOETUS
Ultrasound scanners are routinely used to monitor unborn babies, to check their growth and the development of organs, such as the heart.

X-RAY OF BROKEN ARM ▲
This X-ray shows the badly fractured (broken) radius and ulna bones of the forearm. X-rays are a form of radiation that passes through soft parts of the body, but shows up dense material such as bones and teeth.

FIND OUT MORE ►► Cells 73 • Genetics 209 • Mammals 120–123

Cranium
(skull)

Mandible
(lower jaw)

Clavicle
(collarbone)

Cervical
(neck)
vertebrae

Scapula
(shoulder
blade)

Sternum
(breastbone)

Ribs

Humerus
(upper arm
bone)

Pelvis
(hip bone)

Lumbar
(lower back)
vertebrae

Radius
(thumb side
forearm bone)

Ulna
(forearm bone)

Carpals
(wrist bones)

Metacarpals
(palm bones)

Phalanges
(finger
bones)

Femur
(thigh bone)

e ⏩

skeleton

Patella
(kneecap)

Tibia
(shin bone)

Fibula
(calf bone)

Metatarsals
(foot bones)

Tarsals
(ankle bones)

Phalanges
(toe bones)

SKELETON

The skeleton is the inner framework of ⏩**BONES** that supports and gives shape to the human body. It also protects some of the soft organs of the body – for example, the skull surrounds the brain. Muscles and ligaments pull on the bones of the skeleton at ⏩**JOINTS** to make the body move.

HOW STRONG ARE BONES?
Weight for weight, bone is five times stronger than steel, but it is very light. The skeleton makes up only one sixth of an adult's weight. The skull in particular is very strong, because it has to protect the brain and sense organs, such as the eyes, ears, and nose.

ARE BONES DRY?
Dead bones are dry and brittle, but living bones feel wet and a little soft. They are also slightly flexible, so they can absorb pressure. Like most parts of the body, bones have a network of blood vessels and nerves running through them, and they bleed when broken. Up to one third of the weight of a living bone is water.

The jaw is the only freely moving bone in the skull

The cranium, the part of the skull that protects the brain, is made up of eight bones fused tightly together

HOW DOES A SKELETON GROW?
A newborn baby has more than 300 bones, but many are made of a soft, rubbery material called cartilage instead of bone. Up until the late teens, as a child grows the cartilage lengthens and turns into bone, and some bones fuse together. By adulthood, there are just 206 bones in the skeleton.

SKULL BONES ▲
This coloured X-ray of the skull has an image of the brain placed over it to show the fit. The skull is made up of 22 separate bones, all locked together by immovable joints, except for the jaw.

GROWING HANDS ►
The first X-ray shows the gaps between the bones in a baby's hand that are filled with cartilage. By age 20, the finger bones have grown longer and ossified (turned to bone).

The fingers are now made of mature, hard bone

Cartilage outline is just visible

◄ THE HUMAN SKELETON
Each bone in the body has a scientific name, but many also have everyday names. The largest is the femur, or thigh bone, and the smallest are the tiny ossicle bones in the inner ear. More than half the bones of an adult's skeleton are in the hands and feet.

HAND OF A
ONE-YEAR-OLD

HAND OF A
20-YEAR-OLD

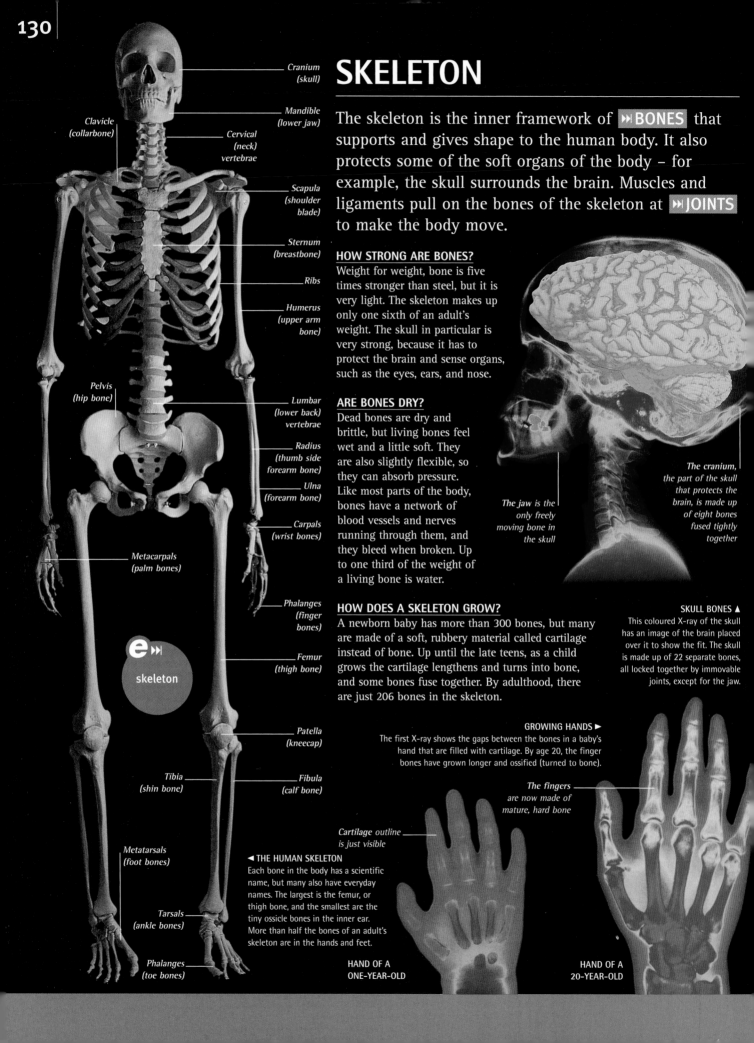

BONE

This strong yet flexible material is a living tissue, made up of bone cells embedded in a matrix of fibres. Bone is not solid – blood vessels and nerves run through tunnels within it, and some areas are a honeycomb of small spaces. In the centre of many bones is a cavity packed with a jelly-like substance called bone marrow.

WHAT IS BONE MADE OF?

The hard matrix of bone is made of crystals of calcium phosphate and other minerals, and fibres of protein called collagen. The minerals make bone hard, while the collagen fibres are arranged lengthways to make bone flexible. Both are produced by cells called osteocytes, found throughout the matrix.

Compact bone

Spongy bone

▲ SECTION THROUGH A BONE
This femur has been cut to show its different layers. Because this is not a living bone the hollow centre has no bone marrow in it.

◄ COMPACT BONE
Densely packed, concentric rings of minerals and collagen give compact bone immense strength. Blood vessels run through tunnels in the centre of each set of rings.

SPONGY BONE ▲
A honeycomb of struts and spaces makes spongy bone lightweight yet resilient. Bone marrow fills the spaces.

WHAT DOES BONE MARROW DO?

Bone marrow makes millions of blood cells every second to replace old, worn-out blood cells, which the body destroys. There are two types of marrow: red and yellow. Red marrow makes blood cells. Yellow marrow is mainly a fat store, but it can turn into red marrow if the body needs extra blood cells. At birth, nearly all bone marrow is red. During the teens, much of it turns into yellow bone marrow.

JOINTS

Bones are joined at joints. Different types of joint allow different movements. Joints are often held together by straps of tough fibrous tissue, called ligaments, and the muscles that cross the joint.

HOW DO DIFFERENT JOINTS WORK?

Most joints are free-moving. These are called synovial joints, and they allow varying degrees of movement. Hinge joints, like those in the fingers, knees, and elbows, can only bend and straighten. Others, such as the ball-and-socket joints in the shoulders and hips, allow movement in all directions.

WHY DON'T BONES RUB AGAINST EACH OTHER?

In synovial joints, the bone endings are covered with a smooth, glossy material called hyaline cartilage, which is slippery yet hard-wearing. This cartilage allows the bone ends to slide smoothly past each other. Also, a capsule of fluid surrounds the joint. The fluid lubricates the joint, reducing friction just as oil helps the movement of a bicycle chain.

Synovial fluid (blue) allows the joint to move more freely

Cartilage (pink) lines the surfaces where the bones meet

The elbow is a hinge joint, allowing the arm to bend and straighten

HINGE JOINT

A column of 24 vertebrae holds the trunk upright, but twists and bends to allow movement

The shoulder is a ball-and-socket joint, which allows the greatest range of movement

BALL-AND-SOCKET JOINT

KNEE JOINT ►
Synovial fluid and cartilage ease movement where the femur (thigh bone) and tibia (shin bone) meet.

◄ ARM MOVEMENT
The joints in the shoulder, elbow, and wrist work together to give the arm an amazing range of movement.

FIND OUT MORE ►► Circulation 134 • Growth 149 • Muscle 132

MUSCLE

Body movement is brought about by muscle, a tissue that can contract. There are three main types: skeletal muscle, smooth muscle, and cardiac muscle. Most muscle is made of elongated cells called ▶▶ MUSCLE FIBRES.

WHAT ARE INVOLUNTARY MUSCLES?

Smooth muscle and cardiac muscle are involuntary – they work automatically, without our conscious control. Smooth muscle is found in the walls of the intestines, stomach, oesophagus, and other organs. It contracts slowly and rhythmically to push food through the digestive system. Cardiac muscle is found in the heart and works continuously without tiring.

HOW DO MUSCLES WORK WITH BONES?

Skeletal muscles move bones by pulling on them. Because we control this movement, they are called voluntary muscles. Muscles can pull but not push, so skeletal muscles are often arranged in pairs that pull bones in opposite directions.

MUSCLE FIBRES

Individual muscle cells are called muscle fibres. Skeletal muscle is made up of thousands of muscle fibres arranged in parallel bundles. Each fibre is thinner than a hair and can measure up to 30 cm (12 in) long.

SKELETAL MUSCLES ▶
The body has some 640 skeletal muscles, accounting for about 40 per cent of body weight. Skeletal muscles are attached to bones by tough fibrous connections called tendons.

Pectoralis major swings the arm

Frontalis wrinkles forehead and lifts eyebrows

Orbicularis oculi closes eyelids

Orbicularis oris purses the lips

Sternocleidomastoid twists and bends neck

Biceps brachii bends arm

TYPES OF MUSCLE FIBRE

The three main types of muscle fibre work in very different ways. Smooth muscle can contract for prolonged periods. Skeletal muscle contracts quickly and powerfully, but only for short periods of time. Cardiac muscle contracts rhythmically and continually without tiring.

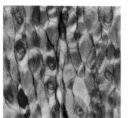

▲ SMOOTH MUSCLE
Smooth muscle has spindle-shaped cells that overlap. It contracts about 50 times more slowly than skeletal muscle.

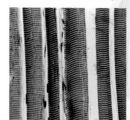

▲ SKELETAL MUSCLE
Skeletal muscle contains very long, slender muscle fibres arranged in parallel, which give it a striped appearance.

▲ CARDIAC MUSCLE
The short, branching fibres of cardiac muscles interconnect. They are packed with energy-releasing mitochondria.

HOW DOES A MUSCLE CONTRACT?

A muscle fibre is made up of myofibrils, which are made of thinner strands called myofilaments. When myofilaments are stimulated by a nerve impulse, they slide over each other, shortening the muscle. The more signals there are, the more the muscle contracts, until it reaches up to 70 per cent of its relaxed length.

e ▶▶
muscle

External oblique twists trunk and bends it sideways

Adductor longus pulls the leg inwards towards the body

FIND OUT MORE ▶▶ Body 128–129 • Heart 135 • Lungs 137 • Skeleton 130–131

SKIN

An outer covering of skin protects the body from injury, germs, water loss, and sunlight. Skin is also an important sensory organ, full of receptor cells sensitive to touch, heat, cold, and pain.

WHAT MAKES SKIN TOUGH?
Skin gets its strength from a supple outer layer called the epidermis, made largely of dead cells packed with a hard protein called keratin. The epidermis is continually wearing away and renewing itself. Its bottom layer of living cells keeps dividing, producing new cells that slowly move to the surface. As they travel up, they flatten, harden, and die.

WHAT'S UNDER THE EPIDERMIS?
Beneath the epidermis is the dermis, a layer of tissue containing blood vessels, nerves, sensory receptors, sweat glands, and hair roots. Under the dermis is a layer of fat cells that cushions the skin and traps heat deep within the body.

HOW DOES SKIN CONTROL BODY TEMPERATURE?
When the body is hot, sweat glands secrete a watery fluid onto the skin. The water draws heat from the skin as it evaporates. At the same time, blood vessels in the skin widen to release excess heat. When the body is cold, the skin's blood vessels narrow to reduce heat loss, and tiny muscles pull hairs erect, trapping warm air over the skin.

Skin surface is made up of dead, flattened cells from the epidermis

Epidermis cells continually divide to produce new skin cells

Dermis is a layer of living tissue below the epidermis full of blood vessels and sensory receptors

Melanocyte cells in this area at the base of the epidermis produce melanin – the pigment that gives skin its colour and filters out ultraviolet light

▲ **A CROSS-SECTION THROUGH THE SKIN**
This highly magnified image shows the layers in healthy skin. The top of the epidermis (red) is made up of flattened dead cells full of keratin. Surface cells continually flake away.

WHY DOES SKIN COLOUR VARY?
Skin colour comes from the pigment melanin, made by cells called melanocytes in the epidermis. Everyone has the same number of melanocytes, but they are much more active in people with dark skin. Melanocytes also become more active after exposure to the sun, producing pigment to protect the skin from damage from the sun.

Hair follicles are rooted deep in the dermis

◄ **FINGERNAILS**
Nails are made of overlapping plates of dead cells filled with the protein keratin. Keratin is tough and waterproof and is also found in hair and skin. Nails protect the sensitive tips of the fingers and toes.

▲ **SWEAT**
Droplets of sweat cover the skin on the back of a hand. The fluid is produced in sweat glands in the dermis, and rises up through pores onto the surface of the skin. Sweat lowers the body's temperature by using its heat to evaporate.

e ▸▸ skin

BEARD STUBBLE ▶
These shafts of hair from a man's beard have been shaved short. Hair is found all over the body to protect the skin and help us feel things that come near to the skin's surface. It is made of dead cells and keratin, and can grow up to 1 cm (1/2 in) a month.

Hair shaft

FIND OUT MORE ▸▸ Body 128–129 • Circulation 134 • Growth 149

CIRCULATION

The heart, ▶▶BLOOD, and blood vessels make up the circulatory system, which supplies the body with oxygen and nutrients, removes waste, distributes heat, and fights disease.

The aorta is the body's biggest artery

Heart

The vena cava is the main vein taking blood to the heart

Veins are shown in blue

Arteries are shown in red

ARE ARTERIES AND VEINS DIFFERENT?
Arteries carry blood from the heart, and veins bring it back. Arteries have thicker walls than veins, to withstand the force of the blood pumping directly out of the heart.

WHAT ARE CAPILLARIES?
About 98 per cent of blood vessels are microscopically thin vessels, called capillaries, that form a network between arteries and veins. Their walls are only one cell thick, so that chemicals can pass between the blood and the body's tissues.

◀ CIRCULATORY SYSTEM
The heart pumps blood continually around the circulatory system. Arteries and veins divide into ever finer branches as they reach throughout the body.

BLOOD CELLS ▶
An adult has about 5 litres (11 pints) of blood. Blood cells are made inside bones, and every second, 2 million red blood cells are made and the same number are destroyed.

BLOOD

A liquid tissue, blood consists of trillions of cells suspended in a watery liquid called plasma. Blood is the body's transport system, keeping all tissues and organs supplied with the chemicals needed for life and removing waste. Plasma makes up 55 per cent of blood, and red cells around 44 per cent. White cells account for less than 1 per cent of blood.

WHAT DO RED BLOOD CELLS DO?
Red blood cells pick up the life-giving gas oxygen in the lungs and release it throughout the body. A single drop of blood contains about five million of these tiny cells. Each cell is packed with the bright red protein haemoglobin, which binds with oxygen and then releases it where it is needed.

WHY DO WE HAVE WHITE BLOOD CELLS?
White blood cells destroy germs and damaged tissue. A drop of blood contains about 7,000 cells, and there are many different types. Some patrol the body like soldiers, swallowing germs. Others produce chemicals, called antibodies, which stick to germs and so make them easier to kill.

◀ BLOOD CLOT
When the skin is cut, a tough protein called fibrin (shown in grey) forms a tangle of solid fibres that traps blood cells and seals the wound.

White blood cells are round with tiny projections on the surface to help them stick to germs

Red blood cells are flexible so they can squeeze through capillaries

e ▶▶
circulation

FIND OUT MORE ▶▶ Respiration 136 • Skeleton 130–131

HEART

Blood is driven around the body by the heart, a powerful muscular pump that never stops beating. The heart is a dual pump. The left side sends blood to the body, while the right sends blood only to the lungs.

WHAT'S INSIDE THE HEART?

There are four chambers in the heart: two on the left and two on the right. The top chambers, called atria, are holding stations for incoming blood. The bottom chambers, called ventricles, pump blood out of the heart. It is the contractions of the atria and ventricles that make the sound of the ▶▶ HEARTBEAT .

WHAT IS THE HEART MADE OF?

The heart consists mostly of cardiac muscle, a special type of muscle that contracts rhythmically of its own accord. A tough membranous bag called the pericardium surrounds the heart, and a smooth membrane, called the endocardium, lines the inner surface.

e ▶▶

heart

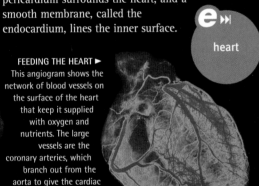

FEEDING THE HEART ▶
This angiogram shows the network of blood vessels on the surface of the heart that keep it supplied with oxygen and nutrients. The large vessels are the coronary arteries, which branch out from the aorta to give the cardiac muscle a direct supply of oxygen-rich blood.

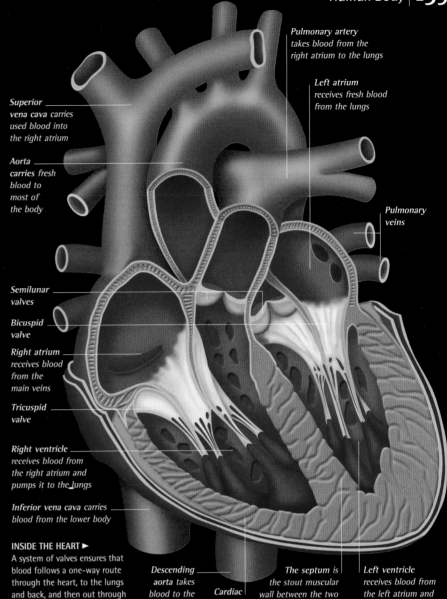

Superior vena cava carries used blood into the right atrium

Aorta carries fresh blood to most of the body

Semilunar valves

Bicuspid valve

Right atrium receives blood from the main veins

Tricuspid valve

Right ventricle receives blood from the right atrium and pumps it to the lungs

Inferior vena cava carries blood from the lower body

Pulmonary artery takes blood from the right atrium to the lungs

Left atrium receives fresh blood from the lungs

Pulmonary veins

Descending aorta takes blood to the lower body

Cardiac muscle

The septum is the stout muscular wall between the two sides of the heart

Left ventricle receives blood from the left atrium and pumps it to the body

INSIDE THE HEART ▶
A system of valves ensures that blood follows a one-way route through the heart, to the lungs and back, and then out through the aorta to the body.

HEARTBEAT

One complete contraction of the heart is called a heartbeat. Each heartbeat involves a sequence of events, with different parts of the heart contracting at different times. The rhythmic "lub-dub" noise of the heartbeat is the sound of valves snapping shut.

HOW IS THE HEARTBEAT CONTROLLED?

A small patch of modified cardiac muscle, the sinoatrial node, is the heart's pacemaker. It sends out a wave of electricity to make the heart's walls contract about 70 times a minute. However, nerve signals from the brain can speed it up during exercise or stress, if necessary.

Right atrium fills with used blood from the body

Oxygen-rich blood fills the left atrium

Semilunar valves

CLOSED VALVE
The semilunar valves close to prevent backflow.

Right atrium contracts

Left atrium contracts

Tricuspid and bicuspid valves open

Full ventricles

Oxygen-rich blood flows to upper and lower body

OPEN VALVE
The force of blood rushing through opens the valve.

Semilunar valves open

Tricuspid and bicuspid valves snap shut

Contracted ventricles

▲ STAGE 1 – THE HEART RELAXES
As the heart relaxes and the atria fill up with blood, the semilunar valves shut, making the "dub" beat.

▲ STAGE 2 – THE ATRIA CONTRACT
The atria contract to push blood into the ventricles. Valves between the atria and ventricles are pushed open.

▲ STAGE 3 – THE VENTRICLES CONTRACT
The ventricles contract to force blood out. The valves between the atria and ventricles shut to make the "lub" beat.

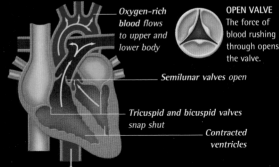

FIND OUT MORE ▶▶ Lungs 137 • Muscle 132 • Respiration 136

RESPIRATION

The process of taking in oxygen and expelling carbon dioxide is called respiration. When you breathe in, oxygen from the air enters the bloodstream. When you breathe out, waste carbon dioxide is removed.

respiration

HOW DOES AIR REACH THE LUNGS?

Air enters the body through the nose and mouth and travels to the pharynx (throat). The pharynx splits into the oesophagus for food, and the trachea (windpipe) for air. The trachea leads to the chest, where it divides into two branches, or bronchi, one to each lung.

Pharynx (throat)

The epiglottis
swings down to cover the larynx when we swallow, to stop food entering the air passages

Vocal cords
in the larynx (voice box) produce sound

The trachea (windpipe) is made up of rings of cartilage that hold the air passage open

▲ CILIA IN THE NOSE
Tiny beating hairs, called cilia, line the inside of the nose. The cilia clean, warm, and moisten the air to protect the sensitive airways of the lungs.

Pulmonary vessels
run throughout the lungs, bringing blood from the heart to pick up oxygen, then taking it back to the heart to be pumped around the body

HOW DO THE AIRWAYS STAY CLEAN?

The inner lining of the airways constantly produces a sticky fluid, called mucus, to trap particles of dirt. The mucus is always moving. In the nose, it is pushed by cilia towards the back of the throat where it is swallowed. Mucus also moves up from the airways of the lungs to the throat to be swallowed.

RESPIRATORY SYSTEM ▶
The respiratory system is made up of many organs, including the lungs, nose, mouth, airways leading to the lungs, and the network of blood vessels running through the lungs.

HOW SOUND IS MADE IN THE LARYNX

Vocal cords

Adam's apple

Ligaments

Cartilage rings of the trachea

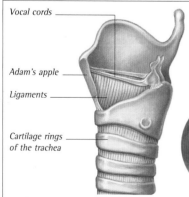

THE LARYNX

The larynx is made up of two pieces of cartilage at the top of the trachea and the two flaps of tissue, called vocal cords, stretched across them. If the vocal cords are open, air passes silently through them. If drawn together, air makes the cords vibrate, creating sound. The tighter the vocal cords, the higher the pitch. The mouth and tongue alter the sound to make words.

VOCAL CORDS CLOSED

VOCAL CORDS OPEN

Bronchi
divide again and again, to form a network of ever smaller airways

Heart

The diaphragm is a dome of muscle between the chest and abdomen

WHY DO WE NEED TO BREATHE?

Breathing is essential to keep us alive, because every living cell in the body needs a continual supply of oxygen. Inside each cell, oxygen combines with food molecules in a chemical reaction called oxidation, which releases energy. This energy powers every process in the human body.

FIND OUT MORE ▶▶ Cells 73 • Mouth 142 • Nose 143 • Sound 176–177

LUNGS

The main organs of the respiratory system are the lungs – two large organs that expand and contract. Each has a network of airways which end in tiny pockets called alveoli, where oxygen enters the blood and carbon dioxide leaves – a process known as ▸▸ GAS EXCHANGE.

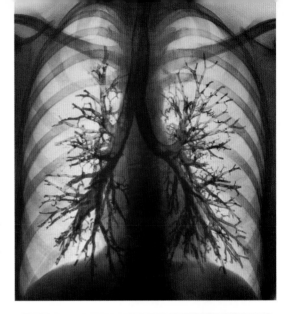

THE BRONCHIAL TREE ▶
In this X-ray, dye has been used to outline the tree-like network of airways in the lungs – the trachea act as the trunk, the bronchi as branches, and the bronchioles as the twigs.

WHAT MAKES THE LUNGS EXPAND AND CONTRACT?
The lungs rely on surrounding muscles to make them expand and contract. Muscles between the ribs pull the ribcage up and out, making the chest expand and drawing air in, or relax to squeeze the lungs and force air out as the ribcage falls down and in. At the same time, the diaphragm (a dome of muscle beneath the lungs) contracts to suck air into the airway, or relaxes and rises up to push air out.

HOW IS OUR BREATHING CONTROLLED?
The respiratory centre of the brain regulates our breathing, even while we sleep, with the help of receptors in some of the large arteries. The receptors monitor the level of carbon dioxide in the blood, which rises when we are active, and tell the brain if we need to breathe faster to get rid of the carbon dioxide.

Ribs provide a flexible framework for the lungs, protecting them, yet allowing them to expand and contract

Intercostal muscles move the ribs making the lungs expand or contract

HOW BREATHING WORKS

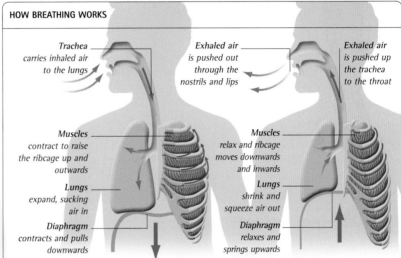

Trachea carries inhaled air to the lungs

Muscles contract to raise the ribcage up and outwards

Lungs expand, sucking air in

Diaphragm contracts and pulls downwards

Exhaled air is pushed out through the nostrils and lips

Muscles relax and ribcage moves downwards and inwards

Lungs shrink and squeeze air out

Diaphragm relaxes and springs upwards

Exhaled air is pushed up the trachea to the throat

▲ INHALATION (BREATHING IN)
To inhale, the intercostal muscles contract, and the diaphragm moves down, making the chest expand. Air is sucked into the lungs, because the pressure in the airways is less than it is outside.

▲ EXHALATION (BREATHING OUT)
When the intercostal muscles and diaphragm relax, we exhale. The ribs fall downwards and inwards, and the diaphragm springs back into a dome shape, gently squeezing the lungs and pushing air out.

GAS EXCHANGE

The passing of gases from the air into the blood, and from the blood back to the air, is called gas exchange. It takes place in the lungs, in tiny air pockets called alveoli.

WHAT ARE ALVEOLI?
Alveoli are like tiny bags of air with walls so thin that gases can pass through them. There are around 300 million alveoli in the lungs. Together they provide an area about as big as a tennis court for gas exchange.

HOW DOES OXYGEN GET INTO THE BLOOD?
Oxygen passes through the walls of the alveoli and the surrounding blood capillaries into the blood. The oxygen enters red blood cells and binds to a chemical called haemoglobin. Carbon dioxide passes out of the plasma (the watery part of blood) to enter the alveoli.

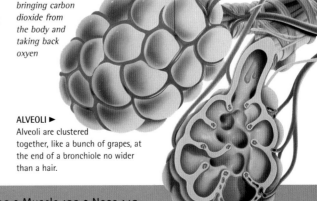

Terminal bronchiole surrounded by blood capillaries

Cluster of alveoli

Capillaries (red and blue) cover the alveoli, bringing carbon dioxide from the body and taking back oxyen

ALVEOLI ▶
Alveoli are clustered together, like a bunch of grapes, at the end of a bronchiole no wider than a hair.

e ▸▸ lungs

FIND OUT MORE ▸▸ Brain 139 • Circulation 134 • Mouth 142 • Muscle 132 • Nose 143

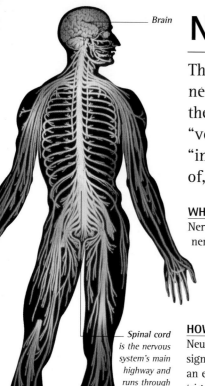

Brain

Spinal cord
is the nervous
system's main
highway and
runs through
a tunnel in
the vertebrae

◄ A NETWORK OF NERVES
Nerves branch from the brain and spinal cord, forming
a tree-like network that runs throughout the body.

NERVOUS SYSTEM

The brain, nerves, and spinal cord make up the
nervous system. It processes information from
the sense organs and controls conscious
"voluntary" actions, such as walking, and
"involuntary" processes we are not aware
of, like reflexes and breathing.

WHAT IS A NERVE?

Nerves are the cables of the nervous system. Each
nerve is packed with hundreds of wire-like cells
called neurons, which carry electric signals to
and from the brain. The brain and spinal cord
form the central nervous system, and the nerves
outside them are the peripheral nervous system.

HOW DO NEURONS WORK?

Neurons work like wires, transmitting electric
signals at speed. When the neuron is resting,
an electric charge builds up inside it. If
triggered, a nerve impulse rushes to the
end of the cell where a chemical
called a neurotransmitter passes
the signal to the next neuron
across a gap or synapse.

The cerebrum
is the largest part
of the human brain,
and is responsible for
voluntary actions, thought,
language, and
consciousness

The cerebral cortex
is the folded surface of
the cerebrum where
information is processed

e ▸▸
nervous
system

The hypothalamus
is a tiny region in the centre of the
brain that controls hormone levels
and regulates sleep, temperature, and
body water levels

Axon
(nerve fibre)

Cell body

Nucleus

Dendrite

◄ MOTOR NEURON
All neurons are similar in
structure to this motor
neuron. The cell body
contains the nucleus
that controls the cell.
Filaments called dendrites
branch out from the cell
body and pick up signals
from other neurons. The
nerve fibre, or axon, takes
the signal and passes it on
to other neurons, muscles,
or glands.

ARE ALL NEURONS THE SAME?

There are three main types of neuron. Sensory
neurons carry incoming signals from sense organs to
the central nervous system. Motor neurons carry
outgoing signals from the brain to the body, usually
to muscle cells. Association neurons form a complex
maze of connections in the brain and spinal cord,
linking sensory neurons to motor neurons.

WHAT IS A REFLEX ACTION?

Reflex actions are involuntary – they happen before
you have time to think. When they happen, a nerve
signal takes a shortcut through the spinal cord
rather than involving the brain. If we touch a very
hot object, a sensory neuron sends a signal
shooting from the hand to the spinal cord.
There an association neuron transmits the
signal to a motor neuron, which tells a
muscle in the arm to move the hand.

◄ NERVE JUNCTION
This highly magnified image shows the
junction, or synapse, between two nerve
cells. In the blue cell, a nerve signal has
stimulated the release of chemicals called
neurotransmitters (pink circles). The
neurotransmitters cross the gap and bind on to
the pink receptor nerve cell to pass on the signal.

FIND OUT MORE ▸▸ Muscle 132 • Respiration 136

BRAIN

The largest organ in the nervous system is the brain. It controls vital involuntary processes, such as breathing, as well as our thoughts, emotions, memories, and sensations. Brain scans can monitor brain activity, called ▸▸ BRAINWAVES .

▲ NEURONS IN THE BRAIN
Brain cells send signals to each other via spindly connections. Each cell has an average of 10,000 connections, which change as the brain learns and adapts.

The cerebellum is involved in the involuntary control of balance and posture, especially during movement

WHY IS THE HUMAN BRAIN SPECIAL?
Relative to body weight, the human brain is the largest in the animal kingdom. Its surface, the cerebral cortex, is also the wrinkliest. During human evolution, the cerebral cortex grew, and so became wrinklier to fit inside the skull. The large cortex, site of unique abilities such as language, is probably what makes humans unusually intelligent.

WHAT IS THE BRAIN MADE OF?
The brain contains more than 100 billion neurons, and a multitude of helper cells, which nourish and support the neurons. The cells are organized into different areas, the largest of which is the cerebrum. The whole brain is surrounded by protective membranes and cushioned by fluid-filled hollows.

◂ BRAIN SCAN
This MRI scan shows how the brain fills the space inside the skull. The cerebrum takes up most of the room, and accounts for nearly 70 per cent of the weight of the nervous system.

HOW DOES THE BRAIN WORK?
Scientists used to think that each part of the cerebral cortex carried out a specific function. Recent research has shown the brain to be more complicated. During speech, for instance, large areas of the cerebral cortex work together in an ever-changing pattern.

◂ PET SCANS OF THE BRAIN
Active parts of the cerebral cortex show as flashes of colour in a PET scan. Scientists use these scanners to carry out research into how the brain works.

The brain stem is an extension of the spinal cord and controls vital involuntary functions such as breathing and heart rate

LISTENING

IN CONVERSATION

e ▸▸
brain

Spinal cord

BRAINWAVES

Doctors can monitor a person's brain by looking at brainwaves, the pattern of electrical activity produced by all the brain's neurons. There are three main types of wave: alpha, beta, and delta. They are detected by an EEG (electroencephalograph).

ALPHA: AWAKE BUT RESTING

IS THE BRAIN ACTIVE WHEN WE SLEEP?
The brain is always active, but the level of activity varies. In deep sleep, when delta waves occur, the brain is working but at its least active. During dreams, the eyes dart about and the brain produces alpha waves and is just as active as during waking hours.

WAVE PATTERNS ▸
When a person is awake but resting, the brain produces a regular pattern of medium-length waves – alpha waves. When alert and concentrating, the brain produces shorter, quicker waves – beta waves. During deep sleep, very long, slow delta waves occur.

BETA: ALERT AND CONCENTRATING

DELTA: SLEEPING DEEPLY

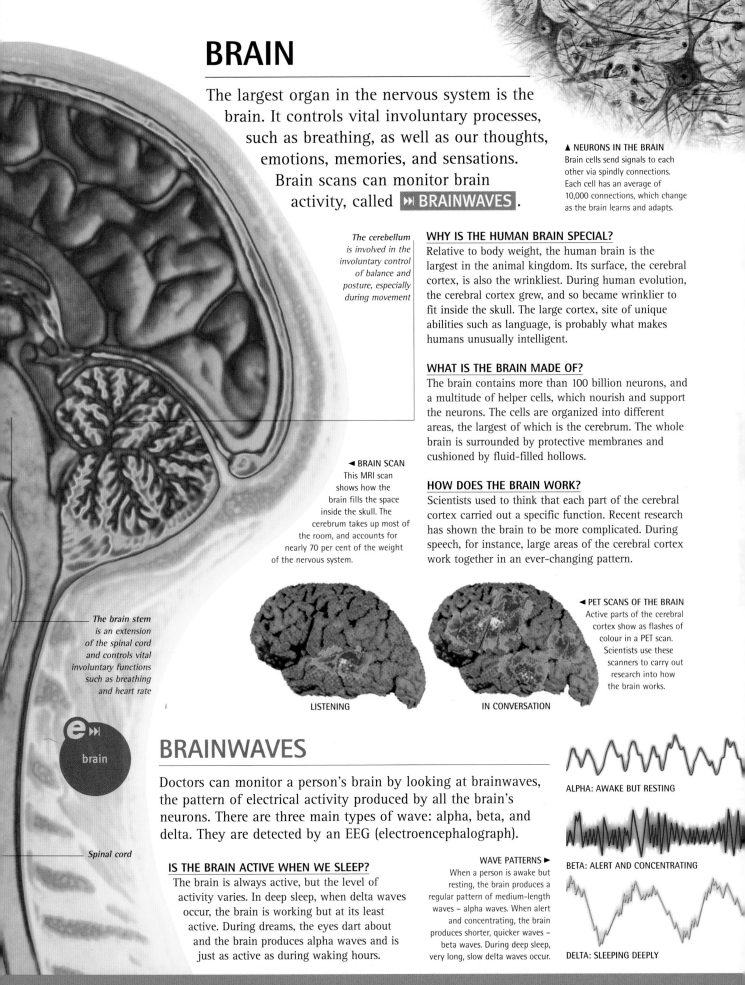

FIND OUT MORE ▸▸ Nervous System 138 • Skeleton 130–131

EYE

Our eyes create the sense of vision. They take in light rays, focus them to create an image, and convert this image into a stream of billions of nerve impulses that travels to the brain. The impulses are interpreted in different parts of the brain, but come together to create the detailed, colour, 3-D image we "see".

WHAT IS THE PUPIL?

The pupil is a hole that lets light enter the eye. It appears black, because light passes straight through it without being reflected. Around the pupil is the iris – a circle of coloured muscle that controls the pupil's size. In dim light the pupil widens to take in extra light. In bright light it shrinks to protect the nerve cells at the back of the eye.

HOW THE EYE FOCUSES

The eye has a curved, transparent lens that bends light rays to create an image. The eye focuses images on the retina, just as a projector focuses images on a screen. To keep the image sharp, the lens changes shape. Muscles around the lens make it fatter for nearby objects and thinner for distant objects.

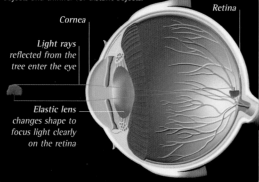

Cornea

Retina

Light rays reflected from the tree enter the eye

Elastic lens changes shape to focus light clearly on the retina

WHY DO WE HAVE TWO EYES?

Each eye sees the world from a different angle, creating slightly different pictures. The brain combines these two pictures into a single, three-dimensional image. This is called binocular vision. Seeing in 3-D helps you to judge the distance and size of objects much more easily.

HOW DO WE SEE IN COLOUR?

The cells in the retina that are sensitive to light are called rods and cones. Rods work best in dim light, but cannot see colour. Cones can detect colours in bright light. There are three types of cone, and each type is sensitive to one of the primary light colours – red, blue, and green. By combining information from all three, we are able to see all the colours of the rainbow.

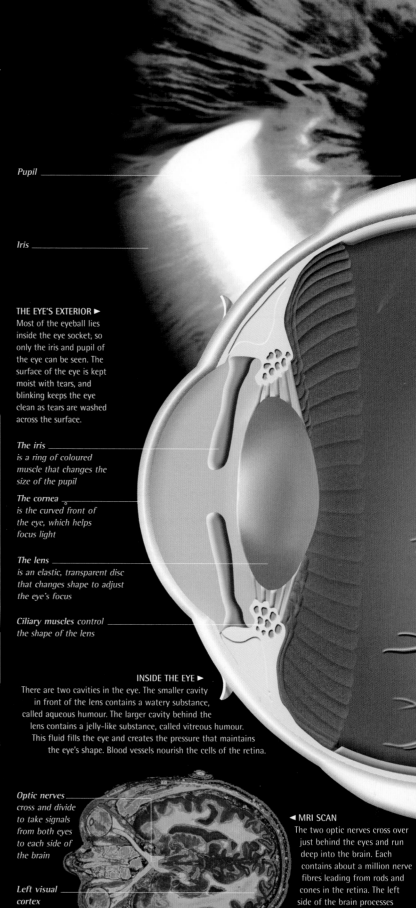

Pupil

Iris

THE EYE'S EXTERIOR ▶
Most of the eyeball lies inside the eye socket, so only the iris and pupil of the eye can be seen. The surface of the eye is kept moist with tears, and blinking keeps the eye clean as tears are washed across the surface.

The iris is a ring of coloured muscle that changes the size of the pupil

The cornea is the curved front of the eye, which helps focus light

The lens is an elastic, transparent disc that changes shape to adjust the eye's focus

Ciliary muscles control the shape of the lens

INSIDE THE EYE ▶
There are two cavities in the eye. The smaller cavity in front of the lens contains a watery substance, called aqueous humour. The larger cavity behind the lens contains a jelly-like substance, called vitreous humour. This fluid fills the eye and creates the pressure that maintains the eye's shape. Blood vessels nourish the cells of the retina.

Optic nerves cross and divide to take signals from both eyes to each side of the brain

Left visual cortex processes signals from the left side of both eyes

◀ MRI SCAN
The two optic nerves cross over just behind the eyes and run deep into the brain. Each contains about a million nerve fibres leading from rods and cones in the retina. The left side of the brain processes signals from the left side of each retina; the right side of the brain processes signals from the right side of each retina.

FIND OUT MORE ▶▶ Brain 139 • Colour 180 • Lenses 181 • Light 178–179 • Nervous System 138

EAR

The ear is the organ of hearing and balance. The outer ear collects sound and directs it to the sensory structures deep inside the skull.

HOW DOES SOUND TRAVEL THROUGH THE EAR?

Sound travels into the ear as vibrations in air. The eardrum picks up the vibrations and transmits them to tiny bones in the middle ear. These bones pass the vibrations to the fluid-filled inner ear and the cochlea.

Outer ear

The middle ear has three tiny bones, which carry vibrations to the inner ear

The inner ear is made up of the tiny organs that detect sound, balance, and movement

The retina is a layer of light-sensitive cells lining the back of the eye

The optic nerve contains nerve cells carrying signals from the retina to the brain

The eardrum passes vibrations to tiny bones inside the middle ear

Ear canal

INSIDE THE EAR ▲
Sound vibrations push the eardrum against the bones of the middle ear, which pass the signals to the inner ear.

WHAT HAPPENS IN THE COCHLEA?

Sound vibrations travel along the cochlea's spiral, fluid-filled tube, creating waves of pressure. These stimulate tiny hair cells on a structure called the organ of Corti, which sends signals to the brain.

HOW DO EARS HELP US BALANCE?

The semi-circular canals contain fluid that moves whenever the head moves, making tiny blobs of jelly sway about and triggering nerve cells. There are also two fluid-filled chambers, called the utricle and saccule, which contain blobs of jelly that sway with gravity, telling the brain which way is up and down.

e ▸▸
eye

◄ RODS AND CONES
Magnified thousands of times, this picture shows rods (in blue) and a shorter cone (in green) in the retina. Each retina has about 130 million rods and 6.5 million cones. The cells are concentrated mainly in an area called the fovea, in the middle of the retina. The fovea creates a detailed image of whatever the eyes are looking at directly.

Semi-circular canals contain balance receptors

Nerve fibres carry signals to the brain

Saccule and utricle detect movement

Cochlea contains receptor cells that detect vibrations

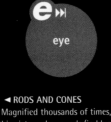

INNER EAR ▲
The inner ear consists of the semi-circular canals, the saccule and utricle, which detect movement, and the cochlea, which contains the sound receptors.

e ▸▸
ear

FIND OUT MORE ▸▸ Brain 139 • Sound 176–177

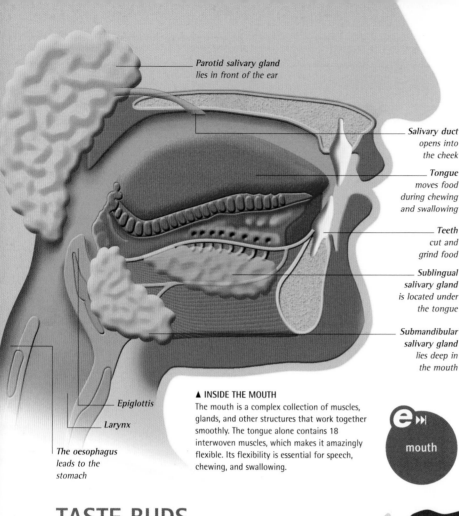

Parotid salivary gland
lies in front of the ear

Salivary duct
*opens into
the cheek*

Tongue
*moves food
during chewing
and swallowing*

Teeth
*cut and
grind food*

Sublingual
salivary gland
*is located under
the tongue*

Submandibular
salivary gland
*lies deep in
the mouth*

Epiglottis

Larynx

*The oesophagus
leads to the
stomach*

▲ INSIDE THE MOUTH
The mouth is a complex collection of muscles,
glands, and other structures that work together
smoothly. The tongue alone contains 18
interwoven muscles, which makes it amazingly
flexible. Its flexibility is essential for speech,
chewing, and swallowing.

e ▶▶
mouth

MOUTH

Food enters the body through the
mouth. The mouth is the first part
of the digestive system, where food
is mashed and moistened so that it
can be swallowed. The mouth also
plays an essential role in speech
and breathing.

WHY IS THE MOUTH ALWAYS WET?
Saliva contains chemicals that kill bacteria, and flows
constantly into the mouth to help keep it free of
disease. The mouth's inner lining also secretes a
lubricating fluid called mucus. Saliva and mucus both
moisten food, making it easier to swallow.

WHAT HAPPENS TO FOOD IN THE MOUTH?
The front teeth cut up food, and the tongue and
cheek muscles push it between the back teeth where
it is ground by the lower jaw. Saliva softens and
moistens food and washes over **▶▶ TASTE BUDS**
in the tongue so that flavours can be identified. The
digestive process also begins in the mouth, as saliva
contains chemicals that break down some foods.

TASTE BUDS

Our sense of taste comes from tiny,
onion-shaped clusters of cells called taste
buds. Most taste buds are scattered across
the surface of the tongue, where there are
around 10,000, but they are also found
in the roof of the mouth and the throat.

WHAT CAN THE TONGUE TASTE?
The tongue is sensitive to four basic tastes: salty,
sweet, bitter, and acidic (sour). The chemicals that
cause these tastes dissolve in saliva on the tongue and
seep into the taste buds, where they trigger receptor
cells that send signals to the brain.

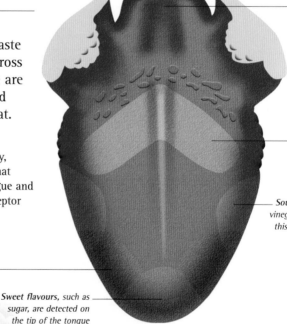

*The epiglottis is a flap that
lowers when we swallow, to
stop food instead of air
going down the larynx*

◄ TONGUE TASTE MAP
Specialized taste buds are clustered in
different parts of the tongue. As a
result, different parts of the tongue
are sensitive to specific tastes.

*Bitter flavours, such as
coffee, are detected towards
the back of tongue*

*Sour flavours, such as
vinegar, are identified in
this area of the tongue*

*Saliva
pours into the gap
between papillae*

*Salty flavours, such as
potato crisps, are identified
by taste buds in this area*

*Sweet flavours, such as
sugar, are detected on
the tip of the tongue*

◄ SURFACE OF THE TONGUE
The surface of the tongue is
covered by tiny bumps called
papillae, which give it a rough
texture to grip food. Most are
small filliform papillae (shown in
blue) that have a sense of touch.
Scattered among these are larger
fungiform papillae (shown in
pink), which contain taste buds.

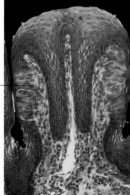

*Taste buds contain
25–30 receptor cells*

TASTE BUDS ▶
This magnified view of papillae
on the tongue shows the taste
buds in their sides. Each taste
bud has a tiny opening, or taste
pore, to let in the dissolved
flavours of food and drink.

FIND OUT MORE ▶▶ Brain 139 • Digestion 144–145 • Respiration 136

TEETH

Anchored firmly in the jaw bones are the teeth. Our teeth are used to tear, chop, and grind food to make it soft enough to swallow and easier to digest.

WHAT ARE TEETH MADE OF?
The white, outer shell of a tooth is made of enamel, the hardest substance in the body. Under the enamel is a softer substance called dentine, and inside this is the soft, living heart of the tooth, called the pulp cavity.

WHY DO TEETH DECAY?
If teeth are not properly cleaned, a mixture of bacteria and food, called plaque, builds up on them. As the bacteria feed on the sugary food debris they produce acid, which dissolves the calcium minerals in enamel and dentine, forming a cavity. If the sensitive dentine layer is exposed, hot and cold foods can cause pain.

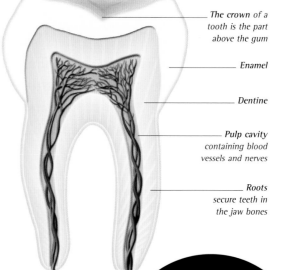

The crown of a tooth is the part above the gum

Enamel

Dentine

Pulp cavity containing blood vessels and nerves

Roots secure teeth in the jaw bones

INSIDE A TOOTH ▶
Beneath the hard outer surface, dentine forms the body of a tooth. Nerves (green) and blood vessels (red and blue) run through the tissue of the pulp cavity and out through root canals at the base of the tooth.

teeth

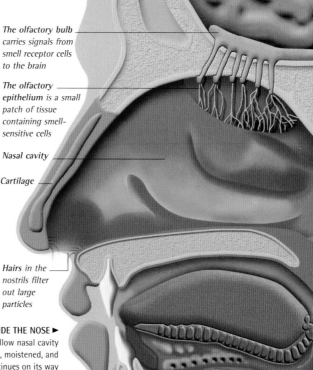

PLAQUE ▶
A sticky deposit called plaque builds up on teeth that are not cleaned regularly. Plaque consists of mucus, food debris, and bacteria that cause tooth decay.

◀ ORAL X-RAY
This X-ray shows all the teeth in an adult's mouth in one picture. It reveals their long roots, usually hidden beneath the gums. The white areas in the crowns are fillings. There are four main types of tooth, each suited to a particular task. Incisors (1) bite and chew, canines (2) pierce and tear, premolars (3) and molars (4) crush and grind.

Plaque (yellow) has built up on the enamel (grey) of this tooth

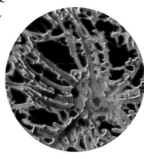

FIND OUT MORE ▶▶ Digestion 144–145 • Micro-organisms 85

NOSE

The main entrance to the body's airways is the nose. It also contains our smell sensors. The outer part of the nose is made mostly of a rubbery tissue called cartilage.

WHY DO WE BREATHE THROUGH THE NOSE?
Breathing through the nose helps to protect the tissues of the lungs from germs, dirt, and very dry or cold air. The moist lining of the nasal passages warms and moistens air. Sticky mucus traps particles of dust, soot, and bacteria. Tiny beating hairs, called cilia, drive the mucus towards the throat to be swallowed.

HOW DOES THE NOSE DETECT SMELLS?
In the roof of each nostril is a small patch of nerve endings, called the olfactory epithelium, covered by mucus. Odour molecules from smells dissolve in the mucus and stimulate the nerve endings, which send signals to the olfactory bulb and the brain. We can recognize more than 10,000 smells and detect just a few molecules of some odours.

▲ SMELL RECEPTORS
This magnified view shows a tangle of cilia (microscopic hairs) emerging from a smell receptor cell in the nose.

nose

The olfactory bulb carries signals from smell receptor cells to the brain

The olfactory epithelium is a small patch of tissue containing smell-sensitive cells

Nasal cavity

Cartilage

Hairs in the nostrils filter out large particles

INSIDE THE NOSE ▶
Inside the nose is the hollow nasal cavity where air is warmed, moistened, and cleaned before it continues on its way down the pharynx (throat) to the lungs.

FIND OUT MORE Brain 139 • Digestion 144–145 • Respiration 136

DIGESTION

The process of breaking down food into molecules the body can absorb is called digestion. The digestive system begins with the mouth and involves many organs in the abdomen. The digestive organs produce **▸▸ ENZYMES** which break down food chemically.

HOW DOES THE STOMACH WORK?
The stomach is a stretchy, muscular bag that stores food and churns it around until it is a thick liquid. Glands in the lining of the stomach secrete gastric juice, which contains pepsin and hydrochloric acid. Pepsin is an enzyme that digests protein molecules; hydrochloric acid kills germs and helps pepsin work.

WHERE DOES FOOD GO AFTER THE STOMACH?
Food is squirted from the stomach into the small intestine. Here it mixes with digestive juices from the liver and pancreas. Bile from the liver breaks up fat. Pancreatic juice neutralizes stomach acid and contains enzymes that digest carbohydrates, proteins, and fats.

▲ VILLI IN SMALL INTESTINE
Finger-like villi line the inside of the small intestine, giving it a velvety texture and increasing the area for absorbing food.

WHY IS THE SMALL INTESTINE SO LONG?
The small intestine measures 6.5 m (21 ft) and is the main organ of digestion and absorption. As food moves slowly along the great length of the intestine, it has plenty of time to break down properly. The size of the small intestine maximizes the area of the inner lining that food passes and the absorbtion of nutrients.

HOW IS FOOD ABSORBED?
The lining of the small intestine is covered with microscopic projections called villi, which dramatically increase its surface area. Molecules of nutrients dissolve in fluids in the intestine and pass into the villi. From there, nutrients pass through the thin walls of the blood vessels in the villi, and into the body.

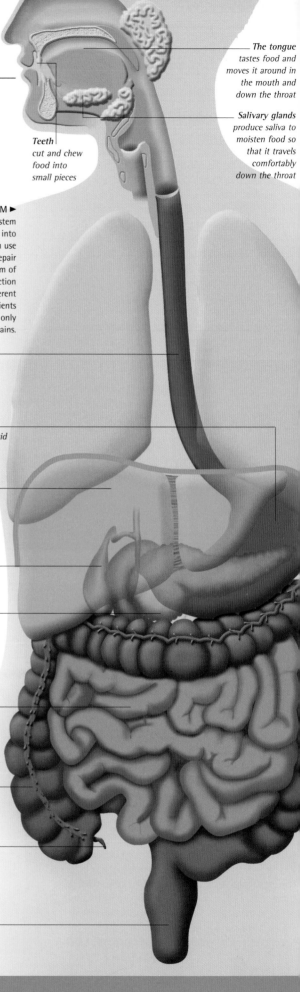

DIGESTIVE SYSTEM ▸
The job of the digestive system is to turn the food we eat into material that the body can use for energy, growth, and to repair itself. It is a long system of different organs, each section working in a slightly different way to extract nutrients and water from food until only waste remains.

The tongue
tastes food and moves it around in the mouth and down the throat

Salivary glands
produce saliva to moisten food so that it travels comfortably down the throat

Teeth
cut and chew food into small pieces

The oesophagus
takes swallowed food to the stomach

The stomach
churns food into a thick liquid and produces acid and an enzyme that digests protein

The liver
produces bile, which breaks down fats

The gall bladder
stores bile and releases it into the small intestine

The pancreas
produces enzymes that digest fat, protein, and carbohydrate in the small intestine

The small intestine
is where most digestion and nutrient absorption take place

The large intestine
is about 1.5 m (5 ft) long and absorbs water from the undigested remains of food

The appendix
is a small dead-end tube with no function

The rectum
stores undigested waste (faeces) until it can be expelled

THE TIMETABLE OF THE DIGESTIVE SYSTEM

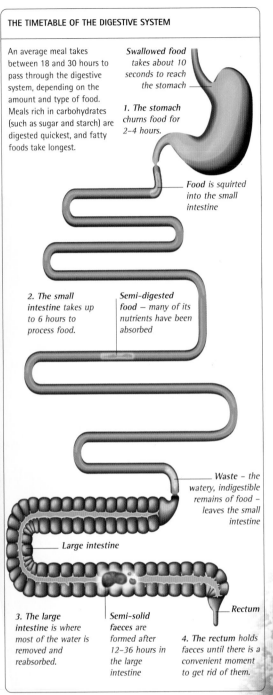

An average meal takes between 18 and 30 hours to pass through the digestive system, depending on the amount and type of food. Meals rich in carbohydrates (such as sugar and starch) are digested quickest, and fatty foods take longest.

Swallowed food takes about 10 seconds to reach the stomach

1. The stomach churns food for 2–4 hours.

Food is squirted into the small intestine

2. The small intestine takes up to 6 hours to process food.

Semi-digested food – many of its nutrients have been absorbed

Waste – the watery, indigestible remains of food – leaves the small intestine

Large intestine

Rectum

3. The large intestine is where most of the water is removed and reabsorbed.

Semi-solid faeces are formed after 12–36 hours in the large intestine

4. The rectum holds faeces until there is a convenient moment to get rid of them.

WHY DON'T THE DIGESTIVE ORGANS DIGEST THEMSELVES?

The lining of the stomach and intestines secretes a thick, slippery liquid called mucus, which helps food slide along and protects the digestive organs from acid and enzymes. Even so, the intestinal lining does gradually wear away, but it continually renews itself by producing new cells, just as skin does.

HOW DOES FOOD MOVE ALONG THE DIGESTIVE SYSTEM?

The oesophagus, stomach, small intestine, and large intestine all have muscular walls. When these muscle walls contract, the hollow organ narrows, pushing the food forward. The contraction happens in waves that move along the organs. This action is called peristalsis.

WHAT HAPPENS IN THE LARGE INTESTINE?

Undigested leftovers pass into the large intestine, which absorbs water and minerals. Harmless bacteria flourish in the waste and produce some vitamins, which are also absorbed. The semi-solid wastes (faeces) collect in the rectum before being expelled.

BACTERIA IN THE LARGE INTESTINE ▶
This image shows rod-shaped bacteria (in pink) on the surface of the large intestine. Billions of useful and harmless bacteria live in the large intestine. This is one of the most common species, which helps release vitamins from food.

Muscles contract to make the intestine narrower

Food

Muscles relax, allowing the intestine to widen

▲ PERISTALSIS
The muscular walls of most sections of the digestive system contract in a wave-like pattern, known as peristalsis, to push food through.

ENZYMES

Most chemical reactions in living organisms are controlled by enzymes. There are many types, each suited to a particular task.

HOW DO ENZYMES WORK?

Enzymes are catalysts, which means that they speed up the rate of a chemical reaction. The molecules of each enzyme have a very particular shape which enables them to bind to a specific molecule in the body and make it react.

WHICH ORGANS MAKE DIGESTIVE ENZYMES?

The salivary glands, stomach, pancreas, and small intestine all produce digestive enzymes. These enzymes break down proteins, carbohydrates, and fats into the units they are made up of – amino acids, sugars, and fatty acids. These tiny units are so small they can pass into the villi lining the intestine.

◀ ENZYMES IN THE PANCREAS
This magnified view shows granules of enzymes (in yellow and orange) made by the pancreas. These will be released into the small intestine to help the digestion of food.

digestion

FIND OUT MORE ▶▶ Liver 146 • Micro-organisms 85 • Mouth 142 • Teeth 143

LIVER

A vital organ, the liver carries out hundreds of essential chemical processes, adjusts the levels of many substances in the blood, and produces a digestive juice called bile. The liver is the body's heaviest organ, weighing about 1.5 kg (3½ lbs).

WHAT IS INSIDE THE LIVER?

The liver is made up of thousands of lobules – tiny hexagonal units about 1 mm (¹/₂₅ in) wide. Each is surrounded by a network of incoming blood vessels. Blood filters through the lobule and drains away through a vein in the middle.

HOW DOES BLOOD GET TO THE LIVER?

Unlike other organs, the liver receives blood from two major blood vessels. The hepatic artery brings oxygen-rich blood from the heart. The hepatic portal vein brings blood rich in digested nutrients from the intestine. This means excess nutrients can be removed and stored before blood circulates round the body.

WHY IS THE LIVER A FACTORY?

The liver carries out so many tasks that scientists compare it to a chemical factory. It filters blood from the intestines and removes excess food and iron for storage or for conversion into other substances. It also removes debris, destroys poisons, worn-out blood cells, and alcohol, and manufactures vitamin A and many other chemicals vital to the body.

▼ LIVER CELLS

This magnified view shows red blood cells flowing through spaces between the cells in a liver lobule. As the blood filters through the lobule, the liver adjusts the levels of many different chemicals.

Red blood cells pass through channels called sinusoids

SCAN THROUGH THE ABDOMEN ▶
This MRI scan shows a vertical slice through the back of the abdomen. Seen from the front, the liver is on the left and the stomach is on the right. This view shows a section of one end of the liver, making it look smaller than it is.

The liver is not seen in full in this image, which shows a cross-section of the back part of the liver

Kidneys lie beneath the ribs at the back of the abdomen

Vertebrae of the spine

e ▶▶ liver

Liver fills the upper-left area of the abdomen

Intestines show up only partially on this scan

Vena cava carries blood to the heart

Aorta carries blood out of the heart

Vertebra

Stomach

▲ HORIZONTAL CROSS-SECTION THROUGH THE BODY
This scan shows a horizontal slice through the abdomen and gives an impression of the liver's size. The liver is the largest organ in the body and takes up most of the space in the upper abdomen, just below the ribs. The blue "hole" in the liver is the inferior vena cava – one of the body's largest veins.

WHAT IS BILE?

The liver makes a greenish-brown liquid called bile, which is stored in a pouch called the gall bladder and emptied into the small intestine, where it makes fats mix with water and so helps digestion. Bile consists of water, bile salts, acid, cholesterol, and a pigment called bilirubin, which gives faeces their colour.

FIND OUT MORE ▶▶ Circulation 134 • Digestion 144–145

KIDNEYS

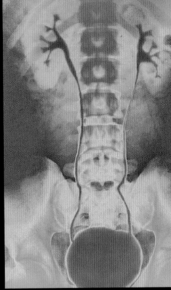

kidneys

The kidneys are two bean-shaped organs at the back of the abdomen that filter and clean the blood, removing chemical wastes and excess water. Wastes drain out of the kidneys as urine.

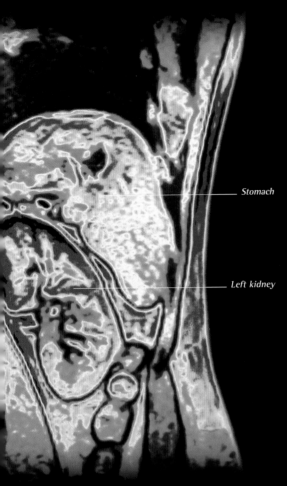

Stomach

Left kidney

WHAT IS INSIDE A KIDNEY?
Each kidney contains about a million tiny filtering units called nephrons. Blood flows through a kind of filter at the top of each nephron and water and small molecules pass through it into a long tube. In the tube useful substances such as glucose and salt are then reabsorbed, and what is left over forms urine.

WHY DOES BLOOD NEED CLEANING?
If the kidneys did not filter the blood, chemical wastes would build up in the body and become poisonous. The kidneys also control the level of water in the blood by varying how much water is reabsorbed in the nephrons. If we drink a lot, the kidneys can excrete the excess to stop the blood becoming diluted.

WHERE DOES WASTE GO?
Urine from each kidney drains through a tube called a ureter and collects in the bladder. As the bladder fills, its muscular wall stretches. When it is full, receptors in the wall send a signal to the brain and trigger the urge to urinate. During urination the muscles that close the bladder exit relax to release the urine.

▲ **A FULL BLADDER**
In this X-ray, dye is used to show urine from the kidneys draining through the ureters to a full bladder. An adult bladder can hold about 0.5 litre (1 pint) of urine.

FIND OUT MORE ▸▸ Brain 139 • Circulation 134

HORMONES

Hormones are control chemicals that trigger major changes in the body. They control many important functions, including body chemistry, growth and sexual development, and the body's response to stress.

HOW DO HORMONES WORK?
Hormone molecules travel in the blood looking for specific cells which they bind on to. This triggers a chain of chemical reactions and changes the cell's job. Some hormones work by switching genes on or off.

PITUITARY GLAND ▶
This 3-D CT reconstruction shows the pituitary gland at the base of the brain. The pituitary gland produces hormones and controls other hormone glands in the body.

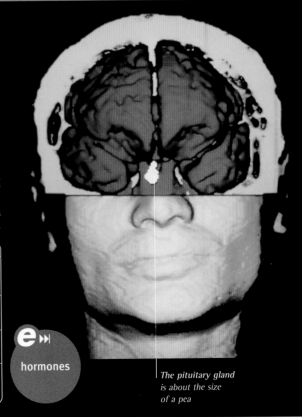

hormones

The pituitary gland is about the size of a pea

HORMONAL GLANDS AND THEIR FUNCTIONS			
Pituitary gland	A key gland that releases nine hormones that control body functions or trigger other glands.	Parathyroid glands	Four small glands that work with the thyroid gland to balance levels of calcium in the blood.
Pancreas	Secretes insulin and glucagon, which control the level of sugar in the blood.	Pineal gland	Secretes melatonin, a hormone that controls the daily rhythm of sleep and waking.
Adrenal gland	Secretes adrenaline, which helps the body cope with fear or excitement, and steroids.	Ovaries (in females)	Make oestrogen and progesterone, which control the development and function of the sex organs.
Thyroid gland	Secretes thyroxine, which speeds up the rate of body chemistry.	Testes (in males)	Secrete testosterone, which controls the development and function of the male sex organs.

FIND OUT MORE ▸▸ Cells 73 • Growth 149 • Reproduction 148

The umbilical cord carries food and oxygen to the baby from the placenta – the organ inside the womb that links the baby to the mother's blood supply

REPRODUCTION

New life is created by reproduction. The mother and father produce sex cells, which join to form an embryo. These sex cells also determine the child's ►► HEREDITY .

WHERE DO SEX CELLS FORM?
Male cells are called sperm. They are produced by the million in the testes – a pair of ball-shaped glands that hang outside the body in the scrotum. A female sex cell is called an ovum (plural ova). A woman's ova form before she is born, in two organs called ovaries, in her abdomen.

HOW DOES AN EMBRYO FORM?
Sperm and ova come together as a result of sexual intercourse (sex). During sex, a man places his penis inside a woman's body. Sperm leave the penis and swim into the woman's reproductive organs. If the ovaries have released an ovum, a sperm cell may fuse with it and form an embryo. This is called fertilization.

Sperm attach to the ovum and try to enter it

▲ HUMAN FOETUS
At five months old, the human foetus weighs under 500 g (1 lb) but has fully developed lips, eyes, fingers, and toes. The mother can feel movements of the foetus inside the uterus (womb).

WHERE DOES THE EMBRYO DEVELOP?
The embryo develops inside an organ called the uterus (womb). It sinks into the soft lining of the uterus and absorbs food from the mother through an organ called the placenta, which develops from the embryo. The uterus has a very stretchy wall so that it can expand as the baby grows.

◄ OVUM AND SPERM
When sperm cells find an ovum, they try to break through its coat. The first to get through fertilizes the egg and the rest die. Nuclei from the sperm and the ovum then fuse to make a single nucleus.

Ovum – ova are the largest cells in the human body

reproduction

HEREDITY

The process of inheriting characteristics from parents is called heredity. Many of our characteristics are passed on through genes – instructions made up of DNA molecules in our chromosomes.

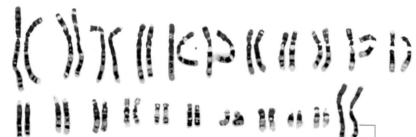

▲ CHROMOSOMES OF A WOMAN
Chromosomes are microscopic threads in our cell nuclei. Each one contains a long DNA molecule. We have 46 chromosomes in 23 pairs. One of each pair comes from our mother and the other from our father.

The sex chromosomes are the only chromosomes that differ between men and women

HOW ARE GENES INHERITED?
People inherit half their genes from their mother and half from their father. The genes are passed on in chromosomes carried by sperm and ova. The chromosomes interact with each other in different ways, so children from the same parents may share characteristics, but are also very different. Apart from identical twins, everyone has a unique set of genes.

HOW DO GENES AFFECT CHARACTERISTICS?
Genes determine most of your physical characteristics, such as eye colour. Eye colour is controlled by only a handful of genes, but other characteristics, such as height, involve lots of genes. Genes can also affect mental characteristics such as personality and intelligence, but these are heavily influenced by your experiences as well. The study of genes and how they affect you is called genetics.

GROWTH

It takes nine months for an embryo to grow into a baby inside its mother's uterus (womb). After birth, the baby keeps growing for another 20 years, changing all the time. Growth is quickest in the first few years of life.

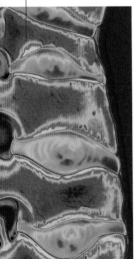

HOW DOES A BABY GROW?

An embryo begins life as one cell. It divides repeatedly to form a ball of cells and starts to change shape. After four weeks it has a brain and a backbone. At six weeks it has limbs and its heart starts beating. At 12 weeks it looks like a miniature baby.

WHAT HAPPENS AS CHILDREN GROW?

Children change shape as they grow because parts of the body grow at different speeds. The brain grows quickest at first, which is why babies have such large heads. Muscles and bones grow later on. The rate of growth slows down during childhood, but shoots up again at puberty.

HOW DO GIRLS CHANGE AT PUBERTY?

The period when a child changes into an adult is called puberty. For girls, puberty usually begins between 10 and 12 years. They grow taller, their breasts develop, and their hips widen. Hair grows under the arms and around the groin. Girls' ovaries start to release ova each month and they have periods.

WHAT HAPPENS WHEN PEOPLE GROW OLD?

After early adulthood, the body gradually begins to decline. The skin loses its elasticity, muscles get weaker, and internal organs become less efficient. Certain diseases become more common as we get older, including heart disease and cancer. Aging is a very slow process, and most people lead active lives well into their 70s and 80s.

MILK TEETH ▲
A human has two sets of teeth in their lifetime. At about six months old, the first set, called milk teeth, begin to appear. Milk teeth start to fall out when we are about six years old as permanent teeth, shown here in green, grow up beneath them. In adult life, most people have a full set of 32 permanent teeth.

This vertebra (coloured red) has shrunk and become wedge-shaped

▲ OSTEOPOROSIS
A natural part of aging is a condition called osteoporosis, which makes bones become weaker and more brittle. Some people with osteoporosis shrink in height or become hunched because the bones of their spine lose shape and crumble.

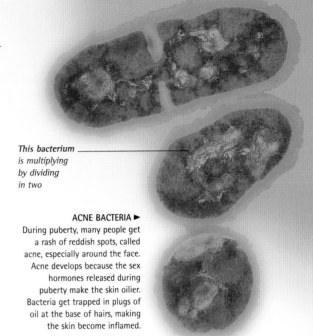

This bacterium is multiplying by dividing in two

ACNE BACTERIA ►
During puberty, many people get a rash of reddish spots, called acne, especially around the face. Acne develops because the sex hormones released during puberty make the skin oilier. Bacteria get trapped in plugs of oil at the base of hairs, making the skin become inflamed.

HOW DO BOYS CHANGE AT PUBERTY?

Boys go through puberty later than girls – between 12 and 14 years. They shoot up in height, and their shoulders and chests get broader. Hair starts to grow on the face, under the arms, around the groin, and sometimes on the chest. The voice gets deeper and the testes start to make sperm.

AGING SKIN ►
These hands of a child and an elderly person show the effects of aging on the skin. The outer layer of skin becomes thinner and loses the protein fibres that make it elastic, causing it to wrinkle. Harmless dark spots also often appear, the result of the overproduction of melanin.

e ⏩ growth

BRAIN AND SKULL DEVELOPMENT

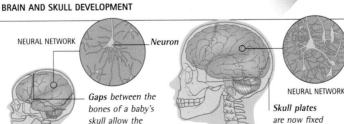

NEURAL NETWORK — *Neuron*

Gaps between the bones of a baby's skull allow the head to grow

NEURAL NETWORK

Skull plates are now fixed at the sutures

NEURAL NETWORK

The facial bones are now mature

AT BIRTH
A baby's brain has a full set of brain cells, but there are few connections between them. The brain grows quickly in the first two years.

AT SIX YEARS
The brain is nearly adult size, but continues to change and learn by growing new connections between the brain cells.

AT 18 YEARS
The brain is fully formed and brain cells have formed billions of complex connections, but we still continue to learn.

FIND OUT MORE ⏩ Hormones 147 • Skeleton 130–131 • Skin 133 • Teeth 143

HEALTH

Being healthy means being free of disease or injury and able to lead a fulfilling, active life. Many factors contribute to a person's health, including genes, the environment, ▸▸ NUTRITION , lifestyle, and luck.

WHAT ARE THE MAJOR HEALTH ISSUES IN THE WORLD TODAY?

In poor countries, dirty water and lack of adequate food are among the main causes of poor health. Infectious diseases such as malaria and AIDS are also major problems, especially in countries that cannot afford modern drugs and medical equipment. In rich countries, health problems are more often caused by people's lifestyle.

CLEAN WATER ▸
A supply of clean drinking water, such as this pump in Cambodia, is vital for good health. In places without a modern sewage system, germs from sewage often contaminate the drinking water supply and cause diseases such as typhoid and cholera.

HOW DOES LIFESTYLE AFFECT HEALTH?

The affluent lifestyle of people in rich countries can increase the risk of serious diseases. Heart disease, obesity (excessive storage of fat), and strokes (blood clots in the brain) are all more common in people who take little exercise or eat too much rich food. Health problems caused by tobacco, alcohol, and drug abuse are also common in rich countries.

e ▸▸ health

LIFE EXPECTANCY

These World Health Organization figures show average life expectancy for babies born in 1999. The life expectancy of people living in the wealthy countries of the world is almost three times that of people in the poorest.

THE TOP FIVE COUNTRIES	THE BOTTOM FIVE COUNTRIES
Japan 74.5 years	Botswana 32.3 years
Australia 73.2 years	Zambia 30.3 years
France 73.1 years	Malawi 29.4 years
Sweden 73 years	Niger 29.1 years
Spain 72.8 years	Sierra Leone 25.9 years

NUTRITION

The process of supplying the body with the nutrients (foods) it needs to stay alive is called nutrition. Eating a variety of foods – a balanced diet – is an important part of keeping healthy.

Cakes, oils, and sweets are rich in fats and sugars that contain useful nutrients but should only be eaten in small quantities

Milk, cheese, butter, and yogurt are good sources of calcium

Meat, eggs, fish, and nuts are rich in protein, vitamins, and minerals, but some kinds of meat contain large amounts of fat, which can cause health problems if eaten in large quantities

Fruit is a good source of water, fibre, and vitamins and contains natural sugars that give us a burst of energy

Vegetables contain vitamins and minerals, and are rich in fibre

Bread, potatoes, rice, and pasta are mostly carbohydrate and are the body's main source of energy

WHAT IS A BALANCED DIET?

A balanced diet includes a mixture of carbohydrates, proteins, fats, vitamins, minerals, and fibre. Sweets and fast food usually contain too much carbohydrate and fat, and little of the fibre needed to keep the digestive system healthy. Fast food that does not contain fresh ingredients is often low in vitamins and minerals.

WHAT IS MALNUTRITION?

Malnutrition means "bad nutrition". This can happen when a person has too little of certain types of food. Lack of protein, for example, can cause stunted growth. Malnutrition can also occur if the diet has excessive amounts of some types of foods – too much fat and sugar, for example, can result in obesity.

WHY IS OBESITY A PROBLEM?

Obesity is increasingly common in wealthy countries. It can lead to medical problems, including diabetes, heart disease, stroke, and high blood pressure. Excess weight can also put strain on the body, causing back pain, shortness of breath, and arthritis.

◂ FOOD PYRAMID
The food pyramid shows the proportions and range of food types that make up a healthy diet. It is important to eat plenty of fresh fruit and vegetables and to reduce the intake of saturated fats and sugar.

FIND OUT MORE ▸▸ Cells 73 • Disease 151 • Genetics 209

DISEASE

Anything that damages the body or how it works can be called a disease. Some diseases are caused by microscopic organisms (germs), others by injury, poisons, or the body itself. Nearly all diseases can be treated by modern ▶ **MEDICINE** to some extent.

WHAT ARE BACTERIA AND VIRUSES?
The most common infectious diseases are caused by bacteria and viruses. Bacteria are single-celled organisms that live outside our cells. They multiply in body fluids and wounds. Many are killed with drugs called antibiotics. Viruses are microscopic particles with their own genetic material. They live in our cells and take them over, but cannot survive without them.

PNEUMONIA BACTERIA ▶
Pneumonia is a lung disease which can be caused by bacteria or a virus. This electron micrograph shows pneumonia-causing bacteria (shown in pink) on the tiny hairs (green) that line the lungs' airways. Pneumonia can affect anyone, but people who are sick and so have a weakened defence system are particularly vulnerable.

◄ HIV VIRUS
The virus that causes AIDS (acquired immune deficiency syndrome) is called HIV (human immunodeficiency virus). The virus invades cells of the immune system, making it more difficult for the body to defend itself from the virus and other diseases.

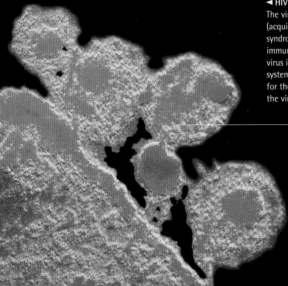

The HIV virus (pink) has taken over a white blood cell of the immune system (yellow and red, bottom left) and tricked it into making more copies of the virus cells

disease

WHAT ARE GENETIC DISEASES?
Genetic diseases, such as cystic fibrosis and muscular dystrophy, occur when a person inherits a particular gene or combination of genes that is harmful. Sometimes the harmful genes are passed on unknowingly by unaffected parents; in other cases the gene changes at conception to become abnormal.

WHY DO SOME PEOPLE SUFFER FROM ALLERGIES?
The body has sophisticated defences for attacking germs, called the immune system, but sometimes the system attacks the wrong targets – people have an allergic reaction when the immune system is triggered by harmless substances like pollen and dust.

WHAT IS CANCER?
There are many different types of cancer, but what they all have in common is that cells start to divide uncontrollably, forming a tumour. The tumour may then prevent part of the body from working normally. This is sometimes caused by agents called carcinogens, such as sunlight or tobacco smoke.

MEDICINE

The study and treatment of disease is called medicine. Modern medicine aims to prevent and cure disease where possible. Some diseases, such as diabetes, are incurable, but medical treatment can still relieve symptoms and improve a patient's quality of life.

CAN DISEASES BE PREVENTED?
Many infectious diseases are prevented by vaccination, which protects the body from specific germs. Screening programmes can detect the early stages of diseases such as cancer. A healthy lifestyle can also help prevent conditions such as heart disease.

HOW ARE DISEASES TREATED?
The body can cope with most illnesses itself, without medical help. We recover from a sore throat, for example. For major problems, a range of treatments can be used, such as drugs, surgery, or radiotherapy (the killing of harmful cells using radiation).

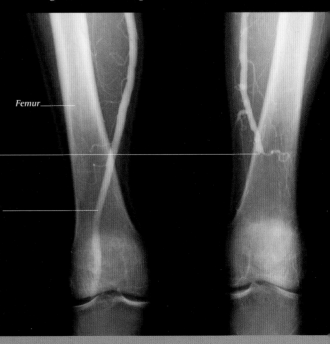

Femur

Blood flow in this femoral artery has stopped just above the knee

Femoral artery with normal blood flow

BLOCKED ARTERY ▶
X-rays are one of the many medical imaging techniques that doctors use to investigate and diagnose disease. This X-ray reveals a blockage in a major artery (yellow) in a person's leg.

FIND OUT MORE ▶ Biotechnology 208 • Body 128–129 • Cells 73 • Micro-organisms 85 • Robots 194

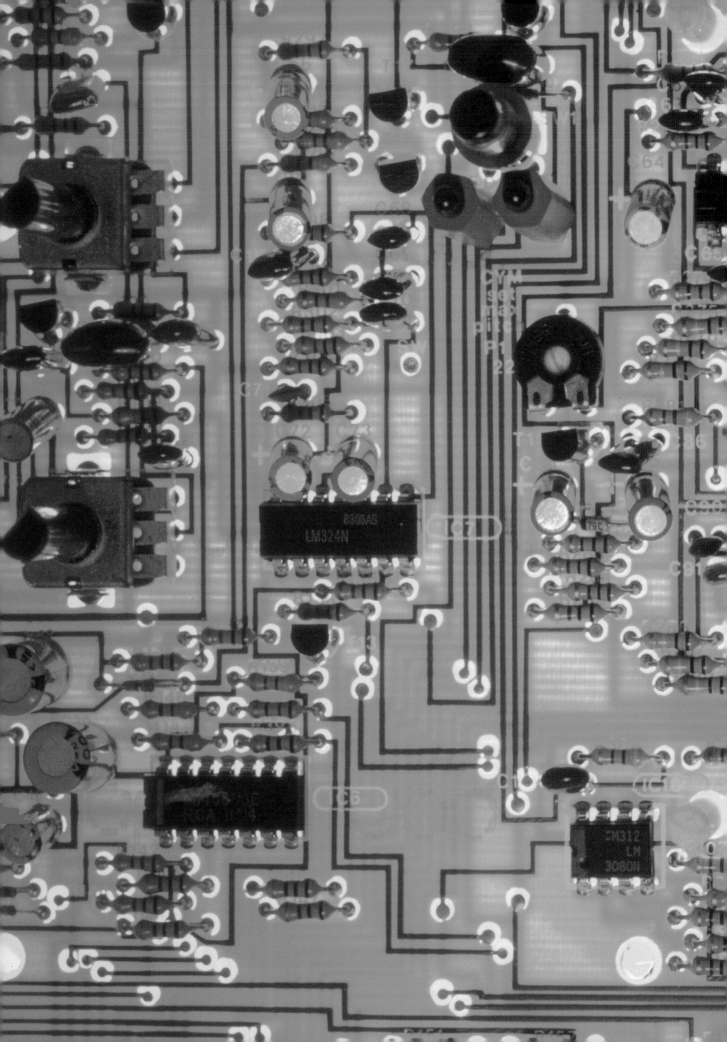

SCIENCE and TECHNOLOGY

SCIENCE

What makes the stars shine?
Why is the sky blue? How did
life start on Earth? Science
explores and tries to understand
everything in the world.

WHAT DO SCIENTISTS DO?
A scientist uses knowledge and a logical approach to
solve a problem or explain an observation. Scientists
use instruments to study forces, disease, and materials.
Without scientists, we would not have gone to the
Moon, discovered penicillin, or developed computers.

WHAT IS SCIENTIFIC METHOD?
Scientists create a theory to explain observations.
Theories are often written as equations. A good
theory makes predictions that can be tested by
further observations and experiments. A trial theory
is called a hypothesis. If its predictions are correct,
the hypothesis is supported.

WHY DO SCIENTISTS PERFORM EXPERIMENTS?
An experiment is a practical test of a theory. By
performing experiments, scientists seek answers to
questions. They use measuring instruments to record
the results of their experiments as numbers.

FIND OUT MORE ▸▸ Biology 72 • Chemistry 162 • Physics 163

Bacteria culture
(growth)
in petri dish

**▲ EXPLORATION
AND DISCOVERY**
From the ocean depths to outer
space, scientists investigate the
natural world by observation
and measurement.

e ▸▸
science

IN THE LABORATORY ▶
Scientists test their theories with
experiments in the laboratory.
This scientist is looking at
bacteria in a petri dish.

TECHNOLOGY

Technology is the practical application of
knowledge and skills to make tools, machines,
buildings, vehicles, and other useful things.

e ▸▸
technology

HOW ARE SCIENCE AND TECHNOLOGY LINKED?
Ancient technologies, such as shipbuilding, were crafts
passed on through generations. Understanding the
materials and forces used came later. Today engineers
use the discoveries and methods of science at every
stage as they solve problems and develop inventions.

▲ BANGLADESHI PANOS STOVE
Appropriate technology fits in
with the environment and
lifestyle of the people using it.
This stove design helps people to
use less wood as fuel, which in
turn conserves forest trees.

◀ COMPUTER-AIDED DESIGN
High-speed computers solve
complex equations. Technologists
simulate (copy) the performance
of aircraft on computers to
improve designs.

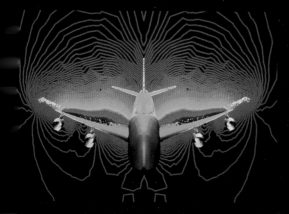

FIND OUT MORE ▸▸ Computers 190 • Design 326 • Machines 196–197

MEASUREMENTS

How big is an ant? How high is a mountain? An observation of a property (characteristic) as a number on a scale of units is a measurement. A child's height may be measured on a metre scale as 1.2 m (4 ft).

BALANCE

STOP WATCH

MEASURING CYLINDERS

THERMOMETER

WHAT IS A MEASUREMENT SCALE?

A simple measurement scale is a series of numbered graduations (marks) on a measuring instrument. Modern electronic instruments often have digital readouts that automatically display the reading.

MEASUREMENT UNITS

QUANTITY	UNIT NAME	SYMBOL
Base units		
Mass	kilogram	kg
Length	metre	m
Time	second	s
Electric current	ampere (amp)	A
Temperature	kelvin	K
Derived units		
Area	square metre	m^2
Volume	cubic metre	m^3
Density	kilogram per cubic metre	kg/m^3
Speed	metre per second	m/s
Acceleration	metre per second squared	m/s^2
Force	newton	N ($kg\,m/s^2$)

▲ MEASURING INSTRUMENTS

Different measuring tools are used to measure different things. Balances measure weight, stop watches measure time, measuring cylinders measure volume of liquids, and thermometers measure temperature.

WHO MADE THE FIRST MEASUREMENTS?

Early people used measurements to build structures such as Stonehenge and the pyramids. Many measurements from this time were based on parts of the body – a cubit was the distance from the elbow to the tip of the fingers on an outstretched hand.

HOW ARE MEASUREMENT UNITS FIXED?

Units are fixed by international agreement. Scientists define a standard against which scales can be calibrated (set and checked). The standard kilogram is the mass of a platinum-iridium cylinder kept at Sèvres in France. The metre is defined as the distance travelled by light in 1/299,792,458 of a second.

measu

FIND OUT MORE ▶▶ Electronics 18₈

MATHEMATICS

Mathematics explores the properties (characteristics) of numbers, shapes, and space. Using maths, scientists can describe patterns they observe in nature, and make models that explain how things behave.

◄ DODECAHEDRON
Geometry is the branch of maths that studies shapes. Engineers use shapes like this to help them create new designs. This shape has 12 identical faces. Each face is a regular pentagon (five-sided flat shape).

mathematics

WHAT ARE MATHEMATICAL MODELS?

Mathematical models are equations that describe real processes. For example, a simple model based on the laws of motion predicts that the speed of a falling stone is equal to the time it has been falling, multiplied by the acceleration due to gravity. The predictions of the model can be compared with real measurements to test the model's accuracy.

WHAT IS SCIENTIFIC NOTATION?

Scientists measure anything, from very large numbers such as the speed of light, to very small numbers, such as the mass of an atom. Scientific notation is a shorthand way of writing these numbers. The speed o light is approximately 300,000,000 metres per second This is shortened to 3.0×10^8 m/s, where ^{8} is the number of zeros that follow the 3.

FIND OUT MORE ▶▶ Physics 16

MATTER

Dust, living things, oceans, mountains, and planets – everything you can touch is made from matter. With electron microscopes scientists can see that all matter is made from particles – tiny specks of matter that stick together like crystals in a cube of sugar.

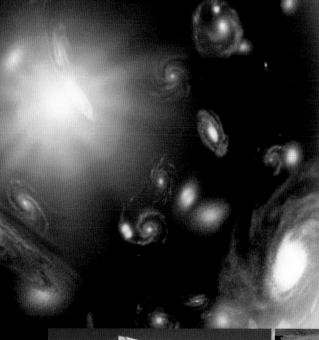

◄ BIG BANG
The Universe is still expanding and cooling today. As it cools, the force of gravity draws floating particles of matter together to form new stars and galaxies.

WHERE DOES MATTER COME FROM?

All matter in the Universe was created by the Big Bang 14 billion years ago. In less than a second, the Universe was filled with vast amounts of energy, such as light and heat. The explosion made the Universe expand. As it expanded, it cooled, and particles with ▶▶ MASS formed and clumped together.

▲ SOLID
Ice is water in the solid state. The ice in this iceberg is at a temperature of 0°C (32°F) or below.

▲ LIQUID
When the temperature rises above 0°C (32°F) ice melts to liquid water. This is water's normal state over most of the Earth.

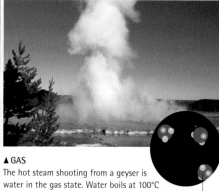

▲ GAS
The hot steam shooting from a geyser is water in the gas state. Water boils at 100°C (212°F), changing from liquid to gas.

Water molecule

PLASMA ▶
A fourth state of matter forms when matter is heated to very high temperatures – like the flame of a welding torch. Plasma glows brightly. Stars and the hottest parts of flames are made from matter in the plasma state.

matter

WHAT ARE STATES OF MATTER?

Most matter on Earth exists in one of three states — solid, liquid, or gas. In a solid, the particles are packed closely together in a rigid pattern. In a liquid, the particles are touching, but tumble freely over each other. In a gas, the particles are widely spaced and move about at random.

WHAT ARE FUNDAMENTAL PARTICLES?

Matter is built from particles. The smallest particles are fundamental particles. Scientists have discovered two kinds of fundamental particle – quarks and leptons. Evidence for quarks and leptons is found by smashing together larger particles at very high speeds. The particles split and new particles are formed.

MASS

Mass is the amount of matter an object contains. All objects with mass have inertia (a force is needed to start, stop, or change their motion), and are attracted to each other by the force of gravity.

CAN MATTER BE DESTROYED?

Matter can be destroyed by changing its mass into pure energy. This can happen when a particle of matter collides with a particle of antimatter. The matter and antimatter annihilate (destroy) each other, and vanish as a flash of radiation.

PARTICLE TRACKS ▶
In a particle accelerator, physicists investigate high-energy collisions between particles. Some particles are destroyed and some are created. Their tracks spread out from the point of impact.

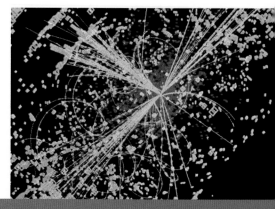

FIND OUT MORE ▶▶ Atoms 157 • Energy 166 • Forces 164 • Heat 168–169 • Motion 165 • Universe 26

ATOMS

All matter is made from particles called atoms. The Ancient Greeks described atoms as the smallest particles that make up everything. We now know that atoms are built from even smaller particles. Atoms link together and make ▶▶ MOLECULES .

HOW BIG IS AN ATOM?
The radius of a typical atom is one tenth of a billionth of a metre. A string of atoms one metre long contains one atom for every person in the world. A cube of sugar contains as many atoms as there are stars in the Universe. The biggest atom (caesium) is about nine times the diameter of the smallest atom (helium).

ATOMIC BOMB ▶
In a nuclear explosion the atom's nucleus (centre) is split. Neutrons are released and hit other nuclei, setting off a chain reaction. The result is a big release of energy in a blast of heat, light, and radiation.

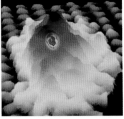

▲ SEEING ATOMS
Electron microscopes can magnify objects 10 million times to show individual atoms. This picture shows a clump of gold atoms (red and yellow) on a regular pattern of carbon atoms (green).

WHAT'S INSIDE AN ATOM?
The particles that make up atoms are electrons, protons, and neutrons. Their position in an atom is the ▶▶ ATOMIC STRUCTURE . Electrons are a type of lepton. Protons and neutrons are made up of three quarks each. Quarks and leptons are fundamental particles – the smallest particles in the Universe.

HOW CAN ATOMS BE SPLIT?
Protons and neutrons are held together in the nucleus at the centre of the atom by a strong force. But this force can be overcome by striking the nucleus with a neutron, a proton, or another particle. The nucleus may split and form new atoms. Atoms are split in this way inside nuclear reactors and during nuclear explosions.

ATOMIC STRUCTURE

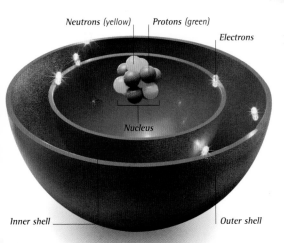

Neutrons (yellow)   *Protons (green)*
Electrons
Nucleus
Inner shell   *Outer shell*

e ▶▶
atoms

Most of an atom is empty space. Protons and neutrons occupy the nucleus at the centre of the atom. Electrons orbit the nucleus like planets around a star. They are grouped in layers called shells.

◀ CARBON ATOM
This model of a carbon atom is split in half to show the inside. The nucleus of a carbon atom contains six neutrons and six protons. Six electrons orbit the nucleus in two shells.

WHAT MAKES ATOMS STICK TOGETHER?
Electrons carry a negative electric charge, protons carry a positive charge. The attraction between them holds electrons in orbits. When atoms come together they share electrons in their outer shells to form chemical bonds.

MOLECULES

Different atoms bonded (stuck) together in particular arrangements are called molecules. Water molecules, for example, have two hydrogen atoms bonded to one oxygen atom.

WHAT SHAPES ARE MOLECULES?
The simplest molecules consist of just two atoms, and are shaped like dumb-bells. But atoms can link together to make molecules of almost any shape imaginable — pyramids, chains, rings, spirals, balls, or tubes.

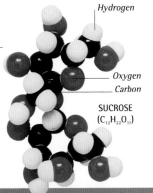

Hydrogen
Oxygen
Carbon
SUCROSE
$(C_{12}H_{22}O_{11})$

Oxygen
Hydrogen
WATER (H_2O)

▲ SIMPLE MOLECULE
A single water molecule consists of three atoms.

◀ COMPLEX MOLECULE
Every molecule of the sugar sucrose is built from 45 atoms linked in an identical pattern.

FIND OUT MORE ▶▶ Electricity 182 • Elements 160–161 • Nuclear Energy 167

TIME

We use time to say when an event happened or how long it lasted. Time seems to pass at the same rate for everyone, but Einstein's theory of ▸▸ RELATIVITY shows that time is not constant throughout the Universe.

HOW DO WE MEASURE TIME?

The steady ticking of a clock marks the passing of time. An accurate clock is controlled by something that repeats at a precise, unchanging interval. Early clocks were set by the swing of a pendulum. Modern clocks are set by the vibrations of a quartz crystal.

DOES TIME BEGIN AND END?

Time began when the Universe was created in the Big Bang about 14 billion years ago. The Universe is currently expanding. Scientists are not sure if the Universe will expand forever, so that time never ends, or if it will collapse in a "Big Crunch", stopping time for good.

▲ ATOMIC CLOCK, USA
This accurate clock uses the regular vibrations of caesium atoms to measure time. It is so accurate, it will be less than three seconds out in a million years.

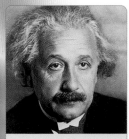

Co-ordinates locate the object's position at a given time

Harbour where the ship is docked

Coastline

▲ RADAR
A radar system locates ships in space and time. Using radars helps to prevent collisions in busy shipping lanes.

time

ALBERT EINSTEIN
German, 1879–1955
Albert Einstein did not do very well at school, but was fascinated by mathematics and science. The Special Theory of Relativity (1905), the General Theory of Relativity (1916), and his work on the quantum theory of light established him as one of the most original and creative thinkers of all time. He was awarded the Nobel Prize for Physics in 1921.

RELATIVITY

Einstein's theory of relativity states that time is not the same for everyone. Time passes more slowly if you are travelling very fast, almost at the speed of light.

HOW DOES RELATIVITY WORK?

If a person watches two identical clocks, one stationary and one travelling at high speed, the moving clock ticks more slowly. To another person travelling with the moving clock, the other clock appears to be moving, and ticking, more slowly.

◂ SHORTCUT THROUGH SPACE AND TIME
Scientists have shown that, in theory, two distant parts of the Universe could be linked by a tunnel through space and time called a wormhole. A wormhole might work as a time machine. By making a return journey through the tunnel you could arrive home before you left.

FIND OUT MORE ▸▸ Light 178–179 • Quantum Theory 159 • Space 10 • Universe 26

QUANTUM THEORY

Quantum theory grew from the ideas of Max Planck. He proposed that atoms could only emit (give out) energy in fixed units called quanta. The theory has been developed to explain the behaviour of particles and the energy they emit.

WHAT IS A QUANTUM?
A quantum is the smallest possible amount of energy. A quantum of light (or other electromagnetic radiation) is called a photon. A photon may be emitted by an electron as it makes a ▶▶ QUANTUM LEAP.

WHY IS QUANTUM THEORY SO STRANGE?
Quantum theory shows that energy behaves as both waves and particles at the same time. Quanta are packets of energy that exist in lumps or units like separate particles – but when they travel, they spread out like waves on the surface of a pond.

HOW DO SCIENTISTS USE QUANTUM THEORY?
Although quantum theory is hard to understand, it is one of the most accurate scientific theories ever developed. With quantum theory, scientists can calculate precisely the properties of atoms, molecules, and materials. Quantum theory is used to design electronic components, new materials, and drugs. Without it there would be no computers, mobile phones, or many other recent inventions.

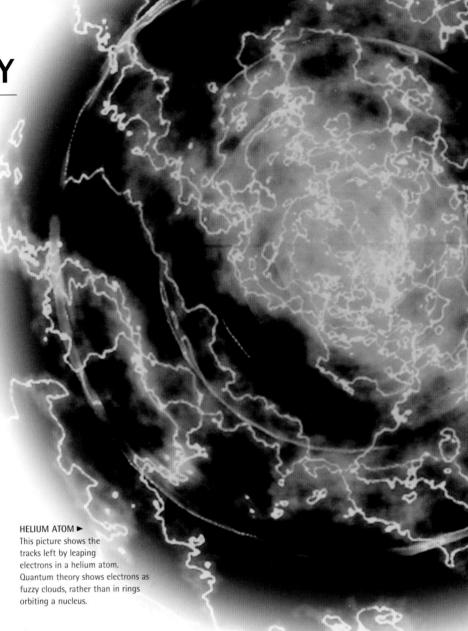

HELIUM ATOM ▶
This picture shows the tracks left by leaping electrons in a helium atom. Quantum theory shows electrons as fuzzy clouds, rather than in rings orbiting a nucleus.

QUANTUM LEAP

Electrons in atoms occupy shells. In each shell an electron has a certain energy. If an electron moves to a higher or lower energy shell, it is said to make a quantum leap.

WHAT IS THE UNCERTAINTY PRINCIPLE?
Quantum theory shows that the position and the speed of a quantum, such as a photon or an electron, cannot both be known exactly. The more accurately we know the position, the more uncertain we are of the speed, and vice versa. The uncertainty principle shows that we can only calculate probabilities, not certainties.

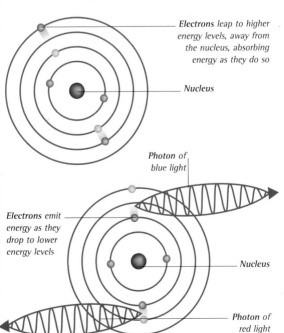

Electrons leap to higher energy levels, away from the nucleus, absorbing energy as they do so

Nucleus

Photon of blue light

Electrons emit energy as they drop to lower energy levels

Nucleus

Photon of red light

◀ ABSORPTION AND EMISSION
When an atom absorbs (takes in) energy, its electrons jump to higher energy levels. As electrons fall back to their original levels they emit (give out) photons. If an electron emits a photon of blue light, it is losing more energy than if it emits a photon of red light.

e ▶▶ quantum theory

MAX PLANCK
German, 1858-1947
Max Planck was born in Kiel, Germany. He was outstanding at all subjects at school and was a talented musician, but he decided to devote his life to physics. Planck's constant (fixed number) is used to calculate the energy of quanta. He was awarded the Nobel Prize for Physics in 1918.

FIND OUT MORE ▶▶ Atoms 157 • Energy 166 • Light 178–179 • Motion 165

ELEMENTS

A substance made up of one kind of atom is an element. Gold is an element because it only contains gold atoms. Water is not an element because it contains hydrogen and oxygen atoms. Scientists list the elements by atomic number in the ▶▶ PERIODIC TABLE . The atomic number is the number of protons in the atom's nucleus.

HOW MANY ELEMENTS ARE THERE?
Scientists have identified 92 elements that occur naturally. Over three-quarters of the natural elements are ▶▶ METALS . The heaviest natural element is the metal uranium. Scientists have created heavier elements in nuclear reactors and particle accelerators.

▼ SUPERNOVA
All the natural elements were created by nuclear reactions that happened inside stars. After burning for billions of years, stars explode as spectacular supernovas, scattering atomic nuclei through space.

METALS

Over 60 elements are metals. They are elements with only one or two electrons in their outer shell. They all share similar properties (characteristics) – they are shiny and strong. Metals also conduct heat and electricity well – they are useful for cooking utensils and electric wires.

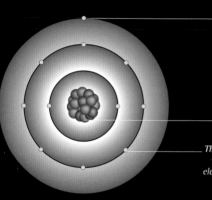

Single electron in outer shell

◄ SODIUM
This metal has one electron in its outer shell.

Nucleus

The middle atomic shell can hold 8 electrons. The inner shell can hold 2

7 electrons in outer shell

The inner shell holds 2 electrons. The middle holds 8

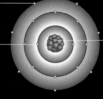

Nucleus

◄ CHLORINE
This non-metal has 7 electrons in the outer shell.

▲ METAL AND NON-METAL
Sodium is a silvery-white metal. It reacts with other elements by giving them its single outer electron. Chlorine is a non-metal. It reacts by accepting an electron. It needs just one more electron to make a stable outer shell of eight. Elements, such as the group of elements called the noble gases, that have eight outer electrons, are particularly stable. They do not lose or gain electrons from other atoms to form chemical bonds.

WHY DO METALS CONDUCT ELECTRICITY?
A metal's outer electrons become detached from their atoms and wander freely through the atoms that make up the metal substance. These free electrons can carry heat and electricity, which explains why metals are good electrical and thermal (heat) conductors.

▼ GOLD
Gold is a transition metal. The transition metals have metallic properties, but they are less reactive than the groups of elements called alkali and alkali-earth metals.

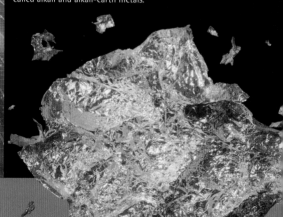

PERIODIC TABLE

The periodic table is a simple list of all the elements. The elements are arranged by their atomic number. The information given for each element includes atomic number, symbol, name, and mass number. The vertical columns of the table are called groups, and the horizontal rows are called periods.

HOW DOES THE PERIODIC TABLE WORK?

The periodic table sets out the elements in a way that highlights similarities and trends in their properties. Elements in the same group (column) have similar properties. The properties change gradually along periods (rows) in the table – elements on the left are metals, elements on the right are non-metals. As you move across periods, the atomic number increases. Also, at the start of a period, elements have one electron in their outer shell – by the end, they have eight.

WHY ARE ELEMENTS IN A GROUP SIMILAR?

The chemical properties of an element depend on the number of electrons in its outer shell. Elements in the same group have the same number of outer electrons. For example, all the elements in Group 1 (alkali metals) have one electron in their outer shells. They are all silvery-white, highly reactive metals.

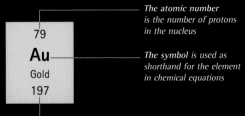

The **atomic number** is the number of protons in the nucleus

The **symbol** is used as shorthand for the element in chemical equations

The **mass number** gives the number of protons and neutrons in the nucleus. The mass numbers given on this page are for the most common isotope (form) of the element

KEY

- Alkali metals
- Alkali-earth metals
- Transition metals
- Rare earths
- Radioactive rare earths
- Poor metals
- Semimetals
- Non-metals
- Noble gases
- Hydrogen does not belong to any one group

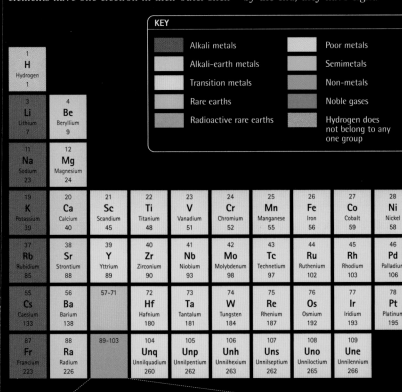

◄ **PERIODIC TABLE**
Russian chemist Dimitri Ivanovich Mendeleyev (1834–1907) drew up the first periodic table in 1869. Gaps in Mendeleyev's table suggested the existence of elements that were not known at the time. The missing elements have all since been discovered – for example, scandium, gallium, and germanium.

WHAT IS AN ISOTOPE?

All elements have several forms called isotopes. Each isotope of an element has the same atomic number, but a different atomic mass. In carbon, 99 per cent of the atoms are isotope carbon 12, and 1 per cent are carbon 13. Both isotopes have six protons, but carbon 12 has six neutrons, while carbon 13 has seven.

WHY IS THE PERIODIC TABLE USEFUL?

Scientists can tell a great deal about the properties of an element, even before they do experiments, by looking at its position in the periodic table. They can decide whether it will be a metal or a non-metal, judge how well it will conduct electricity, and predict how it will react with other elements.

elements

FIND OUT MORE ►► Alloys 174 • Atoms 157 • Electricity 182 • Heat 168–169 • Materials 170 • Matter 156

CHEMISTRY

Chemistry is the science of matter. Scientists study chemicals, their properties, and ▸▸ REACTIONS . ▸▸ BIOCHEMISTRY is the chemistry of living things.

WHAT IS A CHEMICAL?
Chemicals are the basic types of matter. The elements, such as hydrogen and oxygen, are chemicals. So are the compounds, such as water, that are made when atoms of different elements join. Our bodies, food, and the clothes we wear are all made from chemicals.

WHAT ARE CHEMICAL PROPERTIES?
The properties of a chemical describe what it does to other chemicals. Oxygen, for example, makes iron rust, or oxidize, so oxygen is an oxidizing agent.

WHY ARE SOME CHEMICALS DANGEROUS?
Our bodies contain tens of thousands of chemicals that mix and react to give us energy and keep us alive. Toxic (poisonous) chemicals interfere with these reactions. Some chemicals are also corrosive – they eat through solid material.

◀ THE pH SCALE
The pH scale is a measure of acidity. Very strong acids have a pH of 1, neutral chemicals are pH 7, and strong bases, or alkalis, are pH 14.

STRONG REACTION ▶
Chemists use experiments to find out how chemicals react when they are mixed in different ways. Some chemicals react strongly, bubbling, burning, or even exploding. Other chemicals do not react at all.

Two liquids react in a flask

Vapour escapes into the atmosphere

CHEMICAL REACTIONS

A chemical reaction happens when two or more chemicals combine to make new chemical compounds. Many reactions release heat, for example burning.

WHAT ARE ACIDS AND BASES?
Acids are chemicals that react with metals. Strong acids, such as sulphuric, nitric, and hydrochloric acid, are very corrosive. A base is a chemical that neutralizes an acid. When acids and bases react, they form chemicals called salts. Alkalis are bases that dissolve in water.

◀ GRAPHITE
Graphite is a form of pure carbon. The carbon atoms in graphite are bonded in sheets that slide over each other easily. This is why a graphite pencil leaves black marks.

DIAMOND ▶
The carbon atoms in diamond are bonded in a strong 3-D network. This makes diamond the hardest material on Earth.

e ▸▸
chemistry

BIOCHEMISTRY

Biochemistry studies the molecules in living things, including plants, animals, and the human body. These molecules are all compounds of the element carbon.

WHY IS LIFE BASED ON CARBON?
Carbon atoms can link to each other (and to other elements) in many, many ways, including rings and chains of any length. This enormous variety means carbon is the perfect main building block for the complicated molecules of life.

pH column

pH 14

Caustic soda (oven cleaner)
Caustic soda reacts with fat and grease marks, and destroys skin and flesh.

pH 11

Milk of magnesia
This alkali is used to cure indigestion – it neutralizßes the acid in your stomach.

pH 9

Liquid soap
All cleaning products are bases. Like most bases, soap feels slippery.

pH 7.5

Blood
Medical injections contain chemicals called buffers to match the pH of blood.

pH 6–7

Pure water
Pure water is neutral – it is neither an acid nor a base.

pH 4

Oranges
Oranges are mildly acidic, which is why they taste slightly sharp.

pH 3

Vinegar
The acid in vinegar kills bacteria, so it is used in pickling to preserve food.

pH 2

Lemon juice
Lemons taste sour because they contain citric acid. Acid means "sour" in Latin.

pH 1

Hydrochloric acid
This is a strong, corrosive acid. It eats through most metals in a fizzing reaction.

FIND OUT MORE ▸▸ Elements 160–161 • Materials 170 • Matter 156

PHYSICS

Physics is the study of the forces, the energy, and the matter that make up the Universe and everything in it. ▶ APPLIED PHYSICS uses the discoveries of physics in medicine, engineering, and other practical situations.

WHAT DO PHYSICISTS STUDY?

Physicists investigate what atoms are made of, how materials behave, and the forces that keep planets in orbit. They also study heat, light, sound, electricity, and magnetism. They try to discover the basic laws that matter and energy obey. Discoveries are usually written down as scientific ▶ EQUATIONS.

WHAT ARE PHYSICAL PROPERTIES?

Physical properties are features that can be measured as numbers – length, weight, and volume, for example. Other physical properties include hardness, density, elasticity (how flexible a material is), conductivity (how well it conducts electricity or heat), and reflectivity (how much light it reflects).

HOW DO PHYSICISTS WORK?

There are two main types of investigation in physics. Experimental physicists work in laboratories, designing experiments to measure physical properties and processes. Theoretical physicists work with ideas, equations, and models to uncover new laws of physics that can explain or predict the results of experiments.

ROLLERCOASTER ▲
Designers used physics to make sure this rollercoaster is safe, but also fun. They use the basic laws of motion to predict the forces you will experience at every loop and turn of the ride.

EQUATIONS

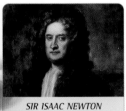

SIR ISAAC NEWTON
English, 1642–1727

Isaac Newton made some of the most important scientific and mathematical discoveries of all time. His laws of motion and theories of gravity explain how all objects from atoms to planets move. His theories of optics (light) show that white light is made of a spectrum of colour light.

An equation is a short way to write a scientific idea. For example, the density of a material is a measure of how tightly packed the matter inside it is. The equation density=mass/volume says that an object's density is its mass divided by its volume.

WHAT DO EQUATIONS TELL US?

An equation states that the amount to the left of the equals sign is the same as the amount on the right. Letters are used for physical properties – in the equation F=ma, F is force, and ma means mass (m) multiplied by acceleration (a). Some equations show the results of an experiment, and others show the predictions of a theory.

$$d = 0.7v + 0.07v^2$$

▲ STOPPING DISTANCE
This equation shows how the stopping distance (d) of a braking car depends on its speed, or velocity (v). The distance has two parts. $0.7v$ (0.7 times the speed) is the distance travelled while the driver is reacting (the thinking distance). $0.07v^2$ is the distance travelled during braking. The symbol ^{2} means the number multiplied by itself.

APPLIED PHYSICS

Applied physicists use the basic laws of the physical world to design useful tools and techniques for many areas of science and technology, including medicine, astronomy, meteorology, materials science, and information technology.

e ▶▶
physics

◀ MRI SCAN
With an MRI (magnetic resonance imaging) scan, a doctor can look inside the body without surgery. MRI is based on the magnetic properties of atomic nuclei, discovered by physicists.

HOW IS PHYSICS USED IN MEDICINE?

Physics has been used to develop many valuable medical instruments and techniques. Scanners, X-ray machines, and laser surgery are based on discoveries made by physicists, as are heart monitors and radiation treatment for cancer.

FIND OUT MORE ▶▶ Energy 166 • Forces 164 • Matter 156 • Measurements 155

FORCES

When you strike a ball with a bat, stretch a rubber band, or lift a suitcase, you are applying a force. All forces are pushes and pulls. Some forces can act over long distances, for example, the force of ▶▶ GRAVITY pulls you down when you jump from a high diving board.

WHAT CAN FORCES DO?

Forces change motion and shape. The force of a boot kicking a ball speeds the ball up. The force of a parachute on a skydiver slows the skydiver down. The force of a string on a whirling ball constantly changes the direction of motion, keeping it moving in a circle. Combinations of forces applied to materials can stretch, twist, and crush them.

HOW CAN YOU MEASURE A FORCE?

Forces are measured by their effects. Spring balances are used to measure the effect of forces. The stronger the force applied to a spring, the more it is stretched. The amount the spring is stretched from its normal size is proportional to the force applied to it. The unit of measurement of force is called a newton. One newton of force increases the speed of a one kilogram mass by one metre per second every second.

WHAT ARE BALANCED FORCES?

Two forces are balanced when they are equal in size and opposite in direction. If the balanced forces are applied to an object, they will have no effect on its motion in a straight line, but may stretch or compress it. If the forces do not act along the same line, they may cause the object to rotate.

FUNDAMENTAL FORCES		
FORCE	*EFFECTS*	*RELATIVE STRENGTH*
Gravity	Gives objects weight	Very weak
	Holds moons and planets in their orbits	
Electromagnetic	Holds electrons in atoms and atoms in molecules	Strong
	Gives materials strength and shape	
	Responsible for electricity, magnetism, light, and other forms of electromagnetic radiation	
Weak nuclear	Involved in radioactivity	Weak
Strong nuclear	Holds protons and neutrons in the nuclei of atoms	Very strong

▲ IMPACT
Forces always come in pairs. As you head a ball, the force on your head is opposite in direction to the force on the ball. During the impact both the head and the ball change shape. Their motion changes in opposite ways. The ball goes away from you as your head goes back.

▲ SKYDIVERS
The force of gravity pulls these skydivers towards the Earth. Their speed increases until their weight is exactly balanced by the force from the air (air resistance), which acts in the opposite direction. They continue to fall, but at a steady rate. By spreading their arms and legs the skydivers use air resistance to steer as they fall, linking hands to make a ring.

e ▶▶ forces

GRAVITY

Gravity is the force that acts between all objects with mass. Gravity always attracts, never repels – it is always a pull and never a push. The strength of the force of gravity increases either when mass is increased or when the distance between the objects is decreased.

WHAT IS THE DIFFERENCE BETWEEN MASS AND WEIGHT?

Mass is the amount of matter in an object. The mass of an object does not change if it is taken from Earth into space. Weight is a force. The weight of an object on Earth is the force acting on it because of Earth's gravity. On the Moon the object weighs less than on Earth since the Moon's force of gravity is less.

WHY DO THINGS FLOAT OR SINK?

If you place a block of wood in water, it displaces (pushes aside) some of the water but floats. A force in the water called upthrust acts upwards on it to counter the downwards pull of gravity. The upthrust equals the weight of the displaced water. When you place a heavy object in water, the weight of the displaced water, which equals the upthrust, is less than the weight of the object, so the object sinks.

MOTION

From molecules in this sheet of paper, to planets in orbits, the objects around us are in constant motion. The simplest motion is in a straight line at constant speed. When the speed or direction change, scientists say that motion is accelerated.

Pendulum

WHAT IS ACCELERATION?
When you drop a stone, it starts from rest (speed equals zero), then speeds up as it falls. The stone is accelerating. A force is always needed to produce acceleration – in this case, it is the force of gravity. Acceleration is slowed by  **FRICTION** – in this case, air resistance.

HOW IS SPEED MEASURED?
Two measurements are needed to find speed – the distance moved, and the time taken. Speed is calculated by dividing the distance by the time. If a runner covers five metres in one second, his or her speed is five metres per second. A car that travels 100 kilometres in two hours has an average speed of 50 kilometres per hour.

PENDULUM SWING ▲
The child on the swing is moving like a pendulum. She kicks to start. Gravity slows her down as she rises, then speeds her up again in the opposite direction. She swings to and fro, until friction and air resistance eventually bring her to rest.

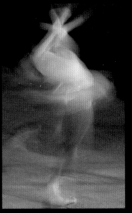

CIRCULAR MOTION ►
Whirling in a circle involves constantly changing direction. The ice skater's arms fly out as she spins. By using a force to bring them straight above her head, she can increase her turning speed.

◄ COMPLEX MOTION
The complicated motion of a gymnast's front handspring combines movement in a straight line and movement in a circle.

FRICTION

The force of friction opposes motion when one surface slides, or tries to slide, over another. You feel friction as you drag your hand across a table. Friction is produced by forces between the molecules in the surfaces. Drag is the friction between a solid object and the fluid it is travelling through.

HOW CAN WE USE FRICTION?
Friction is not always a problem – sometimes we use it to prevent or slow down motion. Without friction your shoes would not grip the ground and you would slip over, and a car's wheels would spin and skid. Friction is increased by making shoe soles and tyres from soft, sticky materials, such as rubber.

HOW CAN FRICTION BE REDUCED?
Friction between parts of machines can damage them by wear and tear. Friction also wastes energy as heat instead of movement. Friction can be reduced by using oil as a lubricant to make a slippery film between surfaces. Machines built with a streamlined shape reduce drag. Aeroplanes are designed to let air flow over them smoothly with the least resistance. The study of air flow is called aerodynamics.

FRICTION BY DESIGN ►
An athlete needs friction between the soles of his shoes and the road to run. Without friction, his feet would slide on the spot.

Soft rubber soles grip the ground

Grooves channel water away

e ▸▸
motion

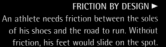

FIND OUT MORE ▸▸ Atoms 157 • Forces 164 • Materials 170

ENERGY

Without energy, the world would be lifeless, dark, and still. When something has energy, it can do work and bring about change. Energy produces light and movement. Energy is required to produce heat, to generate electricity, and to overcome forces such as friction.

WHAT FORMS CAN ENERGY TAKE?
Speeding cars, whizzing rockets, the wind, and waves have ▶▶ KINETIC (motion) energy. A stretched rubber band has potential (stored) energy because of the forces that try to make it return to its original size. Heat is the kinetic energy of particles in materials. Light is radiation energy created by the electromagnetic force.

Kinetic energy increases with speed

Elastic energy is stored by the rope as it stretches

Gravitational potential energy increases with height above the Earth's surface

HOW DOES ENERGY CHANGE FORM?
When something happens, energy is changed from one form into another. When you climb stairs, chemical energy in your food is changed into kinetic energy by your muscles, and into potential energy as you raise your body against gravity. The amount of energy transferred is measured in ▶▶ JOULES.

◀ **BUNGEE JUMP**
A bungee jumper uses gravitational energy to power his dive from a bridge. As he accelerates down, gravitational energy is converted into kinetic energy. As the bungee rope begins to stretch, then slow his fall, kinetic energy is converted into elastic (potential) energy.

DOES ENERGY GET USED UP?
Energy cannot be created or destroyed, it can only change from one form to another. There is always as much energy after an event as there was before, but some of the energy may be wasted as heat that escapes into the surroundings.

KINETIC

Moving and vibrating objects have kinetic energy. The greater the moving object's mass, and the higher its speed, the more kinetic energy it has.

WHY IS IT WORSE TO CRASH AT HIGHER SPEEDS?
You might think a 64 km/h (40 mph) crash is twice as dangerous as a 32 km/h (20 mph) crash. In fact, doubling the speed increases the kinetic energy by four. At 64 km/h (40 mph), there is four times as much energy to cause damage as at 32 km/h (20 mph).

KINETIC ENERGY ▲
Racing cyclists convert food into muscular energy, and then into kinetic energy.

PLAYER POWER ▲
An athlete playing high-intensity sports consumes lots of Calories. He can burn 1,000 Calories an hour during a game. You use just 50 Calories an hour watching TV.

e ▶▶
energy

JOULES

The modern international unit of energy is the joule. One joule is the energy used up when a force of one newton moves through a distance of one metre.

WHAT IS A CALORIE?
The calorie is an old-fashioned unit of heat energy. It is equal to just over four joules. The unit called the Calorie (with a capital C) is still used to give the energy content of foods. One Calorie is equal to 4,200 joules. An active teenager needs between 2,000 and 2,500 Calories of energy a day. The body stores excess Calories as fat.

FIND OUT MORE ▶▶ Electricity 182 • Electromagnetism 186 • Forces 164 • Heat 168–169 • Light 178–179 • Motion 165

NUCLEAR ENERGY

The energy that makes the stars shine and produces the heat inside a nuclear reactor is nuclear energy. It is produced by the strong force that holds protons and neutrons together inside atomic nuclei.

WHAT ARE FUSION AND FISSION?

Two kinds of reaction release nuclear energy. Fusion takes place when two light nuclei combine (fuse) to make a heavier nucleus. This is the process that powers the stars. Fission takes place when an unstable nucleus of a heavy element, such as uranium, splits in two. Fission is used in nuclear power stations.

HOW IS A NUCLEAR REACTION CONTROLLED?

The fission of ▶▶ RADIOACTIVE uranium produces nuclear energy. The process is controlled by adjusting the number of neutrons produced. Control rods that absorb neutrons are inserted between the uranium fuel rods. They are raised or lowered to maintain a steady release of energy.

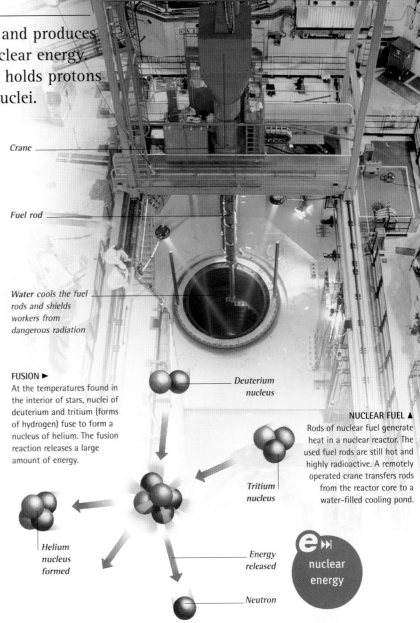

Crane

Fuel rod

Water cools the fuel rods and shields workers from dangerous radiation

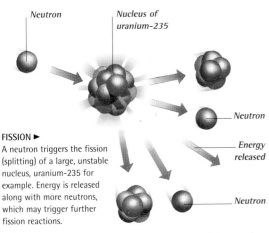

Neutron

Nucleus of uranium-235

FISSION ▶
A neutron triggers the fission (splitting) of a large, unstable nucleus, uranium-235 for example. Energy is released along with more neutrons, which may trigger further fission reactions.

Neutron

Energy released

Neutron

FUSION ▶
At the temperatures found in the interior of stars, nuclei of deuterium and tritium (forms of hydrogen) fuse to form a nucleus of helium. The fusion reaction releases a large amount of energy.

Deuterium nucleus

Tritium nucleus

Helium nucleus formed

Energy released

Neutron

NUCLEAR FUEL ▲
Rods of nuclear fuel generate heat in a nuclear reactor. The used fuel rods are still hot and highly radioactive. A remotely operated crane transfers rods from the reactor core to a water-filled cooling pond.

e ▶▶ nuclear energy

RADIOACTIVITY

Strong forces act inside the nuclei of atoms. Some atoms are unstable – they decay (break down) over time, releasing energy as radiation. These atoms are radioactive. There are three main types of radiation – alpha, beta, and gamma.

HOW IS RADIOACTIVITY USEFUL?

Radioactive substances decay over time in a predictable way. Geologists and archaeologists can date rocks by measuring the radiation they emit. In industry, radiation is used to trace underground pipes and to kill dangerous germs on food before it is packaged. In medicine, radiation treats cancer and sterilizes medical instruments.

WHY IS RADIOACTIVITY DANGEROUS?

To a living cell an alpha particle, beta particle, or a gamma ray is like a bullet from a gun. Its energy damages molecules, disrupting the cell's life processes. Long-term exposure to radiation can cause cancers, such as leukaemia. Exposure to a single, large dose of radiation can produce radiation sickness and death. Radioactive material must be handled with great care.

◀ NUCLEAR WASTE
A nuclear technician checks nuclear waste storage containers for emissions of radiation. The radiation detector records the number of radioactive particles (alpha, beta, and gamma rays) penetrating the thick walls of the storage containers.

MARIE CURIE
French, 1867-1934
Polish-born physicist Marie Curie was one of the first scientists to investigate radioactivity. She discovered the radioactive element radium. She was the first person ever to win two Nobel Prizes. Marie Curie died from leukaemia caused by the radiation she worked with.

FIND OUT MORE ▶▶ Atoms 157 • Energy 166 • Energy Resources 60–61

HEAT

Everything around us contains heat. Heat is a form of energy – the energy of the random jiggling motion of particles that make up all matter. ⏩ TEMPERATURE is a measure of how hot an object is – it can be recorded on a ⏩ THERMOMETER .

HOW DOES HEAT FLOW?

Heat always flows from a higher temperature to a lower temperature. If you stand next to a radiator, the heat from it warms you up. Different materials let heat flow through them at different rates. Metals are the best conductors (they let heat flow easily). ⏩ THERMAL INSULATORS don't conduct heat well.

WHAT ARE THE THREE TYPES OF HEAT TRANSFER?

Conduction is the transfer of heat from one molecule to another. Energetic molecules pass on heat energy when they collide with less energetic molecules. Convection is the transfer of heat through a liquid or a gas as warm fluid rises and cool fluid sinks. These movements are convection currents. Radiation is the movement of heat by electromagnetic rays. All objects emit radiation.

▲ THERMAL-IMAGING
Rescue workers use a thermal-imaging camera to search for survivors in dense smoke or under fallen rubble. A warm body shows up as a bright area in the image.

CAN WE SEE HEAT?

We cannot see heat, but we can see its effects. Convection currents rising from a hot tarmac road make the air above shimmer. A thermal-imaging camera detects radiation emitted by hot objects. Electronics convert invisible electromagnetic rays into an image on a television screen.

Eyes are hot areas because they contain lots of blood vessels

Blue and green regions are coolest

Red and yellow regions are warmest

The nose loses heat easily because it does not contain many blood vessels

THERMOGRAPH ▲
This false-colour image shows the temperature differences over a man's head and shoulders. Thermal imaging cameras installed at airports can spot passengers with a fever (higher than normal temperature) who may be carrying an infectious disease. They are also used at ports to detect people smuggled in vehicles.

TEMPERATURE

The temperature tells us how hot an object is. It is a measure of how fast the particles in the object are moving. The hotter an object, the more vigorously its molecules move. Temperature is measured in degrees on a temperature scale.

WHAT IS ABSOLUTE ZERO?

If you could remove all the heat energy from an object, its molecules would be effectively stationary. The temperature at which molecules are no longer moving is called absolute zero. It is the lowest possible temperature. Absolute zero is equivalent to -273.15°C (-459.67°F).

WHERE IS THE HOTTEST PLACE IN THE UNIVERSE?

The centre of the Sun is 14 million°C (25 million°F). Temperatures 30 times higher are created in laboratories to produce nuclear fusion. But even these temperatures are tiny compared to the Big Bang – this was more than 10 billion billion billon°C!

TEMPERATURE SCALE ▶
Three different temperature scales are commonly used. On the Celsius scale the melting temperature of ice is 0°C. On the Fahrenheit scale the temperature of melting ice is 32°F. On the Kelvin scale ice melts at 273.15 K.

THERMOMETERS

The instrument for measuring temperature is called a thermometer. Most thermometers have a scale with two fixed points – the melting point of ice and the boiling point of water. All temperatures are measured against these points.

HOW DOES A THERMOSTAT WORK?

Thermostats control the temperatures of buildings and machines. A simple room thermostat has a two-metal strip as part of a switch that turns the heat on and off. As the temperature rises, the two metals in the strip expand by different amounts. The strip bends, breaking the circuit and turning off the heat supply. As the room cools, the strip straightens, completes the circuit again, and turns the heat back on.

▲ GLASS THERMOMETER
This thermometer contains liquid in a glass capsule. The liquid expands when heated, and flows up the scale. This gives the temperature of the liquid.

THERMAL INSULATORS

Any material that resists the flow of heat is a thermal insulator. Many animals keep warm because fur is a good insulator – it stops heat flowing away from their bodies.

HOW DOES A VACUUM FLASK WORK?

A vacuum flask is designed to keep hot food hot, or cold food cold. Double walls prevent heat flow in or out by conduction. The walls are coated in shiny silver to reflect electromagnetic rays, reducing heat transfer by radiation. The space between the walls contains air at a low pressure (vacuum). This reduces heat transfer by convection.

Stopper

Flask

Double walls *with* vacuum between

◀ VACUUM FLASK
The vacuum flask has silvered double walls with a vacuum in between. This prevents heat transfer by conduction, convection, and radiation.

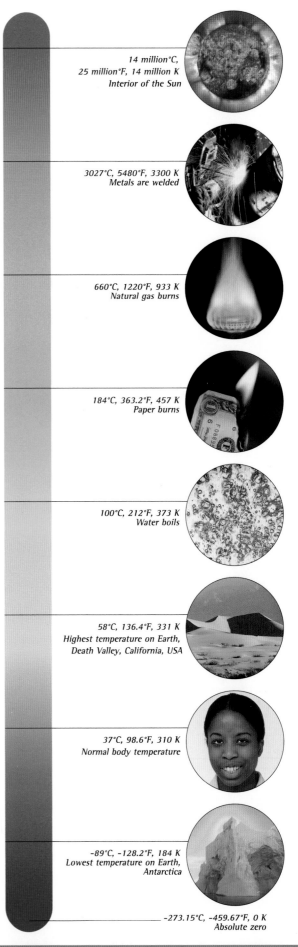

14 million°C, 25 million°F, 14 million K
Interior of the Sun

3027°C, 5480°F, 3300 K
Metals are welded

660°C, 1220°F, 933 K
Natural gas burns

184°C, 363.2°F, 457 K
Paper burns

100°C, 212°F, 373 K
Water boils

58°C, 136.4°F, 331 K
Highest temperature on Earth, Death Valley, California, USA

37°C, 98.6°F, 310 K
Normal body temperature

-89°C, -128.2°F, 184 K
Lowest temperature on Earth, Antarctica

-273.15°C, -459.67°F, 0 K
Absolute zero

FIND OUT MORE ▶▶ Atoms 157 • Circulation 134 • Energy 166 • Sun 15

▲ HEAT-RESISTANT CLOTHING
Many natural and synthetic fibres burn easily, but the fibres used to make a firefighter's suit are heat and flame resistant. The whole suit is coated with a thin layer of aluminium to reflect heat away from the surface, like a mirror.

MATERIALS

Any substance that is used to make something is a material. Natural materials such as stone and wood are used as they are found in nature. ▸▸ SYNTHETIC materials are made from natural materials with the help of heat and chemical reactions.

WHAT ARE MATERIALS' PROPERTIES?
Materials are selected for use according to their properties (characteristics). Mechanical properties, such as strength, are important for materials used in construction. Chemical properties show if a material will react with other materials. Thermal properties show how a material conducts heat.

TENSILE TEST ▶
This machine tests the strength of the plastic toy by using a pulling (tensile) force. If the head comes off easily, the toy is a choking hazard to small children.

HOW STRONG IS A SPIDER'S WEB?
Millions of years of evolution have produced natural materials ideally suited to the jobs they do. A spider's web is, weight-for-weight, 10 times as strong as steel, and far more elastic. Bones, teeth, and tusks are also very strong natural materials. They can be used every day for a hundred years without breaking.

▲ SPIDER'S WEB
A spider weaves its web from silk fibres made from proteins called fibroin. The silk is not easily broken because it is both strong and elastic.

HOW ARE MATERIALS USED?
The chosen materials for a product need to be shaped and joined. Wood is shaped by sawing, planing, and drilling. It is joined with nails, screws, or glue. Metal is bent and hammered into shape – or heated until it melts, and poured into moulds. Metal is joined with nuts and bolts, rivets, or by welding.

SYNTHETICS

A substance made artificially, by heat and chemical reactions, is a synthetic. It may be similar to a natural material, or have completely new properties.

WHAT WERE THE FIRST SYNTHETICS?
Heat melts sand and other minerals to make glass. The first glass bottles were made about 3,500 years ago in Ancient Egypt. The first modern synthetic was made in 1909, when Leo Baekeland, an American chemist, created a plastic called Bakelite.

WHAT IS A COMPOSITE MATERIAL?
Composite materials combine the useful properties of two or more materials in one. Steel is strong and concrete is strong, but steel-reinforced concrete is even stronger. It is used for constructing tall buildings and long bridges.

▲ GLASS-REINFORCED PLASTIC (GRP) CHAIR
A GRP chair is light and tough. It is made from glass fibres in plastic. The fibres stop cracks from spreading through the material, giving it great strength.

FIND OUT MORE ▸▸ Alloys 174 • Chemistry 162 • Heat 168–169 • New Materials 175

CHANGING MATERIALS

We can use chemical reactions and heat to change materials and their properties to our needs. Some changes are ►► PERMANENT , others are ►► REVERSIBLE .

HOW DO CHEMICAL REACTIONS CHANGE MATERIALS?

Chemical reactions take place when existing bonds between atoms are broken and new bonds form. When the gas ethene is heated at high pressure, its molecules join together in long chains to make the plastic polythene. Polythene is used to make washing up bowls, squeezy bottles, and plastic bags.

WHAT MAKES GLUE STICK?

A good glue is a substance that starts as a liquid, but transforms into a solid when exposed to air. As a liquid, the glue can flow into every nook and cranny of the surfaces where it is spread. The glue molecules form bonds with the molecules in the surfaces. As the glue sets, the surfaces are held firmly together.

changing materials

ROT AND DECAY ►
The complex molecules in living things are decomposed by micro-organisms after death.

HOW DOES HEAT CHANGE MATERIALS?

Heat makes many solids, especially metals, softer and easier to shape. As the temperature rises, most solids eventually melt to the liquid state, but some materials react differently to heat. Heat can trigger chemical reactions between mixtures. In an oven heat changes a cake mix from a sticky liquid into a fluffy solid.

RUSTING IRON ▲
Any iron object left outside in the wet becomes covered with an orange-brown substance called rust. Rusting is a chemical reaction between iron, oxygen, and water.

Fungus spores multiply on the nectarine skin, breaking down its structure as they feed

Water escapes into the atmosphere and the nectarine shrivels and dies

FRESH NECTARINE   ROTTEN NECTARINE

REVERSIBLE CHANGES

Melting and boiling are reversible changes produced by heat. Steam from a boiling kettle condenses back into drops of water when it comes into contact with a cold surface, such as a window.

◄ LAVA FLOW
Liquid lava pouring from a volcano is solid rock melted by heat from the Earth's core at about 700°C (1,292°F). The lava's surface cools first, setting into a thin skin that wrinkles as the lava moves. When it is completely cool, it sets back into solid rock.

CAN STONE MELT?

Candle wax melts at 60°C (140°F), lead melts at 327.5°C (621.5°F), iron at 1,540°C (2,804°F). Even stone can melt. The material with the highest known melting temperature is the metal tungsten, which melts at 3,387°C (6,129°F). Tungsten wire is used to make the filaments of electric light bulbs and television tubes.

PERMANENT CHANGES

Burning, rusting, and cooking are permanent changes. They can't be undone by reversing the conditions that brought them about.

HOW DOES CONCRETE CHANGE FROM A LIQUID TO A SOLID?

Concrete is a mixture of sand, gravel, cement, and water. Cement powder contains calcium oxide (lime) and silica or similar chemical compounds (substances that are two or more elements). When cement is mixed with water, the compounds react and set into a solid. The setting cement glues the sand and gravel particles together to make a permanent solid structure.

CONCRETE ►
An electron microscope picture of setting concrete shows the changes that take place as the concrete hardens. As cement reacts with water, crystals form, bonding sand and gravel particles together.

FIND OUT MORE ►► Atoms 157 • Chemistry 162 • Electricity 182 • Heat 168–169 • Matter 156 • Mixtures 172 • Micro-organisms 85

MIXTURES

A mixture is a jumble of different things. Soil is a mixture of sand, clay, stones, roots, and plant and animal remains. The air is a mixture of different gases. Sea water contains a mixture of different chemical compounds in ▶▶ SOLUTION .

WHAT IS THE DIFFERENCE BETWEEN A MIXTURE AND A COMPOUND?

The components of a mixture are physically mixed together, but they have not reacted chemically. When materials react chemically, chemical bonds break and reform, producing compounds with new properties.

DO SOLIDS, LIQUIDS, AND GASES MIX?

All the states of matter can mix, with themselves and each other. Solid powders mix easily. Most rocks are a mixture of different minerals. Some liquids mix easily, and some don't. Water and alcohol mix together, but water and oil do not mix. Gases mix rapidly by ▶▶ DIFFUSION – their molecules can move between each other because gas molecules are widely spaced.

SOLUTION

A solution is a mixture in the liquid state. Molecules of one substance are dispersed (scattered) throughout molecules of another – the substance is dissolved. The amount of a substance that will dissolve in another is called its solubility.

◀ LAYERS OF OIL AND WATER
Oil and water don't mix, and therefore do not form a solution.

DIFFUSION

When two liquids or gases are in the same container, the random motion of their molecules makes them mingle together until the mixture is the same throughout. This is called diffusion.

WHAT IS A RANDOM WALK?

The movement of a single molecule in a liquid or a gas is a zig-zag random walk. The molecule is continually moving and changing direction as it collides with other molecules. A group of molecules that were concentrated in one spot gradually spread apart. This explains how an odour, for example perfume, spreads through a room.

WHY IS IT EASIER TO MIX THAN TO SEPARATE?

It couldn't be easier to mix a bucket of red balls with a bucket of white balls – just tip them together. Mixing makes the balls more jumbled. Scientists say that they have more entropy (disorder). Separating the balls is much harder. To make them ordered again, red balls in one bucket, white in another, you have to pick the balls out one at a time.

◀ LAVA LAMP
The lamp contains two liquids with slightly different densities that do not mix.

▬ *Warm bubbles rise, cool, and sink again*

▬ *Liquid bubbles expand and float up*

▬ *Lamp base contains an electric bulb. This heats the bubbles. The liquid nearer the heat expands, becomes less dense, and rises*

WHY DON'T OIL AND WATER MIX?

Oil is insoluble (does not dissolve) in water because oil and water molecules repel each other. Cooking oil and water can be physically mixed together by shaking them vigorously in a bottle, but when the mixture is left to stand, the oil and water molecules gradually separate again. Oil is less dense (heavy) than water, so the oil floats on top of the water.

e ▶▶
mixtures

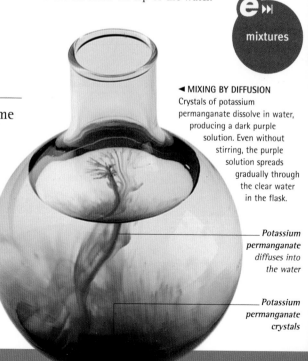

◀ MIXING BY DIFFUSION
Crystals of potassium permanganate dissolve in water, producing a dark purple solution. Even without stirring, the purple solution spreads gradually through the clear water in the flask.

▬ *Potassium permanganate diffuses into the water*

▬ *Potassium permanganate crystals*

FIND OUT MORE ▶▶ Chemistry 162 • Heat 168–169 • Matter 156 • Soil 48

SEPARATING MIXTURES

How do we extract salt from sea water? Methods for separating a mixture depend on differences in the physical properties of its components.

Water boils at 100°C (212°F)

e ▸▸
separating mixtures

HOW CAN SOLIDS BE SEPARATED?

Differences in size, density, solubility, and magnetic properties separate one solid from another. Adding water separates salt from sand – the salt dissolves, the sand does not. ▸▸ FILTRATION separates an insoluble solid (one that does not dissolve) from a liquid.

PANNING FOR GOLD ►
Gold is separated from gravel. Gold is heavier and sinks more quickly to settle in the bottom of the pan.

HOW DOES DISTILLATION WORK?

When a liquid mixture is heated, the liquid with the lower boiling point evaporates (becomes a vapour), leaving behind the liquid with the higher boiling point. Cooling condenses the vapour back to liquid. Fractional distillation separates substances one by one as the temperature rises.

Hot water vapour enters the condenser's inner tube

Vapour rises as water in the mixture boils

Sodium dichromate and water

Water is led off from the outer tube

◄ LABORATORY DISTILLATION
In this laboratory demonstration, the solution to be distilled is boiled by a Bunsen burner. Vapour from the boiling liquid is directed into a water-cooled condenser. The condenser is angled so that gravity causes the condensed liquid (turned from vapour back to liquid by cooling) to run down into the collecting flask.

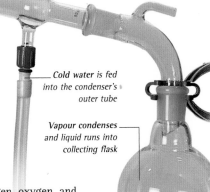

Cold water is fed into the condenser's outer tube

Vapour condenses and liquid runs into collecting flask

HOW ARE GASES SEPARATED?

Air is separated to produce nitrogen, oxygen, and other gases by first cooling it to the liquid state at -196°C (-321°F). The liquid air is fractionally distilled. Gases may also be separated by the rate they diffuse through a barrier. Light molecules diffuse more quickly than heavy molecules.

Bunsen burner gives heat

FILTRATION

Filtration is a method of separating a solid from a liquid by trapping solid particles in a material that only lets the liquid through. A coffee filter separates solid coffee grounds from liquid coffee. The size of the pores (holes) in the filter paper determines which particles will pass through.

CENTRIFUGE ►
A blood sample in a microtube is placed into a centrifuge. The high-speed rotation separates the blood components into layers ready for analysis.

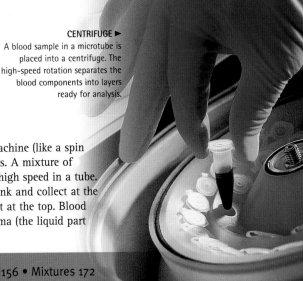

WHAT IS DIALYSIS?

Your kidneys clean your blood. Waste chemicals dissolved in the blood pass through a membrane to be excreted in urine. Blood cells are too big to pass through and are retained in the body. If a patient's kidneys fail they can be treated on a dialysis machine. This uses a synthetic membrane outside the body.

WHAT IS A CENTRIFUGE?

A centrifuge is a spinning machine (like a spin dryer) that separates materials. A mixture of liquids and solids is spun at high speed in a tube. The larger, denser particles sink and collect at the bottom. Light particles collect at the top. Blood cells are separated from plasma (the liquid part of blood) by this method.

FIND OUT MORE ▸▸ Chemical Industry 206–207 • Kidneys 147 • Matter 156 • Mixtures 172

ALLOYS

An alloy is a mixture of metals, or of metals and other substances. Mixing metals and other elements in alloys can improve their properties. The alloy bronze is a mixture of the metals copper and tin. It is resistant to water corrosion and is used in outdoor structures.

METAL TOOLS ▶
The metal for a good tool must be strong enough to take blows, and hard enough to sharpen to a fine cutting edge. Modern tools are still made from iron, alloyed with carbon.

Bronze Age sickle with a wooden handle and a bronze blade

Iron Age sickle made of the metal iron, which is extracted from ores (minerals)

◀ STEEL ALLOY
The Atomium in Brussels, Belgium, is built from steel girders, which give it strength. Steel is a mixture of iron and carbon. The Atomium is covered in aluminium, which protects it from the weather. The nine spheres are arranged like the atoms in iron. There is a science museum inside the spheres.

ARE ALLOYS STRONGER THAN PURE METALS?
A pure metal has identical atoms arranged in regular layers. The layers slide over each other easily. Alloys are harder and stronger because the different sized atoms of the mixed metals make the atomic layers less regular, so they cannot slide as easily.

DO ALLOYS MELT EASILY?
The different sizes of atoms in an alloy make their arrangement less regular than a pure metal. This makes the bonds between the atoms weaker, and lowers the melting point. Alloys that melt easily, such as ▶▶ SOLDER, have important uses.

WHO FIRST USED ALLOYS?
About 6,000 years ago, early peoples made the alloy bronze by roasting together copper and tin ores (minerals). Bronze is stronger and longer-lasting than pure copper. This period in history when bronze was the main material used is called the Bronze Age.

ALLOYS

NAME	MAIN CONSTITUENTS	USES
Brass	copper, zinc	musical instruments, decorative items
Bronze	copper, tin	statues, bearings, coins
Cupronickel	copper, nickel	coins
Duralumin	aluminium, copper, magnesium, manganese	aircraft, bicycles
Nichrome	nickel, chromium	electrical heating elements
Steel	iron, carbon	construction, tools, vehicles
Stainless steel	iron, chromium, carbon	kitchen fittings, cutlery, surgical equipment
Solder	lead, tin	joining metals

SOLDER

Lead is a heavy, soft metal, and melts at a low temperature, 328°C (622°F). By adding tin to make the alloy solder, the melting point is lowered further.

WHAT IS FLUX?
Flux is any substance that stops a metal oxidising (combining with oxygen), such as salt. Most metals oxidise in air – the process is speeded up with heat. When a plumber joins a copper pipe with solder, he coats the surface with flux. Flux stops the copper oxidising. If the copper made an oxide, the solder would not stick, and the pipes could not be joined.

HEATING SOLDER ▲
Solder is melted with a hot soldering iron to connect electronic components on a circuit board.

FIND OUT MORE ▶▶ Circuits 184–185 • Elements 160–161 • First Metalworkers 367

NEW MATERIALS

Materials scientists combine atoms in new ways to produce new materials with ▸▸ SMART properties. Imagine a window that changes colour to control the room temperature, or artificial arteries that pump blood around the body – these new materials are being developed, tested, and used now.

SEAgel is so light, it rests on soap bubbles without popping them

Soap bubbles

e ▸▸ new materials

HOW ARE NEW MATERIALS MADE?
Most new materials are developed from existing materials. Scientists try out new combinations of elements. They apply heat and pressure to materials to obtain new properties.

WHAT PROPERTIES SHOULD NEW MATERIALS HAVE?
Different properties are needed depending on where the materials are used. Materials for use in the human body must be non-toxic and resistant to corrosion by blood and other body fluids. New packaging materials should be cheap to produce, easy to recycle, or biodegradable.

WHY IS CARBON FIBRE SO STRONG?
The latest carbon fibre sports rackets and bicycles are as light as wood, but as strong as steel. Diamond is the hardest material – the bonds between its carbon atoms are strong because they are arranged in a structure like a 3-D honeycomb. Carbon fibres are strings of carbon atoms. The bonds between the atoms give the fibres strength and stiffness.

LIGHTER-THAN-AIR SEAGEL SOLID ▲
This new material is a foam made from agar (jelly extracted from seaweed). It could replace plastic in packaging.

SMART MATERIALS

A material that responds to its environment, like the chameleon's skin, is a smart material. Smart clothes could control your body temperature, light up in the dark, or even keep themselves clean.

◀ SEE-THROUGH CLOTHING
The image on the front of this woman's coat shows what is happening in the street behind her. The coat is covered with tiny reflective beads. A TV image of the scene behind is projected onto the beads. New materials could use this method to provide camouflage for people, vehicles, and buildings.

CAN A METAL REMEMBER?
Alloys of nickel and titanium have shape memory. The pattern of the atoms changes when the metal is bent or twisted, but when the metal is heated, the atoms spring back into their original positions. Some spectacle frames are made from memory alloys.

CAN A TELEVISION SCREEN GET ANY THINNER?
Some new polymers (plastics) conduct electricity. Electric currents may make them emit light as well. Video screens made from these polymers could be as thin and flexible as sheets of paper, and could lead to ultra-thin mobile phone displays. In the future, it may be possible to spray a video screen onto a T-shirt!

FIND OUT MORE ▸▸ Chemistry 162 • Electricity 182 • Elements 160–161 • Materials 170 • Technology 154

FREQUENCY SCALE

BAT 12,000 – 150,000 Hz
Bats hunt and fly at night.
To help them find their way
in the dark, they make a series
of very high-frequency clicks
(which humans cannot hear).
Then they use their sensitive
ears to listen for the echoes
bouncing back off objects
in their path.

**GRASSHOPPER
7,000 – 100,000 Hz**
To attract females, male
grasshoppers make a loud
rasping sound by scraping their
hardened wing cases across a
comb-like series of pegs on
their back legs. Grasshoppers
have ears on their abdomens.

**HOWLER MONKEY
400 – 6,000 Hz**
The loud hooting call of a
howler monkey can travel
for several kilometres
through the dense forest
where it lives. A hollow space
in its neckbones works like an
amplifier to strengthen the
call through resonance.

HUMAN 85 – 11,000 Hz
Human hearing is not as
sensitive as that of a bat or
a dog, but we do make a wide
range of sounds. Using the air
in our lungs, we vibrate the
vocal chords in our throat
to make complicated sound
patterns. We cry, scream,
laugh, sigh, speak, and sing.

FROG 50 – 8,000 Hz
A male frog croaks to attract
a female. The frog puffs up a
pouch of skin under its jaw.
Then it forces air through its
vocal chords to make them
vibrate. The air in the pouch
picks up the vibration and
strengthens it by resonance,
making the sound louder.

ELEPHANT 10 – 10,000 Hz
When an elephant trumpets a
warning, humans can hear it.
But elephants also produce
low-frequency sounds that we
cannot hear. Sounds that
happen outside our frequency
range are called ultrasonic
(higher frequencies), or
infrasonic (lower frequencies).

SOUND

Our world is full of sounds. Sound is a form of energy that travels as ▶▶ SOUND WAVES . As well as making and hearing sounds, we also record them. Today, many recordings are made using ▶▶ DIGITAL SOUND .

HOW ARE SOUNDS MADE?
Sound is made when something moves or vibrates. The movement sets up a sound wave in the surrounding air. Continuous sounds, such as drumming, are made when an object vibrates to and fro. A sudden clap or bang sends out a single sharp pulse of sound called a shock wave. The shock wave from an explosion can knock people over.

HOW DO MUSICAL INSTRUMENTS MAKE MUSIC?
Stringed instruments (such as violins) have a series of stretched strings, which vibrate when they are plucked or stroked. Players of wind instruments (such as flutes) blow across or into a mouthpiece to force columns of air to vibrate in tubes or pipes. Percussion instruments (such as drums) vibrate when they are struck.

WHY ARE SOUNDS DIFFERENT?
Sounds are different because sound waves have different frequencies. The frequency is the number of vibrations or sound waves produced in a second. We sometimes describe frequency as pitch. High-pitched sounds, such as from whistles, have a higher frequency (more waves per second) than low-pitched sounds, such as from bass drums.

WHAT IS RESONANCE?
A wine glass has a natural frequency at which it vibrates. A singer can break the glass by singing a note at the same frequency. Because the frequencies match, energy transfers from the sound to the glass until its vibrations become so strong it shatters. This is called resonance. Resonance is used to strengthen the sound in some types of musical instrument.

*Jet engines w
hardest and make m
noise at take*

*Eardrums need
protection from
very loud sounds*

DEAFENING SOUND ▶
The sound of a jet aircraft at
takeoff is millions of times louder
than the quietest sounds we can
hear. Very loud sounds can cause
us pain and damage our ears.

◀ SOUND FREQUENCY
Frequency (the number of vibrations or waves per second) is measured in hertz (Hz). Low-pitched sounds have low frequencies, high-pitched sounds have high frequencies. There is an enormous variety of sounds in the animal world and different types of animals make, and hear, sounds of different frequencies.

Aircraft in flight give out sound waves in all directions

SOUND WAVES

A vibrating object moves to and fro. As it moves forwards it pushes against the air around it, compressing or squashing it. As it moves backwards it lets the air spread out. These squashing, expanding movements create a sound wave.

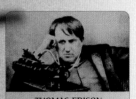

THOMAS EDISON
American, 1847–1931

In 1877, Thomas Edison made the first-ever sound recording. He recited "Mary had a little lamb" into his new invention – the phonograph. This used a vibrating needle to scratch a groove into a wax cylinder.

HOW DOES SOUND TRAVEL?

The energy in a sound wave moves outwards from its source, passing from air molecule to air molecule in a series of pulses called compressions (air is squashed) and rarefactions (air is spread out). Sound travels easily through air.

HOW IS SOUND RECORDED?

A microphone changes sound waves into electrical signals that rise and fall in the same pattern as the sound. Analogue recordings store the pattern as a wavy groove cut into a plastic disc (record), or as a magnetic pattern on a plastic tape.

SOUND BARRIER ▲
A jet travelling faster than sound creates a loud shock wave. This is called breaking the sound barrier.

COMPRESSION   RAREFACTION

◄ SOUND WAVE
In a sound wave, a series of compressions and rarefactions carries the sound energy along.

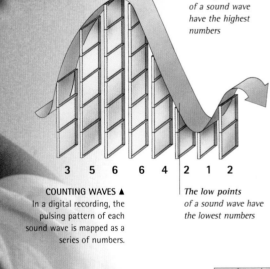

The high points of a sound wave have the highest numbers

3 5 6   6 4 2 1 2

COUNTING WAVES ▲
In a digital recording, the pulsing pattern of each sound wave is mapped as a series of numbers.

The low points of a sound wave have the lowest numbers

DIGITAL SOUND

Sound can be recorded or transmitted as a digital signal. A digital signal holds the pattern of a sound wave as a series of numbers that can be stored on a CD, digital tape, or in a computer. When the signal is played, it changes back into sound waves.

WHY IS DIGITAL SOUND BETTER THAN ANALOGUE?

Analogue recordings rely on making an exact copy of the sound wave pattern. But making more copies of the original recording can distort the pattern and add extra noises (hiss, for example). Because a digital recording is just numbers, it can be copied and corrected, if necessary, over and over again.

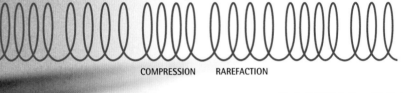

Wave height is turned into binary numbers

3	5	6	6	4	2	1	2

0 1 1 1 0 1 1 1 0 1 1 0 1 0 0 0 1 0 0 0 1 0 1 0

Binary numbers are shown as pits or no pits

◄ RECORDING NUMBERS
The numbers in a digital recording are stored as binary code. This is made up of just two digits, 0 and 1. Each binary number is pressed onto a compact disc (CD) as a series of pits (dents) and no pits.

HOW CAN ONE PERSON PRODUCE THE SOUND OF AN ENTIRE ORCHESTRA?

Different instruments make sounds with a mixture of different frequencies. By making sounds with the right mix of frequencies, an electronic synthesizer can imitate any instrument in an orchestra. A computer helps the player to arrange the sounds into music.

sound

FIND OUT MORE ►► Atoms 157 • Computers 190 • Ear 141 • Musical Instruments 332

Light is a type of energy known as electromagnetic radiation. It is given out by hot objects such as the Sun, light bulbs, and ▸▸ LASERS. When light hits a surface, its energy can be absorbed (soaked up), ▸▸ REFLECTED, or deflected by ▸▸ REFRACTION.

WHAT IS LIGHT?

Light is made up of little packets of energy called photons. Most of these photons are produced when the atoms in an object heat up. Heat "excites" the electrons inside the atoms and they gain extra energy. This extra energy is then released as a photon. The hotter an object gets, the more photons it gives out.

HOW DOES LIGHT TRAVEL?

Light travels as a wave. But unlike sound waves or water waves, it does not need any matter or material to carry its energy along. This means that light can travel through a vacuum – a completely airless space. (Sound, on the other hand, must travel through a solid, a liquid, or a gas.) Nothing travels faster than light energy. It speeds through the vacuum of space at 300,000 km (186,400 miles) per second.

WHAT ARE SHADOWS?

Light waves travel out from their source in straight lines called rays. Rays do not curve around corners, so when they hit an opaque object (one that does not allow light to pass through it), they are blocked from reaching the other side of that object. We see a dark shadow in the area from which light is blocked.

WHAT MAKES SOME MATERIALS OPAQUE?

When light falls on a material, the energy in its photons can affect the atoms in the material. In some materials, such as metal, the atoms absorb some of the photons so light does not pass through them. These materials are opaque. In other materials, such as glass, the atoms cannot absorb the photons and light passes through them. These materials are transparent.

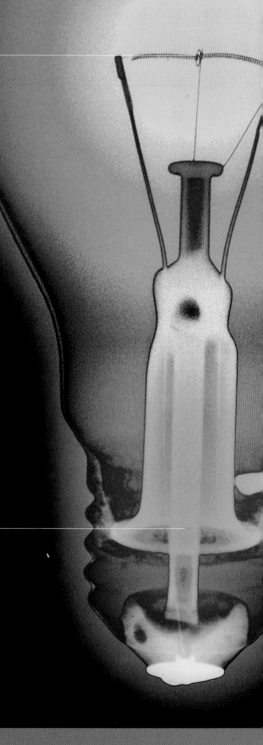

Glass bulb is filled with a mixture of gases that prevent the filament from burning out

Coiled filament is heated up by the electric current flowing through it, and glows brightly

e ▸▸

light

◂ POLARIZING LIGHT
Bright sunlight reflected from the road dazzles our eyes. One way of cutting down the glare is to look through a polarizing filter. Light waves vibrate (shake) in all directions. A polarizing filter lets through light vibrating in only one direction, blocking out the rest and reducing glare.

Electricity flows into the bulb through wires in the filament support

LIGHT BULB ▸
A light bulb produces light when electricity heats up a fine wire filament inside it. The filament in a standard light bulb heats up to about 3,000°C (5,400°F). The surface of the Sun is about 5,500°C (10,000°F).

REFLECTION

Light rays reflect (bounce) off objects. The Moon shines because it reflects light from the Sun. Smooth surfaces, such as mirrors, reflect light in one direction.

A glass mirror is coated on one side with a thin, reflective layer of metal

The beam hits the mirror, and is reflected just like a billiard ball bouncing off the side of a table

LAW OF REFLECTION ▶
The law of reflection says that the angle of the beam bouncing off a mirror will be equal to the angle at which it arrived.

The laser beam travels in a straight line through the air

Multiple reflections alternately flip from left to right

MIRROR MIRROR ▶
If you stand between two mirrors that are directly opposite each other, you will see reflections of your reflection vanishing off into the distance.

Boy looking in mirror

WHAT HAPPENS WHEN YOU LOOK IN A MIRROR?
At first sight your image is identical to you. But a closer look shows that as you lift your right hand your image raises its left. Reflection always flips an image from left to right. If you hold up a sheet of paper with writing on it, the image in the mirror shows the writing back to front.

REFRACTION

Light travels more slowly through some materials than others. The change in speed can cause light rays to change direction. This directional change is called refraction.

◀ SEEING THINGS
Refraction makes this girl's body look closer when it is seen through the surface of the water. This is because the light rays change direction as they travel from water into air.

Laser beam in air

Refracted laser beam inside plastic block

The laser beam leaves the block. It has moved sideways, but is still parallel to the original beam

WHY IS A SWIMMING POOL DEEPER THAN IT LOOKS?
Refraction can make things look closer than they really are. The difference in speed between light travelling through water and through air means that, from the surface, a 4 m (13 ft) pool appears to be just 3 m (10 ft) deep. Glass is another material that refracts light. It is used to make spectacles and other lenses.

▲ REFRACTION
A laser beam is refracted (changes direction) when it passes from air into a block of transparent plastic.

LASER

A laser produces an incredibly powerful, concentrated form of light. Inside a laser, light waves are bounced back and forth between two mirrors to build up energy before being released as a narrow beam.

WHY IS LASER LIGHT SO SPECIAL?
Laser light does not spread out in the way that light from other sources does. All the light waves in laser light are precisely in step with each other. As a result, laser light can be concentrated and controlled far more accurately. It can carry television and other signals over great distances without losing quality.

Fine laser beams can be very precisely controlled

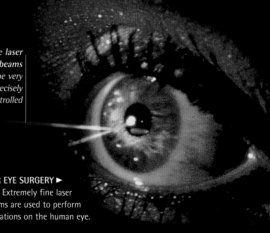

LASER EYE SURGERY ▶
Extremely fine laser beams are used to perform operations on the human eye.

FIND OUT MORE ▶▶ Atoms 157 • Colour 180 • Eye 140 • Lenses 181 • Matter 156

COLOUR

Light has different wavelengths, which we see as colours. The range of wavelengths we see is called the visible spectrum. We separate the colours of the spectrum by ▶▶ DISPERSION .

Beam of white light

WHAT IS THE VISIBLE SPECTRUM?

Light waves are just one type of electromagnetic wave. They belong to an electromagnetic spectrum that includes radio waves, X-rays, and gamma rays. The visible spectrum is the only part the human eye can see. To our eyes, the colours in the visible spectrum range from violet at one end to red at the other.

WHAT ARE PRIMARY COLOURS?

The light-sensitive cells in the human eye react to just three types of light: red, green, and blue wavelengths. These are the three primary light colours. If all three types of wavelength enter the eye with equal strength, we see white light. When just red and green light are present, we see the mixture as yellow.

HOW MANY COLOURS CAN WE SEE?

Different wavelengths of light blend to produce millions of shades of colour. The human eye is able to pick out over 10 million of them – some of which can be shown by a ▶▶ COLOUR TREE . The amount of colour we see depends on how much light there is. In dim light we see no colours at all, only shades of grey.

Some light is reflected off the bottom of the prism

Triangular glass prism

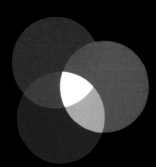

▲ PRIMARY LIGHT
The three primary light colours, red, green, and blue, combine in pairs to create secondary colours. Red and green make yellow, blue and green make cyan, and red and blue make magenta. All three together make white light.

The different wavelengths (colours) in the light beam are refracted at different angles

BENDING LIGHT THROUGH A PRISM ▲
Different wavelengths of light travel at different speeds through glass. A prism refracts (bends) the shortest wavelengths the most. We see these as violet light. The longest wavelengths are refracted the least. We see these as deep red. All the other colours are in between.

DISPERSION

When white light shines through a specially shaped piece of glass called a prism, it separates into its different wavelengths by dispersion. The wavelengths show up as a range of colours called a spectrum. The English scientist Isaac Newton first used a prism to disperse sunlight in the late 1600s.

HOW DOES A RAINBOW FORM?

Rainbows appear when there are water drops in the atmosphere and bright sunshine at the same time. The water drops act like tiny prisms, refracting and reflecting the sunlight, and dispersing it into the colours of the spectrum. To see a rainbow, you have to be standing at a particular angle to the water drops and the Sun.

◀ RAINBOW OF LIGHT
Sunlight is a mixture of all the colours of the spectrum – red, orange, yellow, green, blue, indigo, and violet. Some animals can see colors that we cannot see.

COLOUR TREE

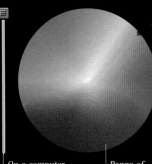

On a computer, moving a slide up or down changes the level of value

Range of colour shades at the highest value level

A colour tree is one way of grading or classifying colours. Using a colour tree, it is possible to describe and then match a particular shade of colour (of paint or fabric, for example).

e ▶▶
visible spectrum

◀ THE MUNSELL COLOUR TREE
This system describes a colour according to three characteristics: its hue (basic colour, such as blue), its chroma (strength of colour), and its value (lightness or darkness). There are ten levels of value going up (like the trunk of a tree) from black to white. At each level, each hue has a range of shades depending on how far out it is from the central trunk. Today, this system is used to specify colour on computers.

HOW IS COLOUR CREATED ON A COMPUTER?

Most computer drawing and graphics programs include an electronic version of a colour tree for choosing colours. This may be done by selecting pre-set colours from a given range, or by setting the percentages of red, green, and blue in the colour.

FIND OUT MORE ▶▶ Eye 140 • Light 178–179

LENSES

When you look through a magnifying glass, or take a picture with a camera, you are using a lens. A lens is a polished piece of glass or transparent plastic with curved surfaces. There are two main shapes of lens, ▶▶ CONVEX and ▶▶ CONCAVE .

WHAT DOES A LENS DO?

A lens changes the direction of light waves by refraction. It may form an image of a scene or an object. The image might be smaller (as in a camera), or larger (as in a microscope). Because a lens is curved, light rays strike different parts of its surface and are bent by different amounts. Depending on the lens shape, this either diverges (spreads out) or converges (concentrates) a beam of light.

WHAT IS THE DIFFERENCE BETWEEN A MICROSCOPE AND A TELESCOPE?

A microscope makes a tiny, nearby object look much bigger. A telescope makes a large, distant object or scene appear much closer and brighter. In both instruments, light from the object passes through two or more lenses to form an image. The shapes of the lenses and the distances between them alter the image that is produced.

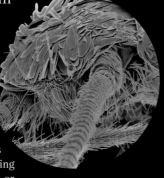

▲ MAGNIFIED IMAGES
Optical microscopes use beams of light, but electron microscopes use beams of electrons to give much greater magnification. The image of this silverfish has been magnified thousands of times.

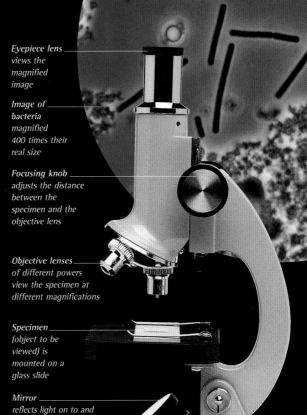

Eyepiece lens views the magnified image

Image of bacteria magnified 400 times their real size

Focusing knob adjusts the distance between the specimen and the objective lens

Objective lenses of different powers view the specimen at different magnifications

Specimen (object to be viewed) is mounted on a glass slide

Mirror reflects light on to and through the specimen

OPTICAL MICROSCOPE ▶
Optical microscopes use light to magnify an image up to 2,000 times. Light from a brightly lit specimen (object) is captured and concentrated by a powerful objective lens to produce a magnified image. The eyepiece lens may then magnify the image further.

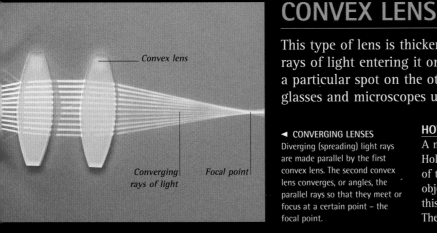

Convex lens

Converging rays of light

Focal point

CONVEX LENS

This type of lens is thicker in the centre than at the edge. Parallel rays of light entering it on one side will converge (meet) at a particular spot on the other side of the lens. Magnifying glasses and microscopes use convex lenses.

e ▶▶ lenses

◀ CONVERGING LENSES
Diverging (spreading) light rays are made parallel by the first convex lens. The second convex lens converges, or angles, the parallel rays so that they meet or focus at a certain point – the focal point.

HOW DOES A MAGNIFYING GLASS WORK?

A magnifying glass makes an object look bigger. Holding it close to an object makes a virtual image of the object form on the same side of the glass as the object. When you look through the magnifying glass, this virtual object seems to be larger than the real one. The thicker the lens, the larger the virtual image.

CONCAVE LENS

A concave lens is thinner at the centre than at the edge. Parallel light rays passing into one side of the lens diverge (spread out) as they emerge from the other side.

HOW DO CONCAVE LENSES HELP YOU SEE?

If you are short-sighted, your eye lens focuses a scene just in front of the retina in your eye and the image you see is blurred. A concave lens spreads out the light rays before they enter the eye, so that they are focused on the retina and the image is sharp.

DIVERGING LENSES ▶
Diverging light rays are made parallel by a convex lens. But when the parallel light rays pass through a concave lens, they diverge (spread out) again.

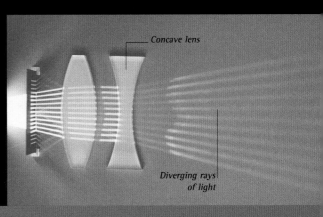

Concave lens

Diverging rays of light

FIND OUT MORE ▶▶ Eye 140 • Light 178–179

ELECTRICITY

A lightning strike demonstrates the incredible energy of electricity. This intense flash of heat and light is created naturally by static electricity. We use this same electric force to provide a clean, controllable power supply to our homes, farms, factories, and cities.

e ▸▸ electricity

Lightning flash heats the surrounding air to 30,000°C (54,000°F)

WHAT IS ELECTRICITY?

The electrons and protons inside every atom carry a property called an electric charge. Electrons have a negative charge and protons a positive charge. These charges either attract or repel each other. Unlike (opposite) charges attract, and like (the same) charges repel. The force they do this with is called electricity.

ELECTRIC LIGHTNING ▶
The build-up of electric charge in a thunder cloud creates an opposite charge in the ground. Eventually, a gigantic electric spark leaps between the two charges in a spectacular release of energy.

HOW MANY FORMS OF ELECTRICITY ARE THERE?

Electricity comes in two forms – as electric current when electric charges flow along wires in a circuit, and as static electricity, when electric charges do not move. Normally, most materials are neutral (have no charge). But if a material gains or loses large numbers of electrons it becomes charged with static electricity.

Lightning stroke between cloud and ground may be up to 14 km (9 miles) long

HOW DO MATERIALS BECOME CHARGED?

Materials can become charged with static electricity by **▸▸ INDUCTION** or by friction. When two materials rub together, friction transfers electrons from one to the other. This gives one material a negative charge, and the other a positive charge. A nylon comb gains a negative charge when it is pulled through hair.

◀ PLASMA GLOBE
A charged metal ball causes electrons to separate from gas atoms inside a glass sphere. The gas gives out light as electrons flow through it.

ELECTROSTATIC INDUCTION

Electric induction is the process by which a charged object can charge another object without touching it. A charged nylon comb, for example, will attract scraps of paper, even though the scraps are not charged themselves.

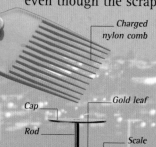

Charged nylon comb

Cap
Rod
Gold leaf
Scale

HOW DOES INDUCTION WORK?

When the comb is brought close to the paper, the negative charge on the comb repels electrons in the paper to the side farthest away from the comb. This creates a positive charge (fewer electrons) on the side of the paper facing the comb. Positive and negative attract, so the paper is pulled towards the comb.

▼ USING ELECTROSTATICS
By making the car body and the paint sprayer oppositely charged, paint drops are attracted into all the bumps and hollows of the surface to be painted.

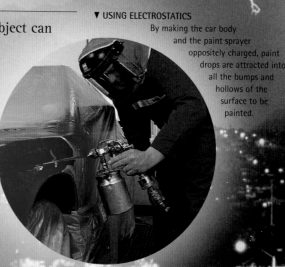

◀ GOLD LEAF ELECTROSCOPE
Electric charge can be measured by an electroscope. One of the simplest is a gold-leaf electroscope. A charged object held near the cap repels like charges to the far end of a metal rod, onto a thin sheet of gold. The charges on the gold leaf and the rod repel each other, and the leaf rises. The amount by which it rises can be measured against a notched scale.

FIND OUT MORE ▸▸ Atoms 157 • Circuits 184–185 • Forces 164 • Motion 165

MAGNETISM

Magnetism is an invisible force that attracts or repels some materials, such as iron and steel, but not others, like plastic and silver. In a magnetic material, the atoms line up in groups or regions called ▸▸ MAGNETIC DOMAINS.

WHAT ARE MAGNETIC POLES?
Every magnet has a north magnetic pole and a south magnetic pole. These are the places where the magnetic force is strongest. The laws of magnetism are that like (the same) poles repel each other, and unlike (opposite) poles attract each other.

WHAT ARE MAGNETIC MATERIALS?
The elements iron, nickel, and cobalt are magnetic materials – they can be magnetized by another magnet. But in their pure form, they easily lose their magnetism by heat or hammering. Permanent magnets are made from mixtures of these elements with others, such as steel (iron and carbon), for example.

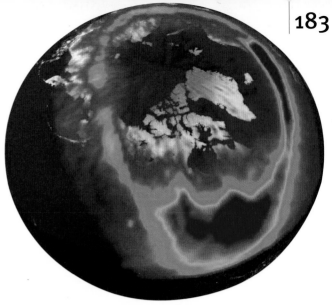

▲ MAGNETIC EARTH
The Earth's magnetic poles attract particles from the Sun that glow when they reach the atmosphere. The Earth's magnetic north and south poles are close to its geographical North and South Poles.

HOW DOES A MAGNETIC COMPASS WORK?
The Earth's core acts as a gigantic magnet with a vast ▸▸ MAGNETIC FIELD. In a magnetic compass, the northern end of the compass needle always points in the direction of the Earth's north magnetic pole. Its other (southern) end always points south.

e ▸▸ magnetism

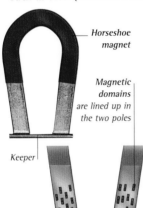

Horseshoe magnet

Magnetic domains are lined up in the two poles

Keeper

Keeper

◀ MAGNETIC POWER
To keep a magnet strong, place a keeper between its poles when it is not in use. A keeper is a piece of soft iron. The poles magnetize the keeper, which in turn keeps the poles' domains pointing in the same direction.

MAGNETIC DOMAINS

Every atom in a piece of iron is a tiny, permanent magnet. These tiny magnets group together in magnetic regions called domains. If the north-south magnetic poles of these domains all point in different directions, they cancel each other's magnetism out.

WHAT MAKES A PERMANENT MAGNET?
In a permanent magnet, the magnetic poles of the domains point in the same direction, so their magnetic fields reinforce one another. Magnetic material can be magnetized by stroking it with a magnet to line up the domains. Heat or hammering shakes the domains out of position, and the material loses its magnetism.

MAGNETIC FIELD

A magnet creates a force in the space around it. The area in which the force operates is the magnetic field. A magnetic field can be imagined as lines of force that spread out from the magnet's poles.

HOW CAN A MAGNETIC FIELD BE SEEN?
If iron filings are sprinkled around a magnet, they will line up along the lines of force of its magnetic field. The pattern made by the filings always shows the lines of force looping outwards between the magnet's north and south poles. The magnetic field gets weaker as it gets farther away from the magnet.

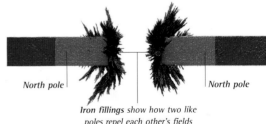

North pole

North pole

Iron filings show how two like poles repel each other's fields

North pole

South pole

Filings show the attraction between unlike poles

MAGNETIC POLES ▲
Iron filings can be used to show the repulsion between two like poles, and the attraction between unlike poles.

FIND OUT MORE ▸▸ Atoms 157 • Electromagnetism 186 • Elements 160–161

CIRCUITS

An electric current flows in a loop – powering bulbs or other electric ▸ COMPONENTS . The loop is an electric circuit. A circuit is made up of various components linked together by wires. The current is driven around the circuit by a power source, such as a ▸ BATTERY .

Plastic does not carry current and can be used to separate different parts of the circuit

WHAT IS AN ELECTRIC CURRENT?
Electric current is a flow of electric charge (usually in the form of electrons) through a substance. The substance or conductor that an electric current flows through is often metal wire, although current can also flow through some gases, liquids, and other materials.

PINBALL MACHINE ▶
A pinball machine uses components wired into parallel circuits to produce light, sound, and movement from electricity. Switches control the circuits – when a switch is off, no current flows. The steel ball turns on switches so that bells ring, lamps flash, and springs and flippers move.

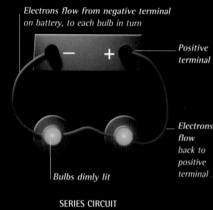

Electrons flow from negative terminal on battery, to each bulb in turn

Positive terminal

Electrons flow back to positive terminal

Bulbs dimly lit

SERIES CIRCUIT

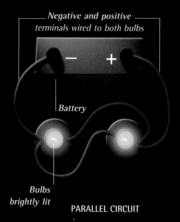

Negative and positive terminals wired to both bulbs

Battery

Bulbs brightly lit

PARALLEL CIRCUIT

e ▸▸

circuits

Flat disc operates a switch when it is hit

▲ IN SERIES AND IN PARALLEL
Circuits can be wired in two ways. In a series circuit, current flows to each bulb in turn. Both bulbs are dimly lit. In a parallel circuit, the current divides and flows directly to both bulbs at the same time. The bulbs are then brighter.

WHEN DOES CURRENT FLOW IN A CIRCUIT?
Current only flows when a circuit is complete – when there are no gaps in it. In a complete circuit, the electrons flow from the negative terminal (connection) on the power source, through the connecting wires and components, such as bulbs, and back to the positive terminal.

WHAT MAKES CURRENT FLOW IN A CIRCUIT?
When a wire is connected to battery terminals, electrons flow from negative to positive. Unlike (opposite) charges attract, like (same) charges repel. Electrons have a negative charge – they are repelled from the negative and attracted to the positive.

BATTERY

A battery is a compact, easily transportable source of electricity. When a battery is connected in a circuit, it provides the energy that drives the electrons along in a current. Batteries contain chemical substances that react together to separate positive and negative charges.

Zinc electrode becomes negatively charged

Wires carry current in circuit

Copper electrode becomes positively charged

Sulphuric acid

Bubbles show chemical action

◀ SIMPLE BATTERY CELL
A simple cell can be made by putting zinc and copper electrodes into a liquid electrolyte, such as sulphuric acid.

WHAT IS INSIDE A BATTERY?
A battery is made of one or more sections or cells. Inside each cell, two chemically active materials called electrodes are separated by a liquid or paste called the electrolyte. Small batteries may have just one cell. Large, powerful batteries may have six cells.

HOW DOES A BATTERY CELL WORK?
Inside a cell the electrolyte reacts with the electrodes, causing electrons to move through the electrolyte from one electrode to the other. One electrode gains a negative charge and the other a positive charge. The two electrodes are the positive and negative terminals.

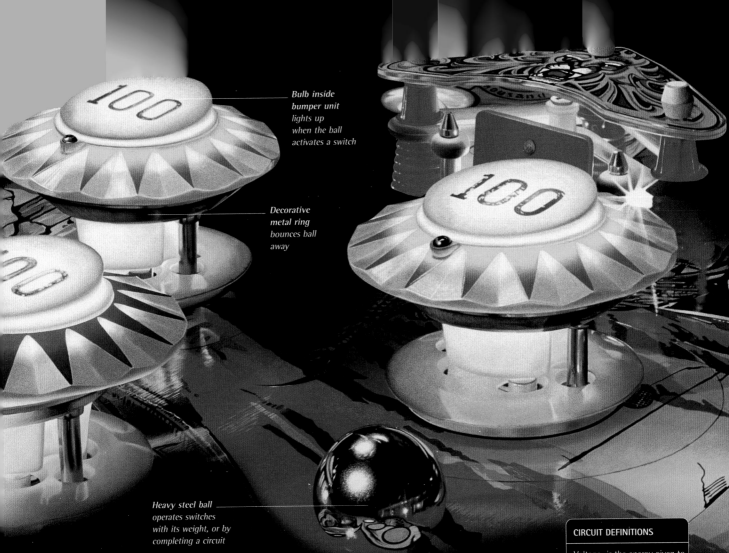

Bulb inside
bumper unit
*lights up
when the ball
activates a switch*

Decorative
metal ring
*bounces ball
away*

Heavy steel ball
*operates switches
with its weight, or by
completing a circuit*

COMPONENTS

The different objects that make up a circuit are called components. A circuit must have a power source, such as a battery, and the current flows through a conductor, such as a wire. Bulbs, buzzers, and motors are components that change electricity into light, sound, and movement.

WHAT IS A CONDUCTOR?

A material that carries a current well is called a conductor. Metals are good conductors because metal atoms readily release electrons to carry the current. Silver and copper are the best conductors, and most electric wires are made from copper. To prevent electric shocks, wires are covered with an insulator.

◄ HEART PACEMAKER
The battery and other components of an artificial heart pacemaker send electric pulses through wires to a patient's heart to keep it beating steadily. A pacemaker is fitted when the heart does not beat steadily by itself.

WHAT IS AN A INSULATOR?

Some materials do not carry current well. They are said to resist (oppose) the flow of current. Materials that do this are called insulators. Plastics, glass, rubber, and ceramics are all good insulators. Insulators are used to cover wires and components to prevent electric shocks, and to stop currents flowing.

HOW DOES A SWITCH WORK?

Switches are like gates that control the flow of electricity in a circuit. When a switch is open, it creates a gap in the circuit and current will not flow. When it is closed, it completes the circuit, and current flows through it. Switches are used in parallel circuits to turn different parts of the circuit on and off.

WHAT IS MAINS ELECTRICITY?

Most of the electricity we use in our homes and workplaces is mains electricity. Mains electricity is produced by machines in power stations called generators. Generators send electric current through a huge network of circuits spread around the country.

CIRCUIT DEFINITIONS

Voltage	is the energy given to each unit of charge that flows in a circuit
Current	is the amount of electric charge flowing past a point in a circuit each second
Wattage	is the amount of electrical energy a circuit uses each second

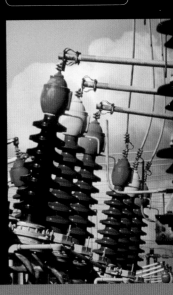

POWER INSULATORS ►
Mains electricity travels around the country in wires called power lines. Giant ceramic insulators prevent the current flowing to the ground.

FIND OUT MORE ▶▶ Chemistry 162 • Electricity 182 • Electricity Supply 187 • Electromagnetism 186

Crane jib
moves magnet
into place

e ▶▶
electromagnet

Electromagnet
hangs from
chains

Cable carries
electric current

ELECTROMAGNETISM

An electric current produces magnetism, and a magnet can produce an electric current. The two forces are so closely connected that scientists talk about the single force of electromagnetism. Without it, we would not have an electricity supply, or ▶▶ ELECTRIC MOTORS.

HOW DOES ELECTRICITY CREATE MAGNETISM?

Each electron is surrounded by a force called an electric field. When an electron moves, it creates a second field – a magnetic field. When electrons are made to flow in a current through a conductor, such as a piece of metal or a coil of wire, the conductor becomes a temporary magnet – an electromagnet.

◄ METAL DETECTOR
A metal detector makes use of electromagnetic effects to find metal landmines hidden under the soil. Wire coils in the detector produce a changing magnetic field, which induces (causes) electric currents to flow in the metal landmines. These in turn produce magnetism that can be sensed by the detector.

Iron and steel scrap
is attracted by the
magnet when it is on

◄ ELECTROMAGNET
Unlike permanent magnets, electromagnets can be switched on and off. This is useful in a scrapyard, where a powerful electromagnet separates iron and steel scrap from other materials.

Non-magnetic scrap
is left behind

HOW DOES MAGNETISM PRODUCE ELECTRICITY?

If a coil of wire is placed near a magnet with an unchanging magnetic field, nothing happens. But if the magnetic field is changed, by moving the magnet back and forth, or spinning the wire, the changing magnetic field produces an electric current in the wire.

WHAT DO GENERATORS DO?

Generators supply us with most of the electric current we use. They turn mechanical energy (movement) into electrical energy. Inside a generator, a coil of wire is spun inside a powerful magnetic field. This creates an electric current in the wire. A large generator can produce enough electricity to run an entire city.

ELECTRIC MOTORS

Electric motors are machines that turn electrical energy into mechanical energy to do work. Electric motors can be small, like the motor that turns the fan in a hairdryer, or huge, like the engine that drives a train.

HOW DO ELECTRIC MOTORS WORK?

A current turns a conductor into an electromagnet. If the current is reversed, the electromagnetic poles will reverse, too. When the electromagnet is placed near to a fixed magnet, the two sets of poles repel and attract each other. This produces a force which makes the conductor rotate (spin) at high speed. This turns a shaft which then drives a machine.

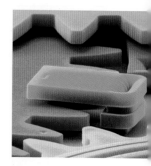

▲ MICRO MOTOR GEARS
In 1960, engineer William McLellan built a motor the size of a full stop from 13 separate parts. Today, engineers are trying to build motors thousands of times smaller. This picture of motor gears is magnified 200 times.

FIND OUT MORE ▶▶ Circuits 184–185 • Electricity 182 • Magnetism 183

ELECTRICITY SUPPLY

Electricity has revolutionized the way we use energy. It can be generated in large ▸▸ POWER STATIONS far away from towns and cities, and distributed cleanly to homes, offices, and factories through a network of power lines.

HOW ARE MOST GENERATORS POWERED?

To make electricity, the coils inside a generator are turned by turbines. Most large generators are powered by turbines spun around by high-pressure steam. The steam is produced in boilers heated by fossil fuels (or in a nuclear reactor). Water turbines are also used to turn the generators in hydroelectric power stations.

WHAT IS THE NATIONAL GRID?

From the power stations, electricity is fed into a vast network of cables and wires called the national grid. Electricity travels through the grid into almost every room in the country. Controlling the power in the grid is complex. Engineers must try to make sure that enough power is available whenever it is needed.

NATIONAL GRID ▶
Electricity generated by the power stations is fed into a national grid of interconnecting power lines. These take the energy wherever it is required. When you switch on a light, you have no way of knowing which power station the electricity came from.

electricity supply

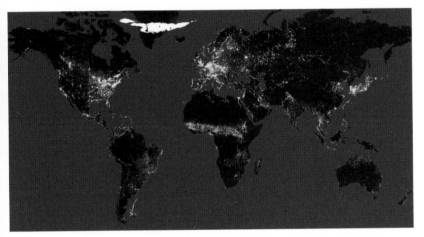

WHAT IS ALTERNATING CURRENT?

Current is produced in two forms: direct current (DC) and alternating current (AC). Direct current (produced by batteries) only flows in one direction. Alternating current (produced by power stations) switches back and forth, reversing direction regularly. An AC current switches back and forth 50 or 60 times a second.

▲ NIGHT LIGHTS
This night-time satellite photograph shows the artificial light produced on Earth by electric road and building lights. North America, Europe, and Japan are the most brightly lit regions. The bright lights at upper left on the map are the Northern Lights.

POWER STATIONS

Power stations work day and night to produce the electricity that provides us with heat and light, and drives all kinds of machines, from hairdryers and refrigerators to televisions and trains.

HOW DOES ELECTRICITY GET FROM THE POWER STATION TO US?

Electricity from a power station is boosted from 25,000 volts to 400,000 volts to travel along power lines. But the voltage must be lowered before it is safe to use. Transformers reduce the voltage in stages to different levels to supply factories, railways, farms, hospitals, offices, homes, and motorways.

FIND OUT MORE ▸▸ Circuits 184–185 • Electricity 182 • Engines 198–199

ENERGY EVERYWHERE

POWER STATION
A large, coal-fired power station like this may produce a continuous flow of up to 1,000 MW (megawatts) of electricity. That's enough power to light 20 million light bulbs, or meet all the power needs of a small city.

POWER LINES
Electric current is carried around the country by power lines. Most power lines are slung high above the ground, on tall metal pylons. In towns or cities, the lines may go underground. Power lines carry electricity at 400,000 volts – thousands of times greater than the voltage received in our homes.

SUB STATION
At various stages along the way, the power lines feed into sub stations. These contain transformers and heavy-duty switching gear that reduce (lower) the voltage to safer levels and direct power to where it is needed.

FACTORIES
Large industrial plants such as this chemical factory use tremendous amounts of electrical energy. Many have their own dedicated power stations.

HOMES
Electric power travels from sub stations to homes through underground cables or lightweight overhead lines. For domestic use, voltage is reduced to 110 or 240 volts. Each house has its own meter to record the amount of electrical energy used.

ELECTRONICS

Electronic circuits operate nearly every modern machine – microwave ovens, cars, and computers. In an electronic circuit, an electric signal carries information. Signals are controlled and changed by components made from materials called ▶▶ SEMICONDUCTORS .

WHAT IS AN ELECTRIC SIGNAL?
A signal is a current or voltage change that carries information. Changes can represent instructions, numbers, sounds, or pictures in the form of a code. A digital signal is either on or off. An analogue signal is continuously flowing electricity, which increases and decreases to represent the information.

WHAT ARE ELECTRONIC COMPONENTS?
Electronic circuits use components (parts) to control electric signals. These include resistors, capacitors, diodes, and transistors. Resistors control how much current flows through them, capacitors store electric charges and release them when necessary, and diodes let current pass through in only one direction.

WHAT IS A TRANSISTOR?
Transistors are electronic components that can change and control electronic signals. A transistor can work as a switch – turning a signal on or off, or as an amplifier – increasing the current or voltage in a circuit.

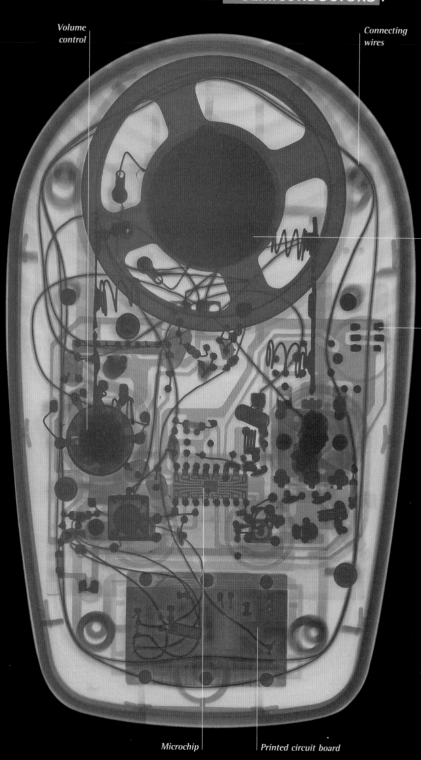

Volume control

Connecting wires

Loudspeaker gives out sound

Capacitors store high voltages

electronics

◀ RADIO
This colourful X-ray picture shows the electronic components of a radio through its casing. The radio receives radio waves from a radio station, translates them into an electric current, and then turns them into sounds, which are produced by its loudspeaker.

Microchip

Printed circuit board

SEMICONDUCTORS

A semiconductor is a material that conducts electricity less well than a metal, but better than an insulator, and can act as both a conductor and an insulator. The chemical elements silicon and germanium are the most important semiconductors for making electronic components.

HOW DOES A SEMICONDUCTOR CONDUCT ELECTRICITY?
The current in a semiconductor is carried by positive holes and by negative electrons. A hole is an empty space left in the orbit of an atom when an electron has escaped. Holes move through a semiconductor in the opposite direction to electrons, hopping from atom to atom.

FIND OUT MORE ▶▶ Circuits 184–185 • Elements 160–161 • Sound 176–177 • Telecommunications 192–193

MICROCHIPS

A microchip is an electronic device built as a single unit from many miniature components, mainly transistors. It is plugged into a socket on a printed circuit board to connect it to other components.

WHAT DO MICROCHIPS DO?

CIRCUIT BOARDS ▲
These technicians are checking the quality of circuit boards before final assembly. Individual microchips are linked on circuit boards to form electronic devices, such as computers.

Each kind of microchip performs a different task, and is identified by a code number. Some microchips work with analogue signals (A microchip with code 741 is an analogue amplifier). Others work with digital signals – to act as  **LOGIC GATES**, or to get digital sound from a CD.

◄ CERAMIC CAPSULE
A microchip is encased in an insulating capsule. This capsule has a transparent cover – the chip is inside. It is a charged-coupled device (CCD) used to take images in digital cameras.

A single CCD is a grid of a million or more transistors

Metal pins plug into a socket on a circuit board

HOW ARE MICROCHIPS MADE?

Microchips are made by building up electronic circuits in a tiny wafer (slice) of pure silicon in a complicated layer-by-layer process. The different circuit components are producing by doping (treating) areas of the silicon with different chemicals.

◄ SILICON WAFER
Hundreds of identical copies of a microchip are made on a slice of pure silicon. The circuits are tested and faulty units rejected. Those that work are linked by gold wires to pins and sealed in their capsules (cases).

WHAT IS BINARY CODE?

Digital microchips send and receive digital electronic signals in binary code. All information is represented by on/off signals. These signals are processed by the transistors on microchips. When a switch is on, it is the digit 1; when it is off, it is the digit 0. The binary code for the letter "a" on a keyboard is 01100001.

LOGIC GATES

A logic gate is a digital circuit that makes a simple decision. Logic gates include AND, OR, NOT, NOR, and NAND gates. Logic gate circuits can be made with individual transistors, or formed on microchips.

HOW ARE LOGIC GATES USED?

You can link logic gates to make complex decisions, or perform difficult calculations. For example, a washing machine will only start when a programme has been selected AND the door is closed AND the water supply is on.

LOGIC GATES ►
A logic gate may have one or two inputs, and an output. Whether the output is on (1) or off (0) depends on the state of the inputs according to the logic set out in the tables.

microchips

INPUT A	INPUT B	OUTPUT
0	0	0
1	0	0
0	1	0
1	1	1

▲ THE "AND" GATE
This has two inputs, A and B. If both inputs are on, then the output is on.

INPUT A	INPUT B	OUTPUT
0	0	0
1	0	1
0	1	1
1	1	1

▲ THE "OR" GATE
The output of this gate is on when either input A, or input B, or both, are on.

INPUT	OUTPUT
0	1
1	0

▲ THE "NOT" GATE
This gate has only one input. The output is on when the input is not on.

COMPUTERS

An electronic machine that uses binary code to store and process data is a computer. Binary code can represent numbers, text, sounds, pictures, and movies. This data is stored in the computer's memory and on magnetic discs, CD-ROMs, and DVDs.

WHAT IS A MICROPROCESSOR?

A microprocessor is a computer's brain. It is an integrated circuit made of millions of transistors. It carries out the instructions (the programs) that make a computer operate. Everything the computer does is broken down into simple steps. The power of a microprocessor is measured by how fast it carries out these instructions.

WHAT IS MEMORY?

Data is stored in binary code on microchips. They are made up of millions of transistors that are on or off – 1 or 0 in binary code. The capacity (size) of a memory chip is measured in megabytes (MB). One byte is an eight-digit binary number. One megabyte is just over one million bytes of information.

HOW IS VIRTUAL REALITY CREATED?

Virtual reality controls what you see, and responds to your movements and actions. When you wear virtual reality goggles, the scene you see changes as you move. Sensors on special gloves, or a body suit, allow you to interact with the scene by pointing or touching. Sounds increase the experience of reality.

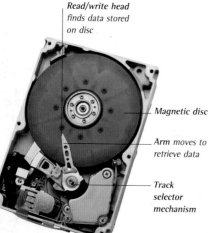

▲ VIRTUAL REALITY
Virtual reality goggles feed slightly different images to the right and left eyes to create a realistic 3-D scene. These goggles help architects visualize plans.

Read/write head finds data stored on disc

Liquid crystal monitor screen

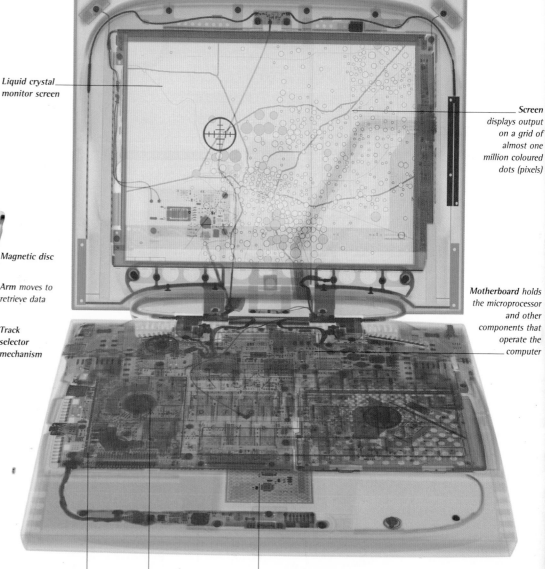

Screen displays output on a grid of almost one million coloured dots (pixels)

Magnetic disc

Arm moves to retrieve data

Motherboard holds the microprocessor and other components that operate the computer

Track selector mechanism

▲ HARD DISC DRIVE
The computer's hard disc is the main storage area for programs, documents, images, and other files. It can hold tens of gigabytes of data (billions of binary numbers). Information is written (put on) and read (taken off) by electromagnetic heads that swing over the disc surfaces as they spin at high speed.

computers

Keyboard used to input letters and other characters

Disc drive reads and writes discs

Touchpad moves the pointer round the screen, like a mouse

▲ LAPTOP COMPUTER
All the components of a personal computer can be built into a convenient folding package the size of a book. Some laptops use wireless technology to interact with printers, scanners, and other devices by radio waves. Through wireless telephone links, you can log onto the Internet to send emails from your laptop.

FIND OUT MORE ▸▸ Electronics 188 • Robots 194

NETWORKS

networks

A network is formed when people, places, or things are linked together. A rail network links towns and cities. A computer network links computers.

◄ NETWORK CONTROL
The global telephone system is the largest communications network on Earth. Engineers at this telecommunications control centre look after network links and control the flow of information.

WHAT IS THE TRAVELLING SALESMAN PROBLEM?
A network of roads connects the towns that a travelling salesman must visit. How does he work out the shortest route to take so that he visits each town only once? This is a difficult mathematical puzzle. The same problem faces engineers designing efficient communications networks.

FIND OUT MORE ►► Internet 191 • Telecommunications 192–193

INTERNET

The global computer network, connecting computers by telephone cables, optical fibres, and microwaves, is called the Internet. The Internet provides almost instant electronic communication around the world.

TIM BERNERS LEE
British, 1955-
MARC ANDREESSEN
American, 1971-

Tim Berners Lee invented the World Wide Web as a source of information for scientists in the 1980s. In 1993, Marc Andreessen developed the first browser program (Mosaic) with text, pictures, and hypertext links.

HOW DOES THE INTERNET WORK?
Every computer linked to the Internet has an address. This is its IP number. When you send a message or request information on the Internet, your computer sends packets of data with the sender's and receiver's addresses attached. Special computers called servers and routers direct the data through the Internet.

WHAT IS THE WORLD WIDE WEB?
The World Wide Web is a library of billions of pages of information, including ►► SEARCH ENGINES, stored on servers connected to the Internet. The pages are written using hypertext, which links them. A program called a browser on your computer uses a web address (URL) to request a page. The request is routed through the Internet to the correct server, and the page is sent back to your computer.

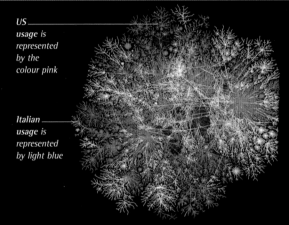

US usage is represented by the colour pink

Italian usage is represented by light blue

INTERNET MAP ▲
This computer graphic illustrates the movement of information around the world over the Internet. Each line shows the route of data sent to 20,000 locations on the network. The lines are colour-coded by country.

WHAT IS HYPERTEXT?
Web pages are written using hypertext. Hypertext links one web page to another. Web pages contain text prepared in a computer language called HTML. Hypertext links special words or phrases to other sections of the document, or to other documents. Clicking on a link takes you to the linked page.

SEARCH ENGINES

If you need to find information on the World Wide Web, you use a program called a search engine. When you enter keywords, the search engine (located on a server) makes a hypertext list of web pages that have the words you are looking for.

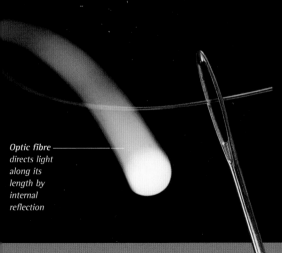

Internet

Optic fibre directs light along its length by internal reflection

◄ FIBRE OPTICS
An optical fibre is a hair-thin strand of pure glass. It carries computer data as pulses of laser light. Reflections stop the light escaping through the fibre walls, so it emerges at the end almost as bright as when it went in.

HOW DOES A SEARCH ENGINE RANK PAGES?
Entering the words "team sports" will produce a list of millions of results from a search engine. The engine tries to place the most relevant pages at the top of the list. Different engines do this in different ways. For example, the engine may check if all the words appear or how many times they appear.

FIND OUT MORE ►► Computers 190 • Light 178–179 • Telecommunications 192–193

TELECOMMUNICATIONS

Telecommunications are messages carried round the world in seconds by electric signals and waves from the ▸▸ ELECTROMAGNETIC SPECTRUM . They include radio and television broadcasts, and telephone conversations.

HOW DOES A TELEPHONE WORK?

A telephone has a microphone and an earpiece. The microphone converts sound into an electric signal. The signal travels at the speed of light along wires, through optical fibres, or via microwaves. A network connects the phones. The earpiece contains a loudspeaker. This changes the signal back into sound.

HOW DOES A RADIO WORK?

Radio broadcasts are made from a central transmitter. Sound signals from microphones in the radio studio are combined with radio waves broadcast from an antenna. Your radio at home has a receiver that separates the sound signal from the radio signal and sends it to a loudspeaker. This is the sound you hear.

GUGLIELMO MARCONI
Italian, 1874-1937
Scientist and inventor Guglielmo Marconi made the first radio transmissions in 1894. His transmitter rang a bell 10 m (30 ft) away. By 1901, he had developed his invention and made the first wireless transmission across the Atlantic Ocean from England to Canada. Marconi was awarded the Nobel Prize for Physics in 1909.

◀ COMMUNICATIONS SATELLITE
A satellite bounces telecommunications signals from one side of Earth to another. The satellite travels in a geostationary orbit so that it stays over the same point on Earth's surface at all times.

HOW DOES A TELEVISION WORK?

An analogue television transmitter sends pictures and sounds as a pattern of radio waves through cables. ▸▸ DIGITAL BROADCASTS transmit the sounds and pictures in binary code through cables and satellites.

telecoms

HOW DOES A MOBILE PHONE WORK?

A mobile (or cell) phone sends and receives signals using microwaves. A phone has a range of only a few miles, so land-based aerials are used. The area that each aerial covers is called a cell. A phone exchanges signals with the nearest aerial. As you move from cell to cell the phone changes aerials. The aerials are connected to the global telephone network.

TELEPHONE TOWER ▶
The BT tower in London, England, provides telecommunications links into and out of the city. It is an electronic communications centre for radio and television broadcasting, telephone services, and digital computer data transmissions.

◀ HIDDEN MOBILE PHONE MAST
To create an effective mobile phone network, mobile phone masts are built at regular intervals nationwide. In some locations, masts spoil attractive views of the countryside or historic buildings. This mast has been disguised as a tree.

Aircraft warning beacons flash on the top and sides of the tower at night

Dish-shaped microwave antennae point towards similar dishes on masts in other cities

ELECTROMAGNETIC SPECTRUM

Electromagnetic rays are waves of electromagnetic force that travel at the speed of light. The full range of rays make up the electromagnetic spectrum.

WHAT ARE RADIO WAVES?
Electrons produce radio waves as they vibrate. They are low-frequency, long-wavelength waves. Radio broadcasts use the lower-frequency range of radio waves, and television broadcasts use the higher range.

HOW ARE DIFFERENT WAVE BANDS USED?
Waves are grouped in wave bands by frequency. Low- to medium-frequency wave bands travel far, and are used for shipping signals. High-frequency waves are used for radio and telephones. The ultra-high to extremely high-frequency bands carry huge amounts of information, including TV, mobile phone, radar signals, and microwave communications.

ELECTROMAGNETIC SPECTRUM ▶
The spectrum arranges the waves according to frequency (number of waves passing a point per second) and wavelength (the distance between the crest of one wave and the crest of the next).

DIGITAL BROADCASTS

Have you seen television pictures as clear as computer graphics? In a digital broadcast, sounds and pictures are converted into streams of binary numbers. The result is higher-quality reception, and many more channels.

▶ DIGITAL BROADCASTING
A TV cameraman records a football match to be broadcast digitally. The image is created with 25 still pictures (frames) each second, 30 in the USA. Only the changes from frame to frame are transmitted.

HOW DOES DIGITAL TV WORK?
Digital TV converts sounds and images into binary code. The code is carried on electromagnetic waves. Digital pictures are clearer because binary code can be compressed (made smaller) to send lots more information about the picture to the receiver. Broadcasters can also send more channels this way.

Gamma rays have wavelengths of up to about 0.01 nm (nanometre — one billionth of a metre)

X-rays 0.001–10 nm

Ultraviolet rays 10–390 nm

Visible light 390–7,000 nm

Infrared rays 700 nm–1 mm

Microwaves 0.3 m–0.001 m

Radio waves 1 mm–1 km+

▲ GAMMA RAYS
Nuclear reactions and radioactive decay emit these high-energy rays.

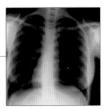
▲ X-RAYS
X-rays go through materials that block light, such as clothing and skin.

▲ ULTRAVIOLET RAYS
These dangerous rays from the Sun can damage your skin.

▲ INFRARED
Night-vision cameras detect infrared rays to see missiles in the dark.

▲ RADAR
Radar systems transmit radio waves to detect moving ships and aircraft.

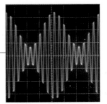
▲ RADIO WAVES
Radio waves are used for radio, TV, telephone, and satellite communication.

FIND OUT MORE ▶▶ Home Entertainment 351 • Internet 191 • Media 298–299 • Networks 191 • Satellites 28 • Sound 176–177

ROBOTS

Robots are automatic machines. Some robots can perform mechanical and repetitive jobs faster, more accurately, and more safely than people. Robots can also handle dangerous materials, and explore distant planets.

WHAT CAN ROBOTS DO?

Robots can sense and respond to their surroundings. They can handle delicate objects or apply great force, for example to perform eye operations guided by a human surgeon, or to assemble a car. With ▸▸ ARTIFICIAL INTELLIGENCE , robots will also be able to make decisions for themselves.

HOW DO ROBOTS SENSE?

Electronic sensors are a robot's eyes and ears. Twin video cameras give the robot a 3-D view of the world. Microphones detect sounds. Pressure sensors give the robot a sense of touch, to judge how hard to grip an egg. Built-in computers send and receive information with radio waves.

HUMANOID ROBOT ▶
This humanoid robot has been built for the entertainment industry. Dressed as pirates or cowboys, robots like this are performers in theme park attractions.

Joints move like a human's

Limbs moved by pipes and pistons

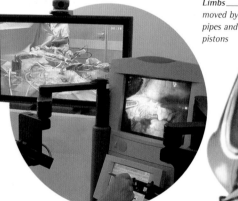

robots

Movements controlled by a computer

▲ ROBOTS IN MEDICINE
Monitoring progress on a TV, a skilled surgeon performs an operation by remote control. Robot instruments carry out his actions on the patient.

ARTIFICIAL INTELLIGENCE

Artificial intelligence attempts to create computer programs that think like human brains. Current research has not achieved this, but some computers can be programmed to recognize faces in a crowd.

CAN ROBOTS THINK?

Robots can think. They can play complex games, such as chess, better than human beings. But will a robot ever know that it is thinking? Human beings are conscious – we know we are thinking – but we don't know how consciousness works. We don't know if computers can ever be conscious.

WILL ROBOTS TAKE THE PLACE OF PEOPLE?

Robots have replaced people performing repetitive jobs, and in dangerous jobs, such as bomb disposal. In future, robots may do housework and other jobs we hate. But will robots replace people in jobs that need kindness or creativity? It's hard to imagine a robot teacher or dancer.

◀ ROBOT CLEANER
This robot vacuum cleaner finds its own way around as it cleans your home. With three computers, and over 70 sensors, it plans an efficient route, remembering where it has been and deciding where to clean next.

FIND OUT MORE ▸▸ Computers 190 • Industry 204 • Machines 196–197

NANOTECHNOLOGY

A nanometre is one billionth of a metre. This is about a million times smaller than the full stop on this line. Nanotechnology aims to make tiny machines measured in nanometers.

nano

WHAT IS A NANOMACHINE?
A nanomachine is built from individual atoms, like the parts of a tiny construction kit, with atomic wheels and motors. A nanomachine will make other products from atoms, such as nanovehicles to transport drugs through the body's bloodstream. Vast armies of nanomachines might even assemble ▸▸ CARBON COMPUTERS , atom by atom.

WHAT IS SELF-ASSEMBLY?
Nanomachines will be designed to build and copy themselves. They will be self-assembling in a similar way to the molecules that make up living things. To build a large structure, such as a car, billions of nanomachines will be organized to work together.

Red blood cells

Nanorobot powered by a propeller

NANOTECHNOLOGY IN MEDICINE ▲
This imaginative artwork shows how nanotechnology might work in medicine – tiny nanorobots the size of cells are programmed to travel through the blood stream, finding and repairing defects in the body's organs and tissues.

NANOTECHNOLOGY BEARING ▶
Before complete nanomachines and robots can be constructed, scientists will build basic machine components, such as levers, gears, bearings, and motors, all at a nano scale. This computer design shows how a frictionless bearing might be assembled from individual atoms.

ARE THERE ANY DANGERS ASSOCIATED WITH NANOTECHNOLOGY?
One danger is that self-assembling nanomachines could multiply and spread out of control – damaging natural materials. They would have to be programmed so that they could not escape into the environment in this destructive way.

CARBON COMPUTER

At an atomic scale, scientists think carbon will have better electrical properties than silicon for making computers. A computer processor could be made by linking individual carbon atoms. Only nanomachines could work at this scale.

HOW COULD NANOTECHNOLOGY BUILD A CARBON CAR?
Nanomachines could make things, such as carbon cars, by linking carbon atoms one at a time into the diamond structure. These new cars will be many times stronger, yet lighter than existing versions made with titanium, aluminium, and steel. A carbon car built by nanomachines would be light enough to lift with one hand.

◀ NANO FLY
Using nano components built from carbon and other atoms, it might be possible to build intelligent robot insects such as this fly – pictured on a computer key. Tiny machines like this could be used for police surveillance.

WHAT HAS NANOTECHNOLOGY ACHIEVED SO FAR?
Nanotechnology is still at a very early stage, but some progress has been made. Simple wheels, axles, and gears have been produced. Scientists have already manipulated individual carbon atoms to produce nano scale numbers and lettering.

FIND OUT MORE ▸▸ Atoms 157 • Machines 196–197

MACHINES

From bottle openers to cranes, machines make work easier. Simple machines include ▸▸ LEVERS , ▸▸ PULLEYS , ▸▸ INCLINED PLANES , and ▸▸ GEARS . They transfer force and movement from one place to another, often magnifying the force or the movement at the same time.

WHAT IS MECHANICAL ADVANTAGE?

The mechanical advantage of a machine is the amount that it magnifies (increases) a force to overcome a load. Nutcrackers have a mechanical advantage of about five. The force you use to squeeze the handles is magnified five times – making it strong enough to crack even the hardest nut.

HOW IS A MACHINE'S EFFICIENCY MEASURED?

The efficiency of a machine is the ratio of the work output to the work input. If the machine is perfect, then all the work (energy) that you put in (the effort) is used to move the load. It would be 100 per cent efficient. In reality, a machine always wastes some energy as a result of friction between its parts.

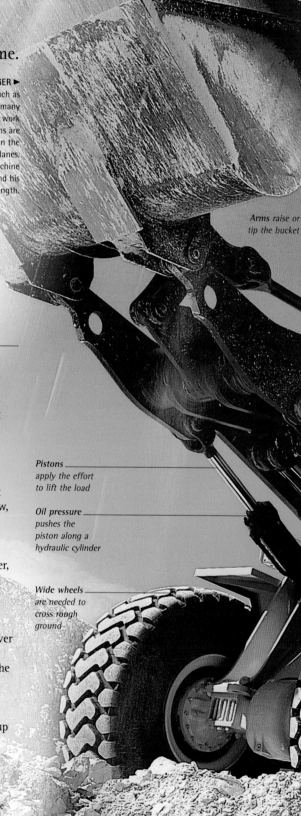

INDUSTRIAL DIGGER ▶
A complicated machine, such as this digger, is built from many simple machines that work together – the digger arms are levers, and the teeth on the bucket are inclined planes. The driver operates the machine to move a load far beyond his own strength.

Load lifted by the digger

Arms raise or tip the bucket

Pistons apply the effort to lift the load

Oil pressure pushes the piston along a hydraulic cylinder

Wide wheels are needed to cross rough ground

machines

LEVERS

A lever is a rod or bar that turns on a pivot (the fulcrum). The effort applied at one place moves a load at another place via the fulcrum. There are three different types of lever, each with the effort, load, and fulcrum in different places.

WHAT ARE THE DIFFERENT CLASSES OF LEVER?

The three classes of lever are suited to carrying out different jobs. In a first-class lever, such as a seesaw, the effort and load are on opposite sides of the fulcrum. In a second-class lever, such as a bottle opener, the fulcrum is at one end, the effort at the other, and the load in between. In a third-class lever, such as chopsticks, the fulcrum and the load are at either end, with the effort in between.

WHAT IS A WHEEL AND AXLE?

The steering wheel of a car works like a circular lever – it magnifies a turning force. Your hands on the wheel move through a much larger distance than the axle (the steering column). The turning effort is magnified to produce enough force to steer the car wheels. A crank is a turning handle that works in a similar way, to raise a heavy bucket of water up a well with a small effort on the winding handle.

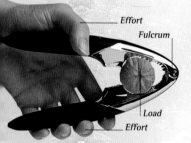

Effort
Load

Fulcrum

Effort

▲ FIRST-CLASS LEVER
These pliers are a pair of first-class levers. The fulcrum is between the load and the effort. The effort is magnified because the load is closer to the fulcrum.

Effort
Fulcrum

Load
Effort

▲ SECOND-CLASS LEVER
These nutcrackers have the fulcrum at one end, the effort at the other, and the load between – ideal for cracking open a nut.

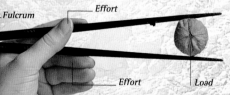

Fulcrum
Effort

Effort
Load

◀ THIRD-CLASS LEVER
In chopsticks, the effort is between the fulcrum and the load. The effort is reduced by this lever, but the movement is magnified. With small movements of the hand, you can pick up anything from a grain of rice to a large nut – but you can't crack a nut.

PULLEYS

A pulley is a grooved wheel that a rope or belt runs over. A single pulley changes the direction of a force, without changing its size – for example, to raise a flag up a pole by pulling down on the rope.

WHAT IS A BLOCK AND TACKLE?
A block and tackle is two sets of pulleys linked by a single rope. Pulling the rope draws the block and tackle together. This magnifies the effort put in so that you can lift or lower a heavy load – a car engine, for example. Block and tackle pulley systems have been used for centuries to raise sails and shift cargo on sailing ships.

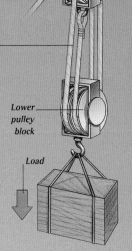

Effort ___
Upper pulley ___
block

A single length of rope ___
runs over four pulleys. The
mechanical advantage of this
pulley system means it can lift
a load that is four times bigger
than the effort applied.

Lower ___
pulley
block

Load ___

BLOCK AND TACKLE ▶
A block and tackle is a pulley system designed to lift a large load with a smaller effort. The crane on the far right is equipped with a block and tackle to move heavy loads, such as steel plates, into position on a building site.

INCLINED PLANES

The first construction machine was probably the inclined plane. Early builders raised loads such as blocks of building stone by pushing them gradually up a slope. The more gradual the slope, the easier it is to raise the load, but the farther you must travel to get to the top.

Cab where the driver operates controls

WHY DOES A SLOPE MAKE IT EASIER TO RAISE A LOAD?
When you push a load up a slope, the weight of the load is shared between your effort and the slope. You do not have to lift the whole weight in one go. However, although the effort is smaller, the distance moved is greater. If you climb a zig-zag path up a mountain, each step is easier, but you take many more steps to reach the top than if you follow a steeper, but more direct route to the top.

WHAT IS A WEDGE?
A wedge is a movable inclined plane. As it is pushed forwards, it pushes a load sideways. The sharper the wedge, the further it must be pushed to produce the same sideways movement, but the greater the sideways force it applies. The blade of an axe is a wedge that produces a splitting force as it cuts into hard materials, such as wood, rock, or ice.

◀ INCLINED PLANE
This road follows a zig-zag path up a hillside. The distance travelled is greater than following the direct route to the top, but the slope is gentler, so less effort is needed.

GEARS

Gears are toothed wheels that transfer turning motion and forces from one place to another, for example from a car engine to the car wheels. The gear teeth mesh (fit together) so that as one gear turns, it forces its neighbour to turn in the opposite direction.

WHAT IS A GEAR RATIO?
If two gears have the same number of teeth then they turn at the same rate and with the same force. If one gear has twice the number of teeth as the other, the gear with more teeth rotates at half the speed of the other gear, but with twice the force.

WATCH GEARS ▶
The gears in this watch carry the turning force from the spring inside the watch to the hands on its face. The gear ratios make each hand turn at the correct rate to keep time.

FIND OUT MORE ➤➤ Engines 198–199 • Forces 164 • Motion 165

ENGINES

A machine that converts energy from a fuel to do work is an engine. Steam engines were the first engines for transport and industry. Internal combustion engines power road vehicles and many trains. Jet engines power aircraft, and ▶ TURBINES drive ships.

WHAT IS A HEAT ENGINE?

Most engines convert heat energy into motion. The heat comes from burning a fuel such as coal, petrol, or hydrogen gas. The heat makes a gas, such as air, expand rapidly. In a piston engine, the expanding gas pushes a piston down a cylinder. The piston moves down on the power stroke, which drives the machine. The amount of fuel an engine uses to run for a given time is called its ▶ FUEL CONSUMPTION .

WHAT IS AN INTERNAL COMBUSTION ENGINE?

In this engine, fuel is burnt in a cylinder. The cylinder draws in air and fuel through a valve as the piston moves down. As the piston moves up, it compresses the air and fuel, causing them to heat up. The fuel combusts (explodes), and the expanding gases from the explosion push the piston down, producing power.

HOW DOES A STEAM ENGINE WORK?

In a steam engine, fuel is burned outside the cylinder – coal heats water in a boiler, which makes steam. Steam is fed into the cylinder, where it expands and pushes the piston. The piston pushes a rod connected to a crank to turn a wheel.

◀ STEAM ENGINE
The first steam engines pumped water from deep mines. Scottish engineer James Watt (1736-1819) introduced many improvements to the steam engine. His ideas led to efficient steam engines that could power factories and drive heavy locomotives, such as this one from Harbin, Manchuria, in China.

Crankshaft turns the wheels

Piston drives the crankshaft as it is forced down by expanding hot gases

Air intake draws in air needed for fuel to burn. A filter traps dust and dirt

Cylinder where the fuel is ignited

Valves open to let fuel and air mixture into cylinder and to let exhaust gases out

Camshaft controls the opening and closing of the valves

Spark plug ignites the fuel and air mixture

PETROL ENGINE

Petrol engines are internal combustion engines. Most modern petrol engines operate on a four-stroke cycle. Fuel and air are drawn into the cylinder, the mixture is compressed, and ignited. The expanding gases push down the piston. As the piston descends, power is applied to the crankshaft, and finally the exhaust gases are forced out. Each cylinder operates out of step with the others, so the four work in sequence. This produces a continuous output of power so that the car runs smoothly.

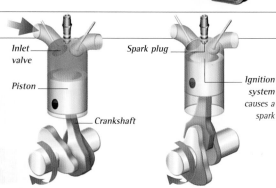

Inlet valve

Spark plug

Piston

Ignition system causes a spark

Crankshaft

INTAKE STROKE
The inlet valve opens. Fuel and air are drawn into the cylinder as the piston descends.

COMPRESSION STROKE
The mixture of fuel and air is compressed as the piston rises. Then, the spark plug ignites the mixture and it explodes.

HOW DOES A JET ENGINE WORK?
Air entering the front of the engine is compressed by rotating blades and fed to a combustion chamber. Jet fuel injected into the chamber mixes with the compressed air, and burns at a high temperature. This makes a jet of gas shoot from the rear of the engine at such speed that it thrusts the aircraft forwards.

Belt drives the alternator to charge the battery

FRANK WHITTLE
English, 1907-1996
Engineer Frank Whittle proposed the idea for jet aircraft in 1928. But it was not until 1937 that he built the first successful engine. His ideas were developed in World War II, and the first Whittle engine jet fighters flew in 1944.

ENGINE DEVELOPMENT

c. AD 60	Steam powers an engine
1698	First practical steam engine
1765–1790	**James Watt** improves steam engines
1804	First steam locomotive
1876	First internal combustion engine
1903	First gas turbine
1937	First jet engine

◄ CAR ENGINE
In this high-performance, six-cylinder car engine, the power strokes from the pistons take place in sequence. The power is transferred smoothly through the crankshaft to the gearbox and wheels.

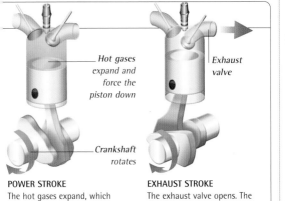

Hot gases expand and force the piston down

Exhaust valve

Crankshaft rotates

POWER STROKE
The hot gases expand, which forces the piston down, transferring power to the crankshaft.

EXHAUST STROKE
The exhaust valve opens. The exhaust gases (waste gases) are forced out of the cylinder as the piston rises.

TURBINES
A turbine is an engine that has a set of blades or paddles, rotated by a moving liquid or gas. Turbines are used in hydroelectric power stations and ships.

WHAT ARE THE DIFFERENT TYPES OF TURBINE?
Water-mills and windmills are examples of water and air turbines. They are not heat engines because they do not rely on heat to produce motion. Gas and steam turbines are powerful heat engines – the turbine blades are spun by hot gases from burning fuel, or by high-pressure steam from a boiler. They are used to drive large ships and turn power station generators.

WHAT MAKES A TURBINE TURN?
The flowing gas or liquid pushes the turbine blades, spinning the shaft. The turbine is connected to a generator. In a modern turbine, the angled blades have a similar shape to aircraft wings to maximize the force generated. The fluid may pass through two, three, or more sets of blades arranged in sequence – to convert as much energy as possible to motion.

▲ STEAM TURBINE
This turbine rotor is spun by high-pressure steam. It turns a generator to produce electricity at a power station. The rotor blades are arranged in stages. Multi-stage turbines are the most efficient as they take all the energy produced by the steam.

FUEL CONSUMPTION
A vehicle's fuel consumption is measured by how much fuel it uses to travel a certain distance. The fuel consumption of a car depends on its engine power, its weight, its aerodynamics (how smoothly it moves through the air), its speed, and how it is driven.

HOW CAN ENGINE EFFICIENCY BE IMPROVED?
The more fuel a car needs to work, the less engine efficient it is. Scientists are developing cars that use less fuel, and therefore do not waste energy or pollute the air. They are also making cars that use different sources of energy, such as solar panels, electric motors, or hydrogen fuel, which is pollution-free.

▼ ELECTRIC CAR
Solar panels in this car's roof feed power to its batteries. Electric cars do not pollute city streets with exhaust fumes.

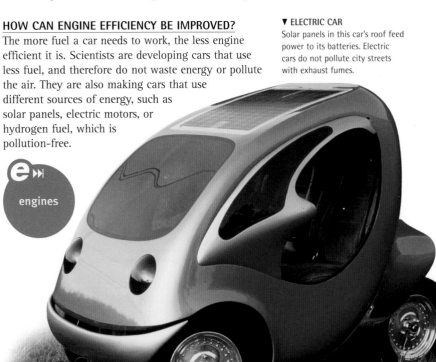

FIND OUT MORE ►► Electromagnetism 186 • Energy 166 • Human Impact 64 • Machines 196–197 • Rockets 28 • Transport 200–201

TRANSPORT

Many people live in one place, but work in another. At local supermarkets, people buy products from other countries. Modern transport – the movement of people and ▶▶ FREIGHT by land, sea, and air – lets us travel all over the world with great speed.

▲ CYCLE PATH
In some cities, dedicated cycle paths keep cyclists and motor vehicles in separate lanes, making cycling safer and more enjoyable.

WHAT IS A TRANSPORT SYSTEM?

Road, rail, sea, and air transport link together to make an integrated transport system. A package sent from the UK can be delivered 24 hours later to an address in the USA. A courier collects the package and takes it by road to the airport. The freight plane flies overnight to the USA. Its cargo is sorted, and the package travels onwards by rail, then road.

▼ AIR TRAFFIC
Demand for air travel is so great that a busy airport can operate flights every minute, 24 hours a day. This can create disturbing noise pollution for people living along the flight path. Night flights are restricted, or banned completely, at many airports.

HOW EFFICIENT ARE DIFFERENT FORMS OF TRANSPORT?

The most fuel-efficient way to transport people and goods is by sea, but journey times are long. Rail is the next most efficient, and safe. Flying is the fastest, but least efficient. The most efficient transport for short journeys is by bicycle or on foot – both are pollution-free, suffer few delays, and keep you fit as you travel.

WHAT IS A SCIENTIST'S ROLE IN TRANSPORT?

Scientists and engineers seek solutions to transport problems. They try to reduce ▶▶ CONGESTION and pollution, and improve ▶▶ ROAD SAFETY . They also work with governments to introduce new scanning equipment to improve security and stop the smuggling of illegal goods across borders.

Flight deck, where the pilot and co-pilot fly the plane

Fuselage (aircraft body) is made from strong but lightweight alloys such as aluminium

e ▶▶
transport

Turbofan engines power the plane at more than 805 km/h (500 mph)

Ground crew guides plane into its docking bay

HOW ARE AIRCRAFT CONTROLLED IN THE AIR?

The pilot and crew use flight deck computers to fly the plane, and radar screens to show their position, and weather conditions ahead. Air traffic controllers on the ground give pilots permission to take off and land, issue flight paths, and make sure that no aircraft come within 16 km (10 miles) of one another horizontally, or 310 m (1,000 ft) vertically.

CONGESTION

Congestion occurs when too many vehicles use the same route at the same time, and traffic slows or comes to a halt. One solution is to build more roads, but some people argue that the number of vehicles grows to fill the roads available. An alternative is to encourage people to use public transport.

TRANSPORT FIRSTS	
3200 BC	Wheels
3000 BC	Sailing ships
1803	Steam train
1807	Steamboat
1839	Bicycle
1885	Car
1903	Aeroplane
1947	Supersonic flight
1952	Commercial passenger flight

WHAT IS GRIDLOCK?
The streets in many modern cities are planned on a grid. At busy times traffic may halt as traffic jams form at junctions. This is called gridlock. Gridlock may be avoided by synchronizing traffic signals from one junction to the next, and by introducing one-way systems.

WHY IS PUBLIC TRANSPORT IMPORTANT?
Public transport is more efficient and less polluting than private cars. Underground rail can transport two million people in and out of a city each day – two million cars can block the roads. City planners also encourage the public to use trams, bicycles, buses, light railways, and ferries to reduce congestion.

▲ TRAFFIC JAM
Managing traffic flow at peak periods and dealing with incidents, such as crashes, are challenging problems for transport planners. Engineers are developing ways to avoid jams – charging road tolls to discourage drivers, introducing in-car navigation systems to warn drivers of jams ahead, and installing synchronized traffic signals.

FREIGHT

When goods are being transported they are called freight. Almost everything you purchase – clothes, electronics, food, and books – has been brought to the store from elsewhere.

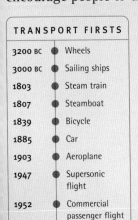

◄ LOADING CONTAINERS
A huge crane called a derrick loads containers onto the ship. The crew are careful that the ship doesn't tilt during loading. They chalk numbers on the floor of the ship so they know where to place the different containers.

HOW IS A CONTAINER SHIP LOADED?
Container ships are loaded at special container ports. The containers are easily transferred from road, to rail, and to ship because each container is a standard size, 2.5 m by 2.5 m by 12 m (8 ft by 8 ft by 40 ft). They stack together like bricks. The largest container ship can carry 4,000 containers.

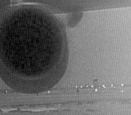

▼ CRASH-TEST DUMMIES
New car models are crash-tested in laboratories before they go into production. Dummies in the car show what happens to passengers in a crash. The impact forces in the crash are monitored with sensors inside the dummies and by high-speed videos.

ROAD SAFETY

Scientists are always looking for ways to improve safety on the roads so that fewer people are hurt or killed in accidents. Millions of people are injured each year in road crashes around the world, but many more injuries are not reported.

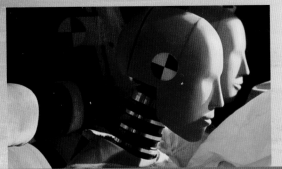

HOW CAN ROAD SAFETY BE IMPROVED?
Driving too fast is a major cause of accidents. Speed increases the severity of accidents. Nine out of ten collisions with a pedestrian at 64 km/h (40 mph) are fatal, but less than one in ten are fatal at 32 km/h (20 mph). Speed bumps and traffic islands help to keep speeds down. Radar speed traps and roadside cameras catch speeding vehicles, encouraging drivers to obey speed limits. Electronic signs on motorways warn drivers to slow down in fog or snow.

FIND OUT MORE ▶▶ Engines 198–199

CONSTRUCTION

From houses and skyscrapers to bridges and highways, our environment is constructed from many different materials. Architects design structures to look good and suit a purpose – ▸▸ ENGINEERS make structures work.

HEMISPHERIUM ▲
An architect explores his new designs inside a virtual reality dome. He uses a joystick to navigate round the view.

WHAT DOES AN ARCHITECT DO?
An architect's job is to design and plan new buildings and structures. Architects must consider the building's use, the choice of materials, and the building's environment. Plans show the exact position and method of fixing every detail, even the electric sockets.

HOW ARE BUILDING MATERIALS CHOSEN?
Most large structures are built with concrete and steel. Concrete is used in huge quantities to make solid foundations. Concrete walls, columns, and arches are reinforced with steel to make them stronger. Wood is still used for many smaller buildings, particularly in ▸▸ MODULAR CONSTRUCTION. It is light yet tough.

HOW IS A ROAD BUILT?
The first stage is planning. The route must not destroy important landscapes or buildings. The design depends on the terrain the road crosses. Tunnels are needed through hills, and bridges across rivers. The site is cleared, foundations are dug, and a stable stone base is laid. The road is paved with concrete or Tarmac.

SKYSCRAPER CONSTRUCTION ▶
When a new building is built in a busy city, the construction company plan carefully so that they do not disrupt the traffic and trade nearby. This skyscraper in Hong Kong's financial district will be 88 stories high when complete.

Giant tower cranes lift building materials

Scaffolding at the top of the building provides a platform for materials and construction workers to build higher

Concrete core reinforced with steel rods

Empty shell does not contain fittings or fixtures, such as carpets, yet

Temporary structures around the main building store equipment, canteens, and washrooms for construction workers

Fence seals off construction site for safety

MODULAR CONSTRUCTION

Large parts of modern buildings can be built away from the site, then delivered ready for assembly. The modules fit together in a pre-planned way. Modular construction reduces construction costs and the time spent at a construction site.

WHAT ARE BUILDING SYSTEMS?
As well as the foundations, walls, and roof, the parts or systems that go into making a building include the heating, lighting, plumbing, and ventilation systems. Usually, these systems are installed when the main structure is complete, but some modules arrive with bathrooms and electrical wiring intact.

▲ MICROFLATS
These modular microflats in Tokyo, Japan, were built to save space in the city. They are cheaper because they are smaller than most houses, and easier to build.

ENGINEERING

An engineer applies the principles of science to the design of structures and machines. Structural engineers, for example, make calculations to predict the stability of structures. Civil engineers plan the construction of railways, roads, and dams.

▼ BRIDGES
These bridges are some of the most beautiful engineering structures. They are carefully designed to carry heavy loads, and survive bad weather.

ARCH BRIDGE

CABLE-STAYED BRIDGE

CANTILEVER BRIDGE

SUSPENSION BRIDGE

Concrete and steel frame will be clad (coated) with glass so that it looks attractive, and windows will be glazed

construction

HOW DOES A BRIDGE CARRY A LOAD?

A straight beam bends in the middle as it supports a load. A beam bridge can carry a load over a narrow gap, but a longer bridge needs a stronger shape. An arch supports the load from beneath – it directs the force around the curve to push against the ground at both sides. A suspension bridge supports a load from above, with cables.

HOW HIGH CAN A SKYSCRAPER GO?

The twin Petronas towers in Kuala Lumpur, Malaysia, are the tallest skyscrapers in the world, 452 m (1,482 ft) high. Engineers could build even taller structures, but higher buildings cost more money and need to be made safe.

WHAT IS THE BEST SHAPE FOR A DAM?

A dam holds back water in a river to form an artificial lake. Water pressure increases with depth, so the greatest pressure on the dam is at its base – the dam wall is much thicker at the bottom than at the top.

▲ CURVED DAM
The curved shape of this concrete dam gives it strength. The water pressure is directed around the curve, which pushes against the high ground at either side, so the ground takes some of the pressure away from the dam.

HOW IS A TUNNEL BORED?

Tunnels are cut with tunnel boring machines (TBMs), burrowing through the ground. As their cutting blades turn, the machines move forward at an average rate of about 1.6 km/h (1 mph). Engineers line the tunnel behind the TBMs with reinforced concrete rings to prevent the roof and walls from collapsing.

▲ TUNNEL DIGGING
Each of the six TBMs used to dig the Anglo-French Channel Tunnel was pushed forwards on rails with a force of 420 tonnes. As the TBM worked, conveyor belts following behind carried away 1,000 tonnes of clay and rubble each hour.

FIND OUT MORE ▶▶ Architecture 328–329 • Computers 190

INDUSTRY

Industry is a general term meaning the businesses and organizations that provide the goods and services we need. There are primary industries, such as agriculture and mining, manufacturing industries, and service industries, such as tourism and banking.

WHAT ARE PRIMARY INDUSTRIES?

Primary industries supply us with food and with the ▶▶ RAW MATERIALS we need to clothe and house ourselves, and to make all the other things we use. For example, agricultural and fishing industries produce food. Forestry supplies wood for making paper and construction. Oil drilling and mining extract fuels to supply energy and materials.

WHERE ARE INDUSTRIES LOCATED?

Industries develop wherever their supplies are found. Steel-making and shipbuilding, for example, need raw materials. Steel plants are often built near coal mines, which supply the fuel they need to produce the steel. Some other industries need lots of workers, so they are often located where labour costs are low.

WHAT IS A COTTAGE INDUSTRY?

A cottage industry is run by an individual or a family, often from their home. Before the Industrial Revolution, most industries were cottage industries. Family names such as Weaver and Potter identified the family trade. Today, new kinds of cottage industry have developed where home-based workers use computers and the Internet to supply their customers.

▲ TEA PRODUCTION
Growing tea is an agricultural industry. Tea leaves are picked by hand so it is labour-intensive – it needs a lot of workers. Many such jobs in agriculture are now done by machine.

MOTOR INDUSTRY ▶
The motor industry is now one of the biggest industries in the world. Each day, thousands of cars roll off the production lines of car plants around the world.

Robot arms, guided by computers, assemble car bodies

Partly-completed cars move steadily along the production line

RAW MATERIALS

Raw materials are the natural sources of fuel and manufacturing materials used by industry. For example, oil supplies energy and also chemicals for making plastics. Metal ores give us metals such as iron. Clay makes pottery, and sand makes glass.

Modern cars consist of a steel shell to which all the other parts are attached

HOW ARE RAW MATERIALS USED?

Many raw materials have to be processed using force, heat, or chemical reactions. Iron ore rock is crushed, then heated with coke (a form of carbon) in a blast furnace. Chemical reactions with the coke and air reduce the ore to liquid iron, which flows from the bottom of the furnace and hardens as it cools.

WHAT ARE BY-PRODUCTS?

A by-product is any useful material that is left over from an industrial process. The slag (crumbled rock) left behind when iron is extracted from iron ore can be used for road-building. Useful amounts of gold, silver, and platinum are left behind as by-products of copper production.

▲ OPENCAST MINING
An opencast mine is a gaping hole in the ground where raw materials are dug. Coal, metal ores, and stone are all used as raw materials for industry.

e ▶▶
industry

FIND OUT MORE ▶▶ Energy Resources 60–61 • Farming 66 • Fishing 67 • Forestry 67 • Materials 170 • Rocks 46–47

MANUFACTURING

From ankle socks to aircraft, almost everything we use has been manufactured. Manufacturing is the process of making products from materials. It may be done by hand, or by computer-controlled ▶ PRODUCTION LINES.

WHERE DO NEW PRODUCTS COME FROM?
Product development begins with an idea – such as a new design for a trainer or an electronic game. If the idea is accepted, working samples are made and tested. Then the samples are shown to the public to get their reaction. If it seems that enough people would buy it, the product is put into production.

▼ TEXTILE MANUFACTURING
At one time, all textiles (fabrics) were spun and woven by hand. Today, machines do the same job in a fraction of the time it once took, and produce a vast variety of fabrics – from cotton and silk to nylon string and carpeting.

HENRY FORD
American, 1863–1947
The son of a farmer, Henry Ford founded the Ford Motor Company in 1903 and introduced production-line methods to car manufacture. For the first time, cars became generally affordable. The first type of car produced in this way was the Model T. Ford. Ford said his customers could have any colour for their car, "so long as it was black".

WHAT IS MASS PRODUCTION?
A product is mass produced when identical copies of it are made in vast numbers by machines. Once, all books were copied by hand. The printing press made it possible for books to be printed quickly and easily, so books became cheaper and more widely available.

PRODUCTION LINE

A production line is a system for mass producing a complicated product efficiently. The idea was first used by Henry Ford as a way of making cars quickly and cheaply, so more people could buy them.

manufacturing

▲ AUTOMATED PRODUCTION
In a bottling factory, bottles are sterilized, filled, and capped by machines. Human workers watch over the process in case there is a problem. People are still better at solving problems than machines.

HOW DOES A PRODUCTION LINE WORK?
On a production line, every stage in the making of a product is a separate workstation. Workers (or machines) at each station do the same task over and over again as partly made products move along a line from station to station. This means that many more products can be completed each day than if groups of workers made one complete product at a time.

WHAT IS QUALITY CONTROL?
Things can go wrong in a complicated production process. Machines break down, the materials may not be available, or they may be the wrong sort. Such problems can lead to faulty products, which must not be allowed to leave the factory or customers will be disappointed. Quality control checks that every finished product is of a sufficiently high standard.

FIND OUT MORE ▶▶ Changing Materials 171 • Materials 170 • Robots 194

CHEMICAL INDUSTRY

Plastics, ▶▶ AGROCHEMICALS, ▶▶ PHARMACEUTICALS, paints, and detergents are just a few of the products of the chemical industry. Chemicals are manufactured in huge chemical plants or extracted at ▶▶ OIL REFINERIES.

ℯ▶▶ chemical industry

WHAT DOES A CHEMICAL PLANT DO?
Chemicals found in nature, such as salt, sulphur, nitrogen, and natural gas, are the raw materials of the chemical industry. At a chemical plant, these materials are mixed, heated, and refined. The chemical reactions that take place transform the raw materials into acids, alkalis, and other valuable chemical compounds.

HOW ARE ACIDS AND ALKALIS USED?
Sulphuric acid is made from sulphur, air, and water. It is the biggest single product of the chemical industry. It is used in batteries, dyes, detergents, fertilizers, and synthetic fibres. Other acids make rocket fuel, varnish, and explosives. Sodium carbonate is a common alkali used to make both soap and glass, for example.

▲ OIL REFINERY
Oil refineries break down crude (untreated) oil into many of the chemical compounds used by the chemical industry. A refinery operates around the clock – at night its illuminated pipes, tanks, and towers look like a small city.

DRILLING FOR OIL ▶
Crude oil is extracted from under the sea bed by offshore oil rigs. These enormous platforms are the largest sea-based structures in the world. Anchored to the sea bed, the rig supports the drill and all the machinery needed to run the drilling operation.

Derrick supports the drill and the drill string (the pipes that lead down to the drill head in the sea bed)

Communication towers keep the rig in constant touch with the mainland

Rig platform supports the derrick, as well as offices, canteens, recreation rooms, and sleeping quarters for the workers

Massive legs support the platform. They may stand directly on the sea bed, or may be filled with air to provide a floating base which is anchored to the sea bed

OIL REFINERY

Crude oil from oil fields around the world is shipped to refineries. The thick, black crude is not a single substance, but a mixture of many different carbon compounds (groups of atoms). At the refinery, the compounds are separated by fractional distillation.

WHAT IS FRACTIONAL DISTILLATION?
At a refinery, crude oil is heated until it boils and turns into a mixture of vapours. Different compounds in the vapours cool and condense at different levels inside a tall distillation tower, allowing them to be separated out. Heavy industrial fuels condense at the bottom of the tower, lighter petroleum fuel at the top.

WHAT CAN WE MAKE FROM OIL?
Using further treatments, lighter compounds can be turned into important fuels, such as petrol and kerosene for motor vehicles and aircraft. They can also make fibres and plastics, solvents for paints, inks, adhesives, cosmetics, and pharmaceuticals. Heavier molecules are used for lubricant oils and bitumen.

AGROCHEMICALS

Plants need minerals from the soil to grow well. But repeated use of soil drains the minerals from it and fewer crops are produced. The farming industry uses agrochemicals to help them improve the quality of the soil, and also to fight off the insect pests, diseases, and weeds that would otherwise destroy their crops.

WHAT IS ORGANIC FARMING?

Because of the effect of artificial sprays and fertilizers on the environment, organic farmers choose not to use them. Instead, they use animal manure and compost, and rotate their crops with beans and peas to replace nitrogen in the soil. They also control pests with natural methods, such as planting onions between carrots to discourage carrot fly.

◄ CROP SPRAYING
Fruit trees in an orchard are sprayed with pesticides to control insects and other pests that would damage the fruit or the trees. At the same time, care must be taken not to kill helpful insects, such as bees.

WHAT ARE SELECTIVE WEEDKILLERS?

In the past, farmers tried to kill weeds with sea salt and other common chemicals. But these substances killed crops as well. Modern herbicides (weedkillers) are organic chemicals designed to limit weed growth. Many are selective, which means that they kill the weeds but do little harm to the crop.

PHARMACEUTICALS

A pharmaceutical is any substance used to treat or prevent disease. Since ancient times, people have experimented with plants as medicines, often poisoning themselves, but sometimes finding substances with real benefits – aspirin, for example. Today, the pharmaceutical industry is based on stricter scientific methods.

HOW ARE NEW DRUGS DEVELOPED?

Now that biochemists understand the chemicals in living cells, they can design molecules to combat illness. Molecules can be made in a laboratory and tested on cells in a culture (in vitro). Successful compounds are then tested on animals (in vivo).

HOW ARE NEW DRUGS TESTED?

When a drug has been tested in a laboratory it is given to patients in tests called clinical trials. In these, some patients are given the new drug while others receive a placebo (a dummy medicine). Because the patients do not know which drug they have received, the test will show if the drug has a genuine effect.

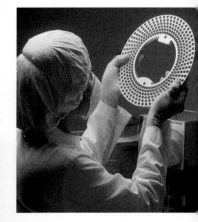

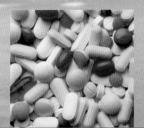

◄ TAKING DRUGS
Most types of drug are taken orally (by mouth) in the form of tablets or pills, or as powders. Some drugs are swallowed in liquid form, and some are injected using a hypodermic syringe. Some drugs can also be absorbed through the skin.

DRUG MANUFACTURE ▲
This mould is used for shaping tablets (pills). Pills contain the drugs prescribed for patients by doctors. Each drug is made into a pill with a different shape, colour, size, or pattern. This makes it less likely that the wrong pill will be taken by mistake.

FIND OUT MORE ►►I Atoms 157 • Cells 73 • Chemistry 162 • Farming 66

BIOTECHNOLOGY

The use of microbes (micro-organisms) to produce and process materials is called biotechnology. Bacteria and yeasts are used to produce products, such as yoghurt, cheese, and wine, by ▶ FERMENTATION.

SIR ALEXANDER FLEMING
Scottish, 1881-1955
Fleming won the Nobel Prize for Medicine in 1945 for the discovery of penicillin. While searching for compounds that would kill bacteria without harming the body, he noticed that bacteria cultured (grown) in a glass dish had died around spots of mould. The mould had blown in through a window. Fleming extracted the antibiotic substance from the mould and called it penicillin.

HOW DO WE USE MICROBES?
Microbes are like tiny chemical factories. They make chemicals called enzymes (biological catalysts) to break down chemicals in their surroundings for food. As microbes feed and multiply, they produce chemical by-products. Yeast cells make an enzyme that turns sugar into alcohol.

◀ PENICILLIN GROWTH
This macrophotograph (close-up) shows a disc-shaped culture (growth) of the green penicillin mould growing on agar jelly in a glass petri dish. Penicillin is an antibiotic substance made by the mould *Penicillium notatum*. It was among the first antibiotics to be discovered, and is still widely used to treat infections.

WHAT ARE ANTIBIOTICS?
Some microbes produce chemicals that kill disease-spreading bacteria. These chemicals are antibiotics. They either destroy the bacteria completely, or stop it multiplying. The first antibiotic, penicillin, was made from a mould that grows on bread. Its antibiotic action was discovered by chance in 1928.

FERMENTATION

Fermentation is the action of yeasts and bacteria on the sugars in fruit, grains, milk, and other food. Yeast cells added to bread dough feed on its natural sugars, turning them into carbon dioxide and water. This makes the dough rise to make light, fluffy bread.

◀ CHEESE-MAKING
The type of cheese made depends on the variety of microbes added, and the conditions of fermentation. As the milk curdles, the curds are separated from the whey. This batch will become Baby Swiss cheeses.

HOW IS MILK TURNED INTO CHEESE?
An enzyme called rennin is added to milk. It ferments the milk sugars to produce lactic acid. The acid separates the milk into solid curds and liquid whey. The curds are pressed into cheeses. Microbes continue to work in the cheese as it ages, making its flavour stronger and changing its texture.

HOW ARE GRAPES MADE INTO WINE?
Natural yeast on grape skins ferments the fruit sugars to produce alcohol. Fermentation stops after 10 to 30 days, when all the sugars have been used up, or when the alcohol content is 12 to 15 per cent, which stops the yeast cells working. The wine is sealed in barrels. If it is exposed to the air, the alcohol is oxidized to acetic acid (vinegar), and the wine turns sour.

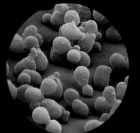

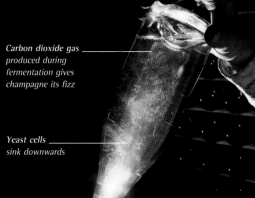

Carbon dioxide gas produced during fermentation gives champagne its fizz

Yeast cells sink downwards

▲ YEAST
This electron microscope picture shows individual yeast cells. Some of the cells are reproducing by budding (producing two cells from one).

◀ WINE-MAKING
In the traditional champagne method for making sparkling (fizzy) wine, the wine continues to ferment after it has been bottled. The bottles are turned upside down to allow the yeast to settle onto the cork. Finally the cork is loosened briefly, and the gas pressure shoots the sediment (settled particles of yeast) from the bottle.

e ▶▶
biotechnolog

GENETICS

Genetics is the study of how living things pass their features from one generation to the next. Your sex and your chances of developing certain diseases are fixed by your genes.

DNA DOUBLE HELIX ▶
This 3-D computer graphic shows a section of the double helix (spiral) of DNA. Individual atoms are shown as coloured balls. These atoms form into groups to create different bases. The two strands of the helix are linked by bases.

FRANCIS CRICK
English, 1916–
JAMES WATSON
American, 1928–

In 1953, inspired by scientist Rosalind Franklin, Crick and Watson built a DNA double helix (spiral) model. They linked the strands of the helix with A, T, C, and G molecules.

WHAT IS THE GENETIC CODE?
The genetic code has four letters, A, T, C, and G. These letters represent groups of atoms called bases, spaced out along the DNA molecule. The make-up of living things is fixed by the order of these bases. Words in the code are three letters, such as TCA. Genes are like long sentences written with these words.

WHAT IS A GENOME?
A genome is the sequence of all the letters of the genetic code on the DNA of a particular organism. The ▶▶HUMAN GENOME has about three billion letters. Scientists have developed special techniques for sequencing (reading) DNA, with the help of powerful computers.

e ▶▶ genetics

HUMAN GENOME PROJECT

The aim of the Human Genome Project is to produce the complete sequence of the genome of the human being.

HOW WILL THE HUMAN GENOME BE USED?
Scientists are using results of the Human Genome Project to study genetic diseases (those that may be inherited), such as cystic fibrosis. By identifying the gene, they should be able to diagnose a disease much earlier, and design more effective treatments. Knowing part of the genome means that scientists can already identify an individual's ▶▶DNA FINGERPRINT.

◀ **HUMAN GENOME**
Each of the wells in this tray contains a different fragment of human DNA. It takes 60 of these trays to hold a complete human genome.

DNA FINGERPRINT

Apart from identical twins, everyone's DNA is different. By scanning about 10 sections (about 500 letters long each) of your DNA, scientists can create your DNA fingerprint.

CAN DNA PROVE WHO COMMITTED A CRIME?
The chance of two individuals having the same DNA sequence in 10 scanned sections is incredibly small. If DNA found at a crime scene, in a hair for example, matches a sample from a suspect to this degree, then it is "beyond reasonable doubt" that the hair is the suspect's.

DNA FINGERPRINT ▲
The pattern and the strength of the bands on this chart represent the DNA sequences of samples taken from individuals.

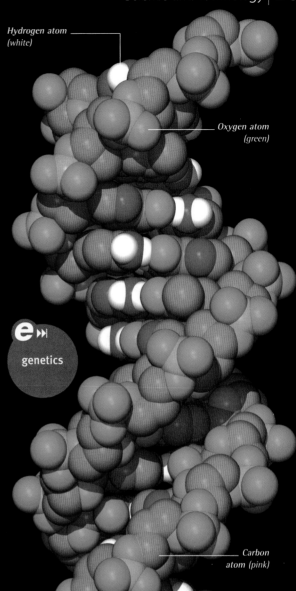

Hydrogen atom (white) · Oxygen atom (green) · Carbon atom (pink) · Nitrogen atom (blue) · Phosphorus atom (orange)

FIND OUT MORE ▶▶ Cells 73 • Genetic Engineering 210–211 • Reproduction 148

GENETIC ENGINEERING

Genetic engineering is the manipulation of genes of living things. Scientists can now insert genes from one organism into another. They do this to grow ▸▸ GM FOOD. They can also ▸▸ CLONE embryos that provide ▸▸ STEM CELLS to repair damaged body tissue.

e ▸▸
genetic engineering

WHAT IS GENETIC VARIATION?

The differences between species and between individuals are explained by the differences in their genes. Sexual reproduction, which randomly mixes genes from parents in their children, produces variation from generation to generation.

HOW CAN WE MANIPULATE GENES?

When dog breeders select puppies with short tails to breed from, they are manipulating the gene for tail length. The gene for short tails is passed on, and the gene for long tails dies out. Now, scientists can select and move genes between organisms in the laboratory. A gene for disease resistance can be "snipped out" from the DNA of one plant and inserted into another.

MICROBE COLONY ▲
Genetic engineering is commonly performed on microbes grown in the laboratory, such as on this fungus. Genes are inserted into microbes to make them produce substances to treat disease.

GM FOOD

The first genetically modified (GM) food went on sale in 1994. It was a variety of tomato called Flavr Savr. The gene that makes the tomato soften had been changed to make it ripen more slowly, so that it would develop more flavour.

GM seedling tolerates pesticides and herbicides

◄ **GM OR NOT?**
GM crops, such as these tomatoes, look just like traditional varieties. The changes produced by gene manipulation are subtle. Genetic modification is more likely to be used to affect the crop's disease resistance or shelf life than its appearance.

Soil with natural nutrients

ARE GM CROPS SAFE?

Some farmers are not keen to grow GM crops. One worry is that genes introduced into the crop will transfer to other species. Another concern is that herbicide- and pesticide-resistant crops encourage farmers to use too many of these chemicals, which might damage wildlife.

GENETICALLY MODIFIED PLANT ▸
This GM seedling has had genetic material from another species inserted into its genetic code. Scientists perform genetic modification on plants to make them more resistant to disease, pests, pesticides, and even bad weather conditions.

WHAT WAS THE GREEN REVOLUTION?

In the 1960s, scientists tried to breed crops suited to conditions in developing countries. The aim was to reduce food shortages by introducing productive crops that were disease-resistant. In India, crop production increased, but in other places, the new crop varieties needed fertilizers that farmers could not afford.

CLONES

Clones are different individuals with the same genes. Clones are common in nature – a bacterium clones itself by splitting in two, producing two identical bacteria. Now scientists have developed artificial cloning techniques that work with mammals.

HOW ARE ANIMAL CLONES PRODUCED?

The first clone made with DNA from an adult animal was Dolly the sheep in 1997. DNA was taken from an adult sheep (Dolly's biological mother) and inserted into an egg cell (with its own DNA removed) from another sheep. The cell started to divide, and the embryo was taken and put into the womb of a third sheep – Dolly's surrogate (birth) mother. Animal clones could be used for medical research.

Leaves designed to grow using less fertilizer

HOW ARE BANANAS CLONED?

Many plants propagate (reproduce) vegetatively (without sex). Each new plant has the same DNA as the parent and is therefore a clone. On a plantation all the banana plants are clones of their parents.

DOLLY THE SHEEP ▲
Dolly's biological mother was six years old when her DNA was cloned to produce Dolly. Sheep can live for 11 to 12 years, but Dolly died when she was six.

COULD HUMAN BEINGS BE CLONED?

In principle, humans could be cloned in the same way as Dolly, perhaps to help a person unable to have a child in any other way. But, as with other aspects of genetic engineering, human cloning is controversial, and has already been banned in many countries.

◄ INTRACYTOPLASMIC SPERM INJECTION (ICSI)
ICSI is used to help couples who have difficulty conceiving a baby. The father's sperm is injected into an egg from the mother. In cloning, the procedure is different. Instead of injecting sperm, the nucleus of the egg cell is removed and replaced with the nucleus of a mature cell from the mother. Sperm is not needed.

STEM CELLS

The starter cells in an embryo are called stem cells. As the embryo grows, stem cells change to become the different cells needed in the body, such as nerve cells and blood cells.

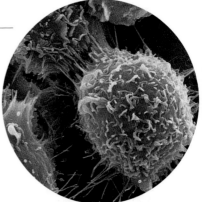

HOW CAN STEM CELL RESEARCH HELP PEOPLE?

Stem cell research is investigating the use of stem cells to repair damaged or diseased tissue. For example, the body cannot repair or replace nerve cells damaged by disease or injury. Transplanted stem cells could be grown to develop into new nerve cells to treat Parkinson's and Alzheimer's diseases.

▲ STEM CELL RESEARCH
This electron microscope image shows stem cells from an adult's bone marrow. These are the only type of stem cells that occur in an adult's body. These stem cells change to produce different blood cells, but only embryo cells can produce all the different cells that make up a human being.

WHY IS THERE CONCERN ABOUT IT?

Stem cell research is controversial because the cells are taken from human embryos that have been fertilized in the laboratory. To avoid rejection of the cells the embryo should ideally have been cloned using the patient's DNA. Many people have concerns about using human embryos in this way.

FIND OUT MORE ▸▸ Cells 73 • Farming 66 • Genetics 209 • Growth 149 • Nervous System 138 • Reproduction 148

PEOPLE and PLACES

PHYSICAL WORLD

Despite being called Earth, more than two-thirds of our planet's surface is covered in water. The rest consists of seven vast expanses of land called continents. The largest of these is Asia, followed by Africa, North America, South America, Antarctica, Europe, and Australasia. They contain an amazing variety of landscapes – mountains, deserts, tropical rainforests, woodlands, and polar ice caps.

▲ **PYRENEES MOUNTAINS**
The Pyrenees stretch for 435 km (270 miles) between the Bay of Biscay and the Mediterranean Sea in western Europe. Like other mountains, the Pyrenees were formed by movements in the Earth's crust, causing the land above to fold and buckle.

ELEVATION

over 4,000 m (13,000 ft)
2,000–4,000 m (6,500–13,000 ft)
1,000–2,000 m (3,300–6,500 ft)
500–1,000 m (1,600–3,300 ft)
250–500 m (800–1,600 ft)
100–250 m (300–800 ft)
0–100 m (0–300 ft)
below sea level

SEA DEPTH

0–250 m (0–800 ft)
250–2,000 m (800–6,500 ft)
2,000–4,000 m (6,500–13,000 ft)
below 4,000 m (13,000 ft)

▲ **NORTHERN HEMISPHERE**
Most of the land on Earth is concentrated in the northern hemisphere, although Europe and North America are the only continents that lie entirely in the north.

e ⏭ physical world

◄ **SOUTHERN HEMISPHERE**
Oceans dominate the southern hemisphere. Australia and Antarctica are the only continental landmasses that lie entirely in the south.

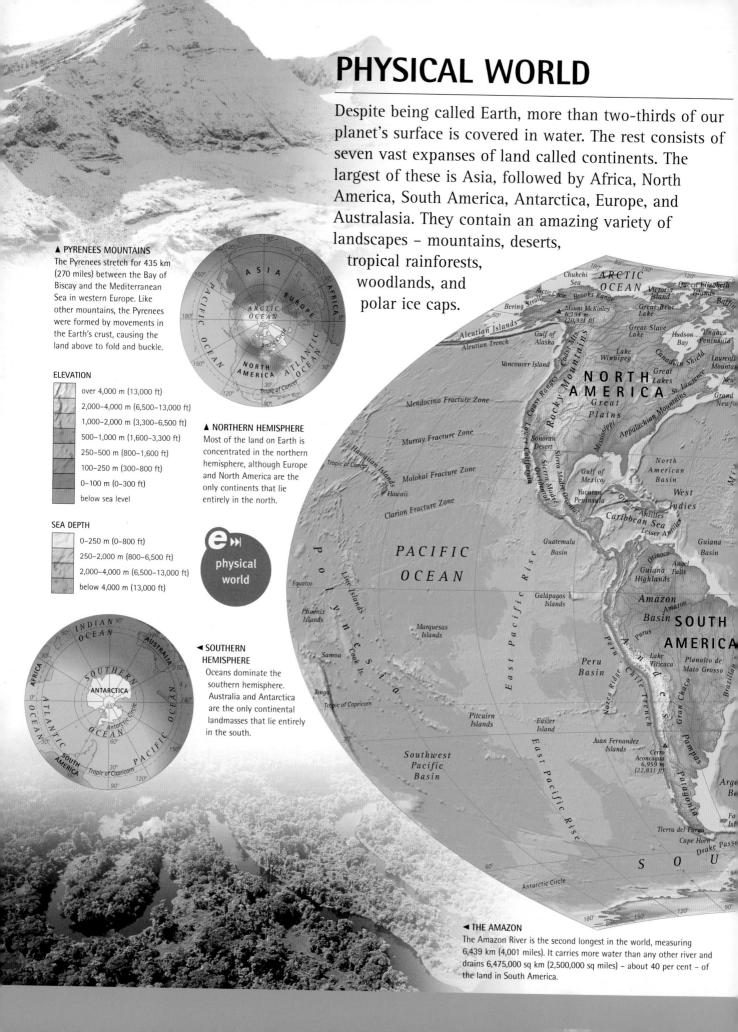

◄ **THE AMAZON**
The Amazon River is the second longest in the world, measuring 6,439 km (4,001 miles). It carries more water than any other river and drains 6,475,000 sq km (2,500,000 sq miles) – about 40 per cent – of the land in South America.

SAHARA DESERT ▶
The world's largest desert is the Sahara, which stretches from the Atlantic Ocean in the west, right across North Africa to the Red Sea in the east.

◀ IGUAÇU FALLS
Lying between Argentina and Brazil, the Iguaçu Falls have two main sections, each containing hundreds of waterfalls separated from each other by rocky islands. The name Iguaçu comes from the Guarani Indian word meaning "great water".

PHYSICAL WORLD

Longest river: Nile
6,695 km (4,160 miles)

Largest lake: Caspian Sea
371,000 sq km
(143,243 sq miles)

Highest point: Everest
8,850 m (29,035 ft)

Lowest point: Dead Sea
-392 m (-1,285 ft)

Largest ocean: Pacific Ocean
165,384,000 sq km
(63,838,000 sq miles)

Largest desert: Sahara
9,065,000 sq km
(3,263,400 sq miles)

Largest island: Greenland
2,175,219 sq km
(839,852 sq miles)

Coldest inhabited place:
Verkhoyansk, Siberia
-70°C in January

Hottest inhabited place: Baghdad, Iraq, 43°C in July–August

Wettest inhabited place: Buenaventura, Columbia, 6,734 cm (2,651 in) of rain per year

Driest place: Aswan, Egypt, 0.5 mm (0.02 in) of rain per year

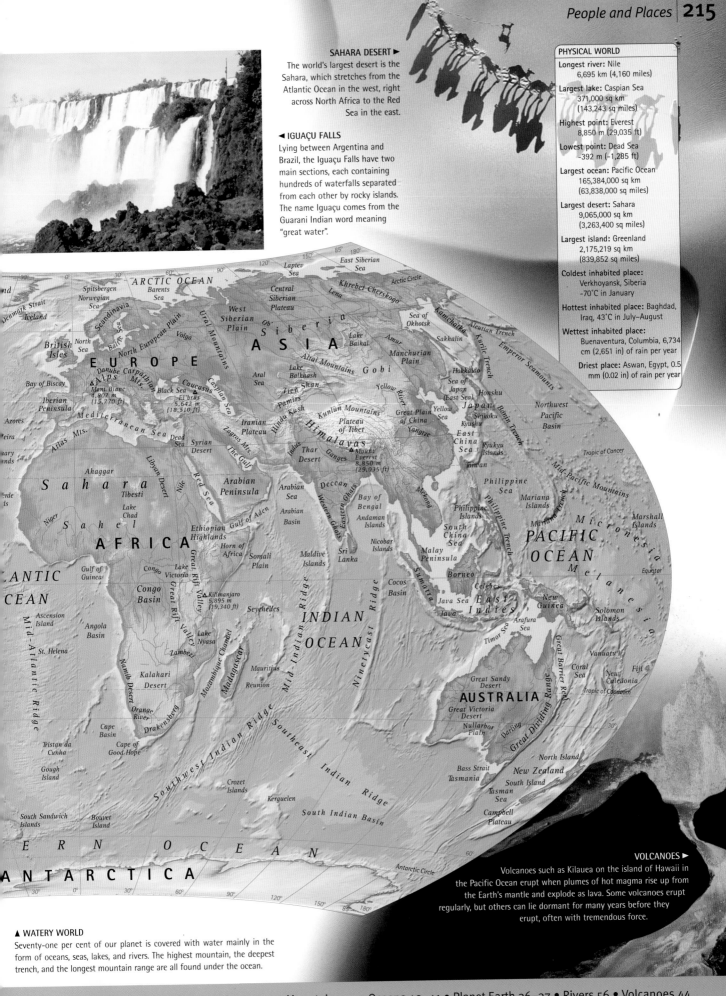

VOLCANOES ▶
Volcanoes such as Kilauea on the island of Hawaii in the Pacific Ocean erupt when plumes of hot magma rise up from the Earth's mantle and explode as lava. Some volcanoes erupt regularly, but others can lie dormant for many years before they erupt, often with tremendous force.

▲ WATERY WORLD
Seventy-one per cent of our planet is covered with water mainly in the form of oceans, seas, lakes, and rivers. The highest mountain, the deepest trench, and the longest mountain range are all found under the ocean.

FIND OUT MORE ▶▶ Continents 39 • Mountains 45 • Oceans 40–41 • Planet Earth 36–37 • Rivers 56 • Volcanoes 44

POLITICAL WORLD

The world today is divided into 193 independent nations, differing from each other in size, shape, population, people, language, government, culture, and wealth. World maps are always changing, as new countries emerge from colonial rule or old ones divide or fall apart. In 1950, there were only 82 independent nations, the rest being colonies or dependencies waiting to gain their independence.

POLITICAL WORLD

Largest country: Russian Federation 17,075,200 sq km (6,592,735 sq miles)

Smallest country: Vatican City 0.44 sq km (0.17 sq miles)

Longest border: USA-Canada 8,893 km (5,526 miles)

Country with most neighbours: China (14), Russia (14)

Oldest country: Denmark, AD 950

Youngest country: East Timor, 2002

e ▸▸
political world

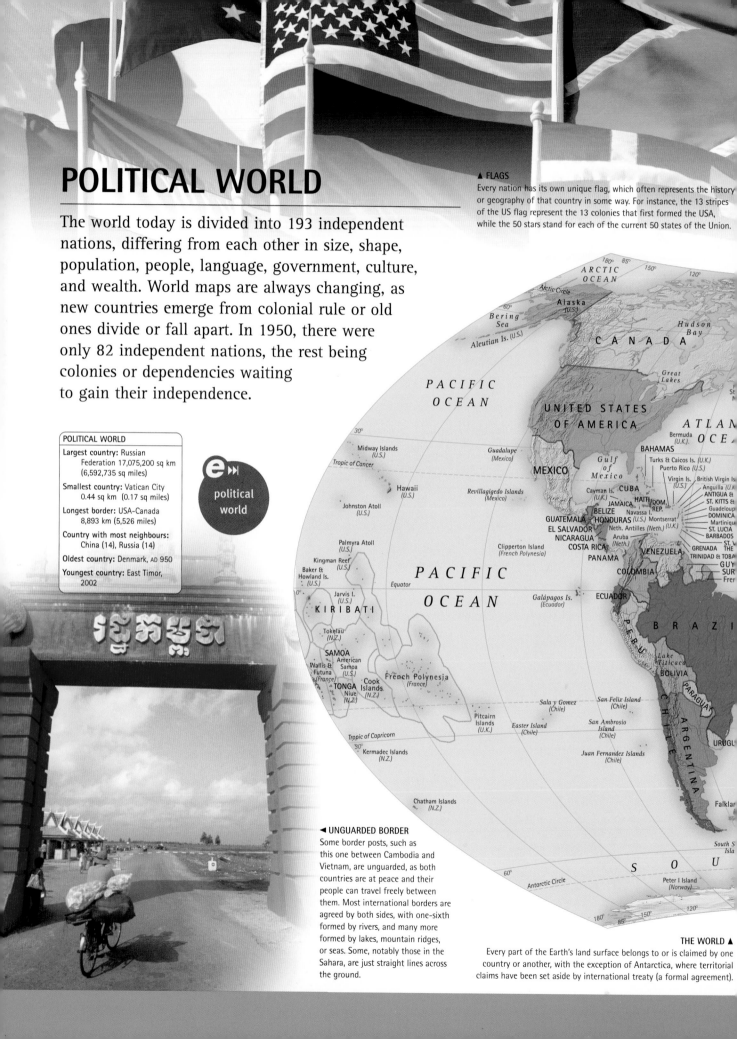

▲ FLAGS
Every nation has its own unique flag, which often represents the history or geography of that country in some way. For instance, the 13 stripes of the US flag represent the 13 colonies that first formed the USA, while the 50 stars stand for each of the current 50 states of the Union.

◀ UNGUARDED BORDER
Some border posts, such as this one between Cambodia and Vietnam, are unguarded, as both countries are at peace and their people can travel freely between them. Most international borders are agreed by both sides, with one-sixth formed by rivers, and many more formed by lakes, mountain ridges, or seas. Some, notably those in the Sahara, are just straight lines across the ground.

THE WORLD ▲
Every part of the Earth's land surface belongs to or is claimed by one country or another, with the exception of Antarctica, where territorial claims have been set aside by international treaty (a formal agreement).

◀ USA-MEXICO BORDER
The international border linking San Diego in the USA with Tijuana in Mexico is crossed by thousands of workers every day. Both countries are part of a free trade area, but their long, joint border is heavily policed to prevent immigrants from Mexico entering the USA illegally in order to seek work and a better standard of living.

GUARDED BORDER ▶
Some borders are disputed and heavily guarded, such as this one between North and South Korea, which was the scene of fierce fighting between the two nations in 1950–53.

FIND OUT MORE ▸▸ Eastern Asia 268–269 • Nations 312 • Politics 306–307 • Social Equality 304–305 • War 313

POPULATION

People have lived on Earth for two million years. For most of that time, the population has remained small, as the number of births has roughly equalled the number of deaths. Improved medicine and health care, better sanitation, improved farming methods producing more and better food, and less physical work have all led to fewer infant deaths and more people living longer. This has caused a massive increase in population over the last 150 years. Today, the world's population is more than 6.4 billion and is rising at the rate of about one million a week.

▲ MULTICULTURAL SOCIETY
A busy street in a large European city, such as Amsterdam in the Netherlands, shows just how multiracial most cities and countries now are. Immigration, international travel, trade, and tourism have all contributed to this great change.

POPULATION

Top five biggest cities and populations:
- Tokyo, Japan 36.5 million
- New York, USA 22.3 million
- Mexico City, Mexico 22.1 million
- Seoul, South Korea 21.7 million
- Mumbai, India 19.5 million

Country with smallest population: Vatican City 911

Most densely populated country: Monaco
16,477 people per sq km
(42,840 people per sq mile)

Least densely populated country: Mongolia
2 people per sq km
(4 people per sq mile)

Country with highest birth rate: Niger
55 per 1,000 population

Country with lowest birth rate: Hong Kong/Macao (China)
7 per 1,000 population

Country with highest death rate: Sierra Leone
25 per 1,000 population

Country with lowest death rate: United Arab Emirates
2 per 1,000 population

Country with the highest life expectancy: Andorra (83)

Countries with the lowest life expectancy: Sierra Leone, Zambia (37)

Richest country (highest GNP*): United States $10,207 billion

Poorest country (lowest GNP*): Tuvalu US$21 million

*GNP = Gross National Product

WORLD POPULATION ▶
The world's 6.4 billion people are not evenly distributed around the planet, but concentrated in areas where the climate is suitable and the land habitable. This concentration of people is measured by population density, which is the average number of people living in each square kilometre.

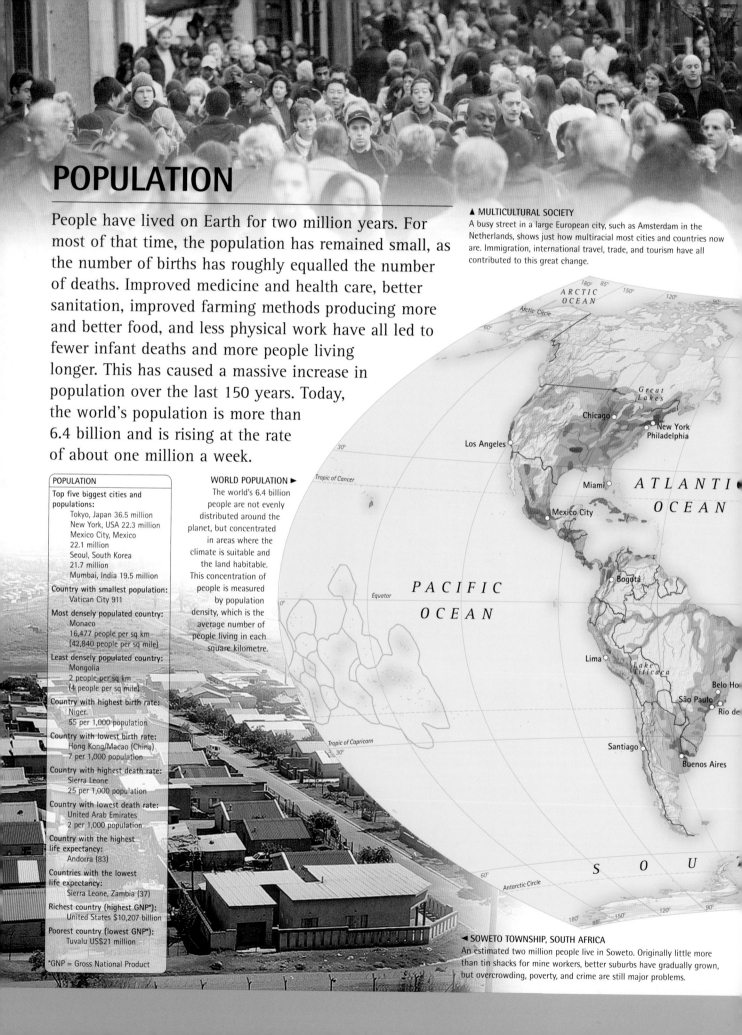

◀ SOWETO TOWNSHIP, SOUTH AFRICA
An estimated two million people live in Soweto. Originally little more than tin shacks for mine workers, better suburbs have gradually grown, but overcrowding, poverty, and crime are still major problems.

KEY

○ City with over
5 million inhabitants

POPULATION DENSITY

People per square km (square mile)

- over 200 (over 520)
- 101–200 (261–520)
- 51–100 (131–260)
- 21–50 (52–130)
- 13–20 (30–51)
- 6–12 (14–29)
- 1–5 (4–13)
- below 1 (below 3)

HONG KONG, CHINA ▶
Cities such as Hong Kong have solved the problem of limited space by building up rather than out. This has led to a growing number of so-called mega-cities, with populations of more than ten million. However, overcrowding, pollution, and a lack of open space make such cities unpleasant to live in.

e ▸▸
population

REFUGEES ▶
Poverty drives many people, such as these Albanians, to flee their country in search of jobs and a better life elsewhere.

FIND OUT MORE ▸▸ Architecture 328–329 • Human Impact 64–65 • International Organizations 434 • Social Equality 304–305

PHYSICAL FEATURES

VICTORIA FALLS
Major waterfalls, such as Victoria Falls on the Zambezi River in Africa, are clearly labelled on the maps in this section. In real life they are dramatic natural features, but on a large-scale continental map they are sometimes too small to pinpoint precisely.

GREAT BARRIER REEF
The Great Barrier Reef is the largest living thing in the world and consists of millions of tiny coral polyps. It runs for about 2,000 km (1,242 miles) along the coast of Queensland in northeast Australia. Major natural features like this are labelled on the maps in this section.

MOUNT KILIMANJARO
Tall mountain ranges are marked on maps in white. Individual peaks, such as Mount Kilimanjaro in Tanzania, Africa, are marked with a special triangular symbol. See the map key on the opposite page for an example.

LAKE CHAD
Rainfall over the land is collected in lakes or underground chambers and drains into the ocean via rivers. Major rivers and large lakes, such as Lake Chad in central Africa, are coloured blue and clearly labelled on the maps here. See the map key on the opposite page for an example.

NAMIB DESERT
Many parts of the world are covered by hot, dry deserts such as the Namib Desert in southern Africa. Deserts often contain sandy soil that can support few plants other than cacti. They are labelled on the continental maps in this section.

PACIFIC OCEAN
Seventy-one per cent of the world's surface is covered by water, mainly in the form of vast oceans such as the Pacific, the largest ocean in the world. The oceans are coloured blue on the maps here and are all labelled.

MAPPING

A map is a picture that represents a particular part of the Earth's surface, usually from above and at a reduced size. It can show the whole world, a single country, or the street where you live. Unlike a photograph, a map can give different kinds of information, such as place names, the height of the land, or where the borders between countries are.

THE OLD WORLD ▶
This world map was drawn in 1584, just 62 years after Ferdinand Magellan and Juan de Elcano completed the first circumnavigation of the world. European mapmakers used their imagination as much as fact when compiling maps, as many parts of the world, such as Australia, the Arctic, and Antarctica, were unknown to them and many coastlines had yet to be fully explored.

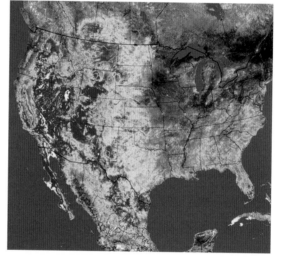

◀ MODERN TECHNOLOGY
Today, cartographers (mapmakers) use sophisticated satellite imaging to accurately map the world. This map of the United States was created from a satellite photograph and clearly shows the contours and vegetation of the land.

TIME ZONES ▼
The world is divided into 24 time zones starting with Greenwich Mean Time (GMT) on the Prime Meridian. Countries to the east of this line are ahead of GMT, those to the west are behind. The 180° line of longitude is called the International Date Line. Places just west of this line are one day ahead of places to the east.

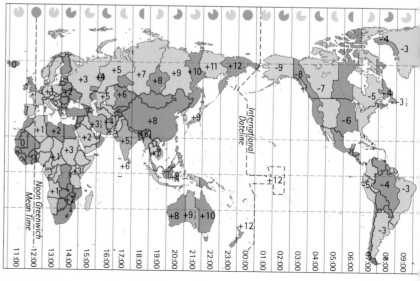

HOW TO USE THE MAPS

This section of the encyclopedia looks at the world and its people. The world has been divided into its seven continents, and each continent is featured with its own map and photographs. Following each continental spread are illustrated double pages that look at each continent in more detail.

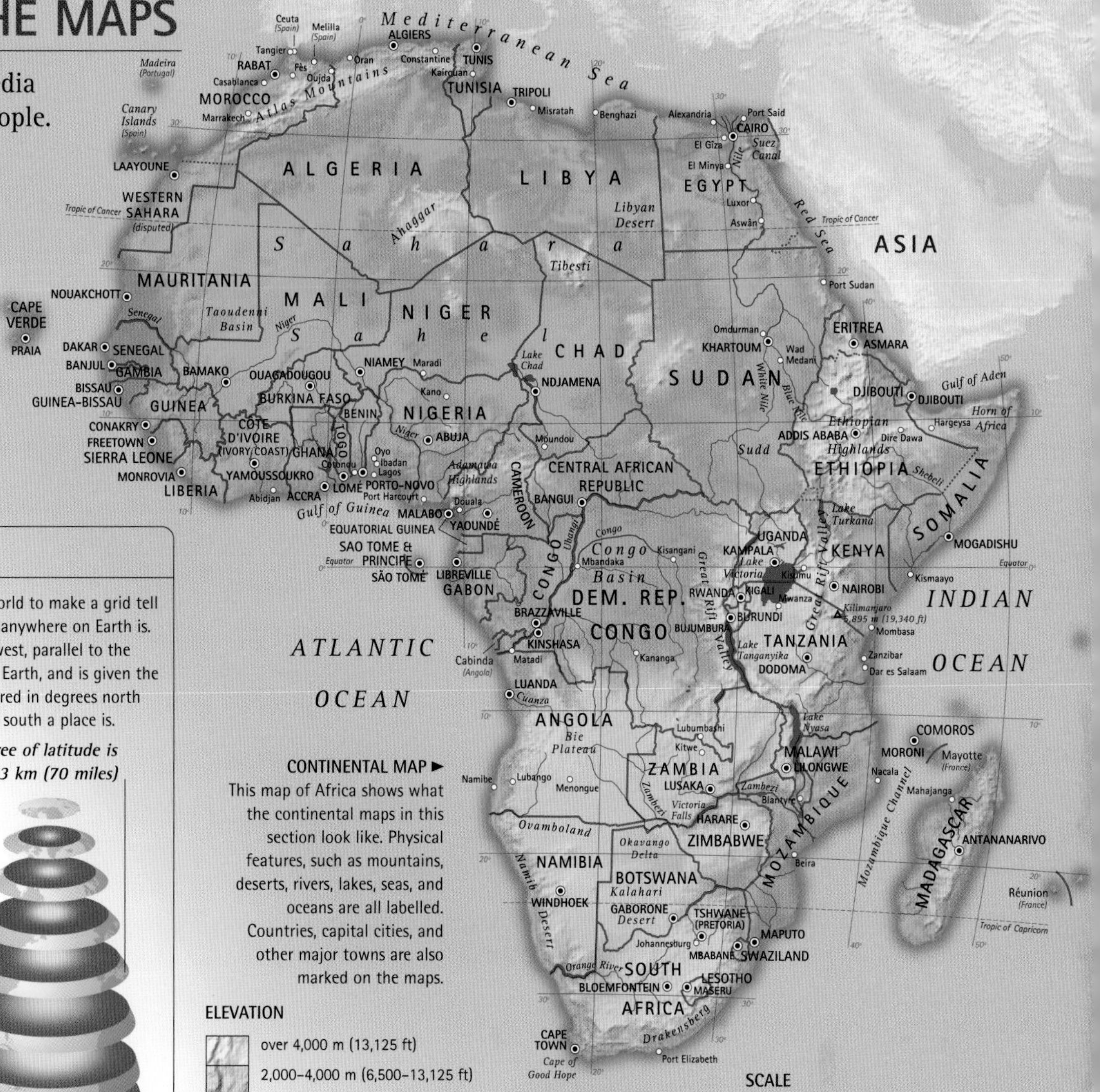

LATITUDE AND LONGITUDE

Latitude Imaginary lines drawn around the world to make a grid tell us exactly how far north, south, east, or west anywhere on Earth is. Horizontal lines of latitude run from east to west, parallel to the Equator which runs around the middle of the Earth, and is given the value 0°. All other lines of latitude are numbered in degrees north or south of it. They measure how far north or south a place is.

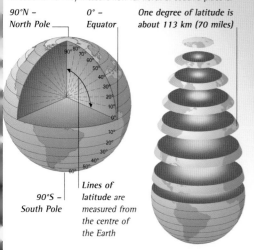

90°N –
North Pole

0° –
Equator

One degree of latitude is
about 113 km (70 miles)

90°S –
South Pole

Lines of latitude are measured from the centre of the Earth

Longitude Vertical lines of longitude run between the North and South Poles. The Prime Meridian (numbered 0°) runs through Greenwich in London, and all other lines of longitude are numbered in degrees east or west of this line. The line opposite the Prime Meridian on the other side of the world is numbered 180°. Lines of longitude measure how far east or west a place is.

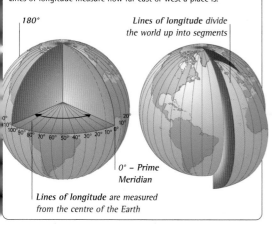

180°

Lines of longitude divide the world up into segments

0° – Prime
Meridian

Lines of longitude are measured from the centre of the Earth

CONTINENTAL MAP ▶
This map of Africa shows what the continental maps in this section look like. Physical features, such as mountains, deserts, rivers, lakes, seas, and oceans are all labelled. Countries, capital cities, and other major towns are also marked on the maps.

ELEVATION

	over 4,000 m (13,125 ft)
	2,000–4,000 m (6,500–13,125 ft)
	1,000–2,000 m (3,300–6,500 ft)
	500–1,000 m (1,600–3,300 ft)
	250–500 m (800–1,600 ft)
	100–250 m (300–800 ft)
	0–100 m (0–300 ft)
	below sea level

MAP KEY

 Congo — River

 Lake Turkana — Lake

 Kilimanjaro △5,895 m (19,340 ft) — Mountain with height in metres

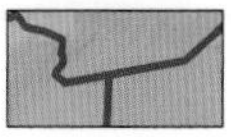

 — International border

 LUANDA — Capital city

 Benghazi — Major town

mapping

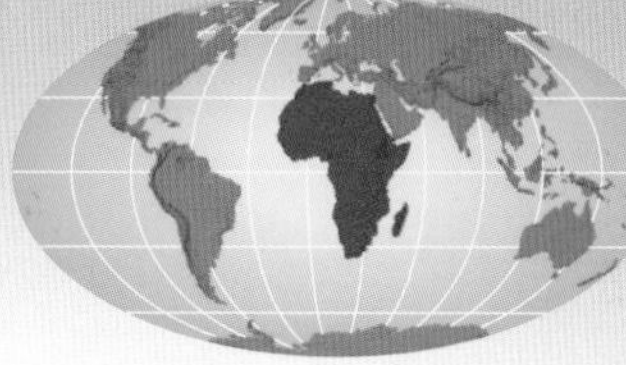

GLOBE LOCATOR ▶
Each of the seven continental map pages has a locator globe showing where in the world the continent is located. The continent is marked in red, the rest of the world in green.

REGION LOCATOR ▶
On the regional pages following each continental page, the location of the region is marked on a locator map: red for the region and green for the rest of the continent.

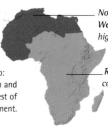

North and West Africa highlighted red

Rest of Africa coloured green

SCALE
0 km   400   800
0 miles   400   800

FIND OUT MORE ▶▶ Exploration 400–401 • Habitats 82–84

Map labels (Africa):

Mediterranean Sea, Ceuta (Spain), Melilla (Spain), Tangier, ALGIERS, Oran, Constantine, TUNIS, Kairouan, TRIPOLI, Misratah, Benghazi, Alexandria, Port Said, CAIRO, Suez Canal, El Giza, El Minya, Luxor, Aswân, Red Sea, Tropic of Cancer, ASIA, Madeira (Portugal), RABAT, Fés, Oujda, Casablanca, MOROCCO, Marrakech, Atlas Mountains, Canary Islands (Spain), LAAYOUNE, WESTERN SAHARA (disputed), ALGERIA, LIBYA, EGYPT, Libyan Desert, Sahara, Ahaggar, Tibesti, MAURITANIA, NOUAKCHOTT, MALI, NIGER, CHAD, SUDAN, ERITREA, ASMARA, Omdurman, KHARTOUM, Wad Medani, DJIBOUTI, Gulf of Aden, Horn of Africa, Hargeysa, Port Sudan, Taoudenni Basin, Senegal, Niger, CAPE VERDE, PRAIA, DAKAR, SENEGAL, BANJUL, GAMBIA, BAMAKO, OUAGADOUGOU, BURKINA FASO, NIAMEY, Maradi, Lake Chad, NDJAMENA, Kano, Sahel, White Nile, Blue Nile, Ethiopian Highlands, ADDIS ABABA, Dire Dawa, ETHIOPIA, Shebeli, SOMALIA, MOGADISHU, BISSAU, GUINEA-BISSAU, GUINEA, CONAKRY, FREETOWN, SIERRA LEONE, MONROVIA, LIBERIA, CÔTE D'IVOIRE (IVORY COAST), GHANA, BENIN, NIGERIA, Oyo, Ibadan, Lagos, ABUJA, Moundou, CENTRAL AFRICAN REPUBLIC, BANGUI, Sudd, Lake Turkana, YAMOUSSOUKRO, ACCRA, LOMÉ, PORTO-NOVO, Port Harcourt, Abidjan, Gulf of Guinea, MALABO, Douala, CAMEROON, YAOUNDÉ, Adamawa Highlands, EQUATORIAL GUINEA, SÃO TOMÉ & PRÍNCIPE, Equator, LIBREVILLE, GABON, CONGO, BRAZZAVILLE, KINSHASA, DEM. REP. CONGO, Cabinda (Angola), LUANDA, ANGOLA, Cuanza, Congo Basin, Kisangani, UGANDA, KAMPALA, Lake Victoria, RWANDA, KIGALI, BUJUMBURA, BURUNDI, KENYA, NAIROBI, Kisumu, Mwanza, Great Rift Valley, Kilimanjaro 5,895 m (19,340 ft), Mombasa, Zanzibar, Dar es Salaam, INDIAN OCEAN, Kismaayo, TANZANIA, DODOMA, Lake Tanganyika, Kananga, Lubumbashi, Kitwe, Lake Nyasa, COMOROS, MORONI, Mayotte (France), Namibe, Lubango, Menongue, Bié Plateau, ZAMBIA, LUSAKA, Zambezi, Victoria Falls, MALAWI, LILONGWE, Nacala, Mahajanga, Ovamboland, Okavango Delta, HARARE, ZIMBABWE, Beira, MOZAMBIQUE, ANTANANARIVO, MADAGASCAR, Mozambique Channel, NAMIBIA, Kalahari, BOTSWANA, WINDHOEK, Namib Desert, GABORONE, TSHWANE (PRETORIA), Johannesburg, MAPUTO, MBABANE, SWAZILAND, Réunion (France), Tropic of Capricorn, Orange River, BLOEMFONTEIN, LESOTHO, MASERU, SOUTH AFRICA, CAPE TOWN, Cape of Good Hope, Drakensberg, Port Elizabeth, ATLANTIC OCEAN

NORTH AMERICA

North America is a continent of enormous contrasts, with vast mountain ranges, huge, flat, grassy plains, hot deserts, and frozen ice caps. In the south lie the tropical islands of the Caribbean and the rainforests of Central America. To the far north a polar ice cap 3 km (2 miles) thick covers most of Greenland. Most North Americans live in the large cities on the east and west coasts. The Great Plains and deserts west of the Mississippi River are sparsely populated, as are the forests and frozen wastes of northern Canada and Alaska.

ARCTIC OCEAN

Bering Strait

Arctic Circle

Bering Sea

Aleutian Islands

Brooks Range

Beaufort Sea

Queen Eliz. Island

Yukon

ALASKA (U.S.)

Mr McKinley
6,194 m
(20,321 ft)

Anchorage

Alaska Range

Mackenzie Mountains

Victoria Isla

Great Bear Lake

YUKON TERRITORY

NORTHWEST TERRITORIES

Gre Slave I

Kodiak Island

Gulf of Alaska

Coast Mountains

Mackenzie

Slave

ROCKY MOUNTAINS

Queen Charlotte Islands

BRITISH COLUMBIA

ALBERTA

SASKAT

Edmonton

Fraser

Vancouver Island

Calgary

Vancouver

PACIFIC OCEAN

Seattle

WASHINGTON

Portland

Salem

OREGON

Boise

IDAHO

Snake

MONTANA

U N I T E
O F A

WYOM

Sacramento

San Francisco

San Jose

Reno

NEVADA

Salt Lake City

UTAH

Den

CO

Central Valley

Colorado

CALIFORNIA

Los Angeles

San Diego

Tijuana

Mexicali

ARIZONA

Phoenix

Las Vegas

Albu

N MEX

Ciudad Juarez

Hermosillo

Chih

N

Sierra Madre

California

Tropic of Cancer

Guad

▲ ROCKY MOUNTAINS

Running down the western side of North America from the Arctic in the north, to Mexico in the south, the Rocky Mountains formed about 80 million years ago. As they are relatively young, the Rockies have not yet worn down, giving them a craggy appearance.

▲ ICE HOCKEY

Ice hockey is Canada's favourite game, with millions of people watching every major game live or on television. Teams of skaters use long, curved sticks to try and get a hard rubber disc, called a puck, into the opposing team's goal. The Canadian men's and women's teams both won gold medals in the 2002 Winter Olympics.

◄ PRAIRIES

The Great Plains, or prairies, of central Canada and the USA lie between the Rocky Mountains and the Mississippi River valley. Vast herds of buffalo once roamed these grassy plains, but today they are largely agricultural, producing wheat in the north and corn in the south.

Map labels

Greenland (Denmark)

Baffin Bay

Baffin Island

Davis Strait

NUUK

NAVUT

Labrador Sea

Hudson Strait

Ungava Peninsula

Hudson Bay

Newfoundland Strait

NEWFOUNDLAND & LABRADOR

St. John's

Cape Race

Newfoundland

St. Pierre & Miquelon (France)

QUEBEC

Laurentian Mountains

PRINCE EDWARD ISLAND

NEW BRUNSWICK

Quebec

Halifax

NOVA SCOTIA

MAINE

D A

TOBA

ONTARIO

Great Lakes

Lake Superior

Thunder Bay

Montreal

Lawrence

NEW HAMPSHIRE

Boston

Cape Cod

MASS.

RHODE IS.

CONNECTICUT

New York

NEW JERSEY

Philadelphia

DELAWARE

WASHINGTON D.C.

MARYLAND

MINNESOTA

MICHIGAN

Lake Huron

Toronto

OTTAWA

VERMONT

NEW YORK

WISCONSIN

Lake Michigan

Milwaukee

Detroit

Cleveland

OHIO

PENNSYLVANIA

Lake Erie

Lake Ontario

Columbus

WEST VIRGINIA

Chicago

INDIANA

Indianapolis

Des Moines

IOWA

innepolis

RICA

ILLINOIS

MISSOURI

KENTUCKY

Nashville

TENNESSEE

Memphis

ARKANSAS

Little Rock

OKLAHOMA

Arkansas

Red River

Dallas

LOUISIANA

New Orleans

Houston

San Antonio

Mississippi Delta

VIRGINIA

Cape Hatteras

NORTH CAROLINA

SOUTH CAROLINA

Appalachian Mountains

Atlanta

GEORGIA

ALABAMA

MISSISSIPPI

Jackson

Jacksonville

Tallahassee

FLORIDA

Tampa

Miami

ATLANTIC OCEAN

BAHAMAS

NASSAU

Tropic of Cancer

Straits of Florida

CUBA

Santa Clara

HAVANA

Santiago de Cuba

Cayman Islands (U.K.)

JAMAICA

KINGSTON

Méda

HAITI

PORT-AU-PRINCE

SANTO DOMINGO

DOMINICAN REPUBLIC

Turks & Caicos Islands (U.K.)

Puerto Rico (U.S.)

British Virgin Islands (U.K.)

Virgin Islands (U.S.)

Anguilla (U.K.)

ST. KITTS & NEVIS

ANTIGUA & BARBUDA

Guadeloupe (France)

DOMINICA

Martinique (France)

Montserrat (U.K.)

ST. LUCIA

BARBADOS

ST. VINCENT & THE GRENADINES

GRENADA

Netherlands Antilles (Neth.)

Aruba (Neth.)

TRINIDAD & TOBAGO

PORT-OF-SPAIN

Caribbean Sea

Luis Potosí

Bay of Campeche

Yucatan Peninsula

MEXICO CITY

Puebla

BELIZE

BELMOPAN

HONDURAS

San Pedro Sula

GUATEMALA

GUATEMALA CITY

TEGUCIGALPA

SAN SALVADOR

EL SALVADOR

MANAGUA

NICARAGUA

SAN JOSÉ

PANAMA CITY

PANAMA

COSTA RICA

SOUTH AMERICA

Gulf of Mexico

Monterrey

CO

Rio Grande

0 km 400 800

0 miles 400 800

Captions

▲ STATUE OF LIBERTY, NEW YORK
The Statue of Liberty was erected in 1886 and stands 93 m (305 ft) tall in New York Harbor. It was the first thing millions of immigrants saw as they sailed into New York in the 1800s and 1900s to start a new life. The statue has become a symbol of freedom and opportunity.

JUNKANOO FESTIVAL ▶
Extravagant carnivals, such as the Junkanoo Festival in the Bahamas, are held throughout the Caribbean. People dress up in flamboyant costumes, stage elaborate parades, and dance in the street in the days before Lent, the 40-day period of fasting and restraint leading up to the Christian festival of Easter.

e ▶▶ North America

NORTH AMERICA
Total land area: 24,238,000 sq km (9,358,340 sq miles)

Total population: 501 million

Number of countries: 23

Largest country: Canada 9,984,670 sq km (3,855,171 sq miles)

Smallest country: St Kitts & Nevis 261 sq km (101 sq miles)

Largest country population: USA 294 million

Largest lake: Lake Superior, Canada/USA 83,270 sq km (32,151 sq miles)

Longest river: Mississippi-Missouri, USA 5,969 km (3,710 miles)

Highest point: Mt McKinley (Denali), Alaska, USA 6,194 m (20,322 ft)

Major deserts: Great Basin, Mojave, Sonoran, and Chihuahuan deserts

Largest island: Greenland 2,175,219 sq km (839,852 sq miles)

FIND OUT MORE ▶▶ American Revolution 414 • Colonial America 409 • Competitions 354–355 • Early Americans 380

CANADA, ALASKA, AND GREENLAND

Northern North America is occupied by Canada, the second largest country in the world, the US state of Alaska, and the Danish self-governing territory of Greenland. Much of Greenland is covered by ice and all these regions are sparsely populated, although there are several large cities in Canada. These are mainly in the south of the country and on the Pacific coast near the stunning Rocky Mountains. Huge oil and mineral reserves have brought wealth to both Canada and Alaska.

▲ TRANS-ALASKAN PIPELINE
The Trans-Alaskan pipeline runs 1,270 km (789 miles) from the oilfields of Prudhoe Bay in the Arctic Ocean, south to the ice-free port of Valdez. The pipeline is raised on stilts above the ground to prevent disruption of moose and caribou migration routes and to stop the oil from freezing.

HOW DID ALASKA BECOME PART OF AMERICA?
Alaska was part of Russia until 1867, when it was sold to the USA for $7.2 million. Most Americans thought this was a huge waste of money until gold was discovered there in 1896, attracting many people hoping to make their fortune. The discovery of oil in the Arctic Ocean in 1968 brought great wealth to the state, and tourism is also a major source of income.

▼ NATIVE PEOPLES
The Aleut and the Inuit, the native peoples of Alaska and northern Canada respectively, have adapted to their harsh environment, combining modern technology with a traditional lifestyle of hunting and fishing.

FISHING, NEWFOUNDLAND ▶
Fishing has traditionally been a major industry of Newfoundland, with huge stocks of fish once found off the east coast. Sadly, over-fishing has greatly reduced these stocks, and catches are now severely restricted.

e ▸▸
Alaska

Sled races between rival teams are fiercely contested

Team of huskies pulls a sled across the ice

WHO ARE CANADA'S NATIVE PEOPLES?
The First Nations and the Inuit peoples lived in Canada long before Europeans began settling there in the 17th century. They number about 900,000 people, or 4 per cent of the population, and have kept many of their traditional customs and traditions. In 1999, the self-governing Inuit homeland of Nunavut was created in the north of Canada.

WHAT IS LIFE LIKE IN GREENLAND?
Greenland is the world's largest island, but has a population of less than 60,000 because its climate is so harsh and cold. Most live in small settlements along the coast, making a living from catching fish, shrimp, and seals. There is a small network of roads, but dog sleds and planes are more reliable than cars for getting around.

Greenland

CANADA, ALASKA, & GREENLAND	
ALASKA (US STATE)	🇺🇸
Capital city: Juneau	
Area: 1,477,268 sq km (570,374 sq miles)	
Population: 643,000	
Official language: English	
Major religion: Christian	
Currency: US dollar	
CANADA	🇨🇦
Capital city: Ottawa	
Area: 9,984,670 sq km (3,855,171 sq miles)	
Population: 31.5 million	
Official languages: English and French	
Major religion: Roman Catholic	
Currency: Canadian dollar	
GREENLAND	
Capital city: Nuuk (Godthab)	
Area: 2,175,219 sq km (839,852 sq miles)	
Population: 56,385	
Official languages: Greenlandic and Danish	
Major religion: Lutheran	
Currency: Danish krone	

WHY IS CANADA BILINGUAL?

Until the middle of the 18th century, large parts of eastern Canada were ruled by France and many French people settled there, mainly in Quebec. Today, one-quarter of Canadians speak French as their first language. Canada is officially bilingual and recognizes both English and French as its official languages, but some French speakers in Quebec want to leave Canada and set up their own independent state.

▲ TORONTO, CANADA
The Toronto skyline is dominated by the CN Tower, currently the world's second-tallest free-standing structure at 555 m (1,822 ft). Toronto is Canada's biggest city and its main commercial and industrial centre.

▼ NIAGARA FALLS
About 180 million litres (40 million gallons) of water plunge over Niagara Falls every minute. The falls are 58 m (190 ft) high, and lie between lakes Erie and Ontario on the border between the USA and Canada.

▲ BANFF, CANADA
Spectacular scenery like this is one of the reasons Canada is such a popular tourist destination. Banff National Park, in Alberta, is in the majestic Rocky Mountains.

Canada

Rainbows
often form
in the mist

HOW DO CANADIANS COPE WITH THE COLD?

One-third of Canada lies within the Arctic Circle, and much of the land is permanently frozen. Farming in the north is therefore impossible, and food supplies are flown in from outside. Houses are built on stilts above the snow, and pipes are heavily insulated against the cold. Further south, large cities such as Montreal and Toronto have underground shopping centres so that shoppers can stay inside during winter.

FIND OUT MORE ▸▸ Canada 417 • Fishing 67

EASTERN USA

The eastern half of the USA is the most heavily populated part of the country, with many Americans living in the large cities along the east coast. The national capital, Washington, D.C., is situated here, as are the 13 original states that founded the country in 1776. To the north, the Great Lakes and St Lawrence River separate the region from Canada.

WHO IS THE CAPITAL NAMED AFTER?

Washington, D.C., (the D.C. stands for District of Columbia) is named after George Washington, commander-in-chief of the American army in the Revolutionary War against Britain, and first president of the USA. Washington is the political capital of the USA, and the home of the American president.

WHAT ARE THE EVERGLADES?

This huge expanse of marsh and swampland in southern Florida is a haven for many rare creatures, such as the Florida panther and the manatee. Drainage schemes to create more land for building and farming threaten to reduce the size of the Everglades and destroy the habitat of these creatures forever.

▲ EVERGLADES, FLORIDA
During the wet summer months, alligators, snakes, and other inhabitants of the Everglades can move freely throughout the national park. In contrast, the dry winter months reduce their habitat to the areas around the few remaining water holes.

WHY IS THE USA KNOWN AS A MELTING POT?

The USA calls itself a melting pot of different peoples because, over the centuries, people from all over the world have come to the USA to join the original American Indian population. Some came as slaves from Africa, others fled religious or political persecution in Europe, and many more escaped poverty to start again. The USA is proud of its rich mix of peoples, although racial tension and segregation continue to be major problems.

◄ FALL LEAVES, NEW ENGLAND
The large deciduous forests that cover much of New England turn vibrant shades of red, orange, and yellow during the fall, or autumn season. Tourists come here to see this spectacular display of colour, as well as to fish, hike, ski, or just enjoy the scenery.

▼ NEW YORK CITY
The Manhattan skyline in New York is one of the most famous in the world, with huge skyscrapers towering over the city's streets. New York is the business centre of the USA, as well as its cultural capital.

WHAT IS THANKSGIVING?

The first Thanksgiving feast was held in 1621 as a gesture of friendship between the Pilgrim Fathers (immigrants from England) and American Indians, after their first successful joint harvest. Ever since, Americans have celebrated Thanksgiving in November with a traditional meal of turkey and other food.

WHY IS THE USA SO POWERFUL?

The economic strength and wealth of the USA have made it the most powerful nation on Earth. It uses its huge wealth to maintain vast armed services and employ the latest military technology, making it the world's only superpower. US companies dominate the international economy, while American popular music and films have a major impact on global culture.

SHUTTLE, FLORIDA ▶
The Kennedy Space Center at Cape Canaveral, Florida, is the launch site for the space shuttle and the rest of the US space programme. Staff have to check the runway for stray alligators and bobcats before the shuttle can land safely after its mission.

External fuel tank and solid rocket booster lift shuttle into space

Space shuttle, or orbiter, has three main engines and carries seven crew members

USA

Discovery

e ▶▶
eastern US

WHY DO ROCKETS BLAST OFF FROM FLORIDA?

NASA (the National Aeronautics and Space Administration) blasts its rockets, shuttles, and satellites into space from Cape Canaveral on the east coast of Florida. The site was chosen because it enjoys year-round good weather, and its remoteness means that few people are disturbed by the noise of a launch.

WHAT HAPPENS WHEN THE MISSISSIPPI FLOODS?

The Mississippi river causes huge destruction every time it floods, inundating towns and farmland, killing livestock, ruining crops, and causing billions of dollars-worth of damage. The floods occur naturally through heavy rain and snowfall, but deforestation and intensive cultivation have made the problem worse.

▲ THE GREAT LAKES
The five Great Lakes–Superior, Michigan, Huron, Ontario, and Erie–mark the border between the USA and Canada. The lakes are linked by the St Lawrence Seaway to the Atlantic Ocean, so cargo can be carried far inland.

USA
Capital city: Washington, D.C.
Area: 9,629,091 sq km (3,717,792 sq miles)
Population: 294 million
Dominant language: English
Major religion: Protestant
Currency: US dollar

NEW YORK YANKEES ▶
Major League baseball teams such as the New York Yankees have a huge following throughout the country. The game is one of the most popular spectator sports in the USA, along with American football and basketball.

THE CAPITOL, WASHINGTON, D.C. ▲
The Capitol in Washington, D.C. is the home of Congress, the US legislature, or parliament. Congressmen and senators represent every state and region of the USA and meet to pass laws and oversee the president and Supreme Court. The president of the USA lives a short distance away on Pennsylvania Avenue in the White House.

FIND OUT MORE ▶▶ American Revolution 414 • Colonial America 409 • Space Shuttle 32

WESTERN USA

Beyond the Mississippi valley, the western USA rises gently through the vast expanses of the Great Plains until it reaches the Rocky Mountains. The land then drops down again to the coastal ranges and plains of the Pacific coast, where there are forests, fruit groves, and farms, as well as deserts and rocky, flat-topped hills. Most people live in the southwestern states, or in cities along the Pacific coastline.

LOS ANGELES ▶
The best way to get around most American cities is by car. Freeways such as this six-lane highway in Los Angeles (LA) carry thousands of cars every day. Combined with sun, heat, and fog, their pollution produces the brown smog for which LA is famous.

◀ SAN FRANCISCO
Cable cars run throughout the hilly Californian city of San Francisco. The cars fasten onto a constantly moving wire cable, gripping it tightly on the way up a hill, and then releasing it to glide down the other side.

HOW FERTILE IS THE WEST COAST?
The Pacific coast is hugely productive. Its soils are rich, its rivers provide extensive irrigation, and the sun shines all year. Apples are grown in Washington State, while California produces vegetables and citrus fruit, as well as Napa Valley grapes that make some of the best wines in the world.

▼ YOSEMITE NATIONAL PARK
The first national park to be created in the USA was Yosemite, in central California. Its scenery is spectacular, with towering cliffs, tumbling waterfalls, and more than 2,000 varieties of plants and animals, including brown bears.

WHY DOES LOS ANGELES HAVE TROUBLE WITH POLLUTION?
Los Angeles is the centre of a sprawling built-up area with a total population of 15 million people. Public transport is limited, so everyone travels by car. As the city is sandwiched between the coast and a ring of surrounding mountains, air pollution is extremely high.

DO AMERICAN INDIANS HAVE THEIR OWN LAND?
The American Indians who once wandered freely across the whole of the USA, hunting buffalo and living off the land, now live mainly on reservations. Here they control their own affairs, but the land is often poor and jobs are scarce, so many leave the reservations to live and work elsewhere.

WHY IS THE PACIFIC COAST A DANGEROUS AREA TO LIVE IN?
The San Andreas, San Fernando, and Santa Monica fault lines cause frequent earth tremors and sometimes earthquakes, especially in the San Francisco area. Long periods without rain often lead to serious bush fires that threaten the West Coast's big cities, and flooding is a major problem because of sinking coastal areas.

WHAT IS DEATH VALLEY?

Sheltered by mountains from the Pacific coastline are some of the driest, hottest regions of North America. One of these, Death Valley in California, has very little rainfall and temperatures that soar to 57°C (134°F). Its landscape is bleak but magnificent, attracting tourists to see its many canyons and strange rock formations.

▲ COWBOY RODEO
The vast cattle ranches that stretch from Montana down to Texas still need cowboys to watch over their cattle, although today, trucks and even helicopters are used alongside horses. Traditional cowboy skills are still celebrated at rodeos and stampedes.

◄ MONUMENT VALLEY
Millions of years of erosion have created the amazing cliffs and rock pinnacles of Monument Valley in northern Arizona. The area is a centre of Navajo culture. It has also starred as the backdrop for many films.

George Washington   *Thomas Jefferson*   *Theodore Roosevelt*   *Abraham Lincoln*

MOUNT RUSHMORE ▲
The faces of four great US presidents gaze out from a granite cliff on Mount Rushmore in South Dakota. The four faces, each about 18 m (60 ft) high, were carved between 1927 and 1941 by 400 workers.

WHAT MAKES TEXAS RICH?

The wealth of Texas comes mainly from oil, which was discovered there in 1901. As well as being the second largest oil-producing state in the USA after Alaska, Texas is rich in iron ore, magnesium, uranium, and other minerals. Cattle ranching and cotton farming also help make it one of the wealthier states.

CAN YOU SEE THE GRAND CANYON FROM SPACE?

The Grand Canyon is the largest land gorge on Earth, and is easily visible from Space. The canyon runs through northern Arizona and is more than 1.6 km (1 mile) deep and 446 km (277 miles) long. It was formed by the Colorado River cutting through a rocky plateau for over a million years, exposing at its lowest point some of the oldest rocks in North America.

western US

FIND OUT MORE ▶▶ American Indians 408 • Earthquakes 43

MEXICO, CENTRAL AMERICA, AND THE CARIBBEAN

From the high snowy mountains and hot arid deserts of northern Mexico, south to the lush tropical forests of Nicaragua's Atlantic coast, this is a region of great contrasts. Central America consists of seven small countries on the thin land bridge between Mexico and South America. To its east lie the beautiful tropical islands of the Caribbean Sea.

TELESCOPES, MEXICO ▶
The clean air and high altitude of the Sierra Madre in Mexico make it an ideal location for radio telescopes. They tune into radio waves from Space, which are then converted into electronic images.

CARIBBEAN ISLANDS ▶
The sandy beaches of the Caribbean islands are popular destinations for tourists avoiding winter in the USA or Europe. Cruise ships also visit the many islands, their passengers helping to support local economies.

◀ AZTECS, MEXICO
Buildings and remains from the Aztec Empire, such as this imposing statue, still exist throughout central Mexico. Most of the Aztec capital, Tenochtitlan, is buried beneath Mexico City.

PANAMA CANAL ▶
More than 80 km (50 miles) long, the Panama Canal connects the Atlantic and Pacific Oceans. More than 14,000 ships a year sail through it, from tankers and cargo vessels to cruise liners.

e ▶▶
Mexico

WHAT REMAINS OF MAYA AND AZTEC CIVILIZATIONS?

The Mayan and Aztec empires no longer exist, but both civilizations have left behind the ruins of many amazing buildings. Mayan temples and cities can be found in the forests of Belize and Guatemala, and ancient Aztec remains are still being uncovered beneath the buildings of Mexico City.

WHAT IS THE DAY OF THE DEAD?

Every year, on 1 November, Mexicans honour their dead family and friends in a celebration called the Day of the Dead. They believe death is a part of life and should be celebrated. They decorate the streets with flowers and hang up ghoulish papier-mâché skeletons. Families gather together to pray to the dead and visit family graves.

DO NATIVE PEOPLES STILL LIVE IN CENTRAL AMERICA?

Native peoples lived in Central America for centuries until Europeans conquered the region during the 1500s. As a result, many people today are mestizos (of mixed European and Native American descent). Native peoples themselves make up less than 10 per cent of the total population.

DIA DE LOS MUERTOS ▼
On the Day of the Dead, people dress up as skeletons and dance in huge parades. At home, families make small altars which they decorate with flowers, candles, food, and photographs of those they want to remember.

▲ CARIBBEAN BANANAS
Caribbean islands such as Dominica, St Lucia, and St Vincent are heavily dependent on the export of bananas to the USA and Europe for their income. The loss of these markets to cheaper bananas from Central America threatens many farmers' livelihoods.

WHAT ARE THE CARIBBEAN'S BIGGEST EXPORTS?

The Caribbean islands export sugar, bananas, tobacco, coffee, rum, and more recently illegal drugs. But its biggest exports are people and culture. Poverty led many islanders to migrate to the USA or Europe, taking with them an extraordinarily vibrant culture.

WHY ARE THERE SO MANY ISLANDS IN THE CARIBBEAN?

The eastern Caribbean islands sit on the edge of a small plate (section) of the Earth's crust surrounded by bigger plates. As these plates were forced into each other over millions of years, they created a chain of volcanic islands. Most of the volcanoes are now extinct, but some, such as Soufrière Hills volcano in Montserrat, have erupted recently.

WHY ARE MANY CENTRAL AMERICAN COUNTRIES POOR?

In recent years, Central American nations have lost a lot of income as the prices for exports of coffee, bananas, and other cash crops have fallen. At the same time, they borrowed money from abroad to pay for new roads, hospitals, and other projects, leaving them heavily in debt. Political instability and civil war have helped keep countries in this region very poor.

WHAT IS LIFE LIKE IN MEXICO CITY?

Life is tough in Mexico City, as housing is often poor and earthquakes are a constant threat. The city is home to more than 20 million people, making it one of the largest cities in the world. It is very polluted because a ring of mountains surrounds it, stopping polluted air from cars and factories escaping.

e ▶▶
Central America

e ▶▶
Caribbean

MEXICO CITY ▶
Despite being a huge, bustling city, the lack of environmental controls and poor public transport give Mexico City one of the worst air qualities of any city in the world. Children sometimes have to wait until after the rush hour to go to school, to avoid car fumes.

NORTH AMERICA	
MEXICO	
Capital: Mexico City	
CENTRAL AMERICA	
GUATEMALA	
Capital: Guatemala City	
BELIZE	
Capital: Belmopan	
EL SALVADOR	
Capital: San Salvador	
HONDURAS	
Capital: Tegucigalpa	
NICARAGUA	
Capital: Managua	
COSTA RICA	
Capital: San José	
PANAMA	
Capital: Panama City	
CARIBBEAN ISLANDS	
CUBA	
Capital: Havana	
BAHAMAS	
Capital: Nassau	
JAMAICA	
Capital: Kingston	
HAITI	
Capital: Port-au-Prince	
DOMINICAN REPUBLIC	
Capital: Santo Domingo	
ARUBA	
Capital: Oranjestad	
PUERTO RICO	
Capital: San Juan	
ST KITTS & NEVIS	
Capital: Basseterre	
ANTIGUA & BARBUDA	
Capital: St John's	
GUADELOUPE	
Capital: Basse-Terre	
DOMINICA	
Capital: Roseau	
MARTINIQUE	
Capital: Fort-de-France	
ST LUCIA	
Capital: Castries	
BARBADOS	
Capital: Bridgetown	
ST VINCENT & THE GRENADINES	
Capital: Kingstown	
GRENADA	
Capital: St George's	
NETHERLANDS ANTILLES	
Capital: Willemstad	
TRINIDAD & TOBAGO	
Capital: Port-of-Spain	

FIND OUT MORE ▶▶ Astronomy 11 • Aztecs 403 • Continents 39 • Islands 42 • Maya 381

SOUTH AMERICA

The triangular-shaped continent of South America stretches from north of the Equator almost down to the Antarctic Circle. It contains three very different landscapes. In the west, the Andes tower up 6,959 m (22,833 ft) in height, forming a backbone down the entire length of the continent along the Pacific Ocean coast. Dense rainforests in the humid Amazon valley and along the Caribbean coast cover much of the north and northeast. In the south, windswept grasslands and dry pampas roll down to the cold, rocky point of the continent at Cape Horn.

◄ **ATACAMA DESERT**
The Atacama Desert in northern Chile is the driest place on Earth – in places it has not rained at all for a century. When rain does fall, devastating flash floods are often the result. There are huge deposits of copper under its sun-baked rocks and shifting sands.

▲ **SÃO PAULO, BRAZIL**
One of the biggest cities in the world and also one of the fastest growing, greater São Paulo has a population of around 20 million people. Because much of the interior of South America is uninhabitable, all its biggest cities are on the coast. Many people move to these cities in search of work and a better standard of living.

PERUVIAN TEXTILES ►
The hand-woven, brightly coloured woollen textiles worn by these Peruvian women are based on traditional Indian designs that have been handed down through the generations.

▲ **THE ANDES**
The world's longest mountain chain, the Andes, runs 7,250 km (4,505 miles) down the western edge of South America. Its steep slopes are terraced to grow barley, potatoes, and wheat on its colder, upper slopes, and coffee, tobacco, and corn on the warmer, lower slopes.

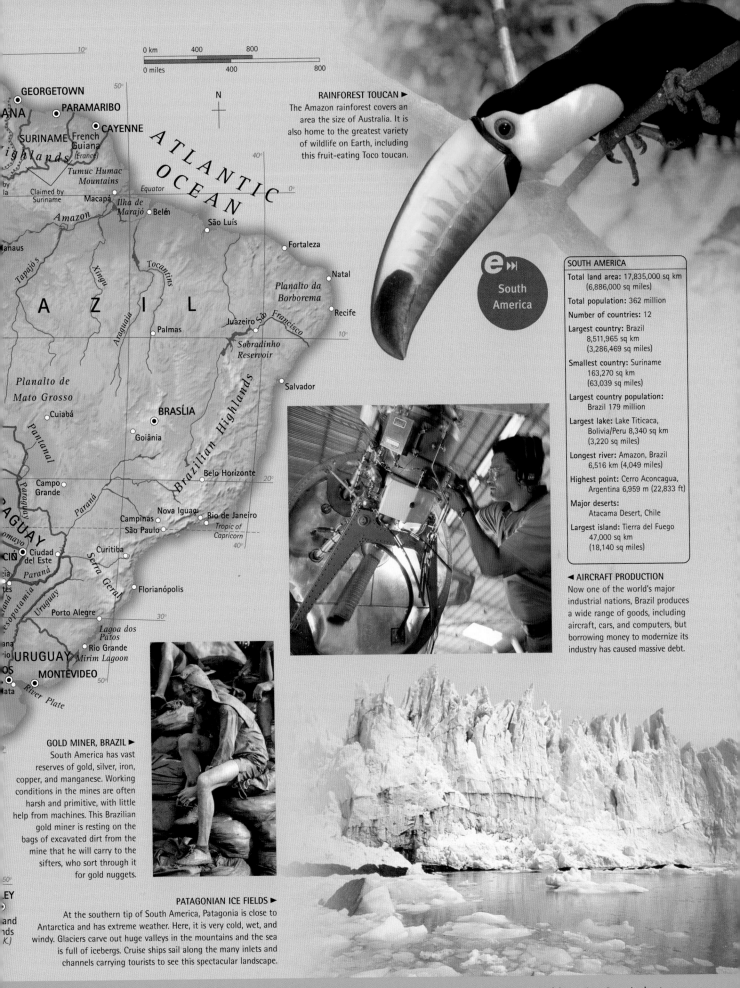

0 km   400   800
0 miles   400   800

GEORGETOWN
PARAMARIBO
CAYENNE
SURINAME   French Guiana (France)
Highlands
Tumuc Humac Mountains
Claimed by Suriname
Macapá
Amazon   Ilha de Marajó   Belém
Manaus
São Luís
Tapajós
Xingu
Tocantins
Fortaleza
Natal
Planalto da Borborema
Recife
B R A Z I L
Araguaia
Juàzeiro   São Francisco
Palmas
Sobradinho Reservoir
Planalto de Mato Grosso
Salvador
Pantanal
Cuiabá
BRASÍLIA
Goiânia
Brazilian Highlands
Campo Grande
Belo Horizonte
Paraná
PARAGUAY
Campinas
Nova Iguaçu
Rio de Janeiro
Tropic of Capricorn
São Paulo
Ciudad del Este
Curitiba
Serra Geral
Paraná
Florianópolis
Uruguay
Porto Alegre
Lagoa dos Patos
URUGUAY
Rio Grande
Mirim Lagoon
MONTEVIDEO
River Plate

ATLANTIC OCEAN
Equator

N

RAINFOREST TOUCAN ▶
The Amazon rainforest covers an area the size of Australia. It is also home to the greatest variety of wildlife on Earth, including this fruit-eating Toco toucan.

e ▶▶
South America

SOUTH AMERICA
Total land area: 17,835,000 sq km (6,886,000 sq miles)

Total population: 362 million

Number of countries: 12

Largest country: Brazil 8,511,965 sq km (3,286,469 sq miles)

Smallest country: Suriname 163,270 sq km (63,039 sq miles)

Largest country population: Brazil 179 million

Largest lake: Lake Titicaca, Bolivia/Peru 8,340 sq km (3,220 sq miles)

Longest river: Amazon, Brazil 6,516 km (4,049 miles)

Highest point: Cerro Aconcagua, Argentina 6,959 m (22,833 ft)

Major deserts: Atacama Desert, Chile

Largest island: Tierra del Fuego 47,000 sq km (18,140 sq miles)

◀ AIRCRAFT PRODUCTION
Now one of the world's major industrial nations, Brazil produces a wide range of goods, including aircraft, cars, and computers, but borrowing money to modernize its industry has caused massive debt.

GOLD MINER, BRAZIL ▶
South America has vast reserves of gold, silver, iron, copper, and manganese. Working conditions in the mines are often harsh and primitive, with little help from machines. This Brazilian gold miner is resting on the bags of excavated dirt from the mine that he will carry to the sifters, who sort through it for gold nuggets.

PATAGONIAN ICE FIELDS ▶
At the southern tip of South America, Patagonia is close to Antarctica and has extreme weather. Here, it is very cold, wet, and windy. Glaciers carve out huge valleys in the mountains and the sea is full of icebergs. Cruise ships sail along the many inlets and channels carrying tourists to see this spectacular landscape.

FIND OUT MORE ▶▶ Exploration 400–401 • Habitats 82–84 • Industry 204

One of the two mountain peaks that overlook this high city

NORTHERN SOUTH AMERICA

Spanish influence remains strong in the four countries in this region that were once Spanish colonies (Peru, Ecuador, Colombia, and Venezuela). The others were colonized by Britain (Guyana), the Netherlands (Suriname), and France (French Guiana) – the last European colony. The people are a mix of native peoples, Europeans, and descendants of African slaves.

◄ **MACHU PICCHU, PERU**
The ancient Inca city of Machu Picchu, high up in the Andes in Peru, was never discovered by the Spanish conquerors and gradually fell into ruin. It was found in 1911 and is now a major tourist sight.

SALT MINING, COLOMBIA ►
Along Colombia's flat Caribbean coast, workers remove sand to create tidal pools, which are flooded at high tide. The sun dries them out, leaving sea salt behind.

Steep hillsides are terraced for housing and farming

More than 3,000 steps connect the different levels

Temples, homes, and other ceremonial buildings are built around a central square

WHAT IS LATIN AMERICA?
South America is sometimes called Latin America because most South Americans speak the Latin-based languages Spanish and Portuguese. They learned these from Spanish and Portuguese invaders, who conquered and settled most of South America in the 16th century. Many strong ties of language, culture, and religion still link Latin America, Spain, and Portugal.

HOW DO PEOPLE MAKE A LIVING IN THE ANDES?
Most people in the Andes are farmers. Because fertile land is scarce, they cut terraces into the steep hillsides. Crops are chosen to suit either the hot, humid climate of the lower slopes or the cooler climate higher up. Animals such as the llama and alpaca are also kept for food and wool, which is used for clothing.

HAVE NATURAL RESOURCES HELPED NORTHERN SOUTH AMERICA?
This region has immense oil and mineral wealth: the oil reserves in Venezuela are the biggest outside the Middle East, and Colombia produces over half the world's emeralds. But despite this wealth, public services have been neglected, and many people remain poor because the dangerous mining work is low-paid.

ARE ECUADOR'S MANGROVE SWAMPS IN DANGER?
The mangrove swamps of Ecuador's Pacific coast teem with shrimp, and are a vital source of food, firewood, and timber for local people. Shrimp are Ecuador's second biggest export after oil, but while large shrimp farms have created much-needed jobs, they are slowly destroying the environment on which they depend.

e ►► northern South America

▲ TOMATO HARVEST, ECUADOR
The hot, humid coastal plain of Ecuador has an ideal climate for growing tomatoes and other important crops, such as bananas, coffee, and cocoa, which are produced on an industrial scale for export.

WHAT IS HAPPENING TO SOUTH AMERICA'S RAINFORESTS?

About 30 per cent of all the world's plant and animal species live in the Amazon rainforest in Brazil, as well as many native Indian tribes. Since 1970, vast swathes of forest have been cut down for timber, or to clear land for cattle pasture or new roads. Similar problems are facing the forests of Colombia and Ecuador.

◄ BOGOTÁ, COLOMBIA
The Colombian capital of Bogotá lies on a plateau in the eastern Andes and has a cool, damp climate. The city is the financial centre of the country and home to about five million people.

▲ ROCKETS, FRENCH GUIANA
French Guiana, the only remaining European colony in South America, is home to the European Space Agency launch site. From here, Ariane rockets carry satellites into space.

WHAT REMAINS OF THE INCA CIVILIZATION IN SOUTH AMERICA?

The Spanish destroyed the Inca Empire in the 1530s, but many buildings and some towns survived, such as the hilltop city of Machu Picchu. The Quechua Indians were the most powerful Incas, and groups of them still live on the high plains in the Andes.

WHAT ARE THE LOST WORLDS OF VENEZUELA?

More than 100 flat-topped sandstone hills called tepuis tower up to 1,000 m (3,300 ft) above Venezuela's rainforests. They are called "lost worlds" because their remoteness has meant that unique animals and plants have evolved there.

HOW DO THE OTAVALO INDIANS MAKE A LIVING?

Ecuador's Otavalo Indians have adapted to modern life and are one of wealthiest Indian groups in South America. They weave colourful ponchos, blankets, and rugs, which are in great demand in the USA and Europe. The income this generates enables the Otavalo to continue their traditional way of life.

Llama carries heavy loads at high altitudes

Quechua Indian woman wearing a distinctive hat with a four-quarters-of-the-world design

NORTHERN SOUTH AMERICA

PERU

Capital city: Lima

Area: 1,285,000 sq km (496,141 sq miles)

Population: 27.2 million

Official languages: Spanish and Quechua

Major religion: Roman Catholic

Currency: New sol

ECUADOR

Capital city: Quito

Area: 283,560 sq km (109,483 sq miles)

Population: 13 million

Official language: Spanish

Major religion: Roman Catholic

Currency: US dollar

COLOMBIA

Capital city: Bogotá

Area: 1,138,910 sq km (439,733 sq miles)

Population: 44.2 million

Official language: Spanish

Major religion: Roman Catholic

Currency: Colombian peso

VENEZUELA

Capital city: Caracas

Area: 912,050 sq km (352,143 sq miles)

Population: 25.7 million

Official language: Spanish

Major religion: Roman Catholic

Currency: Bolívar

GUYANA

Capital city: Georgetown

Area: 214,970 sq km (83,000 sq miles)

Population: 765,000

Official language: English

Major religion: Christian

Currency: Guyana dollar

SURINAME

Capital city: Paramaribo

Area: 163,270 sq km (63,039 sq miles)

Population: 436,000

Official language: Dutch

Major religions: Hindu, Protestant, Roman Catholic, and Muslim

Currency: Suriname dollar

FRENCH GUIANA

Capital city: Cayenne

Area: 90,000 sq km (34,749 sq miles)

Population: 186,917

Official language: French

Major religion: Roman Catholic

Currency: Euro

◄ PERUVIAN WOMAN
The Quechua Indians keep llamas and alpacas – close relatives of the camel – which thrive in the high Andes of Peru and Bolivia. Alpacas are kept for their long, soft wool, and llamas carry loads and provide wool, milk, and meat.

SOUTHERN SOUTH AMERICA

Brazil is the giant of South America, occupying almost half the continent and containing more than half its people. Once-rich Argentina has been impoverished by corrupt government, and all six countries in this region have had long periods of military or dictatorial rule in recent years, although all now have elected governments.

HOW LONG IS THE AMAZON RIVER?

The Amazon River is 6,516 km (4,049 miles) long, which makes it the longest river in South America and second longest in the world after the Nile. It flows from the Peruvian Andes eastwards across Brazil to the Atlantic Ocean. The Amazon carries one-fifth of the world's fresh water and discharges so much water into the Atlantic that seawater 180 km (112 miles) out to sea is still only slightly salty.

WHAT ARE THE PAMPAS?

The Pampas are vast, fertile grasslands that stretch across Argentina and Uruguay. This land is ideal for growing wheat and other cereals and for feeding vast herds of sheep and cattle, all of which are extremely important to the two national economies. Gauchos (cowboys) rode the Pampas for 300 years, working on cattle ranches, but there are few left now as their role has largely disappeared.

▲ GAUCHOS
These cowboys look after cattle on ranches. The name comes from a South American Indian word for "outcast", as they used to live outside towns and cities and beyond the law.

◀ FAVELAS, BRAZIL
Living conditions are poor in the crowded favelas, or slums, that surround the main cities of Brazil. Many inhabitants suffer from bad health due to inadequate drainage and sanitation.

RIVER AMAZON ▶
The Amazon is an important waterway for Brazil. Ships can travel inland as far as Manaus, about 1,600 km (994 miles) from the sea, and floods deposit fertile silt on the land.

WHAT ARE FAVELAS?

The favelas are the sprawling shanty towns around most of the big cities in South America, notably Rio de Janeiro and São Paulo in Brazil. Overcrowding and the lack of affordable housing in the cities force poor people to build their own homes from scrap metal and junk. The favelas have little running water or sanitation. Recent self-help schemes have begun to introduce some basic amenities, but progress is slow.

DO NATIVE INDIANS STILL LIVE IN THE RAINFORESTS?

There were once more than two million native Indians living in the Amazon rainforest, but today only about 240,000 survive. Most of them were wiped out by western diseases such as influenza and measles. Deforestation, farming, and gold prospecting are a threat to the habitat of many tribes, although some, like the Xingu, now live in protected areas.

KAYAPO INDIAN ▶
The headdress of this Kayapo Indian elder from the Amazon rainforest is made of feathers from the macaw and the stork. Unfortunately, both birds are now endangered species in Brazil.

▲ CAR INDUSTRY, BRAZIL
Brazil is a major industrial nation, producing iron, steel, computers, aircraft, and cars, such as this Volkswagen/Audi assembly line at San Jose dos Pinhais. The country is also rich in minerals and is a major exporter of coffee, sugar, and other products.

WHAT IS SOUTH AMERICA'S MOST SOUTHERLY TOWN?

The town of Ushuaia lies at the southern tip of Argentina, so close to the Antarctic that it is bitterly cold for much of the year. The town is situated on a chain of islands called Tierra del Fuego, or "land of fire" in Spanish, named after the Indian fires seen there by the first explorers. Once a port for whaling ships, Ushuaia is now a bustling modern town.

WHY HAVE SO MANY EUROPEANS SETTLED IN ARGENTINA?

About 98 per cent of the population in Argentina are descended from European settlers. This includes the descendants of the two million people who came from Italy to escape poverty in the years before World War I and many people from Wales. Immigrants were attracted by the relative wealth of the country and the almost unlimited areas of fertile land for farming.

WHAT IS THE NATIONAL DANCE OF ARGENTINA?

The tango began in the slums of the Argentine capital Buenos Aires in the late 1800s, but is now danced worldwide. It is a passionate dance for two people and has a distinctive stop-start rhythm. It was traditionally accompanied by a type of concertina known as a bandoneon, together with a piano and a violin.

◄ SANTIAGO, CHILE
Although the Chilean capital of Santiago is a rich and modern city, wealth is unevenly distributed and one-third of all Chileans live on or below the poverty line.

southern South America

BRAZILIAN FOOTBALL ►
Football is an all-consuming passion for Brazilians. From an early age, Brazilians play on every back street and open space, and footballers like Pelé, Ronaldo, and Ronaldinho are national heroes. In 2002 Brazil won the World Cup for a record fifth time.

SOUTHERN SOUTH AMERICA

BRAZIL
Capital city: Brasília
Area: 8,511,965 sq km (3,268,470 sq miles)
Population: 179 million
Official language: Portuguese
Major religion: Roman Catholic
Currency: Real

CHILE
Capital city: Santiago
Area: 756,950 sq km (292,258 sq miles)
Population: 15.8 million
Official language: Spanish
Major religion: Roman Catholic
Currency: Chilean peso

BOLIVIA
Capital city: La Paz (administrative); Sucre (judicial)
Area: 1,098,580 sq km (424,162 sq miles)
Population: 8.8 million
Official languages: Spanish, Quechua, and Aymara
Major religion: Roman Catholic
Currency: Boliviano

ARGENTINA
Capital city: Buenos Aires
Area: 2,766,890 sq km (1,068,296 sq miles)
Population: 38.4 million
Official language: Spanish
Major religion: Roman Catholic
Currency: Argentine peso

PARAGUAY
Capital city: Asunción
Area: 406,750 sq km (157,046 sq miles)
Population: 5.9 million
Official language: Spanish
Major religion: Roman Catholic
Currency: Guaraní

URUGUAY
Capital city: Montevideo
Area: 176,220 sq km (68,039 sq miles)
Population: 3.4 million
Official language: Spanish
Major religion: Roman Catholic
Currency: Uruguayan peso

FIND OUT MORE ►► • Dance 336–337 • Endangered Species 124 • Politics 306–307 • South American Independence 420

AFRICA

Africa is the second-largest continent in the world after Asia. About 849 million people live there – more than one in eight of the world's population. The majority of Africans are Muslim or Christian, although there are many local religious beliefs and customs. Most people live in small towns or villages, where they grow crops, tend livestock, and sometimes work in tourism and other industries. Rapid population growth means that people often need to move to cities in search of food or work. They also move to escape the civil wars, droughts, and famines in rural areas.

Nomad with a camel train crossing the desert

ATLANTIC

OCEAN

DISAPPEARING WILDLIFE ▼
These Namibian elephants, like much of Africa's wildlife, are in danger of extinction from hunters who kill the animals for their ivory, hides, or meat. Game reserves now protect these creatures, and tourists can see them in their natural habitat.

SAHARA DESERT ▲
Africa has three huge deserts: the Kalahari and Namib in the south, and the Sahara in the north. The Sahara is the world's largest desert, and few animals other than camels can survive its intense heat.

JOHANNESBURG ▼
This is the commercial and industrial capital of South Africa and the centre of its gold and diamond production. Despite the city's great wealth, many of its inhabitants still live in primitive shanty towns around its edge, because housing is scarce and wages are low.

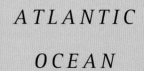

NORTH AFRICAN MARKETS ▲
Markets like this one in Morocco are called souks and are the bustling heart of every town in North Africa. Here, farmers sell vegetables and fruit, while traders sell a variety of items from natural dyes, herbs and spices, and rolls of cloth, to fine silver jewellery and hand-crafted leather goods.

Paintings of houses decorate this Ndebele home

AFRICA
Total land area: 30,335,000 sq km (11,712,434 sq miles)
Total population: 849 million
Number of countries: 53
Largest country: Sudan 2,505,810 sq km (967,493 sq miles)
Smallest country: Seychelles 455 sq km (176 sq miles)
Largest country population: Nigeria 124 million
Largest lake: Lake Victoria, Kenya/Tanzania/Uganda 68,880 sq km (26,560 sq miles)
Longest river: Nile, Uganda/Sudan/Egypt 6,695 km (4,160 miles)
Highest point: Kilimanjaro, Tanzania 5,895 m (19,341 ft)
Major desert: Sahara Desert
Largest island: Madagascar 587,040 sq km (226,656 sq miles)

NDEBELE STYLE ▲
The Ndebele people of South Africa are renowned for their distinctive sense of colour and pattern. Their houses are brightly decorated with strong, geometric shapes. The women are responsible for the upkeep of their houses and they repaint the walls each spring.

e ▶▶ Africa

VICTORIA FALLS ▶
In its long course from Zambia down to the Indian Ocean, the Zambezi River plummets 108 m (354 ft) at the Victoria Falls. This magnificent waterfall creates so much noise and spray that locals call it "the smoke that thunders". The falls were officially named after Queen Victoria, as they were first discovered by a European (British explorer David Livingstone) in 1855, during her reign.

FIND OUT MORE ▶▶ Age of Empire 422–423 • Christianity 288 • Islam 290 • Local Religions 283 • Medieval Africa 394–395

Map labels:

an Sea
20°
tah, Benghazi, Alexandria, Port Said
30°
CAIRO
30°
El Gîza, Suez Canal
El Minya
BYA
EGYPT
Luxor
Libyan Desert
Aswân
Tropic of Cancer
a
Red Sea
ASIA
ibesti
20°
Port Sudan
40°
CHAD
Omdurman
ERITREA
KHARTOUM, Wad Medani, ASMARA
50°
JAMENA
SUDAN
White Nile
Blue Nile
DJIBOUTI, DJIBOUTI
Gulf of Aden
10°
CENTRAL AFRICAN REPUBLIC
Sudd
Ethiopian Highlands
ADDIS ABABA, Dire Dawa, Hargeysa
Horn of Africa
ndou
ETHIOPIA
Shebeli
ngui
SOMALIA
Congo
Ubangi
Congo Basin
Kisangani
Mbandaka
Lake Turkana
UGANDA
KAMPALA
Lake Victoria
Kisumu
RWANDA
KIGALI
Mwanza
KENYA
NAIROBI
MOGADISHU
Equator 0°
DEM. REP.
BURUNDI
BUJUMBURA
Great Rift Valley
Kilimanjaro 5,895 m (19,340 ft)
INDIAN
CONGO
HASA
Kananga
Lake Tanganyika
TANZANIA
DODOMA
Mombasa
Zanzibar
Dar es Salaam
OCEAN
VICTORIA
SEYCHELLES
NGOLA
Bie Plateau
Lubumbashi
Kitwe
Lake Nyasa
COMOROS
MORONI
Mayotte (France)
10°
MALAWI
LILONGWE
Nacala
ZAMBIA
LUSAKA
Zambezi
Blantyre
Mahajanga
Victoria Falls
HARARE
MOZAMBIQUE
boland
Okavango Delta
ZIMBABWE
Beira
MADAGASCAR
ANTANANARIVO
60°
AMIBIA
BOTSWANA
Kalahari
PORT LOUIS
20°
NDHOEK
GABORONE
TSHWANE (PRETORIA)
MAPUTO
Réunion (France)
MAURITIUS
60°
Johannesburg
MBABANE, SWAZILAND
Orange River
SOUTH
LESOTHO
Tropic of Capricorn
50°
APE OWN
BLOEMFONTEIN, MASERU
AFRICA
Drakensberg
30°
30°
40°
Cape of d Hope
Port Elizabeth

0 km 400 800
0 miles 400 800

NORTH AND WEST AFRICA

The Sahara desert is vast and covers most of north and west Africa, stretching from the Atlantic Ocean in the west to the Red Sea in the east. Few people live in this desert area, which separates the Arab and Berber peoples of the north coast from the mainly Black African peoples to the south. Most of the 63 million Africans who inhabit this region live on the narrow coastal plain where the climate is milder.

WHAT INFLUENCE HAS ISLAM HAD?

During the 7th century AD, Arabs from the Arabian peninsula swept across north Africa bringing their new religion of Islam with them. Today, most north and west Africans are Muslims, speak a common Arabic language, and share a culture based on the Islamic faith. Every town has at least one mosque, where the faithful are called to prayer.

WHO LIVES IN THE SAHARA?

Few people live in the Sahara because it regularly has temperatures of over 50°C (122°F) and water is very scarce. People such as the Tuareg have learned how to survive in these extreme conditions, and live by trading salt and other goods across huge distances. Camels are their transport and also provide them with milk, meat, and hides. However, long droughts and other hardships have led many to give up desert life.

◄ MINARET
Beside every mosque is a thin minaret, or tower, from which the muezzin (Muslim official) calls all Muslims to prayer five times a day. Minarets are often beautifully decorated with engravings and elaborate stone work. They are usually the tallest buildings in a Muslim town.

TUAREG NOMADS ►
The Tuareg are a nomadic (wandering) tribe who live in the Western Sahara. In the past they travelled in great camel trains that crossed the desert to the Mediterranean, carrying slaves, ivory, gold, and salt. Today, some still follow this way of life, but most have now become settled farmers.

DATES FROM ALGERIA ►
The giant date palm is found near the oases (watering holes) scattered across the hot, dry Sahara, and its sweet fruit is known as the "bread of the desert". Highly nutritious, dates provide food for people and animals, while every part of the palm tree itself has some use.

WHAT IS DESERTIFICATION?

This is the name for the growth of the world's deserts. It means that good farmland is turning into dry wasteland, which causes famine. It begins when expected rains fail to arrive in areas near the desert. Crops are still grown but the soil becomes infertile, and as the plants die, it turns to dust. With the Sahara spreading south, huge areas are under threat.

▲ CAIRO, EGYPT
The Egyptian capital of Cairo is the largest city in Africa, and has a population of about 7 million people. This huge, modern city on the River Nile is also the site of historic monuments built during its long history, such as the colossal statue of Rameses II.

Distinctive blue robes are specially dyed

e ▸▸
north Africa

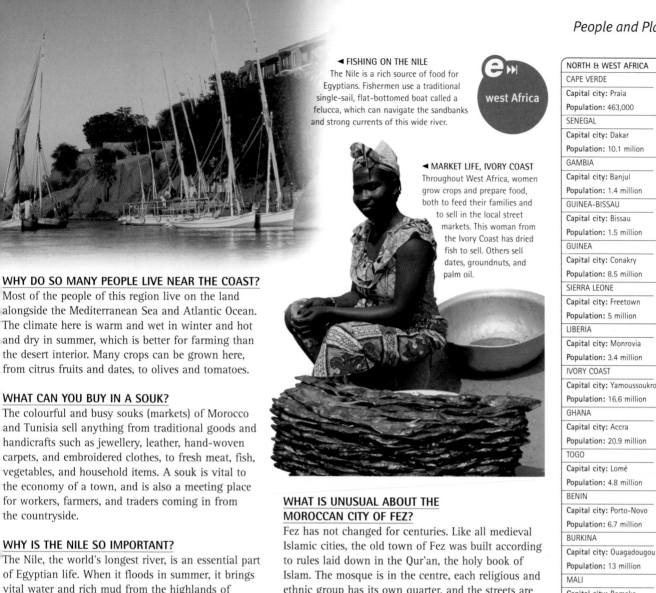

◄ FISHING ON THE NILE
The Nile is a rich source of food for Egyptians. Fishermen use a traditional single-sail, flat-bottomed boat called a felucca, which can navigate the sandbanks and strong currents of this wide river.

◄ MARKET LIFE, IVORY COAST
Throughout West Africa, women grow crops and prepare food, both to feed their families and to sell in the local street markets. This woman from the Ivory Coast has dried fish to sell. Others sell dates, groundnuts, and palm oil.

e ▸▸ west Africa

WHY DO SO MANY PEOPLE LIVE NEAR THE COAST?
Most of the people of this region live on the land alongside the Mediterranean Sea and Atlantic Ocean. The climate here is warm and wet in winter and hot and dry in summer, which is better for farming than the desert interior. Many crops can be grown here, from citrus fruits and dates, to olives and tomatoes.

WHAT CAN YOU BUY IN A SOUK?
The colourful and busy souks (markets) of Morocco and Tunisia sell anything from traditional goods and handicrafts such as jewellery, leather, hand-woven carpets, and embroidered clothes, to fresh meat, fish, vegetables, and household items. A souk is vital to the economy of a town, and is also a meeting place for workers, farmers, and traders coming in from the countryside.

WHY IS THE NILE SO IMPORTANT?
The Nile, the world's longest river, is an essential part of Egyptian life. When it floods in summer, it brings vital water and rich mud from the highlands of Ethiopia and Sudan to its deserts, creating a fertile valley for crops. It also provides drinking water for those who live alongside it, and money from tourists who visit the many ancient sites along its banks.

WHAT IS UNUSUAL ABOUT THE MOROCCAN CITY OF FEZ?
Fez has not changed for centuries. Like all medieval Islamic cities, the old town of Fez was built according to rules laid down in the Qur'an, the holy book of Islam. The mosque is in the centre, each religious and ethnic group has its own quarter, and the streets are narrow enough to give shade and wide enough for two fully laden camels to pass through.

ABU SIMBEL, EGYPT ▶
The magnificent temple of Abu Simbel was built during the reign of Pharaoh Rameses II more than 3,200 years ago. During the 1960s the rising waters of Lake Nasser behind the new Aswân Dam threatened the temple, so it was dismantled and rebuilt at a higher and safer location.

▲ DOGON VILLAGE, MALI
Many African people build their homes from whatever local materials are at hand. The Dogon of Mali, for instance, construct tall, thin houses from local sandstone topped with conical reed roofs. This village is surrounded by stone walls for defence, and the only entrance is through a narrow doorway.

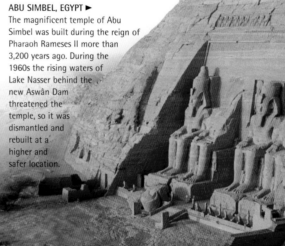

NORTH & WEST AFRICA	
CAPE VERDE	
Capital city: Praia	
Population: 463,000	
SENEGAL	
Capital city: Dakar	
Population: 10.1 million	
GAMBIA	
Capital city: Banjul	
Population: 1.4 million	
GUINEA-BISSAU	
Capital city: Bissau	
Population: 1.5 million	
GUINEA	
Capital city: Conakry	
Population: 8.5 million	
SIERRA LEONE	
Capital city: Freetown	
Population: 5 million	
LIBERIA	
Capital city: Monrovia	
Population: 3.4 million	
IVORY COAST	
Capital city: Yamoussoukro	
Population: 16.6 million	
GHANA	
Capital city: Accra	
Population: 20.9 million	
TOGO	
Capital city: Lomé	
Population: 4.8 million	
BENIN	
Capital city: Porto-Novo	
Population: 6.7 million	
BURKINA	
Capital city: Ouagadougou	
Population: 13 million	
MALI	
Capital city: Bamako	
Population: 13 million	
MAURITANIA	
Capital city: Nouakchott	
Population: 2.9 million	
MOROCCO	
Capital city: Rabat	
Population: 30.6 million	
ALGERIA	
Capital city: Algiers	
Population: 31.8 million	
TUNISIA	
Capital city: Tunis	
Population: 9.8 million	
LIBYA	
Capital city: Tripoli	
Population: 5.6 million	
EGYPT	
Capital city: Cairo	
Population: 71.9 million	

FIND OUT MORE ▸▸ Ancient Egypt 370–371 • Islam 290 • Islamic Civilization 386–387 • Medieval Africa 394–395

EAST AND CENTRAL AFRICA

Central Africa is a hugely fertile region, with abundant grasslands, vast tropical rainforests, and many rivers and lakes. Both Niger and Chad are mostly desert, however, and in recent years, Lake Chad has shrunk to one-tenth of its former size as the rivers that feed it have dried up. Although many of the countries have great agricultural and mineral wealth, political instability and civil wars have kept people in this region in great poverty.

▲ RWANDAN REFUGEES
Since 1993, at least one million lives have been lost and many more people injured in fighting between the majority Hutu and minority Tutsi tribes in Burundi and Rwanda. The conflict has ruined both countries' economies and created nearly two million refugees.

HOW CAN THE ANIMALS BE PROTECTED?
Governments have established huge national parks and wildlife reserves, such as the Masai Mara in Kenya and the Serengeti in Tanzania. Here, tourists can go on safari to view the animals in their natural habitat, contributing much-needed income to both local and national economies.

WHAT IS THREATENING AFRICA'S WILDLIFE?
Africa has an amazing variety of wildlife, but in recent years many species have come under threat from hunters. Elephants are prized for their ivory tusks, black rhinoceroses for their horns. These and other species are now threatened with extinction, while some species have been lost forever.

RIVER NIGER ▲
The River Niger flows east through Guinea, Mali, and Niger before turning south into Nigeria and the Gulf of Guinea. It is a means of transport for people living along its banks.

▼ GORILLAS
The gorillas that live in the forests of Rwanda, Uganda, and elsewhere in East Africa are in danger of extinction, especially from hunters. Their habitat is threatened by farming, although some are now protected in national parks.

e ▸▸ east Africa

RIFT VALLEY ▶
The Great Rift Valley stretches for 4,830 km (3,000 miles) from Syria in western Asia south through the Red Sea and East Africa to Mozambique. Its landscape is extraordinary, with many deep lakes, steep-sided valleys, vast plateaux, and volcanic peaks.

▼ NIGERIAN OIL
Nigeria is one of the main producers and exporters of oil in the world, and has substantial reserves of natural gas. When oil prices fell in the 1980s, efforts were made to develop other products so that Nigeria's economy was not so dependent on oil.

HOW DOES THE EQUATOR AFFECT THE LANDSCAPE?
Africa is the only continent through which the Equator and both tropics (Capricorn and Cancer) run. Around the Equator itself, high rainfall has created a watery landscape of lakes, rivers, and lush tropical rainforest. Either side of the Equator, the climate and vegetation roughly mirror each other, with great deserts forming in the hot and rain-starved land around each tropic.

WHAT WORK DO PEOPLE DO IN THIS REGION?
Most rural Africans live off the land, tending herds of cattle, sheep, and goats, and growing food crops such as maize, cassava, and yams. In East Africa, many also work on the tea and coffee plantations or earn a living from tourism in the many wildlife reserves. The oil industries of Nigeria and Cameroon and the mineral mines of Congo employ thousands of people.

WHAT DO LOCAL PEOPLE CALL THE CONGO RIVER?
The Congo River is known locally as the Zaire. It runs in a huge, upturned U-shape through the Democratic Republic of Congo, previously known as Zaire. The river is a lifeline for the Congolese people, providing fresh water, fish, irrigation for crops along its banks, and a vital transport system.

WHY DOES FAMINE KEEP OCCURRING?
Ethiopia and Somalia have both endured lengthy civil wars in recent years, leaving many people homeless and destitute and creating millions of refugees. Both countries have also been affected by drought, crop failure, and the over-farming of poor or exhausted land. This intense pressure on hugely over-stretched resources means that famine occurs regularly.

IS NIGERIA RICH?
Nigeria is potentially the richest nation in Africa, with huge reserves of oil, natural gas, coal, tin, and iron ore. It also has abundant fertile land, capable of growing cotton, coffee, sugar, and many other crops. However, corruption and bad government have meant that the money earned from these natural resources has not been used properly, and most Nigerians remain very poor.

Cattle are kept for milk and blood, which the Masai drink mixed together

MASAI PEOPLE ▶
The Masai are a semi-nomadic people who live in the Great Rift Valley in Kenya and Tanzania. They keep cattle, goats, and sheep, although some are settled farmers. The Masai once had a fearsome reputation as warriors, although today they live at peace with their neighbours.

e ▶▶
central Africa

Children wear home-spun cotton clothes

FIND OUT MORE ▶▶ Conservation 125 • Endangered Species 124 • Energy Resources 60–61 • Weather 50

SOUTHERN AFRICA

This part of Africa has a narrow coastal plain running up to a ridge of hills surrounding a huge central plateau of high land. The eastern coast is sub-tropical, the south has a Mediterranean-style climate, where fruit and other crops can be grown, and the interior is desert or dry grassland. South Africa is highly industrialized and there are large mineral mines in Namibia and Zambia.

◄ BUSHMEN
The Kalahari Bushmen live and work together in tightly knit communities. Traditionally, they moved from place to place searching for insects and edible plants and hunting small animals with poisonous arrows. Many now live a more settled existence.

CAN ANYONE LIVE IN THE KALAHARI DESERT?
Only one tribe lives in this desert, which covers much of Botswana, Namibia, and northwest South Africa, and is one of the most inhospitable places on Earth. The Bushmen, or San people, have managed to live here for thousands of years searching for their food instead of growing it. People, plants, and wildlife must be able to withstand drought conditions for up to ten months of the year.

HOW HAVE BORDERS MADE LIFE DIFFICULT?
The national borders of some African nations follow natural features, such as rivers and lakes, but many were drawn as straight lines on maps by the European nations who divided Africa up between them in the late 19th century. As a result, many African peoples are split between several countries and do not feel part of any of them. This has caused great unrest and even civil war in some areas.

◄ RING-TAILED LEMUR, MADAGASCAR
The ring-tailed lemur is one of many species that can only be found on Madagascar. The fourth largest island in the world, Madagascar is remote from the mainland of Africa and, as a result, many unique plants and animals have evolved here. In fact, two-thirds of all the chameleons in the world live on the island.

WHERE ARE GOLD AND DIAMONDS FOUND?
Vast deposits of gold and diamonds were first found in South Africa in the late 19th century and have made the country rich. One-third of the world's gold is still produced in the Witwatersrand goldfield around Johannesburg. Its neighbouring country Namibia is also rich in diamonds and other minerals, such as copper and tin. In fact, minerals make up 90 per cent of Namibia's total income from exports.

RUGBY ►
Here, Bolla Conradie plays for the Springboks, South Africa's national rugby team. The team has enjoyed huge worldwide success, winning the 1995 World Cup and many international matches.

WHAT ARE THE SPRINGBOKS?
The South African national rugby team are named after the springbok, a fast-running local antelope. Rugby is one of the two national games of South Africa, with cricket also attracting a large following. Under apartheid the national rugby team was all-white. Today, the team is multiracial and has huge support from all South Africans.

▲ BLACK RHINOCEROS

This baby rhinoceros will grow into a huge 3.6-m (12-ft) long adult with a 50 cm (20 in) ivory horn. Although it can run extremely fast – 48 km/h (30 mph) – it is endangered because its valuable horn makes it a target for ivory hunters unless it can be protected in a wildlife park.

SOUTH AFRICAN TOWNSHIPS ▲

Under apartheid, many black people were forced from their homes and made to live in "townships" on the edge of cities, often far from their work. The biggest of these was Soweto, short for Southwestern Township. Living conditions here are poor, with few facilities.

WHAT IS APARTHEID?

The word apartheid means "apartness" in the Afrikaans language. It was a policy introduced into South Africa by the government (in which only white people were allowed to participate) in 1948 that said that black and white people must live and work separately. It caused great hardship to black people and was widely condemned. Apartheid was abolished in 1994 when South Africa became a multiracial state.

NELSON MANDELA ▶

A leading member of the African National Congress party, Nelson Mandela spent 27 years in prison for his opposition to the whites-only South African government. He was released in 1990, and after winning the Nobel Prize for Peace in 1993, led his party to victory in the first ever multiracial elections in South Africa in 1994. He remained president of his country until 1999.

IS SOUTHERN AFRICA CHANGING?

The end of apartheid in South Africa has led to huge changes in the region. Although the old conflict between black and white peoples has been replaced by a desire to work together, poverty, violence, and high crime rates are widespread. With thousands of people currently dying each day from AIDS, many families are left without a main earner.

e ▶▶
southern Africa

▼ TABLE MOUNTAIN

The flat-topped Table Mountain overlooks Table Bay and the South African city of Cape Town. The parliamentary capital of South Africa, Cape Town is also a major port and a tourist destination for visitors from all over the world.

FIND OUT MORE ▶▶ Decolonization 434 • Endangered Species 124 • Medieval Africa 394–395 • Social Equality 304–305

EUROPE

Europe is the world's second smallest continent with the third highest population. The landscape ranges from the frozen tundra and forests of the north to the hot, dry hills of the Mediterranean region. Vast fertile grasslands stretch between the mountains of the Alps in the west and the Ural Mountains in the east, which separate Europe from Asia. Europe is a crowded continent with over 40 different countries, and conflicts in the past century have often erupted into war. Today, the majority of people live in cities and many enjoy a high standard of living thanks to their countries' abundant natural resources, successful agriculture, and modern industries.

◄ GREEK ORTHODOX CHURCH, SANTORINI, GREECE
Greek Christians belong to the Eastern Orthodox Church, a 700-year-old branch of the Christian community. Christianity has been the dominant religion of Europe for 2,000 years. It has had a major influence on the region's art, architecture, and culture.

▲ COUNCIL OF EUROPE
Institutions such as the Council of Europe, set up in Strasbourg, France in 1949, have helped to bind the nations of Europe together after nearly a century of war. Other Europe-wide organizations include the European Union (EU), which has many different roles, and covers economic, political, agricultural, social, and cultural matters. It is run by the EU Commission in Brussels, Belgium.

The Louvre's historical buildings contain fine paintings, sculptures, and antiquities

The steel and glass pyramid entrance was added in the 1980s

◄ THE LOUVRE, PARIS, FRANCE
The glass entrance hall to the Louvre Museum in Paris symbolizes the old and the new in contemporary Europe. Many of the continent's oldest towns are now dynamic cities that combine historic landmarks with a vibrant multicultural life.

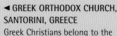

Map labels:
Arctic Circle
REYKJAVÍK — ICELAND
Faeroe Islands (Denmark)
Shetland Islands
Outer Hebrides
Orkney Islands
British Isles
Scotland
Glasgow
Northern Ireland
Edinburgh
Belfast
Great Britain
IRELAND
DUBLIN
Liverpool — Manchester
Celtic Sea
Wales — Birmingham
UNITED KINGDOM
Cardiff
LONDON
England
English Channel
Channel Islands (U.K.)
le Havre
Rennes
PARIS
Seine
Nantes
Loire
Orléans
Strasbourg
Bay of Biscay
A Coruña
Bordeaux
Massif Central
Garonne
Lyon
Pyrenees
Toulouse
Bilbao
Porto
Duero
PORTUGAL
LISBON
Iberian Peninsula
MADRID
Zaragoza
Tagus
SPAIN
Guadalquivir
Seville
Strait of Gibraltar
Málaga
Gibraltar (U.K.)
Ceuta (Spain)
Melilla (Spain)
Ebro
ANDORRA
Barcelona
Valencia
Palma
Balearic Islands
ATLANTIC OCEAN
Norwegian Sea
Trondheim
Bergen
OSLO
Stavanger
Vänern
Gothenburg
Ålborg
DENMARK
COPENHAGEN
Odense
North Sea
NETHERLANDS
AMSTERDAM
THE HAGUE
Rotterdam
Hamburg
Hannover
BERLIN
BELGIUM
BRUSSELS
Bonn
Liège
GERMANY
LUX.
LUXEMBOURG
Frankfurt am Main
Stuttgart
LIECH.
Zürich
BERN
SWITZERLAND
Munich
Innsbruck
AUSTRIA
SLOVENIA
LJUBLJANA
Mont Blanc 4,807 m (15,770 ft)
Milan
Po
Turin
Venice
Trieste
Marseille
MONACO
Corsica
Pisa
Bologna
SAN MARINO
ROME
ITALY
HER.
VATICAN CITY
Sardinia
Cagliari
Mediterranean Sea
Tyrrhenian Sea
Palermo
Sicily
VAL
MALTA

SCALE

0 km 200 400

0 miles 200 400

N

North Cape

Barents Sea

Ostrov Kolguyev

Arctic Circle

EUROPE

Total land area: 10,498,000 sq km
(4,053,309 sq miles)

Total population: 774 million

Number of countries: 43

Largest country: Russian
Federation (European part)
3,955,818 sq km
(1,527,341 sq miles)

Smallest country: Vatican City
0.44 sq km (0.17 sq miles)

Largest country population:
Russian Federation (whole
country) 143 million

Largest lake: Ladoga, Russian
Federation 18,390 sq km
(7,100 sq miles)

Longest river: Volga, Russian
Federation 3,688 km
(2,290 miles)

Highest point: El'brus, Caucasus
Mountains, Russian
Federation 5,642 m (18,510 ft)

Murmansk

Kola
Peninsula

White
Sea

Archangel

Northern Dvina

Lapland

FINLAND

Ural Mountains

R U S S I A N

F E D E R A T I O N

Gulf of Bothnia

Tampere

Turku

HELSINKI

Åland

HOLM

ESTONIA

Lake Onega

Lake
Ladoga

Saint Petersburg

TALLINN

tic Sea

LATVIA

RÍGA

Vologda

Perm

Yaroslavl'

Kazan'

Ufa

Nizhniy
Novgorod

Ul'yanovsk

Orenburg

Samara

Ural

60°

LITHUANIA

VILNIUS

Vitsyebsk

MOSCOW

Central

Russian

Upland

Volga Uplands

Volga

European Plain

RUSS.
FED.

Kaunas

Kaliningrad

MINSK

Homyel'

Voronezh

BELARUS

dgoszcz

LAND

Brest

Pripet

Marshes

Bug

WARSAW

Vistula

Kraków

L'viv

Carpathian Mountains

Dniester

Dnieper Lowlands

Kharkiv

Dnipropetrovs'k

Donets'k

Don

Volgograd

Astrakhan'

KIEV

UKRAINE

Dnieper

Chernivtsi

Rostov-na-Donu

Caspian Sea

OVAKIA

ISLAVA

BUDAPEST

GARY

Cluj-Napoca

MOLDOVA

CHISINAU

Odesa

Sea of
Azov

Stavropol'

▲ FLAMENCO DANCER, SPAIN

Spain is famous for flamenco
dancing, which was developed by
gypsies in the south of the
country in the 15th century.
Europe is a small continent, but
its many countries reflect a rich
mix of cultures and traditions.

▲ OLIVE GROVES, GREECE

Much of Europe has rich, fertile
soils and more than half the land is
used for farming. Olive trees grow
around the Mediterranean, where
the summers are hot and dry.

ROMANIA

BELGRADE

Brasov

BUCHAREST

Crimea

Simferopol'

Caucasus

El'brus
5,642 m
(18,510 ft)

SERBIA &
ONTENEGRO

Danube

Constanta

Black Sea

KORJE

BULGARIA

Varna

SOFIA

Balkan Mts.

Burgas

BANIA

MACEDONIA

TURKEY

*The Matterhorn in
Switzerland has a
pyramid-shaped peak*

Aegean
Sea

GREECE

Piraeus

ATHENS

Peloponnese

Crete

Irákleio

THE ALPS ►

The Alps, Europe's highest mountains,
sweep from the southeastern corner of
France through Switzerland and Italy, and
into Austria. Over millions of years, ice has
moulded the scenery, carving peaks, ridges,
waterfalls, and basins filled with lakes.

FIND OUT MORE ▶▶ Architecture 328–329 • Christianity 288 • Dance 336–337 • Mountains 45 • World War II 432–433

SCANDINAVIA AND ICELAND

Scandinavia, the most northerly region in Europe, is made up of Norway, Sweden, Denmark, and Finland. Together with the volcanic island of Iceland, this is a sparsely populated land of mountains, pine forests, and unpolluted lakes. In the far north, snow falls for six months of the year. Parts of Scandinavia are highly industrialized, but agriculture is important in Denmark and parts of Finland, where the flatter land is more suitable for farming.

WHY IS TIMBER SO IMPORTANT TO FINLAND?

Trees are Finland's most important natural resource. About three-quarters of the country is covered in forests of pine, spruce, and birch. The softwood timber they provide supplies the building and furniture industries, and accounts for about a third of the country's exports. In addition, Finland is the world's largest producer of plywood, wood pulp, and paper.

▲ TIMBER STACK, FINLAND
Finland is a forested country and timber is its largest industry. As old trees are felled new ones are planted, creating sustainable forests.

DO SCANDINAVIANS HAVE A GOOD STANDARD OF LIVING?

The people of the region enjoy high living standards. All Scandinavian countries have small populations, and provide good child-care facilities, schools and universities, and health care for all. With low levels of unemployment, these services are funded through high taxation.

DO SCANDINAVIANS PROTECT THE ENVIRONMENT?

People in Scandinavia value their unspoilt countryside and work hard to protect it. They avoid pollution by recycling waste materials and making use of natural sources of energy. Electricity is generated by wind power in Denmark, geothermal power in Iceland, and hydroelectric power across the whole region.

▲ WINTER SNOW, NORWAY
Log cabins, made of horizontal logs with a sloping roof, are built to withstand heavy winter snowfalls.

WHERE DO MOST SCANDINAVIANS LIVE?

Most Scandinavians live in the south of the region, away from the harsh northern climate. Towns, cities, roads, and railways have been built on flat land in valleys, beside lakes, and along coasts. Many coastal towns, including all the capital cities, are important ports. Scandinavia has so many lakes and rivers that boats are a vital form of transportation for people and their goods.

Scandinavia

Glass walls make the most of the sun's warmth and light

Colourful houses and market stalls line the harbour quayside

◄ SCANDINAVIAN HOUSE
Scandinavia is famous for its architectural design. Local materials, such as timber and glass, are used to create modern, well-insulated homes that sit in harmony with the environment. Many houses are powered by solar panels that transform sunlight into heat.

▲ COPENHAGEN, DENMARK
Copenhagen, the capital of Denmark, lies on the coast of the island of Sjaelland. It is the largest city in Scandinavia and a busy trading centre. Many old buildings and historic churches line its canals, alleyways, and pedestrianized streets.

▲ FROZEN COAST, SWEDEN
Winters are extreme in the north of Sweden, where there are six months of snow. The freezing temperatures cause the sea in the Gulf of Bothnia, which divides Sweden and Finland, to ice over.

WHERE IS THE LAND OF THE MIDNIGHT SUN?

The far north of Scandinavia is known as the land of the "Midnight Sun". In midsummer the sun never sets and there are nearly 24 hours of sunlight. During midwinter, the sun hardly rises and there are just a few hours of natural daylight. The darkness has an effect on some of the population, who suffer from seasonal affective disorder, or SAD.

WHAT IS LAPLAND?

Lapland is a region that stretches across the northernmost parts of Norway, Sweden, and Finland, deep inside the Arctic Circle. The Sami people have lived in Lapland for centuries, surviving the long, harsh winters by herding reindeer for meat, milk, and skins. Today, the Sami still keep their own language and customs, but increased development is threatening their traditional way of life.

Reindeer
feed on lichens
under the snow

Sami herders
wear thick boots
and traditional dress

REINDEER HERDER, LAPLAND ▲
The Sami people live in the inhospitable Arctic region of northern Scandinavia. For thousands of years, they have raised reindeer for their meat and rich, creamy milk.

SCANDINAVIA & ICELAND	
DENMARK	
Capital city: Copenhagen	
Area: 43,094 sq km (16,639 sq miles)	
Population: 5.4 million	
Official language: Danish	
Major religion: Evangelical Lutheran	
Currency: Danish krone	
FINLAND	
Capital city: Helsinki	
Area: 337,030 sq km (130,127 sq miles)	
Population: 5.2 million	
Official languages: Finnish and Swedish	
Major religion: Evangelical Lutheran	
Currency: Euro	
ICELAND	
Capital city: Reykjavik	
Area: 103,000 sq km (39,768 sq miles)	
Population: 290,000	
Official language: Icelandic	
Major religion: Evangelical Lutheran	
Currency: Icelandic króna	
NORWAY	
Capital city: Oslo	
Area: 324,220 sq km (125,181 sq miles)	
Population: 4.5 million	
Official language: Norwegian	
Major religion: Evangelical Lutheran	
Currency: Norwegian krone	
SWEDEN	
Capital city: Stockholm	
Area: 449,964 sq km (173,731 sq miles)	
Population: 8.9 million	
Official language: Swedish	
Major religion: Evangelical Lutheran	
Currency: Swedish krona	

▲ GEOTHERMAL POOL, ICELAND
Bathers on the volcanic island of Iceland swim in the warm, mineral-rich waters of a natural, geothermal pool. The nearby power station uses the underground heat to power its turbines and produce electricity.

Steam billows
from the pool's
warm water

e ▸▸
Iceland

HOW DOES ICELAND USE ITS ACTIVE VOLCANOES?

Iceland has more than 100 volcanoes. At least 20 of these are active and could erupt at any time. The underground heat created by volcanoes is known as geothermal power and is used to produce electricity. Geothermal power stations are clean, cheap, and also provide hot water and heating. Together with the electricity from water-powered stations, they supply all of Iceland's energy needs.

Deep sheltered water
makes a natural harbour
for ships and boats

NORWEGIAN FJORD ▶
Norway's west coast is heavily indented with long, deep inlets called fjords. These were carved out by glaciers during past ice ages. Today, the fjords shelter villages and towns and make perfect natural harbours.

FIND OUT MORE ▸▸ Energy Resources 60–61 • Forestry 67 • Vikings 388 • Volcanoes 44

BRITISH ISLES

The British Isles is made up of two separate nations:
The United Kingdom of Great Britain and
Northern Ireland (the UK) and Ireland. These
islands have a rugged coastline and a
varied landscape of mountains,
moorlands, marshes, and fertile,
rolling farmland. In past centuries,
Britain controlled a vast empire and so
English is now spoken around the world.

◄ LONDON EYE
The London Eye, a huge wheel
standing 135 m (443 ft) high, gives
passengers a 360° panoramic view of
London and its landmarks, including
St Paul's Cathedral, Buckingham Palace,
and the Houses of Parliament.

WHY IS LONDON A LEADING FINANCIAL CENTRE?
The city of London is home to the country's banking
and financial services. London is conveniently located
midway between the important financial centres of
Tokyo and New York, meaning more currency changes
hands in London each day than in any other city.

*The Eye
is over 200
times the size of
a bicycle wheel*

*32 glass
capsules
carry up
to 15,000
passengers
a day*

▲ CITY OF LONDON, ENGLAND
London is an historic, multicultural city and a leading financial centre. It
remains the ruling capital of the UK in spite of some devolved powers
passing to the new Scottish Parliament and the Welsh National Assembly.

◄ TRINITY COLLEGE, DUBLIN, IRELAND
Ireland's most famous university is a well-known
landmark in the Irish capital. In the past, its graduates
often had to leave the country to find jobs elsewhere.
Today, many are choosing to stay in Ireland, because
since becoming a member of the European Union, the
country's economy has become very strong.

e ▸▸
British Isles

WHAT IS GREAT BRITAIN?
The countries of England, Scotland, and Wales make
up the island known as Great Britain. Wales was
united with England in 1536 and Scotland in 1707.
All three nations have separate identities, customs,
and traditions. English remains the main language,
but Welsh is widely spoken in Wales, and Gaelic is
spoken by some people in Scotland.

WHY IS IRELAND KNOWN AS THE EMERALD ISLE?
Ireland was named the "Emerald Isle" because of its
lush, green hills. Pastures thrive in the mild, wet
climate and provide grazing for the breeding of cattle
and racehorses. Since joining the European Union in
1973, Ireland's largely agricultural society has become
a modern, technologically advanced economy based
on industries such as finance, electronics, and tourism.

IS THE UK A MULTICULTURAL SOCIETY?
The UK is home to a multicultural population, where
one in 20 people are from ethnic minorities. Since the
1950s, many people from the country's former
colonies in Africa, India, and the Caribbean have
settled in the UK. Recent refugees from the world's
trouble spots have also brought with them their
culture and traditions. This multiracial population is
largely integrated into British life.

▲ MILLENNIUM STADIUM, CARDIFF, WALES
Wales's new national stadium is a highly visible icon in its capital,
Cardiff. Built to seat up to 74,000 spectators, the stadium has a
retractable roof and hosts many big sporting events.

◄ NEWCASTLE, ENGLAND
Northern towns like Newcastle and Manchester have been transformed by wealthy investors turning industrial buildings into businesses and homes. This has created vibrant, lively cities in which to live and work.

HOW DO THE WELSH CELEBRATE THEIR CULTURAL HERITAGE?

Welsh people celebrate their ancient culture in annual arts festivals called eisteddfods, where poets, dramatists, performers, and choirs compete with each other. The Welsh are renowned for their singing, and male-voice choirs can be found in factories, villages, and towns. The country's national sport is rugby, and the Welsh team now play in the Millennium Stadium, which opened in Cardiff in 1999.

BRITISH ISLES

IRELAND
Capital city: Dublin
Area: 70,282 sq km (27,135 sq miles)
Population: 4 million
Official languages: Irish, English
Major religion: Roman Catholic
Currency: Euro

UNITED KINGDOM
Capital city: London
Area: 244,820 sq km (94,525 sq miles)
Population: 59.3 million
Official language: English
Major religions: Anglican and Roman Catholic
Currency: Pound sterling

WHY DO SO MANY TOURISTS COME HERE?

Over 23 million tourists visit the British Isles each year, attracted by their history and heritage. Visitors flock to the medieval cities of Oxford and Cambridge, the Roman city of Bath, Shakespeare's home town of Stratford-upon-Avon, and the beautiful scenery of Ireland, Wales, and the Scottish Highlands. Royal palaces and traditions are also a major attraction.

HOW HAS THE DECLINE IN NORTH SEA OIL AFFECTED JOBS IN SCOTLAND?

After rich reserves of oil and natural gas were found under the North Sea in the 1960s, the energy industry boosted the Scottish economy by creating work on oil rigs and in refineries. With reserves now running low, employment is in decline. However, developing industries such as petrochemicals, electronics, and textiles are creating new jobs.

◄ WELSH FARM
The cool, wet climate and hilly landscape of Wales make it unsuitable for growing crops. Instead, sheep are reared on remote farms throughout the country, and Welsh lamb, fattened on the lush pasture, is highly prized.

HIGHLAND GAMES, SCOTLAND ►
Scotsmen in traditional tartan kilts participate here in a "tug of war". Scotland has a strong sense of national identity, which is kept alive by customs such as these Highland Games. Scottish kilts are pleated skirts made of the special tartan that belongs to each family "clan" or tribe.

▼ SCOTTISH LOCH
The spectacular scenery of the Scottish Highlands attracts many tourists to the north of the country. Beautiful lochs, empty hills, and romantic castles make up for the region's cool, damp summers and long, harsh winters.

FIND OUT MORE ►► Age of Empire 422–423 • Energy Resources 60–61 • Farming 66 • International Organizations 434

WESTERN EUROPE

Many countries of western Europe combine successful industry with abundant agriculture and a booming tourist trade. As a result, most people here enjoy high living standards. The region, which has a long history, includes world-famous cities, such as Paris and Rome, a landscape of rolling farmland, high mountains, and a beautiful coastline along the Mediterranean Sea.

western Europe

▲ VENICE CANALS, ITALY
Venice is one of Europe's most beautiful cities. Every year, thousands of tourists visit its palaces, churches, and galleries, and take a boat ride on its canals.

▲ THE ALGARVE, PORTUGAL
The villages and beaches of Portugal's Algarve coast are a magnet for European tourists. Portugal is one of the poorer countries in this region, so tourism provides a welcome economic boost.

WHY DO TOURISTS FLOCK TO THE REGION'S BEACHES?
Every year, millions of tourists travel to the beaches of the Mediterranean Sea to enjoy the sunny climate, warm waters, and beautiful scenery. Tourism has led to heavy development along many parts of the coast, such as the Algarve in Portugal, the Costa del Sol in Spain, and the Riviera in Italy and France.

WHY IS FISHING UNDER THREAT IN SPAIN AND PORTUGAL?
Fishing is at risk in Spain and Portugal because years of over-fishing in the North Atlantic Ocean, and recent marine pollution, have reduced fish stocks to an all-time low. In 2002, a vast oil spill in northwest Spain brought fishing there to a halt. Both countries have well-developed fishing industries – Spain has the largest fishing fleet in Europe – which provide the fish for paella and other popular regional dishes.

WHAT DO FARMERS GROW IN ITALY?
Italian farmers grow lots of cereals, fruit, vegetables, and vines. Agriculture is very important to Italy's economy and, although most farms are small and family run, the country is a leading producer of oranges, lemons, wine, olives, and olive oil. The best farming region lies in the north, in the flat, fertile valley of the River Po. Higher land offers pasture for cows and sheep, whose milk makes delicious cheeses.

◄ TOUR DE FRANCE
The world-famous cycle race, the Tour de France, celebrated its centenary in 2003. Riders cover about 4,800 km (3,000 miles) of beautiful French countryside in gruelling one-day stages in a contest that lasts three weeks.

FRENCH VINEYARDS ►
French pickers empty baskets of grapes ready for wine-making. France's first vines were planted by the Romans about 2,000 years ago. Since then, the country has become one of the world's leading wine producers.

WHY IS FRANCE FAMOUS FOR FOOD AND WINE?
A range of climates and landscapes enable France, Western Europe's largest country, to produce many different foods, including wheat, sunflowers, olives, grapes, and dairy products. These foods help to make the regional dishes, cheeses, and wines for which France is famous. The country's vineyards produce a quarter of all the world's wine.

WHY IS SWITZERLAND ONE OF THE WORLD'S WEALTHIEST COUNTRIES?

Switzerland's is one of the world's richest countries thanks to a successful financial industry. The country has neutral status and has enjoyed peace and political stability for nearly 200 years, partly due to its refusal to take part in wars since 1815. This fact, combined with low taxes, and strict secrecy laws, has made Switzerland a major banking centre.

▲ **FARMING IN SWITZERLAND**
The lush, green pastures on Switzerland's mountains are used for grazing cattle. The milk the cows produce is used to make Emmental cheese, and chocolate, two of the country's best-selling exports.

WHY DOES THE SMALL ISLAND OF MALTA HAVE AN IMPORTANT SEAPORT?

Malta has an important port because the island lies on major trade shipping routes between Europe, Africa, and Asia. In the past, Malta's strategic position has led to invasions by Roman, Arab, French, Turkish, Spanish, and British forces, who have all wanted to control the island. Independent since 1964, Malta's main income comes from its port facilities and tourist industry.

▲ **VATICAN CITY, ROME**
St Peter's Square lies in front of the Basilica in the middle of the Vatican. On important feast days, it fills with Roman Catholic pilgrims and tourists who gather to hear the word of the Pope.

WHAT IS THE WORLD'S SMALLEST INDEPENDENT STATE?

Vatican City, situated in the heart of Italy's capital, Rome, is a state in its own right, yet it's no larger than the size of a city park. This tiny state is the headquarters of the Roman Catholic Church and the home of the Pope, who is also head of state. The Vatican City has its own flag, national anthem, stamps, and radio station – even though its population numbers under 1,000.

GUGGENHEIM MUSEUM, BILBAO, SPAIN ▶
The sleek lines of Bilbao's Guggenheim Museum house a collection of modern art. The museum opened in 1977, adding to the cultural life of Spain's most important port.

Gleaming titanium tiles on a strong steel frame

Curved walls make the building look like a sculpture

WESTERN EUROPE

PORTUGAL
Capital city: Lisbon
Area: 92,391 sq km (35,672 sq miles)
Population: 10.1 million
Official language: Portuguese

SPAIN
Capital city: Madrid
Area: 504,782 sq km (194,896 sq miles)
Population: 41.1 million
Official languages: Spanish, Galician, Basque, Catalan

ANDORRA
Capital city: Andorra la Vella
Area: 468 sq km (181 sq miles)
Population: 69,150
Official language: Catalan

FRANCE
Capital city: Paris
Area: 547,030 sq km (211,209 sq miles)
Population: 60.1 million
Official language: French

MONACO
Capital city: Monaco
Area: 1.95 sq km (0.75 sq miles)
Population: 32,130
Official language: French

SWITZERLAND
Capital city: Bern
Area: 41,290 sq km (15,942 sq miles)
Population: 7.2 million
Official languages: French, German, Italian

ITALY
Capital city: Rome
Area: 301,230 sq km (116,305 sq miles)
Population: 57.4 million
Official language: Italian

VATICAN CITY
Capital city: Vatican City
Area: 0.44 sq km (0.17 sq miles)
Population: 911
Official languages: Italian, Latin

SAN MARINO
Capital city: San Marino
Area: 61 sq km (23.6 sq miles)
Population: 28,119
Official language: Italian

MALTA
Capital city: Valletta
Area: 316 sq km (122 sq miles)
Population: 394,000
Official languages: Maltese and English

CENTRAL EUROPE

Nine very different countries form the heart of Europe.
Germany, Luxembourg, and the Netherlands have
thriving economies, but others, such as Poland,
Slovakia, and the Czech Republic, face huge
challenges as independent states after 40 years of
Communist rule. Most of the region is flat and
rolling, with some major rivers flowing to the North Sea.

◀ SKIING IN THE ALPS
Skiing and snow-boarding are popular winter sports in Chamonix,
St Moritz, and other Alpine resorts. The mountains are also busy in
summer, with the beautiful scenery and picturesque towns attracting
many visitors.

HOW DOES SKIING IN THE ALPS DAMAGE THE ENVIRONMENT?
Over 100 million tourists visit the Alps each year, and
hotels, ski runs, lifts, and roads have all been built to
cater for them. This has had a harmful effect on the
Alpine environment. The destruction of forests,
meadows, and grassy slopes threatens the survival of
plants and animals and opens routes for
dangerous avalanches. In recent
years, creating national parks has
helped conserve unspoilt areas.

central Europe

WHY IS LUXEMBOURG VITAL TO THE EUROPEAN UNION?
Luxembourg, one of the smallest countries in Europe, is home to the headquarters
of the European Parliament and the European Court of Justice, two institutions of
the European Union (EU). The EU encourages free trade and economic co-operation
between its 25 members, 12 of whom share a common currency, the euro.

WHICH COUNTRIES ARE KNOWN AS THE LOW COUNTRIES?
Belgium, the Netherlands, and Luxembourg are known as the low countries,
because much of their land is flat and very low-lying. Almost one-third of the
Netherlands has been reclaimed from marshland and the sea, and is enclosed by
earth barriers called dykes. The drained soil is extremely fertile.

▼ ROTTERDAM HARBOUR, THE NETHERLANDS
The Erasmus Bridge spans the River Rhine in the major industrial port of
Rotterdam. The port lies at the mouth of the Rhine, a vital trade route
for countries in this region. Many imports and exports travel through
Rotterdam on vast container ships that call in daily to load or unload
their cargo. Each year, 110,000 barges stop at the port.

WHICH COUNTRY IS EUROPE'S LARGEST FLOWER PRODUCER?
The Netherlands is a major producer of fresh flowers,
which are exported daily to cities around the world.
The country is famous for its cultivation of flower
bulbs, such as crocuses, hyacinths, daffodils, and
tulips, which have been grown here for over 400
years. Fields of Dutch tulips flower in the spring and
are a major tourist attraction.

▲ TULIP FIELDS, THE NETHERLANDS
Vast fields of tulips and other bulbs bloom in the
Netherlands in the spring. Tulips were first
brought to the country from Turkey in the
1630s. Today, they are probably its
most famous export.

▲ POTSDAMER PLATZ, BERLIN, GERMANY
Newly-built skyscrapers in Potsdamer Platz, Berlin's commercial centre, are signs of the economic activity in Germany's reunified capital. New government, commercial, and tourist-oriented buildings are part of a major building boom.

HOW HAS REUNIFICATION AFFECTED GERMANY?

When East and West Germany became one country in 1990, a period of great change was introduced. After World War II, democratic West Germany became a wealthy, industrialized nation. In contrast, East Germany, run by the former Soviet Union, had little investment and inefficient industry. Since 1990, however, East Germany has slowly been modernized.

▲ POZNAN, POLAND
Poland has many beautiful old towns, such as Poznan, its ancient capital. Many of its buildings date back to the Middle Ages, including these houses on the market place, once the homes of wealthy residents.

▼ CASTLE, RIVER RHINE, GERMANY
The Stahleck Fortress is just one of many castles that overlook the southern part of the River Rhine. Tourists take cruise boats along the river to view the vineyards, scenery, and romantic castles on the river banks.

WHICH COUNTRIES ARE HEAVILY INDUSTRIALIZED?

Poland and the Czech Republic are major producers of iron, steel, cars, and industrial machinery. Poland is also a major shipbuilder and exporter of coal and metals. Factories in these former Communist countries are old, poorly equipped, and pollute the environment, but their governments are slowly trying to make them cleaner and more productive.

▲ PRAGUE, CZECH REPUBLIC
Every year, visitors flock to Prague, the historic capital of the Czech Republic, to visit its beautiful streets and squares. The city is a booming commercial centre, although its ageing factories cause air pollution.

WHY IS THE RIVER RHINE SO IMPORTANT TO EUROPE?

The Rhine is one of Europe's most important trade routes. Huge barges use the waterway to transport heavy freight such as timber, coal, and grain. The river starts in the Swiss Alps and flows northwest for 1,320 km (820 miles) through Germany and France. It empties into the North Sea at Rotterdam in the Netherlands, the world's second-largest port.

11th-century castle on a hill overlooking the River Rhine

CENTRAL EUROPE

BELGIUM
Capital city: Brussels
Area: 30,510 sq km (11,780 sq miles)
Population: 10.3 million
Official languages: Dutch, French, and German
Major religion: Roman Catholic

NETHERLANDS
Capital cities: Amsterdam; The Hague (administrative)
Area: 41,526 sq km (16,033 sq miles)
Population: 16.1 million
Official language: Dutch
Major religions: Roman Catholic and Protestant

LUXEMBOURG
Capital city: Luxembourg-Ville
Area: 2,586 sq km (998 sq miles)
Population: 453,000
Official languages: French, German, and Luxembourgish
Major religion: Roman Catholic

GERMANY
Capital city: Berlin
Area: 357,021 sq km (137,846 sq miles)
Population: 82.5 million
Official language: German
Major religions: Protestant and Roman Catholic

LIECHTENSTEIN
Capital city: Vaduz
Area: 160 sq km (62 sq miles)
Population: 33,145
Official language: German
Major religion: Roman Catholic

AUSTRIA
Capital city: Vienna
Area: 83,858 sq km (32,378 sq miles)
Population: 8.1 million
Official language: German
Major religion: Roman Catholic

CZECH REPUBLIC
Capital city: Prague
Area: 78,866 sq km (30,450 sq miles)
Population: 10.2 million
Official language: Czech
Major religion: Roman Catholic

POLAND
Capital city: Warsaw
Area: 312,685 sq km (120,728 sq miles)
Population: 38.6 million
Official language: Polish
Major religion: Roman Catholic

SLOVAKIA
Capital city: Bratislava
Area: 48,845 sq km (18,859 sq miles)
Population: 5.4 million
Official language: Slovak
Major religion: Roman Catholic

FIND OUT MORE ►► Industry 204 • Medieval Europe 390–391 • Politics 306–307 • Rivers 56 • World War II 432–433

SOUTHEAST EUROPE

The countries of southeastern Europe, once called the Balkans, hold a variety of peoples, religions, and languages. Tensions led to war in the 1990s, resulting in smaller countries being formed. This region of ancient towns and old traditions has picturesque landscapes of forested mountains, deep valleys, fertile plains, and lakes. Its long, indented coastline leads to the peninsula and many islands of Greece.

Church building dating back to the Middle Ages

e ▶▶
southeast Europe

WHERE IS THE VALLEY OF THE ROSES?

In the foothills of the Balkan Mountains near Kazanluk, in Bulgaria, lies the Valley of the Roses. Here, vast fields of roses are grown to produce an essential oil called attar, which is important in the making of perfume. Fragrant rose petals are harvested by hand and dried in the sun. Bulgaria produces most of the world's attar, which is worth its weight in gold.

▲ VALLEY OF THE ROSES, BULGARIA
Women rise at dawn to pick damask roses in the vast rose fields of central Bulgaria. Attar, the essential oil they are grown for, is one of the country's most important exports.

▲ LAKE OHRID, MACEDONIA
This Eastern Orthodox Church (a branch of Christianity popular in this region) sits on the banks of Lake Ohrid, which lies in the beautiful mountains of southwest Macedonia. Once popular with tourists, ethnic tensions and recent outbreaks of violence now keep visitors away.

HOW DID THE RECENT CIVIL WAR IN FORMER YUGOSLAVIA AFFECT THIS REGION?

Croatia, Bosnia and Herzegovina, Macedonia, and Slovenia were once part of the communist country of Yugoslavia. When Yugoslavia split up in 1991, the differences between its ethnic peoples exploded into civil war. Thousands were killed or lost their homes, and the economies of these countries were badly affected.

WHY WAS ALBANIA CUT OFF FROM THE WORLD FOR 50 YEARS?

From 1944 to 1991, Albania was under a communist dictatorship that isolated it from the rest of Europe. Free speech and religion were forbidden by law, and private cars were banned. The country is now a democracy and is slowly emerging from isolation, but it remains poverty stricken.

DUBROVNIK, CROATIA ▶
The ancient walled city of Dubrovnik and the beautiful Adriatic coast are once again drawing tourists to Croatia. Tourism is helping to revitalize the country's economy after the recent war.

▲ THE ACROPOLIS, ATHENS, GREECE
Just as in ancient times, the Acropolis dominates the city of Athens.
The rocky hill is crowned by the ruins of the Parthenon temple, which is
over 2,400 years old.

▲ ROMANIAN FARMERS
Hay is harvested on this Romanian farm as it has been for centuries.
Romania is a rich farming country – wheat, maize, potatoes, and fruit
are all grown on its fertile land.

WHICH COUNTRY IS MADE UP OF 2,000 SCATTERED ISLANDS?

Hundreds of small Greek islands dot the Aegean and
Ionian Seas. Every year, more than nine million tourists
visit Greece for its warm blue waters, beautiful scenery,
ancient ruins, and sunny climate. Demand for hotels
and restaurants has made tourism more profitable
than the more traditional farming and fishing.

WHY ARE CARS OFTEN BANNED FROM ATHENS?

In order to protect the ancient buildings of Athens
from damaging lead fumes, cars are sometimes
banned from the streets of the Greek capital. Traffic
produces toxic fumes that create a thick smog of air
pollution. This obscures the view of the Acropolis and
the Parthenon, Athens' most famous ancient ruins,
and destroys the carving on their marble statues.

WHICH TWO COUNTRIES ARE SEPARATED BY THE RIVER DANUBE?

Bulgaria and Romania are divided by the River
Danube, which forms a border between them. The
fertile plain on each side of the river is used as
farmland for grazing sheep, goats, and cattle, and
for growing crops like sunflowers, wheat, maize,
potatoes, and fruit.

▲ LESBOS HARBOUR, GREECE
Fishing boats shelter in this harbour on the Greek island of Lesbos.
Fishing is an important part of the Greek islands' economy, and fresh
fish features on the menu of every restaurant.

◄ THERMAL SPRINGS, BUDAPEST, HUNGARY
Many baths and spas are built around Hungary's warm natural springs,
whose mineral waters are believed to cure bathers of their ailments.
Some bathe for so long that they have time to play a game of chess!

WHICH COUNTRY IS FAMOUS FOR ITS HOT SPRINGS?

Hungary is famous for its thermal springs. These warm
mineral waters rise naturally from the ground and are
said to have medicinal properties. Baths and spas have
been built over the hot springs since Roman times.

SOUTHEAST EUROPE

ALBANIA
Capital city: Tirana
Area: 28,748 sq km
(11,100 sq miles)
Population: 3.2 million
Official language: Albanian

BOSNIA & HERZEGOVINA
Capital city: Sarajevo
Area: 51,129 sq km
(19,741 sq miles)
Population: 4.2 million
Official language: Serbo-Croat

BULGARIA
Capital city: Sofia
Area: 110,910 sq km
(42,822 sq miles)
Population: 7.9 million
Official language: Bulgarian

CROATIA
Capital city: Zagreb
Area: 56,542 sq km
(21,831 sq miles)
Population: 4.4 million
Official language: Croatian

GREECE
Capital city: Athens
Area: 131,940 sq km
(50,942 sq miles)
Population: 11 million
Official language: Greek

HUNGARY
Capital city: Budapest
Area: 93,030 sq km
(35,919 sq miles)
Population: 9.9 million
Official language: Hungarian

MACEDONIA
Capital city: Skopje
Area: 25,333 sq km
(9,781 sq miles)
Population: 2 million
Official languages: Macedonian
and Albanian

MONTENEGRO
Capital city: Podgorica
Area: 14,026 sq km
(5,415 sq miles)
Population: 630,500
Official language: Serbian

ROMANIA
Capital city: Bucharest
Area: 237,500 sq km
(91,699 sq miles)
Population: 22.3 million
Official language: Romanian

SERBIA
Capital city: Belgrade
Area: 88,361 sq km
(34,116 sq miles)
Population: 9.4 million
Official language: Serbo-Croat

SLOVENIA
Capital city: Ljubljana
Area: 20,253 sq km
(7,820 sq miles)
Population: 2 million
Official language: Slovene

FIND OUT MORE ▶▶ Islands 42 • Olympics 356–357

EASTERN EUROPE

Once part of the former Soviet Union, the countries o eastern Europe are now independent republics. The region stretches from the Arctic in the north to the Crimea in the south, and from the Baltic Sea in the west to the Ural Mountains in the east. Much of the landscape is forested. There are also hills and lakes in the Baltic area, marshes in Belarus, and rolling plains in Ukraine and Russian Federation.

The tower of Tallinn's Oleviste church dominates the picturesque skyline

▲ TALLINN, ESTONIA
Tallinn, the capital of Estonia, is an important Baltic port with regular ferries to Scandinavia. Its modern facilities contrast with the city's historic area, whose ancient walls, turrets, towers, and narrow, cobbled streets date back to medieval times.

WHAT ARE THE BALTIC STATES?
Latvia, Lithuania, and Estonia are known as the Baltic States because they border the Baltic Sea. Coastal ports provide access to shipping trade routes between northern and eastern Europe, but the sea ices up during the cold winter months. In summer, the long coastline attracts many tourists from Finland and Scandinavia. They come to enjoy the area's unspoilt beaches, sand dunes, and islands.

WHY WAS UKRAINE ONCE KNOWN AS A BREADBASKET ?
Ukraine is the second largest country in Europe. It was known as a "breadbasket" because it once supplied grain to the former Soviet Union and provided this vast population with its bread. The country is covered by flat, fertile plains known as the steppes. Here, large farms still produce huge quantities of wheat, maize, barley, oats, buckwheat, and rye. Ukraine broke away from Soviet Union control in 1991.

▲ POTATO FARMING, UKRAINE
Potatoes, carrots, and other root crops are harvested throughout Ukraine. Vegetables form an important part of the Ukrainian diet and the country is famous for its borscht, a warming beetroot soup.

WHY DO MOST PEOPLE LIVE IN THE EUROPEAN PART OF THE RUSSIAN FEDERATION (RUSSIA)?
Over 100 million people live in the European part of Russia because it has a milder climate, there is fertile farmland, and it's highly industrialized. Most people live in big cities, such as St Petersburg and the capital, Moscow. The Russian Federation is the world's largest country. Two-thirds of it lie in Asia but vast expanses are uninhabited because the climate is so harsh.

IS RUSSIA RICH IN NATURAL RESOURCES?
The Russian Federation has huge natural resources. The land is rich in minerals and has many mines from which diamonds, gold, nickel, copper, iron, and other metals are extracted. The country is also a leading producer of oil and gas and has enormous reserves of coal.

◄ MINING, RUSSIAN FEDERATION
Mining is important in the European part of Russia, where there are rich reserves of minerals. Some of these remain unexploited because of poor investment and a lack of technology.

e ▸▸
eastern Europe

▲ RUSSIAN BALLET
Russia is famous for its ballet, a popular form of entertainment. The Bolshoi Ballet company of Moscow and the Kirov Ballet of St Petersburg are renowned throughout the world.

WHY DO PEOPLE VISIT THE CRIMEA IN UKRAINE?

The Crimea is a peninsula in southern Ukraine that juts into the Black Sea. The region's warm summers and mild winters attract many tourists who cram onto the crowded beaches. Holiday resorts, such as Yalta and Sevastopol, cater for visitors who come for a healthy regime of massage, exercise, and rest.

WHERE ARE EUROPE'S LARGEST MARSHLANDS?

Vast areas in the south of Belarus are low-lying and covered by swampy marshland, fed by the Byerazino and Dneiper Rivers. The Pripet Marshes stretch for 40,000 sq km (15,444 sq miles) and form the largest expanse of wetland in Europe. The marshes and surrounding forests are a haven for wildlife, including elk, lynx, wild boar, and grouse.

▲ PRIPET MARSHES, BELARUS
Horses graze on the Pripet Marshes, in southern Belarus. This vast area of marshland gives way to huge forests of alder, pine, and oak, which are home to mink and deer.

WHICH PRECIOUS MATERIAL IS FOUND ALONG THE BALTIC COAST?

Two-thirds of the world's amber is found washed up on the shores of the Baltic Sea in chunks of different shapes and sizes. Amber is the fossilized sap of ancient pine trees. It forms over millions of years buried in sediments under the sea. The most sought-after amber is collected in shades of yellow, orange, or gold and is cut and polished to make jewellery.

WHICH CROPS ARE GROWN IN MOLDOVA'S FERTILE FARMLAND?

Moldova's fertile black soil enables farmers to grow a variety of crops, such as wheat, maize, and sunflowers. The country's mild climate is also well suited to growing fruit and grape vines, which are used to make wine.

▼ THE KREMLIN, RUSSIAN FEDERATION
Moscow's Kremlin, or fortress, has witnessed many political changes. Initially, it was the residence of the Russian emperors called the tsars, then the headquarters of the world's first Communist government in 1917. Today, it is the symbolic home of the new leaders of the Russian Federation.

The Cathedral of the Annunciation is situated inside Moscow's Kremlin

This gilt-domed chapel of the tsars was built in 1449

EASTERN EUROPE

ESTONIA
Capital city: Tallinn
Area: 45,226 sq km (17,462 sq miles)
Population: 1.3 million
Official language: Estonian
Major religion: Evangelical Lutheran
Currency: Kroon

LATVIA
Capital city: Riga
Area: 64,589 sq km (24,938 sq miles)
Population: 2.3 million
Official language: Latvian
Major religion: Lutheran
Currency: Lats

LITHUANIA
Capital city: Vilnius
Area: 65,200 sq km (25,174 sq miles)
Population: 2.4 million
Official language: Lithuanian
Major religion: Roman Catholic
Currency: Litas

BELARUS
Capital city: Minsk
Area: 207,600 sq km (80,154 sq miles)
Population: 9.9 million
Official languages: Belarussian and Russian
Major religion: Russian Orthodox
Currency: Belarussian rouble

UKRAINE
Capital city: Kiev
Area: 603,700 sq km (233,089 sq miles)
Population: 47.7 million
Official language: Ukrainian
Major religion: Ukrainian Orthodox
Currency: Hryvna

MOLDOVA
Capital city: Chisinau
Area: 33,843 sq km (13,067 sq miles)
Population: 4.3 million
Official language: Moldovan
Major religion: Eastern Orthodox
Currency: Moldovan leu

RUSSIAN FEDERATION
Capital city: Moscow
Area: 17,075,200 sq km (6,592,735 sq miles)
Population: 143 million
Official language: Russian
Major religion: Russian Orthodox
Currency: Russian rouble

FIND OUT MORE ▶▶ Cold War 435 • Habitats 82–84 • Revolutionary Russia 428 • Rocks 46–47

ASIA

Asia is the world's biggest continent and covers almost a third of the Earth's land surface. The landscape includes the frozen tundra in the north, the baking deserts of the Middle East, a vast coniferous forest, and the Himalayas – the world's highest mountains. Large areas of Asia are uninhabitable, but there are huge grassy plains and fertile valleys beside the Indus, the Mekong, and other mighty rivers. In the southeast of the region, there are thousands of tiny, volcanic islands, many of which are covered by tropical rainforests. Two-thirds of the world's population lives in Asia, reflecting a great variety of cultures, lifestyles, and religions.

SIBERIAN TIGER ▲
The rare Siberian tiger, the largest and most powerful of all the big cats, lives in mountain forests in eastern Russia. Up to 300 tigers are thought to remain in the wild and they are rigorously protected.

▲ FLOATING MARKET, BANGKOK, THAILAND
Flat-bottomed boats, called sampans, are still used to transport fruit and vegetables from the countryside into the city of Bangkok, where they form a floating market. The Thai capital is built on a river and its streets were once canals.

Fresh produce is brought in from outlying farms

▼ MOUNT EVEREST, HIMALAYAS
Standing tall at 8,850 m (29,035 ft), Mount Everest is the world's highest peak. It lies in the Himalayas, a mountain range that forms a natural barrier between the Indian subcontinent and northern Asia.

VOLCANIC ERUPTION, LUZON, PHILIPPINES ▶
The biggest-ever eruption of Mount Pinatubo in 1991 brought destruction to the island of Luzon in the Philippines. Families rescued their belongings and escaped their homes before they were buried by ash and rocks.

Asia

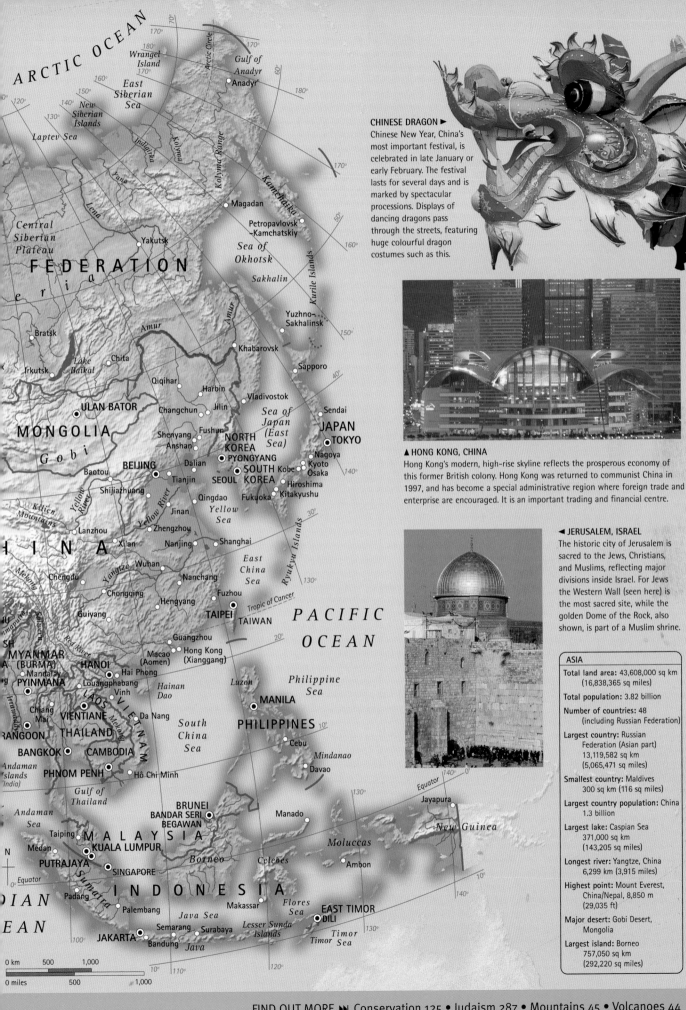

CHINESE DRAGON ▶
Chinese New Year, China's most important festival, is celebrated in late January or early February. The festival lasts for several days and is marked by spectacular processions. Displays of dancing dragons pass through the streets, featuring huge colourful dragon costumes such as this.

▲ HONG KONG, CHINA
Hong Kong's modern, high-rise skyline reflects the prosperous economy of this former British colony. Hong Kong was returned to communist China in 1997, and has become a special administrative region where foreign trade and enterprise are encouraged. It is an important trading and financial centre.

◀ JERUSALEM, ISRAEL
The historic city of Jerusalem is sacred to the Jews, Christians, and Muslims, reflecting major divisions inside Israel. For Jews the Western Wall (seen here) is the most sacred site, while the golden Dome of the Rock, also shown, is part of a Muslim shrine.

ASIA

Total land area: 43,608,000 sq km (16,838,365 sq miles)

Total population: 3.82 billion

Number of countries: 48 (including Russian Federation)

Largest country: Russian Federation (Asian part) 13,119,582 sq km (5,065,471 sq miles)

Smallest country: Maldives 300 sq km (116 sq miles)

Largest country population: China 1.3 billion

Largest lake: Caspian Sea 371,000 sq km (143,205 sq miles)

Longest river: Yangtze, China 6,299 km (3,915 miles)

Highest point: Mount Everest, China/Nepal, 8,850 m (29,035 ft)

Major desert: Gobi Desert, Mongolia

Largest island: Borneo 757,050 sq km (292,220 sq miles)

FIND OUT MORE ▶▶ Conservation 125 • Judaism 287 • Mountains 45 • Volcanoes 44

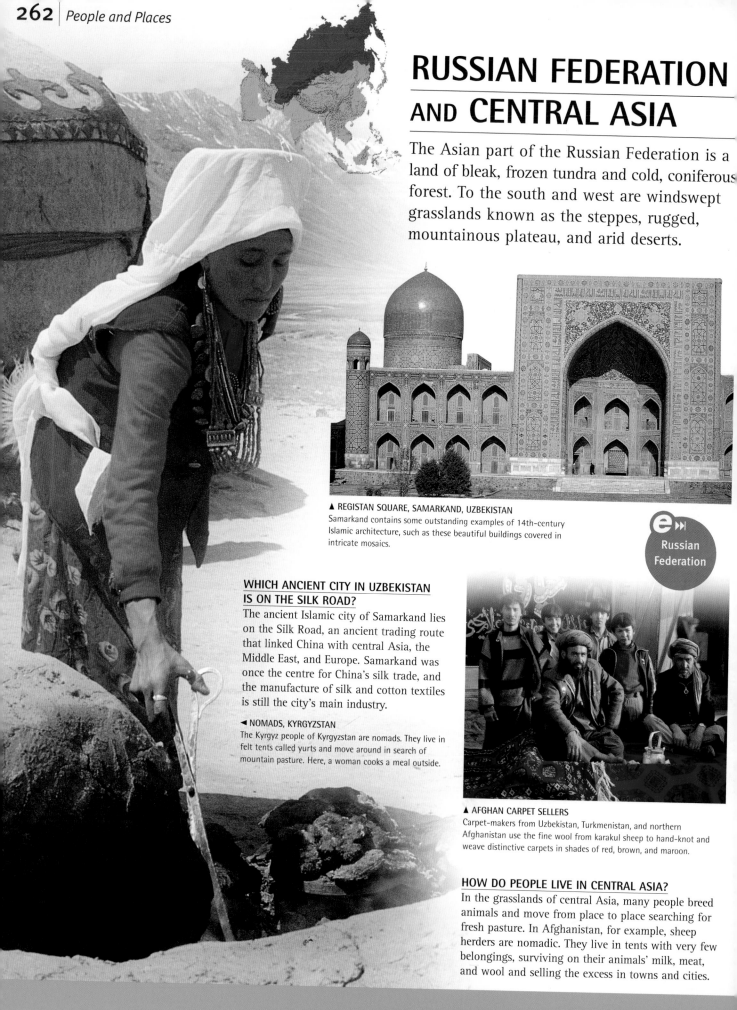

RUSSIAN FEDERATION AND CENTRAL ASIA

The Asian part of the Russian Federation is a land of bleak, frozen tundra and cold, coniferous forest. To the south and west are windswept grasslands known as the steppes, rugged, mountainous plateau, and arid deserts.

▲ REGISTAN SQUARE, SAMARKAND, UZBEKISTAN
Samarkand contains some outstanding examples of 14th-century Islamic architecture, such as these beautiful buildings covered in intricate mosaics.

e ▶▶
Russian Federation

WHICH ANCIENT CITY IN UZBEKISTAN IS ON THE SILK ROAD?
The ancient Islamic city of Samarkand lies on the Silk Road, an ancient trading route that linked China with central Asia, the Middle East, and Europe. Samarkand was once the centre for China's silk trade, and the manufacture of silk and cotton textiles is still the city's main industry.

◀ NOMADS, KYRGYZSTAN
The Kyrgyz people of Kyrgyzstan are nomads. They live in felt tents called yurts and move around in search of mountain pasture. Here, a woman cooks a meal outside.

▲ AFGHAN CARPET SELLERS
Carpet-makers from Uzbekistan, Turkmenistan, and northern Afghanistan use the fine wool from karakul sheep to hand-knot and weave distinctive carpets in shades of red, brown, and maroon.

HOW DO PEOPLE LIVE IN CENTRAL ASIA?
In the grasslands of central Asia, many people breed animals and move from place to place searching for fresh pasture. In Afghanistan, for example, sheep herders are nomadic. They live in tents with very few belongings, surviving on their animals' milk, meat, and wool and selling the excess in towns and cities.

◄ **NENET PEOPLE, SIBERIA, RUSSIAN FEDERATION**

The Nenet people live in a cold, inhospitable Arctic region of the Russian Federation. This Siberian community traditionally survived by herding reindeer or trapping wild animals. Today, however, the region is being developed for its huge reserves of gas.

▼ **RUSSIAN SPACE CENTRE, KAZAKHSTAN**

A rocket is towed to the launch pad of the Russian Space Centre at the Baykonur Cosmodrome in Kazakhstan. From here, the Russians launched the world's first artificial satellite, *Sputnik 1*, in 1957, and the first person in space, Yuri Gagarin, in 1961.

DO MANY PEOPLE LIVE IN SIBERIA?

Siberia, a vast, bitterly cold region of tundra, pine forest, rivers, and lakes, is sparsely populated. The Yakut and other native peoples survive there by hunting, fishing, and herding reindeer. Siberia stretches from the Ural Mountains in the west to the Pacific Ocean in the east. The region is rich in natural resources, such as coal, oil, gas, diamonds, and gold.

WHY IS THE ARAL SEA SHRINKING?

The Aral Sea in Uzbekistan and Kazakhstan was once the world's fourth largest freshwater lake. Today, it is shrinking at an alarming rate because the rivers that feed it, the Syr Darya and the Amu Darya, have been diverted to irrigate cotton fields. A fishing village that once stood on the lake's banks now stands 48 km (30 miles) from the shore.

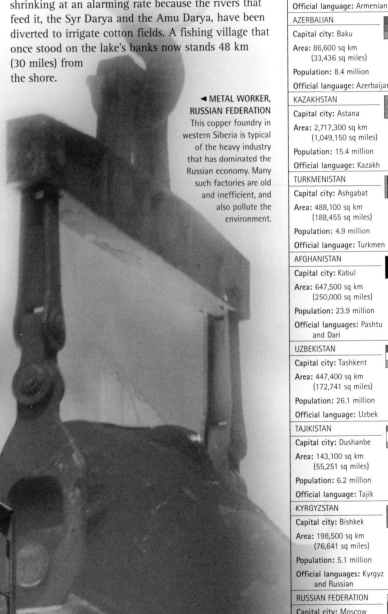

◄ **METAL WORKER, RUSSIAN FEDERATION**

This copper foundry in western Siberia is typical of the heavy industry that has dominated the Russian economy. Many such factories are old and inefficient, and also pollute the environment.

WHERE IS THE WORLD'S LONGEST RAILWAY?

The Trans-Siberian Railway, the world's longest continuous rail line, crosses the Russian Federation. It starts in Moscow and runs 9,446 km (5,870 miles) to the Pacific port of Vladivostok. The whole journey crosses eight time zones and takes eight days to complete.

▶▶ **Central Asia**

RUSSIAN FEDERATION & CENTRAL ASIA

GEORGIA
Capital city: T'bilisi
Area: 69,700 sq km (26,911 sq miles)
Population: 5.1 million
Official languages: Georgian and Abkhazian (in Abkhazia)

ARMENIA
Capital city: Yerevan
Area: 29,800 sq km (11,506 sq miles)
Population: 3.1 million
Official language: Armenian

AZERBAIJAN
Capital city: Baku
Area: 86,600 sq km (33,436 sq miles)
Population: 8.4 million
Official language: Azerbaijani

KAZAKHSTAN
Capital city: Astana
Area: 2,717,300 sq km (1,049,150 sq miles)
Population: 15.4 million
Official language: Kazakh

TURKMENISTAN
Capital city: Ashgabat
Area: 488,100 sq km (188,455 sq miles)
Population: 4.9 million
Official language: Turkmen

AFGHANISTAN
Capital city: Kabul
Area: 647,500 sq km (250,000 sq miles)
Population: 23.9 million
Official languages: Pashtu and Dari

UZBEKISTAN
Capital city: Tashkent
Area: 447,400 sq km (172,741 sq miles)
Population: 26.1 million
Official language: Uzbek

TAJIKISTAN
Capital city: Dushanbe
Area: 143,100 sq km (55,251 sq miles)
Population: 6.2 million
Official language: Tajik

KYRGYZSTAN
Capital city: Bishkek
Area: 198,500 sq km (76,641 sq miles)
Population: 5.1 million
Official languages: Kyrgyz and Russian

RUSSIAN FEDERATION
Capital city: Moscow
Area: 17,075,200 sq km (6,592,735 sq miles)
Population: 143 million
Official language: Russian

FIND OUT MORE ▶▶ China's First Empire 378 • Habitats 82–84 • Islam 290 • Space Stations 33

WESTERN ASIA AND THE MIDDLE EAST

The Middle East is the name given to the area of land between the Red Sea and the Gulf, from Israel in the west to Iran in the east. Along with western Asia, much of this land is inhospitable, with dry desert in the Arabian Peninsula, and mountains in Iran and Iraq. Turkey is dominated by a high plateau, but has plenty of fertile farmland. There are snow-capped mountains in north Lebanon and Israel, which drop down to fertile plains along the coasts.

▲ SOUK STALL, SYRIA
A stall sells fresh fruit in the sou or marketplace, of Syria's capital Damascus. The souk's narrow, bustling alleyways are packed with workshops and stalls offerin all kinds of foodstuffs and crafts.

HOW HAS OIL CHANGED THE GULF REGION?
The discovery of oil in the Gulf has brought enormous wealth to Saudi Arabia, Iraq, Kuwait, and other desert countries, which now supply 30 per cent of the world's oil. Fleets of oil tankers have made the Gulf one of the world's busiest seaways. The presence of oil has increased this area's international importance and its influence on world affairs.

WHY IS THE MIDDLE EAST CALLED A TROUBLE SPOT?
There have been many recent conflicts in the Middle East. In 1975, Lebanon suffered a violent civil war between the Christian and Muslim populations. In 1990 and 2003, international forces led by the USA invaded Iraq, eventually deposing President Saddam Hussein's regime. Today, huge tensions exist between Israelis and Palestinians, who lost their homes in 1948 when Israel was created as a homeland for the Jews.

▲ BEIRUT, LEBANON
Modern tower blocks stand alongside ruins in Beirut, the capital of Lebanon. This elegant city was almost completely destroyed in the civil war of 1975–89 that raged between the Christian and Muslim populations. Once a dangerous destination for visitors, the rebuilt city is now attracting increasing numbers of tourists.

WHICH TURKISH CITY LIES HALF IN ASIA AND HALF IN EUROPE?
Istanbul is the only city in the world to lie in two continents. Split by a narrow channel of water called the Bosporus Strait, the European and Asian parts of the city are linked by a number of bridges. Istanbul is Turkey's largest city and home to nearly 9.4 million people. Once known by the name of Constantinople, Istanbul was Turkey's capital from AD 330–1923.

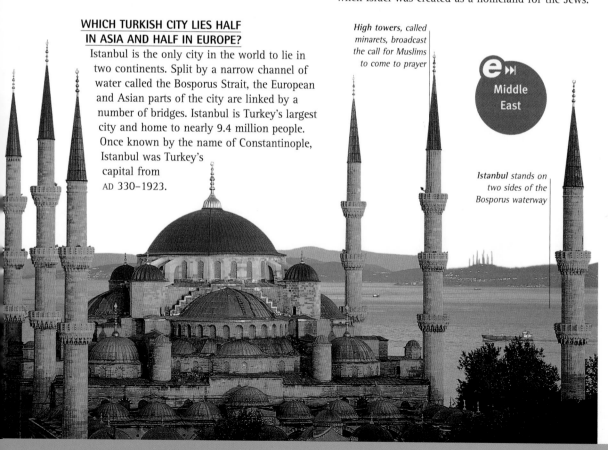

High towers, called minarets, broadcast the call for Muslims to come to prayer

e ▶▶
Middle East

Istanbul stands on two sides of the Bosporus waterway

▲ PETRA, JORDAN
The ancient city of Petra in Jordan dates from the 4th century BC. Its temples and other spectacular buildings were cut out of pink limestone rock deep inside a desert canyon. Bedouin nomads still travel around the Syrian Desert using camels, cars, and trucks.

◄ BLUE MOSQUE, ISTANBUL, TURKEY
Istanbul's Blue Mosque is an outstanding example of Islamic architecture. It stands in a city where East meets West: the mosque's graceful minarets and domed roof rub shoulders with bustling bazaars, designer shops, restaurants, and high-rise blocks.

SAUDI ARABIAN DESERT ►
Over 95 per cent of Saudi Arabia is dry, inhospitable desert, where daytime temperatures reach 48°C (118°F) and plunge to near freezing at night. The extreme temperatures and wind-borne sand wear down the desert rocks. The southern desert covers 650,000 sq km (250,000 sq miles) and is the largest expanse of sand in the world.

e ▸▸
western Asia

HOW DO DESERT COUNTRIES OBTAIN FRESH WATER?

Many desert countries have no reliable source of fresh water and have to process sea water in desalination plants for domestic and agricultural use. Water is carefully managed throughout the region. Saudi Arabia's huge irrigation programme waters the wheat, fruit, and vegetable crops that are grown in the desert.

WHERE IS THE LOWEST PLACE ON EARTH?

At 392 m (1,285 ft) below sea level, the Dead Sea is the lowest place on Earth. This vast lake, 74 km (46 miles) long, lies on the border between Israel and Jordan. Its water is so salty that nothing can live in it, which is how the lake got its name. However, the mud on its shore is rich in minerals, and is said to have healing properties.

WHO ARE THE KURDS?

The Kurds are a stateless people, whose mountainous homeland of Kurdistan straddles the borders of Turkey, Syria, Iraq, and Iran. For many years, the Kurds have wanted self-government and tried to form a Kurdistan state, but their attempts have been put down with violence and bloodshed. Many Kurds now live as refugees.

▲ KURDISH REFUGEES, TURKEY
Years of dictatorship and conflict in Iraq have led to thousands of Kurds leaving the country for refugee camps in Turkey. The Kurds, who number about 25 million, are one of the largest stateless peoples in the world.

DUBAI, UNITED ARAB EMIRATES ►
Dubai, one of the United Arab Emirates, has been rebuilt with wealth generated by oil revenues. Like other nations in the Gulf, the United Arab Emirates is a prosperous country and most of its people enjoy a high standard of living.

United Arab Emirates' wealth is reflected in its glittering buildings

Dubai's skyline is dominated by high-rise apartments, offices, and banks

WESTERN ASIA & MIDDLE EAST

TURKEY
Capital city: Ankara
Population: 71.3 million
Official language: Turkish

CYPRUS
Capital city: Nicosia
Population: 802,000
Official languages: Greek and Turkish

LEBANON
Capital city: Beirut
Population: 3.7 million
Official language: Arabic

ISRAEL
Capital city: Jerusalem (not internationally recognized)
Population: 6.4 million
Official languages: Hebrew and Arabic

JORDAN
Capital city: Amman
Population: 5.5 million
Official language: Arabic

SAUDI ARABIA
Capital city: Riyadh; Jedda (administrative)
Population: 24.4 million
Official language: Arabic

YEMEN
Capital city: Sana
Population: 20 million
Official language: Arabic

SYRIA
Capital city: Damascus
Population: 17.8 million
Official language: Arabic

IRAQ
Capital city: Baghdad
Population: 25.2 million
Official language: Arabic

KUWAIT
Capital city: Kuwait City
Population: 2.5 million
Official language: Arabic

BAHRAIN
Capital city: Manama
Population: 724,000
Official language: Arabic

QATAR
Capital city: Doha
Population: 610,000
Official language: Arabic

UNITED ARAB EMIRATES
Capital city: Abu Dhabi
Population: 3 million
Official language: Arabic

OMAN
Capital city: Muscat
Population: 2.9 million
Official language: Arabic

IRAN
Capital city: Tehran
Population: 68.9 million
Official language: Farsi

FIND OUT MORE ▸▸ Energy Resources 60–61 • Habitats 82–84 • Islam 290 • Mesopotamia 368 • Middle East 435

SOUTHERN ASIA

Southern Asia, home to over one-fifth of the world's population, is bordered by the sea to the south and the Himalayan mountains to the north. The region has a great variety of landscapes and climates with dry, sandy desert in the northwest, and tropical rainforests in the south.

In the east, three major rivers – the Brahmaputra, the Meghna, and the Ganges – flow together towards the Bay of Bengal where they form the world's largest delta.

▲ GANGES RIVER, INDIA
Hindus bathe in the sacred Ganges River from one or more of the 40 ghats (stone steps) along the river in Varanasi. Hindus believe that Varanasi is the earthly home of the god Shiva, creator of the world.

WHY DO HINDU PILGRIMS GATHER AT VARANASI?
The city of Varanasi is sacred to Hindus, who form 90 per cent of India's population. Every year, millions of pilgrims gather on the stone steps called ghats along the high banks of the Ganges River. Here they pray, meditate, and purify themselves in the river's holy waters. The dead are cremated on funeral pyres and their ashes are sprinkled onto the surface of the water.

HOW ARE TREKKERS DAMAGING THE HIMALAYAS?
The large number of trekkers visiting the Himalayas each year are damaging the fragile mountain environment and threatening its ecology. Every year, 300,000 tourists visit Nepal to walk on the slopes of Mount Everest and other major peaks. These visitors erode mountain trails and often leave behind vast quantities of rubbish.

Bangladeshi houses are raised on stilts above the flood plain

southern Asia

▲ FLOODING IN BANGLADESH
Water levels in Bangladesh rise 6 m (20 ft) above normal during the annual monsoon rains. Flood waters can destroy animals, crops, and homes, and spread disease. More than 50 per cent of Bangladeshis live in extreme poverty and the country is too poor to invest in large-scale flood defences, such as dams.

WHY IS BANGLADESH PRONE TO FLOODING?
Large parts of central and southern Bangladesh are flat, low-lying river plains, which flood during the summer monsoon rains. In good years, the floods water the crops and fertilize the fields. In bad years, they cause devastation by surging over flood defences and sweeping away villages, livestock, and crops.

WHICH ISOLATED COUNTRY IS RULED BY THE DRAGON KING?
Bhutan is a small Buddhist kingdom in the Himalayas, ruled by a monarch called the Dragon King. The country has little contact with the outside world, although television was introduced in 1999. Most of the population makes a living from farming.

◄ HIMALAYAN MOUNTAIN CLIMB
The Sherpa people of Nepal are skilled climbers, who act as guides and porters for the tourists and mountaineers visiting the Himalayas. Trekking provides a welcome boost to Nepal's economy.

Stilts are handed down from father to son

HOW DID BRITAIN INFLUENCE INDIA?
India was a British colony from the mid-19th century until 1947, when it gained its independence. British influences can still be seen in the region today, such as the widespread use of English, the European style of architecture, the vast rail network, the passion for cricket, and in the legal and political systems.

◄ REPUBLIC DAY, INDIA
Parades in New Delhi mark the anniversary of Republic Day, when India became a republic on 26 January 1950.

MUMBAI, INDIA ►
Mumbai, on India's western coast, has a modern, high-rise skyline. Here, extreme wealth is seen alongside extreme poverty: 100,000 people live on the city's streets.

Mumbai's rich live in elegant housing that overlooks the Arabian Sea

WHAT IS CITY LIFE LIKE IN INDIA?
India's two largest cities are crowded, bustling places where modern, high-rise office buildings stand next to ancient temples, monuments, and mosques. Calcutta is a major industrial city, and Mumbai (Bombay) is the centre of India's huge film industry. As more people move from the countryside in search of work, overcrowding in the cities' slums is a growing problem.

WHICH CROP IS IMPORTANT TO SRI LANKA?
The island of Sri Lanka has over 2,000 tea plantations and is the world's largest tea exporter. The best tea grows on the hillsides in the cooler, central highlands. Tea is harvested by hand, as machines would bruise the fragile leaves and spoil their delicate flavour. The leaves are then rolled, dried, and packed for export.

Stilt fishing is thousands of years old

▼ FISHING IN SRI LANKA
Stilt fishing is famous in Sri Lanka. The fishermen perch on poles embedded in the seabed, and fish with a rod and line. The small fish that swim in the shallow waters are a valuable catch.

SOUTHERN ASIA

PAKISTAN
Capital city: Islamabad
Area: 803,940 sq km (310,401 sq miles)
Population: 154 million
Official language: Urdu
Major religion: Sunni Muslim
Currency: Pakistani rupee

INDIA
Capital city: New Delhi
Area: 3,287,590 sq km (1,269,338 sq miles)
Population: 1.07 billion
Official languages: Hindi and English
Major religion: Hindu
Currency: Indian rupee

MALDIVES
Capital city: Male'
Area: 300 sq km (116 sq miles)
Population: 318,000
Official language: Dhivehi
Major religion: Sunni Muslim
Currency: Rufiyaa

SRI LANKA
Capital city: Colombo
Area: 65,610 sq km (25,332 sq miles)
Population: 19.1 million
Official languages: Sinhala, Tamil, and English
Major religion: Buddhist
Currency: Sri Lanka rupee

NEPAL
Capital city: Kathmandu
Area: 140,800 sq km (54,363 sq miles)
Population: 25.2 million
Official language: Nepali
Major religion: Hindu
Currency: Nepalese rupee

BANGLADESH
Capital city: Dhaka
Area: 144,000 sq km (55,598 sq miles)
Population: 147 million
Official language: Bengali
Major religion: Muslim (mainly Sunni)
Currency: Taka

BHUTAN
Capital city: Thimphu
Area: 47,000 sq km (18,147 sq miles)
Population: 2.3 million
Official language: Dzongkha
Major religion: Mahayana Buddhist
Currency: Ngultrum

FIND OUT MORE ►► Age of Empire 422–423 • Cinema 346–347 • Hinduism 286 • Winds 51

EASTERN ASIA

The harsh landscapes of Eastern Asia include remote mountains, cold deserts, and the vast, dry grasslands of Mongolia and northern China. In the southeast of China, there are wide plains and valleys, watered by mighty rivers. North and South Korea form a peninsula, where the land is mountainous and thickly forested, as are the neighbouring islands across the sea that make up Japan.

HOW LONG IS THE GREAT WALL OF CHINA?
The wall stretches over 6,400 km (3,980 miles) through the mountains and deserts of northern China. It is the longest structure ever to be built by hand. Work began over 2,200 years ago by order of the first Chinese emperor, Qin Shi Huangdi. Most of the wall was built by slaves in the 15th century to keep out Mongolian invaders.

▲ HONG KONG, CHINA
A traditional Chinese junk sails into Hong Kong harbour. Hong Kong is not only a leading financial centre, and a major manufacturer of textiles and electronics, but also one of the world's busiest ports.

▼ THE GREAT WALL OF CHINA
The Great Wall of China is made up of two high walls sandwiched together with earth. The top is paved with stone slabs, making a roadway about 4 m (13 ft) wide. Along its length, there are 25,000 square watch towers.

Guards sat in towers along the wall, watching for signs of danger

WHEN WAS HONG KONG A BRITISH COLONY?
Hong Kong was returned to China in 1997 having been a British colony for 99 years. With a population of over 6.5 million people, this small territory lies in southeast China and comprises a mountainous mainland area and 236 offshore islands.

WHERE DO CHINA'S 1.3 BILLION PEOPLE LIVE?
About 80 per cent of China's vast population live in small, rural villages, and work on the land. The rest live in overcrowded cities, where housing is scarce. With the world's largest population, China has a huge task to provide all its citizens with food and education.

▲ MONGOLIAN HORSEMAN
Mongolians are some of the world's most accomplished horse riders. Here, a Kazakh horseman hunts with a trained golden eagle. Kazakhs are the largest of Mongolia's ethnic minorities.

eastern
Asia

◀ SHANGHAI, CHINA
International trade is
transforming the east coast
port of Shanghai, China's
largest city. Home to more
than nine million people,
Shanghai is a leading
industrial and commercial
centre with the world's busiest
port. Its modern skyline is
crowded with high-rise office
buildings, convention centres,
and modern shopping malls.

EASTERN ASIA

CHINA
Capital city: Beijing
Area: 9,596,960 sq km
(3,705,386 sq miles)
Population: 1.3 billion
Official language: Mandarin
Chinese
Major religion: Majority are
non-religious
Currency: Renminbi (called yuan)

MONGOLIA
Capital city: Ulan Bator
Area: 1,565,000 sq km
(604,247 sq miles)
Population: 2.6 million
Official language: Khalkha
Mongolian
Major religion: Tibetan Buddhist
Currency: Tugrik

NORTH KOREA
Capital city: Pyongyang
Area: 120,540 sq km
(46,540 sq miles)
Population: 22.7 million
Official language: Korean
Major religion: Most non-religious
Currency: North Korean won

SOUTH KOREA
Capital city: Seoul
Area: 98,480 sq km
(38,023 sq miles)
Population: 47.7 million
Official language: Korean
Major religions: Mahayana
Buddhist and Protestant
Currency: South Korean won

TAIWAN
Capital city: Taipei
Area: 35,980 sq km
(13,892 sq miles)
Population: 22.6 million
Official language: Mandarin
Chinese
Major religion: Buddhist
Currency: Taiwan dollar

JAPAN
Capital city: Tokyo
Area: 377,835 sq km
(145,882 sq miles)
Population: 128 million
Official language: Japanese
Major religions: Shinto and
Buddhist
Currency: Yen

WHY ARE FISH IMPORTANT TO THE JAPANESE?
The mountainous islands of Japan have limited
farmland, so the people depend on the sea for food.
The fishing fleet, which is the largest in the world,
catches about 6 million tonnes (6 million tons) of
fish each year. Fresh fish forms the basis of most
Japanese cooking, and much of it is eaten raw.

*A kimono
is fastened by
a broad sash
called an obi*

▲ JAPANESE CHILDREN WEARING KIMONOS
The Japanese often wear kimonos for special occasions. These
traditional, wide-sleeved, wrap-around robes are made from
colourful printed silks and tied at the back with a sash.

WHAT IS UNUSUAL ABOUT THE GOBI DESERT?
Unlike most deserts, the Gobi desert in Mongolia has
hot summers, but icy winters. The Bactrian camels
that live in the Gobi have adapted by growing thick
winter coats that moult in the spring. The desert, the
fourth largest in the world, is made of rock and sand.
It is famous for the discovery of fossilized bones and
eggs of dinosaurs that lived here 85 million years ago.

WHICH STAPLE FOOD IS GROWN IN THE REGION?
Rice is the staple food of eastern Asia and the region's
farms must produce enough to feed the vast
populations. The fertile, flooded rice fields of southern
China produce two harvests every year. Planting and
harvesting are still done by hand, and water buffaloes
or oxen pull farm machinery. In contrast, rice is
intensively farmed in Japan with modern machinery.

◀ SEOUL, SOUTH KOREA
A busy shopping street in
night-time Seoul. South Korea's
thriving capital is home to a
quarter of the country's
population.

WHY ARE THERE TWO KOREAS?
Korea was a single country until the end of World War II, when it was occupied by
Russian and American forces. In 1948, it was divided in two and democratic South
Korea separated from its communist neighbour. Hostilities between these countries
led to the Korean War (1950–53). Today, South Korea specializes in producing and
exporting manufactured goods. North Korea remains a politically isolated regime.

FIND OUT MORE ▶▶ Cold War 435 • Dinosaurs 78–79 • Farming 66 • Fishing 67 • Imperial China 393

SOUTHEAST ASIA

Southeast Asia is made up of a large mainland peninsula, and a maritime area with 20,000 islands scattered through the Pacific and Indian Oceans. Much of the land in this region is mountainous and covered in dense, tropical forest.

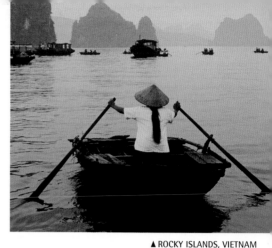

▲ ROCKY ISLANDS, VIETNAM
A Vietnamese woman rows her boat among the rocky limestone islands of Ha Long Bay. The beauty of the coastline draws many tourists to this area on the Red River delta.

HOW DOES DEFORESTATION AFFECT THE REGION?
Deforestation in Indonesia, Thailand, Burma, and Laos has destroyed the habitats of many rare plants and animals, such as tigers and wild elephants. It has also caused flooding and soil erosion. Some trees, such as teak, are logged for their timber; others are felled to create farmland and replanting is rare. Thailand took the step of banning commercial logging in 1989.

HOW IS RICE FARMING CHANGING IN THE REGION?
In the last 20 years, rice farmers have been planting new species of high-quality rice, which produce a greater yield. These, along with new, intensive rice-planting programmes and sophisticated machinery, have helped countries, such as Indonesia, to become self-sufficient. Rice is a staple food of the region and grows well in the warm, humid climate.

WHY DOES SOUTHEAST ASIA HAVE A RICH TRADITION OF PERFORMING ARTS?
The music, dance, and drama of southeast Asia derive from the region's religious traditions. Cambodia's highly stylized classical dances are based on 12th-century Hindu dances, while much of Indonesian drama re-tells Hindu myths. Indonesia is also famous for its shadow puppet shows.

e ▸▸
southeast
Asia

A rich head-dress and jewellery transform the dancer into a goddess or other divine being

Hand gestures convey a specific meaning

CAMBODIAN CLASSICAL DANCER ▶
In her traditional, close-fitting, silk costume, a dancer performs the graceful movements of a classical Cambodian dance.

Terraces were cut by hand about 2,000 years ago

Stone walls prevent major soil erosion on the hillsides

▲ RICE TERRACES, PHILIPPINES
The stone walls on these ancient rice terraces in the Philippines help to retain the water in the fields at each level. Rice has been cultivated in southeast Asia for 7,000 years.

WHAT IS THE MAIN RELIGION ON THE MAINLAND?

Buddhism is the most important religion in mainland
southeast Asia, and the area has thousands of
monasteries and ornate Buddhist temples. In
Thailand, 95 per cent of the people are Buddhist
and nearly every village has its own temple or wat,
which is the centre of village life.

◄ BUDDHIST MONK,
BANGKOK, THAILAND
This Thai man's orange robes and
shaven head signify that he is a
Buddhist monk. He kneels at the
feet of a statue of the Buddha
inside a Bangkok temple.

*Two 88-storey towers
are linked by a skybridge
on the 42nd floor*

WHERE IS THE RING OF FIRE?

The "Ring of Fire" is an arc of active volcanoes
running through maritime southeast Asia and around
the Pacific Ocean. The volcanoes sit along the edges
of two plates that make up the Earth's crust. When the
plates move against each other they cause earthquakes
and volcanic eruptions on the islands of this region.

WHAT WAS THE ASIAN TSUNAMI?

On 26 December 2004, an undersea earthquake in
the Indian Ocean set off a tsunami (giant wave),
up to 30 m (100 ft) high. The so-called Asian
Tsunami devastated the shoreline of many Asian
countries, including parts of Indonesia, Sri
Lanka, Thailand, and southern India, killing
more than 280,000 people.

WHO ARE THE LITTLE TIGERS?

Many southeast Asian countries, such as Singapore,
the Philippines, Malaysia, and Indonesia, are known
as "Little Tigers" because of their fast-growing "tiger"
economies and industrial enterprise. These countries
benefit from cheap, plentiful labour, and export
manufactured goods such as clothes and electronics.

◄ JAKARTA, JAVA, INDONESIA
Jakarta, the capital of Indonesia,
is a crowded, modern city. Once
part of the Dutch Empire, its old
colonial buildings are now
overshadowed by the skyscrapers
of a modern economy.

▲ PETRONAS TOWERS,
KUALA LUMPUR, MALAYSIA
At 452 m (1,483 ft), the
Petronas Towers are among the
tallest buildings in the world.
They contain shops, businesses,
a museum, and a mosque.

SOUTHEAST ASIA

MYANMAR (BURMA)
Capital city: Rangoon
(Yangon)
Area: 678,500 sq km
(261,969 sq miles)
Population: 49.5 million

THAILAND
Capital city: Bangkok
Area: 514,000 sq km
(198,455 sq miles)
Population: 62.8 million

LAOS
Capital city: Vientiane
Area: 236,800 sq km
(91,428 sq miles)
Population: 5.7 million

VIETNAM
Capital city: Hanoi
Area: 329,560 sq km
(127,243 sq miles)
Population: 81.4 million

CAMBODIA
Capital city: Phnom Penh
Area: 181,040 sq km
(69,900 sq miles)
Population: 14.1 million

MALAYSIA
Capital city: Kuala Lumpur;
Putrajaya (administrative)
Area: 329,750 sq km
(127, 316 sq miles)
Population: 24.4 million

SINGAPORE
Capital city: Singapore
Area: 647.5 sq km
(250 sq miles)
Population: 4.3 million

BRUNEI
Capital city: Bandar Seri
Begawan
Area: 5,770 sq km
(2,228 sq miles)
Population: 358,000

INDONESIA
Capital city: Jakarta
Area: 1,919,440 sq km
(741,096 sq miles)
Population: 220 million

PHILIPPINES
Capital city: Manila
Area: 300,000 sq km
(115,830 sq miles)
Population: 80 million

EAST TIMOR
Capital city: Dili
Area: 14,874 sq km
(5,743 sq miles)
Population: 778,000

FIND OUT MORE ▸▸ Buddhism 289 • Continents 39 • Farming 66 • Islands 42 • Volcanoes 44

AUSTRALASIA AND OCEANIA

The sparsely populated continent of Australasia is made up of Australia, New Zealand, Papua New Guinea, and several nearby islands. It is the world's smallest continent, but includes a range of landscapes from tropical rainforest and arid desert, to volcanoes and dry grasslands. Oceania consists of about 25,000 volcanic or coral tropical islands, scattered over a vast area of the Pacific Ocean. The islands are divided into three groups: Melanesia, Micronesia, and Polynesia. Some of the islands are mountainous and densely forested, and many are uninhabited.

AUSTRALASIA & OCEANIA

Total land area: 8,508,238 sq km
(3,285,048 sq miles)

Total population: 31.4 million

Number of countries: 14

Largest country: Australia
7,686,850 sq km
(2,967,893 sq miles)

Smallest country: Nauru
21 sq km (8.1 sq miles)

Largest country population:
Australia 19.7 million

Largest lake: Lake Eyre, Australia
9,583 sq km
(3,700 sq miles)

Longest river: Murray-Darling,
Australia
3,750 km (2,330 miles)

Highest point: Mt Wilhelm,
Papua New Guinea
4,509 m (14,794 ft)

Major desert: Great Victoria
Desert, Australia

Largest coral reef: Great Barrier
Reef, Australia
2,000 km (1,242 miles)

e» Australasia

◄ SYDNEY HARBOUR
BRIDGE, AUSTRALIA
This huge landmark bridge carries road and railway traffic over the harbour of Australia's biggest city.

0 km   400   800
0 miles   400   800

▲ TROPICAL ISLAND, TONGA

Thousands of tiny tropical islands lie in the Pacific Ocean, circled by the coral reefs that grow off-shore. Many islands are covered in coconut trees that thrive throughout the region in spite of the poor soil and a lack of fresh water. Their fruits provide islanders with food and coconut milk, and husks to make rope and matting.

e ►► Oceania

PACIFIC OCEAN

Hawaiian Islands (U.S.)

Ratak Chain

Ralik Chain

MAJURO

BAIRIKI

Tarawa

Tungaru

Kiritimati

Line Islands

Equator

K I R I B A T I

Phoenix Islands

TUVALU

FONGAFALE

International Dateline

Tokelau (New Zealand)

Northern Cook Islands

Manihiki

Penrhyn

Santa Cruz Islands

Millennium Island

Marquesas Islands

Wallis & Futuna (France)

APIA

American Samoa (U.S.)

SAMOA

PAGO PAGO

Vanua Levu

VANUATU

Malekula

Efate

PORT VILA

Tango

Tanna

Viti Levu

SUVA

FIJI

Vava'u Group

TONGA

NUKU'ALOFA

Tongatapu Group

Niue (New Zealand)

ALOFI

Southern Cook Islands

Cook Islands (New Zealand)

Rarotonga

AVARUA

Society Islands

Tuamotu Islands

PAPEETE

Tahiti

French Polynesia (France)

Îles Australes

Îles Gambier

Pitcairn Islands (U.K.)

Tropic of Capricorn

Caledonia

PACIFIC

OCEAN

P o l y n e s i a

International Dateline

Marotiri

N

North Cape

Auckland

North Island

NEW ZEALAND

WELLINGTON

Cook Strait

Christchurch

South Island

Dunedin

Invercargill

SOUTH ISLAND, NEW ZEALAND ►

This lush, empty landscape is typical of the northern tip of New Zealand's South Island. The country as a whole is sparsely populated and its unspoilt scenery attracts many tourists.

FIND OUT MORE ►► Australia 425 • Habitats 82–84 • Islands 42 • New Zealand 425 • Volcanoes 44

AUSTRALIA AND NEW ZEALAND

Australia is both an island country and continent, lying between the Pacific and Indian Oceans. Its varied landscapes include a hot, dry centre (known as the outback), tropical rainforests, snow-capped mountains, and beautiful beaches. New Zealand lies about 1,500 km (932 miles) southeast of Australia. On the North Island there are forests, volcanoes, and hot springs. South Island is more mountainous with glaciers, fjords, and lakes.

WHAT IS UNIQUE ABOUT AUSTRALIA'S WILDLIFE?

Many of the animals in Australia are found nowhere else in the world. Marsupial mammals, such as kangaroos, koalas, and wombats, and egg-laying mammals, such as the duck-billed platypus, are unique to this country. These creatures evolved here because they were isolated by vast oceans for 30 million years.

▲ ABORIGINAL WAY OF LIFE
Some Aboriginals still live a traditional life, travelling through the outback on foot in search of food. The men hunt animals, such as kangaroos and possums, with boomerangs and spears.

▲ KANGAROOS, AUSTRALIA
Kangaroos, the largest of Australia's marsupial mammals, can reach speeds of 56 km/h (35 mph). The animals live in herds in the outback, sheltering from the Sun by day and feeding on grass at dusk.

SYDNEY, AUSTRALIA ▶
Sydney is Australia's largest city. It is an important cultural centre and home to four million people. The landmark Sydney Opera House stands on the harbour. Its roof design mirrors the sails of passing boats.

WHICH SPORTS ARE POPULAR IN AUSTRALIA?

Outdoor sports are a large part of the Australian lifestyle. The majority of Australians live near the coast where the sunny climate, sandy beaches, and warm water make sailing, swimming, surfing, and diving popular activities. Australians also enjoy spectator sports, and their tennis players and cricket and rugby teams all enjoy great international success.

Australia

WHO LIVES IN AUSTRALIA?

Australia has a diverse, multicultural society. Many people are of European origin, but the population also includes people from China, Indonesia, and Vietnam. Australia's oldest inhabitants are the Aboriginal people who settled here over 40,000 years ago.

WHICH GIANT DESERT ROCK IS A SACRED SITE?

The giant block of red sandstone named Uluru, meaning "great pebble", stands in the middle of Australia's desert. The rock is held sacred by the Aboriginals of this region and features in their beliefs about the creation of the world.

▲ ULURU, AUSTRALIA
Uluru was formed more than 570 million years ago. This giant rock rises 867 m (2,844 ft) above the desert and is 3.6 km (2.2 miles) long. The rock seems to glow and turn orange at sunrise.

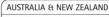

New Zealand

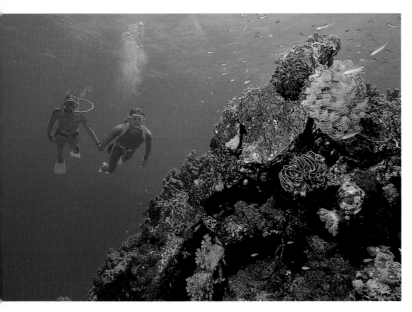

◄ **GREAT BARRIER REEF, AUSTRALIA**
The Great Barrier Reef stretches for 2,000 km (1,242 miles) in the Pacific Ocean. It is a major attraction to tourists in glass-bottom boats and divers, who come to see the huge variety of wildlife. This includes 350 species of brightly coloured corals, 1,500 species of fish, sea anemones, giant clams, and many different types of sponge.

AUSTRALIA & NEW ZEALAND	
AUSTRALIA	
Capital city: Canberra	
Area: 7,686,850 sq km (2,967,893 sq miles)	
Population: 19.7 million	
Official language: English	
Major religions: Roman Catholic and Anglican	
Currency: Australian dollar	
NEW ZEALAND	
Capital city: Wellington	
Area: 268,680 sq km (103,737 sq miles)	
Population: 3.9 million	
Official languages: English and Maori	
Major religions: Anglican and Presbyterian	
Currency: New Zealand dollar	

WHY IS THE GREAT BARRIER REEF UNDER THREAT?
Each year, thousands of tourists visit the Great Barrier Reef, causing damage and pollution to what is the largest coral reef in the world. The fragile reef lies off the northeast coast of Australia, and is home to a huge variety of underwater life. Constructed by tiny creatures over thousands of years, the reef is also threatened by infestations of the crown of thorns starfish, which devours large areas of coral in a day.

WHO WERE THE FIRST PEOPLE IN NEW ZEALAND?
New Zealand was uninhabited until the Maori people came to settle from Pacific islands over 1,000 years ago. Later in the 19th century, European settlers arrived in the country. In recent years, there has been an influx of non-Maori Polynesians and Asians, adding to this multicultural society. Today, Maoris – the original inhabitants – make up about 12 per cent of New Zealand's total population.

WHAT SIGHTS CAN YOU SEE IN NEW ZEALAND'S NATIONAL PARKS?
Nearly 13 per cent of New Zealand's land lies inside national parks. The rugged mountains, huge glaciers, lakes, fjords, and forests are ideal for trekking, sailing, white-water rafting, and other outdoor pursuits. The spectacular scenery also includes active volcanoes, spouting geysers, and boiling mud pools.

GEYSERS, NEW ZEALAND ►
Geysers are found where volcanic rocks inside the Earth heat water in underground chasms to boiling point. It erupts as a fountain of scalding water and steam up to 460 m (1,509 ft) high.

◄ **NEW ZEALAND SHEEP**
Since the introduction of refrigerated ships, New Zealand sheep have been raised for meat. Frozen lamb is a major export to Asia, Europe, and the USA.

WHY ARE THERE SO MANY SHEEP IN THE REGION?
New Zealand's damp climate and rich pasture make sheep farming the country's biggest industry. With over 44 million sheep (about 11 sheep for every person), wool and lamb are major exports. Australia is the world's chief wool-producing country. Its 120 million sheep are raised on huge farms called stations, where farmers use light aircraft to patrol up to 15,000 sq km (5,792 sq miles) of land.

FIND OUT MORE ►► Cnidarians 103 • First Modern Humans 362–363 • Islands 42 • Mammals 120–123 • Polynesia 396

ANTARCTICA

The freezing, inhospitable continent of Antarctica was the last place on Earth to be explored. It is a vast, mountainous land mass at the South Pole, buried under an ice sheet up to 4 km (2.5 miles) thick, and surrounded by frozen seas.

Antarctica has no countries and no permanent population. With winter temperatures falling to −80°C (−112°F), its sole inhabitants are visiting research scientists.

WHO OWNS ANTARCTICA?

Antarctica does not belong to any nation, but is governed under an international treaty that bans countries from owning or exploiting its land. The 1959 Antarctic Treaty, signed by 45 nations, suspended the claims of seven countries for territory in the region. Today, Antarctica is designated as "a continent for science", and only used for peaceful purposes.

WHAT DO SCIENTISTS STUDY IN ANTARCTICA?

Scientists from all over the world visit Antarctica to study the climate, weather, geology, and wildlife of this unique region. Their research has helped to highlight global problems, such as climate change. During the summer, about 3,700 scientists work in the 46 or more scientific research stations scattered across the continent. Only about 1,200 scientists remain in winter because of the intense cold.

◄ PENGUIN COLONY, ANTARCTICA
Emperor penguins feed on fish and spend most of the year at sea. They come onto the ice to breed in huge colonies called rookeries.

◀ **AMUNDSEN-SCOTT BASE**
The American-owned Amundsen-Scott research station, named after two Antarctic explorers, is situated at the South Pole. It is insulated against the intense cold and parts are built below the surface in order to conserve heat.

ANTARCTICA
Total land area: 14 million sq km (5.4 million sq miles)

Total population: no indigenous inhabitants, but there are seasonally staffed research stations

Number of countries: 0

Highest point: Vinson Massif 4,897 m (16,066 ft)

Major deserts: the continent is technically a desert

Largest island: Alexander Island

Lowest temperature on Earth: -89.2°C (-128.6°F) recorded at Vostok Station

ARCTIC

The Arctic region lies at the North Pole. It is a small, frozen ocean surrounded by the northern edges of Europe, Asia, and North America, whose flat, bleak landscape is known as the tundra. The region is a cold and hostile environment and few people live there. The Arctic Ocean, however, teems with wildlife.

◀ **POLAR BEAR ON ARCTIC ICE**
A polar bear's thick white fur protects it from the cold and provides camouflage as it hunts for seals and other animals.

WHICH ANIMALS CAN SURVIVE IN THE ARCTIC?
The Arctic Ocean is home to seals, walruses, and many species of whale, which thrive in the icy waters protected by thick layers of blubber. In the warmer summer months, animals such as reindeer, musk oxen, hares, and Arctic foxes hunt for food on land, but migrate south during the harsh winter.

Arctic

Antarctica

0 km 800
0 miles 800

SOCIETY and BELIEFS

ABBREVIATIONS

The dates in this section are followed by the letters CE or BCE, which mean "Common Era" and "Before Common Era". These terms replace BC and AD – "Before Christ" and Anno Domini ("In the Year of Our Lord") – but refer to the same periods.

RELIGION

Religion involves belief in divine beings along with a set of practices and a moral code that help to reinforce that belief. A religion's teachings, usually written down in a holy book, and its stories, are intended to help people to understand the meaning of life. Each religion has its own idea of the ultimate goal of life, its own place for worshipping ▸▸ **GOD** or gods, its own rituals, and its own rules for living.

◀ **HOLY RIVER**
The River Ganges, also worshipped as the goddess Ganga, is considered the holiest of all rivers by Hindus. Pilgrims drink, bathe, and scatter their loved ones' ashes in the sacred waters in an act of spiritual purification.

▲ **ILLUMINATED GOSPEL**
Before printing was invented, holy books were beautifully written out by scribes. Christian Bibles, like this 1503 New Testament in Ancient Greek from Moldavia in present-day Romania, were all hand-copied in monasteries by monks.

Hindu pilgrims ritually wash themselves in the Ganges during a religious festival in the holy city of Varanasi (Benares)

ARE THERE MANY RELIGIONS?
Religions are not easy to count. Islam, Judaism, and Christianity share some common origins, but are all separate. Each of these may contain more recent differences, such as Sunni and Shia Muslims, or Catholic and Protestant Christians.

GOD

Most religions believe in one or many gods. A god is an all-knowing, all-powerful being, who can help or hinder humans. In some religions, believers pray to their god or gods for help. In others, they use meditation to help them focus on their duties.

DO ALL FAITHS HAVE A GOD?
Although Buddhists share common roots with Hindus, they worship no gods but instead use Buddha's teachings to encourage spiritual progress. Confucians strive for cosmic harmony by creating a society based on order and virtue. Many local religions worship spirits that inhabit the natural world around them.

WHY IS THERE SUFFERING IN THE WORLD?
Each religion has its own explanation for suffering. Often it is seen as punishment for sin, or bad behaviour. People may be tricked into being bad by a devil figure, or they may be misled by their own desires. Western religions generally see suffering as the result of human failing. Eastern religions see it as the result of human ignorance.

WHO DOES NOT HAVE FAITH?
Atheists reject all belief in supernatural beings. Agnostics accept the possibility of God, but cannot commit themselves. Humanists replace faith with human reason. Many people are non-religious, but may describe themselves as having spiritual beliefs.

HOW DO WE LEARN A RELIGION?
Young people usually learn a religion by following the same beliefs and rituals as their parents. Most religions use teachings and stories to inform children about, for example, ▶◀ CREATION. Some religions also try to convince other people to join their faith.

DO RELIGIONS HAVE ALL THE ANSWERS?
As people grow up, they start to ask all sorts of questions: "What is the meaning of life?"; "Why do people suffer?"; "Does God exist?" The world's religions have all sought in different ways to provide answers to these questions. Where Western religions tend to focus on obedience to God and salvation from sin, Eastern religions tend to focus on self-knowledge and release from the cycle of rebirth.

WHY DO PEOPLE BECOME RELIGIOUS?
The mysteries of the natural world and the Universe have inspired religious feelings throughout time. Today, science can explain much but not everything, and people still use religion to help them explain events and their place in the world.

FAITHS AND FOLLOWERS (A ROUGH GUIDE BASED ON CENSUSES)	
BELIEFS	*NUMBER OF FOLLOWERS*
Christianity	1.9 billion
Islam	1.2 billion
Non-religious	920 million
Hinduism	780 million
Confucianism/Taoism	540 million
Buddhism	330 million
Shintoism	110 million
Sikhism	19 million
Judaism	14 million
Zoroastrianism	150,000

▲ RELIGIOUS UNITY
These religious leaders are marching for peace in the world. They include a Jewish rabbi, a Muslim sheikh, a Christian bishop, and a Japanese Buddhist monk, showing how universal goals can rise above religious differences.

religion

CREATION

Many religions have their own story about the origins of the Universe and of humankind. Called creation stories, these often pass on ancient insights about humanity and its relation to the natural world. Some view the scientific Big Bang theory as another creation story.

HOW DID THE WORLD BEGIN?
Some religions have complex stories about the gods who gave birth to the world. Australian Aboriginal beliefs recount a Dreamtime when mythic ancestors roamed the Earth, creating the landscape by their actions. Judaism and Christianity describe a world that was created in seven days by God's command.

DO RELIGIONS BELIEVE IN EVERLASTING LIFE?
Most religions follow their own calendar. The Mayan calendar of Central America predicts that the current epoch will end in 2012. Hindus and Buddhists believe that time is cyclical, so everything is reborn over and over again, including the world. Christians and Muslims believe that time is linear and that the world will end with a Day of Judgement.

▲ NAVAHO YEI RUG
The Yei figures in this American Indian rug were originally only shown during the healing Night Chant ritual, when medicine men (healer-priests) created their images on the ground with coloured sand.

Yei are sacred beings, possibly ancestors, worshipped by the Navaho

FIND OUT MORE ▶▶ Southern Asia 266–267 • Universe 26

ANCIENT RELIGIONS

Some religions have died out, along with the cultures that practised them. We know about them and their practices, such as belief in the ▸▸ AFTERLIFE , through their buildings and artefacts. The best-known are from Egypt, Greece, and Central America.

WHO WAS RA?
The Egyptian sun god Ra could be shown with the head of a falcon, a ram, or an old man. Like many long-lived religions, Ancient Egyptian beliefs combined gods from several local religions.

WHO WORSHIPPED A FEATHERED SNAKE?
The greatest god of the Aztec religion was Quetzalcoatl, creator of the world, who was depicted as a snake with Quetzal feathers. When the Spanish conquistador Cortés landed in Mexico, the Aztec ruler believed he was the returning Quetzalcoatl.

ARE THE OLD GODS STILL WITH US?
The names of the Ancient Roman and Greek gods are still used in Western naming systems. All the planets of the Solar System (apart from Earth) are named after Roman gods. The swift-footed messenger god Mercury gives his name to a silvery liquid metal.

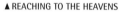

▲ MARS, GOD OF WAR
Mars, the Roman god of war, gave his name to the fourth planet of the Solar System, the month of March, martial arts (fighting skills), and martial law (military rule).

▲ REACHING TO THE HEAVENS
Central American cultures such as the Zapotecs (forerunners of the Aztecs) built huge pyramid temples with stairs leading up to platforms for human sacrifice (top). Mount Fuji (above) is sacred to Shintoism.

AFTERLIFE

The idea of an afterlife – what happens to people after they die – has been around as long as the oldest religions. Ancient rulers were often buried with large numbers of useful items, such as model boats and food, to help them live on in the next world.

ancient religions

WHAT IS A SOUL?
Many religions believe that there is an eternal, godlike part in people, called a soul or spirit. Some religions, such as Hinduism, believe this soul inhabits all living things. After death, the soul returns to Earth in a new body, or goes on to inhabit heaven or hell.

WHAT WERE THE PYRAMIDS?
Some Ancient Egyptian pharaohs were buried in huge pyramids. These monumental tombs symbolically pointed to the stars to guide the pharaoh's soul on its journey to the heavens. The most famous are the three found at Giza, near Cairo.

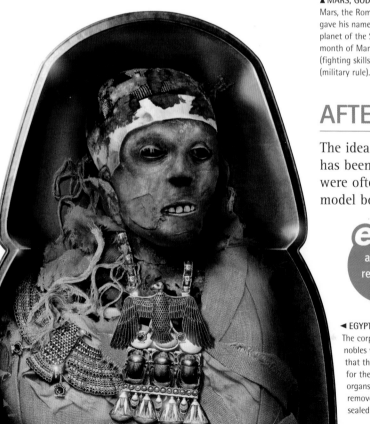

◀ EGYPTIAN MUMMY
The corpses of Egyptian nobles were mummified, so that they were preserved for the afterlife. Internal organs were carefully removed and kept in sealed jars near the body.

FIND OUT MORE ▸▸ Ancient Egypt 370–371 • Conquistadors 405

LOCAL RELIGIONS

Local religions are unique to tribal or cultural groups living apart from modern societies. They are not taught through texts, but through story-telling, art, songs, and ▶▶ RITUALS. Many honour their ancestors as well as gods or natural spirits.

◀ ULURU ▶
This huge red rock (also known as Ayers Rock) in the heart of the Northern Territory, Australia, is the most sacred place for the Aboriginal people.

WHY ARE SOME PLACES SACRED?
Sacred places always have a special importance to the life of the tribe. They may be a source of water, a gathering point, a site of ancestor activities, or a border with another group's territory. Sometimes they are used as burial grounds for the dead.

WHO WORSHIPS ANCESTORS?
Offering gifts and prayers to dead ancestors is a common feature of local religious ritual throughout the world, especially in Asia. The dead are believed to help their living relatives, and to intervene with the gods on their behalf.

WHAT IS A FETISH FOR?
Fetishes are portable, carved, and customized objects that are believed to be the home for a spirit or magical powers. The owner of the fetish may use it to borrow the powers of that spirit or simply as protection against bad luck or bad health.

TOTEM POLE ▶
Totem poles are mainly found among the tribal peoples of the northwest coast of America. The carvings represent the different clans (symbolized by animal spirits) to which the owner belongs.

RITUALS

Like all world religions, local religions have rituals – special performances of words and actions that help to bind the community together in a common identity. Rituals may mark a rite of passage, such as marriage, or be a call for help from the spirit world.

ARE SHAMANS MAGICIANS?
Most local religions have a shaman, or medicine man, who possesses secret knowledge and uses spells, rituals, and traditional knowledge of medicinal plants or animals to help those who need healing or spiritual help.

SHAMAN DANCING ▶
This Dayak shaman from Indonesia is performing a ceremonial dance. Shamans often use dance to enter altered states of consciousness in order to communicate with the spirit world.

e ▶▶
local
religions

FIND OUT MORE ▶▶ Canada, Alaska, and Greenland 224–225

ZOROASTRIANISM

Zarathustra lived around the 13th century BCE in Iran. He taught that people should choose between the opposing forces of good and evil. His teachings were highly influential on later religions.

WHAT MAKES A PARSI?

Zoroastrianism was the official religion of the Persian Empire. When that empire fell, some of its followers, after a period of much religious persecution, moved to India, where they became known as Parsis ("people from Persia"). Young Parsis are initiated into the faith at the age of seven, in a ceremony called Navjote.

NAVJOTE INITIATION ▶
A young initiate receives the kusti, or sacred thread, which is wrapped three times around the waist, and undone during prayers.

HOW DO PARSIS WORSHIP?

Zoroastrian religious buildings are called Fire Temples. Zoroastrians perform prayer rituals before a sacred fire, where incense and sandalwood are burnt. This is believed to represent the god Ahura Mazda, source of light and life. Zarathustra's teachings are read or sung from the sacred Avesta scripture.

Three layers of feathers on the wings represent good words, good thoughts, and good deeds, while the three layers on the tail represent the opposite

Zoroastrianism

FARAVAHAR ▶
This symbol, known as the faravahar, represents the immortal human soul, and by extension the Zoroastrian religion. Its human face indicates its connection to humankind.

FIND OUT MORE ▶▶ Persian Empire 375 • Western Asia and the Middle East 264–265

SHINTO

Shinto ("the way of the gods") is Japan's oldest religion and centres on the worship of kami, or spirits. These are believed to inhabit any powerful or impressive natural phenomena, such as the wind or Mount Fuji.

WHEN DID SHINTO BEGIN?

No-one knows how old Shinto is, for its origins lie deep in prehistory. Its main elements probably appeared from the 4th century BCE onwards. Although most Shinto worship relates to earthly kami, Shinto texts written around 700 CE also mention heavenly kami, who are responsible for creating the world.

▲ MATSURI PARADE
The matsuri festival is a shrine's most important annual event. Local people carry an image of the local kami through the streets in a portable shrine or mikoshi. The ceremony blesses both the neighbourhood and the carriers.

TORII GATE ▲
The distinctive torii arch symbolizes the border between the human world and the kami world. The best-known example is the floating torii off the island of Miyajima, near Hiroshima.

◀ AMATERASU EMERGES
The most important kami is the sun goddess Amaterasu, who is also associated with the imperial family. Here she is shown emerging from her cave and restoring sunlight to the world.

Shinto

WHAT MARKS A SACRED PLACE?

Followers of Shinto consider nature to be sacred, so their places of worship are often found in beautiful natural settings. Natural sacred places are marked with a thick rope (shimenawa) tied around a tree or rock. Shinto shrines, which are built to house at least one kami, are marked by a simple torii, or gateway.

FIND OUT MORE ▶▶ Eastern Asia 268–269 • Local Religions 283

CONFUCIANISM

Kong Fuzi ("Master Kong"), known as Confucius to Western cultures, was a wise man who lived in China from 551 to 479 BCE. His teachings focused on the proper relationships between people, including respect for one's parents and ancestors, and the creation of a harmonious society based on virtue.

Confucius carries the five classic scrolls

Confucianism

DO PEOPLE WORSHIP CONFUCIUS?

Kong Fuzi made no claim to holiness, and taught that living a good life is its own reward. After his death, his teachings were developed by his followers and spread to Korea, Japan, and Vietnam. His followers worship his soul as a great ancestor.

WHAT ARE THE FIVE CLASSICS?

Confucianism consists of five classic texts – *History*, *Poetry*, *Rituals*, *Seasons*, and the *I Ching*, or *Book of Changes*. The *I Ching* helped people cope with uncertainty by offering them the chance to predict the future.

◄ CONFUCIAN TEMPLE
Although Confucians do not worship gods, they honour their ancestors in temples, like this one in Taiwan.

CONFUCIUS ►
The writings of Confucius were originally intended as advice for the rulers of China. One of his most famous lines was: "Rule by the power of moral example."

FIND OUT MORE ▶▶ China's First Empire 378

DAOISM

Dao ("the way") is the organizing principle of the Universe. The best way to act or think is wuwei, or effortless activity. Not trying to resist or control events helps peace and harmony to be created within oneself and within the world.

Laozi carries a scroll of the Daode Jing

◄ YIN AND YANG
The Daoist Universe is made up of two opposite but balancing forces. Yin is female, dark, fluid, and low energy. Yang is male, fiery, solid, and high energy.

Daoism

WHO FOUNDED DAOISM?

Laozi ("the old master"), who lived in China in the 6th century BCE, wrote the *Daode Jing*, whose teachings form the cornerstone of Daoism. According to tradition, Laozi served as archivist in the royal court and knew Confucius. When Laozi decided to go on a spiritual pilgrimage, he was not allowed to leave China until he had written down all his teachings.

◄ LAOZI ON A BUFFALO
There are several legends about the life of Laozi, but very little is known of him for certain. He is said to have travelled around China on the back of a water buffalo.

WHAT IS QI?

The principle of Qi lies at the root of Chinese life and belief. It is the vital substance that makes up the Universe and is composed of two complementary energy forces: yin and yang. The Chinese believe that Qi runs through energy lines in our bodies and that when these lines are blocked, ill health results. Acupuncture uses needles to unblock them.

FIND OUT MORE ▶▶ China's First Empire 378

HINDUISM

Hinduism is one of the world's oldest religions and the main religious tradition of India. More a way of life than a set of beliefs, it has no individual founder. It developed slowly over a long period of time out of a variety of local religions.

WHAT IS BRAHMAN?

Many Hindus believe that beneath this variety there is one unchanging reality known as Brahman, the eternal creative force which made the Universe and to which all things return. Hindus believe that human souls are reborn in cycles of **▶▶ REINCARNATION**.

DO HINDU GODS LIVE IN STATUES?

Images are powerful symbols of the presence of a god and offerings are often made before them. The most popular gods include the elephant-headed Ganesh, symbol of wealth and success, and the monkey god Hanuman, symbol of heroism and loyalty.

▲ SACRED SOUND
The sacred symbol Om (or Aum) is a mantra (repeated sound) that represents Brahman and is often used to help meditation.

SHIVA THE DANCER ▶
The god Shiva symbolizes both destruction and creation. He is shown here dancing on the body of a demon, with a hoop of flames around him to represent the energy of the Universe.

▲ FESTIVAL OF COLOUR
Holi marks the start of spring. During the day, people visit and greet one another, and commemorate the mischievous pranks of the god Krishna by throwing coloured water and powder over one another.

Hinduism

▲ "HAIL TO KRISHNA"
Hare Krishnas belong to a branch of Hinduism that was established in America in the 1960s by A.C. Bhaktivedanta. They honour Krishna, one of Vishnu's incarnations, and their name comes from the devotional mantra they chant: "Hare Krishna" ("Hail to Krishna").

BRAHMA ▶
Brahma the creator (not to be confused with Brahman) has four heads, in order to see in all directions. Together with Vishnu the preserver and Shiva the destroyer, these gods are known to Hindus as the Trimurti, or "three forms".

◀ HOLY SADHU
Sadhus are wandering holy men who have cut all family ties, own nothing, and live on alms. They devote their life to gaining wisdom and achieving moksha (release from the cycle of rebirth).

REINCARNATION

Hindus believe that living things do not have just one life but are trapped in a cycle of death and rebirth, known as samsara. People are reborn into higher or lower social positions depending on their actions in their current life.

DID BUDDHISM LEARN FROM HINDUISM?

Buddhism is not interested in whether God exists, or how and why the world was created. Instead, it focuses on the Hindu idea of the cycle of rebirth and how to achieve nirvana, or release from this cycle, by freeing its followers from greed, hatred, and ignorance.

FIND OUT MORE ▶▶ Buddhism 289 • Southern Asia 266–267

JUDAISM

Judaism is the world's oldest religion based on belief in one God. Jews believe that God made them his chosen people and promised them a land of their own, Israel, in return for following his commandments. These are laid down in the sacred text of the ▶▶ TORAH.

The rabbi is the spiritual leader of the synagogue

A yarmulka, or kippah, is a skull-cap used to cover the head as a sign of respect for God

A tallit is a prayer shawl with knotted fringes

HOW MANY TYPES OF JUDAISM ARE THERE?

Religious Jews are divided into two main groups: Orthodox and Non-Orthodox. Orthodox Jews unquestioningly obey the Torah and all its rules. Non-Orthodox Jews try to adapt Judaism to modern life. Both groups observe the Jewish ▶▶ HOLY DAYS.

HOW DO YOUNG BOYS COME OF AGE?

At the age of 13, a boy is considered an adult and becomes bar mitzvah ("son of the covenant") after a ceremony of the same name. This takes place in their place of worship, the synagogue, and is followed by a big party to celebrate the occasion.

STAR OF DAVID ▶
This six-pointed Star of David was adopted as a symbol of Judaism about 200 years ago. The star has 12 sides, symbolizing the 12 tribes of Israel unified by King David. Today, it is the main symbol on the Israeli flag.

BAR MITZVAH ▲
When a boy attends his bar mitzvah, he reads from the Torah scroll in the synagogue for the first time.

Yad is the silver pointer used to follow the text

The Sefer Torah, or Torah scroll, is the most sacred object in Judaism

TORAH

The most sacred texts of Judaism are the first five books of the Hebrew Scriptures, which are known as the Torah or Book of Law. Orthodox tradition believes that God spoke the words of the Torah directly to Moses. Every synagogue keeps a beautifully hand-written Torah scroll in an ark (cupboard) facing Jerusalem.

IS THE TORAH JUDAISM'S ONLY SCRIPTURE?

The Hebrew Bible (known to Christians as the Old Testament) consists of the Torah and two other books: The Prophets and The Writings. The Talmud, which contains Jewish law and writings of the ancient rabbis, is also important.

Judaism

HOLY DAYS

Jewish families come together to mark major festivals throughout the year, including Yom Kippur (Day of Atonement), Pesach (Passover), and Rosh Hashanah (New Year). One of the most important commandments is to observe the Sabbath as a day of rest.

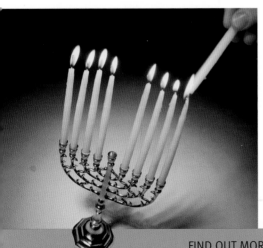

◀ LIGHTING THE MENORAH
The eight-day celebration of Hanukkah, or festival of lights, is marked by lighting one extra candle each night on the menorah (a nine-branched candlestick).

WHAT IS THE SABBATH?

The Sabbath (Shabbat in Hebrew) is the Jewish holy day. It begins at sunset on Friday and lasts until sunset on Saturday. It is a day for rest when no work – even cooking – may be done. It honours the belief that God rested on the seventh day of Creation.

FIND OUT MORE ▶▶ Christianity 288 • Middle East 264–265 • Middle Eastern Empires 372–373

CHRISTIANITY

Christians believe in one God with three aspects: God the father, God the son (Jesus Christ), and God the Holy Spirit. Jesus's role as the Messiah, who lived around 2,000 years ago, is revealed in the ▶▶ BIBLE.

▲ THE CROSS
Jesus was nailed to a wooden cross by the Romans and left to die – a method of execution known as crucifixion.

WHY IS JESUS CALLED KING OF THE JEWS?
Judaism teaches that a Messiah, or holy king, will come to Earth to complete God's plan for humankind. Christians believe that Jesus (who was born a Jew) is this Messiah, while Jews believe he was a prophet, preparing the way for a Messiah yet to come.

WHAT DOES THE CROSS MEAN?
The cross symbolizes the death and ▶▶ RESURRECTION of Christ. Christians believe that Jesus's death brought salvation, by taking away their sins. When Christians are baptized they are marked with the sign of the cross in remembrance of this sacrifice.

Flag with a red cross is a symbol of Christ's resurrection

I · AM · THE · RESVRRECTION · AND · THE · LIFE

Angels are God's messengers and helpers

THE RESURRECTION ▲
This 19th-century stained-glass window from Lincoln Cathedral shows Jesus rising from the dead. Christians celebrate this event during the Easter festival.

Jesus rising from the tomb

Wounds on Jesus's hands and feet show where he was nailed to the cross

e ▶▶
Christianity

▲ ST BASIL THE BLESSED, MOSCOW
This distinctive 16th-century Russian cathedral belongs to the Orthodox tradition of Christianity. This tradition, based in eastern Europe, split from the Roman Catholic Church, and its leader the Pope, in the 11th century.

RESURRECTION

Christians believe that Jesus Christ came to life three days after his death and rose up to heaven to live again at the right hand of God. His resurrection is a symbol of hope for all Christians.

HOW LONG DID JESUS LIVE ON EARTH?
Jesus Christ lived in Roman-occupied Palestine. His mother was the Virgin Mary and his earthly father was Joseph. He worked as a carpenter before becoming a religious teacher. His teachings upset the Roman and religious authorities and he was executed at the age of 33.

BIBLE

The Christian scripture is called the Bible. It combines the Jewish Bible (Old Testament) with a Christian Bible (New Testament) that includes accounts of Jesus's teachings and those of his followers.

DO CHRISTIANS THINK THE BIBLE IS TRUE?
Many Christians regard the Bible as the sacred word of God and literally true. Others view it as a mixture of history, stories, poems, and parables that can be interpreted in a more symbolic way.

MANUSCRIPT BIBLE ▶
Before the age of printing, the Bible was carefully hand-copied in Latin or Greek, usually by monks in monasteries, and sold to rich, well-educated people.

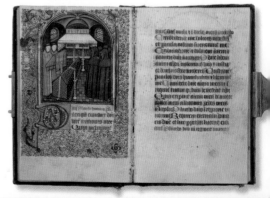

FIND OUT MORE ▶▶ Crusades 389 • Judaism 287

BUDDHISM

Buddhism was developed in India about 2,500 years ago by Siddhartha Gautama, or Buddha ("the enlightened one"). He reinterpreted Hindu ideas about ▶▶ KARMA and rebirth to show how suffering could be avoided. His teachings spread throughout eastern Asia.

WHAT IS MEDITATION FOR?

The Buddha is believed to have found nirvana (enlightenment) while meditating under a bodhi tree. Meditation involves emptying the mind of all thoughts and distractions in order to achieve inner peace and greater understanding.

DO BUDDHISTS HAVE SACRED BUILDINGS?

Many Buddhists visit temples or shrines to pay homage to Buddha or ask for his help. The oldest style of Buddhist shrine is called a stupa (a bell-shaped mound) and holds holy relics. Chinese and Japanese shrines are multi-storeyed towers, known as pagodas.

▲ BUDDHA'S FOOTPRINTS
This relief sculpture shows Buddha's footprints on a pillar at the Great Stupa of Sanchi, India, built by King Ashoka.

▲ BUDDHIST MONKS
These young monks from Thailand wear distinctive saffron-coloured robes and live in a monastic community called the Sangha. Monks and nuns may start their training as early as five years old.

Buddhism

KARMA

Karma refers to the idea that a person's good or bad actions have consequences in this and future lives. Buddhists believe that the inequality of mankind is the result of karma accumulated over many lives, but that it is always open to change.

WHAT IS NIRVANA?

Nirvana is enlightenment, which means freedom from the cycle of rebirth and suffering, and is imagined as a blissful, everlasting state. This is reached when a person is completely free from greed, hatred, and ignorance, and attachments to the human world. Unlike Hindus, Buddhists do not believe in an everlasting soul.

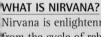

TIBETAN PRAYER WHEEL ▶
The wheel contains hundreds of mantras (short prayers) written on a paper scroll. Spinning the wheel releases these mantras into the world.

▲ MANDALA
A mandala is an image of the heavenly realm used to help focus meditation. Monks made this mandala over many months by sprinkling coloured sand on the ground. They made it for a young monk's initiation ritual and will destroy it at the end.

◀ ENLIGHTENED BUDDHA
Many statues of Buddha capture his enlightenment and usually show him sitting cross-legged or lying on his side. This 30-m (98-ft-) high statue is one of four at Kyaikpun pagoda in Bago, Myanmar (formerly known as Burma).

FIND OUT MORE ▶▶ Southern Asia 266–267 • Hinduism 286

ISLAM

Islam means obedience to the will of Allah (God) and honours the laws and teachings revealed to his prophet Muhammad in the sacred book known as the ▶▶ QUR'AN. Followers of Islam are called Muslims ("obedient ones").

WHERE DO MUSLIMS WORSHIP?

Muslims can pray anywhere, but often gather in a mosque to pray together. A mosque usually has a minaret tower, from which a muezzin (caller) chants a call to prayer five times a day. All Muslims pray facing east towards Mecca and a small niche (mihrab) is always set into the mosque wall nearest Mecca.

WHY DO MUSLIMS PRAY TOWARDS MECCA?

Mecca in Saudi Arabia is Muhammad's birthplace and the holiest city of Islam. In 610 CE, Muhammad received the first of his revelations from God on a mountain outside Mecca. All Muslims are supposed to make the ▶▶ HAJJ at least once a lifetime, if they can.

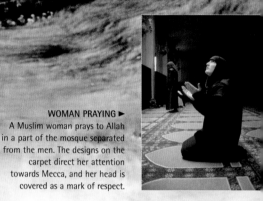

▲ KA'BA
When Muslim pilgrims arrive in Mecca, they must walk seven times around the Ka'ba, a shrine covered in a black cloth.

WOMAN PRAYING ▶
A Muslim woman prays to Allah in a part of the mosque separated from the men. The designs on the carpet direct her attention towards Mecca, and her head is covered as a mark of respect.

▲ MOSQUE AT DJENNE, MALI
Like most world religions, Islamic architecture tends to adapt to its surroundings. This 14th-century African mosque in Djenne, once a major centre of trade and learning, is built of mud and shaped like a fort.

▲ CRESCENT MOON
The hilal, or crescent moon, has become the recognized symbol of Islam. It has ancient connections with Islamic dynasties and also links the lunar calendar to Muslim religious life.

HAJJ

The Hajj is a pilgrimage to Mecca made once in every Muslim's lifetime, if it is possible. It is one of the five Pillars of Islam – which also include the statement of faith, daily worship, charity, and fasting.

WHAT IS THE KA'BA?

The Ka'ba is a holy shrine at the heart of Mecca's Sacred Mosque. Muslims believe it was originally built by Ibrahim (Abraham) on a site made holy by the first man, Adam. In the pre-Islamic period it was a shrine to 360 Arabic deities. In 630 CE, Muhammad rededicated the shrine to Allah.

QUR'AN

Also spelled Koran, this is Islam's holiest text, believed to have been revealed to Muhammad by Allah. The Qur'an unites all Muslims in a single language, as they must learn Arabic to read Allah's original words.

HOW DOES THE QUR'AN SPEAK?

The Arabic name Qur'an means "the recital". Muhammad's first revelation began with the angel Gabriel's instruction, "Recite!" The verses (Ayat) and chapters (Surahs) are arranged to help reading aloud. Marks show when to breathe at the end of each verse.

Islam

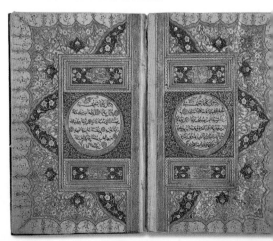

DECORATED QUR'AN ▶
Many copies of the Qur'an are precious works of art, such as this 17th-century example. Making the word of Allah beautiful is an act of worship in itself.

FIND OUT MORE ▶▶ Judaism 287 • North Africa 240–241

SIKHISM

Sikhism was founded about 500 years ago in the Punjab region of India, by a man who became known as ⏩ GURU Nanak. He taught that all religions share the same essential truth and that holiness is to be found within. Sikh literally means "disciple".

◀ **THE KHANDA**
The khanda symbol represents many of the core Sikh beliefs. The khanda (two-edged sword) symbolizes belief in the power of truth. The circle represents unity and eternity. The curved swords stand for the warrior spirit.

The Akal Takht stores the sacred book overnight

The Causeway connects the temple to the pavement surrounding the lake

The Harimandir (Golden Temple) houses the sacred book, the Guru Granth Sahib

The Lake of Immortality was built by Guru Ram Das

The Darshani Deorhi is the gateway to the temple complex

WHERE IS THE CENTRE OF SIKHISM?

The Harimandir, or Golden Temple, has become the symbol of the Sikh religion and their most important pilgrimage site. The fourth Guru, Ram Das, built a city and sacred lakes at Amritsar, in the Punjab, where Guru Nanak once meditated. The fifth Guru, Arjan, built the Golden Temple and collected the teachings of the Gurus into a sacred book, the Granth Sahib.

HOW DO SIKHS WORSHIP?

Guru Nanak taught that "the only temple that matters is inside oneself". Sikhs pray at home, and also worship together, with hymns read from the sacred book. The focus of worship is on Nam, the divine name which lives within everyone. Sikh gurdwaras (temples) have a langar, or eating space, where Sikhs can share a communal meal, with anyone who comes.

▲ **GOLDEN TEMPLE, AMRITSAR**
The Golden Temple, or Harimandir Sahib (House of God), has been rebuilt many times since its completion in 1601. "Sahib" is a title of respect that Sikhs use for places as well as people.

GURU

As with Hindu traditions, guru means wise teacher, or more literally, "revealer of light and darkness". Sikhism regards its Ten Gurus as a single living spiritual flame, passed down from God, through Guru Nanak onwards, and eventually reaching all Sikhs.

WHO WAS GURU GOBIND SINGH?

Guru Gobind Singh, the tenth Guru (1666–1708), founded the Khalsa, or community of Sikhs, in 1699 to protect them against religious persecution. He called for volunteers who were prepared to die for their faith. All Sikhs wear five symbols, known as the five "Ks", as a sign of their allegiance to the Khalsa. These include the kirpan (dagger) and kangha (comb).

WHERE IS THE SACRED BOOK KEPT?

The tenth Guru, Gobind Singh, appointed the sacred Adi Granth ("First Book") as his successor, so that after him there would be no more human gurus. It became known as the Guru Granth Sahib and copies are kept with great care at temples and treated with the respect a human guru would be given.

Sikhism

THE TEN GURUS ▶
This picture honours the Ten Gurus, and shows Guru Nanak (top), Guru Gobind Singh (top right), and Guru Granth Sahib (centre). The boy guru is Har Krishnan, who died after defying the orders of a Mughal emperor who objected to Sikhism.

PHILOSOPHY

Philosophy comes from the Ancient Greek words for "love of wisdom". It is the search for truth based on reason rather than religious teaching. Most philosophy is concerned with questions of being, knowing, and acting, such as: "Why are we here?"; "What is real?"; and "How should we behave?"

FAMOUS SAYINGS BY FAMOUS PHILOSOPHERS	
Man is the measure of all things	Protagoras c. 5th century BCE
Knowledge is power	Francis Bacon 1561–1626
I think, therefore I am	René Descartes 1596–1650
[Without] law, there is no freedom	John Locke 1632–1704
Man was born free, and everywhere he is in chains	Jean-Jacques Rousseau 1712–1778
Man makes himself	Jean-Paul Sartre 1905–1980

WHO WERE THE FIRST PHILOSOPHERS?

We do not know when philosophy began. The Western tradition originates with the writings of Ancient Greek thinkers, such as Plato and Aristotle, from 500 BCE onwards. Plato and Aristotle's thoughts on logic, science, classification, ethics, and politics have guided Western thought for over 2,000 years.

IS PHILOSOPHY LIKE RELIGION?

Like religion, philosophy tries to explain the mystery of the world and of human existence. Unlike religion, which relies on faith, philosophy applies reasoned thought to its problems, such as the question of moral obligation or free will.

WHAT IS LOGIC?

In philosophy, logic is the search for a way of distinguishing good from bad thinking. The classic example given by Aristotle shows how a conclusion may be drawn from two facts. If "Socrates is a man", and "All men are mortal", then "Socrates is mortal".

◄ HUMAN PROPORTIONS
One of philosophy's main objectives has been to understand humankind's place in the Universe. Renaissance artist Leonardo da Vinci's drawing, *Vitruvian Man*, showed how the arms and legs of a human figure could be fitted in a square and a circle. He believed these two shapes formed the basis of the Universe.

philosophy

SCHOOL OF ATHENS
This 16th-century fresco from the Pope's library in the Vatican, Rome, was painted by the Italian artist Raphael. It shows wise men from different eras as colleagues in a timeless academy. At its centre, Plato and Aristotle can be seen deep in discussion.

Socrates in animated discussion with Xenophon and Alexander the Great (in armour)

Plato points up to represent the Universe and abstract thought

Aristotle gestures down to represent the Earth and ethical thought

Flaming torch represents freedom

*Spiked crown
represents the
seven continents*

WHY DOES TRUTH MATTER?

The question of truth – what it is and how to
recognize it – is among the oldest and most
controversial in philosophy. Some philosophers believe
that the abstract rules of mathematics are a kind of
absolute truth. Others believe there is no such thing
as absolute truth, only the relative truth of individual
or cultural viewpoints – that "Man is the measure of
all things".

WHAT IS FREE WILL?

The question of free will – a major concern of many
religions, too – revolves around the question of what
controls our lives. Can we choose our own destiny, or
are our actions limited by what has gone before
(determinism) or by God's will (predestination)?

▲ **ARJUNA AND KRISHNA**
The Bhagavad Gita ("the Song of the Lord")
features many philosophical discussions between
Krishna (Vishnu in human form) and Arjuna, his
close friend. Krishna's practical advice guides the
soldier Arjuna in his actions.

WHAT IS ETHICS?

Ethics, or moral philosophy, is the
study of how people create moral
systems and judge right and wrong
behaviour. Does good behaviour come
from duty to God or a person's own sense
of how to live a proper life? Not all societies
share the same ethical truth – in general,
Eastern societies place more emphasis on
collective duty than Western societies.

*Zoroaster (holding a
celestial globe) discusses
geography with Ptolemy*

FIND OUT MORE ►► Ancient Greece 376–377 • Hinduism 286

SOCIETIES

Throughout time and in every part of the world, people have organized themselves into groups with common rules of living. A society is the name we give to the organization of such a group.

WHAT DO SOCIETIES HAVE IN COMMON?
Certain institutions are found in every society, such as the family, marriage, kin relationships, childcare, and the division of work according to age or gender (between male and female). Even so, the customs that govern social behaviour vary greatly worldwide.

HOW ARE SOCIETIES ORGANIZED?
All societies are organized around a division of labour and decision-making. Modern societies are expected to provide their members with protection, law and order, economic security, and a sense of belonging. Trying to understand how societies organize themselves is the goal of the ▶▶ SOCIAL SCIENCES.

Cash suggests that society is ruled by the wealthy

Rulers appear to be the sole decision-makers

Church leaders support those above them, not beneath them

The military protect the rulers from rebellious workers

Workers struggle to provide for the rest of society's needs

The middle class rely on the workers' labour for their wealth and lifestyle

1912 AMERICAN ELECTION POSTER WOOS THE WORKERS' VOTE

◀ ONCE DIVIDED, NOW UNITED
In 1989, Germans celebrated as the Berlin Wall, separating the societies of East and West Germany, was torn down.

▲ CAKE FOR A FEW, CRUMBS FOR THE REST
Some people think that society should work for the good of all its members. This picture illustrates the socialist viewpoint that society only works for the benefit of one group of people and should be changed.

DO SOCIETIES EVOLVE?
Societies usually adapt to changes around them, such as the environment or technology. Most change happens gradually, but some major events, such as war or revolution, can completely transform societies.

societies

SOCIAL SCIENCES

Social scientists study how people live together in societies. Economists study commercial activities and relate them to human behaviour. Sociologists study the social structures of modern societies and relate them to human behaviour. Anthropologists focus on the cultures and social structures of traditional societies.

▲ MARKING A BOY'S PASSAGE TO MANHOOD IN SOUTH AFRICA
While each society has its own customs, many celebrate the same thing in their own unique way. One of the most common customs is the "coming-of-age" ritual which marks a child's transition to adulthood.

▼ A GLOBAL COMMUNITY
Today, improved communications mean that very few societies are completely isolated from others. Most people – from villagers to city-dwellers – depend on economic and technological systems that connect the world, creating a global community.

WHY ARE THE SOCIAL SCIENCES USEFUL?
During the Industrial Revolution of the 1700s and 1800s, rapid economic growth brought huge social change. Social sciences evolved to help explain the effects of these changes and to collect social data. Today, they help us to understand complex social issues, from cultural differences to race relations.

DO OUR GENES AFFECT SOCIETY?
For many years, scientists have debated about what has more influence on society: nature or nurture, biology or culture. Sociobiologists argue that genes, which determine our physical characteristics, are responsible for most human behaviour. Other scientists argue that culture is mostly responsible.

WHAT IS ANTHROPOLOGY?
Physical anthropology looks at human evolution and biological differences, such as genetic variety. Social anthropology looks at the wide range of human languages, beliefs, and behaviour, known collectively as culture, especially among local societies. The aim is to reach a better understanding of the "human family" to which we all belong.

▲ ANIMAL SOCIETIES
Ants are among many animal groups that live in societies. Because their society's "rules" are encoded in the queen ant's genes and passed down, ant societies cannot learn or adapt.

MARGARET MEAD
American, 1901-1978
This pioneering anthropologist studied social behaviour, especially rites of passage and child-rearing, in Samoa, New Guinea, and Bali. Her main conclusion was that personality was culturally and not biologically determined. She also analysed US society.

FIND OUT MORE ▶▶ Culture 296–297 • Economy 302–303 • Families 300 • Genetics 209 • The State 308–309

CELEBRATING CULTURE ACROSS THE GLOBE

DAY OF THE DEAD
In this Mexican festival, held on All Souls' Day, people pray to the souls of their dead relatives, inviting them to return to the land of the living for one more celebration. These are festival-goers in Los Angeles, USA, a city that has a large Hispanic-American population.

MAASAI DANCE
The Maasai men of east Africa live in age groups called brotherhoods. The members of a brotherhood practise this Eunoto ritual, in which the men dance with straight-legged jumps. This is to mark the passage from warrior age to husband age.

INDEPENDENCE DAY
Each year, on the fourth of July, Americans of all cultural backgrounds mark the anniversary of US freedom from British rule. Annual festivals that mark special moments in a nation's history encourage citizens to take pride in their country.

DUSSEHRA FESTIVAL
The story of Rama's victory over Ravana, a battle between good and evil, is celebrated in this colourful Hindu festival in India. Elephants are decorated and painted, like those used in India's past to carry kings to war.

TROOPING THE COLOUR
An annual parade in London marks the official birthday of Queen Elizabeth II, Britain's head of state. The time-honoured rituals, uniforms, flags, and the monarch's horse-drawn carriage highlight tradition and stability.

HANDS UP
Spectators at this American football game rise to their feet to ripple a "Mexican wave" around the stadium. Joining a large audience at sports events, or supporting a sports team, gives people a powerful sense of community.

CULTURE

Culture is made up of all the shared values, customs, and beliefs that give a society a common identity. It includes the **▶▶ LANGUAGE** a society uses, along with its rituals, fashions, arts, food, stories, and lifestyles.

DO ALL MEMBERS OF A SOCIETY SHARE ONE CULTURE?

Traditional societies usually share a common culture. People who live in larger, more diverse societies share a mainstream culture, with which most people can identify. Societies may also have **▶▶ SUBCULTURES**, alongside their normal cultures, often based on shared values or interests, especially among immigrants and young people.

IS THERE A GLOBAL CULTURE?

Cultures spread and influence one another as a result of increased trade and communication, and modern technology has brought the world's cultures closer than ever. Some cultural events, such as a Hollywood movie, are shared across the world – but local aspects of culture, such as language or myth, remain the most powerful cultural influences in most people's lives.

▲ **AMISH CULTURE**
North America's Amish people choose to separate themselves from mainstream US culture. Most Amish live without modern innovations such as electricity or engines, because their religion encourages them to question the need for change. Like their plain clothing, this sets them apart from those outside their culture.

◀ **PATCHWORK OF CULTURE**
Each of these cultures is unique. Together, they build a vast global culture. A greater understanding of the world's cultures means that people can be influenced by many different ways of life.

DO CULTURES CHANGE?

Cultures emerge from the growing history and experiences of a society, or its **▶▶ TRADITION**. Rapid social change and revolution can cause changes in culture. Cultures also change as people make contact with other cultures. Greater global communications and opportunities to travel allow people across the world to study and learn from other cultures.

HOW DO WE LEARN A CULTURE?

Most people grow up immersed in their culture. They absorb it from their family, through rituals and customs, through language, through the arts, through social habits, and through a shared history. People also learn about culture through school, friends, television, and books.

TRADITION

Tradition generally refers to patterns of customs and beliefs, which reflect a group's common identity. Tradition is passed down from one generation to the next through teaching and practice.

WHY DO WE HAVE TRADITIONS?

Traditions often come from deep-rooted beliefs, or are simply invented at a certain point in history. Special events, such as royal pageants in the UK, Thanksgiving Day in the USA, and Bastille Day in France, help people to remember certain times and traditions, giving them a sense of a shared cultural history.

TEA CEREMONY (CHAJI) ▶
A Japanese woman in traditional dress performs a tea ceremony in front of honoured guests. The ceremony is highly complex with many rules to follow. Originally, this tradition was part of the formal welcoming of guests.

LANGUAGE

Each culture communicates through language – a set of words and grammar, signs and symbols. There are some 5,000 different languages in the world.

STOP SIGN ▶
This stop sign gets its message across in Arabic and English. Its distinctive shape and colour also help to convey the meaning.

HOW DO LANGUAGES CHANGE?

Languages evolve in the same way as cultures – through interaction with other languages. Languages adopt new words and lose old words all the time. Sometimes, old words take on new meanings. Local variations of the same language are known as dialects. These may occur when a group of speakers moves away from their homeland, such as the Spanish settlers in South America, or when they become isolated from other speakers of the same language.

SUBCULTURE

Many complex societies encourage diversity by allowing smaller groups to form their own subcultures, with their own distinct behaviour, beliefs, and attitudes. Through fashion, music, and art, subcultures often influence mainstream culture.

WHAT IS GANG CULTURE?

People looking for excitement, a strong identity, and a code to live by may choose to join a gang, such as the Hells Angels bikers or Japanese Yakuza. These gangs usually create their own subculture, complete with dress-codes, tattoos, slang, and music. These highly visible signs show the members' loyalty and pride in belonging to the gang. Mainstream music, such as "gangsta rap", is often influenced by gang culture.

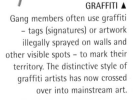

GRAFFITI ▲
Gang members often use graffiti – tags (signatures) or artwork illegally sprayed on walls and other visible spots – to mark their territory. The distinctive style of graffiti artists has now crossed over into mainstream art.

WHO JOINS A SUBCULTURE?

Many people, especially younger people, choose to join a subculture to express their interests and identity. Teenagers and young adults often feel a lack of identification with the values or interests of mainstream society, so they seek out groups of like-minded people – with similar musical, sporting, or political interests – to give them a sense of belonging. Subcultures can even be based around hobbies such as folk-dancing or pigeon racing.

▲ ANARCHY IN THE UK?
The punk subculture appealed to teenagers in the late 1970s, inspired by its raw, fast rock music and angry lyrics. Punk fashions, such as dyed hair and facial piercings, represent a rejection of mainstream cultural values, perfect for shocking or rebelling against parents and society.

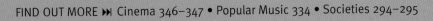

FIND OUT MORE ▶▶ Cinema 346–347 • Popular Music 334 • Societies 294–295

MEDIA

The media (sometimes called mass media) includes all the institutions and technology that communicate news and entertainment to society. They include print media (the ▶ PRESS), ▶ BROADCAST media (television and radio), and new media, such as the Internet.

WHO PAYS FOR THE MEDIA?

Media can be state-owned, such as the British Broadcasting Corporation (BBC), or owned by a private company. Media consumers normally pay a small fee to access information, although private companies meet most of the cost from businesses or sponsors who buy ▶ ADVERTISING space.

WHAT EFFECTS DO MASS MEDIA HAVE?

People depend on media for everything from the latest headlines to yesterday's sports results. At its best, the media educates, provokes, and entertains. Yet mass media can also be used for propaganda purposes to sway public opinion and distort the truth.

HOT OFF THE PRESS ▶
Newspapers must be written by journalists, printed in vast quantities, and distributed – all before their news is out of date. A typical daily paper must meet a 1am deadline so that its 6am first edition hits the newsagent.

SUPERMAN

◢ HOLLYWOOD FILMS
The American film industry depends on populist movies, with plenty of action, comedy, or romance, to capture the interest – and ticket sales – of a global audience. Blockbusters, such as the *Superman* series, enable studios to cover their huge production costs of making the films.

IS THE INTERNET DIFFERENT TO OTHER MEDIA?

In most mass media, information flows in one direction only, from its creators to the public. The Internet, however, has created a "virtual" community that can share information, views, and experiences with each other via emails, weblogs, and message boards. While Internet sites are not checked for accuracy or fairness, they can provide a balanced and informal alternative to the official media by letting diverse voices be heard.

◀ THE WORLD IS JUST A CLICK AWAY
Over three-quarters of a billion people worldwide use the Internet. Its technology enables us to access information wherever we find a computer, a modem, and a phone link, provided we can pay. Mobile phone technology can allow people to log on from almost anywhere.

PRESS

Newspapers, magazines, and the journalists who write for them, are known collectively as the press. One in every six people reads a daily newspaper. The world's leading newspaper, Japan's *Yomiuri Shimbun*, sells over 14 million copies a day.

HOW DO PEOPLE CHOOSE A PAPER?

Readers often pick a newspaper that reflects their own interests and political views. Each newspaper has its own editorial standards, which shape how the news is presented. Some newspapers present a more serious coverage; others are more sensational. Readers may buy a different paper if it has an exclusive story.

PRESS GANG ▶
Newspapers often buy photos from paparazzi, people who take unofficial pictures of the rich and famous.

▲ SELF-POWERED RADIO
This Burundian girl lives in a refugee camp in Tanzania. As there is no school, she listens to lessons on a battery-free radio. These economical radios are solar powered or can be charged by winding them up.

BROADCAST

Broadcast media send information to a wide audience using advanced electronic technology. Radio was first broadcast in the 1920s, and television in the 1930s. In recent years, digital technologies have created a huge expansion in the number of channels of all kinds.

WHO LISTENS TO THE RADIO?

Radio is a truly global medium for talk, news, and music. More than 300 million battery-powered radios are sold every year, providing a cheap and accessible alternative to television. Television is often less easily available to many in developing countries, especially for those without access to electricity.

ADVERTISING

Producers of goods and services use the media to encourage people to buy their products. They buy space in any media that reach their target consumers, in order to advertise, or promote, their goods in a way that appeals to them.

DOES ADVERTISING WORK?

Although consumers rarely admit to being influenced by adverts, effective advertising does increase sales. Global industry pours more than £200 billion into advertising every year, with around 40 per cent of the total budget dedicated to TV coverage.

media

ADVERTISING ICON ▶
Coca-Cola™ is one of the world's most successful products. Its soft drinks are sold almost everywhere, and its distinctive logo is recognized worldwide.

FIND OUT MORE ▶▶ Cinema 346–347 • Internet 191 • Printing 339 • Telecommunications 192–193

FAMILIES

The family is a basic social unit that exists in every culture, although its structure varies widely. The main purpose of families, which are usually created by marriage, is for ▶▶ PARENTING children.

WHAT IS A NUCLEAR FAMILY?

The term "nuclear family" refers to two married adults and their children. It has been the main family unit of Western society since the Industrial Revolution. Recent social changes, such as divorce and remarriage, have resulted in many single-parent and step families.

▲ IN THE FAMILY

Extended families, such as this group of yak herders in Bhutan, work together like a miniature society. They share domestic and work duties, childcare, and care of the elderly for the benefit of all the members.

WHAT ARE EXTENDED FAMILIES?

In most societies, especially in pre-industrial, traditional communities, it is usual for a wide circle of relatives from one or both sides of the family to live together in the same household. This type of family is known as an extended family.

ARE ALL FAMILIES BASED ON MARRIAGE?

Most societies have an elaborate religious ritual to celebrate marriage. Some couples may choose to reject this tradition and marry in a civil ceremony. Others may choose to create a family outside marriage.

families

◀ OLDER AND WISER

Much of the world's population is living longer as health care improves. While many families still care for their elderly, some states also provide some housing and financial support.

Red is the most common colour for a Hindu bride

A veil of beaded strings shields the bride from evil

A sherwani is embroidered with golden thread

HINDU MARRIAGE ▲

A traditional Hindu marriage ceremony is not just a bond between husband and wife. Members of both families play an important part in the life of the new family afterwards.

Groom wears an elaborate turban

PARENTING

Parents and children, whether united by birth or by adoption, share a unique bond. Parenting means providing food, shelter, and emotional support for children, as well as preparing them for a role in adult society. Sometimes children are looked after by their legal guardians.

WHY DO CHILDREN NEED PARENTS?

Children enter the world without the skills or ability to look after themselves. Parents must protect and nurture children during their early years, as they develop and grow. In later years, parents lay down guidelines for behaviour, so children learn how to be responsible for themselves. As children grow older, parents continue to support them, emotionally and financially, as they take their first tentative steps towards adulthood.

▲ CLOSE TIES
This South American girl will rely on her family's care until she reaches adulthood. In some societies, a parent's role can also extend to providing education or teaching a trade or skill.

FIND OUT MORE ▶▶ Hinduism 286 • Industrial Revolution 418–419 • Societies 294–295

CIVIL SOCIETY

Many people see themselves joined by common interests to a social network that extends beyond their immediate families. People get together to promote causes and to organize sports and other leisure activities.

civil society

WHY DO PEOPLE FORM SOCIETIES AND CLUBS?

In wealthier societies especially, people have time for interests, such as sport, that fall outside their main economic and family roles. Joining a club or society with others who share the same interests provides a common bond among people. Some groups, called charities, exist to provide support for those in need.

▲ INDIAN WOMEN'S TRADE CO-OPERATIVE
Wealthy people and companies sometimes use part of their wealth to set up charities, called foundations. A foundation provides financial support for good causes, such as development aid or the environment.

WHAT IS VOLUNTEERING?

Clubs, societies, and charities often rely on the work of unpaid helpers, or volunteers, to achieve their goals. People volunteer because they agree with the aims of the group, and find satisfaction in helping others. Volunteering can also bring people new friendships, or improve their work skills.

▲ "FEED THE WORLD!"
In 1985, a charity called Live Aid staged twin concerts in the UK and USA to raise money for African famine victims. Millions of people pledged money during its broadcast, raising £40 million in aid.

FIND OUT MORE ▶▶ Hinduism 286 • Societies 294–295

ECONOMY

People work together to grow things, extract raw materials from the Earth, manufacture objects that are sold to ▶▶ CONSUMERS , and help to organize our lives through services like banking. The ▶▶ PRODUCTION and distribution of all these things make up the economy.

WHAT IS SUPPLY AND DEMAND?

In an economy, there are people who supply goods and services at a price, and people who demand those goods and services and pay for them. The laws of supply and demand try to explain how and why prices change and how producers and consumers behave. For example, if there is a lot of demand, prices increase. If supply is high, prices go down.

WHAT IS THE MARKET?

In economics, the market is a place, or a network, where buyers and sellers exchange goods and services for money. All activity in the market depends on the supply of, and demand for, these goods and services.

▲ DOMESTIC WORK
This woman in India handwashes her family's clothes in the nearest river. This kind of domestic work is not considered part of the economy.

WHAT TYPES OF ECONOMIES ARE THERE?

In traditional economies, people produce the goods they need on a small scale, and sell the surplus (the amount they do not need) at local trading centres, known as markets. In command economies, most economic activity is controlled by the government rather than private companies or market forces. In a mixed economy, some industries are privately owned by companies and others, such as public transport, are publicly owned and run by the government.

WHAT IS NOT PART OF THE ECONOMY?

Domestic work, such as housework, is not considered part of the economy, unless someone is paid to do it. The portion of a nation's income that is (illegally) not declared for tax is known as the black economy.

Computers
store details of the best time to buy and sell shares according to their price. This means that some trading can happen automatically

Paper slips are dropped to the floor after being used by traders to scribble down prices of the deals they have made

NEW YORK STOCK EXCHANGE ▶
Big companies are usually owned by thousands of people, who each hold a stake in the company called a share. Shares are traded through a stock exchange. People invest their money in shares to claim a portion of a company's profits if the company does well. However, they risk losing money if the company does badly and the share price goes down.

PRODUCTION

Production involves the use of Earth's raw materials and human labour to make useful things. Every society uses its land, people, skills, and tools to make products, from petrol to stainless steel and running shoes. In modern economies, companies aim to maximize profits by keeping their production costs down and sales up.

WHAT IS ECONOMIC GROWTH?

An economy grows when its production increases in quantity. Growth in the economy can lead to more jobs and more income for consumers to spend. It also frees resources for other uses, such as science, the arts, or sport. However, economic growth can also create difficulties, such as environmental problems and the gap between rich and poor.

economy

Video screens display the latest share prices of different companies

SALES OF TOP 1,000 COMPANIES (US$ BILLION)	
Consumer luxuries	2,807
Industrials	1,777
Information technology and telecoms	1,751
Consumer basics (such as food)	1,364
Energy	1,318
Utilities (water, gas, electricity)	954
Health care	685

MASS PRODUCTION ▲
These cars are produced on a state-of-the-art factory production line. Automated assembly lines help to cut production costs. Sometimes, producers pass these savings along to consumers in the form of lower prices, hoping to sell more cars than their competitors.

Traders buy and sell shares on behalf of companies and investors

CONSUMERS

Someone who buys goods and services is called a consumer. Most people are consumers, because they need to buy basic goods, such as food, shelter, and clothing, in order to live. Producers need to predict what consumers want, so that they can make goods that will sell.

WHAT GIVES CONSUMERS POWER?

Consumers need a way to pay for goods before they can decide which goods to buy. Their buying power comes from income (wages earned by working) or investment (profits made from owning shares or property). A wide choice of products gives consumers some power over producers, since a company will go out of business if consumers do not buy its product.

▲ CONSUMER POWER
Consumers have the most power in markets where there are many traders. It is easy to check and choose between many products and prices on display, such as on a fruit and vegetable stall.

WHAT ARE CONSUMER GOODS?

Consumer goods are products manufactured to satisfy personal needs. Goods that are required for the production of other goods and services, such as paper or coal, are known as producer or capital goods. Consumer goods can include anything from clothing and CDs to children's toys and Coca-Cola™. Demand for consumer goods is often created by advertising and by technological changes.

◄ ON THE ROAD
These cars will be shipped around the world to meet consumer demand. Sometimes it is cheaper for producers to manufacture goods in one place. Sometimes it is cheaper to manufacture them in several locations.

FIND OUT MORE ►► Human Impact 64–65 • Industry 204 • Manufacturing 205

SOCIAL EQUALITY

Sociologists have shown that all societies are stratified or divided into layers, based on caste, class, ethnicity, or gender. As a result, some people in a society have more advantages than others, leading to social inequality.

WHY ARE SOME SOCIETIES DIVIDED?

Some basic differences between people may affect their place in the social hierarchy. ▶▶ GENDER divisions are common because of the different roles men and women play in bearing and raising children. Other divisions come from the unequal distribution of ▶▶ WEALTH , or attitudes to ▶▶ ETHNICITY .

CROSSING BARRIERS ▶
When people use their talents and skills to cross physical and social barriers, it provides inspiration to others. Singer Stevie Wonder and former US President Bill Clinton both overcame obstacles to achieve their success.

WHAT ARE THE CASTE AND CLASS SYSTEMS?

The caste system is an ancient, inflexible system of social and economic hierarchy, closely aligned with some Hindu beliefs. In the caste system, fixed social roles are inherited. While this often guarantees employment, it also means that caste members cannot improve their social status. In most other societies, people are born into a social position or class, depending on the property, employment, or wealth of their family. However, education and economic success can help people improve their social position.

CAN SOCIAL DIVISIONS CHANGE?

Societies can change when the roles dividing people, such as the division of labour, are shared more equally. For example, peace-making efforts between Catholics and Protestants in Northern Ireland are directed at sharing political power and job opportunities fairly.

HOW CAN PEOPLE BE TREATED EQUALLY?

In recent history, many societies have passed laws that prohibit discrimination against people based on race, gender, or age. These ensure that all people are treated equally by employers, governments, and other members of society. These laws have primarily been won by struggle, protest, and organisation.

◀ EDUCATIONAL GOALS
All children deserve a good education to help them achieve their full potential. Wealthy people often choose to buy a better education for their children, giving them access to a full range of activities outside the classroom, such as sports or music. Many developing countries cannot afford to provide any education after primary level.

▲ BASIC NEEDS
This Peruvian boy is one of billions of people around the world who live in poverty, without enough money to meet their basic needs – around a third of the world's population, according to the United Nations. Poor people often have limited access to healthcare and education.

WOMAN IN A MAN'S WORLD
...aditionally, men have monopolized jobs which required greater physical strength. However, improved ...chnology means that there are fewer jobs which rely on muscle power alone. Women like Space Shuttle ...tronaut Mary Ellen Weber have broken barriers by choosing careers once held exclusively by men.

GENDER

Gender division is the social recognition and reinforcement of sexual differences between men and women. This might take the form of an unequal division of labour, reduced social opportunities, or social discrimination.

DO WOMEN HAVE EQUAL RIGHTS?

Although women have won important rights over the last 100 years, gender inequality is still commonplace in most parts of the world. While countries with equal rights laws have improved women's access to politics, jobs, and property, women are still not equally represented in government and business, and are often paid less for doing the same jobs as men.

WEALTH

A few people in each society earn large amounts of money, or inherit fortunes handed down through their families. Their wealth gives them access to more economic and social opportunities than others, and can give them more influence over society as a whole.

HOW DOES WEALTH DIVIDE PEOPLE?

Wealth gives people power in a society, because wealthy people can buy and use other people's time. This can be seen as a reward for individual success. However, if only the rich can enjoy such success, there can be no social equality. The numbers on the chart below illustrate the huge – and growing – gap between the world's rich and poor.

TABLE OF GLOBAL WEALTH	
$US (excluding homes)	*Number of people*
Above $1bn	480
$5m–$1bn	483,000
$1m–$5m	6,500,000
$100,000–$1m	25,000,000
$10,000–$100,000	180,000,000
$0–$10,000	5,700,000,000

▲ **WHAT IT MEANS TO BE RICH**
Wealth allows people to choose their own lifestyles, free of the limits most people face. The wealthy may also make choices which affect other people's lives, such as where to spend, donate, or invest money.

social equality

ETHNICITY

Ethnicity refers to a group's cultural and linguistic habits, as well as its race. The term "race" is now considered to be an outdated concept for distinguishing groups of people who share common physical characteristics, such as black skin or blonde hair.

◄ **ETHNIC DIVIDE**
In South Africa, the white minority imposed years of enforced separation on black people, denying them basic rights. This policy, known as apartheid, ended in 1993.

WHAT IS A MULTI-ETHNIC SOCIETY?

Societies made up of several ethnic groups, each with their own cultural traditions, are called multi-ethnic societies. During the 20th and 21st centuries, many multi-ethnic societies have searched for ways to promote respect for these different groups, often passing laws to promote equal opportunities for all.

FIND OUT MORE ▶▶ Decolonization 434 • Human Rights 317 • Societies 294–295

POLITICS

Politics is the process of obtaining and using power to shape and execute the rules that govern a society. It can involve elected politicians in a ▶ DEMOCRACY , or the unelected members of a ruling elite.

WHY DO PEOPLE CARE ABOUT POLITICS?
Political decisions affect people's daily lives in two very important ways. They decide how much money the state will take from people in the form of taxes to spend on public projects such as health care, education, or defence. Political decisions make the laws affecting people's lives.

▲ HOUSES OF PARLIAMENT, LONDON
Government in the UK is divided into three areas: Parliament, who write and pass laws; the judiciary, who ensure the laws are applied fairly; and the Cabinet and civil service (the executive) who carry out the laws.

CAN POLITICS CHANGE SOCIETY?
Political ideas alone do not change society, but when enough people with the same ideas form a ▶ PARTY , they can influence how society changes. Sometimes the process of change can be gradual, sometimes it comes from violent revolution, fuelled by new political ideas. This happened in countries such as the USA, France, and Tsarist Russia.

DOES EVERYONE HAVE A SAY?
There are two main types of government: democratic and authoritarian. In democratic societies, adults have a role in shaping how their country is run, by voting in free elections for a political party. This is part of their ▶ CIVIL RIGHTS .

▲ HEATED DEBATE
Arab-Israeli and Jewish Labour Party politicians have an angry exchange in the Knesset, Israel' parliamentary chamber. Workin out differences of opinion through debate can provide an alternative to violent conflict.

▼ INSIDE THE BUNDESTAG
In the Bundestag, or German parliament, deputies are electe by proportional representation. The Bundestag moved to Berlin 1991, following the reunificatio of East and West Germany.

Cabinet members run the government

President of the chamber oversees debates

Deputies sit in party groups and vote electronically

DEMOCRACY

Democracy (from the Greek for "rule by the people") is a way that people can choose their government from a range of political parties. In republics, or countries without monarchies, the electors vote for a head of state, or president, as well as the government.

HOW MANY TYPES OF DEMOCRACY ARE THERE?

There are two main types of democracy: presidential, where voters elect a president, who then appoints the government, such as in the USA or France; and parliamentary, where voters directly elect the government of their choice, such as in the UK. Sometimes a president may rule yet represent a minority party.

WHAT IS A REFERENDUM?

Sometimes a political decision is too important to be left to elected politicians, so the issue is decided by voters, normally with a simple yes or no answer to a direct question. A referendum is typically used for a decision that affects people's basic rights, or the sovereign (independent) status of a nation.

politics

▲ NELSON MANDELA CASTING A VOTE IN SOUTH AFRICA'S ELECTIONS
During elections, each citizen may vote anonymously for the candidate of their choice by marking an "X" against the candidate's name on the ballot slip and placing it in a sealed ballot box. Sometimes electors vote for individuals, sometimes they vote for parties.

CIVIL RIGHTS

Citizens of democratic societies expect equal participation in political, social, and economic life. These freedoms are called civil rights. They are meant to guarantee that society is fair to everyone.

DO DEMOCRACIES NEED CIVIL RIGHTS?

Sometimes laws that represent the will of the majority can restrict the freedom of others and exclude minorities from full political and social participation and threaten the idea of democracy. Civil rights protect the freedoms of all people within society.

MARTIN LUTHER KING, JR
American, 1929–1968
"We know through painful experience that freedom is never voluntarily given by the oppressor; it must be demanded by the oppressed." In the 1950s and 1960s, King campaigned against racial injustice and for civil rights for all black Americans.

WOMEN DEMONSTRATING ▶
Women in Aceh, Indonesia, protest against the introduction of sweeping emergency laws by the government in 2002, issued to combat rebel groups. These laws took away many basic civil rights.

PARTY

Political parties are formed to represent different interests. These may be economic, social, or religious – each with its own ideas about how society should be ruled.

HOW ARE POLITICAL PARTIES CREATED?

A new party is created when people who share common political beliefs feel unrepresented and decide to compete for political power. They agree a name for themselves, and draw up a list of their ideas, called a manifesto, for voters to consider. Party members normally vote to choose their leader.

◀ POLITICAL RALLY
Parties often hold large meetings, such as this convention of Democratic Party supporters in the USA. The meetings help choose party leaders, reward their supporters, and publicize their interests.

FIND OUT MORE ▶▶ Decolonization 434 • French Revolution 415 • Revolutionary Russia 428 • The Law 310–311 • The State 308–309

THE STATE

A state is a territory where one central culture, a set of ideals, and a set of laws has been imposed. A modern state has its own government, armed forces, and a civil service, which carries out the work of the government. The state generally manages the police and other emergency services, the departments of health, education, and ▶ WELFARE. It also has a ▶ CENTRAL BANK.

WHO WORKS FOR THE STATE?

A state employs a large workforce of civil servants to carry out its many functions. These state employees include police officers, health inspectors, teachers, and office workers. Together, they represent a large part of the total workforce. In the UK, for example, 17 per cent of all workers are employed by the state.

WHY ARE STATES FORMED?

States were first created many thousands of years ago, mainly to fight wars and defend territory. Today, states do more than this. They provide a form of central control for public services, and look after the welfare of their citizens.

TOP 8 INDUSTRIALIZED STATES: ANNUAL STATE SPENDING PER CITIZEN	
Germany	10,067 (in US$)
Italy	9,189
United Kingdom	9,037
United States	5,908
Japan	5,633
Canada	5,124
France	4,060
Russian Federation	300

The hammer and sickle was the official symbol of the former Soviet Union

HOW DOES A STATE PAY FOR ITS SERVICES?

Each year, a government decides how much money the state will need to pay for its public services. Most of this is raised via a ▶ TAX on its citizens and businesses, but states can also charge for services – for example, through road tolls. If a state gets into debt, it may also borrow money from private corporations or from wealthier nations.

e ▶▶
the state

◀ STATE DEPARTMENT
In the Russian Federation, the state has a say in many aspects of society. Many civil servants work to carry out government policy in huge offices, such as this Ministry of Foreign Affairs in Moscow.

▲ ARMED FORCES
The state pays to staff and equip its armed forces. This American F-22 Raptor jet cost around 70 billion US dollars to design. Although made by a private company, the jet could not be built without state money.

▲ EDUCATION
States have funded education, from nursery schools to universities, since the 19th century. Investment in education results in a better-educated society, which in turn creates steady economic growth for the state.

▲ TRANSPORTATION
Roads and bridges are complicated and expensive to build. States pay for transport networks, such as this road system in Shanghai, China, to improve communications and to encourage more economic activity.

▲ ARTS
The Sydney Opera House in Australia was built with state money. States give money to support the arts – especially orchestras, opera and ballet companies, theatre groups, and museums – as symbols of national pride.

TAX

Tax is the money that citizens and companies have to pay to the government, helping the state raise the funds it needs to operate. A state may impose direct taxes on an individual's income or property, or indirect taxes on business trade in goods and services.

WHAT ARE TAX INCENTIVES?
A state can use tax incentives to encourage its citizens to make certain economic choices. Most people try to avoid paying large amounts of tax, so a state can actually encourage participation in an activity by lowering or removing the tax on it. The opposite is true when a state raises taxes. For example, some governments impose high taxes on cigarettes and alcohol to discourage people from consuming these harmful products, which are known to create health risks.

DO TAXES MAKE SOCIETIES MORE EQUAL?
Whether taxation can make societies more equal depends on the mix of taxes raised by the state. Progressive taxes, such as income tax, take more from the rich than the poor. Other taxes, such as flat rate taxes, take more from the poor than the rich. This is called regressive taxation.

▲ TAXING CONSUMERS AT THE PETROL PUMP
If a government sees private transport and car use as bad for society, it can discourage car use by raising tax on petrol purchases. High petrol taxes encourage people to buy smaller cars that consume less fuel.

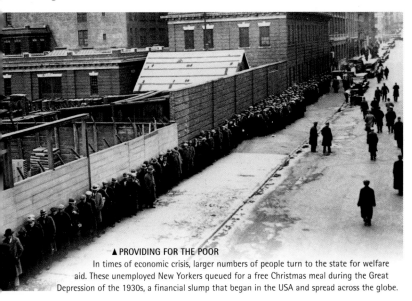
▲ PROVIDING FOR THE POOR
In times of economic crisis, larger numbers of people turn to the state for welfare aid. These unemployed New Yorkers queued for a free Christmas meal during the Great Depression of the 1930s, a financial slump that began in the USA and spread across the globe.

WELFARE

Welfare is the financial assistance that a state provides to help people in need. Government welfare support may include payments to unemployed workers, disabled people excluded from the workplace, or pensions to the elderly. Welfare benefits can also be provided to all citizens in forms such as public education.

HAVE ALL COUNTRIES CREATED A WELFARE STATE?
Each nation makes a political decision about how much welfare to provide to its citizens. Politicians debate over how much a person's welfare is their own responsibility, or the responsibility of the state. Some developing countries have little money for welfare, and the needy must rely on charity for help instead.

CENTRAL BANK

A state that possesses its own currency has a central bank, which prints money. A central bank tries to regulate the state's economy by influencing interest rates. The aim is to ensure economic stability and prevent sharp swings between growth and decline.

WHAT IS INTEREST?
Interest is what money costs. People pay a price to borrow money – for example, to make a large consumer purchase – and that price is called interest. The central bank issues a basic interest rate called the base rate, which private banking companies follow when people arrange to borrow money from them.

▲ US GOLD BULLION DEPOSITORY, FORT KNOX, KENTUCKY, USA
Different countries have different currencies, or money. One of the tasks of the central bank is to determine how much currency should be in circulation (in use) at any given time. Until 1971, the value of each US dollar in circulation was backed up by a dollar's worth of gold, some of which was stored at Fort Knox.

FIND OUT MORE ▸▸ Culture 296–297 • The Depression 430 • Economy 302–303 • The Law 310–311

THE LAW

Laws are the formal rules that society makes for itself.
They are made for various reasons: for example, to
settle arguments and maintain a peaceful social order.
Some laws are made by governments. Others are set
down by custom or religion.

Blindfold *protects
from the risk
of prejudice*

*Sword
represents
punishment
for the guilty*

*Scales help to
weigh both
sides of a
dispute fairly*

WHO MAKES THE LAW IN A DEMOCRATIC SOCIETY?
In a democracy, the power to make laws is held by a branch of the government
called the legislature. In the legislative chamber, politicians (usually elected to
represent the views of the voters) introduce new laws and debate them. Through
discussion and compromise, they try to gain support for a law and organize a vote
on it. The majority of members must approve a law before it can be put into effect.

CAN POLITICIANS MAKE ANY LAW THEY LIKE?
Politicians in different countries have different
law-making powers. In some cases, a head of state
can refuse to accept a law. Sometimes, political leaders
may put forward a law that would weaken rights or
freedoms that have been promised to all citizens. Such
laws can be challenged by citizens in ▸▸ COURT .

WHY DO PEOPLE OBEY THE LAW?
Most people obey the law because they believe it
results in a peaceful society. The law is enforced by
the ▸▸ POLICE . The risk of being caught by the police
and punished reminds most people to obey the law.
But some political activists deliberately break laws they
disagree with – an act called "civil disobedience".

▲ A SYMBOL OF JUSTICE
Law courts across the world
feature images of the Greek
goddess Themis ("Justicia", in
Roman religion), goddess of
justice. Themis is always seen
holding the scales of justice.

HOW IS CRIMINAL LAW DIFFERENT TO CIVIL LAW?
Criminal law defines a person's responsibility towards
society as a whole. Breaking a criminal law is an
offence against the public good, so the state pursues
criminals in the name of the public. Civil law deals
with a person's responsibility towards another person.
Civil laws cover agreements between people such as
property ownership, contracts, or marriage.

DO DIFFERENT COUNTRIES HAVE DIFFERENT LAWS?
Because law-making is part of national politics, most countries have quite different
laws. But there are also many similarities. English-speaking countries around
the world share ideas laid down in the common law of Britain. French-speaking
countries share parts of the law codes set down in France by Napoleon. There
are also international agreements that many countries treat as laws, such as those
to do with human rights.

US SUPREME COURT ▶
Most countries have a high
court to make decisions about
its most important legal
problems. In the USA, the
Supreme Court is made up of
nine justices. The justices hear an
average of 6,500 cases a year,
mostly appeals from lower
courts. A majority vote decides
the outcome of each case.

e ▸▸
law

POLICE

Every modern state has created a police force to find law breakers, charge them with crimes, and bring them to court for a trial. The police are entrusted with enforcing the law, as well as protecting the rights of citizens.

WHY DON'T CITIZENS POLICE THEMSELVES?
In small societies, rule-breakers are usually discovered and punished by their fellow citizens. In complex, mobile societies, there are often weaker social links between people. This makes it harder for communities to police themselves. Some crimes also require the work of specially trained detectives.

WHAT IS A THREAT TO PUBLIC ORDER?
Police forces in countries such as the UK and the USA were created in around the 1840s, to control street fighting between urban groups. Today, public order usually involves controlling large crowds, or political protestors, and protecting property. Police are allowed to use force, if necessary, to maintain public order.

CAN POLICE FORCES PREVENT CRIME?
Police forces invest time in advising citizens how to prevent crimes – for example, by fitting locks to stop burglars. Crimes can be prevented if the risk of being caught is increased. The percentage of crimes in which a criminal is caught varies. Generally, more resources are used to solve serious crimes than petty crimes.

▲ CROWD CONTROL IN JAPAN
Large crowds – such as those that assemble at big sporting events, pop concerts, or a rush-hour tube platform – can be dangerous. These Japanese policemen are creating a barrier to keep a crowd back, to protect those in front from being trampled or forced onto the tracks.

▲ POLICE IN THE COMMUNITY
This US police officer addresses school children during a drug awareness and education programme. These programmes show children that there is an alternative to gangs and violence.

COURT

A person accused of law-breaking is tried in a court, a public hall of justice presided over by a state official called a judge. The court hears the evidence both against and in favour of the accused. If the court finds the person guilty, it can impose a penalty.

WHY DO WE HAVE JURIES?
A jury is a panel of usually 12 citizens selected from the general population. They hear all the evidence and decide whether they think an accused person is guilty or innocent. Juries represent the public during a trial, bringing with them a democratic power to balance the powers of state officials.

HOW ARE LAW-BREAKERS PUNISHED?
Different legal systems use different punishments to deter crime and discipline a law-breaker. Legal systems based on traditional rules tend to prefer penalties which cause physical injury to the guilty person (corporal punishment). Modern systems tend to prefer detention in prison or cash fines.

PRISON ▶
The law sets down which types of crime deserve shorter or longer prison terms. The risk of losing personal and economic freedoms while locked away in a prison such as this one can deter law-breaking. However, prisons can also brutalize and dehumanize inmates.

◀ COURT OF LAW
Some cases are tried in front of a panel of judges, rather than a jury of citizens. This trial of a US serviceman, accused of a crime in Japan, was too politically sensitive for a normal jury to hear.

PRISON POPULATION		
COUNTRY	PRISONERS	PER 100,000 CITIZENS
USA	2,100,000	726
Russia	805,000	564
Singapore	17,000	392
South Africa	156,000	344
UK	77,000	145
China	1,550,000	118
Germany	80,000	97
France	53,000	88
Japan	76,000	60
India	322,000	31

FIND OUT MORE ▶▶ Global Protest 316 • Human Rights 317 • Politics 306–307 • Society 294–295 • The State 308–309

NATIONS

A nation (from the Latin for "birthplace") is defined as a large group of people unified by a common language or culture. Nationalism is the belief that people sharing national characteristics should be able to form their own independent state, surrounded by a ▸▸ BORDER.

WHAT ARE NATIONS FOR?
Modern nation-states were created to give people sharing a common language and cultural characteristics the right to govern themselves as they choose. Nations provide protection against external threats and can ask their citizens to perform tasks, such as military service, in return. The more powerful a nation's military and economic power, the more it can promote its own interests.

▲ DIALOGUE BETWEEN NATIONS
Cuba's Fidel Castro (left) meets the USSR's Nikita Khrushchev (right) to seal a friendship treaty between their two countries in 1963. Treaties like this help to establish trust between nations.

HOW DO NATIONS FORM?
Throughout history, nations have formed in several ways. Some were established as a result of geographic isolation, such as England. Others, such as Australia, were created as the result of emigration and imperial conquest, often displacing existing nations. Others again were created from the break-up of larger empires or from peace treaties, such as Croatia. Some nations, such as the Kurds or the Palestinians, are still fighting to create their own nation-states.

◂ A NATION WITHOUT A HOME
These Kurds have no territory. Their homelands lie within the borders of five other nations.

HOW DO NATIONS DEAL WITH OTHER NATIONS?
Nations interact on many levels. Trade agreements allow businesses from different nations to buy and sell their goods and services with each other. Formal agreements, signed by political leaders or their diplomatic representatives, reinforce friendly relations and allow co-operation in different areas, such as military know-how. International agreements ensure that all member nations abide by the same rules.

BORDERS

A border is a line marking where the territory of one nation-state ends and another begins. Borders are clearly marked on maps, but those between friendly nations may often be unmarked on the ground. Borders under dispute are often heavily guarded and have strictly controlled border crossings.

WHY DO NATIONS ARGUE OVER BORDERS?
Nations often contest their borders, because of the need for land and valuable raw materials, such as oil, which are important to a nation's wealth. Borders are often redrawn as a result of wars. Sometimes nationals end up on the wrong side of the border, such as in the former Yugoslavia, and this can lead to conflict too.

DO NATIONS END AT THE COAST?
The open sea is considered public territory apart from a strip of water extending 5 km (3 miles) from a nation's coastal shoreline. Nations seeking to mine wthe sea floor or fish the waters beyond these borders should have this agreed by treaty.

nations

▲ SYMBOLIC BORDER MARKER
This Peace Arch marks the border between the USA and Canada, which is unmarked for most of its 8,893-km (5,526-mile) length. The USA's southern border with Mexico is more difficult to police. It is one of the busiest land borders in the world, with around 500 million people making the crossing each year.

FIND OUT MORE ▸▸ International Organizations 434 • Nationalism 421 • New World Order 314–315 • Political World 216–217

WAR

When nations fail to settle their arguments by peaceful means, they often turn to war, or the use of armed conflict. War is also caused by some states pursuing a policy of active imperial conquest. Civil war is war between people within a nation. It can happen when political or ethnic differences become too great.

DO WARS HAVE RULES?
Henri Dunant founded the Red Cross as a medical service to care for the war wounded. In 1864, the first Geneva Convention was signed, guaranteeing their protection. Later treaties attempted to minimize the suffering of war and ensured that prisoners and civilians are treated with respect. Groups using ▶▶ TERRORISM to reach their goal do not obey rules.

HOW DO WARS END?
Wars between nations end when the leaders of one side agree to surrender to prevent further destruction. Wars also end when leaders perceive there is a military stalemate, or when they are threatened with revolt from below by their disaffected people.

▲ ARMED PROFESSIONALS
Nations at war rely on their armed forces – army, navy, and airforce – to fight the opposing side. Some nations, such as the USA or UK, employ professional full-time soldiers. Others, such as China or Israel, rely on conscription, or forced service.

▲ WEAPONS OF WAR
Expensive, state-of-the-art military equipment allows wealthy nations to engage in warfare far from their own borders. This Typhoon class Russian submarine is the world's largest underwater vessel. It is 170 m (558 ft) long and holds 150 crew.

TERRORISM

If a group feels it cannot achieve its goals under the normal rules of a nation or of international politics, it may resort to terrorism. Terrorists use or threaten violence to make their demands. Some groups target only political enemies, others target anybody.

HOW IS TERRORISM SET APART FROM WARFARE?
Terrorism has been around since the time of the Ancient Greeks. Today, it can be difficult to separate terrorism from other forms of warfare. Guerilla fighters, small bands who attack larger armies, often use terrorist tactics. Governments may also use illegal violence as part of their secret service operations.

war

▲ TERROR AGAINST TERROR
The use of terrorist tactics – surprise, boldness, and a willingness to target the innocent – is becoming increasingly common in conflicts across the globe. These Amal fighters (a Syrian-backed militia) are launching missiles into a refugee camp in Lebanon, trying to target a Palestinian terror group hiding there. Thousands of refugees with no links to terrorism have died in such attacks.

FIND OUT MORE ▶▶ New World Order 314–315 • Political World 216–217

◄ ZEMIN AND BUSH
President Jiang Zemin of China and President George W. Bush of the USA met in October 2001 to improve links between their countries. During the Cold War, China and the USA were enemies.

NEW WORLD ORDER

After 1945, two powerful and opposing nations emerged within the ▶ INTERNATIONAL COMMUNITY : the Soviet Union and the United States. When the Soviet Union fell apart in 1991 and the Cold War ended, a new order began with the USA as the world's only superpower.

WHAT IS THE NEW BALANCE OF POWER?

The USA is now the world's most powerful country, giving it a leading role in global issues. Its global leadership is balanced by regional powers, such as the nations of the European Union (EU), the Middle East's Arab League, and the Association of South East Asian Nations (ASEAN). Their relationships are marked by both co-operation and conflict.

IS THE NEW ORDER STABLE?

The Cold War order was made stable by ▶ SECURITY alliances between nations, to align themselves with the might of the two superpowers. Nations must now find other reasons to work together, because stability will depend on countries agreeing shared goals.

WHAT TRENDS WILL AFFECT THE NEW ORDER?

Trends such as ▶ GLOBALIZATION will affect how economic power is shared between nations. Regional powers, such as the European Union, may become stronger to counter US power. Security issues such as terrorism may remain a focus worldwide.

DEVASTATION IN CHECHNYA ►
As the Soviet Union's power crumbled at the end of the Cold War, many new conflicts emerged at its borders. In Chechnya, the new leaders in Russia waged war to stop a movement for national independence.

▲ FACTORIES ABROAD
Sights such as this German car-making factory in Shanghai, China, are now more common. Companies can set up factories wherever there is a workforce.

GLOBALIZATION

When the Cold War ended, a vast global economy emerged. Trade and migration between countries became easier, and big businesses set up bases across the world – bringing new wealth, but also new problems, to the world. Globalization also describes the spread of Western culture.

WHAT ARE THE RISKS OF GLOBALIZATION?

Creating a truly global market that includes every nation could make business more efficient, improving everyone's quality of life. But if some people are excluded, the gap between the rich and poor of the world could grow. Governments must also make sure that the economic power of a huge business does not undermine the rights of individual people.

WHEN DID GLOBALIZATION BEGIN?

The term "globalization" was first used in the 1980s, but trade on a global scale has been going on for centuries. In the 16th and 17th centuries, Portugal, Spain, the Netherlands, and Britain built up trading empires that spanned the world. The Industrial Revolution of the 19th century also helped to unite the world's markets. Global trade slowed down during the two World Wars, but began to build up again in the late 1980s, towards the end of the Cold War.

CAN INDIVIDUAL NATIONS AFFECT GLOBAL TRENDS?

Individual nations may not have much power on their own, but they can open up their economies to the world as a whole by working as part of larger organizations. Nations can also work together to agree on a set of international rules, which should apply to businesses wherever they are based and control their conduct for everyone's benefit.

INTERNATIONAL COMMUNITY

Representatives of the world's 193 countries meet and talk in different forums, such as the United Nations (UN) and the World Bank. These countries make up a community of nations, which can act together to deal with global problems.

UN flag's olive branches symbolize global peace

WHAT ARE THE GOALS OF THE UNITED NATIONS?
The major goals of the United Nations are defined in its charter. The first is to recognize each nation's sovereignty, or the right to govern itself. The second is to encourage a policy of non-intervention in each other's affairs. The UN also seeks to prevent conflict by providing a forum for co-operation.

CAN THE COMMUNITY HELP THE WEAK?
The international community aims to maintain global peace, which is vital for social progress. It also provides aid for countries facing great difficulty – for example, those devastated by famine, debt, or war. Aid might come in the form of food or medical packages, or a deal to cut a nation's debt to another.

Vehicles painted white to show they belong to UN forces

Soldiers in UN forces wear blue helmets

▼ UN PEACEKEEPERS
The United Nations Security Council can ask member nations to send troops to war zones to keep the peace. UN soldiers do not normally fight, but they do try to keep enemies apart.

new world order

National badge shows a soldier's home nation

KENYA

SECURITY

The government of every country needs a security system to protect its citizens. Governments must have the resources to defend the country from attack, and gather good information to warn against future attacks. Under the new world order, the need for global security requires nations to work together.

IS SECURITY NEEDED IN THE NEW WORLD ORDER?
After the Cold War, many nations hoped to cut military spending and put the money into social projects, such as poverty relief, instead. However, the new world order created new tensions and pockets of resistance across the globe, and defence spending started to grow again in 1995.

WHAT DOES SECURITY COST?
The cost of protecting the world by military and other means is enormous. Military spending around the world is roughly $1,000,000,000,000 (one trillion) per year, or about 2.5 per cent of the global economy. US spending makes up a third of the global total.

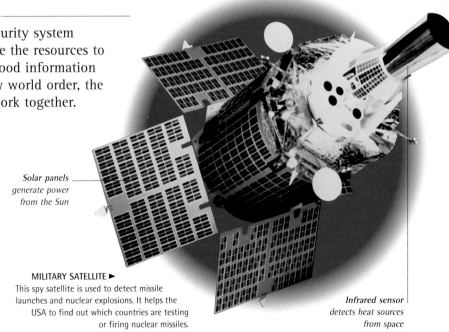

Solar panels generate power from the Sun

MILITARY SATELLITE ▶
This spy satellite is used to detect missile launches and nuclear explosions. It helps the USA to find out which countries are testing or firing nuclear missiles.

Infrared sensor detects heat sources from space

FIND OUT MORE ▶▶ Cold War 435 • Industrial Revolution 418–419 • International Organizations 434 • Satellites 28

GLOBAL PROTEST

People who object to their government's policies may gather together in protest. But many issues, such as ⏩ DEBT and the ⏩ ENVIRONMENT, affect people across the globe. In the 1990s, global protest groups emerged, uniting voices of protest from all nations.

HOW DO GLOBAL PROTESTORS GET ORGANIZED?

Cheaper travel and improvements in communications, such as the development of the Internet, have made it easier for people from different countries – already united by shared opinions – to meet and plan political action or demonstrations.

WHAT CAN PROTESTORS ACHIEVE?

By questioning decisions made or actions taken by world leaders and big business, protesters can draw other people into a wider discussion of the issue. This democratic debate can influence global as well as national decisions. Protestors can also share knowledge with others about how such issues affect their own countries.

◀ ON THE MARCH
Protests can alert the wider public to issues that demand action. This protest in Seattle, in 1999, drew media attention to issues being discussed by the World Trade Organization, and inspired more people to support global protest in other countries.

WHAT ARE THE PROTESTS AGAINST?

Although global protests express many different concerns, an issue at the root of many protests is equality. For example, some protestors feel that people in poor countries are treated unfairly in the global community, because international rules are made by powerful countries to help their own economies.

DEBT

Wealthy countries have loaned money to the governments of poor countries. As a result, debt payments cost the world's poorest people US$100 million a day, on top of the cost of basic survival. This makes it difficult for the poor to escape poverty.

CAN DEBT BE CANCELLED?

About five per cent of the debt of developing countries has been cancelled by wealthy countries. In return for this, countries in debt had to agree to open their economies to the global market. People fighting to reduce such debt want more of it cancelled faster, with fewer controls placed on the countries in debt.

e ⏩
global protest

ENVIRONMENT

Companies desperate to compete in the global market often do not respect the natural world, or the environment. Protesters campaign to protect the environment from human damage, such as pollution or habitat destruction, by setting up international controls.

WHAT IS SUSTAINABLE DEVELOPMENT?

In the past, Western countries have often achieved wealth by using up natural resources such as coal or forests, without considering the future effects on the environment. Sustainable development aims for growth that works with nature rather than against it – for example, replanting logging areas with new trees.

GM CROP PROTEST ▶
Greenpeace activists attack a field of genetically modified (GM) crops in the UK. They aim to persuade more people that GM plants are a hazard to the environment.

FIND OUT MORE ⏩ Economy 302–303 • Human Impact 64–65 • New World Order 314–315

HUMAN RIGHTS

The laws that establish a balance between the powers of a state and the individual rights of its citizens are known as human rights. After World War II, the United Nations (UN) drew up a list of human rights to protect all citizens and promote the rights of each individual.

DOES EVERYONE AGREE OVER HUMAN RIGHTS?

Some human rights are accepted by almost all cultures and political parties, while others are still disputed. For example, rights supporting political freedoms, such as the right to vote in elections, are more widely accepted than those supporting economic and social freedoms, such as equal rights for women.

WHAT IS SOVEREIGNTY?

Nations have rights, just as citizens within nations do. The right for nations to make decisions free from outside control is called sovereignty. Sovereignty can be a barrier to ▶▶ HUMANITARIANISM, if a nation refuses to admit to its human rights problems.

▲ UN UNIVERSAL DECLARATION
On 10 December, 1948, world leaders announced that the UN had voted to support a single human rights law for all humanity. The Soviet Union, South Africa, and Saudi Arabia chose not to vote on this issue.

◀ RIGHTS CAMPAIGNERS
Groups like Amnesty International help to defend human rights worldwide. This banner was raised in Pakistan to challenge those who supported the Taliban's rule in neighbouring Afghanistan.

e ▶▶
human rights

CAN HUMAN RIGHTS ABUSERS BE PUNISHED?

International law on human rights allows the international community to punish politicians if they abuse the rights of their citizens. But many states reject this use of international law, because they suspect that it could be used to control a country, rather than to improve its human rights.

▲ INTERNATIONAL COURT OF JUSTICE, THE HAGUE
Nations can bring a complaint to the International Court of Justice in The Hague, in the Netherlands, about crimes committed by another nation. This 1999 sitting of the court found NATO countries not guilty of a complaint by Yugoslavia that it had been illegally bombed.

HUMANITARIANISM

The goal of humanitarianism is to put human welfare above all things. In warfare, for example, the humanitarian approach is that doctors should treat wounded enemy soldiers as well as their own, without concern for the political issues involved. Humanitarian organizations provide vital sources of aid in times of war or crisis.

WHAT IS IMPARTIAL AID?

Humanitarian organizations, such as the Red Cross, are able to enter war-torn areas to get help to the people who need it most. All sides trust them to give impartial aid during a conflict – to help any human being who needs it, whichever political side they may be on. Some humanitarian aid agencies prefer to be partial, giving aid only to the people whose political positions they share.

▲ FOOD AID REACHES THE HUNGRY
In 2001, wealthier countries gave food to thousands of Afghan refugees through the World Food Program. Refugees from wars or government repression urgently require access to food, clean water, and shelter.

FIND OUT MORE ▶▶ Cold War 435 • International Organizations 434

ARTS and ENTERTAINMENT

PAINTING

Painting is the art of creating pictures by applying colour to a surface. Paintings can record events, capture a likeness of a person, place, or object, tell stories, decorate walls, and illustrate texts. Paintings can express emotions and ideas, or simply be enjoyed for their beauty.

WHAT KINDS OF PAINTS DO ARTISTS USE?

Paint is made by mixing a pigment (coloured powder) with a medium (liquid substance) such as water. Egg is the medium for tempera painting, linseed oil for oil painting, and acrylic resin for acrylic painting. In fresco wall paintings, pigments are applied to wet plaster. Watercolours are made by mixing pigments with a water-soluble binder such as gum.

HOW AND WHEN DID PAINTING BEGIN?

Some 20,000 years ago, early humans ground up earth, charcoal, and minerals, and used the coloured powders to create images on cave walls. Sometimes the powders were mixed with saliva or animal fat to form a fluid, which was blown through reeds, or applied with fingers. The first paintings were of hunting scenes.

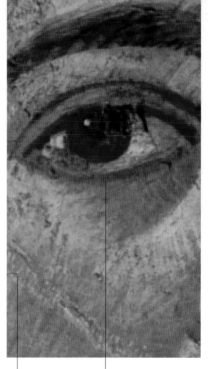

Individual, parallel brushstrokes

Strong outline adds emphasis to eye

Craquelure (cracks) caused by drying and ageing of paint

Sfumato (smoky) technique blends tones and blurs lines

Cracks in plaster on which fresco painting was created

Stylus (writing tool) held by wife indicates status

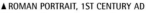

Rocky landscape, often a feature in Leonardo's paintings

Calm pose with folded hands resting on chair arm

▲ ROMAN PORTRAIT, 1ST CENTURY AD
This fresco, by an unknown artist, was rescued from the ruins of Pompeii, Italy. It shows the Roman painter's ability to create a realistic portrait, and also his interest in depicting the social position of the young couple, believed to be a lawyer and his wife.

▲ *MONA LISA*, c. 1503–1506
Mona Lisa by Leonardo da Vinci (1452–1519) is probably the most famous painting in Western art. Set against a misty mountain background, a young Florentine woman gazes at us with a mysterious smile that has fascinated generations of viewers.

▲ *KANGAROO DREAMING*, MICHAEL NELSON JAGAMARA, 2000
Traditionally, the paintings of Aboriginal Australians tell stories of sacred ancestors. The apparently abstract symbols at the centre represent fire and rain. The snakes are a supernatural being called the Rainbow Serpent.

OCULUS, GONZAGA PALACE, MANTUA, ITALY ▼
In this example of illusionism, Andrea Mantegna (c. 1431–1506) painted a fake oculus (circular opening) on the palace ceiling, so that the room seems to open on to the sky. Figures peer over, and a plant pot delicately balances.

WHAT SUBJECTS DO ARTISTS PAINT?

Some artists paint aspects of the visible world, such as people, landscapes, still-lifes of tableware, fruit, and flowers, or scenes from history, literature, and the imagination. Such paintings are realistic – they look like something real. Other paintings are abstract – they are not meant to look like anything from the real world, but use colours, shapes, and lines to express feelings, moods, or ideas.

Leaves *are painted with feathery brushstrokes*

Oil paint *is diluted with turpentine for luminous effect*

Canvas texture *shows through beneath the paint*

Swirls *are thickly applied paint that is not fully blended*

Overhanging foliage *frames the sitter's head*

Relaxed hands *and outstretched legs create an informal pose*

Colours *are not realistic, but express emotion*

Red of beard *contrasts with dominant greens and blues*

▲ *MRS RICHARD BRINSLEY SHERIDAN, c.* 1785
This lovely full-length portrait was painted by Thomas Gainsborough (1727–1788), who excelled at both portraiture and landscape painting. The beauty of the sitter is enhanced by the delicately painted woodland setting. Mrs Sheridan was a famous singer.

▲ *SELF-PORTRAIT,* 1889
One of many self-portraits by Vincent van Gogh (1853–1890), this powerful image was painted while he was living at a mental asylum. The acid colours, thick swirling brushstrokes, and intense, staring eyes express the artist's inner suffering.

A cherub *leans over and looks at other cherubs peeping out*

Stone parapet *creates the illusion of 3-D architecture*

e ▶▶ painting

WATERCOLOUR ▶
Before photography, watercolour painting was the most common way to record images of plants and animals. The great illustrator Pierre-Joseph Redouté (1759–1814) produced many exquisitely detailed watercolour studies such as this wild rose.

WHAT IS ILLUSIONISM?

Since paintings are two-dimensional (flat) and the real world is three-dimensional, artists use methods such as perspective to create the illusion that painted objects are real. One form of illusionism is *sotto in sù*, Italian for "from below upwards". Used on ceilings, it shows objects from below so that they appear to exist above the viewer's head.

PERSPECTIVE

In painting, perspective is a system for representing three-dimensional space on a flat surface. In the real world, objects seem to be smaller the further away they are from the viewer, and parallel lines appear to converge (meet). Perspective mimics this.

WHO INVENTED PERSPECTIVE?

Perspective was developed in the Italian Renaissance by two painters, Leon Battista Alberti (1404–1472) and Filippo Brunelleschi (1377–1446). They created a mathematical system and experimented with it. Before the invention of perspective, artists could not accurately represent how objects looked in space. Now they could paint a consistent, convincing illusion.

Vanishing point

Horizon line

▲ *THE AVENUE, MIDDELHARNIS,* MEINDERT HOBBEMA,1689
This Dutch landscape is famous for its use of a deep, central perspective scheme. The parallel lines of the straight avenue and the trees converge towards the vanishing point on the horizon. The lines superimposed show the mathematical framework used to create perspective.

WHAT IS THE VANISHING POINT?

The vanishing point is the spot where lines that would be parallel in reality appear to converge in the distance on the painting's horizon line (where the sky meets the land). As the converging lines move inwards towards the vanishing point, they lead the viewer's eye into the picture's imaginary depth. By focusing on the tiny figure on the road, just beneath the vanishing point, the viewer feels it is almost possible to step into the painted landscape.

KEY SCHOOLS OF PAINTING		
SCHOOL	*CENTURY*	*KEY WORKS*
Gothic	13th–15th	*The Annunciation,* Simone Martini
Renaissance	14th–16th	*The Arnolfini Marriage,* van Eyck *School of Athens,* Raphael
Baroque	17th–18th	*The Descent from the Cross,* Rubens
Rococo	17th–18th	*The Swing,* Fragonard
Neoclassicism	18th–19th	*The Oath of the Horatii,* David
Romanticism	18th–19th	*The Raft of the Medusa,* Géricault
Impressionism & Post-Impressionism	Late 19th	*Dance at the Moulin de la Galette,* Renoir; *Mont Ste Victoire,* Cezanne
Cubism	20th	*Les Demoiselles d'Avignon,* Picasso

FIND OUT MORE ▶▶ Artists 324 • Drawing 322 • First Modern Humans 362–363 • Renaissance 398

DRAWING

Drawing uses lines, dots, or similar marks to create pictures and designs. Artists often use drawings as preparations for paintings and sculptures, but drawings can also be finished works of art in their own right.

▲ *DANCERS*, EDGAR DEGAS, *c.* 1900
Degas (1834–1917) often worked with pastels, sticks of powdered colour. Pastels lie on the borderline between drawing and painting.

IS DRAWING ALWAYS BLACK AND WHITE?
Artists draw in a variety of coloured media, including colour pencils, wax crayons, inks, chalks, and pastels. Some artists, such as Degas, are as famous for their pastels as for their paintings.

WHAT DO ARTISTS DRAW WITH?
Artists draw with many different tools, including pencils, pen and ink, fibre-tip pens, chalk, charcoal, crayons, and pastel. In Western art, before graphite (lead) pencils were introduced in the 17th century, artists drew in silverpoint, using a silver-tipped rod on specially prepared paper.

WHAT DO THE NUMBERS AND LETTERS ON PENCILS MEAN?
Drawing pencils are coded according to how hard and how dark they are. HB, for example, is medium-hard and creates a thin line, while 6B is softer and darker – good for ▶▶ SHADING.

Precisely drawn lines describe the armour in detail

▲ *PROFILE OF A WARRIOR*, *c.* 1475
Leonardo da Vinci (1452–1519) made drawings of all kinds of subjects, including this imaginary warrior in fantastical armour.

SHADING

Shading is the way tone – the lightness or darkness in a picture – is created. There are many shading techniques in drawing. Hatching uses a series of parallel or roughly parallel lines to create shading. An artist can also rub charcoal with his finger to make lighter or darker effects on paper.

▲ SHADED FACE
Light falling on the face creates highlights and shadows. The artist reproduces this effect to create the illusion of solid form on paper.

HOW DOES HATCHING WORK?
In hatching, varying the width, weight, and closeness of parallel lines can create depth in a shadow. In cross-hatching an artist draws a set of closely spaced parallel lines and then applies another set over the top at a different angle. This technique is often used in printmaking where a design is cut on metal or wood.

drawing

FIND OUT MORE ▶▶ Design 326 • Painting 320–321 • Renaissance 398

SCULPTURE

Sculpture is three-dimensional art. Traditionally, there are two main methods: carving material such as wood or stone, and modelling forms by adding pieces of material such as clay. Modern artists have explored new materials and techniques.

Sculpture is 4.1 m (13 ft 6 in) high

The cobra is the serpent demon, representing evil

WOODEN MASK ►
Wood is carved to make sculptures or functional objects such as this Sri Lankan dancer's mask, created from carved and painted wood.

WHAT DOES THREE-DIMENSIONAL MEAN?
The term refers to the three dimensions of space – length, breadth, and depth. It is a useful way of distinguishing between art such as painting, drawing, and prints, which are two-dimensional (flat) and sculpture, which is three-dimensional.

HORSES OF SAN MARCO ▼
Four life-size horses stand atop the Basilica de San Marco, Venice. They date from the the 4th century BC to the 4th century AD. They were taken to Italy from Constantinople in the 13th century.

Material is steel mesh sprayed with expanding foam, covered with fibre-glass skin, and topped with ceramic tiles for mosaic effect

▲ RELIEF CARVING
This detail is from an ancient Hindu relief carving cut into a massive rock in Tamil Nadu, southern India. It was made during the 7th or 8th centuries.

IS SCULPTURE ALWAYS VIEWED FROM ALL SIDES?
Not all sculptures are carved in the round. Relief sculptures are carved on one side only, and stand out from a background surface. Relief panels have been used since ancient times, often to decorate important buildings, such as temples and churches.

HOW IS SCULPTURE MADE?
Techniques depend upon the materials used. When carving stone or wood, the sculptor chips away with a hammer and chisel. When sculpting clay, artists may use their hands. Clay models may be cast in bronze to create a strong, permanent sculpture. Other techniques include welding metal, moulding plastic or concrete, and using fibre-glass.

Big face decorates most of Halpern's sculptures, often inspired by Picasso

sculpture

◄ OPHELIA, DEBORAH HALPERN, 1996
Australian artist Deborah Halpern (1957–) creates public art, sculptures created for outside. This one adds colour and exuberance to city life in Melbourne.

Bronze consists of copper mixed with small amounts of lead and tin. This bronze is overlaid with gold

ARTISTS

Artists are people who create art. Although some of them have no formal training, most great artists have studied art. Today artists can study at art schools, but in the past they learned by apprenticeship, working with more experienced artists. Every culture and period of history has its great artists.

WHERE DO ARTISTS WORK?
Most artists have a studio – a room or other place where they make their art. Many also work outside. For example, landscape painters might make sketches in the open air, and complete the work in their studio. Other artists work mainly in the landscape, completing paintings outside, or creating land art within the natural environment.

HOW DO ARTISTS EARN A LIVING?
Sometimes artists receive commissions (orders) for work from a patron – an individual or an institution. Sometimes existing work is bought by an individual, an institution, or a ▸▸ **GALLERY**. Earning a living as an artist is not easy. Vincent van Gogh (1853–1890), whose works now sell for vast sums of money, sold hardly any paintings during his lifetime.

▲ *SURROUNDED ISLANDS*
Christo and Jeanne-Claude surrounded these Florida islands i 1983 with floating pink fabric.

▲ *THE ARTIST'S STUDIO,* JAN VERMEER, *c.* 1665
This Dutch artist (1632–1675) gives us a glimpse of how and where he worked. Seated at his easel, he paints a female model, who poses as Clio, the muse of history.

▲ PABLO PICASSO MIXING PAINTS IN HIS STUDIO
Some artists become celebrities. One of the most versatile and influential artists of the 20th century was the Spanish painter Picasso (1881–1973), who became a world-famous personality.

▲ BARBARA HEPWORTH CARVING IN WOOD
The achievement of women artists has often been overlooked. The British sculptor Hepworth (1903–197 was one of the most famous artists of the 20th centur

▲ METROPOLITAN MUSEUM
In this tour at the Metropolitan Museum in New York City, a guide shows visitors around the different galleries and explains the history of the paintings.

GALLERIES

A gallery is an exhibition space where works of art are shown. Galleries show all sorts of art and craft – including painting, sculpture, ceramics, installations, video, and photography. They can be public institutions (which are like museums) or privately owned.

DO ALL GALLERIES BUY AND SELL ART?
Privately owned commercial galleries sell the works they exhibit. This type of gallery often specializes in certain types of art – such as contemporary art, or traditional landscape painting. Public galleries acquire works of art to add to their permanent collections – not to sell, but to show to the public.

e ▸▸

artists

GREAT GALLERIES OF THE WORLD	
LOCATION	*MAJOR GALLERIES*
London	National Gallery, Tate, Victoria & Albert Museum
Madrid	Prado
New York	Metropolitan Museum of Art, Museum of Modern Art
Paris	Louvre, Musée d'Art Moderne, Musée d'Orsay
Rome	Vatican Museums

FIND OUT MORE ▸▸ Drawing 322 • Painting 320–321 • Sculpture 323

PHOTOGRAPHY

The word photography comes from two Greek words meaning light and drawing. Photography is the process and the art of creating fixed images using the action of light on a chemically prepared surface.

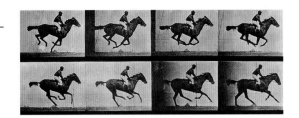

WHO INVENTED PHOTOGRAPHY?

Joseph Nicéphore Niépce (1765–1833) took the first photograph c. 1827. However, his process needed eight hours of exposure to light, and the picture was fuzzy. In 1837 Louis Daguerre (1787–1851) created a sharp but one-off image in a few minutes. In 1839 William Henry Fox Talbot (1800–1877) presented negative film and prints – still the basis for today's photography.

WHEN DID CAMERAS BECOME PORTABLE?

In the early days of photography, cameras were large and cumbersome, and pictures were made on individual glass plates. The big breakthrough came when George Eastman (1854–1932) invented flexible film. In 1888, he introduced the Kodak camera – it was small, light, and loaded with a roll of film. The craze for snapshot photography soon spread.

▲ MOTION IN PICTURES
Eadweard Muybridge (1830–1904) developed a technique for taking a rapid sequence of photographs, which revealed surprising truths about the way animals moved. Before his photographs were published, painters wrongly depicted galloping horses with all four legs outstretched.

▲ LANDSCAPE BY DENNIS STOCK
In this coloured landscape, American photographer Dennis Stock (1928–) uses the effects of the stormy sky to create atmosphere. Dark foreground shadows contrast with the trees and path, which glow in shafts of light.

▲ INTERIOR BY EUGENE ATGET
The French photographer Atget (1857–1927) recorded the changing face of 19th- and 20th-century Paris in more than 10,000 photos. His work is both art and social document.

HAS PHOTOGRAPHY INFLUENCED PAINTING?

The influence has always worked both ways. In the early days of snapshots, for example, Impressionist painters were inspired by their accidental effects, such as the blurring of moving figures, and figures being cropped by the photo's edge. Photographic portraits and landscapes are often inspired by painted ones.

HOW DOES COLOUR PHOTOGRAPHY WORK?

In photography all colours can be made up from mixtures of red, blue, and green. Colour film has three layers of light-sensitive material, each one of which reacts to one of these colours. Coloured dyes are produced in each layer, which combine to make the photographic image.

photography

◄ *AFGHAN GIRL* BY STEVE MCCURRY
This photograph of an Afghan girl in a Pakistani refugee camp was taken in 1984 and appeared on the cover of *National Geographic* magazine. It shows her as ragged and scared, yet dignified, gazing directly at the photographer and the viewer. In its way, it is as unforgettable a portrait as the *Mona Lisa* by Leonardo da Vinci.

WHAT DO DOCUMENTARY PHOTOGRAPHERS DO?

Since the 19th century, documentary photographers have recorded the experiences of others. Photographs of Victorian street-sellers and poverty-stricken US farmers in the Great Depression made a huge impact on public awareness. Tragic images of the Vietnam War reduced public support for the war in the USA.

FIND OUT MORE ▶▶ Colour 180 • Lenses 181 • Light 178–179 • Media 298–299• Painting 320–321

DESIGN

Design is the way something is planned, arranged, and made. A designer aims to create things that look good, and do their job well. Most man-made objects – including the page you are reading, the chair you are sitting on, and the clothes you are wearing – have been designed. Increasingly, computers are used in design.

Mazes create visual intrigue and entertainment

Plants are evenly spaced within a geometric layout

▲ GARDEN DESIGN
This wonderful Renaissance garden at the Villa d'Este in Tivoli, Italy, is a strictly geometric, formal design. Garden designs may be formally planned – like this one with fountains and mazes – or more relaxed and natural.

WHAT MAKES A GOOD DESIGN?
The successful combination of form (how good something looks) and function (how well it works) is the basis of good design. A chair, for example, should look good and be fit for its purpose – which is to provide a safe, comfortable support for a person to sit on. There are many institutions that award prizes for brilliant designs.

WHY DO DESIGNS CHANGE?
Designs change as lifestyles and tastes change, and as new materials and technologies develop. For example, in the 20th century, eating styles became less formal, and people wanted convenience. At the same time, new materials such as stainless steel became available. As a result, kitchen products became more streamlined and more desirable.

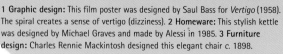

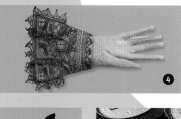

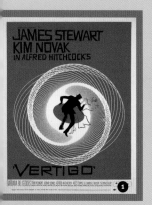

Whistle is plastic bird

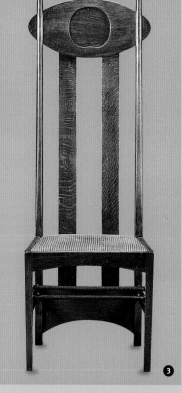

1 **Graphic design:** This film poster was designed by Saul Bass for *Vertigo* (1958). The spiral creates a sense of vertigo (dizziness). 2 **Homeware:** This stylish kettle was designed by Michael Graves and made by Alessi in 1985. 3 **Furniture design:** Charles Rennie Mackintosh designed this elegant chair c. 1898.

4 **Fashion design:** This 16th- or 17th-century leather glove is trimmed with tapestry woven in silk and gold. 5 **Brand design:** This is the logo of Apple Macintosh, the first firm to design personal computers in bright colours. 6 **Product design:** The ring-pull for cans is convenient. 7 **Fashion design:** Twiggy models a new look in 1967. 8 **Car design:** The 1998 Volkswagen Beetle updates the original car, designed in the 1930s.

HOW OLD IS FASHION DESIGN?
Some 40,000 years ago people sewed hides together to fit the body, using needles made from mammoth ivory and reindeer bone. This was mainly for survival, but gradually more emphasis was placed on the decorative value of clothing. In many ancient cultures, such as Egypt, Greece, and Rome, fashion was linked to wealth and social status.

HOW IS A PRODUCT DESIGNED?
Designers sketch out ideas on paper, decide on materials, and then make detailed drawings. They also make sketches on a computer to create images of three-dimensional models, which the designer can then manipulate and view from all angles. Usually a prototype (trial product) is built and fully tested before being manufactured.

design

FIND OUT MORE ▶▶ Architecture 328–329 • Cinema 346–347 • Construction 202–203 • Renaissance 398 • Technology 154

DECORATIVE ARTS

In contrast to the fine arts of painting and sculpture, this term refers to the design of everyday objects that are turned into works of art. These objects are often purely ornamental. The decorative arts include textiles, jewellery, glasswork, and ceramics.

WHO ARE THE GREAT DECORATIVE ARTISTS?

The most famous is probably William Morris (1834–1896). He believed that the craftsmanship of decorative art improved the lives of those who made everyday objects and those who used them. His firm produced furniture, tapestry, stained glass, fabrics, carpets, and wallpapers – all still popular today. Other famous names include Clarice Cliff (1899–1972) and Louis Comfort Tiffany (1848–1933).

STARBURST WALL CLOCK, 1953 ▶
This clock by American designer George Nelson has 12 colourful rays, each representing an hour.

Minute hand

Materials used are beech, metal, and acrylic laquer

Bold simplicity of line and colour are part of the appeal that keeps this clock in production today

Shape of the vase is both beautiful and functional

Illustration depicts one of the 12 Labours of Hercules

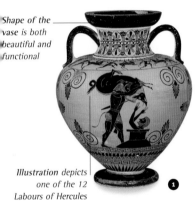

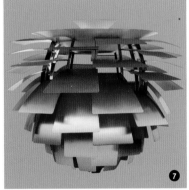

1 **Ceramics:** Ancient Greek painted vase. 2 **Ceramics:** This Art Deco plate was hand painted by Clarice Cliff in a pattern called *Autumn*. 3 **Textiles:** Finnish designer Maija Isola created this flowery fabric pattern in the 1960s. 4 **Textiles:** William Morris's 19th-century wallpaper is still manufactured in the 21st.

5 **Textiles:** Detail from a Persian Bidjar rug *c.* 1890. 6 **Jewellery:** Art Deco enamelled brooch *c.* 1925. 7 **Metalwork:** The *Artichoke* lampshade was designed by Paul Henningsen in 1958. Manufactured from copper and steel by Louis Poulsen, it is still popular today. 8 **Glasswork:** This beautiful glass table lamp with *Poppy* motif was designed in the Art Nouveau style by American glass designer Louis Comfort Tiffany.

WHAT IS ART DECO?

This decorative style spread through all areas of decorative art between World Wars I and II – from jewellery to ceramics, from furniture to architecture. Combining varied influences from Cubist paintings to ancient Egyptian and Aztec jewellery, Art Deco's vivid style was characterized by sleek lines, bold colours, and geometric forms.

WHY IS SOME POTTERY CALLED CHINA?

People sometimes use the term china to mean crockery, but china is a special type of ceramic called porcelain. First produced in China in the 7th or 8th century it is hard and translucent (light can shine through it). Europeans did not discover how to make it until the 18th century, at Meissen, Germany, which is still famous for its china.

FIND OUT MORE ▶▶ Ancient Greece 376–377 • China's First Empire 378 • Sculpture 323

ARCHITECTURE

Architecture is the art of designing buildings. Architects design buildings in different shapes and sizes, from single-storey garden sheds to soaring ▸▸ SKYSCRAPERS . The combination of form and function is vital, since buildings have to be safe as well as good-looking and fit for their purpose.

WHY DO BUILDINGS LOOK SO DIFFERENT?

The way a building looks depends on several factors: the materials and technology available, its particular architectural style, and its purpose. Domestic buildings, corporate offices, and sacred architecture, for example, have entirely different functions which are reflected in their size, form, and content.

Natural daylight reflects down into the building, which means less artificial light is needed

Central cone is made of 360 laminated glass mirrors that reflect everything around them

Cone inside the building supports the dome on top of the building (see image below)

REICHSTAG, BERLIN ▸
Germany's parliament building, the Reichstag, was partially destroyed by a fire in 1933. When it was renovated by the British architect Norman Foster in the 1990s, the use of glass symbolized the openness of democracy.

e ▸▸
architecture

Visitors walk up the ramp that spirals up the glass dome

Marble facing over brick   *Gothic pointed window arch*   *Statues of saints stand in alcoves*

▲ DUOMO, MILAN
One of the world's largest cathedrals, Duomo was designed to hold 40,000 people. Begun in the 14th century, it was not finished until the 19th. The façade reflects many styles, including Gothic and neoclassical.

WHAT IS SUSTAINABLE ARCHITECTURE?

Sustainable buildings aim to be environmentally friendly. The construction and running of buildings causes pollution and uses up energy and resources. Buildings made with renewable materials, non-toxic paints, solar panels, good insulation, and even toilets that use less water all help to preserve the planet.

HOW DO ARCHITECTS WORK?

A client briefs the architect about the type of building they want and how much they can pay. The architect then makes designs, and works out detailed technical drawings, often using computer programs. Engineers check the plans and any models to make sure that the building will be structurally sound.

New glass dome rises from the shell of the 19th-century building

EXTERIOR OF REICHSTAG

SAPPORO DOME, HOKKAIDO ▶
Built by Japan for the 2002 World Cup, this futuristic stadium has a translucent domed roof made from Teflon-coated glass-fibre. Its natural turf football pitch can be moved inside or outside by floating it on a cushion of air.

WHAT MATERIALS DO ARCHITECTS USE?

Traditional building materials are stone, wood, brick, and concrete. However, as technology develops, so do new materials. Steel and glass are commonly used. Fabrics are created by coating glass-fibre with a durable plastic such as Teflon to make a membrane (skin) that can be attached to a steel framework.

WHAT DOES CLASSICAL ARCHITECTURE MEAN?

The architecture of the Ancient Greeks and Romans, which was based on balanced, harmonious proportions, is known as classical architecture. It has had a huge influence on the history of Western architecture. Some modern architects still use elements of the classical tradition today.

▲ PARTHENON (447–432 BC), ATHENS
This temple's Doric columns once supported beams and a richly carved triangular pediment at each end of its roof. Though now in ruins, the Parthenon is the most famous example of classical architecture.

THE CLASSICAL ORDERS

The Ancient Greeks designed buildings in three orders (styles). Each had its own design rules, such as features for columns. The shaft of the column is topped by a capital.

Capital is a circle topped by a square

Shaft is fluted

DORIC

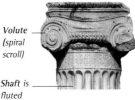

Volute (spiral scroll)

Shaft is fluted

IONIC

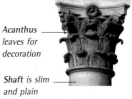

Acanthus leaves for decoration

Shaft is slim and plain

CORINTHIAN

SKYSCRAPERS

The term skyscraper became popular in the USA in the 1880s to describe a new type of tall office building in Chicago and New York City. They rose up to 12 storeys, a startling height at the time.

WHAT IS THE WORLD'S TALLEST BUILDING?

Buildings could only rise as high as about 75 m (250 ft) until the invention of steel-frame construction. In 1998 Chicago's Sears Tower – at 442 m (1,450 ft), the world's tallest building since 1974 – was overtaken by the Petronas Towers in Kuala Lumpur, Malaysia, which stands at 452 m (1,483 ft).

CHRYSLER BUILDING, NEW YORK CITY ▶
Completed in 1930, this Art Deco masterpiece was briefly the tallest building in the world at 319 m (1,048 ft). In 1931 the nearby Empire State Building overtook it, rising to 381 m (1,250 m).

FIND OUT MORE ▶▶ Ancient Greece 376–377 • Construction 202–203 • Design 326

Music is the art of making sounds and arranging them in an entertaining way. People create and listen to music for pleasure, celebration, and to express ideas and feelings. Types of music include classical, folk, and pop.

HOW IS MUSIC CREATED?

Instruments generate sounds, as does the human voice. Some sounds with a specific ▶▶ PITCH are called notes. These sounds are then grouped to create ▶▶ RHYTHM and ▶▶ MELODY . Some music is created spontaneously, and some is composed over many years. Musicians compose alone and in groups.

▲ WOODSTOCK, NEW YORK, USA, 1969
Joe Cocker's band prepare to perform to a huge crowd at the Woodstock music festival. Around 500,000 fans attended the event, which featured 30 top bands and musicians. It was the first festival for popular music.

HOW DO WE REMEMBER PIECES OF MUSIC?

Music can be memorized, written down, or recorded on to a format such as CD. There are several systems for writing music. The most common is to create a score. A score is a page with a series of five-line grids called staves. Using notation (symbols), a composer writes the melody and rhythm of a piece of music.

RHYTHM

The basis of all music is its beat, which divides it into units of time. Composers and musicians group these beats together, decide how long each beat is, and place accents on some for emphasis. This creates the basic rhythm of a piece of music.

WHAT ARE THE BASIC RHYTHMS?

The most basic rhythm is a group of two beats (1, 2) as in the act of walking or the sound of a heartbeat. Another basic rhythm is a group of three beats (1, 2, 3), as in a waltz. Both groups have the accent on the first beat. These two basic rhythms can be multiplied or combined to create more complex rhythms. A group of beats repeated in a regular rhythm is a bar.

LIVE PERFORMANCE ▶
Live performance takes place on stage in front of an audience. Although more people listen to recorded music (on CD, radio, and in clubs), watching the skill of musicians playing live together creates a great atmosphere.

Double bass has four strings, but a fifth can be added to play lower notes

Plucking the strings by hand produces a stronger rhythm than using a bow

music

Fret is wooden – pressing the string against the fret changes the pitch

▲ SNARE DRUM AND STICKS
Drummers tap rhythm with sticks, by hand, or with a foot pedal.

PITCH

Pitch is the height or depth of a particular note or sound. When two or more different notes are played at once, the sound produced is called harmony. Harmonies can change the mood of a piece of music, giving it a bright or a dark feel.

WHY ARE NOTES AT DIFFERENT PITCHES?
The pitch of a note depends on the speed its sound vibrates at: a fast speed of vibration produces a high note, a slow speed produces a low note. The rate of vibration per second is called the frequency of the note. In the West, concert pitch is the standard to which instruments are usually tuned for performance.

▲ DIDGERIDOO
The sounds made by blowing into a didgeridoo have a slow speed of vibration, creating low notes.

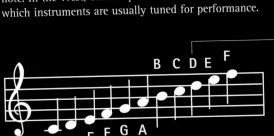

A letter labels each of the eight notes in this octave, which climbs from C to C – where a new octave begins at a higher pitch

◄ SCALE IN KEY OF C MAJOR
A scale shows the rising or falling pitches of notes. It usually contains one octave (eight notes). A key is a group of notes based on a particular note, such as C major.

MELODY

The arrangement of differently pitched notes one after the other creates a melody, or tune. Simple melodies consist of just a few notes, but more complex ones are created using many different notes, rhythms, and harmonies. Good melodies tend to be catchy.

HOW MANY MELODIES ARE THERE?
The world never seems to run out of new tunes, although echoes of one tune often turn up in another. There are only eight notes in the Western scale, but the way notes are combined into patterns and harmonies, and grouped into rhythms creates countless melodies. Other cultures in the world have more complex scales that create even more melodies.

▲ RAVI SHANKAR
Indian classical musicians, such as sitar player Ravi Shankar (1920–), use sets of notes called ragas, melodic scales. There are about 130 ragas. Each has its own mood.

◄ BILLIE HOLIDAY
This jazz singer (1915–1959) sang hundreds of songs. As the songs were not her own, the melodies were often familiar to audiences. However, the way she used her voice made each song unique.

Saxophone is a woodwind instrument not brass, because its mouthpiece is a reed

FIND OUT MORE ▶▶ Composition 333 • Musical Instruments 332 • Musicals 338 • Opera 338 • Orchestra 335 • Popular Music 334

MUSICAL INSTRUMENTS

We use a huge range of instruments to produce sounds and make music. Some are simple pieces of solid wood or hollowed-out seashells. Others are highly technical or electric. Instruments vary around the world and each has its own character.

HOW ARE MUSICAL INSTRUMENTS CATEGORIZED?

Acoustic instruments generate sound physically and electronic instruments create sound electrically. There are four acoustic groups: percussion (hit or shaken), wind – woodwind and brass – (blown), string (bowed or plucked), and keyboard (played with fingers).

Cymbal

Tom-tom

Snare

Hi-hat

Floor tom

Bass drum

▲ DRUM KIT
Drums belong to the percussion family. This standard kit is used in popular music, such as jazz and rock. A drummer needs coordination and energy as they often hit several drums at once using different rhythms.

HOW DO INSTRUMENTS GENERATE SOUND?

An instrument creates sound when part of it vibrates rapidly. The column of air inside a wind instrument, the string of a string instrument, or the stretched skin of a drum all vibrate when played. This vibration produces sound waves in the air, which we hear as musical notes.

Tuning peg

Violin bow

◄ VIOLIN
Like most string instruments, the violin has four strings, each tuned to different notes. It is played either with a bow or by plucking it with the fingers.

▲ GRAND PIANO
When a musician hits a key, a hammer strikes a string inside the piano. The string vibrates, making a sound. In a grand piano the strings are arranged horizontally. In an upright piano they are arranged vertically, to save space.

Keyboard has 88 keys. The difference between each is called a semitone

Tuning pin adjusts the tautness of the string to produce the correct pitch

Felt-covered hammer makes the string vibrate

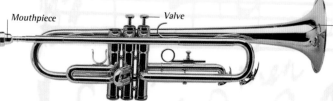

Mouthpiece

Valve

Wide, flared bell to broadcast the sound

e ▸▸ instruments

▲ TRUMPET
This brass instrument is played by blowing air through the mouthpiece into a narrow metal tube. Pressing the valves alters the length of the column of air, producing different notes.

HOW DO ELECTRONIC INSTRUMENTS WORK?

Electronic instruments – such as electronic keyboards – do not make actual sounds in the way an acoustic instrument does. An electronic instrument produces an electric signal that is transmitted to an amplifier and then broadcast through a loudspeaker. Using a process called synthesis, electronic instruments imitate acoustic instruments or create their own noises.

FIND OUT MORE ▸▸ Music 330–331 • Orchestra 335 • Sound 176–177

COMPOSITION

Most music is imagined first and then written down as a composition in a **SCORE**. The music might be vocal or instrumental, for a single singer or a big orchestra, and might last for a few minutes or a few hours. A pop single in the charts, a film soundtrack, and a Mozart symphony are all compositions.

WHERE DO COMPOSERS GET THEIR IDEAS?
Sometimes composers are inspired by an existing melody or just a few notes that they have heard. Sometimes composers express the mood or emotions they are feeling at that time. People, plays, poems, novels, paintings, and landscapes can all give composers ideas for music. In sacred music, inspiration is believed to come from God.

WHAT ARE THE PARTS OF A COMPOSITION?
Compositions are lyric (with words) or instrumental (without words). A song usually consists of several verses and a repeated chorus. An instrumental may have more than one movement (section). A concerto, for an orchestra and one or more soloists, usually has three movements. A symphony, a large-scale orchestral composition, has four or five movements.

WHAT COMES FIRST – WORDS OR MUSIC?
Some composers write the music first, inspiring their lyricist (songwriter) to then write the words. Other composers rely on words to give them the inspiration to write music. Words and music can also be written together by a single composer or a team of musicians.

IS ALL MUSIC COMPOSED?
Some music, such as jazz, is largely improvised (made up on the spot). The musicians start with an agreed written melody but then individually or collectively use it as a basis to create new, unwritten music. Improvisation has always been part of folk and blues, where lyrics and melodies are often improvised.

▲ SINGER/SONGWRITER
Alicia Keys (1981–), the American rhythm and blues singer, writes the music and words to most of her own songs. Other singers, such as the jazz vocalist Ella Fitzgerald (1917-1996), were famous for interpreting other people's songs.

KEY COMPOSERS

1567–1643	Claudio Monteverdi
1685–1750	Johann Sebastian Bach
1685–1759	George Frideric Handel
1756–1791	Wolfgang Mozart
1770–1827	Ludwig van Beethoven
1882–1971	Igor Stravinsky

▲ MUSIC TECHNOLOGY
Computers have made composition faster. Composers can use software to notate a score instead of writing by hand. They can also record melodies using electronic instruments and build up a piece gradually.

SCORE

A score is the written document of a composition. It shows the tempo (speed), rhythm, key, and instruments. Scores used to be written out by hand, but most are now produced on computer.

WHAT ARE PARTS?
A full score is the complete composition for every musician while the parts of a score are just those notes an individual musician or singer has to perform. The conductor uses a comprehensive copy of the entire composition but each musician or singer only requires the part that shows their role.

e ▸▸ composition

Rest symbol indicates that no notes are played here

Stave consists of two five-line grids. For this piece, the right hand plays the top or treble line, and the left hand plays the bottom or bass line

HANDWRITTEN SCORE ▶
This score by J S Bach is for a well-known piano work titled *Well-Tempered Clavier*. It is a fugue written in the key of C minor. A fugue is a variation of the main melody that is played at a higher or lower pitch.

FIND OUT MORE ▸▸ Cinema 346–347 • Music 330–331 • Opera 338 • Orchestra 335 • Poetry 343

POPULAR MUSIC

Popular, or pop, music is largely vocal and appeals to a mass, mainly teenage audience. It was originally available as single or long-playing (LP) vinyl records, but is now almost entirely sold on compact discs (CDs). Its popularity is measured by ▶▶ **THE CHARTS**.

Acoustic guitar was replaced with an electric guitar in Elvis's later career

Glamorous outfits, such as this satin cowboy shirt, were part of Elvis's image

e ▶▶
popular
music

WHEN DID POPULAR MUSIC BEGIN?
Popular music began in the USA in the 1930s with a lively new music called swing. Bing Crosby and Frank Sinatra sang with big swing bands and later became solo stars. During the 1950s rock and roll – a louder and more exciting type of pop music – emerged with songs about youthful rebellion and teenage love.

WHAT STYLES OF POPULAR MUSIC ARE THERE?
The main form of popular music is pop itself. Pop bands usually have singers, guitarists, keyboard players, and percussists. Rock music has a heavier sound and is guitar-led. Reggae from Jamaica, country from the USA, and national folk music, such as rai from Algeria, are also popular around the world.

◀ POP STAR
Popular singers such as Britney Spears sell millions of copies of their records around the world and are international celebrities.

GOLD DISC ▶
A record company awards a gold-plated disc to an artist when they reach certain sales figures for an album or a single. This disc was given to the Swedish band ABBA.

THE CHARTS

The charts measure the popularity of a record by the number of copies it has sold in a given period, usually a week. Most pop musicians dream of reaching number one. Charts show top sellers, highest new entries, fastest climbers, and records on the way down.

WHY ARE THERE SO MANY CHARTS?
Music magazines, radio and television companies, and other organizations all compile their own charts. The best-known charts are the weekly pop charts for albums and singles, but there are also charts for different types of music, such as classical or jazz. Charts cover different regions, such as a country, and different periods, such as a month or a year.

▲ THE BEATLES AT ABBEY ROAD
The *Abbey Road* album was reco[r] the Abbey Road studios in Londo 1969 it reached number one in t album charts in both the USA an It stayed in the UK charts for 81

HOW DO YOU GET TO NUMBER ONE?
A record gets to number one because it has sold more copies than any other record over a specified time. In case a record company or performer tries to influence the charts by artificially boosting sales (with reduced prices or other tricks), all charts are independently checked to ensure their accuracy.

▲ ELVIS PRESLEY
Elvis Presley (1935–1977) is the most famous face of rock and roll and one of the best-selling singers of all time. He was as well known for his outrageous dancing as for his rich, distinctive singing voice. The songs Elvis sang were taken from the American country and blues tradition.

FIND OUT MORE ▶▶ Composition 333 • Music 330 • Musicals 338

ORCHESTRA

An orchestra is a group of musicians playing together under the direction of a conductor. The musicians perform music specially composed for specific instruments in an orchestral performance. They play as soloists, in small groups, and all together, which creates a tremendous sound.

▲ GAMELAN PERCUSSION ORCHESTRA
The gamelan orchestras of Bali in Indonesia use a wide range of percussion instruments, such as gongs, chimes, marimbas, and drums, as well as strings and woodwind. They create an amazing rhythm-driven sound totally unlike that achieved by Western symphony orchestras.

HOW MANY MUSICIANS PLAY IN AN ORCHESTRA?
A full-scale orchestra playing a symphony includes at least 90 musicians, while a smaller orchestra playing a chamber piece ranges from 15 to 45. Sections of the orchestra can perform separately – a string orchestra, for example, includes about 60 musicians.

HOW ARE THE MUSICIANS ARRANGED?
The musicians are arranged into four sections. The strings – such as violins and cellos – sit at the front. The woodwind – such as oboes, clarinets, and bassoons – and brass – such as trumpets and French horns – sit in the middle. Percussion – such as kettledrums and a xylophone – sit at the back.

WHAT DOES A CONDUCTOR DO?
A conductor's job is to make sure that the musicians play perfectly together. A conductor keeps time using a baton (stick) to clearly count out each individual beat in the tempo (speed) the music is to be played.

▲ SIR SIMON RATTLE
The conductor of the Berlin Philharmonic Orchestra uses hand gestures and facial expressions to show how music should be played.

TWO BEATS   THREE BEATS

FOUR BEATS   FIVE BEATS

▲ BEAT PATTERNS
The conductor uses baton patterns to count out beats.

Brass

Percussion, including loud drums

Woodwind

e ▸▸
orchestra

▲ ORCHESTRA
An orchestra with every musician playing together is one of the greatest sounds in classical music.

Conductor stands on a raised platform

String section

FIND OUT MORE ▸▸ Composition 333 • Musical Instruments 332 • Opera 338

DANCE

When people move in time to music, they are dancing. As they dance, they organize their body movements into rhythmic and visual patterns. These dance patterns may be formal, with structured steps and movements, or informal, a natural style of dance known as ▸▸ IMPROVISATION .

WHY DO PEOPLE DANCE?

People have a natural urge to move in time to music. They dance to celebrate an event, or for entertainment and relaxation. Dance is an important part of many religions. Around the world many folk dances (popular, local dances) mark the stages of life, such as birth and death.

WHAT IS CLASSICAL DANCE?

Classical dance is historic and takes many years to learn. Western classical dance is called ballet and combines dance with mime (silent acting). It began in Europe in the 15th century. Countries such as India and Thailand also have great classical dance traditions. ▸▸ CHOREOGRAPHY is used to create classical dance.

Each mudra, or hand gesture, carries a specific meaning

INDIAN CLASSICAL DANCE ▶
Bharat natyam is a classical dance from south India. Most Indian dances act out stories from Indian mythology. The movements are often slow, graceful, and controlled.

Feet and hands are decorated with jewellery and red henna, a plant dye

◀ WHIRLING DERVISH ▶
The Sufi sect of Islam uses dance and music to worship Allah, or God. Some dancers, known as whirling dervishes, spin around in a trance to empty the mind and help them concentrate on God.

DANCE SHOES

BALLET SHOES
Pointe shoes are made stiff with paper and hessian (a plant fibre) to allow ballerinas to dance on tiptoe.

FLAMENCO SHOES
Flamenco dancers wear shoes with hard soles and metal on the heels to stamp out the rhythms noisily.

IMPROVISATION

Unlike classical dance, improvised dance has no formal steps, although it can be choreographed. Improvisation is the basis of contemporary, or modern, dance. In it, dancers express their feelings in their movements to create a highly personal, natural performance.

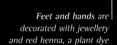
e ▸▸
dance

◀ CONTEMPORARY DANCE
These contemporary dancers work closely together, combining their body movements to create interesting shapes and sequences. Each time they perform this improvised dance, it will be slightly different.

Contemporary dancers often wear everyday clothes and dance barefoot to feel natural

WHEN DID CONTEMPORARY DANCE START?

Contemporary dance began at the start of the 20th century when the American dancer Isadora Duncan (1878–1927) broke away from ballet and developed her own, more natural style. Contemporary dance has many different styles, some of them closely linked to music, such as jazz, rock and roll, and hip-hop.

CAN ANYBODY DANCE?

Anybody can dance, no matter how young or old they are, or how physically fit. People in wheelchairs can move and spin in time to the music, while those who are immobile can move their hands or heads. Deaf people can feel the vibrations of music and respond.

CHOREOGRAPHY

Choreography is the arrangement of dance steps and movements into an organized sequence (order). This means that every dancer knows exactly what steps to perform throughout the performance. Dance is usually choreographed to music.

ARE FOLK DANCES CHOREOGRAPHED?
Folk dances, such as Scottish reels and Spanish flamenco, are not choreographed. However, they do have traditional steps that have developed over centuries and have been passed down through the generations to the present day. Each dancer learns the dance by heart and knows which moves to make in time to the music.

HOW ARE DANCE STEPS RECORDED?
Choreographed dance steps must be written down so that they can be remembered over time. The most common recording system, called Benesh Movement Notation, was developed in the 1940s by Rudolf and Joan Benesh. Each movement is recorded with symbols on a five-line diagram. The diagram is combined with the musical notation so that both can be read together.

HOW DOES A CHOREOGRAPHER WORK?
A choreographer works closely with a dance group to create a new dance, designing steps that show off the skills and strengths of the individual dancers. Steps are memorized by counting them out into sequences. Choreographers have usually been dancers themselves.

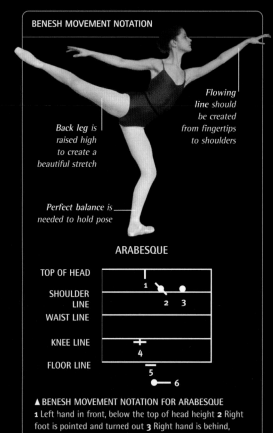

BENESH MOVEMENT NOTATION

Back leg is raised high to create a beautiful stretch

Flowing line should be created from fingertips to shoulders

Perfect balance is needed to hold pose

ARABESQUE

TOP OF HEAD
SHOULDER LINE
WAIST LINE
KNEE LINE
FLOOR LINE

▲ BENESH MOVEMENT NOTATION FOR ARABESQUE
1 Left hand in front, below the top of head height **2** Right foot is pointed and turned out **3** Right hand is behind, above shoulder height **4** Left knee is bent and turned out **5** Left foot is on the floor **6** Dancer is facing stage left

▲ IRISH FOLK DANCE
Folk dances, such as this Irish jig, are often performed in costumes. This dancer wears soft shoes, but some Irish dances use hard soles.

Hair must be tied back in a neat style

SWAN LAKE ►
Swan Lake (1895) is a famous ballet and was created by the French choreographer Marius Petipa, the Russian choreographer Lev Ivanov, and the music composer Pyotr Tchaikovsky. Based on a German fairy tale, it tells the story of Princess Odette, who is turned into a swan by an evil magician.

The thumb is slightly spread from the fingers for a graceful effect

The ballerinas (female ballet dancers) wear identical white costumes to help them to look like the swans in the story

A tutu is a traditional stiff skirt worn by ballerinas

Toes are pointed and feet arched to create a perfect line along the leg

FIND OUT MORE ▶▶ Composition 333 • Music 330–331 • Musicals 338

OPERA

An opera is a drama set to music. It is performed and sung by singers who act out different roles. Opera is often staged in a grand opera house or theatre with lavish costumes and magnificent stage designs. The songs are full of passion and emotion. Opera began in Europe during the Renaissance.

opera

WHAT ARE THE DIFFERENT VOICES IN OPERA?

Opera is technically difficult and takes years of training. The female range covers soprano (high pitch), mezzo-soprano (middle), and contralto (low). The male voice covers tenor (high), baritone (middle), and bass (low).

WHAT ARE THE PARTS OF OPERA?

An opera opens with an overture (an instrumental piece of music). The songs sung by the soloists are arias (Italian for air). Recitatives are speech-like passages between arias that move the plot along. A long opera may be broken into several acts.

▼ *LA TRAVIATA*
One of the most famous operas is *La Traviata* (*The Woman Who Strayed*) written by the Italian composer Giuseppe Verdi (1813–1901). It tells the tragic love story of Violetta and Alfredo

Leading man often has tenor voice and leading lady is usually soprano

Dance reflects opera's origins as a court event with ballet

The chorus is a group of performers who sing in unison

FIND OUT MORE ▶▶ Music 330–331 • Theatre 344–345

▲ *SINGIN' IN THE RAIN*
This 1952 film musical, starring Gene Kelly, is most famous for its title tune, *Singin' in the Rain*. During this song, Kelly sings and dances his way down a street from lamppost to lamppost in the pouring rain.

MUSICALS

Musicals are plays with song and dance. Their stories are fast-paced and dramatic, and the songs are catchy. Musicals are performed in theatres, or made into films. These big productions need hundreds of cast and crew. A popular musical can run at a theatre for many years.

WHERE DID MUSICALS ORIGINATE?

Musicals began in Britain in the late 19th century by combining the comic stories of operetta (short operas) with the songs and dances of the music hall. It was in the Broadway theatre district of New York City in the early 20th century that musicals developed into their modern form: a highly entertaining music and dance show.

HOW ARE MUSICALS PRODUCED?

Musicals are spectacular productions with large choruses of singers and dancers. Film musicals can require hundreds of extras. A composer writes the music and songs, and a choreographer creates the dance sequences. Singing and dancing coaches help the performers learn their parts. The sets built for musicals are often largescale and visually stunning.

musicals

FIND OUT MORE ▶▶ Cinema 346–347 • Dance 336–337

WRITING

Before writing, people had to store information in their heads. Writing was invented to record information so that it could be passed on to other people. Later it became a means of personal expression.

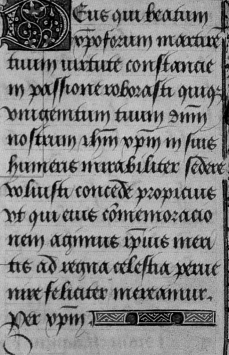

WILL HANDWRITING ALWAYS EXIST?

Writing has changed throughout history. Early writing was created by scratching in clay. Later, Ancient Egyptians used feathers or sticks dipped in berry juice. Neither of these forms exists today, and the spread of word processing may one day replace handwriting.

WHAT IS CREATIVE WRITING?

Creative writing is using the imagination to write stories, describe events and places, and express thoughts. It is different to writing that records facts and events, such as history or biography. Creative writing includes poems, plays, short stories, and novels, and may also include diaries.

Decorated initial with an image inside opens the page

Borders contain elaborate colour illustrations, such as flowers

Latin script describes the life and death of Saint Sebastian

BOOK OF HOURS ▶
These medieval prayer books, often made by monks, were for private reading and meditation at various hours of the day. They were beautifully written on parchment (animal skin) and decorated in brightly coloured inks to glorify God. This one was created in 1470 for a French noblewoman, Margaret de Foix.

This hieroglyph was carved in stone in the 7th century AD at the royal palace at Palenque, Mexico

◀ MAYAN WRITING
Mayan writing was hieroglyphic, using pictures or symbols to record objects or ideas. This hieroglyph shows four pictograms.

writing

WHAT IS LITERACY?

Literacy is the ability to read, write, and use language. Without this skill, people are at a disadvantage. They cannot find out information from printed sources (such as books or the Internet), and they cannot fill in forms, or write letters, text messages, and emails.

FIND OUT MORE ▶▶ First Scripts 369 • Writers 348

PRINTING

Printing is the mass production of the written word. The Chinese invented wooden print blocks in the 8th century. In the West, all books were written by hand until Johann Gutenberg invented movable type around 1450.

printing

▲ EARLY PRINTING SHOP
This painting shows a 17th-century printing shop in France. The printers first arranged the type (letters) into words on a frame, then added ink. The paper and type were put into a wooden press and squeezed together by turning a screw so that the ink printed on the paper.

HOW DID PRINTING DEVELOP?

Movable metal type – letter moulds that can be put together to make words, then taken apart and reused – made printing faster. Combined with the spread of literacy and the new affordability of books, this made information and literature available to the masses. Today, computers and digital technology have replaced movable type and speeded up printing again.

𝕿   **T**   **T**

OLD ENGLISH   TIMES   UNIVERSE

▲ TYPEFACES
The alphabet has been designed in many different styles, known as typefaces. Historic typefaces tend to have more detail, while modern styles are simpler and easier to read. Each typeface has a name.

FIND OUT MORE ▶▶ Design 326 • Industrial Revolution 418–419 • Reformation 399

LITERATURE

Literature uses words to create works of art. It is usually written, but some works are passed on by word of mouth. There are several different forms of writing, such as poetry, drama (plays), or ▶▶ NOVELS, but they can all offer insights into people's innermost thoughts and feelings.

WHAT WERE THE FIRST WORKS OF LITERATURE?
The earliest written works were epic poems – long stories or ▶▶ MYTHS about the adventures of heroes. The Indian epics Ramayana and Mahabharata (c. 500 BC) are still read today. Two famous Greek poems, Homer's *Odyssey* and *Iliad*, were first written down from the spoken tradition in the 8th century.

IS LITERATURE DIFFERENT AROUND THE WORLD?
Literature differs from country to country because of the language it is written in. Some forms of literature come from one country, such as Japanese haiku poetry. However, the themes of love, revenge, and death are found everywhere.

◀ *1,001 NIGHTS*
1,001 Nights (also called *The Arabian Nights*) is a collection of traditional folk tales from the Middle East. Scheherazade tells her husband, the sultan, 1,001 wonderful stories to save her life. The tale of Aladdin and his magic flying carpet is one of the stories.

The monsters seem fierce, but Max can tame them with a single look

Set design and costumes were amazing in this 1999 opera staging of the book

Max is given the name "wild thing" by his mother for being a naughty boy

◀ *WHERE THE WILD THINGS ARE*
Maurice Sendak's tale was thought too scary for children when it was first published in the USA in 1963. In it, a boy called Max sails to the Land of the Wild Things, where he meets monsters and becomes king. However, Max's travels are imaginary, and the smell of his supper brings him back to reality.

The Hatter with the March Hare and Dormouse

Alice is invited to a mad tea party at the March Hare's home

▲ *THE ADVENTURES OF ALICE IN WONDERLAND*
This fantasy of a young girl's adventures down a rabbit hole was written by English author Lewis Carroll in 1865, and illustrated by John Tenniel. It is a witty commentary on society and education in Victorian times.

WHY DO PEOPLE WRITE LITERATURE?
Creative people who have something to say need to find a means of expression. Painters use paint, and writers use words. Authors write to inform, explore, amuse, inspire, and to tell a good story. They also write ▶▶ NON-FICTION to record events and lives.

IL POSTINO ▶
Il Postino (1994) was a film of a novel called *Burning Patience* (1983), written by Chilean author Antonio Skarmeta. The story, set in Italy, tells how a humble postman is inspired by poetry to win the woman of his dreams and to express his political beliefs.

▲ *THE TALE OF GENJI*
This early form of the novel was written by a Japanese noblewoman, Lady Murasaki, in the 11th century. It is about the life of a prince called Genji and describes the daily activities of the Japanese royal court.

NOVELS

Novels are stories in prose (not verse) that explore people and society using imaginary characters. They are structured around ▶▶ PLOTS and are usually more than 50,000 words in length. Novels are organized into categories of fiction called ▶▶ GENRES.

WHAT WERE THE EARLIEST NOVELS?

One of the earliest novels was *Don Quixote* (1605) by the Spanish writer Miguel de Cervantes (1547–1616). Around 100 years later, the novel became popular when *Robinson Crusoe* (1719) was published. Written by English author Daniel Defoe (1660–1731), it is the story of a shipwrecked man alone on an island.

▲ PAPERBACKS
Most books had hard covers until the first paperback novels were published by Penguin in 1935. Paperbacks were cheap and made books more affordable.

GENRES

Genres are categories of fiction (imaginative stories), depending on what the story is about. A love story belongs to the romance genre. A murder story is categorized as crime. Stories can belong to more than one genre.

WHY DO DIFFERENT GENRES EXIST?

Authors, like readers, have their favourite interests and will only write on a subject they feel connected to. Categorizing a book means that readers know what to expect and where to look for it in a bookshop or library. Changing social trends and tastes can inspire new genres.

1 CRIME   **2 ROMANCE**   **3 HORROR**

1 The first popular detective in fiction was Sherlock Holmes, created by Arthur Conan Doyle (1859–1930). 2 *Gone with the Wind* is a classic romance written by Margaret Mitchell (1900–1949). 3 The blood-sucking Count Dracula from Transylvania was created by Bram Stoker (1847–1912).

SCIENCE FICTION ▶
Science fiction (stories about the future and space travel) was a particularly popular genre in the 1950s. It reflected a real interest in space at the time.

PLOTS

The plot is what happens in a story. Most plots have a beginning, a middle, and an end, and contain problems that are eventually solved. Writers usually invent plots, although some authors, like William Shakespeare, may take them from history.

WHAT MAKES A GOOD PLOT?

A good plot grabs the reader's interest and captures his or her emotions right to the end. The writer uses suspense and surprise to control the pace of the plot. Sometimes flashbacks (returning to the past) gradually fill in the background to a story.

▲ *A MIDSUMMER NIGHT'S DREAM*
A Midsummer Night's Dream (c. 1595) by Shakespeare is a comedy. The plot has many fantastic and funny twists, and a happy ending.

e ▶▶
literature

MYTHS

All cultures have myths – stories that reflect religious and social beliefs. These stories feature gods and superhumans and explore the great questions of life – such as "Where do we come from?", "Why are we here?", and "Why does evil exist?"

WHAT IS A HERO?

Mythic heroes are humans with superhuman powers, often because one of their parents was a god or goddess. They have to show tremendous courage in overcoming spiritual and physical challenges to save an individual, their family, or an entire nation.

▼ *BHAGAVAT PURAN*
This sacred Hindu text contains Indian history and mythology. Here the god Rama (a form of the supreme god, Vishnu) and his human wife, Sita, are seated on a five-headed serpent.

▲ THE GREEK MYTH OF PERSEPHONE
The goddess Persephone is kidnapped and taken to the underworld. While she is gone, her mother – the corn goddess, Demeter – grieves, and the fields lie barren. In spring Persephone returns, and so do the crops.

Rama's blue skin shows he is a form of the god Vishnu

Lotus flower is a Hindu symbol of divine beauty

Sita is a human form of the goddess of wealth, Lakshmi

Rama's half-brother, Lakshmana, becomes a snake to make a bed for the couple

WHY DO MYTHS EXIST?

Although myths are old, they still appeal to us because they contain lasting truths about the way people feel. The myth of Persephone, for example, is about the annual crop cycle, but also illustrates the strength of the bond between mother and daughter.

WHAT IS THE ORAL TRADITION?

The oral (spoken) tradition is literature that has not been written down but passed on from one storyteller to another over many years. Myths began in this way. The oral tradition continues today with storytelling, folk tales, and children's stories.

NON-FICTION

Non-fiction deals with facts and real events, and is written in prose. It includes histories, essays, travel-writing, letters, biographies, and diaries. The first known work of prose was a history of the Persian wars, written by Herodotus *c.* 430 BC in Ancient Greece.

IS ALL NON-FICTION LITERATURE?

Much non-fiction is written for reference (information) only, and is not considered to be literature because the author's style and point of view are irrelevant. Compare this with a biography where the author's writing style and interpretation of facts is essential to the understanding of the subject.

WHY ARE DIARIES IMPORTANT?

A diary is a daily record of a person's thoughts and experiences, often not intended for publication. The great English diarist Samuel Pepys (1633–1703) wrote in code. His diary records a mixture of great public and intimate personal events and builds up a vivid picture of the times in which it was written.

▲ *THE DIARY OF ANNE FRANK*
This young Jewish girl recorded how she and her family hid from the Nazis in Amsterdam during World War II. She gave a moving account of the difficulties of her life, but also her friendship with the son of the family hiding with them. Anne Frank died in a concentration camp in 1945.

▲ WILD TURKEY BY JOHN JAMES AUDUBON
Audubon (1785–1851) was an American natural history author and illustrator who wrote *The Birds of America*. His detailed observations included beautiful hand-coloured engravings.

FIND OUT MORE ▶▶ Theatre 344–345 • Writers 348 • Writing 339

POETRY

Poetry (verse) is literature that works through sounds and images. It was originally recited (spoken aloud) to an audience, and its rhythms and sounds affect the meaning of the words. Poetic language is concentrated (it says a lot in few words) and expresses feelings and ideas.

▲ *THE TYGER* BY WILLIAM BLAKE
Blake (1757–1827) was a painter and a poet. This powerful poem asks questions about the creation of the world and good and evil.

ARE THERE DIFFERENT TYPES OF POETRY?
The epic was the earliest type of poem, presenting a long narrative (story) of amazing heroic deeds. Lyric poetry, originally a song for a lyre (an ancient musical instrument), is short and often expresses the poet's own ideas or feelings. Dramatic poetry is written in the voices of different characters and can be acted.

WHAT IS THE OLDEST POEM?
The oldest written poem is the *Epic of Gilgamesh* from Babylon. It is about 4,000 years old and tells the story of a king, Gilgamesh, who was half-man, half-god. The oldest poem in English is *Beowulf*, written in the 8th century AD. This 3,000-line epic is about a Scandinavian hero, Beowulf, who saves the Danes from two monsters – Grendel and its mother.

WHAT IS METRE?
Metre is the rhythm of a poem. Rhythm is created by the stressed (long) and unstressed (short) syllables (parts of a word) in a line. Short and long syllables are arranged in fixed patterns known as feet. A foot with a long and a short syllable is called a trochee. A line with ten syllables is called a pentameter.

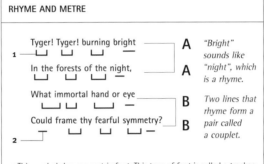

RHYME AND METRE

1 Tyger! Tyger! burning bright   **A**   *"Bright" sounds like "night", which is a rhyme.*

   In the forests of the night,   **A**

   What immortal hand or eye   **B**   *Two lines that rhyme form a pair called a couplet.*

   Could frame thy fearful symmetry?   **B**

2

1 This symbol shows a metric foot. This type of foot is called a trochee and contains a stressed syllable ("Ty-") and an unstressed one ("-ger").
2 This symbol shows a syllable or word that stands alone.

DO POEMS ALWAYS HAVE RHYME AND RHYTHM?
Rhyme (when words sound the same) does not always suit the subject or feeling of a poem, so many poets write poetry that does not rhyme, called blank verse. *Paradise Lost*, the epic poem by John Milton (1608–1674), does not rhyme but has a particular metre (rhythm). Poetry without metre is called free verse.

IS A VERSE THE SAME AS A STANZA?
Verse can mean poetry in general, or it can mean a paragraph of poetry, also called a stanza. Traditionally, a stanza contains no more than 12 lines. A two-line stanza is called a couplet, a four-line couplet is a quatrain.

▲ 18TH-CENTURY HAIKU
This is a simple form of poetry from Japan that contains only 17 syllables. A haiga is a painting of the words and image of a haiku.

▲ POETRY IN PERFORMANCE
Poems are often best appreciated when read aloud. Here the English poet Benjamin Zephaniah recites his poetry at a concert. Popular music that uses the spoken word, such as rap and hip-hop, is a new type of poetry.

WHAT ARE POETIC DEVICES?
Poetic devices are the special tricks and techniques that make poetry different from everyday language. Alliteration repeats consonants, as in "slithering snake" – the repeated use of the "s" makes us think of the sound a snake makes, which strengthens the image. Other common devices are metaphor and simile, both forms of comparison. A simile uses "like" or "as": "My love is like a red, red rose." A metaphor does not: "My love is a red rose."

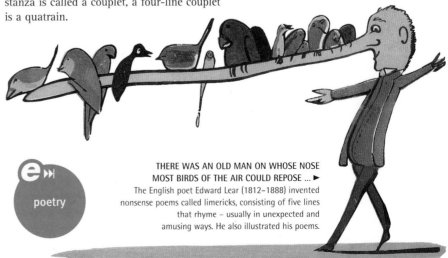

e ▸▸ poetry

THERE WAS AN OLD MAN ON WHOSE NOSE MOST BIRDS OF THE AIR COULD REPOSE ... ▶
The English poet Edward Lear (1812–1888) invented nonsense poems called limericks, consisting of five lines that rhyme – usually in unexpected and amusing ways. He also illustrated his poems.

FIND OUT MORE ▸▸ Theatre 344–345 • Writers 348

THEATRE

Theatre is the performance of a drama (play) on a ▸▸ STAGE in front of an audience. The Ancient Greeks were the first to build theatres where people could watch the two main types of drama: ▸▸ TRAGEDY and ▸▸ COMEDY .

e ▸▸
drama

WHAT WERE THE FIRST PLAYS?
The first plays developed from religious rituals where a chorus (a group of performers) recited stories of the Greek gods and heroes. In the 6th century BC, a Greek poet, Thespis, became the first actor to recite lines by himself.

WHO IS INVOLVED IN MAKING A PLAY?
The director is the person who chooses the play and tells everyone what to do. The actors become the characters in the play by acting out the plot (story). Other people design and make the set and costumes, and create lighting and sound effects.

KABUKI ▸
Kabuki is traditional Japanese theatre with an all-male cast. (Men play the female roles.) The highly dramatic plots rely on skills in dancing and singing, as well as acting.

Distinctive make-up style is called kumadori. Deep red on a white face symbolizes rage mixed with cruelty

◂ THE ZULU MACBETH
Shakespeare's *Macbeth* (1606) is updated from historic Scotland to 20th-century Africa, illustrating the timeless theme of ambition.

Assistant works on stage, performing costume transformations

A hakama is a divided skirt, worn here by a samurai (warrior). Each character has a specific costume

▲ ELIZABETHAN COSTUME
Ben Jonson's *Volpone* (1606) was one of many great English plays written during or shortly after the reign of Queen Elizabeth I (1558–1603). To conjure up the period the designer recreates Elizabethan costumes.

WHAT IS MIME?
Mime expresses a mood or an idea through gestures and facial expressions, without using words. The well-known mime characters Harlequin and Pierrot developed in Italian theatre during the 16th century, and later gave rise to the clown. In China, drama contained no words until the 19th century.

IS DRAMA ALWAYS PERFORMED IN A THEATRE?
Street theatre is performed in public places and is often free to those who watch. It aims to bring plays to people who would not generally get the chance to go to a theatre, and is a direct way of communicating with local people about issues that affect them.

KEY PLAYWRIGHTS

16–17th century	Shakespeare (England)
17th century	Molière (France)
18–19th century	Goethe (Germany)
19th century	Wilde (England)
19–20th century	Chekhov (Russia)
19–20th century	Ibsen (Norway)
20–21st century	Miller (USA)
20–21st century	Soyinka (Nigeria)

TYPES OF STAGE ▶
The arena stage is modelled on the Greek theatre. The thrust stage was very popular in the Elizabethan period.

■ STAGE   ■ AUDIENCE

TRAGEDY

Tragedy is a sad story with an unhappy ending. It originated in Greece in the 5th century BC. In classical tragedy, the main character is noble and good, but has a flaw (weakness) which causes his or her downfall.

WHY DO PEOPLE WATCH TRAGEDY?
According to the Greek scholar Aristotle (384–322 BC), the audience shares in the sadness and fear of the characters they are watching. At the end of the play, the audience feels emotionally purified and uplifted by the release of tension. This process is called catharsis.

ARE THERE MODERN TRAGEDIES?
There are modern tragedies, but not many are similar to Greek plays. Today tragedy is often the unhappy story of an ordinary person with many faults. The tragedy occurs, not because a hero has a tragic flaw, but because beliefs or illusions are destroyed.

▲ FARCE
Noises Off (1982) by English writer Michael Frayn is a farce, a type of comedy with very silly behaviour.

▲ GREEK CHORUS
In Greek tragedy the chorus was a group of performers who spoke in unison and performed ritual dance steps together. The role of the chorus was to provide a commentary on the main action.

COMEDY

Comedy is a play that makes us laugh. It deals with people and their relationships to each other. By laughing at the actors on stage and through wit (jokes), we reach an understanding of the characters' foolishness.

IS SATIRE A TYPE OF COMEDY?
Satire is a cruel form of comedy that criticizes society by showing the weaknesses of public figures. Satire uses caricature (exaggeration of a person's character) and mockery (making fun of someone). The first great writers of satire were the Ancient Romans.

STAGE

In the theatre, a stage is a platform where plays are performed. The Ancient Greeks watched drama in round, open-air theatres. The Romans built roofed theatres, which had permanent stage scenes and complex machinery for sound and lighting effects.

ARE ALL STAGES THE SAME?
The most common type is the proscenium stage, where the audience is separated from the framed, raised stage by a curtain. It was invented in Italy in the 18th century. Other stage designs try to bring the audience and actors closer together.

ARENA

THRUST

PROSCENIUM

FIND OUT MORE ▸▸ Opera 338 • Writers 348

CINEMA

Cinema is a hugely popular modern art form that uses moving pictures to tell a story. Early films were in black and white, and silent. *The Jazz Singer* (1927) was the first "talkie", and colour films appeared in the 1930s. Today many films use ▶▶ SPECIAL EFFECTS .

WHERE ARE FILMS MADE?

Films are made in studios using sets – life-sized models of buildings or places. Underwater scenes are sometimes filmed in huge tanks. Films are also shot on location (outdoors or in a real building). Location filming in towns or cities is often done early in the morning when the streets are empty.

▲ SHOOTING A SCENE
The famous director Alfred Hitchcock (second from right) works with actor Paul Newman (left) and crew on *Torn Curtain* (1966). The camera sits on a dolly (a wheeled platform) so it can move smoothly.

WHAT DOES A DIRECTOR DO?

Directors decide which script the film will be based on and use their personal vision to create the overall style. They advise the actors on how to play the characters and tell the camera crew when and how to film. They also choose the music for the film.

HOW OLD IS CINEMA?

Motion pictures were invented in 1889 in the USA by Thomas Edison. In 1895 in France, the Lumière brothers projected films for the first time to a paying audience. Within 20 years ▶▶ HOLLYWOOD dominated the film industry around the world.

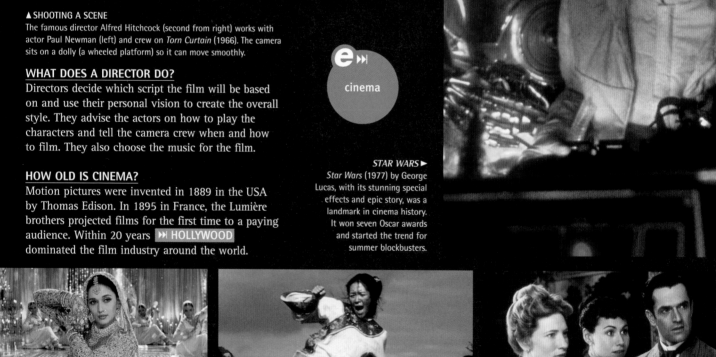

Spaceship set was amazing at the time. The director, George Lucas, drew his ideas from science-fiction books and films

C-3PO is an android, an intelligent robot. He has a smaller companion called R2-D2.

Princess Leia (Carrie Fisher) is a rebel leader fighting against the evil Galactic Empire. She is helped by the smuggler Han Solo (Harrison Ford), shown right

e ▶▶
cinema

STAR WARS ▶
Star Wars (1977) by George Lucas, with its stunning special effects and epic story, was a landmark in cinema history. It won seven Oscar awards and started the trend for summer blockbusters.

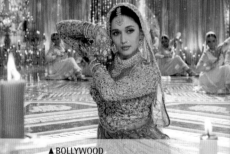

▲ BOLLYWOOD
Bollywood is the nickname of the Indian film industry, centred in Mumbai (Bombay). The films are often romantic, with singing and dancing.

▲ STUNTS
Most stunts, such as fast car chases, are done by doubles of the lead actors. However, in *Crouching Tiger, Hidden Dragon* (2000) Zhang Ziyi, playing the Jade Fox, did all her own martial art fights.

▲ ADAPTATIONS
Many films are based on books. *An Ideal Husband* (1999) was taken from the 1895 play by Oscar Wilde. Films that re-create a historical period are called costume dramas.

HOLLYWOOD

Hollywood – a suburb of Los Angeles, USA – is the centre of the world film industry. The Californian sunshine attracted early movie makers, because the film they used at the time worked best in strong light. The varied landscape also provided good locations.

WHY IS HOLLYWOOD SO FAMOUS?

The big Hollywood studios controlled the industry for many years, because they not only made films but also owned most of the cinemas. They used their power to turn their actors into worldwide stars. Hollywood studios today fund and distribute films made by smaller companies too. While Hollywood remains dominant, other cinema cultures, such as the Indian film industry, also have a big following.

OSCAR STATUETTE ▶
This trophy is given to winners of categories (such as Best Actor) in the annual Academy Awards for film. It shows a knight with a sword standing on a film reel.

© A.M.P.A.S. ®

LEONARDO DICAPRIO   KATE WINSLET

TITANIC

WINNER OF 11 ACADEMY AWARDS
INCLUDING BEST PICTURE

TITANIC ▲
Titanic (1997) is a blockbuster – a spectacular film that attracts huge audiences and makes millions of dollars. Alongside *Ben-Hur* (1959), it holds the record for winning the most Oscars – 11.

SPECIAL EFFECTS

These are techniques used to create illusions (images that are not real). Hidden wires make it look like an actor is flying. A train crash can be filmed with tiny models. Most effects today are computer-generated.

WHAT WERE THE EARLY SPECIAL EFFECTS?

Moving scenery was projected on a screen behind the actors. This made it look like a car was driving along a road when, in fact, it was stationary in a studio. Another effect was to mask part of the camera, so that the same piece of film could be used twice. In this way, actors could be superimposed on backgrounds.

MAKE-UP ▲
Arnold Schwarzenegger is being made up for *The Terminator* (1984). Gory face paints create a fake wound and make it look like he has robot parts beneath his skin.

GENRES
...enre is a category of film, such as a western. The ...ollywood western *The Magnificent Seven* (1960) was ...ased on Japan's *The Seven Samurai* (1954) (above).

▲ SPECIAL EFFECTS
Computers have revolutionized special effects. This spectacular explosion in *The Rock* (1996) was filmed and then enhanced by computer-generated imagery to make it even more breathtaking.

▲ STUDIO SETS
A submarine enters the specially built set in the James Bond film *The Spy Who Loved Me* (1977). This costly set recreates the inside of a warship.

FIND OUT MORE ▶▶ Animation 349 • Literature 340–342 • Musicals 338

WRITERS

Writers express themselves in words. There are many different kinds of writers – for instance, journalists who report for newspapers, and technical writers who explain how machines work. However, many of the best-known authors write fiction and are valued for the way they tell stories and how they use language.

Manuscript was typed on a typewriter

▲ ERNEST HEMINGWAY
The American author Ernest Hemingway (1899–1961) is famous for his novels and short stories. His economical style (expressing many ideas in a few words) has made him a widely admired and imitated writer.

▲ WILLIAM SHAKESPEARE
Shakespeare (1564–1616) was an English playwright and poet. His work deals with human nature so convincingly that it is understood around the world. Although his plays are around 400 years old, they are still produced today.

writers

WHAT MAKES A GOOD WRITER?

A good writer has a style of writing that grips your attention, whether in a long novel or a short poem. Style includes creation of characters, use of dialogue (conversation), descriptive language, and how a piece of work is structured. Some writers experiment with language, such as Irish author James Joyce who invented a highly individual form of English in his novel *Finnegans Wake* (1939).

DO WRITERS GO OUT OF FASHION?

Different writers are appreciated at different times. In the 18th century, writers copied the style of the Greeks and Romans. The early 19th-century Romantic writers, such as the English poet John Keats (1795–1821), valued nature and personal experience. They later gave way to the Realists, such as the French writer Victor Hugo (1802–1885), who wrote about politics and the daily struggles of ordinary people.

IS WRITING FOR CHILDREN DIFFERENT?

Children's writers feature children as main characters, and write from the point of view of a child. Children's stories often appeal to the imagination and have a lot of humour. Children's authors choose subjects that are part of a child's world, such as school, as in the *Harry Potter* series by J K Rowling (1965–); or the family, as in *Little Women* by Louisa May Alcott (1832–1888). However, many themes of children's writing appeal to all ages, such as love, friendship, and adventure.

▲ ARUNDHATI ROY
This Indian writer (1961–) won the British Booker Prize in 1997 with her first novel, *The God of Small Things*. Key literary prizes are the Nobel Prize for Literature, the Pulitzer Prize, and the Commonwealth Writers Award.

▲ J K ROWLING
English writer J K Rowling was a struggling author when she wrote her first *Harry Potter* novel, published in 1997. Today she has sold hundreds of millions of books globally and is a multimillionaire and celebrity.

WHAT IS A NARRATOR?

In fiction, the narrator is the person who tells the story. This can be the author or one of the characters. First-person narration is when the narrator speaks from the "I" point of view about events in which he or she has been personally involved.

WHY DO SOME WRITERS BECOME FAMOUS?

Some writers are famous because they sell lots of books. Some cause controversy (public debate). Others win prizes, such as the Nobel Prize for Literature, or have a successful film made of their book. Writers are also promoted in schools, colleges, and universities.

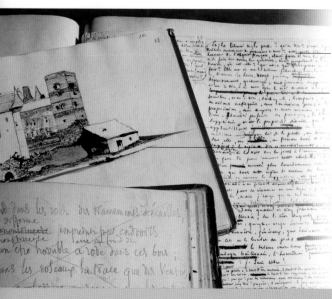

Handwritten manuscript

Editing is when a writer reads back over what they have written and makes changes to improve it

Ink sketch, one of many that Hugo produced

◄ VICTOR HUGO'S DESK
The French writer made sketches and notes that were the basis of his manuscripts (the final text). This manuscript records a journey on the river Rhine, Germany. It shows how he edited his work before publication.

FIND OUT MORE ▶▶ Literature 340 • Poetry 343 • Writing 339

ANIMATION

Animation is an illusion made with a sequence of still pictures that are each slightly different. The pictures are shown at speed to give an impression of movement. Animation is generally filmed at 24 frames per second (fps) and 12 fps. The main types are cel, stop-frame, and ▶▶ **COMPUTER ANIMATION**.

▲ **BUILDING A MODEL**
Animation models are made with clay or latex (a rubber and plastic compound). They are built up on a simple metal skeleton called an armature, which can be moved.

WHAT IS CEL ANIMATION?
An animator produces a sequence of pencil drawings on paper. These are traced onto clear sheets called cels, and coloured in with paints. Each cel is placed on a background and filmed as one frame. The background remains constant while the cels are changed.

HOW DOES STOP-FRAME ANIMATION WORK?
Stop-frame animation is made using models. A miniature set is built to represent a room or a street. Puppets are placed in the set, moved small amounts, and filmed one shot at a time. Modern stop-frame animation also uses computers.

▲ *AN AMERICAN TAIL*
This 1986 feature animation was made on cel and directed by the famous US animator Don Bluth. It tells the story of Russian Jewish mice who flee to America, only to discover that cats live there too!

e ▶▶ animation

▲ *CHICKEN RUN*
The set for *Chicken Run* (2000), made by animation firm Aardman, was built in a warehouse. The team of 40 animators moved each model a tiny amount for each of the 24 shots needed to produce one second of film.

COMPUTER ANIMATION

Computer animation was first used in video games, but as the technology developed, it spread to film and television for special effects and animated features. Computer animation has evolved from both cel and stop-frame animation techniques.

HOW IS COMPUTER ANIMATION MADE?
Using 3-D computer software, models can be built, coloured, and animated in a virtual environment. Computer animation, unlike stop-frame animation, does not need the model placed in every position of a movement. Instead, key poses are set and the computer creates the positions in-between.

CAN COMPUTERS ANIMATE BY THEMSELVES?
Computer software can calculate and re-create the physical movement of objects dropping, bouncing, and even knocking into each other. However, the personalities and emotions of people and creatures are too complex for a computer to understand. The human animation artist is still a vital part of the process.

ANTZ ▶
Antz (1998) by Dreamworks was the second fully computer-animated movie ever made. The characters are individually animated but the film used a crowd animation system so that scenes could contain thousands of ants.

FIND OUT MORE ▶▶ Cinema 346–347 • Home Entertainment 351

TOYS

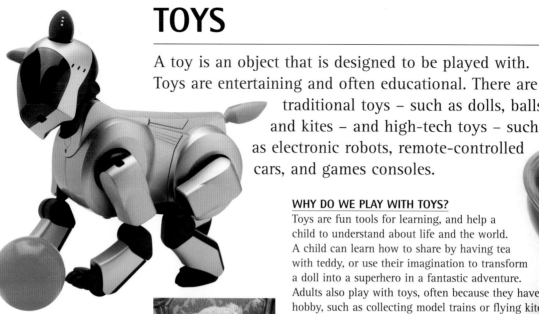

A toy is an object that is designed to be played with. Toys are entertaining and often educational. There are traditional toys – such as dolls, balls, and kites – and high-tech toys – such as electronic robots, remote-controlled cars, and games consoles.

toys

WHY DO WE PLAY WITH TOYS?

Toys are fun tools for learning, and help a child to understand about life and the world. A child can learn how to share by having tea with teddy, or use their imagination to transform a doll into a superhero in a fantastic adventure. Adults also play with toys, often because they have a hobby, such as collecting model trains or flying kites.

WHAT ARE THE OLDEST TOYS?

One of the oldest toys is the spinning top. The first tops were natural objects like shells and acorns. These later developed into clay tops like those discovered in the ancient city of Ur in Mesopotamia. Village squares in 18th-century England often featured giant tops that were played with for physical exercise. Yo-yos existed in Ancient Egypt and in Ancient Greece, where they were believed to bring protection from the gods.

▲ SONY "AIBO"
This battery-operated robot dog imitates real animal instincts that change over time. It can play with a ball or ask to be fed.

ANTIQUE TEDDY BEAR ►
The German firm Steiff began making bears in 1903. Steiff bears are famous for their high quality.

▲ SPINNING TOP
The most common top today has a mechanical plunger. Simple tops, spun between the fingers, require more skill to set off.

FIND OUT MORE ▸▸ Musical Instruments 332

GAMES

A game is a competition between two or more people who play to a set of rules. A player may need skill, as with chess, or rely on the luck of the dice. Games are for the fun of the players or to entertain an audience.

HOW OLD IS CHESS?

It is thought that chess began in China or India around 1,400 years ago. From there it spread to North Africa and eventually to Europe. The modern form of chess emerged in the 16th century and remains one of the world's most popular games. Today, computers can be programmed to play chess against humans.

WHO INVENTS GAMES?

Big companies employ workers to invent new games, but many games are invented by ordinary people with a good idea. An unemployed architect thought up Scrabble in 1931. Monopoly was invented in 1933 during the Great Depression by an American salesman. The dice game Yahtzee was invented in 1956 by a Canadian couple to play on their yacht.

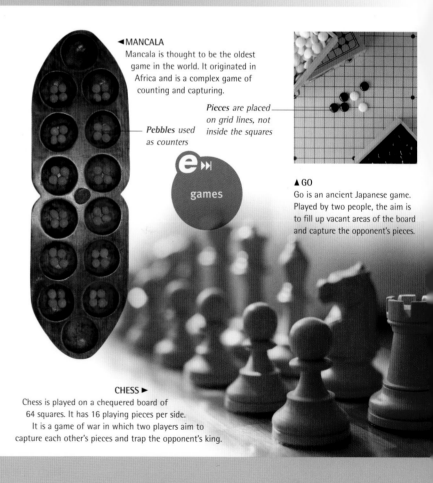

◄MANCALA
Mancala is thought to be the oldest game in the world. It originated in Africa and is a complex game of counting and capturing.

Pebbles used as counters

Pieces are placed on grid lines, not inside the squares

games

▲ GO
Go is an ancient Japanese game. Played by two people, the aim is to fill up vacant areas of the board and capture the opponent's pieces.

CHESS ►
Chess is played on a chequered board of 64 squares. It has 16 playing pieces per side. It is a game of war in which two players aim to capture each other's pieces and trap the opponent's king.

HOME ENTERTAINMENT

Home entertainment is how we have fun and relax at home. Today it is dominated by technology, especially television. Watching videos, playing computer games, and listening to music are all home entertainment. So are reading books, playing cards, and storytelling.

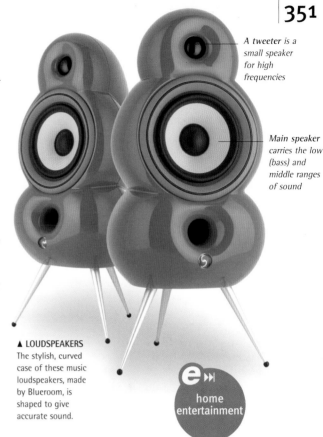

A *tweeter* is a small speaker for high frequencies

Main speaker carries the low (bass) and middle ranges of sound

WHAT DID PEOPLE DO BEFORE TV WAS INVENTED?

People had to make their own amusement by playing games, singing, or reading stories. The invention of the radio and the gramophone at the beginning of the 20th century meant that people could listen to music and programmes at home. Just as we sit in front of the TV to watch our favourite shows, people in the past sat around the radio or listened to the gramophone.

WHAT IS HOME CINEMA?

Home cinema is an attempt to bring the look, the sound, and the excitement of cinema to the home. A basic kit includes a widescreen television, a DVD (digital video disc) player, and speakers positioned around the room to give surround sound. For a more cinematic effect, a wall-mounted digital projector and projection screen can be used instead of a TV.

1960s HOME LISTENING
Electric record players were popular and played two sizes of vinyl disc, a 12-inch and a 7-inch.

▲ LOUDSPEAKERS
The stylish, curved case of these music loudspeakers, made by Blueroom, is shaped to give accurate sound.

e ▸▸
home entertainment

  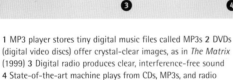 

① **②** **③** **④** **⑤**

1 MP3 player stores tiny digital music files called MP3s 2 DVDs (digital video discs) offer crystal-clear images, as in *The Matrix* (1999) 3 Digital radio produces clear, interference-free sound 4 State-of-the-art machine plays from CDs, MP3s, and radio 5 Flatscreen TVs do not distort the picture like curved TVs

Information screen shows which part of the system is selected

Control buttons for functions such as volume

Arrow keys for radio and TV channel navigation

IS DIGITAL BROADCASTING HERE TO STAY?

Digital broadcasting has many advantages over the old analogue system. Information is compressed (made smaller), producing more channels and better quality pictures and sound. Digital technology makes TV and radio more interactive for the audience.

WHAT IS MUSIC HI-FI?

Music hi-fi is recorded music. Hi-fi is short for high fidelity, which means that the recording is an accurate copy of the original music. Hi-fi was first developed using vinyl records, then magnetic tape (cassettes). It is now recorded using digital media – CDs, mini discs, and MP3 files.

◄ REMOTE CONTROL
This is for a combined system that covers music, TV, satellite, DVD, video, CD, radio – and room lights!

SUPER MARIO BY NINTENDO ►
Since his first game, *Donkey Kong* (1981), Super Mario has appeared in more than 30 video games and starred in his own movie.

FIND OUT MORE ▸▸ Cinema 346–347 • Sound 176–177 • Telecommunications 192–193

SPORTS

Sports are any competitive game that has set rules and involves physical exertion or coordination. There are ▸▸ TEAM SPORTS, individual sports, winter sports on snow and ice, motor sports with cars and motorbikes, sports with horses and dogs, and ▸▸ EXTREME SPORTS.

HAVE PEOPLE ALWAYS PLAYED SPORTS?
People of all cultures and times have played games to test skill and athleticism. Some early ball games used balls made from straw or an inflated animal's bladder. Games were often linked to social and religious rituals. It is only within the last 150 years or so that games with rules have been played regularly for competition.

WHEN DID SPORTS BECOME ORGANIZED?
The first set of rules for golf were drawn up in Scotland in the 18th century. Many other sports – such as soccer, baseball, cricket, and American football – acquired formal rules from the mid-19th century onwards. Some games are relatively recent – basketball was invented from scratch in 1891.

WHAT ARE PROFESSIONAL SPORTS?
In professional sports, competitors are paid prize money or wages, or both. In amateur sports competitors are not paid. Before sports like rugby union and track and athletics became professional, many amateurs had to work part-time in other professions to support themselves.

▲ FORMULA ONE
The Formula One Grand Prix is the most important race in motor sport. Here, Michael Schumacher (1969–) drives his Ferrari in 2002.

▲ TIGER WOODS
Tiger Woods (1975–) has become a superstar in golf. He is the first and only player to have held all four major championship titles at once – the Masters Tournament, PGA, US Open, and British Open.

SNOWBOARDING ▲
Snowboarding was invented in the USA in the 1960s, using skis tied together, with ropes attached for steering. The first custom-made snowboard, modelled on a surfboard, was built in 1966.

Snowboard size depends on the rider's height, build, and shoe size

sports

TEAM SPORTS

Team sports involve more than one person per side and require the members of a team to co-operate with one another to win the game. Nearly all team sports are ball games. Teams are organized into clubs, which attract more long-term interest and support than individuals – clubs and teams outlast their star players.

▲ RUGBY
Rugby union is a hugely popular team sport in Australia and South Africa as well as western Europe. Here, Australia (in the yellow shirts) play South Africa at Ellis Park, Johannesburg, in 2002. South Africa won.

WHAT ARE THE WORLD'S MOST POPULAR TEAM SPORTS?

Football is the world's biggest team sport. American football and baseball are the most popular in the USA. Ice hockey, cricket, and rugby are strong in other nations. Hockey, handball, netball, and volleyball get less media coverage but are widely played.

Helmet helps prevent injury to the head when the rider falls

Goggles protect the eyes from the glare of the snow

▲ BASEBALL
Baseball is the national sport of the USA. The base man for the New York Yankees dives to catch the ball in his mitt (glove) in a game against the Los Angeles Dodgers.

▲ BASKETBALL
Michael Jordan (1963–) is often called the greatest basketball player of all time. The 1.83-m (6-ft-6-in) player was with the Chicago Bulls in 1984–1994 and 1995–1998, with a year off in between as a baseball player.

WHAT DOES A TEAM COACH DO?

A coach trains the individual players to work together as a successful team. Coaches motivate the players to keep up the discipline and focus required during training. They also create strategies for winning. During a game a coach may substitute players who are performing badly or are injured.

EXTREME SPORTS

Extreme sports are events that are a deliberate extension or intensification of older games. Extreme sports are dangerous, challenging, and sometimes bizarre. They have few rules and are usually not team-based. Players use their skills to control the risks.

WHAT ARE THE X GAMES?

The X stands for extreme. The X Games began in 1995 in the USA. They are now the biggest annual international event for extreme sports. Summer events are inline skating, skateboarding, stunt biking, and motocross. Winter events are snowboarding and skiing. In the past, competitions were also held for skysurfing (with parachutes), barefoot waterskiing, ice-climbing, and mountain biking in the snow.

ROCK CLIMBING ▶
France's Catherine Destivelle (1960–) climbs a steep rock cliff in Spain. Unlike traditional rock climbing where the climber uses safety ropes fixed in place with bolts, she has no ropes to guide her.

FIND OUT MORE ▶▶ Competitions 354–355 • Olympics 356–357

COMPETITIONS

Competitions define the highest level of achievement, and exist in every major sport. American football has the ▸▸ SUPER BOWL ; football has the ▸▸ THE WORLD CUP . The most prestigious competitions attract global media coverage and huge ▸▸ SPONSORSHIP deals.

▲ THE ASHES
This urn is given to the winner in cricket's Test Series. It is said to hold the ashes of the wickets used in the first Test match in 1882.

WHAT WERE THE FIRST GREAT COMPETITIONS?
Although the Oxford and Cambridge rowing race in London, England, has been running since 1829, organized sporting competitions began to develop in the late 19th century. The English Football Association Cup in soccer began in 1872. The first American National Baseball League began in 1876.

WHY ARE SOME COMPETITIONS SO FAMOUS?
Competitions become famous when they have continued for many years and have an exciting history filled with sporting legends. Over time they attract loyalty and respect from fans. Some competitions have sponsorship deals and as a result receive publicity from advertisers and broadcasters.

TOUR DE FRANCE ▸
American cyclist Lance Armstrong leads the way in the Tour de France in 2000. The yellow jersey is worn by the current leader of the Tour during each of its many stages. The competition began in 1903.

THE WORLD CUP

First held in 1930, the FIFA (Fédération Internationale de Football Associations) World Cup is the most important tournament for national football teams. It is held every four years and has grown from just 11 teams in 1930 to 32 teams in 2002.

e ▸▸
competitions

HOW MANY PEOPLE WATCH THE WORLD CUP?
There are seats for around one million people at a modern World Cup and it now attracts more than 60 billion television viewers around the world. This means that, on average, every person on the planet watches ten games. The 1950 final in Rio de Janeiro, Brazil, saw the biggest attendance at any football game in history– more than 200,000 people.

WHICH TEAM HAS WON THE MOST WORLD CUPS?
Brazil has won five World Cups (1958, 1962, 1970, 1994, and 2002). Two nations have won three titles each – Italy (1934, 1938, 1982) and Germany (1954, 1974, 1990). Uruguay (1930, 1950) and Argentina (1978, 1986) have each won it twice, and England (1966) and France (1998) have won once each.

WORLD CUP WINNERS 2002 ▸
The Brazilian captain, Cafu, lifts the trophy after Brazil beat Germany 2-0 in Yokohama, Japan. Brazil is the only team to win the title outside their own continent (in Sweden in 1958, and Japan in 2002).

SUPER BOWL

The Super Bowl is the biggest event in the American sporting year. It is a one-off game between the winners of the NFL (National Football League) and the winners of the AFL (American Football League) to decide the national champion.

WHEN DID SUPER BOWL START?

The NFL was started in 1920 and was the only national football league until the AFL began in 1960. In 1967, the two leagues merged for a single end-of-season play-off between the two champions. The first Super Bowl was won by Wisconsin's Green Bay Packers, who beat the Kansas City Chiefs 35–10.

WHO ARE THE BIGGEST SUPER BOWL TEAMS?

The two most successful teams are the Dallas Cowboys and the San Francisco 49ers, who have each won five Super Bowls. The Pittsburgh Steelers have won four, and the Green Bay Packers and Washington Redskins three each. Fans support their teams by wearing hats, t-shirts, and even face paints in the team's colours.

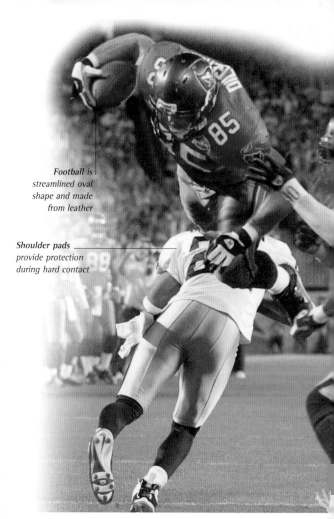

Football is streamlined oval shape and made from leather

Shoulder pads provide protection during hard contact

SUPER BOWL XXXVII ▶
The Tampa Bay Buccaneers (in white) won their first Super Bowl in San Diego, January 2003. They beat the Oakland Raiders 48–21. XXXVII is 37 in Roman numerals, and means the 37th year of the competition.

SPONSORSHIP

Big sporting events need lots of money to organize, promote, and pay prize money and wages. Companies pay competition organizers, venues, teams, and individual sports stars to display their logos and advertising. Sponsors also use their connections with sports stars to promote their brands in the media in general.

HOW BIG ARE SPONSORSHIP DEALS?

The biggest personal sponsorship deals are with the clothing firm Nike. The golfer Tiger Woods has a deal worth US $125 million (£75 million) over five years, and the basketball star LeBron James is receiving US $90 million (£54 million) over seven years. Nike also has the biggest deal with a team – sponsoring Brazil's football team for US $100 million (£60 million).

HOW MUCH INFLUENCE DO SPONSORS HAVE OVER SPORTING COMPETITIONS?

Many organizations now design their events to attract sponsors and TV audiences. In the USA, basketball introduced a rule called the 24-second shot – a team has to shoot within 24 seconds of getting the ball. This increased the pace and excitement of the game, and made it more appealing to TV broadcasters.

▲ SERENA WILLIAMS, 2003 AUSTRALIAN OPEN CHAMPIONSHIP
In 1998 this American tennis star signed a five-year deal with clothes firm Puma for US $11.7 million (£7.2 million). The deal was dependent on her becoming one of the world's top ten players, which she did.

FIND OUT MORE ▶▶ Olympics 356–357 • Sports 352–353

OLYMPICS

The Olympic Games are the world's biggest sporting spectacle. They are divided into a summer and winter Games, held every four years by a single city. Athletes with disabilities compete at the Paralympics. More than 10,000 athletes take part in the summer events alone.

▲ OLYMPIC RINGS
Baron de Coubertin was said to have seen the five rings on an ancient Greek artefact. The rings symbolize the unity of the world's five continents (Europe, Asia, Africa, Oceania, and the Americas). Every national flag in the world contains at least one of the five colours.

Olympic flame has an ancient counterpart – a sacred flame lit in honour of the goddess Hera

Olympic torch was first used in modern Games in 1936, carried by runners from Greece to Berlin

◀ BERLIN OLYMPICS, 1936
The 1936 Olympics is opened as the runner lights the Olympic flame. Organized by the Nazi government, the Berlin Olympics were the first to be openly linked to political propaganda.

e ▶▶ olympics

WHO INVENTED THE MODERN OLYMPICS?
In the 19th century archaeological discoveries revived interest in the ▶▶ ANCIENT OLYMPICS. The Greeks tried to re-create the Games in Athens in 1859 and 1870. However, the major force behind the modern Olympics was the French aristocrat Baron de Coubertin (1863–1937). In 1894 he organized an international conference in Paris to support a revival of the Games.

WHO RUNS THE OLYMPICS NOW?
De Coubertin's 1894 conference created the International Olympic Committee (IOC), which has run the Games ever since. The IOC chooses the host cities and sets the rules for competing. In recent years, its reputation has been hurt by scandals over corruption and bribery in the selection of the host cities.

WHAT IS THE OLYMPIC IDEAL?
Baron de Coubertin saw the Olympics as a place in which sporting excellence could be celebrated. The ideal was to build international understanding and co-operation. The Olympic code promotes amateurism – performance without payment – and professionals are allowed to participate only under certain rules.

ANCIENT OLYMPICS

The Ancient Olympics celebrated the god Zeus and were held every four years at Olympia, Greece. Winners received an olive wreath. The date of the first Games is unclear, but the first recorded Olympic champion was Koroibos, who won a sprint in 776 BC.

WHAT TOOK PLACE AT THE ANCIENT OLYMPICS?
The events at Olympia in 776 BC were sprints and horse races. Later, longer races were added, including sprints wearing full armour. Chariot racing and combat sports such as boxing and wrestling were soon regular features. All events were held in a stadium. The open-air track for horse racing was called a hippodrome.

WHY DID THE ANCIENT OLYMPICS END?
The Romans invaded Olympia in 85 BC. The Games continued under Roman rule, but were disrupted by a Germanic invasion around AD 300. The Games became part of a pagan festival until the Christian emperor Theodosius I ordered the closure of all pagan events in 393.

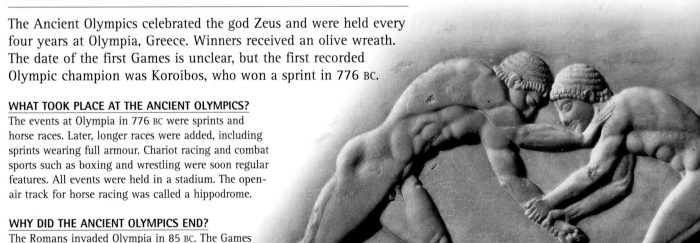

▲ ATHLETES WRESTLING
This carving from Athens dates from c. 510 BC. Athletes mostly competed naked. Women were not allowed to take part or watch.

IS IT EXPENSIVE TO HOST THE OLYMPICS?

The summer and winter Games each cost around US $3.2 billion (£2 billion) to host. Cities must house hundreds of thousands of visitors and provide security and transport for them. The host city must also build world-class stadiums and facilities. All this bankrupted the 1976 host, Montreal. Costs are met by the income from television sponsorship and tourism.

HAVE NEW EVENTS BEEN ADDED SINCE 1896?

The Olympics have changed a lot since 1896, when there were no women's events at all. The winter Games only began in 1924. ▶▶ ATHLETICS remains the focus of the summer Games, but many events have come and gone, such as the tug-of-war. Recent additions include volleyball, canoeing, and cycling.

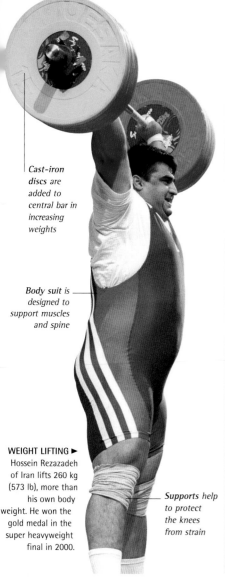

Cast-iron discs are added to central bar in increasing weights

Body suit is designed to support muscles and spine

WEIGHT LIFTING ▶
Hossein Rezazadeh of Iran lifts 260 kg (573 lb), more than his own body weight. He won the gold medal in the super heavyweight final in 2000.

Supports help to protect the knees from strain

▲ OLYMPIC EVENTS, SYDNEY, 2000
1 The Chinese gymnast Xuan Liu reaches for the asymmetric bars. **2** Liuhui Kong concentrates hard to take the gold medal for China in the men's table tennis singles final. **3** Holland's Pieter van den Hoogenband (right) and Australia's Ian Thorpe race to the finish in the 200-m freestyle swimming final. Van den Hoogenband took the gold medal.

ATHLETICS

Athletics is the popular term for track and field events. These were the core of the Ancient Olympics and included running, throwing, and jumping, which combined into multi-event competitions – the pentathlon (five events) and the decathlon (ten events). Today, athletics also includes pole-vaulting, hurdling, and relay racing.

WHAT MAKES A GREAT ATHLETE?

Great athletes, like all great sports competitors, require fitness, dedication, natural ability, and luck. What lifts some athletes above others is a relentless will to win, psychological strength, and the capacity to produce their best performance under any circumstances.

HOW DO ATHLETES KEEP SETTING NEW RECORDS?

With sponsorship, athletes have more resources and time to devote to sport. High-tech running tracks, clothing, and shoes have improved performance. So have new techniques such as the flop in high jumping. However, performance-enhancing drugs damage the Olympic ideals and the competitors' health.

RELAY RACING ▶
The American team pass the baton (stick) at the 2000 Games in the 4 x 100-m relay race.

FIND OUT MORE ▶▶ Ancient Greece 376–377 • Competitions 354–355 • Sports 352–353

HISTORY

HISTORY

History is a record of what happened in the past. It is all about people – how they lived and worked, where they travelled, why they went to war, and what they thought and believed.

WHY DO PEOPLE STUDY HISTORY?
The past is full of adventures. In fact, the word history comes from the ancient Greek for "story". Historians work like detectives. They gather ▶◀ EVIDENCE , search for lost treasures, and report their finds. Their studies can explain why things happen, and how change occurs.

▲ ETRUSCAN WALL PAINTING, ITALY
The dancers in this Etruscan fresco (wall painting) look just as lively as when they were first painted, almost 2,500 years ago. To us, pictures such as this are like windows into the past.

Death mask of gold, to place over dead man's face

Detailed metal-working shows beard

DEATH MASK, GREECE ▶
This mask was found in the AD 1870s, in a grave at Mycenae. It was discovered by the German archaeologist Heinrich Schliemann, who originally claimed that it belonged to Agamemnon, a Mycenaean king described in the poems of Homer. Experts first thought that it was from around 1500 BC, but modern dating techniques suggest that it is older.

HOW IS HISTORY USED?
History helps us to understand our own times, and to plan for the future. Learning about the past shapes our sense of who we are, and a knowledge of past injustices often inspires people to fight for change.

DO HISTORIANS AGREE WITH ONE ANOTHER?
Historians frequently have different opinions about the past, and some may also be influenced by their own religious or political views. In their studies, historians use new evidence and ideas to challenge existing theories about historical periods and events.

EVIDENCE

Anything that survives from the past can be used as evidence (proof) of what happened long ago. Some evidence comes from written documents such as letters, diaries, or government records. Other forms of evidence are still standing – such as old buildings, statues, or grand monuments – while much of it lies hidden in the ground, yet to be discovered.

◀ MAGNA CARTA, ENGLAND
This great document records an agreement made in AD 1215 between King John and a group of nobles. It sets out the laws and customs the king had to respect in dealing with his subjects. It still influences English law today.

HOW DO HISTORIANS STUDY EVIDENCE?
Historians study many different forms of evidence, preserved in libraries, archives, and museums. Often, they have to learn dead languages so that they can read and understand ancient documents. They also rely on the techniques of other subjects, such as ▶◀ ARCHAEOLOGY and ▶◀ ANTHROPOLOGY .

ARCHAEOLOGY

Archaeology involves studying the past through the analysis of physical remains. These include stone or flint objects, metal items, pottery, paintings, tools, weapons, and textiles, as well as fields, towns, and ruined buildings.

WHAT TECHNIQUES DO ARCHAEOLOGISTS USE?

Today's archaeologists locate sites using aerial photography, satellite pictures, and a satellite system called GPS. Then, they excavate (dig up) the sites to uncover buried remains, and record the details of any finds using photos, drawings, charts, and maps. They scan and X-ray their finds to investigate them without harming them, and use computer modelling to create reconstructions of damaged objects and buildings.

PEWTER JUG FROM THE *MARY ROSE*, ENGLAND ▶
This jug, encrusted with barnacles, was salvaged in 1982. It is part of the remains of the wrecked English warship, the *Mary Rose*, which had been built for King Henry VIII. The ship sank in 1545.

WHERE DO ARCHAEOLOGISTS LOOK FOR REMAINS?

Archaeologists search for remains in many different places, including shipwrecks, tombs, caves, and even rubbish tips. They survey towns and villages – recording the location of all historic sites – and examine the soil to find any traces of past fires, fields, and buildings. They study animal bones and seeds to find out what people ate and what the climate was like.

HOW DO ARCHAEOLOGISTS DATE THEIR FINDS?

Archaeologists have many ways of dating finds. Fragments of pottery, or coins, can show when people lived on a site, and tree rings in timber can reveal when a building was made. These experts can also measure the level of radioactive carbon or magnetic energy in an object to calculate its age.

Noose around neck shows Tollund Man was strangled

TOLLUND MAN, DENMARK ▲
This man was thrown into a bog around 2,000 years ago, as a sacrifice to the gods. The acidic earth in the bog preserved his body. Because of this, archaeologists have been able to work out his age, health, height, weight, and social status – and even what he ate for his last meal.

ANTHROPOLOGY

Anthropology is the study of humankind. It often focuses on people living today – especially groups that follow ancient customs and traditions, or still use ancient forms of technology. Anthropologists visit these people to ask them questions, and observe their family life, social customs, and religious rituals. They record their songs, myths, legends, and beliefs.

HOW DOES ANTHROPOLOGY HELP HISTORY?

The study of anthropology can help historians to understand how ancient objects were used, or why ancient beliefs were so important, by comparing evidence from the past with observations made today. It is especially useful to historians investigating past civilizations that have left no written records.

history

Head made of stone – face may represent an ancestor

◀ BURIAL HEAD, USA
This head was found in a burial mound in Ohio, and dates from around 300 BC. It was carved by descendants of the Hopewell culture. Today's anthropologists study the religious customs of present-day cultures in Ohio, USA. Their studies help historians to understand the various uses of figures such as this one.

FIND OUT MORE ▶▶ Ancient Greece 376–377 • Early Americans 380 • First Metalworkers 367 • Prehistoric Pottery 367

FIRST MODERN HUMANS

Homo sapiens (modern humans) first evolved between 200,000 BC and 100,000 BC. They were like ourselves, physically, and had the same brain power. They developed many skills of survival, and advanced ▶▶ FLINT-KNAPPING techniques for making better tools.

WHERE DID THE FIRST MODERN HUMANS LIVE?

Most archaeologists think that *Homo sapiens* first lived in Africa, and that our direct ancestor was *Homo habilis* ("handy man"), who evolved about 2.5 million years ago. But some believe our ancestor was *Homo ergaster* ("work man"), who developed around 1.9 million years ago and settled in different parts of the world.

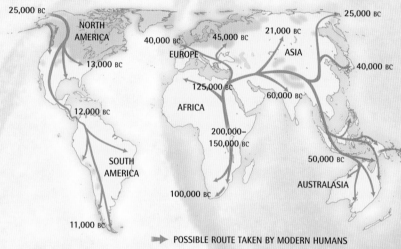

25,000 BC
NORTH AMERICA
25,000 BC
40,000 BC
45,000 BC
21,000 BC
EUROPE
ASIA
13,000 BC
40,000 BC
125,000 BC
60,000 BC
AFRICA
12,000 BC
200,000–150,000 BC
SOUTH AMERICA
50,000 BC
AUSTRALASIA
100,000 BC
11,000 BC

➡ POSSIBLE ROUTE TAKEN BY MODERN HUMANS

▢ EXTENT OF ICE SHEETS c. 10,000 BC

▲ THE SPREAD OF MODERN HUMANS
The arrows on this map show how modern humans may have spread out from Africa. The dates record the age of the earliest modern-human bones and tools found on each continent.

WHO WERE NEANDERTHALS AND WHY DID THEY DISAPPEAR?

Like us, Neanderthals are a subspecies of *Homo sapiens* ("wise man"). They lived in Europe and Asia from *c.* 130,000 BC to *c.* 28,000 BC. The spread of modern humans may have been the cause of their extinction.

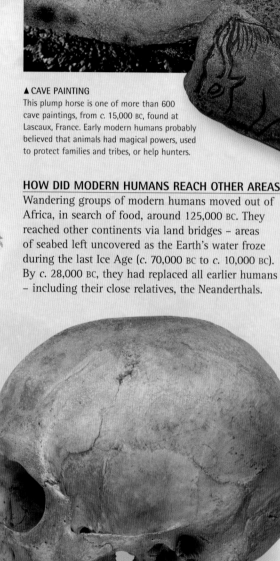

▲ CAVE PAINTING
This plump horse is one of more than 600 cave paintings, from *c.* 15,000 BC, found at Lascaux, France. Early modern humans probably believed that animals had magical powers, used to protect families and tribes, or help hunters.

HOW DID MODERN HUMANS REACH OTHER AREAS

Wandering groups of modern humans moved out of Africa, in search of food, around 125,000 BC. They reached other continents via land bridges – areas of seabed left uncovered as the Earth's water froze during the last Ice Age (*c.* 70,000 BC to *c.* 10,000 BC). By *c.* 28,000 BC, they had replaced all earlier humans – including their close relatives, the Neanderthals.

Thick ridge above brow

Smaller jaw – large jaw not needed as today's humans do not eat tough roots and leaves

▲ MODERN HUMAN SKULL
The first modern humans were tall, and had slender bones, high-domed foreheads, smooth brows, and small jaws. Their muscles were not as well developed as those of the Neanderthals, and their eyesight was weaker.

◀ NEANDERTHAL SKULL
Neanderthals had larger brains than modern humans. Their short, stocky build and broad nose helped them to conserve body heat in Europe's chilly Ice-Age climate. They relied more on strength than brain power.

FLINT-KNAPPING

Early and modern humans used a technique called flint-knapping to make stone tools. They chipped flakes off one piece of flint (a hard, glassy stone) by striking it with another piece. This required great patience and skill. ▸▸ ABORIGINALS still practise flint-knapping today.

WHAT KINDS OF TOOLS DID EARLY HUMANS USE?

Early humans used five main kinds of flint tools – knives for cutting, scrapers for removing flesh from hides, burins (small, pointed tools) for carving, awls for piercing holes, and points or tips for fitting on to spears. They also used flint hand-axes for chopping wood and butchering animal carcasses.

ark made good container or hazelnuts nd blackberries

▲ STORING FOOD
In late summer and autumn, women and children gathered large quantities of nuts, fruits, and berries, then dried them over fires to preserve them for the winter. Archaeologists have found remains of food preserved 12,000 years ago.

Bison grazing

Hunter crawls along ground

FEATHERED ARROW ▲
Hunters fitted a flight of duck feathers to each arrow to make it travel further. This way, they could attack their prey from afar.

STALKING BISON ▲
The picture on this fragment of bone was carved in France between 15,000 BC and 10,000 BC. Teams of people worked together to catch large animals by stampeding them over cliffs or trapping them in narrow valleys.

◀ CRAFTWORKER'S BURIN
This sharp-pointed flint tool, known as a burin, was made around 35,000 BC. Burins were probably used for engraving bone or adding grooves to leather. The craftworker would guide the point using their index finger.

Rounded shape fits worker's hand

Spur

CLOVIS POINT ▶
Ice-Age hunters in North America used a curved piece of flint, known as a clovis point, to make a spear. Two small spurs (spikes) at the rear of the point made it easier to fix on to a wooden shaft, using animal sinew or plant twine.

SPEARHEAD ▶
This leaf-shaped blade was once part of a hunting spear made in France between 20,000 BC and 15,000 BC. It is beautifully shaped, using the pressure-flaking technique developed around 35,000 BC. This technique allowed craftworkers to shape their tools much more precisely.

Design resembles leaf of a laurel tree

ABORIGINALS

Aboriginals, also known as indigenous Australians, were the earliest inhabitants of Australia. Until the 20th century, they followed a lifestyle similar to that of earlier humans. Their skills helped archaeologists understand evidence about the distant past.

HOW DID ABORIGINALS SURVIVE?

In 10,000 BC, sea levels around Australia rose and Aboriginal people were forced to move further inland, where conditions were harsh. To survive, they used fire to clear bushland so that wild food plants could grow, hunted kangaroos with boomerangs, weaved traps for fish, and dug grubs from deep underground.

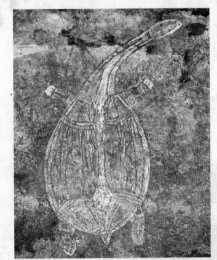

e ▸▸
first modern humans

◀ ABORIGINAL ART
Aboriginals created art on rocks, such as this turtle on Ubirr Rock at the Kakadu National Park in Australia's Northern Territory. Some of their paintings are more than 20,000 years old.

FIND OUT MORE ▸▸ Africa 238–239 • Australia and New Zealand 274–275 • Evolution 74–75

EARLY FARMING

Farming began *c.* 10,000 BC on land that became known as the ▸▸ **FERTILE CRESCENT**. Hunter-gatherers, who had travelled to the area in search of food, began to harvest (gather) wild grains they found growing there. They scattered spare grains on the ground to grow more food.

HOW DID FARMING CHANGE PEOPLE'S LIVES?

Before farming, people lived by hunting wild animals and gathering wild plants. When supplies ran out, these hunter-gatherers moved on. Farming meant that people did not need to travel to find food. Instead, they began to live in settled communities, and grew crops or raised animals on nearby land. They built stronger, more permanent homes and surrounded their settlements with walls to protect themselves.

Plaster spread over real human skull

Eyes made of shells from the Red Sea

MOULDED HEAD ▸
This human head statue, from around 7000 BC, was probably made to show respect for an ancestor. Many statues like this have been found at Jericho. They give us clues as to how people in early farming communities lived.

▲ THE WALLS OF JERICHO
The settlement of Jericho was founded *c.* 9000 BC by farmers, who built walls 3 m (10 ft) thick around it, with a tower 9 m (30 ft) high. Jericho was close to a natural spring, which provided water for their fields.

Base of round tower that formed part of Jericho's ancient walls

early farming

HOW DID PEOPLE BECOME BETTER FARMERS?

By around 9000 BC, people were storing grains during the winter, then sowing them in specially cleared plots. By 8000 BC, the farmers had discovered which grains gave the best yields and selected these ones for planting. They produced more food than they needed and were able to feed non-farmers such as craftworkers and traders. The farmers exchanged their food for various kinds of useful or decorative goods.

▼ FOOD GRAINS
Einkorn and emmer produce grains (seeds) that fall from the ear (seed head) when they are ripe. Seeing this happen probably inspired the first farmers to experiment with different methods of scattering and planting grains.

EINKORN

WHICH PLANTS DID THE FIRST FARMERS GROW?

In the Fertile Crescent, farmers grew tall, wild grasses, including an early type of barley, and primitive varieties of wheat called emmer and einkorn. These naturally produced large grains (seeds) that were tasty and nourishing. In other parts of the world, between 8000 BC and 3000 BC, farmers discovered how to ▸▸ **DOMESTICATE** their own local plants and animals.

Ripe grains from ear of einkorn

Ear of einkorn

EMMER

DOMESTICATION

Domestication is the process of making wild plants and animals more useful to humans, through selective breeding. Farmers select and plant only the best seeds from their last crop. Wild cattle are selectively bred to make a herd docile (easy to control).

WHAT WERE THE FIRST DOMESTICATED ANIMALS?

Dogs were the first animals to be domesticated, c. 12,500 BC. They were descended from wild wolf cubs that had learned to live with human families, who fed and petted them. By 10,000 BC, hunters were managing wild herds of gazelle, sheep, and goats, watching over them and killing the weakest for food. Around 7500 BC, farmers were taking the best animals from their herds to breed them for meat and milk.

◄ HERDED ANIMALS
This seal came from the ancient city of Susa, north of the Persian Gulf, and was made around 3000 BC. By this time, herding animals was a way of life for farmers. Cattle were also being used to prepare the land where farmers grew crops. Sheep with longer hair had been selectively bred to develop fleecy coats, which the farmers used to make wool.

Seal (stamp) engraved with rams and goats

Cutting edge of blade slices wheat and barley stalks

FERTILE CRESCENT

Archaeologists use the name Fertile Crescent to describe an area to the east of the Mediterranean Sea, where farming first developed. It was a crescent-shaped strip of land that stretched across the Levant region (now known as Israel, Lebanon, and Syria), and around the edges of the Tarus and Zagros mountains.

WHY DID FARMING BEGIN HERE?

The Fertile Crescent had regular rainfall, making it ideal for growing grains such as emmer and einkorn, and for raising herds of grass-eating animals such as sheep and goats. In nearby Mesopotamia, where the soil was more fertile, farming was only possible once irrigation methods had developed to supply the land with water.

◄ STONE SICKLE
This sickle has a wooden handle and a sharp flint blade, carefully shaped by a stoneworker around 6,000 years ago. Farmers used sickles to cut ripe ears of grain from the stalk.

Stone is rolled backwards and forwards to crush grains

HAND MILL ►
This is a hand mill known as a quern. It consists of a curved slab of stone and a ball-shaped stone roller. Querns were used by farming women, between c. 6000 BC and 4000 BC, to grind grains of wheat and barley into flour.

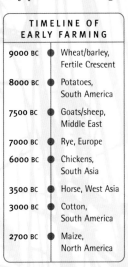

TIMELINE OF EARLY FARMING	
9000 BC	Wheat/barley, Fertile Crescent
8000 BC	Potatoes, South America
7500 BC	Goats/sheep, Middle East
7000 BC	Rye, Europe
6000 BC	Chickens, South Asia
3500 BC	Horse, West Asia
3000 BC	Cotton, South America
2700 BC	Maize, North America

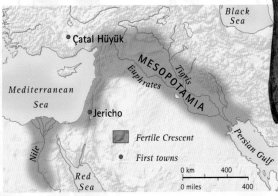

▲ HOME OF THE FIRST FARMERS
The Fertile Crescent stretched in a crescent-shaped curve from the northern tip of the Red Sea around to the Persian Gulf. Some of the world's first settlements, including Jericho, were built in this region. Important trading centres, like Çatal Hüyük, also developed nearby.

WHY WAS ÇATAL HÜYÜK SO PROSPEROUS?

Çatal Hüyük was founded in around 7000 BC, and grew to be the largest settlement in the Middle East. Its wealth came from farming and trade. The farmers kept cattle and grew wheat, barley, and peas. Çatal Hüyük made itself especially prosperous by controlling the trade in obsidian (a coarse, glassy rock), which came from a nearby volcano. Craftworkers used this volcanic glass to make high-quality tools.

ÇATAL HÜYÜK HOMES ►
Excavation of the Çatal Hüyük site found mud-brick houses closely packed together, without any streets. Access to each home was by ladders leading up to doorways on a flat roof. Rooms had hearths for heating, benches for sitting and sleeping on, and ovens for baking bread. When family members died, they were buried under the floor.

FIND OUT MORE ►► Early Americans 380 • Farming 66 • Maya 381 • Western Asia and the Middle East 264–265

MEGALITHIC EUROPE

Between c. 3200 BC and 1500 BC, peoples in northwest Europe began to build monuments from massive stones known as megaliths. Some were arranged in circles or lines, pointing to the sky. Others, called ▶▶ CHAMBER TOMBS, were buried under the earth.

WHO BUILT MEGALITHIC MONUMENTS?

Megalithic monuments came in many different shapes and sizes. Most were quite small, and could easily have been assembled by a family over a few seasons. Large monuments, like Stonehenge and Carnac, were probably built by powerful chiefs who could command their subjects to work on the monuments.

WHAT WERE STONE CIRCLES USED FOR?

Stone circles were probably used for religious ceremonies or for astronomy. Most of them line up with the Sun, Moon, and stars on special days. For example, the rising Sun shines through the centre of Stonehenge, England, at midsummer, and lights up a chamber tomb in Newgrange, Ireland, at midwinter.

▲ CARNAC'S MEGALITHS
These rows of standing stones at Carnac, France, are arranged in parallel lines that run for about one kilometre (two-thirds of a mile) and link two stone circles. Carnac also has many separate standing stones, chamber tombs, and barrows (earth mounds).

Trilithon – a stone arch made of two upright stones and a horizontal stone on top. Five stand at Stonehenge.

▲ STONEHENGE, ENGLAND
In around 3000 BC, workers at this site built a henge (circular ditch and earth bank) and a ring of timber posts. These were later replaced by huge sarsen (upright) stones. In c. 1550 BC, smaller bluestones, from Wales, were added to finish it off.

CHAMBER TOMBS

Megalithic tombs with several chambers (rooms) were built using massive stone slabs, then covered with an earth mound called a barrow. Each one could be used as a burial place for hundreds of years.

WHO WAS BURIED IN THE CHAMBER TOMBS?

Archaeologists are not certain for whom the chamber tombs were made, because they were robbed long ago. From their design, it seems likely that they were used to bury rich, powerful leaders, who controlled vast areas of farmland and the people living in the region.

e ▶▶
megaliths

Vaulted roof made of strips of stone

◀ MAES HOWE TOMB
This tomb, on Mainland island in the Orkney Islands, Scotland, was built in around 2700 BC. The main chamber is reached through a long passageway lined with stone. Square holes in the chamber's walls lead to smaller side rooms, which were also used for burials.

FIND OUT MORE ▶▶ Rocks 46–47

PREHISTORIC POTTERY

Pottery-making was invented in Japanese fishing communities, in *c.* 10,500 BC. When they cooked, people noticed that the clay soil underneath their fires baked and became hard. They soon began to shape clay into pots, cook them on bonfires, and leave them to cool.

Paintwork helps place and date the urn

BURIAL URN ▲
Pottery was often used in religious rituals. This Banshan Era burial urn, from China's Yangshao culture, was made in around 2500 BC.

WHY WERE THE FIRST POTS SO IMPORTANT?

Unlike earlier containers – made from leather, woven twigs, bark, and string – clay pots were heatproof and waterproof. They made it possible to cook soups and stews, brew drinks such as wine and beer, and store grain and oil for long periods. The remains of pots help archaeologists to identify different peoples.

e ⏩
prehistoric pottery

▲ JAPANESE POTTERY JAR
This rope-patterned pot was made between 10,500 BC and 7500 BC. A craftworker shaped it by hand using coils of clay.

FIND OUT MORE ⏩ Rocks 46–47 • Sculpture 323

FIRST METALWORKERS

From around 9000 BC, people in different lands began to work with nuggets of soft metals, such as copper. Later, they discovered how to extract metals, such as tin, from rocks by smelting (heating). Finally, they discovered how to melt metals together to make new materials called alloys, such as bronze.

e ⏩
first metalworkers

SOME OF THE FIRST METALWORKERS	
9000 BC	Hammered copper, central Asia
5000 BC	Gold/copper, Europe
4000 BC	Bronze, Middle East
2300 BC	Bronze, Europe
1500 BC	Iron, western Asia
1000 BC	Iron, Europe

Face perhaps represents revered ancestors

WHAT WAS BRONZE USED FOR?

Bronze is a mixture of copper and tin. It is much harder than either metal, and can be sharpened to make a cutting edge. It was used to create more powerful and long-lasting weapons, tools, and farm implements. Craftworkers also used it to make intricate castings – objects made by pouring melted bronze into a mould.

Handle at either end made vessel easier to carry

HOW WAS BRONZE FIRST MADE?

Bronze-workers heated copper and tin in a furnace fuelled by charcoal. When the two metals melted they combined to form liquid-hot bronze, which ran down a clay pipe into containers made of clay or sand. When cold, these ingots (solid blocks of metal) were re-melted and poured into different-shaped moulds.

▲ BRONZE ARCHER
This bronze statue was made in around 600 BC on the Mediterranean island of Sardinia. Bronze was also used to make sharp arrowheads, spear-tips, and sword blades.

WHO MADE THE FIRST BRONZE OBJECTS?

The technique of making bronze objects – by pouring molten (melted) metal into moulds – was invented in western Asia in around 3000 BC. It was also discovered, separately, in China in around 2000 BC. The Chinese bronze-makers developed their skills to create much more elaborate patterns and designs.

RITUAL VESSEL ▶
This bronze vessel was made while the Shang dynasty ruled China (1650–1027 BC). It was used for cooking ritual meals in honour of the spirits of dead ancestors.

Leg shape possibly derived from that of an animal

FIND OUT MORE ⏩ Alloys 174

MESOPOTAMIA

Mesopotamia is the land between the Tigris and Euphrates rivers. Farmers used the river water to irrigate fields and grow plentiful crops. Around 3500 BC, the Sumerians in southern Mesopotamia built the world's first cities, including Ur, Uruk, and Eridu.

HOW WERE THE SUMERIAN CITIES RULED?

Mighty kings, who commanded large armies, had strong cities, great palaces, and magnificent royal tombs made. The kings were assisted by priests and well-trained scribes, who collected taxes, controlled irrigation projects, and took charge of laws governing city crafts and trade. Priests also served the gods in ziggurats (temples).

Bull's head made of gold

HOW WERE THE ZIGGURATS BUILT?

Mesopotamian builders built ziggurats and houses from bricks made of mud mixed with chopped straw (left to dry and harden in the sun). Teams of workmen moved huge loads of bricks using sleds on wooden rollers, or carried smaller quantities in baskets on their backs. Mud was used as a mortar to bind the bricks.

Mesopotamia

▼ ZIGGURAT AT UR
Ziggurats were holy mountains, where people could get closer to the gods. The ziggurat at Ur (in modern Iraq) was built in around 2100 BC. Originally, it had three tall terraces (raised levels), one on top of the other, which were planted with trees and flowers. A shrine to Nanna, the Moon god, stood at the top. Today, only the temple's lower section survives.

▲ QUEEN'S TREASURE
This bull's head decorates a harp from the tomb of Queen Shub-ad of Ur, who died in around 2500 BC. The harp-player's skeleton was found close by, still holding the harp strings. She had been buried alive to entertain the queen in the afterlife.

FIND OUT MORE ▶▶ Ancient Religions 282 • Western Asia and the Middle East 264–265

INDUS VALLEY

Between around 3500 BC and 2000 BC, people in the Indus Valley built more than 100 towns. The largest were Mohenjo-Daro and Harappa, with populations of 40,000. These towns had large temples, granaries, brick-built houses, and streets laid out in neat grid patterns.

HOW DID THE PEOPLE OF THE INDUS VALLEY LIVE?

Farmers grew wheat, barley, cotton, and rice on land fertilized by yearly River Indus floods. They also raised animals. In towns, people made cloth, pottery, metalwork, and jewellery. On the coast, they went abroad to trade.

Indus Valley

CARVING OF ROYAL PRIEST ▶
This figure, carved from limestone in around 2500 BC, was found at Mohenjo-Daro.

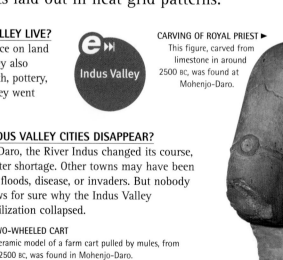

WHY DID INDUS VALLEY CITIES DISAPPEAR?

At Mohenjo-Daro, the River Indus changed its course, causing a water shortage. Other towns may have been destroyed by floods, disease, or invaders. But nobody knows for sure why the Indus Valley civilization collapsed.

◀ TWO-WHEELED CART
This ceramic model of a farm cart pulled by mules, from around 2500 BC, was found in Mohenjo-Daro.

FIND OUT MORE ▶▶ Western Asia and the Middle East 264–265

EGYPTIAN HIEROGLYPHS ▲
These hieroglyphs form part of the *Book of the Dead*, found inscribed on the walls of the tomb of Pharaoh Rameses VI (r.1156–1148 BC) in Egypt's Valley of the Kings.

FIRST SCRIPTS

Writing was invented in Mesopotamia, around 3400 BC. Cities had grown so big that people could no longer do business by keeping every detail in their heads. Rulers needed to keep track of who had paid their taxes, which craftworkers had been given rations, and how many goods they had made.

WHAT WERE EARLY FORMS OF WRITING LIKE?
The first writing was made up of pictograms – small pictures representing objects or expressing actions or ideas. These writing systems, which included ▶▶ CUNEIFORM , were complicated, and few people managed to learn them.

WHERE ELSE DID PEOPLE USE PICTOGRAMS?
Different forms of picture-writing developed in Egypt, China, and Meso (Middle) America. In the Indus Valley, scribes used pictures combined with symbols – a system that today's experts have still not explained.

e ▶▶
first scripts

Pattern of cracks on heated bone gave an answer to a question

ORACLE BONE ▶
In around 1500 BC, priests carved questions in Chinese characters on to bones.

CUNEIFORM

Cuneiform is the name given to the wedge-shaped script, written using trimmed reeds, developed by scribes in Sumer around 2900 BC. It was borrowed by other Middle Eastern peoples to write and develop their own languages, before the ▶▶ ALPHABET was developed.

CUNEIFORM SCRIPT ▲
This Mesopotamian clay tablet, made soon after 2900 BC, lists details of fields and crops. The cuneiform script is very neatly written, with wedge-shaped symbols formed in straight rows.

Smooth clay surface for writing on

Clear cuneiform marks left on clay

HOW WAS THE FIRST SCRIPT WRITTEN?
The first pictograms were scratched on to tablets of wet clay, using stalks from reeds that grew beside Mesopotamian rivers. The tablets were then dried in the sun to preserve the written text. Scribes (people trained to copy manuscripts) soon began to trim the reeds to make a triangular tip, which created clear, wedge-shaped marks.

ALPHABET

The world's first alphabet was invented in around 1000 BC by the Phoenicians, who lived in the eastern Mediterranean region. Unlike pictogram scripts, the alphabet used letters that stood for individual sounds.

WHY WAS THE FIRST ALPHABET SO IMPORTANT?
The Phoenicians discovered that letters could be put together in different combinations to spell almost all known words. Alphabetic writing needed fewer than 30 letters, compared with the 600 cuneiform symbols used by Sumerian scribes, or the 5,000 characters used by Chinese scholars. This made it much easier to learn, so literacy (reading and writing) became much more widespread in societies using alphabetic scripts.

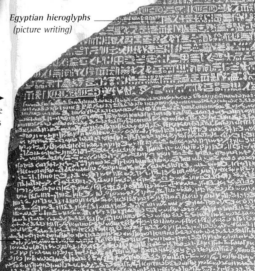

Egyptian hieroglyphs (picture writing)

ROSETTA STONE ▶
In 196 BC, Egyptian scribes carved the same text in three different scripts on this stone. It was discovered at Rosetta, Egypt, in AD 1799, and provided the key to translating Egyptian hieroglyphs.

Egyptian demotic (picture-based script used for writing quickly)

Ancient Greek (written using an alphabet)

FIND OUT MORE ▶▶ Ancient Egypt 370–371 • Writing 339

ANCIENT EGYPT

From around 3100 BC to 30 BC, the dry desert land of Egypt was home to an advanced civilization. The Ancient Egyptians produced massive ▸▸ PYRAMIDS, fabulous golden treasures, and wonderful works of art. They invented hieroglyphs, and were expert engineers.

Uraeus (cobra), symbol of Lower Egypt (in the north) _____

Vulture, symbol _____ *of Upper Egypt (in the south)*

Nemes _____ *headdress made of solid gold and bands of coloured (dark blue) glass paste*

WHY WERE NILE FLOODS IMPORTANT?
The River Nile flows through Egypt on its way to the sea. Every year, between June and October, it flooded the surrounding desert and covered the land with fertile silt (fine mud). Ancient Egyptian farmers were able to grow excellent crops on this land, including wheat, barley, grapes, figs, and many different types of vegetables.

◄ THRESHING WHEAT
These farm workers are threshing wheat to separate the ripe grains from the stalks. This picture decorated the walls of an Egyptian tomb built in around 1400 BC.

WHO DID THE EGYPTIANS WORSHIP?
The Egyptians worshipped hundreds of gods and goddesses. Gods like Osiris, ruler of the underworld, looked human. Others were shown as animals, such as the cat-goddess Bastet, who brought fertility. The most important was ram-headed Amun, king of the gods.

WHY DID EGYPTIAN CIVILIZATION LAST SO LONG?
Egypt became wealthy through farming and trade. Its power was built up by strong governments, led by ▸▸ PHARAOHS and staffed by well-trained scribes (officials). The nation was defended by huge armies.

Golden ball representing life-giving Sun pushed along by scarab

▲ SACRED SCARAB
This gold bracelet, from the tomb of Amenemope, is decorated with a scarab (dung beetle) made from blue lapis lazuli, a semi-precious stone. For the Egyptians, scarabs symbolized the life-giving Sun.

PHARAOHS

Ancient Egypt was ruled by powerful kings called pharaohs, who took the roles of chief priest, war-leader, and head of government. Egyptians believed that the pharaohs were living links between people and gods, and that they actually became gods after death.

WHAT DOES "PHARAOH" MEAN?
The name pharaoh came from two Egyptian words, *per-aa*, meaning "great house" or "palace". Later, the name for such a building was also used to refer to the king living there. It was used to show great respect.

e ▸▸
Ancient Egypt

FUNERAL BOAT ►
Model boats like this one were buried with the pharaohs in royal pyramid tombs.

Pharaoh's spirit carried through world of the dead

GOLDEN MASK ►
This portrait mask covered the face of the mummified body of Pharaoh Tutankhamen (r. 1336–1327 BC). The tomb of Tutankhamen was discovered in the Valley of the Kings, Egypt, in 1922.

PYRAMIDS

Massive stone tombs protected the bodies of dead pharaohs. These pyramids represented stairways leading to the sky. They took great skill to plan and build, and were designed to keep out robbers – but no pharaoh's ▶▶ MUMMY has ever been found inside one.

▲ PYRAMIDS AT GIZA
These pyramids were built in around 2500 BC for the pharaohs Khufu, Khafra, and Menkaura. They were originally covered in limestone and topped with gold. The tallest, the Great Pyramid, is 147 m (482 ft) high.

WHO BUILT THE PYRAMIDS?
The pyramids were constructed by teams of skilled professional builders, such as stone masons, who were paid very well for their work. During the flood season, when the River Nile washed over the farmlands, royal officials commanded peasant farmers to assist the professional workers in building the pyramids.

MUMMIFICATION

A mummy is a dead body that has been carefully preserved, or mummified. Workers removed organs that might rot, then dried the body with natron (salty crystals) and wrapped it in resin-soaked bandages.

WHY WERE PEOPLE MUMMIFIED AFTER DEATH?
Ancient Egyptians thought that people were made up of five elements. These elements were the body, its ka (spirit), ba (personality), name, and shadow. By preserving the body, the Egyptians believed that they could keep the other four elements alive. If the body decayed, to them the person would stay dead for ever.

MUMMY COFFIN ▶
This wood-and-plaster coffin protected the mummified body of a man who died around 700 BC. It is decorated with images of gods.

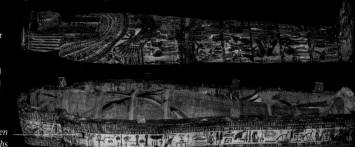

Collar *made up of gold and semi-precious stones*

Magic spells *written in hieroglyphs*

EGYPT'S HISTORY	
5500–3100 BC	Pre-Dynastic Period: before the time of the Pharaohs
3100–2686 BC	Early Dynastic Period: Upper and Lower Egypt are united – Menes becomes first pharaoh
2686–2181 BC	Old Kingdom: age of the pyramids
2181–2055 BC	First Intermediate Period: breakdown of centralized government
2055–1650 BC	Middle Kingdom: Egypt reunited
1650–1550 BC	Second Intermediate Period: invasion of Hyksos people, who are then defeated
1550–1069 BC	New Kingdom: Egypt at its greatest
1069–747 BC	Third Intermediate Period: breaks into small states
747–332 BC	Later Period: invaded by Assyrians, then Persians
332–30 BC	Ptolemaic Period: conquered by Alexander the Great and ruled by his general's family
30 BC–AD 395	Roman Period: Egypt part of Roman Empire

FIND OUT MORE ▶▶ Ancient Religions 282 • First Scripts 369 • North and West Africa 240–241

Bull, symbol of god Addad

Dragon, symbol of god Marduk

MIDDLE EASTERN EMPIRES

From around 2000 BC, rival peoples in the Middle East fought to either conquer or defend land. Some, like the ➤ BABYLONIANS and ➤ ASSYRIANS, were based in magnificent cities. Others, like the ➤ HITTITES and ➤ HEBREWS, arrived to settle and found new kingdoms.

WHY WAS THE MIDDLE EAST SUCH A RICH PRIZE?

Kings and peoples wanted to live in the Middle East because of its fertile farmland. The best land lay beside the Euphrates and Tigris rivers of Mesopotamia, but there were also fields, forests, and orchards in mountain valleys to the north and south. People also competed to control the long-distance trading routes that passed through the Middle East, linking Europe with Asia.

▲ CLAY MAP
Made by Babylonian scholars in around 600 BC, this was one of the first maps of the world.

BABYLONIANS

Babylon became powerful around 1792 BC, under King Hammurabi. From 1595 BC, its people came under the rule of invaders. In 625 BC, a general called Nabopolassar drove out the foreigners and became king. Under his son, King Nebuchadnezzar (r. 605–562 BC), a great new empire emerged.

HOW DID THE BABYLONIANS MEASURE TIME?

Babylonians built mud-brick monuments and used them as sundials. They observed stars and planets, predicted their movements, and compiled calendars. They based their calculations on units of 60 – which we still use today to measure minutes and seconds – and recorded all their findings in cuneiform writing.

KING HAMMURABI
r. 1792–1750 BC
King Hammurabi (pictured standing before the Sun god Shamash) conquered all of Mesopotamia to create a new kingdom, which was named after its chief city – Babylon. He introduced a strict code of law, and many crimes were punished by death. After he died, the empire weakened.

▲ ISHTAR GATE
This gateway, named after the Babylonians' goddess of love and war, was the main entrance to the city of Babylon from around 600 BC. It led to the Hanging Gardens of Babylon, built by King Nebuchadnezzar.

HITTITES

The Hittites were people who settled in Anatolia (now Turkey), in around 1700 BC. They could smelt iron, so they were able to make stronger weapons than their enemies. Around 1400 BC, Hittite city-states joined forces to create a powerful kingdom.

HOW DID THE HITTITES FIGHT THEIR WARS?

Fast, two-wheeled war chariots – pulled by horses – were first used by Hittite warriors around 1800 BC. Armed with bows and arrows, the charioteers would charge at ranks of enemy soldiers to scatter them. The Hittites also attacked enemy cities with the help of siege engines such as tall towers. The Hittites had two great enemies: the Ancient Egyptians and a war-like people from the state of Mitanni, in Mesopotamia.

◀ HITTITE GOD
This war-like god was carved on a gateway in the Hittite capital city of Bogazkoy (now in Turkey) in around 1300 BC.

Battle-axe raised to strike enemies

WHY DID HITTITE POWER COLLAPSE?

The Hittites and their enemies fought to win the eastern Mediterranean region, with its forests, farms, and rich trading ports. In around 1200 BC, the Hittites were also attacked by invaders from Mediterranean islands, known as Sea Peoples, and by nomad tribes from the east. These wars, plus famine, destroyed Hittite power.

HEBREWS

The Hebrews were shepherds and farmers in Canaan, at the eastern end of the Mediterranean Sea. Sea Peoples also settled there. Around 1020 BC, the Hebrews conquered these peoples and founded a powerful new kingdom, led by great kings. Saul was the first king. He was succeeded by David, and then Solomon.

WHERE WAS THE PROMISED LAND?

The Hebrews believed that God had promised them a home in Canaan. According to the Bible, the prophet Moses led them to this land in around 1200 BC. Later, in 922 BC, the Hebrew kingdom of Canaan divided into two separate nations – Israel in the north and Judah in the south. The people of Judah became known as Jews.

Hebrews' valuable farm animals also taken into captivity

Middle Eastern empires

Crown is symbol of power

Human head represents intelligence

◄ **HEBREW PRISONERS**
The Assyrians besieged the town of Lachish, in Judah, in 701 BC. This carving shows Jewish prisoners being led away by Assyria's King Sennacherib (r. 705–681 BC). The picture once decorated the king's palace in the Assyrian city of Nineveh.

Wings of an eagle, the most powerful creature in the sky

ASSYRIANS

The Assyrians lived in northern Mesopotamia. They grew crops in irrigated fields and built fine cities. From around 900 BC, they conquered an empire stretching from Egypt to the Persian Gulf. It collapsed when the Babylonians and Medes attacked in 612 BC.

Bull's legs and body symbolized strength

HOW DID THE ASSYRIANS FIGHT THEIR BATTLES?

The first Assyrian soldiers were farmers, who left their fields when called up to fight. But by around 740 BC, the Assyrian kings had developed fierce new armies made up of captured foreigners. They fought with swords, spears, bows and arrows, and battering rams. They demanded tributes of timber, metal, and horses from weaker peoples.

King Ashurnasirpal II

PRACTISING FOR WAR ►
This stone carving shows the Assyrian King Ashurnasirpal II and his soldiers practising combat skills by hunting lions. It comes from the king's palace at Nimrud.

Wheeled war chariot copied from Hittite armies

GATEWAY GUARDIAN ►
This is one of a pair of huge stone figures that adorned the gateway of the palace of Assyrian King Sargon II (r. 722–705 BC), at Khorsabad (now in Iraq). They represented the might of Assyria and guarded the palace.

FIND OUT MORE ►► Western Asia and the Middle East 264–265

MEDITERRANEAN SEAFARERS

From around 2000 BC, people living close to the Mediterranean Sea, such as the ⏵⏵ MINOANS, Mycenaeans, and ⏵⏵ PHOENICIANS, built strong wooden ships powered by sails and oars. They established long-distance sea routes linking Europe, Africa, and Asia, and became wealthy sea traders. Later, they sailed to explore and set up colonies.

WHAT MADE THE TRADERS SO PROSPEROUS?

Traders braved the stormy Mediterranean waters to earn as much as possible through overseas business. The most profitable cargoes included silver from Spain (used to make coins), tin from Britain, and copper from Cyprus. The tin and copper metals were smelted to make bronze. Phoenician cloth, coloured purple with a dye made from shellfish, was so expensive that only kings and queens could afford to buy it.

seafarers

Octopus design shows importance of the sea for food

◄ MYCENAEAN VASE
This jar, made between around 1400 BC and 1300 BC, was found in a Mycenaean trading settlement on the Greek island of Rhodes. Traders used pots like this one to carry goods such as olive oil. Scholars believe that the Mycenaeans took over the Minoans' sea trade.

MINOANS

From 2000 BC to 1450 BC, Minoan kings ruled the eastern Mediterranean area from the island of Crete. The kings grew rich by trading with other islands and demanding offerings from less powerful peoples. They lived in vast, elegantly decorated palaces.

WHY DID MINOAN POWER COLLAPSE?

In *c.* 1450 BC, the Mediterranean island of Thera (now Santorini) was destroyed by a volcanic eruption. At nearby Crete, sea levels rose, dust blotted out the Sun, and the Minoans' crops died out. Then, the palace at Knossos, Crete, was attacked by the Mycenaeans. By *c.* 1100 BC, the Minoan civilization had disappeared.

▲ BULL-LEAPING
This fresco (wall painting) from the palace at Knossos, Crete, shows the sport of bull-leaping. Young Minoans vaulted over the backs of charging bulls as part of a religious ceremony. Afterwards, the bull was sacrificed.

PHOENICIANS

The Phoenicians lived on the eastern shores of the Mediterranean Sea, and were powerful from around 1000 BC to 500 BC. They lived as farmers, foresters, and craftworkers who were highly skilled in woodworking, glass-making, and textile production.

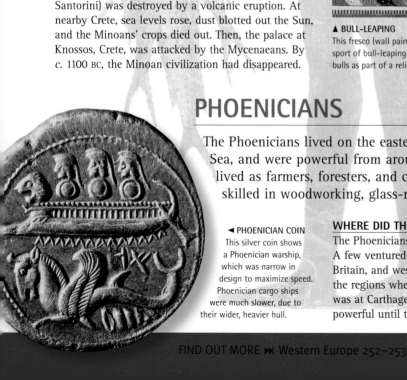

◄ PHOENICIAN COIN
This silver coin shows a Phoenician warship, which was narrow in design to maximize speed. Phoenician cargo ships were much slower, due to their wider, heavier hull.

WHERE DID THE PHOENICIANS TRAVEL TO TRADE?

The Phoenicians sailed all over the Mediterranean Sea. A few ventured further – to western Spain, southwest Britain, and western Africa – and built new cities in the regions where they traded. Their most famous city was at Carthage, in North Africa, which remained powerful until the Romans destroyed it in 146 BC.

FIND OUT MORE ⏵⏵ Western Europe 252–253

PERSIAN EMPIRE

From 539 BC to 331 BC, the Persian Empire was the most powerful state in the world. Ruled from Persia (now Iran), it stretched from Egypt to India. It had rich resources of water, fertile farmland, and gold. The Persians worshipped a fire god, Zoroaster.

▼ ROYAL PALACE
In 520 BC, King Darius gave orders for a magnificent new palace to be built at Persepolis, in Persia. He commanded leaders from all over the empire to bring tributes (forced gifts) to him there.

GOLDEN ARMLET ►
Persia was rich in gold. This armlet was found near the Oxus River, in modern Afghanistan.

Persians

Stairway carving of ambassadors from Media (north Iran) carrying tributes

HOW WAS THE PERSIAN EMPIRE GOVERNED?

Persian rulers claimed the proud title of "King of Kings" and demanded total obedience from their subjects. Under King Darius, the empire was divided into 20 provinces to try and stop any single region from becoming too powerful. Each province was ruled by a governor, called a ►► SATRAP.

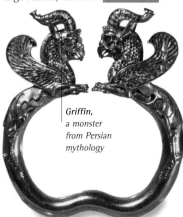

Griffin, a monster from Persian mythology

WHAT WAS THE ROYAL ROAD?

This was the longest highway in the Persian Empire. It ran for more than 2,500 km (1,550 miles) – from Sardis, in western Turkey, to the empire's capital, Susa, near the Persian Gulf. A giant network of roads linked the empire's provinces. Messengers travelled on horseback to deliver urgent royal commands or news, while merchants used camel trains to transport goods.

KING DARIUS I
r. 522–486 BC

Known as Darius the Great, Darius I reorganized the Persian government, won great victories in Turkey, and led an invasion of Greece. But his army was defeated by Greek soldiers at the famous battle of Marathon in 490 BC. This started a long-lasting war with the Greeks that eventually brought down the Persian Empire.

SATRAPS

Satraps were local rulers appointed by the king to govern individual provinces. Their job was to enforce law and order, and to collect taxes and tributes. They worked with Persia's army commanders to defend the empire's frontiers from enemy attack.

COULD THE SATRAPS BE TRUSTED?

Persian kings did not trust the satraps. They employed special spies, known as "the king's ears", to make sure that the satraps were not stealing taxes and tributes. But some satraps did become powerful, and plotted against the king. Some joined up with enemies of the empire, such as Alexander the Great – the Greek leader who conquered the Persian Empire in 331 BC.

FIND OUT MORE ►► Western Asia and the Middle East 264–265

ANCIENT GREECE

Greece was home to a rich civilization that reached its peak between 500 BC and 300 BC. Its people lived by farming, fishing, crafts, and trading. They built 300 ►► CITY-STATES and settled in colonies. In 146 BC, Greece was conquered by Rome, but many aspects of Greek culture still shape our world.

WHAT DO WE KNOW ABOUT MYCENAEAN KINGS?

Mycenaean kings were powerful from 1600 BC to 1200 BC. They were warrior chieftains who lived in fortress-like cities and ruled small kingdoms. Their name comes from the richest of these – Mycenae, in southern Greece. They employed skilled artists and craftworkers to make fine pottery and magnificent gold jewellery. They owned fleets of trading ships that sailed to many ports.

▲ LION GATE, MYCENAE
This gate, built in c. 1550–1100 BC, formed part of a fortress-like wall that surrounded the ancient city of Mycenae. Mycenae was the centre of the richest and most important kingdom of its time.

Ancient Greece

Gold decoration depicts lion hunt

▲ BRONZE DAGGER BLADE
This blade, made in around 1500 BC, was found in a tomb in Mycenae. Mycenaean kings were often buried along with their weapons, and dressed in their finest jewellery.

Hunters armed with spears and shields

Columns are 11 m (35 ft) tall and made of Parian marble

Scaffolding in place for renovation

WHO DID THE ANCIENT GREEKS WORSHIP?

The Ancient Greeks worshipped many different gods and goddesses. They believed that these gods had magic powers and that they were human in form, but bigger and more beautiful. Each god or goddess controlled a different aspect of life. The supreme god Zeus led all other gods. His brother Poseidon ruled the sea, and another brother, Hades, ruled the underworld.

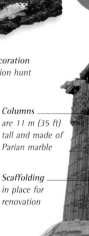

◄ SACRIFICE TO THE GODS
This marble carving is part of a frieze that decorated the Parthenon temple in Athens. It features Athenians leading a bull to be sacrificed to the goddess Athena. The Greeks regularly offered their gods and goddesses gifts of food, drink, and flowers as sacrifices. They hoped for help in return.

Bull being led to a temple for sacrifice

WHAT WERE ANCIENT GREEK PLAYS ABOUT?

Greek tragedies and comedies re-told stories about gods and goddesses, or made fun of people such as politicians. Only men watched the plays. They thought women would find them too rude or upsetting. The plays of Sophocles, Aeschylus, and Euripides are still performed today.

AMPHITHEATRE ►
This semi-circular theatre was built at Epidaurus, southern Greece, in c. 350 BC. Greek actors (all male) wore masks to portray different characters, and recited their words to music. A chorus of junior actors sang, danced, and commented on the action.

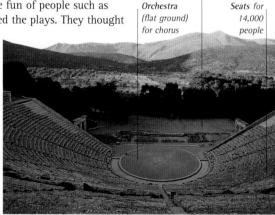

Stage

Orchestra (flat ground) for chorus

Seats for 14,000 people

▼ THE PARTHENON

Temples were homes for the gods and goddesses, and status symbols for cities. The Parthenon, Athens, was built in c. 480 BC, when Greek architecture was at its peak. It is one of the world's most famous buildings and was made from 22,000 tonnes (21,650 tons) of marble. This temple was dedicated to the goddess Athena. Inside stood a 12-m- (40-ft-) tall carved statue of Athena, with solid gold armour.

Frieze shows birth of Athena, and her battle with Poseidon over the Attica region

ALEXANDER THE GREAT
356–323 BC

Alexander was ruler of Macedon, north of Greece. As a young man he conquered many lands, including some of the Greek city-states. When he died, his vast empire stretched from Egypt to Pakistan.

WHY DID THE GREEKS VALUE SPORT?

Sport was good training for war, but city-states also organized sports competitions to form part of their religious festivals. The most famous was the Olympic Games, held every four years to honour the god Zeus. Competitors came from all over Greece. Victorious athletes won praise for themselves, and prestige for their families and towns.

GREEK DISCUS THROWER ▶

Greek artists often used top athletes as models. This statue, c. 450 BC, depicts a discus thrower. Discus throwing was an early Olympic sport.

CITY-STATES

A city-state was made up of a town and all the land near to it. Each one had its own government, laws, and way of life. City-states often fought each other, using troops of ▶▶ **HOPLITES** and huge warships.

HOW DID ATHENIAN DEMOCRACY WORK?

In Athens, all adult male citizens could listen to debates in the Assembly, which met on most days. Here, they could elect and expel city leaders, and vote to decide on government policies. Women, slaves, and foreigners were not able to vote. Three of the world's most famous philosophers – Socrates, Plato, and Aristotle – lived and taught in Athens.

◀ ATHENIAN COIN

This picture of an owl symbolizes Athena, the goddess of wisdom and guardian of Athens. Ancient Greek coins also showed many different local products or gods.

Olives and olive oil were valuable Greek exports

HOPLITES

Hoplites were trained foot-soldiers, who fought for their city-states using swords and spears. Their name came from the round hoplon (shield) that they carried for protection in battle. They also wore helmets, body armour, and plated greaves (shin guards).

HOW DID THE ANCIENT GREEKS FIGHT?

The Greeks used a battle formation called the phalanx. Soldiers stood side by side in rows, overlapping their shields to make a solid wall of defence as they advanced towards the enemy. Their commanders rode in horse-drawn chariots to overlook the battlefield. City-states also hired foreign experts, such as archers from Scythia, and used warships called triremes.

HOPLITES IN CLOSE COMBAT ▶

This picture of hoplites in combat appears on a pottery vase made at Athens in around 530 BC. Only men from wealthy families could be hoplites. Poor men could not afford the weapons and armour.

Soldier dead on battlefield

FIND OUT MORE ▶▶ Ancient Rome 382–383 • Southeast Europe 256–257

CHINA'S FIRST EMPIRE

China was a collection of kingdoms ruled by rival dynasties (powerful families) until 221 BC, when one king conquered the others and became the first emperor. The name "China" comes from his title, Qin Shi Huangdi, which means "first emperor of Qin".

China's first empire

HOW DID THE FIRST EMPEROR UNITE CHINA?
Qin Shi Huangdi defeated his rivals and united China with the help of armies of soldiers like the ▶▶ TERRACOTTA WARRIORS who guard his tomb. China was also united by new laws enforcing the same system of writing, weighing, and measuring.

HOW DID CHINA FEED ITS PEOPLE?
In north China, farmers cut terraces on steep hillsides, to grow millet and wheat. In south China, they dug irrigation ditches and invented machines to carry water from rivers, to grow rice in flooded fields. By AD 2, the Chinese population numbered 57 million.

▲ MODEL RIVER BOAT
This earthenware model of a sampan (river boat) is an artefact from an ancient Chinese tomb. For centuries, boats like this travelled along China's two great natural waterways, the Yellow and Yangtze rivers.

WHAT WAS CHINA'S BEST–KEPT SECRET?
Around 2500 BC, Chinese farmers discovered how to rear silkworms and unwind the fine thread of their cocoons. Women wove the thread into shimmering fabric, and coloured it with brilliant dyes. To preserve the value of silk, the Chinese government tried to keep the processes involved in making it a secret.

▲ STANDARD WEIGHT
Weights like this were used by officials in the vast civil service set up by the Han dynasty, which ruled China after the Qin dynasty.

▲ BURIAL BANNER
This silk banner is from the tomb of Lady Dai of the Han dynasty, who died around 160 BC. It is said to show her journey to heaven.

Real gold wire joined the jade pieces together

Over 2,000 pieces of precious jade

◀ FUNERAL SUIT
A princess of the Han dynasty was buried in this suit, which took 10 years to make. Jade was thought to have magical qualities that would preserve bodies after death.

TERRACOTTA WARRIORS

When Qin Shi Huangdi died in 210 BC, his body was buried with over 7,000 life-size warriors made of terracotta (baked clay). There were also foot-soldiers, horses, and chariots. The underground tomb took 700,000 slave labourers 36 years to build.

WHY WERE THE WARRIORS MADE?
The terracotta warriors were designed to guard the emperor's body, and serve his spirit in life after death. The tomb entrance was defended by crossbows, set to fire automatically if robbers broke in. The Chinese buried all important people with food and drink, and killed servants to care for them.

Jade is carefully cut so pieces fit together

▲ TERRACOTTA GUARDS
Each clay soldier guarding Qin Shi Huangdi's tomb has an individual face, possibly copied from real members of the emperor's army. They all stand facing east in 11 rows, stretching for more than 200 m (656 ft).

FIND OUT MORE ▶▶ Imperial China 393 • Revolutionary China 429

MAURYAN INDIA

The Maurya dynasty ruled India from 322 BC to 185 BC. Its greatest king was Ashoka (273–232 BC). He began his reign as a warrior but after becoming a Buddhist he tried to pursue peaceful policies.

WHAT WERE THE CITIES OF MAURYAN INDIA LIKE?
Mauryan cities were defended by steep banks of earth and timber walls. At Ashoka's capital, Pataliputra (near modern Patna), they stretched for 14 km (9 miles). Inside were temples, reservoirs, palaces, store-houses, and workers' houses.

HOW DID ASHOKA SPREAD BUDDHISM?
Ashoka set up tall stone pillars in important places, carved with Buddhist teachings and his own promises to rule well. He tried to make peace between different peoples in his empire, but after he died the empire split into smaller states, until a new empire emerged under the Guptas.

Stupa

North gate
carved with
guardian spirits
and scenes from
Buddhist legends

Mauryan India (e ▸▸)

LION PILLAR ▶
These lions stand at the top of the first carved pillar set up by Ashoka, at Sarnath, in north India. A wheel at each lion's feet symbolizes Buddhist teachings.

GREAT STUPA AT SANCHI ▲
Ashoka encouraged his subjects to build stupas (domed monuments), like this one in central India, as reminders of the Buddhist faith.

FIND OUT MORE ▸▸ Buddhism 289 • Mughal India 407

GUPTA INDIA

The Gupta dynasty was founded by the Hindu king Chandragupta I in AD 320. From their home in northeast India, the Gupta kings won control of a large empire, which lasted for more than 200 years.

WHY IS GUPTA INDIA CALLED A GOLDEN AGE?
The art, architecture, science, music, literature, and dance of northern India flourished under the generous and tolerant Gupta kings. Gupta mathematicians developed the number system used all over the world today, and invented the concept of zero.

WHAT IS THE MAHABHARATA?
The Mahabharata, or "Great Epic of India", is the world's longest poem. It tells the story of five Hindu princes who lose their kingdom and struggle to win it back. Written in Sanskrit, it is one of the most important works of Hindu literature.

Headdress
with skull,
sign of death

Trident,
symbol of
Shiva's
destructive
power

Nandi, a
white bull,
symbol of
fertility

◀ SHIVA IN STONE
Fine sculptures, such as this statue of the Hindu god Shiva, were created during the golden age of the Guptas.

Gupta India (e ▸▸)

▲ CAVE MONKEY
Gupta artists decorated the walls of Buddhist temples in caves at Ajanta. They painted pictures of Indian animals and plants.

FIND OUT MORE ▸▸ Age of Empire 422–423 • Hinduism 286 • Mughal India 407

EARLY AMERICANS

The first Americans crossed the land bridge that linked Siberia with Alaska during the last Ice Age. Gradually, they spread through the continent. By around 8000 BC there were people in almost every part of the Americas.

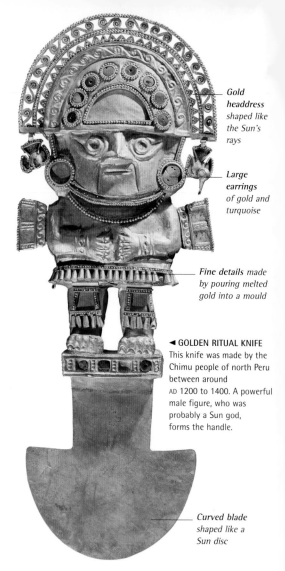

Gold headdress shaped like the Sun's rays

Large earrings of gold and turquoise

Fine details made by pouring melted gold into a mould

◀ GOLDEN RITUAL KNIFE
This knife was made by the Chimu people of north Peru between around AD 1200 to 1400. A powerful male figure, who was probably a Sun god, forms the handle.

Curved blade shaped like a Sun disc

HOW DID EARLY AMERICANS LIVE?
The first Americans were hunters, gatherers, and fishermen, and this way of life continued in tropical rainforests and cold northern woods. Other peoples became farmers. In the Andes of South America they grew potatoes and herded llama. In fertile river valleys, ▶▶ MOUND BUILDERS grew corn (maize), beans, and squash. In semi-deserts, the ▶▶ PUEBLO people farmed irrigated fields.

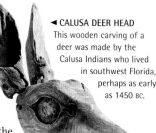

◀ CALUSA DEER HEAD
This wooden carving of a deer was made by the Calusa Indians who lived in southwest Florida, perhaps as early as 1450 BC.

HOW DID EARLY AMERICANS HONOUR THEIR GODS?
The rituals of early Americans were closely connected with persuading the gods, or spirits, to continue to provide sunshine and rain. With gifts of blood and food, and sacrifices of animals and young people, they honoured the gods on whom life depended.

◀ BURIAL OFFERING
This clay bowl from the Mimbres Valley, Arizona, was made around AD 1000. It has been pierced to ward off spirits.

WHICH METALS DID EARLY AMERICANS TREASURE?
Around 1500 BC, craftworkers in South America discovered how to shape nuggets of gold, silver, and copper by hammering them, stretching them into wire, or melting them and casting them in moulds. They crafted jewellery, ritual objects, and images of gods.

PUEBLOS

From around AD 800, in parts of southwest North America, rooms were stacked on top of each other to make villages called pueblos. People living in these apartments also became known as Pueblos.

◀ CLIFF DWELLING
The Mesa Verde pueblo, Colorado, was built in the alcove of a cliff. Pueblos were made of adobe (sun-dried mud bricks) and stone. They were abandoned, probably because of drought, by AD 1400.

HOW MANY PEOPLE LIVED IN A PUEBLO?
Some pueblos, like that at Pueblo Bonito, in New Mexico, may have had as many as 650 rooms, and more than 30 ceremonial chambers (kivas). Each room could house a whole family, so the population of a pueblo could have been well over 3,000.

MOUND BUILDERS

Between 700 BC and AD 550, Adena and Hopewell peoples in the Ohio Valley built huge earth mounds. Some were meeting places for long-distance traders. Others were holy monuments or tombs.

WHERE WERE NORTH AMERICA'S FIRST CITIES?
Around AD 800, mound builders by the River Mississippi also began to build cities. The largest was Cahokia, near St Louis. It covered almost 16 sq km (6 sq miles) and had over 120 earth mounds. About 10,000 people lived there by 1200.

e ▶▶ early Americans

Dead king and servants were buried deep inside

Royal palace and temple stood on top of the mound

CAHOKIA MOUNDS ▶
A king was buried under this mound at Cahokia, together with 300 young women killed to serve him in the afterlife.

FIND OUT MORE ▶▶ American Indians 408 • Indian Wars 417

MAYA

The Maya lived in Central America and were powerful from around AD 250 to 900. Farmers and traders, they built spectacular cities and developed a system of writing that used picture symbols called ▶▶ GLYPHS .

WHO RULED MAYAN KINGDOMS?

The Maya were divided into kingdoms, each of which had a city and a ruler, who acted as war-leader, law-maker, and chief priest. After 900 Mayan civilization declined, possibly because their farming methods led to exhausted fields and failing crops.

RAIN GOD ▶
This is a statue of Chac, the Mayan god of rain, who made all living things grow. According to myth, Chac broke open a giant rock to uncover the first corn (maize) plant.

In his left hand Chac carries a ceremonial bowl – in his right hand Chac has a ball of smoking incense

WHY DID THE MAYA BUILD PYRAMIDS?

Pyramids were the largest buildings in Mayan cities and were built as temples and royal tombs. Shrines where sacrifices were made to the gods were at the top, while burial chambers were hidden deep inside. The pyramids were built of stone, and covered with red-painted plaster, but this plaster has not survived.

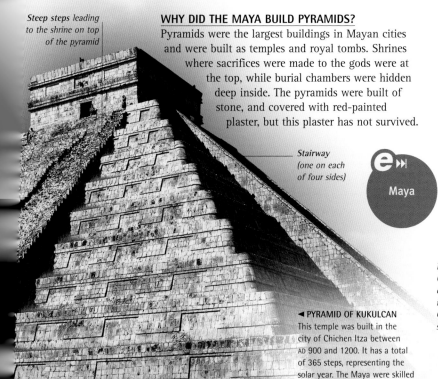

Steep steps leading to the shrine on top of the pyramid

Stairway (one on each of four sides)

e ▶▶ Maya

◀ PYRAMID OF KUKULCAN
This temple was built in the city of Chichen Itza between AD 900 and 1200. It has a total of 365 steps, representing the solar year. The Maya were skilled astronomers and mathematicians.

MAYAN GLYPHS

Mayan glyphs were painted on walls and pots, and carved into pieces of jade and monuments of stone. They were also written into books called codices, which were made out of long strips of bark paper that folded up like screens. This complex writing system was controlled by scribes of very high rank.

WHEN WAS THE RIDDLE OF THE GLYPHS SOLVED?

The study of Mayan hieroglyphs began 200 years ago. By the 1950s, scholars had worked out the glyphs for the names of rulers and animals. Then, in 1960, it became clear that most Mayan inscriptions are historical. They record important events, such as the births, marriages and deaths, and the victories in battle, of the god-like Mayan kings.

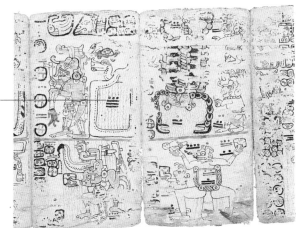

Glyphs stood for names, objects, or ideas

CALENDAR OF PREDICTIONS ▶
Four Mayan codices have survived. This codex was compiled between AD 1300 and AD 1400. It contains information that enabled priests to predict lucky and unlucky dates.

FIND OUT MORE ▶▶ Aztecs 403 • Conquistadors 405 • Incas 402

ANCIENT ROME

Rome began, around 1000 BC, as a settlement of farmers and shepherds in central Italy. Over the course of the next thousand years, it developed into a powerful city-state, and became the capital of an empire that stretched from Britain in the north to Arabia in the southwest.

MORTAL COMBAT ▶
In this Roman mosaic, made around AD 300, a gladiator tackles a leopard. Gladiators were mostly slaves or criminals who had been trained in special schools.

HOW DID ROME EXPAND?
Gradually, the Roman Republic conquered its neighbours until, by 260 BC, it controlled all of Italy. Next, the Romans defeated the Carthaginians, which by 100 BC gave Rome control of the Mediterranean. At the heart of the government of this expanding Roman Republic were the politicians called ▶▶ SENATORS .

WHAT WAS THE RELIGION OF ANCIENT ROME?
Jupiter, Minerva, Vesta, and Mars were among the chief gods and goddesses of ancient Rome. On special occasions animals were sacrificed to them in temples. Before going into battle, for example, a public sacrifice would be made to Mars, the god of war. Throughout the empire a wide range of non-Roman religions were tolerated, so long as they did not disrespect official Roman gods and the ▶▶ EMPERORS .

COLOSSEUM RUINS ▼
Opened by Emperor Titus in AD 80, the Colosseum was the largest amphitheatre in Rome. For the blood-thirsty "games" staged here, gladiators and animals were imported from every corner of the empire.

▲ ROMAN WOMEN
The grand ladies depicted in this Pompeii wall painting are having their hair dressed by skilled slaves. First and foremost, Roman women were expected to be mothers, but rich widows had some freedom.

HOW WERE ROMAN SOLDIERS RECRUITED?
In the early days of Rome every citizen had to be prepared to fight, but soldiers of the Roman imperial army were paid, highly trained professionals who signed on for 20-25 years of service. The ordinary foot-soldier was equipped with a short sword, two javelins, and a heavy shield of leather and wood. When he wasn't at war, he was building forts and roads.

SENATORS

The Roman Republic was ruled by the Senate, the council of noblemen that controlled all the top jobs in the government and army. After 27 BC, when the Roman Republic was replaced by the Roman Empire, the Senate continued to play an important part in politics.

e▶▶ Ancient Rome

WHY WAS JULIUS CAESAR MURDERED?
In 44 BC, five years after he had become the sole ruler of Rome, Julius Caesar was murdered in the Senate building. His assassins were a group of senators who thought he had become too powerful. They also resented the fact that Julius Caesar had rewarded hundreds of his supporters by making them senators. As a result, the Senate, which for most of its history had between 300 and 600 members, was packed with 900 senators.

◀ BRONZE COIN FEATURING JULIUS CAESAR
The profile on this coin is evidence of Julius Caesar's haughty style. He was much too king-like for the proud Roman senators.

FIND OUT MORE ▶▶ Age of Migrations 384 • Byzantine Empire 385

EMPERORS

After Julius Caesar's death, Rome was divided by civil wars. By 27 BC, his adopted son Octavian was master of the Roman world. Under the title Augustus, which means "revered" in Latin, he became the first Roman emperor. His reign brought peace and prosperity to a war-weary world.

WHY DID ROMANS GET BREAD AND CIRCUSES?

Rome was the largest city in the world. By AD 300, it had a million inhabitants, many of whom were hungry and unemployed. To stop them from rioting they were given "bread and circuses". The "bread" was the regular ration of grain issued to Roman citizens and the "circuses" were the free entertainments and chariot races provided by politicians and emperors.

Canvas stretched over the top provided shade

STATUE OF FIRST EMPEROR ▲
Augustus reigned for nearly 50 years. He reorganized coins, laws, and taxation, and transformed the Roman army into a peace-keeping force, designed to protect the empire's expanding frontiers.

Stone and concrete made strong walls

Statues would have stood in arches

CELTS

The tribespeople who lived in western Europe before the Roman conquest were called Celts. Each tribe was made up of three main classes – druids, warriors, and farmers – and the largest settlements were hilltop forts.

GOLD TORC ▶
The Celts were skilled metalworkers. Weapons and tools were made of iron but this torc (neck ring), found in Britain, was made from twisted strands of gold wire.

WHAT WERE CELTIC WARRIORS FAMOUS FOR?

Celtic warriors were famous for their love of feasting, fighting, and jewellery. They daubed their faces with a blue war paint made from woad (plant that produces a blue dye) and yelled at the tops of their voices as they rode into battle. But the terrible look and sound of a Celtic army was no match for the discipline of highly trained Roman legions.

e ⏭
Celts

WHO WERE THE DRUIDS?

After studying everything from herbalism to astronomy for up to 20 years, druids served Celtic society as priests and judges. At sacred pools, or groves of oak trees, they led religious rites that sometimes involved human sacrifice. Unlike most Celts, many druids could read and write.

▲ DUN AENGUS CELTIC FORT, IRELAND
Celtic tribes fought each other, and also battled against invaders. As refuges for themselves and their cattle, they built forts on easily defended sites such as hilltops, and cliffs by the sea.

FIND OUT MORE ⏭ First Metalworkers 367 • Holy Roman Empire 385

AGE OF MIGRATIONS

In AD 285 the Roman Empire divided into eastern and western parts, each with its own emperor. Despite this re-organization, by around AD 400 the western empire could no longer hold out against waves of invading barbarian tribes from northeastern Europe. In 410, Rome itself was attacked.

Hun warriors practically lived in the saddle

▲ ATTILA THE HUN
This bronze plaque of a nomad warrior on horseback was found in Switzerland. It may represent Attila, the brilliant but ruthless leader of the Hun army.

e ▸▸
migrations

WHO WERE THE BARBARIANS?
For the Romans, the Germanic tribes moving across the empire were destructive, disorderly "barbarians". Over time, these migrant peoples did settle down, eventually giving their names to their new homelands: the Franks in France, the ▸▸ ANGLES AND SAXONS in England, the Lombards in northern Italy, and so on.

WHO WERE THE HUNS?
The Huns were a nomadic people from today's Turkestan. Mounted on swift ponies, and armed with bows and arrows, Hun armies rode deep into the Roman Empire in search of plunder. They were not interested in conquering land.

BARBARIAN ATTACKS	
AD 235	Germanic tribes start to invade
410	Visigoths capture Rome
435	Vandals take Roman North Africa
451	Hun invasions
455	Vandals destroy Rome
476	Last western emperor deposed

Strong iron base, decorated with gold, silver, and garnets

Bird of prey – its outstretched wings protect the wearer's brow

Side-pieces protect ears

◄ KING'S HELMET
This helmet was found in a ship grave at Sutton Hoo, in eastern England. It probably belonged to Raedwald, a powerful Anglo-Saxon king who died around 625. His grave treasures also included a sword, shield, gold coins, and silverware.

ANGLES AND SAXONS

Angles and Saxons, who were later known as Anglo-Saxons, lived along the North Sea coast. They began to raid Britain while it was under Roman rule. After 410, when the Roman army left, they arrived in larger numbers to settle, and gradually took over much of eastern Britain.

WHO WAS BURIED IN SHIPS?
The Angles and Saxons were pagan, seafaring people and ships played an important part in their culture. They believed that boats could ferry a dead person's spirit to the next world. People who had been wealthy when they were alive were buried in ships, together with the comforts and treasures they were expected to enjoy in the next world. Poorer Anglo-Saxons were sometimes buried with a few ship's planks.

WHY DID ANGLES AND SAXONS MOVE TO BRITAIN?
Around 200, the climate became warmer and sea levels rose, which made life more difficult for the Angles and Saxons living by the North Sea coast. At the same time, they were being squeezed by other westward-moving Germanic peoples. Some of the first Anglo-Saxons in Britain may have been soldiers, hired to protect villages against other raiders.

FIND OUT MORE ▸▸ Ancient Rome 382 • Normans 389

BYZANTINE EMPIRE

In AD 324 the emperor Constantine reunited the Roman Empire. By then Rome was too difficult to defend against barbarian attacks, so he moved his capital east to Byzantium, renaming it ▶▶ CONSTANTINOPLE.

▲ POPE AND PATRIARCH
In 1054, the Church in the west, led by the Pope, separated from the Church in the east, led by the Patriarch of Constantinople. The eastern, Orthodox Church used Greek rather than Latin.

WHO RULED THE BYZANTINE EMPIRE?
From Constantinople (now Istanbul), Constantine ruled over the entire Roman world, but eventually the empire split again. In 476, the western Roman empire was swept away. However, the eastern empire, which is called the Byzantine Empire, endured until 1453, when it was conquered by the Ottoman Empire.

CONSTANTINOPLE

In 330, Constantinople was proclaimed capital of the Roman Empire. The new city's splendid public buildings, which included a forum, were adorned with treasures from all over the empire.

WHY WAS CONSTANTINOPLE SO PROSPEROUS?
Constantinople was a meeting point for long-distance trade routes linking Europe, Asia, and the Middle East. Merchants brought silks from China, pearls and perfumes from Arabia, spices from southeast Asia, and fine wool and furs from Europe to sell in its markets.

e ▶▶ Byzantine Empire

BYZANTINE ART ▲
This mosaic shows Christ washing the feet of his disciples. It is in the Hosios Loukas Monastery in Boeotia, Greece, which was built in the early 11th century. Christianity was central to Byzantine life and the chief purpose of art and architecture was to glorify God.

FIND OUT MORE ▶▶ Christianity 288 • Ottoman Empire 397

HOLY ROMAN EMPIRE

On Christmas Day, AD 800, Charlemagne, the King of the Franks, was crowned Holy Roman Emperor by the Pope. Under Charlemagne, much of western Europe was ruled as one vast country, but within 40 years of his death, in 814, the Holy Roman Empire had fragmented.

WHY WAS THE EMPIRE FOUNDED?
Charlemagne was a brilliant leader and his kingdom stretched from the North Sea to Italy. As Holy Roman Emperor, he was expected to rule Europe like a Roman emperor, but with a new responsibility for the safety and prosperity of the Church and the Pope.

e ▶▶ Holy Roman Empire

HOW DID CHARLEMAGNE WORK WITH SCHOLARS?
Charlemagne was a great patron of learning, inviting the most famous scholars of the day to his main court at Aachen. His advisers and friends included Peter of Pisa, Agobard of Lyons, and Alcuin of York. Under Charlemagne, rare manuscripts were collected, the text of the Bible was revised, and grammars, history books, and ballads were published.

WHAT HAPPENED TO THE TITLE?
By 843 Charlemagne's empire had split into three kingdoms, each of which was ruled by a member of his family. Following Charlemagne, there was no Holy Roman Emperor until Otto I was crowned in 962. After 1438, all but one of the holders of the prestigious title were Habsburg monarchs. In 1806 Napoleon abolished the title.

STAINED-GLASS WINDOW ▲
At Chartres Cathedral, France, Charlemagne is shown with Constantine (right).

FIND OUT MORE ▶▶ Medieval Europe 390–391 • Napoleonic Wars 416

ISLAMIC CIVILIZATION

In AD 610, an Arab merchant called Muhammad founded a new religion called Islam. His teachings inspired the Arab peoples and by AD 750 Muslims (followers of Islam) had conquered an area stretching from Afghanistan to ▶▶ AL ANDALUS in southern Spain. Trade, science, and culture thrived in this Islamic empire.

e ▶▶
Islamic
civilization

WHAT WAS LIFE LIKE IN MUSLIM LANDS?

Newly conquered lands were united by Islam, and by common tax systems, coinage, and laws. Jews and Christians sometimes paid higher taxes but they were free to run their own religious affairs so long as they did not insult the Prophet Muhammad.

HOW DID ISLAM SPREAD SO QUICKLY?

Islam brought a new sense of unity and purpose to the traders and tribespeople of the Arabian Peninsula. Led by the ▶▶ CALIPH , Arab armies spread Islam in the Middle East and beyond. It helped that their main enemies, the Sassanids in Iran and the Byzantines in eastern Europe, were weakened by fighting each other. Islam was also spread by Muslim traders.

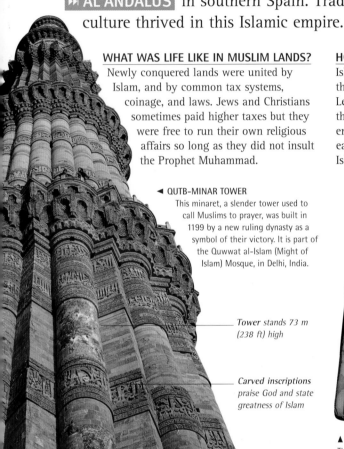

◀ QUTB-MINAR TOWER
This minaret, a slender tower used to call Muslims to prayer, was built in 1199 by a new ruling dynasty as a symbol of their victory. It is part of the Quwwat al-Islam (Might of Islam) Mosque, in Delhi, India.

Tower stands 73 m (238 ft) high

Carved inscriptions praise God and state greatness of Islam

Maps show the position of stars at night

Stars forming the constellations are shown in red

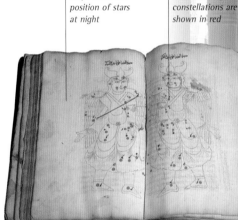

▲ THE BOOK OF THE FIXED STARS
This guide to the constellations was compiled by a famous Arab astronomer, Abd al-Rahman ibn Umar al-Sufi, in the 10th century. Arabic names for stars are still used today.

CALIPHS

After the death of Muhammad in 632 Muslims were ruled by caliphs. As Islam spread, the caliphs had great political as well as spiritual authority. In the reign of the fourth caliph, from 656 to 661, two rival traditions of Islam emerged: the Sunni and the Shi'a. This division meant it was no longer possible for the whole Islamic world to be ruled by a single caliph.

WHO WERE THE UMAYYADS AND THE ABBASIDS?

The Umayyads and Abbasids were dynasties of caliphs. From 661, Islam was ruled by the Umayyads, based in Damascus (in Syria). In 750, a new dynasty, the Abbasid, seized power, although a branch of the Umayyad continued to rule Muslim Spain. The Abbasid caliphs were based at Baghdad, which became the prosperous centre of a huge trading empire and the artistic capital of the Muslim world.

HARUN AND THE BARBER ▶
Harun-al-Rashid was the most famous Abbasid caliph. His court at Baghdad inspired many classic tales. This miniature painting illustrates a story in which Harun notices that his barber never moves from one spot. He has the floor removed and finds treasure beneath it.

Delicate plaster, carved in Muslim geometric patterns

Roof supported by 124 columns of white marble

Cooling fountain at centre of courtyard

◄ THE COURT OF THE LIONS
The Court of the Lions, part of the Alhambra palace, which was built in 1238–1354 for the ruling family of Granada, the last Moorish kingdom in Spain. The central water basin is surrounded by 12 stone lions, each fitted with a water spout. Soothing, cooling water was an essential ingredient of Islamic architecture.

AL ANDALUS

Muslim armies conquered southern Spain in 711. They called it Al Andalus and it became the richest country in Europe. The Muslims, or Moors as they are sometimes called, brought new crops, such as oranges, almonds, and cotton, and new technology, such as water wheels. In 1492, Granada, which was the last surviving Islamic kingdom in Spain, fell to Christian rulers.

HOW DID AL ANDALUS LINK EAST AND WEST?
During the 10th century reign of Abd al-Rahman, Cordoba was the capital of Al Andalus. With its lavishly endowed libraries, it was a magnet for scholars and acted as the door through which the science of the East reached Christian scholars in western Europe. After 1031, when the ruling dynasty changed, Cordoba's golden age ended. In 1236 it was reconquered by Christian Spanish forces.

WHERE DID MUSLIMS TRAVEL?
Muslim pilgrims, traders, soldiers, scholars, and government officials made long journeys across the Islamic empire, and beyond. One of the most famous explorers, Ibn Battuta, set out on a pilgrimage to Mecca in 1325. He spent the next 25 years travelling, crossing the Sahara, and even reaching China before returning to Morocco to write his story.

▲ RIDING THE MONSOON
For voyages of exploration and trade, Arab sailors used boats called dhows, which can be handled by a small crew. The voyages of real sailors inspired the imaginary adventures of Sinbad the Sailor.

WHY WERE TEXTILES SO IMPORTANT?
Many of the first Muslims were nomads, who needed to be able to pack up and move all their belongings quickly. Traditionally, woven cloth was used for tents, bags, clothes, cushions, bedding, and kelims (rugs). The art and craft of making textiles continued to be important in the Muslim world, which gave us the words for damask (from Damascus), muslin (from Mosul), and cashmere (from Kashmir).

CORDOBA'S GREAT MOSQUE ►
A mihrab is a niche that faces Mecca, the holiest city of Islam. This is the mihrab of the Great Mosque (Mezquita) of Cordoba, one of Islam's greatest architectural legacies to Europe. It was begun by the city's rulers in 785 and enlarged over the following two centuries.

FIND OUT MORE ►► Crusades 389 • Islam 290 • Medieval Africa 394–395 • Ottoman Empire 397

VIKINGS

Late in the 8th century, Viking raiders from Norway, Denmark, and Sweden began to sweep across Europe. In their versatile ▸▸ LONGSHIPS , the Vikings sailed vast distances. Their golden age of trade, exploration, and colonization lasted until AD 1100.

Tall prow stopped ship diving into waves in rough seas

WHERE DID THE VIKINGS TRAVEL?
The Vikings raided and settled along the coasts of Britain, Ireland, and continental Europe. They crossed the Atlantic to reach Iceland, Greenland, and Newfoundland. Viking merchants travelled through Russia to Constantinople, exchanging the amber, furs, and whale oil of the north for wine, silks, spices, and silver coins from the Middle East.

HOW DID THE VIKINGS GET THEIR FIERCE REPUTATION?
The Vikings were not Christian and they saw isolated monasteries and churches as easy targets for hit-and-run raids. But the first people to write about the Vikings were monks who had suffered in these raids. As a result, Viking atrocities were better recorded than Viking achievements.

HOW DID THE VIKINGS WORSHIP THEIR GODS?
The Vikings worshipped their gods in the open air, choosing natural landmarks such as big rocks, unusual trees, and waterfalls. Their most important gods were Odin, the god of knowledge, Thor, the god of metalwork and thunder, and Frey, the goddess of fertility. After around 1000, Viking peoples became Christian.

▲ CARVED SILVER CHARM
This silver head of a bearded man, wearing a Viking helmet, was made to hang from a chain, probably as a good luck charm. The Vikings prized silver. We do not know whose face it is meant to represent.

e ▸▸
Vikings

▼ VIKING WEAPON
This sword from Denmark has a double-edged iron blade. Viking warriors took great pride in their swords, which were handed down through families, and sometimes placed in graves.

ROUND TOWER AT ARDMORE ▲
This tower stands in a cemetery at Ardmore, County Waterford, Ireland. It was built around 1100 by monks, as a refuge from Viking raiders. The doorway is 4.5 m (15 ft) above the ground, and was reached by a ladder that could be pulled inside.

LONGSHIPS

Viking ships were the best in Europe. Besides the longships used for raiding and war, they had special fishing boats. For long-distance voyages, they built deeper, broader ships called knorrs.

HOW WERE VIKING SHIPS BUILT?
Viking ships were made of planks of oak or pinewood, nailed to a heavy central keel (supporting timber). This made them strong but flexible. The mast was made from a tall tree trunk and supported a huge square sail. There were oars for each crew man, to row the ship when there was no wind.

◄ REPLICA OF A VIKING LONGSHIP
The shallow hull of a longship made it less likely to capsize. It could be sailed in shallow water close to land, to make a surprise attack. Its planks overlapped for extra strength. Tarred wool was crammed between the planks to keep water out.

CARVED PICTURE STONE ▶
Stones like this, showing the brave deeds and epic voyages of Viking heroes, were raised by proud relatives.

FIND OUT MORE ▸▸ Byzantine Empire 385 • Exploration 400–401

NORMANS

The Normans were descended from Viking warriors who settled in Normandy, northwest France, in AD 912. They conquered large areas of Europe, from England to southern Italy. Norman kings were strong rulers.

WHAT HAPPENED IN 1066?

The Normans invaded England in 1066. They were led by the Duke of Normandy, William the Conqueror, who became king of England. He removed English nobles, and gave their land to Normans. Norman nobles ran the government, and Norman priests led the Church. Norman rulers spoke French, and built castles. They imposed heavy taxes and harsh laws.

CATHEDRAL AT MONREALE ▶
This cathedral in Sicily was built in 1174–1189, in a mixture of Byzantine, Arabic, North African, and Norman styles. The Normans built castles and cathedrals in all the lands they conquered.

Normans

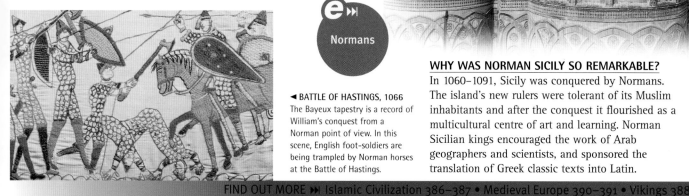

◀ BATTLE OF HASTINGS, 1066
The Bayeux tapestry is a record of William's conquest from a Norman point of view. In this scene, English foot-soldiers are being trampled by Norman horses at the Battle of Hastings.

WHY WAS NORMAN SICILY SO REMARKABLE?

In 1060–1091, Sicily was conquered by Normans. The island's new rulers were tolerant of its Muslim inhabitants and after the conquest it flourished as a multicultural centre of art and learning. Norman Sicilian kings encouraged the work of Arab geographers and scientists, and sponsored the translation of Greek classic texts into Latin.

FIND OUT MORE ▶▶ Islamic Civilization 386–387 • Medieval Europe 390–391 • Vikings 388

CRUSADES

In 1095, Pope Urban II called for a war against the Muslim rulers of Jerusalem. This was the First Crusade. Over the next two centuries, Christian armies from Europe fought more crusades, but none was successful.

Crusades

WHY WAS THE FIRST CRUSADE CALLED?

For centuries, Christian pilgrims had been visiting the Holy Land, where Jesus had lived and which had been ruled by Muslims since 637. The First Crusade happened because, by the 11th century, the region's rulers were less sympathetic to Christian pilgrims.

WHAT DID THE CRUSADERS BRING BACK TO EUROPE?

Crusaders returned with apricots, lemons, rice, dyes, spices, perfume, soap, and glass mirrors. They also brought back a musical instrument, the ancestor of the modern guitar.

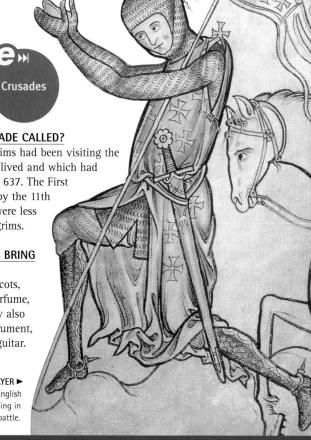

▲ CRUSADERS ATTACK CONSTANTINOPLE
In 1204, crusaders from western Europe sailed to Constantinople. Having captured and looted the city, they then ruled it for nearly 60 years. This Fourth Crusade never reached the Holy Land.

SOLDIER IN PRAYER ▶
This Crusader, featured on an English manuscript of around 1200, is kneeling in prayer before a battle.

FIND OUT MORE ▶▶ Islamic Civilization 386–387 • Medieval Europe 390–391

MEDIEVAL EUROPE

Between AD 1000 and 1500, a lively society developed in Europe. Although most people still worked on the land, this was also the age of ▶▶ CASTLES , cathedrals, and growing towns. Gradually, the traders and craftsmen of the towns began to have more influence on government.

WHO WAS POWERFUL IN MEDIEVAL EUROPE?
Kings led armies of ▶▶ KNIGHTS and foot-soldiers. They made laws, collected taxes, and encouraged trade. Nobles ran great estates, given to them on condition that they would help the king rule. The Church was important in every area of life, providing medieval Europe with its schools, hospitals, and universities.

WHAT DID MEDIEVAL PEOPLE BELIEVE?
Medieval Europeans believed that God had made the world, and ruled it through his Church and the king. Few people, apart from priests and monks, could read and write. Ordinary people learned the stories of the Bible and the saints from preachers, and the pictures painted in their churches.

Medieval queens were the mothers, sisters, and daughters of kings

Bishops were the local lords of the Church

e ▶▶ medieval Europe

▲ MEDIEVAL CHESS PIECES
These chess pieces, made in Scandinavia around 1200, show the most important people in a medieval kingdom (from left to right): a queen, king, bishop (Church leader), and knight (who was always a nobleman).

CASTLES

A castle is a huge, fortified building, or set of buildings. The first castles, built around 900, were made up of a wooden fortress on top of an earth mound. Later, castles built of stone had towers, battlements, moats, and strong defensive walls. They also became prestigious homes.

WERE CASTLES ONLY USED IN WARTIME?
The first castles were built to shelter nobles, ▶▶ KNIGHTS , and soldiers in a war. After around 1200, in times of peace, each castle had its own nobleman and his family living in it. Comfortable private rooms were added for important guests.

HOW DID GUNPOWDER AFFECT CASTLES?
From around 1300, gunpowder for firing cannons began to affect warfare in Europe. Cannon balls could smash through stone walls, making castles less useful as safe strongholds. Castles continued to be built, but for show. They were intended as impressive residences rather than indestructible fortresses.

▲ ROCHESTER CASTLE, ENGLAND
The main building of a castle was its keep (central tower). This one was built around 1130. Its stone walls would not burn, and were very hard to knock down.

TILLING AND SOWING ▶
This medieval painting shows an October scene outside Paris. Peasants are tilling the ground and sowing seed against the background of the French king's castle. The scarecrow is dressed as an archer.

HOW DID MEDIEVAL TOWNS DEVELOP?

Many towns grew up around markets, where farm produce was exchanged for the goods and services of specialist craftsmen, such as shoemakers and weavers. Through their guilds, traders and craftsmen regulated prices and organized the training of their apprentices.

WHAT WAS LIFE LIKE FOR PEASANT FAMILIES?

Most peasants worked on their local lord's fields in return for their own plots of land. Some, called serfs, were not free, and could not travel, or marry, without their lord's permission. Skilled men could be thatchers or carpenters. Women might weave cloth or brew ale.

Towers originally for defence, now for decoration

Plague victim, wrapped in shroud. Once infected, there was little hope of survival

▲ THE BLACK DEATH
This stained-glass window shows the impact of the Black Death, the plague that killed more than a quarter of Europe's population in AD 1347-1349. It was spread by fleabites and contact with infected people.

KNIGHTS

Knights were warriors on horseback. They came from noble families and were trained from boyhood to handle weapons, wear armour, and ride heavy war horses. Some knights owned castles and land, and kept local order. Others served in the private armies of great lords. Each knight had his own coat of arms, helping him to tell friend from foe in battle.

Metal helmet protects head

Metal breastplate and chain-mail tunic

Pointed sword digs between armour

HOW DID KNIGHTS FIGHT?

Knights charged into battle on horseback, spearing enemy soldiers with their long lances, or slashing at them with heavy swords, maces, and battle-axes. On foot, they fought with daggers and short swords.

WHAT WAS THE CODE OF CHIVALRY?

Knights were bound by a solemn promise to be loyal to their king. They were also meant to respect women, protect the weak, and defend the Church. This code became known as chivalry.

Metal greaves (shin pieces)

Even the feet are protected by armour

▲ ITALIAN KNIGHT
This suit of armour, worn around AD 1380, gave good protection while the knight was on horseback, but was hot and heavy when fighting on foot.

Knight kneels in front of a noble lady

A TOURNAMENT SHIELD ▶
This ornamental shield was made for a tournament parade. Tournament contests gave knights a chance to practise their skills. Their lives and loves were celebrated in the songs and poems of travelling minstrels called troubadours.

FIND OUT MORE ▶▶ Crusades 389 • Normans 389 • Reformation 399 • Renaissance 398

MONGOLS

The Mongols were nomadic tribes from the steppes, or grasslands, of central Asia. In AD 1206 they proclaimed Genghis Khan as their supreme ruler. He led their conquest of an empire that, by 1279, included all of China and nearly all of Russia, as well as central Asia, Iran, and Iraq.

GENGHIS KHAN
r. 1206–1227
Genghis Khan began his career as Temujin, the brilliant, ambitious chieftain of one Mongol tribe. He was chosen as supreme ruler, and given the title Genghis Khan, by a gathering of all the Mongol tribes. After his death, in 1227, his empire was divided among his sons.

WHAT WAS SPECIAL ABOUT MONGOL ARMIES?
Mongol military might was based on the speed and ferocity of mounted archers. From galloping horses, Mongol archers let loose arrows that could pierce armour. The riders and the horses were tough, capable of covering more than 160 km (100 miles) a day.

WHO WANTED TO RULE THE WORLD?
Genghis Khan wanted to live up to his title, which means "prince of all that lies between the oceans". He aimed to conquer the world and was proud of the fact that, eventually, it took almost a year to ride from one end of his realm to the other.

◄ **TIMUR IN INDIA**
In 1398, another Mongol warlord called Timur, or Tamerlane, invaded India and sacked Delhi.

e ►►
Mongols

FIND OUT MORE ►► Imperial China 393 • Mughal India 407

SAMURAI

Samurai were warriors from Japanese noble families, who served in private armies recruited by daimyo (local lords). They fought in civil wars that raged in Japan from around 1159. In 1603, the Tokugawa ►► SHOGUNS restored peace. Samurai then became local officials and administrators.

WHAT WAS THE WAY OF THE WARRIOR?
Samurai swore a solemn oath of loyalty to their comrades and their lord. They aimed to follow a code, called the bushido (the way of the warrior). This called for self-discipline, skill, bravery, honour, obedience, and self-sacrifice. Many samurai also followed the teachings of Zen Buddhism.

e ►►
samurai

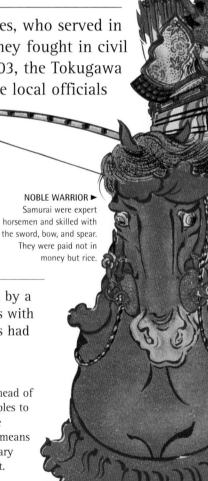

NOBLE WARRIOR ►
Samurai were expert horsemen and skilled with the sword, bow, and spear. They were paid not in money but rice.

SHOGUNS

From 1192 to 1867, Japan was ruled by a series of powerful army commanders with the title of shogun. Japan's emperors had great prestige but little real power.

WHO WAS THE FIRST SHOGUN?
In 1192, the warlord Yoritomo, who was the head of the mighty Minamoto clan, defeated rival nobles to become the most powerful man in Japan. The emperor gave him the title of shogun, which means "great general". Yoritomo set up a new, military government, far away from the imperial court.

▲ **PORTRAIT OF YORITOMO**
Minamoto Yoritomo claimed to be descended from the Japanese imperial family. When he died, in 1199, he passed the title of shogun on to his sons, who ruled until 1219.

FIND OUT MORE ►► Buddhism 289

IMPERIAL CHINA

For more than 2,000 years, from 221 BC until AD 1912, China was ruled by emperors. In that time, the capital city and the imperial dynasty (ruling family) changed. There were periods of unrest and of invasion by fierce tribes, including the Mongols, but the same system of government continued.
Imperial China was a remarkably stable civilization, which led the world in art and technology, with inventions including paper, ▶▶ **PORCELAIN**, and gunpowder.

▲ GREAT WALL OF CHINA
The Great Wall snakes across the mountains north of Beijing. Defensive walls were being built since ancient times, but most of the Great Wall as it still stands was built under the Ming emperors.

Palaces and halls were surrounded by gardens

A red-robed senior official of the imperial household

An official greets others outside the gates

e ▶▶
Imperial China

THE FORBIDDEN CITY ▲
A Ming painting on silk of the Forbidden City. The compound was closed, forbidden to ordinary people, and the emperors hardly ever left it.

CHINA'S RULERS	
221 BC	Qin dynasty
206 BC	Han dynasty
AD 221	Time of disunity
581	Sui dynasty
618	Tang dynasty
907	China divided into five dynasties
960	Song dynasty
1279	Yuan dynasty (Mongol)
1368	Ming dynasty (last Chinese dynasty)
1644 1912	Qing dynasty (Manchu dynasty from Manchuria)

WHY WERE EXAMS IMPORTANT IN CHINA?
The first Han emperor set up a civil service to run China. Before getting a job in the civil service, officials had to pass a series of difficult exams. Those who passed the top exams could expect jobs as government ministers, and marriage to princesses.

HOW DID BEIJING BECOME CHINA'S CAPITAL?
After invading China in 1279, the Mongol (Yuan) emperors established their capital at Beijing, which was just inside the Great Wall, in what was then the far north of China. In 1368, a new dynasty, the Ming, came to power. They kept Beijing as the capital, rebuilding and expanding the city.

WHO LIVED IN THE FORBIDDEN CITY?
The imperial palace at Beijing is called the Forbidden City. Enclosed by a moat and high brick walls, this complex of palaces, halls, gardens, offices, and storehouses was built under the Ming dynasty. The imperial family lived there, along with nobles, servants, and officials.

PORCELAIN

Porcelain is a transluscent (semi-transparent) ceramic material, made of fine white clay mixed with crushed stone. It can be shaped on a potter's wheel, or moulded by hand. When fired (baked) at extremely high temperatures it becomes waterproof, and so hard that steel cannot scratch it.

WHY WAS PORCELAIN SO PRECIOUS?
Porcelain was first made by Chinese potters during the Tang dynasty. It was a luxury product, for the use of nobles and emperors, and for centuries no one but the Chinese knew how to make it. Seventeenth-century Dutch sailors brought the first porcelain "china" to Europe, where it was a prized commodity.

Dragon design is painted with brush over smooth surface

◀ PORCELAIN BOWL
This delicate bowl was made during the Ming dynasty. Designs like this, in blue and white, became very popular. Millions of porcelain items were specially made to be sold overseas.

FIND OUT MORE ▶▶ China's First Empire 378 • Revolutionary China 429

MEDIEVAL AFRICA

From around AD 750 to AD 1500, lands to the south of Africa's Sahara Desert were home to many thriving civilizations. Muslim kings ruled in cities like ▶ TIMBUKTU , and chiefs called ▶ OBAS were powerful in rainforest kingdoms. ▶ SWAHILI peoples became rich through trade.

HOW DID TRADERS CROSS THE SAHARA DESERT?

Traders from North Africa crossed the Sahara together in a group called a caravan. They led as many as 10,000 camels, heavily laden with goods, in a long line known as a camel train. At the southern edge of the Sahara, the goods were transferred to donkeys or human porters, to be carried further south.

WHICH AFRICAN GOODS WERE HIGHLY PRIZED?

Gold, ivory, ebony, and slaves from west African kingdoms such as Ghana, Mali, and Songhai were sold in North Africa and the Middle East. They were traded for salt and copper, mined in the Sahara. Later, European traders came for gold, ebony, and slaves.

◀ ELMINA CASTLE AND FORT, GHANA
This castle and fort were built by the Portuguese in 1482. Portuguese, and later Dutch and English, traders used it as a base for dealing in slaves, gold, and imported European artefacts. The Europeans set up many trading posts in West Africa.

Crown of Portuguese heads

e ▶▶ **medieval Africa**

TIMBUKTU

Timbuktu (in central Mali) was one of the most important cities on the edge of the Sahara. After Muslim scholars brought the religion of Islam to the region, around 900, it became a great centre of Muslim learning, with schools, a university, and a special market where valuable, handwritten books were sold.

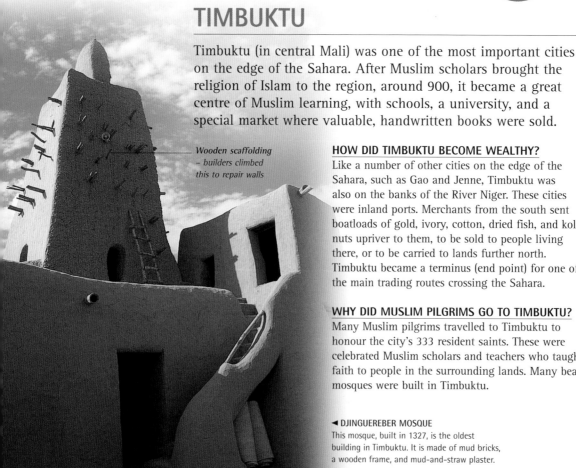

Wooden scaffolding – builders climbed this to repair walls

HOW DID TIMBUKTU BECOME WEALTHY?

Like a number of other cities on the edge of the Sahara, such as Gao and Jenne, Timbuktu was also on the banks of the River Niger. These cities were inland ports. Merchants from the south sent boatloads of gold, ivory, cotton, dried fish, and kola nuts upriver to them, to be sold to people living there, or to be carried to lands further north. Timbuktu became a terminus (end point) for one of the main trading routes crossing the Sahara.

WHY DID MUSLIM PILGRIMS GO TO TIMBUKTU?

Many Muslim pilgrims travelled to Timbuktu to honour the city's 333 resident saints. These were celebrated Muslim scholars and teachers who taught their faith to people in the surrounding lands. Many beautiful mosques were built in Timbuktu.

◀ DJINGUEREBER MOSQUE
This mosque, built in 1327, is the oldest building in Timbuktu. It is made of mud bricks, a wooden frame, and mud-and-straw plaster.

SWAHILI

Swahili became the main language used by different peoples on the coast and islands of East Africa. Many of its words were taken from Arabic – the language of traders who sailed across the Indian Ocean, linking India and Arabia with East Africa's ports such as Mogadishu, Gedi, and Kilwa.

WHO DID THE SWAHILI PEOPLES TRADE WITH?

East Africans produced valuable goods, such as leather, frankincense, leopard skins, ivory, iron, copper, and gold. They sold these to Indian Ocean traders. From around 1071, they sent ambassadors to trade with China, and, from 1418, welcomed Chinese merchant ships to East Africa's ports.

ZANZIBAR ▼
The island of Zanzibar, off the coast of East Africa, is where Swahili was first spoken. It became a major trading centre for slaves, ivory, and cloves.

OBAS

From around 1250 to 1800, a number of different kingdoms made up what is now southwest Nigeria, in west Africa. Each of these was ruled by an oba. The obas were both religious and political leaders. Their subjects, the Yoruba people, lived as farmers, and built city-states surrounded by massive walls of earth.

Oba's cap would have been made from beads

WHERE WERE MANY STATUES OF OBAS MADE?

People living in the rainforest kingdom of Benin, now in south Nigeria, were expert metalworkers and cast elaborate portrait heads of their obas, as well as decorative plaques and ceremonial objects. These were made from brass or bronze and were used for ancestor worship, or to decorate the rulers' palaces.

Elaborate metalwork collar

◄ OBA MASK
This mask of an oba is from around 1500. Cast in brass, it is decorated with a crown of small heads, portraying Portuguese people who first arrived in Yoruba lands around 1430. These look weak and unimportant, compared with the impressive size and proud expression of the oba.

WHAT HAPPENED TO THE KINGDOMS OF THE OBAS?

The power of the obas and other African rulers was weakened by the arrival of Europeans. Portuguese, Dutch, and British traders took back news to their countries of the riches of Africa. Explorers were encouraged to travel there and, by 1900, almost all of Africa was ruled by European powers.

▲ STATUE OF OBA FROM BENIN
Most Benin bronzes, like this one, were in fact made of brass. Obas commanded large armies, and controlled trade in ivory, palm oil, pepper, and slaves.

FIND OUT MORE ►► Africa 238–239 • Age of Empire 422–423 • Exploration 400–401 • Islamic Civilization 386–387

POLYNESIA

Polynesia is a group of scattered islands in the vast Pacific Ocean. Around 2000 BC, families made long, dangerous journeys to settle there. The settlers arrived with pigs, dogs, and hens. They built thatched wooden houses, gathered bananas, coconuts, and breadfruit, and fished.

▲ THE POLYNESIAN TRIANGLE
The islands of Polynesia cover an area of over two million sq km (over 800,000 sq miles). Roughly shaped like a triangle, New Zealand, Hawaii, and Easter Island are at its points. It took many days to sail between groups of islands. Settlers carried farm tools and food plants, to help them survive when they landed.

e ▶▶
Polynesia

WHERE WERE POLYNESIANS FROM?
The settlers' ancestors came from southeast Asia, and had lived there for at least 30,000 years. Slowly, they moved to islands in the Pacific. By 1200 BC, they reached Tonga and Samoa, on the western edge of Polynesia. Around 300 BC, they began to sail further across the ocean.

WHY DID PEOPLE SET SAIL FOR POLYNESIA?
The islands in southeast Asia, where settlers travelled from, were probably over-populated. This would have meant the farmland was exhausted, forests had been cut down, and the soil had eroded away. There may also have been wars between rival islanders, competing for food and land. But some sailors may have been adventurous, eager to explore new lands.

HOW DID THE SETTLERS NAVIGATE?
Settlers travelled in double-hulled canoes, which had sails made of matting. They observed stars, clouds, ocean swells, migrating birds, and te lapa (rays of light reflected underwater from land), and made maps from sticks, pebbles, and shells. Using these techniques, they reached distant islands like Hawaii, and also New Zealand, where settlers called themselves ▶▶ MAORIS.

STONE STATUES ►
Easter Island (also called Rapa Nui) was the furthest east that the settlers reached. They arrived in AD 500. Using simple tools of stone and wood, they built many moai (stone statues). Some were 10 m (33 ft) high.

Statues portray ancestors, or gods

MAORIS

Settlers first reached New Zealand around AD 800. At first they lived in small, peaceful groups but, as the population grew, they became more war-like. Around 1500, they began to build fortified hilltop settlements, called pa. They decorated buildings with woodcarvings, and tattooed their skins with swirling designs.

WHAT WAS LIFE LIKE FOR MAORIS?
The climate of New Zealand was colder and wetter than the settlers' home islands, so they had to adapt to their new environment. They hunted giant flightless birds, called moa, in the forests. They killed seals and gathered shellfish around the coast.

◄ HEITIKI IN SHAPE OF HUMAN FIGURE
This heitiki (greenstone neck ornament) was a sacred heirloom – it symbolized the mana (prestige) of the clan. It was also meant to link humans with gods.

ASIAN TEMPLE KINGDOMS

Between AD 700 and AD 1300, powerful kingdoms, including the Khmer, Pagan, and Sukhothai, emerged in different parts of southeast Asia. They grew rich from growing rice, selling valuable spices, and controlling merchants' sea routes. Their rulers built great temples.

e ⤻ Asian temple kingdoms

▲ BUDDHIST TEMPLE
This is one of over 5,000 temples built in 1000–1200 in the Pagan kingdom, now in Myanmar.

WHY DID ASIAN RULERS BUILD TEMPLES?
Rulers organized thousands of workers to build Hindu and Buddhist temples for worship. The Buddhist religion became much more popular, so many more Buddhist temples were built. The temples brought religious merit to rulers, prestige to their kingdoms, and displayed each ruler's wealth and power.

WHO INFLUENCED THE TEMPLE KINGDOMS?
Buddhist monks and Hindu holy men travelled from India to southeast Asia. They offered advice to kings and led religious rituals. Prayers, offerings, and festivals became an important part of people's lives.

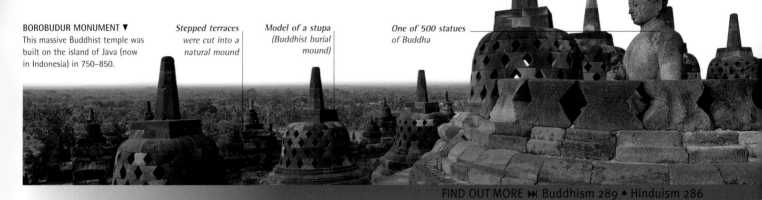

BOROBUDUR MONUMENT ▼
This massive Buddhist temple was built on the island of Java (now in Indonesia) in 750–850.

Stepped terraces were cut into a natural mound

Model of a stupa (Buddhist burial mound)

One of 500 statues of Buddha

FIND OUT MORE ⤻ Buddhism 289 • Hinduism 286

OTTOMAN EMPIRE

Around AD 1300, a new Muslim empire ruled by Turkish leaders called sultans was founded. At its largest extent, in 1700, it covered vast areas of Europe, Africa, and Asia. It lasted until the end of World War I (1918). Today's republic of Turkey was founded in 1923.

e ⤻ Ottomans

SULTAN OTHMAN I ▲
The first sultan, Othman I (1259–1326), was the son of a Turkish chieftain. He led an army of ghazis (warriors fighting for the Muslim faith).

▲ CERAMIC TILES FROM THE BLUE MOSQUE, ISTANBUL
The vibrant, tiled walls of the mosque of Sultan Ahmed, built in 1609–1619 and popularly known as the Blue Mosque. By endowing Istanbul with magnificent mosques and public buildings, the sultans aimed to surpass the achievements of the Byzantine emperors.

WHY WAS SULEIMAN I MAGNIFICENT?
The greatest of the Ottoman sultans was Suleiman the Magnificent. During his reign (1520–1566), the Ottoman Empire reached its greatest extent. He was also a poet and a patron of the arts, adorning Istanbul and other Ottoman cities with glittering mosques.

HOW DID CONSTANTINOPLE BECOME ISTANBUL?
In 1453, after a seige during which its walls were pounded by a battery of cannons, Constantinople was captured by Sultan Muhammad II. Renamed Istanbul, the old capital of the Byzantine Empire then became the new capital of the expanding Ottoman Empire.

WHERE DID JANISSARIES COME FROM?
Janissaries were elite soldiers, who started as non-Turkish Christian boys from the Balkans. They were trained in Istanbul, where they converted to Islam.

FIND OUT MORE ⤻ Crusades 389 • Islamic Civilization 386–387

RENAISSANCE

One of the most creative periods in history occurred in Europe around 1350–1550. This cultural revival is known as the Renaissance (meaning "rebirth"). It was inspired by the civilizations of Ancient Greece and Rome.

WHERE DID THE RENAISSANCE TAKE PLACE?
Italy was the powerhouse of the Renaissance. At that time it was divided into independent states, where wealthy rulers offered ▶▶ PATRONAGE to great artists. The Renaissance also spread through southern France and Spain, and influenced northern Europe.

WHAT WAS THE RENAISSANCE VIEW OF THE WORLD?
There was a passion for knowledge. Scholars had mostly studied the teachings of the Church, but they now rediscovered ancient philosophers. Artists became fascinated by the human body. To celebrate its beauty, they turned away from the formal drawing style of the Middle Ages and adopted a more realistic, natural style.

LEONARDO DA VINCI
1452–1519
Leonardo was a genius. Writer, painter, sculptor, engineer, and architect, he left behind a wealth of sketches and what has become the world's best-known painting – the portrait of a mysterious, smiling woman known as Mona Lisa.

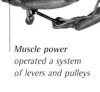

Muscle power operated a system of levers and pulleys

The wood, rope, and other materials available in Leonardo's day were too heavy for practical flight

▲ FLIGHTS OF FANCY
Leonardo da Vinci was a brilliant inventor. This reconstruction shows a flying machine which first appeared in his sketchbooks, alongside futuristic plans for a helicopter, tank, and diving suit.

Retinue includes portraits of the Medici family

Servants carry bows and spears for hunting

PROCESSION OF THE MAGI ▶
This painting of 1459 is by Benozzo Gozzoli. It is one of a series in the Medici family's private chapel in Florence, Italy. Although based on a Biblical scene, it shows the dazzling splendour of a Renaissance court.

FIND OUT MORE ▶▶ Artists 324 • Painting 320–321 • Philosophy 292–293

Wings are powered by pushing the pedals

Biblical king is shown as a Renaissance prince

▲ NORTHERN FRINGES

In Poland, rulers and merchants looked south to Italy and admired the architecture of the Renaissance. This classical facade is in the town of Zamosc, founded in 1579 by Jan Zamoysky, who had studied in Padua.

WHAT CAN WE SEE OF THE RENAISSANCE TODAY?

Many Italian cities still have splendid palaces, churches, libraries, and public squares built during the Renaissance. Visitors to Rome can wonder at the ceiling of the Sistine Chapel, created by Michelangelo, or the masterpieces painted by Raphael.

PATRONAGE

Patronage is the support given by the wealthy to artists, writers and musicians. Renaissance patrons included the French royal family and powerful Italian nobles such as the Sforzas, the Medicis, and the Borgias.

WHY DID FLORENCE FLOURISH?

The Renaissance was a period of great social change, when more and more political power came from money and trade. The Italian city of Florence was a European centre of banking. Its leading family, the Medici, loaned money to popes and kings. It was the Medici fortune which paid the wages of artists such as Michelangelo and Leonardo da Vinci.

e ▶▶ Renaissance

REFORMATION

The Reformation was a Christian movement of the 1500s. Its followers criticized the Catholic Church for corruption and called for radical reform. These protestors became known as Protestants.

WHO LED THE REFORMATION?

The Reformation began in 1517 when a German monk, Martin Luther, nailed a list of complaints to the church door in Wittenberg. Other preachers spread the Protestant message across northern Europe. They called for simpler forms of worship and personal faith.

WHAT WERE THE RESULTS OF THE REFORMATION?

The success of the Protestants aroused fear and anger among Catholics in Rome. A period of religious strife began, which tore Europe apart for hundreds of years. Each side murdered its opponents. Churches and monasteries were destroyed. Civil and national wars caused devastation and streams of refugees.

▲ PRINTED SCRIPTURE

This Bible was printed by a German man called Johannes Gutenberg in about 1455. Printing with movable type made it possible to distribute the Bible and other works to large numbers of ordinary people. Martin Luther later translated the Bible from Latin into German.

Latin was rejected by Protestants because few could read it

e ▶▶ Reformation

RELIGIOUS CONFLICT, EUROPE 1517–1568	
1517	German monk Martin Luther demands reform
1518	Swiss preacher Ulrich Zwingli calls for change
1541	John Calvin founds a Protestant Church, Geneva
1545	Catholics launch a Counter-Reformation
1560	John Knox founds Protestant Church of Scotland
1562	Wars between Catholics and Protestants in France
1568	Dutch Protestants begin revolt against Catholic Spain

FIND OUT MORE ▶▶ Christianity 288 • Printing 339

EXPLORATION

People have always set out to discover new lands and oceans. The greatest age of world exploration began in the 15th century and lasted over four centuries. The Arabs and Chinese had already made improvements in ship design and ▸▸ NAVIGATION . These were now developed further by European seafarers.

e ▸▸
exploration

Brazil, in South America, was discovered by accident in 1500 – its coastline is not yet complete on this map

At Tordesillas in 1494 Spain and Portugal agreed to divide the newly discovered lands in the Americas between them

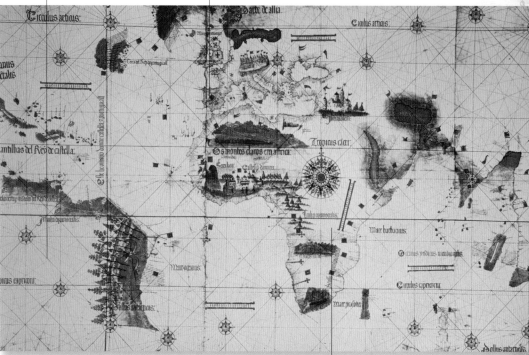

Africa's interior remained unexplored by Europeans until the 1800s

▲ MAPPING THE WORLD
This map was drawn up in 1502 and shows the world known to European seafarers at that time. The coasts of Europe, Africa, and western Asia have been charted, but those of the Americas are only just beginning to take shape.

WHY DID PEOPLE EXPLORE THE WORLD?
The most common reason was trade. The ▸▸ OLD WORLD wanted Asian spices, African ivory, and gold. European traders were soon also seizing lands and trying to convert the local populations to the Christian faith. Many explorers, though, were driven by a sense of adventure or scientific inquiry.

HOW DID EXPLORATION AFFECT THE WORLD?
European countries brought many lands under their control. The world was opened up and new crops were introduced from one land to another. However, there were some disastrous effects. In the ▸▸ NEW WORLD , many native peoples died because they had no resistance to the European diseases that explorers and crews brought with them.

▲ POINTING THE WAY
This type of mariners' compass first came into use in about 1250. This one dates from the 16th century.

EXPLORATION	
1405–1433	Chinese fleets explore the Indian Ocean
1486	Diaz rounds southern Africa
1492	Columbus reaches the Caribbean
1497	John Cabot reaches Canada
1498	Columbus reaches South America
1498	Vasco da Gama sails to India
1500	Pedro Cabral reaches Brazil
1522	Magellan's crew sail around the whole world
1606	Willem Jansz reaches Australia

OLD WORLD

Europe, Asia, and Africa had been known to geographers since ancient times. They became known as the Old World after the European discovery of the Americas.

WHO EXPLORED THE OLD WORLD?

In the Middle Ages, the Venetian Marco Polo and the Moroccan Ibn Battutah travelled east to China. The Chinese admiral Zheng He sailed west to Africa in the 15th century. By the 16th century, Portuguese and Dutch ships were trading in southeast Asia.

TREASURES FROM THE EAST ▶
Silk reached Europe from China along the overland trading routes followed by Marco Polo. Porcelain became a major Chinese export as east–west shipping routes were opened up in the 16th and 17th centuries.

NAVIGATION

Navigation is any method used to find one's way or hold a ship on course. In the 16th century, sailors had various kinds of instruments to help them cross the oceans.

WHAT INSTRUMENTS WERE USED?

Sailors used a compass to check the direction they were travelling. They could also work out a ship's position by measuring the angle of the Sun or stars above the horizon. They did this with a metal plate called a quadrant, a disc called an astrolabe, or a simple stick called a cross-staff.

HOW WAS DISTANCE MEASURED?

Distances travelled at sea were calculated from speed and time. To measure these, a wooden log was thrown overboard. The crew called out the time it took the log to pass between two measuring points on the ship. The ship's course and progress were measured on a peg-board.

HENRY THE NAVIGATOR
1394–1460
This Portuguese prince founded an observatory and a school of navigation on Cape St Vincent, Portugal. Here, a new type of ship, called a caravel, was designed. Henry also sponsored voyages along the coast of West Africa.

NEW WORLD

The New World was one of the terms which came to be used by Europeans to describe the newly discovered lands of North and South America.

WHY DID COLUMBUS SAIL WEST?

In 1492, Christopher Columbus persuaded King Ferdinand and Queen Isabella of Spain to sponsor a voyage westwards. Its aim was to find a new trading route to Asia. Columbus landed in the Bahamas, starting a new age of exploration and invasion.

◀ LANDFALL IN A NEW WORLD
Columbus and his crew meet the Taino people of the Bahamas, believing them to be Asians. The conquered Tainos had to give gold to the Spaniards as tribute. Columbus' discovery brought huge wealth to Spain, but spelt disaster for the native peoples of the Caribbean.

▲ FORTRESS ISLAND
Spain invaded Puerto Rico in 1508. Defences were first built at San Felipe del Morro (above) in 1540. Spain's colonies soon came under attack from rivals such as the English.

FIND OUT MORE ▸▸ Mapping 220–221 • Mediterranean Seafarers 374

Incas

Chimu goldsmiths from the northern part of the empire created this mask

The mask would be placed over the face of a dead nobleman as a funeral ritual

Beaten gold was a sacred metal to the Incas

▲ GOLD MASK
Craftsmen had privileged status in Inca society. Metalworkers from various parts of the empire made masks of shining gold. It was greed for such gold and treasure that lured Spanish invaders to Peru in 1532.

INCAS

The Inca people lived in the Andes mountains of Peru. Between the 12th century and 1532 they conquered an empire that was only 320 kilometres (200 miles) wide, but that stretched for 3,600 kilometres (2,240 miles) from Colombia to Chile.

WHO RULED THE INCA EMPIRE?
The Incas formed a ruling elite. They were a small highland tribe who came to govern 12 million people, speakers of 20 different languages. Conquered chiefs were allowed to keep some local power, provided they adopted the Inca way of life.

HOW DID INCA SOCIETY FUNCTION?
Nobles who were loyal to the emperor were made governors, generals, or priests. They wore golden earplugs as a badge of rank. Most citizens were poor farmers, but they also had to serve the state as soldiers, builders, or labourers.

WHO WAS DESCENDED FROM THE SUN AND MOON?
The Inca emperor claimed descent from Inti, the Sun god, and the empress from Mamakilya, the Moon goddess. Other gods and goddesses represented the sea, thunder, and the goodness of the Earth. The Incas also revered the holy places used by earlier Andean peoples.

◄ MACHU PICCHU
The Inca town of Machu Picchu was built on a remote mountain ridge in about 1450. Its buildings included a palace, housing, temples, army barracks, and craft workshops. The town was abandoned after the Spanish invaded and only rediscovered in 1911.

A big square at the centre of the town was for religious ceremonies

The town is 2,743 metres (9,000 ft) above sea level

Inca walls were strong and earthquake-proof

FIND OUT MORE ▸▸ Ancient Religions 282 • Conquistadors 405

AZTECS

The Aztec, or Mexica, people founded the last of the great civilizations that existed in Mexico before the Spanish invasion. Their powerful empire lasted from around 1325 to 1521. The Aztecs were farmers, warriors, and builders of great cities.

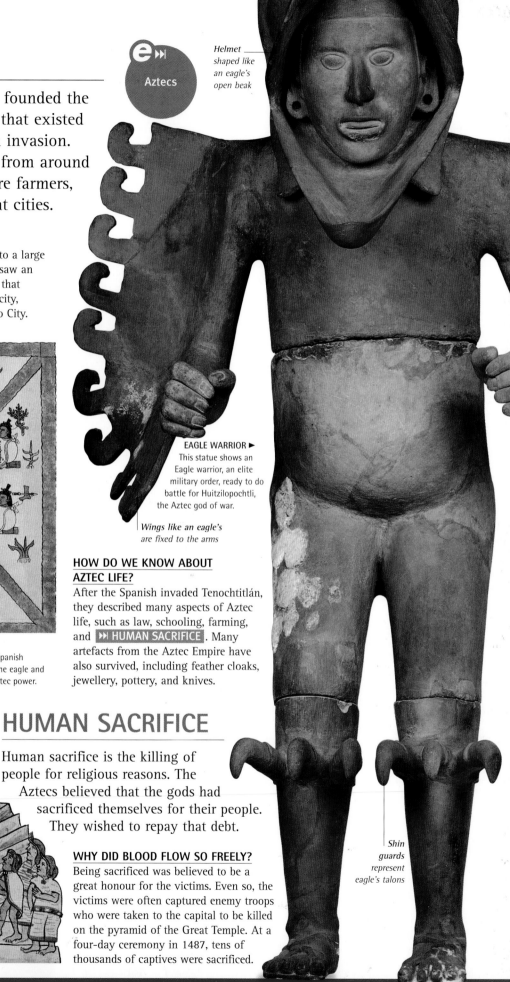

Helmet shaped like an eagle's open beak

e ▶▶ Aztecs

WHERE WAS THE CITY IN THE LAKE?
In 1325, a band of migrating Aztecs came to a large island in Lake Texcoco. When their priests saw an eagle land on a cactus there, they declared that this was the place to build a splendid new city, Tenochtitlán. This is now the site of Mexico City.

▲ AN AZTEC HISTORY
This is part of a codex, or manuscript, painted after the Spanish conquest. The blue square represents Lake Texcoco, and the eagle and cactus represent Tenochtitlán. The shield is a badge of Aztec power.

EAGLE WARRIOR ▶
This statue shows an Eagle warrior, an elite military order, ready to do battle for Huitzilopochtli, the Aztec god of war.

Wings like an eagle's are fixed to the arms

HOW DO WE KNOW ABOUT AZTEC LIFE?
After the Spanish invaded Tenochtitlán, they described many aspects of Aztec life, such as law, schooling, farming, and **▶▶ HUMAN SACRIFICE**. Many artefacts from the Aztec Empire have also survived, including feather cloaks, jewellery, pottery, and knives.

TEMPLE OF DEATH ▶
The emperor or his priest cuts the living heart from the victim with a sharp knife. Blood pours down the steps of the temple pyramid.

HUMAN SACRIFICE

Human sacrifice is the killing of people for religious reasons. The Aztecs believed that the gods had sacrificed themselves for their people. They wished to repay that debt.

WHY DID BLOOD FLOW SO FREELY?
Being sacrificed was believed to be a great honour for the victims. Even so, the victims were often captured enemy troops who were taken to the capital to be killed on the pyramid of the Great Temple. At a four-day ceremony in 1487, tens of thousands of captives were sacrificed.

Shin guards represent eagle's talons

FIND OUT MORE ▶▶ Ancient Religions 282 • Conquistadors 405 • Maya 381

TUDOR AGE

The Tudors were a family of Welsh, French, and English descent. From 1485 to 1603 they ruled England, Wales, and rebellious Ireland. The Tudor kingdom became a powerful force in Europe and the New World.

HOW DID TUDOR MERCHANTS BECOME WEALTHY?
The Tudor economy depended on wool and the cloth trade, which was centred in the English region of East Anglia. To expand their trade, merchants and ships' captains began to seek new business in distant lands.

WHY DID HENRY VIII QUARREL WITH THE POPE?
King Henry VIII married his elder brother's widow, a Spanish princess called Catherine of Aragon. Although she had a daughter, Mary, she did not produce the male heir Henry wanted. The king fell in love with a beautiful courtier called Anne Boleyn. When the Pope refused him a divorce, Henry VIII made himself head of a ▶▶ CHURCH OF ENGLAND.

WHO WAS THE GREATEST TUDOR MONARCH?
Henry VIII was followed as ruler by his three children, Edward VI, Mary I, and Elizabeth I. Elizabeth was a strong and popular ruler, and a shrewd politician. She never married. Her reign saw battles with Spain, exploration of the New World, and a flowering of poetry and theatre.

HENRY VIII
1491–1547

As a young man, Henry was handsome and intelligent. He loved hunting and dancing, and also composed music. As king, he became increasingly arrogant, selfish, and overweight. He married six times and had two of his wives executed. His reign was marked by political plotting, religious strife, and rebellion.

Spanish Armada, or war fleet, is shown nearing England in 1588

Crown is a symbol of royal power

e ▶▶

Tudor age

Globe suggests England's growing role overseas

Spanish Armada is attacked by English ships and scattered by storms

◀ PORTRAIT OF POWER
This image of Elizabeth I shows her as a powerful and confident ruler. She liked to wear elaborate dresses and jewels and was the centre of a sophisticated court.

TUDOR MONARCHS

1485	◆	Henry VII wins throne from Richard III
1509	◆	Henry VIII is crowned king
1547	◆	Rule of the boy king Edward VI
1553	◆	Reign of Mary I
1558	◆	Elizabeth I becomes queen
1603	◆	Death of Elizabeth I

CHURCH OF ENGLAND

Henry VIII finally broke with the Roman Catholic Church in 1534. However, he also rejected the Protestant teachings of Martin Luther. In 1559, after years of religious conflict, Elizabeth I created a reformed Church of England which contained both Catholic and Protestant elements. It was, and still is, headed by the monarch.

WHY DID RELIGION TROUBLE THE TUDORS?
Henry VIII's political quarrel with the Pope coincided with the bitter religious quarrels of the Reformation in Europe. Edward VI and Elizabeth I were both Protestant, while Mary I was an ardent Catholic. Many ordinary people were tortured and executed for having a different faith to the reigning monarch.

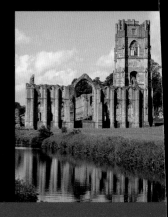

FOUNTAINS ABBEY, YORKSHIRE ▶
Roman Catholic monasteries and convents were closed down or "dissolved" by an order of 1539. Many were ransacked and today lie in ruins.

FIND OUT MORE ▶▶ Monarchy 410 • Reformation 399

CONQUISTADORS

In the 16th century, Central and South America were invaded by Spanish soldiers called conquistadors, who overthrew the Aztec and Inca empires. Many went in search of a rich land called ▸▸ EL DORADO.

WHO WAS THE GOD FROM THE SEA?
In 1517, Aztec spies saw conquistadors on the coast and relayed news of these pale, bearded strangers to Emperor Moctezuma II. He believed that their arrival marked the return of a long-departed god and king called Quetzalcoatl.

HOW DID THE CONQUISTADORS DEFEAT SO MANY PEOPLE?
The conquistadors were few in number but they had ships, horses, armour, and deadly firearms. In Mexico they increased their numbers by joining up with native peoples rebelling against Aztec rule.

▲ SPANISH HELMET
Conquistadors were protected from the spears and clubs of native warriors by tough steel helmets and breastplates.

HERNÁN CORTÉS
1485–1547
Cortés was born in Spain. In 1518 he was given command of a force of 550 soldiers. He landed in Mexico, and reached the Aztec capital in 1519. He was greeted peacefully, but soon there was bitter fighting. In 1521 Cortés destroyed the city and in 1522 became governor of this newly conquered land for Spain.

The Aztecs had no effective defence against steel swords and firearms

WHO KILLED THE INCA EMPEROR?
In 1532, a band of conquistadors led by Francisco Pizarro met the Inca emperor Atahualpa. They tricked him into being captured and demanded a vast ransom of silver and gold for his release. It was paid, but in 1533 they executed him anyway.

e ▸▸
conquistadors

TERROR UNLEASHED ▶
In 1520, Pedro de Alvarado was left in charge of Tenochtitlán. His brutality caused an uprising. The Spanish fled, but recaptured the city in 1521.

EL DORADO

El Dorado means "the golden one" – it is the Spanish name for a mythical land in South America, said to be rich in gold beyond all dreams.

WHY DID THE CONQUISTADORS SEEK EL DORADO?
Conquistadors were often brave, but they were also quarrelsome and violent, driven by a desperate lust for gold and power. Many died in remote jungles, still vainly searching for the riches of El Dorado.

Ornamental tweezers, made in Peru by a Moche goldsmith

GOLDEN TREASURE ▶
Conquistadors looted precious gold statues and ornaments from temples and palaces all over Central and South America. Many were melted down and shipped back to Spain.

FIND OUT MORE ▸▸ Aztecs 403 • Incas 402

THIRTY YEARS' WAR

The Thirty Years' War engulfed Europe between 1618 and 1648. It was a clash between Protestants and Catholics in Germany, which spread into a wider conflict involving Denmark, Sweden, and France.

THIRTY YEARS' WAR	
1618	Protestant revolt in Prague
1625–1629	Denmark enters war for the Protestants
1630	Sweden joins Protestant cause
1635	France joins the war as Sweden's ally
1646	France and Sweden invade Bavaria
1648	Treaty of Westphalia ends the war

WHO WAS THROWN FROM A WINDOW IN PRAGUE?
The Catholic Habsburg family ruled the Holy Roman Empire and Spain. When the Habsburgs tried to place a Catholic on the throne of Protestant Bohemia, their representatives were hurled from a window of Prague castle. Rebellion spread across Germany as Protestant princes within the empire challenged its authority.

WHO WAS THE LION OF THE NORTH?
The war was part of a wider struggle between the Holy Roman Empire and its enemies. Denmark, Sweden, and France all opposed the Empire. The Swedish king Gustavus Adolphus, "Lion of the North", was victorious at Lützen in 1632, but died in battle.

e ►► Thirty Years' War

MAGDEBURG DESTROYED ►
In 1631, the German city of Magdeburg was burnt down by Holy Roman Empire forces. Peace brought more religious freedom and greatly weakened the Holy Roman Empire.

FIND OUT MORE ►► Holy Roman Empire 385

ENGLISH CIVIL WAR

From 1642 to 1648 people in the British Isles were split by a war between King Charles I and Parliament. The king was said to be influenced by his wife, a French Catholic. He brought in unpopular taxes and tried to force his will on Parliament. This led to civil war.

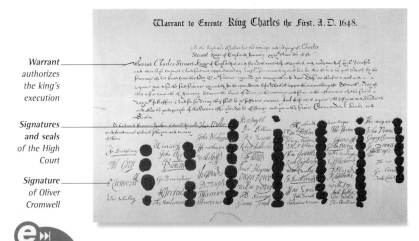

Warrant authorizes the king's execution

Signatures and seals of the High Court

Signature of Oliver Cromwell

e ►► English Civil War

▲ DEATH WARRANT OF CHARLES I
Convicted as a traitor to his people, King Charles I was beheaded in Whitehall, London, on 30 January 1649, by order of the English Parliament. News of this event shocked the whole of Europe. Many people believed that kings ruled by divine right, or the will of God – so the execution was regarded as a terrible sin.

WHO WAS "OLD IRONSIDES"?
Oliver Cromwell (1599-1658) was a farmer and Member of Parliament. In the Civil War he proved himself to be a brilliant soldier. He and his armoured troopers became known as Ironsides. Cromwell led a savage invasion of Catholic Ireland in 1649.

WHO WERE ROUNDHEADS AND CAVALIERS?
The forces of Parliament included many of the more extreme Protestants called Puritans (also known as Roundheads, because of their short haircuts). The royalists were called Cavaliers (meaning "knights"). Their war ended with the capture of Charles I.

WHO WERE THE DIGGERS AND LEVELLERS?
The leaders of the Parliamentary forces were mostly country landowners, squires and merchants. Many of the poor people who fought for them wanted the land to be shared out and equal rights for all. Cromwell crushed these Diggers and Levellers in 1649.

WHAT WAS THE COMMONWEALTH?
In 1649 a republic, or Commonwealth, was declared. There was now a Council of State instead of a king. However the army was impatient for greater change, so in 1653 power was handed over to Oliver Cromwell, who was given the title "Lord Protector". Cromwell died and under his son the Commonwealth soon collapsed. In 1660 the monarchy was restored, but with limited powers.

FIND OUT MORE ►► Monarchy 410

MUGHAL INDIA

The Mughal Empire, founded in 1526, was the most powerful Islamic state to rule in India. It was at its most prosperous during the 1600s, when fine buildings such as the ▶▶ TAJ MAHAL were constructed.

WHO WERE THE MUGHALS?
Mughal means "Mongol". Babur, the Asian invader who founded the empire, was descended from Mongol warlords. Under the Mughal emperors, roads were built, trade prospered, and the arts flourished.

WHERE WAS THE MUGHAL EMPIRE?
The Mughals governed northern India, and at times their rule extended from Afghanistan in the west to Bengal in the east. The emperor Aurangzeb moved the capital from Agra to Delhi and pushed the empire's borders far to the south.

THE MUGHAL EMPIRE	
1526	Babur founds Mughal Empire
1556	Akbar the Great begins reign
1605	Jahangir becomes emperor
1628	Shah Jahan comes to power
1659	Aurangzeb seizes the throne
1675	Sikhs rise against Mughal rule
1707	Start of Mughal decline
1857	Last emperor

Gold hilt studded with gems

MUGHAL DAGGER ▶
The Mughal emperors owned magnificent daggers and swords, hunting weapons, precious jewels, gold, and ivory. They wore splendid silks and brocades. Their court was famed around the world for its luxury.

WHO CHALLENGED MUGHAL RULE?
The Mughals had to fight against Afghans and many regional Hindu rulers. The early Muslim emperors allowed all kinds of religious worship, but Aurangzeb offended Hindus and caused the Sikhs to rebel. He also clashed fiercely with the west coast kingdom of the Marathas and its ruler, Sivaji. However, it was the growing political power of British traders in India that brought about the final decline and collapse of the Mughal Empire in the 18th century.

e ▶▶ Mughal India

▲ MUGHAL MINIATURE
This painting of about 1590 shows Akbar's palace being built. Mughal art was often in miniature, combining Persian and Indian styles.

TAJ MAHAL

The most famous monument of Mughal architecture is the Taj Mahal. It was built in the 17th century by Shah Jahan as a tomb for his beloved wife, Mumtaz-i Mahal, who died in childbirth.

HOW LONG DID IT TAKE TO BUILD THE TAJ MAHAL?
The Taj Mahal was begun in 1632 and completed 22 years later. About 20,000 people were employed, including Asia's finest craftsmen. Famous for its perfect symmetry, it is exactly as wide as it is high, and the dome is the same height as its façade.

◀ INSCRIPTIONS
Beautifully intricate inscriptions in the Persian style adorn the arches of the Taj Mahal. Many of them are verses from the Qur'an, the holy scripture of Islam.

TAJ MAHAL ▶
The domes, minarets, and arches of the Taj Mahal are reflected in still water. The walls of white marble are inlaid with over 43 varieties of precious stones.

FIND OUT MORE ▶▶ Gupta India 379 • Mauryan India 379

AMERICAN INDIANS

The lands of North America were originally occupied by a wide variety of American Indian peoples, each with their own language and culture. Ways of life varied from one region to another, according to the environment – some peoples lived in farming villages, while others hunted buffalo. Their worlds were changed forever by the European invasion.

WHAT WAS THE LEAGUE OF FIVE NATIONS?

Five American Indian nations in the northeast – the Seneca, Cayuga, Onondaga, Oneida, and Mohawk – made a powerful alliance, called the Iroquois Confederacy. It was founded in about 1570 by a prophet called Deganawida. The League's aims were co-operation and mutual defence. A council met each year to discuss their laws.

Decorative bead headband

e ▸▸
American Indians

Resin made the canoe waterproof

Birch bark was stitched over a light timber frame

▲ **CANOE BUILDERS**
American Indians built all kinds of boats, using tree trunks, reeds, or buffalo hide. Birch bark canoes were used on northeastern lakes and rivers.

▲ **EAGLE FEATHERS**
Among many hunters of the Great Plains, such as the Lakota (or Sioux), war bonnets indicated rank and bravery in battle. This one is made of eagle feathers, porcupine quills, buckskin, ermine tails, and horsehair.

HOW DID PEOPLE IN THE NORTHWEST LIVE?

The northwest (in what is now both the USA and Canada) was an area with a large American Indian population. Many peoples there lived by salmon fishing or whaling, and by gathering fruits and berries. They lived in large houses, which were built of red cedar-wood. Cedar was also used to make hats, boats, rope, cloth, boxes, and baskets.

WHY DID FARMERS BECOME HUNTERS?

As Europeans invaded the northeast, many American Indian peoples were forced to retreat westwards. Some had to give up farming. Instead they became buffalo hunters on the Great Plains, the grasslands which make up the prairie regions of the central part of the modern United States and Canada.

▼ **BUFFALO HUNTERS**
For generations, Plains Indians had hunted buffalo, both on foot and on horseback. In the 19th century, the great herds were almost completely destroyed by the arrival of the railroads, which prevented the free grazing of the herds and brought with it the guns of white hunters.

AMERICAN INDIANS

1547	Horses introduced to North America by the Spanish
c. 1570	The Iroquois Confederacy is founded
1626	Manhattan Island is sold to the Dutch
1648	The Iroquois–Huron War
1722	The Tuscarora join the Iroquois Confederacy
1763	Pontiac, chief of the Ottawa, unites tribes against British troops

FIND OUT MORE ▸▸ Early Americans 380 • Indian Wars 417 • Western USA 228–229

COLONIAL AMERICA

From the 16th to 18th century, European nations invaded and settled large areas of North America. The colonists often attacked and dispersed the American Indians, and fought each other for control of the territory.

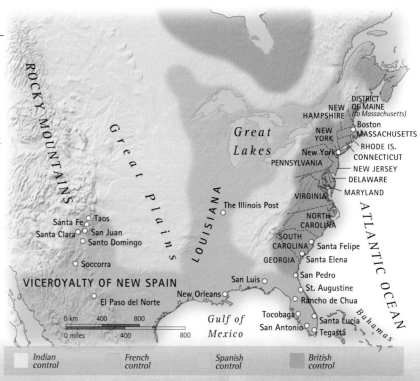

WHO BUILT ST AUGUSTINE?

The Spanish reached Florida in 1513, and in 1565 founded St Augustine, the first European settlement in what is now the USA. They were the first Europeans to see the Mississippi River and to reach Kansas. The Spanish also extended Mexico northwards into Texas, New Mexico, and California. These territories would become part of the USA in the 19th century.

| Indian control | French control | Spanish control | British control |

▲ SAMOSET AND THE PILGRIMS
In 1620, a ship called the *Mayflower* landed a group of settlers at Plymouth in New England. They were religious refugees from England and became known as Pilgrims. They nearly starved to death in their first winter, but a friendly Pemaquid chief called Samoset helped them to survive. By 1625, they had taken over much of his land.

WHERE WAS LOUISIANA?

In 1682, the French explorer Robert de la Salle claimed all the lands around the Mississippi River for France. The region was named Louisiana, after King Louis XIV of France. Most of the eastern part passed to Spain and then to the USA, while the western part was purchased by the USA from the French in 1803.

WHERE DID THE BRITISH SETTLE?

The English seafarer Sir Walter Raleigh organized three expeditions to North America after 1584. He named Virginia after Elizabeth I of England, known as the "Virgin Queen" because she never married. In 1607, Jamestown in Virginia became the first British settlement on the Atlantic coast and became wealthy through the export of tobacco.

▲ NEW WORLD ORDER
This map shows early settlements around the Gulf of Mexico, as well as the 13 British colonies on the Atlantic coast, which later created the United States of America. There was European settlement on the Pacific coast too, with the Russians settling Alaska in 1784.

colonial America

▼ NEW AMSTERDAM
In 1626, the Dutch purchased the island of Manhattan. Its port was named New Amsterdam. It was captured by the British in 1664 and renamed New York.

Buildings were in the Dutch style

Ships anchored at the mouth of the Hudson river

WHO WERE THE SETTLERS?

Europeans settled in the New World for many reasons. Some were religious refugees, such as Quakers, who were unable to worship freely in their own lands. Some were convicted criminals, sent to work in the colonies as a punishment. Some were outlaws or pirates. Others were farmers or business people looking for good land and opportunities.

FIND OUT MORE ▶▶ American Revolution 414 • Indian Wars 417

MONARCHY

Monarchy means rule by a single person, such as a king or a queen. Normally, rule passes from one generation to the next within the same family, or 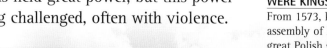 DYNASTY . In the 17th century monarchs held great power, but this power was increasingly being challenged, often with violence.

WHAT WAS THE DIVINE RIGHT OF KINGS?
This was the belief that monarchs were appointed by God to rule, and therefore had a right to impose their will on their subjects. This made it almost impossible to criticise or oppose the monarch.

WERE KINGS EVER ELECTED?
From 1573, kings of Poland were elected by an assembly of lords, called the Republic of Nobles. The great Polish soldier Jan Sobiewski was elected king in 1674, after defeating invading Turks. Many of those chosen as king were foreigners.

◀ HALL OF MIRRORS
This dazzling hall at Versailles was designed to reflect royal power and glory, impressing all visitors.

monarchy

COURTYARD AT VERSAILLES ▶
In 1668, the most luxurious palace in the world was Versailles, the glittering royal court of Louis XIV of France.

DYNASTIES

Dynasties, or royal families, often held power for hundreds of years. Many became hugely wealthy. Their rule came to an end if there were no children or relatives to inherit the throne, or if a monarch was overthrown by rivals or revolutions.

WHICH IS THE WORLD'S OLDEST DYNASTY?
The same dynasty has ruled Japan for 2,000 years or more. Legend states that it is even older, having been founded by Jimmu in 660 BC. However, the emperors have not always held great power. Sometimes, real power was held by military governors called shoguns.

▲ HABSBURG 1273–1918
The Habsburgs ruled Austria and at times the Holy Roman Empire, the Netherlands, and Spain. Charles V reigned 1516–1556.

▲ STUART 1371–1714
The Stuarts ruled Scotland and, after 1603, England, Wales, and Ireland. Charles II reigned 1660–1685.

▲ BOURBON 1589–1830
The Bourbons ruled in France, Navarre, Naples, and Spain. Louis XIV (above, costumed as the Sun) was King of France 1643–1715.

▲ QING 1644–1912
The last dynasty of the Chinese Empire was founded by Manchurian invaders. Emperor Qianlong ruled 1711–1799.

▲ ROMANOV 1613–1917
The Romanovs were the last Russian dynasty. Catherine the Great married into the family and was empress 1762–1796.

FIND OUT MORE ▶▶ English Civil War 406 • Samurai 392 • Tudor Age 404

SCIENTIFIC REVOLUTION

The 18th century was a period of remarkable scientific breakthroughs. This began with the scientific advances of the 16th and 17th centuries, when people began to reject unproven theories and superstition in favour of careful observation, and carried out experiments to test ideas.

WHO DISCOVERED HOW BLOOD CIRCULATES?
In 1597, English student William Harvey went to Padua in Italy, which was then a centre for studying the human body. He returned to become royal doctor, and in 1628 declared that blood was pumped around the body by the heart. Many doctors ridiculed his views, but Harvey was correct. His discovery changed our understanding of the human body forever.

NEW SCIENCE

1609	●	Johannes Kepler works out how planets move
1638	●	Galileo Galilei publishes his theories of mechanics
1687	●	Isaac Newton publishes his three Laws of Motion
1753	●	Carl Linnaeus works out a way of classifying species
1774	●	Joseph Priestley researches into oxygen

WHO WAS THE FIRST PERSON TO SEE GERMS?
The first microscopes were made in the Netherlands in about 1590. Their design was improved by Robert Hooke and Anton van Leeuwenhoek. Van Leeuwenhoek made many important observations and in 1675 was the first person to see bacteria, or germs.

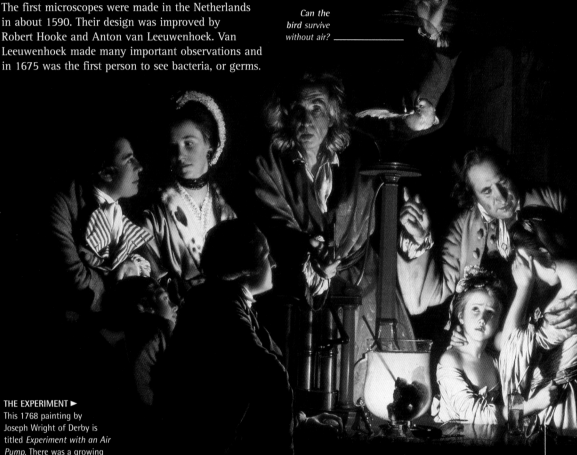

Can the bird survive without air?

ROBERT BOYLE
1627–1691
Irish chemist and physicist Robert Boyle experimented with gases and with vacuum (in which gases are pumped out of a space). He introduced the idea of chemical elements, essential to the development of chemistry as a science.

THE EXPERIMENT ►
This 1768 painting by Joseph Wright of Derby is titled *Experiment with an Air Pump.* There was a growing public interest in science and the ways in which it could be applied to industry.

The girls fear the worst

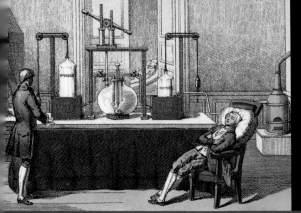

WHO WERE THE FIRST CHEMISTS?
From the Middle Ages to the early 18th century, alchemists believed they could turn ordinary metals into gold, and so find the secret of everlasting life. Although this was impossible, alchemy did provide a basis for useful experiments in chemistry, and inspired the genuine research of Robert Boyle.

◄ LAVOISIER'S LABORATORY
This the laboratory of Antoine Lavoisier, one of the founders of modern chemistry. He continued the work of Englishman Joseph Priestley into oxygen.

REFLECTING TELESCOPE ►
Telescopes were invented in the Netherlands in about 1608. In 1668, Isaac Newton was the first to use mirrors to improve the image seen through the telescope.

e ►►
Scientific Revolution

FIND OUT MORE ►► Chemistry 162 • The Enlightenment 416 • Science 154

AGRICULTURAL REVOLUTION

The 18th and 19th centuries saw great changes in Europe and North America in the way people farmed. Scientific methods were used to improve crop yields and breed better livestock. ▶▶ MECHANIZATION made farming more efficient.

WHY DID CHANGES TAKE PLACE IN FARMING?
At this time there was a new interest in science and technology. Many old crafts were becoming modern industries and farming was no exception. This was necessary, as cities were growing and their populations needed more food. In France, an inefficient farming system had resulted in famine and political unrest.

▲ BRINGERS OF CHANGE
Landowners wishing to improve their estates were at the forefront of change. They experimented with new breeds of cattle, and also learned how to change crops year by year to preserve the goodness of the soil.

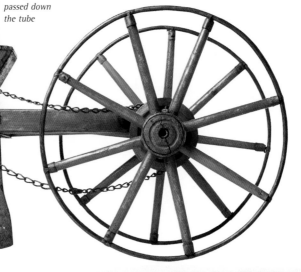

◄ SEED DRILL
Seeds had been scattered by hand until Jethro Tull's seed drill (developed in about 1701) made it possible to plant seeds in rows, which could then be easily hoed.

Seed placed here passed down the tube

Agricultural Revolution

WHO WORKED ON THE LAND?
In many parts of Europe, farming had changed very little since the Middle Ages. Peasants laboured in the fields in great poverty and often had little freedom to move away from their villages. In Britain, farm work was increasingly carried out by large numbers of low-waged labourers.

THOMAS WILLIAM COKE
1752–1842
Thomas Coke was one of the new landowners determined to improve agriculture. He replaced rye with wheat on his land in Norfolk, England, and bred cattle, sheep, and pigs. He also became a Member of Parliament.

MECHANIZATION

In the 1800s, new machines, such as reaping and threshing machines, were invented to do jobs that had previously been done by hand.

DID MACHINES REPLACE PEOPLE?
These new inventions were brought in to make farming easier and also to reduce costs. By the 1830s, English farm labourers were beginning to worry that mechanization would lead to loss of jobs. They protested by smashing new machinery and burning hay ricks. Their fears were founded. In the next 150 years, the number of farm workers declined rapidly.

AGRICULTURAL SHOWS ▶
The Royal Agricultural Society meets at Bristol, England, in 1842. After 1839, the Society helped to spread knowledge of crops, livestock breeding, and new machinery among farmers.

FIND OUT MORE ▶▶ Early Farming 364–365 • Ecology 80–81

SLAVE TRADE

People have been bought and sold as slaves around the world through much of history. This trade reached new heights in the 16th to 19th centuries, as Arabs and Europeans plundered Africa. In the 18th century, it is believed that up to eight million Africans were shipped across the Atlantic Ocean.

TOUSSAINT L'OUVERTURE
1746–1803
Toussaint was a freed slave from the French colony of St Dominque (Haiti). He joined a slave uprising in 1791. When revolutionary France abolished slavery, Toussaint became a respected leader. However, after a change of government he was seized and imprisoned.

◄ SLAVE CHAINS
Slaves were transported to the Americas in chains. Many Europeans and Americans campaigned against slavery. It was abolished in the British Empire in the 1830s and in the USA in 1865.

Iron chains could be fixed around necks or ankles

e ▸▸
slave trade

HOW WAS THE SLAVE TRADE ORGANIZED?
West African slaves were normally captured by African raiders. At the coast they were exchanged for European guns or textiles. The European traders packed the slaves into ships and sailed for the New World. Once the Africans were sold, the European captains picked up cargoes before sailing home.

HOW WERE SLAVES TREATED IN THE NEW WORLD?
After the ordeal of the Atlantic crossing, the slaves were prepared for auction. Once sold, they were forced to work long hours on ▸▸ PLANTATIONS for no pay. Many slaves were treated with cruelty, and were chained and branded. Those who tried to escape were punished by whipping or even hanging.

◄ AUCTIONED LIKE CATTLE
Slaves are auctioned off to plantation owners in the southern USA. They were examined to see if they were strong and fit. Families might be split up, never to see each other again.

PLANTATIONS

Slaves in the Caribbean and the US were forced to work on plantations – estates where sugar cane, cotton, or other crops were grown. The owners paid workers no wages, so their profits were huge.

WHY WERE PLANTATIONS CREATED?
Plantations in the New World marked the start of farming on an industrial, global scale. Plantations produced cash crops – crops grown for sale and export rather than local use. The use of slave labour reduced costs.

PLANTATION IN GEORGIA ▶
This is a cotton plantation in Georgia, USA, in 1895 – thirty years after the abolition of slavery. The work is still exhausting in the heat of the day, the hours still long.

FIND OUT MORE ▸▸ American Civil War 424 • Medieval Africa 394–395

AMERICAN REVOLUTION

e ▶▶ Americ Revolut

The period 1765-1788 saw great changes in North America. The 13 eastern colonies demanded democratic government, and went to war against Britain in 1775. In 1776 they issued a ▶▶ **DECLARATION OF INDEPENDENCE** and in 1781 the British command surrendered the fight.

WHY DID THE COLONISTS REVOLT?

The people who had settled in North America valued personal freedom. Many of them had left Europe because of their strong religious or political views. They protested when the British government imposed taxes on them without consulting the local governing bodies of the colonies.

WHAT WAS THE BOSTON TEA PARTY?

Taxes paid on imported goods were very unpopular. In 1773, colonists disguised as American Indians boarded an English ship in Boston harbour and threw its cargo of highly taxed tea overboard. This became known as the Boston Tea Party.

WHO FOUGHT IN THE WAR?

British troops, including German mercenaries, were supported by colonial loyalists. The rebellious Patriots formed a Continental Army after 1775, defeating the British at Saratoga Springs in 1777. The French sent 6,000 troops to fight the British.

▼ SIEGE OF YORKTOWN, 1781
In 1781, George Washington and the French commander, the Comte de Rochambeau, besieged and finally defeated the British at Yorktown, Virginia.

DECLARATION OF INDEPENDENCE

In 1774, Patriots convened the first in a series of Continental Congresses in Philadelphia, Pennsylvania, to co-ordinate their struggle against the British. The 1776 Congress issued a Declaration of Independence, laying down its principles of freedom. A full United States government was founded in 1788.

◀ LIBERTY BELL
This bell hung in the Pennsylvania State House. It was rung to mark both the Boston Tea Party and the first public reading of the Declaration of Independence.

WHO CALLED FOR FREEDOM?

The 1776 Declaration of Independence was issued in Philadelphia, in the name of John Hancock, president of the Continental Congress. It was written by Thomas Jefferson, who later became the third US president. It declared that "all men are created equal" and have a right to "life, liberty, and the pursuit of happiness". These ringing words inspired revolutionaries around the world.

GEORGE WASHINGTON
1732–1799

Born in Virginia, Washington was a wealthy landowner and served with the British army. In 1775 he was chosen to command the rebel American army, which he led to victory in 1781. He oversaw the new constitution and in 1789 became the first US president.

FRENCH REVOLUTION

The years 1789 to 1799 marked a turning point in European history. In France, calls for political reform were overtaken by a revolution which swept away the monarchy, the aristocracy, and the power of the Church. The revolution was followed by a ▸▸ **REIGN OF TERROR**.

WHY DID THE FRENCH RISE UP?

In 1789, the French aristocracy and leading churchmen led privileged lives and had great power. However, the middle classes wanted more power for themselves. Taxes were high, the country was bankrupt, and the poor were starving. King Louis XVI failed to bring in reforms in time to stop a revolution.

WHAT HAPPENED ON 14 JULY?

On 14 July 1789, the people of Paris were afraid that the army had been ordered to attack them. They armed themselves and marched to the Bastille, a royal fort used as a prison, in search of gunpowder. They attacked and captured the fort. The revolution had begun.

▲ DOOMED MONARCHS
King Louis XVI came to the throne in 1774, but failed to solve his country's problems. Queen Marie-Antoinette was disliked for her extravagance. She showed personal courage during the revolution, but was executed in 1793.

MAXIMILIEN DE ROBESPIERRE
1758–1794

Robespierre became one of the most radical leaders of the revolution. He whipped up a climate of fear and soon his opponents were being sent to the guillotine. He himself was seized and beheaded without trial in 1794.

e ▸▸
French Revolution

◀ MARCH TO VERSAILLES
In October 1789, the poor women of Paris led an angry mob to the royal palace of Versailles and demanded bread for their hungry families. The king agreed to their demands, but the crowd grew and fighting broke out. The next day the king was forced to return to Paris.

REIGN OF TERROR

The French Revolution succeeded in overthrowing a corrupt and unjust system of government, but it soon ran out of control. First aristocrats were executed and then the revolutionaries turned on each other in a bloodbath. The Reign of Terror had begun, in which the state governed by fear.

◀ THE KING'S HEAD
King Louis XVI was accused of treason by the National Convention. He was executed in January 1793, ending over a thousand years of monarchy in France. The Revolutionaries' guillotines were claiming more and more victims.

HOW MANY PEOPLE DIED?

During the Reign of Terror (1793–1794), about 40,000 people were executed or murdered. A guillotine was set up in the Place de la Révolution in Paris. This wooden frame contained a sharp blade which dropped on to the victim's neck. Although it was supposed to be a humane method of execution, its efficiency meant that hundreds were dying every day.

WHEN DID THE TERROR END?

The creator of the Reign of Terror, Robespierre, was seized by his opponents in the National Convention and beheaded in 1794. In 1795 there were major uprisings. Order was restored by a soldier called Napoleon Bonaparte. Power passed to a five-man group called the Directory and by 1799 Napoleon had seized power for himself. The revolution was over.

FIND OUT MORE ▸▸ Monarchy 410 • Napoleonic Wars 416

THE ENLIGHTENMENT

Scientific advances of the 17th and 18th centuries encouraged new ideas, and this led European philosophers to declare that humans progressed by using reason and logic, rather than faith or superstition. This period became known as The Enlightenment, or Age of Reason.

A statue of Wisdom replaced a statue of Atheism

Enlightenment

◄ A NEW RELIGION?
In 1794, Robespierre organized a festival of the Supreme Being. Although he was not an atheist, he disliked the rituals and doctrines of the Church.

WHO PUT TOGETHER A GREAT BOOK OF KNOWLEDGE?
New information systems were needed for this new age. Dictionaries began to appear and a 17-volume encyclopedia, edited by Denis Diderot, was published in France in 1751–1772. Its contributors included thinkers such as Montesquieu, Rousseau, and Voltaire.

WHO ABOLISHED GOD?
In 1793, the French National Convention abolished the worship of God and forbade what it regarded as superstitious festivals. A new calendar was drawn up which did not begin with the birth of Christ but with a current human event, the French Revolution.

FIND OUT MORE ▶▶ Scientific Revolution 411

NAPOLEONIC WARS

During the French Revolution, France was at war with its neighbours in Europe. These wars resumed in 1800 under the leadership of Napoleon, who was crowned as French emperor in 1804. A series of great victories soon brought much of Europe under his control.

WHERE DID NAPOLEON'S ARMIES MARCH?
Napoleon was a brilliant soldier. He defeated Austria. He invaded Spain in 1808 and his armies reached Moscow in 1812, only to be beaten back by the harsh winter weather. He made his relatives rulers in Spain, Italy, and Westphalia. He was finally defeated by Britain and Prussia at Waterloo, Belgium, in 1815.

Napoleonic Wars

EUROPE AT WAR	
1805	French victory at Austerlitz
1805	British victory at Trafalgar
1808–1814	Peninsular War
1812	France invades Russia
1815	Napoleon defeated

WHAT WAS NAPOLEON'S LEGACY?
Napoleon (1769–1821) died in exile. He is remembered as the man who brought the French Revolution to a close and as a military genius. He was a skilled administrator whose system of law, the *Code Napoléon*, gave the poor people of France some of the rights they had demanded in the revolution. The *Code* was also welcomed in many of the lands he invaded.

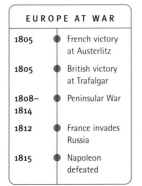

A CORSICAN HERO ▶
Napoleon Bonaparte came from the Mediterranean island of Corsica. He was a hero to his followers and his troops, but aroused fear among his enemies in countries such as Britain.

FIND OUT MORE ▶▶ French Revolution 415

CANADA

European fishermen and fur traders visited Canada from the 16th century onwards. They bought furs from the local people, who were related to the other native peoples of North America. France established colonies in Canada in 1608 (Quebec) and 1642 (Montreal), while the British claimed a vast territory around Hudson Bay after 1670.

JACQUES CARTIER
1491–1557
This French navigator made three voyages to North America between 1534 and 1541. He was the first European to see the St Lawrence river and claimed the land for France.

▼ DEATH OF THE GENERALS
The British general James Wolfe lies dying in 1759, having captured Quebec and defeated the French. The French general, Montcalm, was also killed.

Canadian history

WHO FOUGHT TO CONTROL CANADA?
The French and British fought each other for Canada. Both wanted its furs, timber, and rich fishing grounds. The French were defeated in 1759 and Canada became a British colony four years later. Many American colonists who had remained loyal to Britain during the American Revolution fled to Canada in the 1780s.

Both armies used native warriors as scouts and guides

WHEN DID CANADA BECOME A NATION?
In 1791, the areas of Canada settled by Europeans were divided between Upper (English-speaking) and Lower (French-speaking) Canada. These were reunited in 1841. Canada became a self-governing dominion of the British Empire in 1867. Settlement spread westwards as Europeans arrived.

FIND OUT MORE ▸▸ Canada, Alaska, and Greenland 224–225

INDIAN WARS

For much of the 19th century, especially between 1860 and 1890, a tragic conflict took place in the United States. Settlers and soldiers fought against American Indians. They seized their lands and herded the American Indians into camps known as reservations.

◄ GHOST DANCE
In 1890, many Indians on reservations had strange visions. They began to perform a magical "ghost dance", which they believed would return their land to them. It did not. Many were later gunned down or died of disease.

WHAT WAS THE TRAIL OF TEARS?
In the 1830s, gold was found in Cherokee territory in the southeastern USA. About 16,000 Cherokees from the region were rounded up by the US army and forced to travel west in 1838 on a "Trail of Tears". Over 4,000 Cherokees died on the journey.

WHAT WAS CUSTER'S LAST STAND?
In 1876, General George Custer led the United States Seventh Cavalry into the prairie lands around the Little Bighorn River, in Montana. Stumbling upon a big assembly of Sioux and Cheyenne warriors, Custer's force was defeated and killed. It was the last American Indian victory.

Indian Wars

FIND OUT MORE ▸▸ American Indians 408

INDUSTRIAL REVOLUTION

The Industrial Revolution changed the way things were made as new machines invented in the 1700s and 1800s meant it was possible to mass produce goods in factories. Starting in Britain and spreading through Europe and North America, a period of rapid social and economic change began, with widespread ▸▸URBANIZATION.

▲ STEAM HAMMER
During the 1830s–1840s, James Naysmith of Manchester, England, developed a massive steam-powered hammer.

▲ CITY SLUMS
The growth of cities during the 19th and 20th centuries meant many families in Europe lived in run-down, unhealthy housing.

▲ ON THE BRIGHT SIDE
Technology transformed public life after the 1880s. Electric street lamps lit up cities in Europe and North America.

▲ THE GREAT EXHIBITION
This international showcase for manufacture and trade was held in London in 1851, in a glass building called the Crystal Palace.

HOW WERE FACTORIES POWERED?
During the 18th century water was an important source of power for industry and many machines were driven by waterwheels. Steam power was also developed at this time. Steam engines were used to pump water out of mineshafts and to power new ▸▸TRANSPORTATION systems. Engines and furnaces were all fuelled by coal. By the 19th century, coal was being transported to the factories by ship or rail.

WHY WERE GOODS MASS PRODUCED?
Before the Industrial Revolution, most goods were produced in small workshops or at home. Mass production in factories made it possible to manufacture goods more cheaply and quickly. Huge markets for these goods were opening up in the new cities, and in the lands that the European nations were conquering and settling overseas.

HOW DID WORKING CONDITIONS CHANGE?
The factory age meant that workers no longer owned the means by which they made a living. Some factory owners pushed up their own profits by pushing down the wages of their workers. Men, women, and children worked long hours for little pay, often in dangerous conditions. It took many years for wages and working environments to improve.

ISAMBARD KINGDOM BRUNEL
1806–1859

Brunel was born of a French father in Portsmouth, England. An engineering genius, he helped to shape the industrial age. He built tunnels, docks, and suspension bridges. He was appointed chief engineer of England's Great Western Railway and also designed steamships for crossing the Atlantic Ocean.

Work in a textile mill could be monotonous and noisy

Industrial Revolution

KING COTTON ▶
This photograph of a spinning mill in the United States dates from about 1890. New technology for spinning and weaving had marked the start of the Industrial Revolution in the 18th century. The 19th century saw cotton become the chief industrial textile. It was often produced in mills in Manchester, England, with raw cotton imported from the southern United States or India.

▲ WORKERS UNITED
London dockers strike in 1889. The appalling working conditions of the early Industrial Revolution gradually improved as workers banded together in trade unions and campaigned for better wages. Some were socialists or communists, demanding political reform or revolution.

Children worked in factories and often went barefoot

TRANSPORTATION

The Industrial Revolution depended on transport to move raw materials, goods, and people. Canals were dug in the 18th century. In the 19th, it was the turn of the railways.

WHEN DID THE RAILWAY AGE BEGIN?
The first steam locomotive to run on rails was seen in Wales in 1804. Designs were greatly improved in the 1820s by English rail pioneer George Stephenson. Railways were soon opening up the world.

▲ ACROSS THE USA
Locomotives belch smoke at a busy junction in the USA in 1886. Railways opened up new continents, crossing Europe, Asia, Africa, South America, and Australia. Railway companies made their fortunes.

URBANIZATION

Urbanization means the spread of towns. Between 1700 and 1900 the world's population grew from 679 million to 1,633 million. Many people were city dwellers.

WHAT KIND OF CITIES WERE BUILT?
Cities grew up around coalfields or factories, at important seaports and railway junctions. They provided cheap housing for the industrial workers. New British cities were often rows of terraced houses built of brick and slate, with small yards and alleys.

▲ GLASGOW SKYLINE
Smoke from factory chimneys darkens the sky in Glasgow. This Scottish city grew rapidly after the River Clyde was deepened in 1768, making it more accessible to shipping.

FIND OUT MORE ▶▶ Agricultural Revolution 412 • Industry 204 • Manufacturing 205

SOUTH AMERICAN INDEPENDENCE

The American empires founded by Spain and Portugal broke up in the 19th century. These European countries were no longer powerful and their colonies struggled to break away. Wars brought liberation, but independence was often followed by strife between the new nations.

WHO WAS KNOWN AS THE LIBERATOR?

Simón Bolívar, "the Liberator", helped to free much of South America. He fought in Venezuela and ruled Colombia and Ecuador. He freed Peru, and Bolivia was renamed in his honour. Other freedom fighters included Bernardo O'Higgins and José de San Martín, who fought in Argentina, Chile, and Peru.

WHO ENDED PORTUGUESE RULE IN BRAZIL?

When Portugal was invaded by the French emperor Napoleon in 1807, the Portuguese royal family fled to their colony of Brazil. King John VI returned home in 1821, leaving his son Pedro to rule Brazil for him, but in 1822, Pedro declared himself to be emperor of an independent Brazil.

WHEN DID ARGENTINA BECOME INDEPENDENT?

The capital city of Argentina, Buenos Aires (meaning "fair winds"), was founded by the Spanish in the 16th century. In 1810, its people rose up against Spanish rule, gaining their independence in 1816. There followed a civil war between the city dwellers and the ranchers of the provinces. The country was finally united in 1861.

▲ GAUCHOS OF ARGENTINA
The Gauchos were Argentine cowboys, of part Spanish, part Indian descent. These daring, hard-living rogues opposed the new Buenos Aires government, backing their own leaders in a struggle for power.

WHAT WERE SOUTH AMERICA'S NEW ECONOMIES?

In the 19th century, South America's gold and silver mines began to run out. A new source of wealth was needed. In Brazil, plantations of coffee and rubber were set up, while Argentina's grasslands supported sheep and cattle. When refrigeration was invented, huge amounts of beef were exported from Buenos Aires.

e ▸▸ South American independence

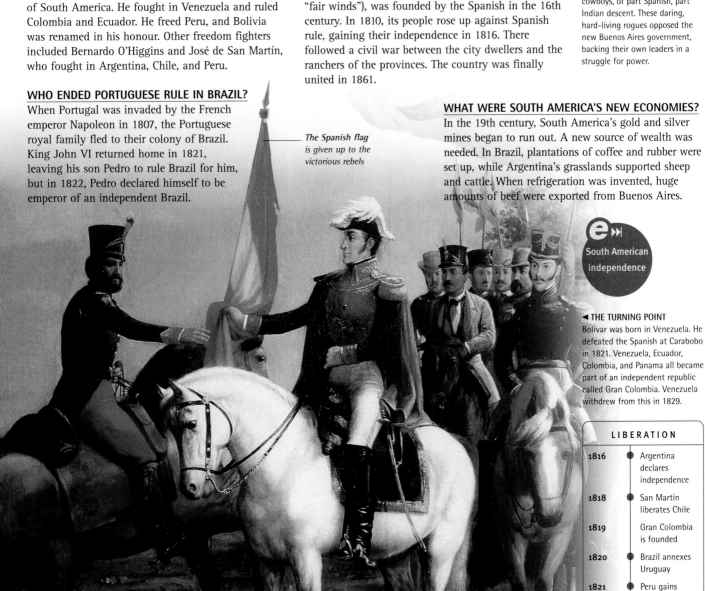

The Spanish flag is given up to the victorious rebels

◂ THE TURNING POINT
Bolivar was born in Venezuela. He defeated the Spanish at Carabobo in 1821. Venezuela, Ecuador, Colombia, and Panama all became part of an independent republic called Gran Colombia. Venezuela withdrew from this in 1829.

LIBERATION	
1816	Argentina declares independence
1818	San Martín liberates Chile
1819	Gran Colombia is founded
1820	Brazil annexes Uruguay
1821	Peru gains independence
	Venezuela and Ecuador are liberated
1822	Brazil breaks away from Portugal
1825	Bolivia is liberated

FIND OUT MORE ▸▸ South America 232–233

NATIONALISM

Nationalism means the wish of a people to govern themselves as a nation. This ideal reshaped the map of Europe in the 19th century. Later in the century, nationalism took on a second meaning – an exaggerated belief in the superiority of one's own nation.

WHY WAS POLAND IN REVOLT?

Between 1772 and 1795 Poland was divided between Russia, Prussia, and Austria. There were nationalist uprisings against the Russians in 1830 and 1863, but independence was not regained until 1918.

▲ THE GREEKS RISE UP
This postage stamp commemorates the 150th anniversary of the Greek uprising (1821-1827) against Turkish rule. The savage response of the Turks gained the Greek rebels sympathy across Europe.

WHEN DID GERMANY COME INTO BEING?

Since the Middle Ages, Germany had been a patchwork of free cities and small states within the Holy Roman Empire. In the 19th century, these came together, first economically, then politically. In 1871, Wilhelm I of Prussia became emperor of a united Germany.

NEW NATIONS	
1830–1831	● Nationalist agitation; calls for democratic reform across Europe
1832	● Greece recognized as independent from Turkey
1848	● Nationalist and liberal uprisings across Europe
1871	● Germany unites as an empire
1871	● Italy becomes a single nation

IRISH BOMB BLAST ▶
Ireland became part of the United Kingdom in 1801. A nationalist organization, the Irish Republican Brotherhood (or "Fenians"), was founded in New York in 1857 to campaign for a free Ireland. It launched attacks in Manchester and London in 1867.

The red shirt became a symbol of freedom

WHO WERE THE REDSHIRTS?

Giuseppe Garibaldi (1807-1882) dreamed of uniting Italy and freeing it from foreign rule. In 1860 he assembled 1,000 volunteers, who wore red shirts as a uniform. They sailed from Genoa to Sicily and joined an uprising against that kingdom's French rulers. They then crossed to southern Italy. Garibaldi later tried to march on Rome, and fought against Austria.

◀ ITALIAN FREEDOM FIGHTER
Garibaldi leads his Redshirts into battle. As a young man, Garibaldi had joined the "Young Italy" movement. Forced to flee to South America, he fought against dictatorship and injustice there before returning to Italy in 1847.

OTTO VON BISMARCK
1815–1898
Bismarck was a Prussian politician, a conservative, and a royalist. He opposed the liberal nationalists who demanded democratic change in Germany in 1848, but played a major role in creating the German Empire of 1871.

nationalism

FIND OUT MORE ▶▶ Holy Roman Empire 385 • Thirty Years' War 406

AGE OF EMPIRE

From the 19th until the early 20th century, much of the world was governed by a few very powerful European nations. The ▶▶ BRITISH RAJ controlled the riches of India. The ▶▶ FRENCH FOREIGN LEGION defended remote forts in the Sahara desert, and there was a ▶▶ SCRAMBLE FOR AFRICA by empire-builders.

WHY DID EUROPEANS WANT TO RULE THE WORLD?
The reasons were many. The factories of the newly industrialized lands needed resources, such as rubber. Some empire-builders wanted land for settlement, others were praying for converts to Christianity.

HOW WERE PEOPLE TREATED BY THEIR RULERS?
Most empire-builders claimed to be bringing civilization to peoples whom they believed to be inferior. Although the ruling countries did build towns, ports, and railways, in some colonies the local peoples were treated little better than slaves.

THE WORLD IN 1900 ▶
The chief empire-builders were the French, British, Germans, Danish, Belgians, Dutch, Spanish, and Portuguese. The United States and Japan were also gaining overseas territories. The Russian Empire now ruled the whole of northern Asia. However, the Chinese Empire was losing territory to foreign powers.

BRITISH RAJ

By the 19th century, real power in India was held by the British East India Company. Following an uprising by Indian soldiers in 1857, British government rule, or Raj, was imposed on India in 1858.

WHO BECAME EMPRESS OF INDIA?
Queen Victoria (1819–1901) was declared Empress of India in 1876. Under her rule Great Britain became the world's most powerful nation. Victoria had a shrewd grasp of politics and took a keen interest in her government's foreign policy. India was believed to be one of the most important parts of the British Empire. The two countries had a great cultural influence on each other.

◀ VICTORIA AT WORK
Queen Victoria, Empress of India, is attended by her Indian servant as she writes letters and reads state papers in 1893.

SCRAMBLE FOR AFRICA

As explorers discovered new lands in Africa, European powers rushed in to take them over. The French clashed with the British in Sudan, and the Germans gained lands in East and West Africa.

WHAT HAPPENED IN BERLIN IN 1884?
From 1884 to 1885 the world's most powerful nations held a conference in Berlin, the capital of Germany. They divided between themselves vast regions of Africa. They knew little of these distant lands and did not consult the peoples living there. Borders were drawn up to serve their own political needs.

STANLEY FINDS LIVINGSTONE ▶
David Livingstone was a Scottish missionary and explorer who wanted to open trading routes through Africa. Held up by illness in 1871, Livingstone was found by H.M. Stanley, an explorer hired by the *New York Herald* paper.

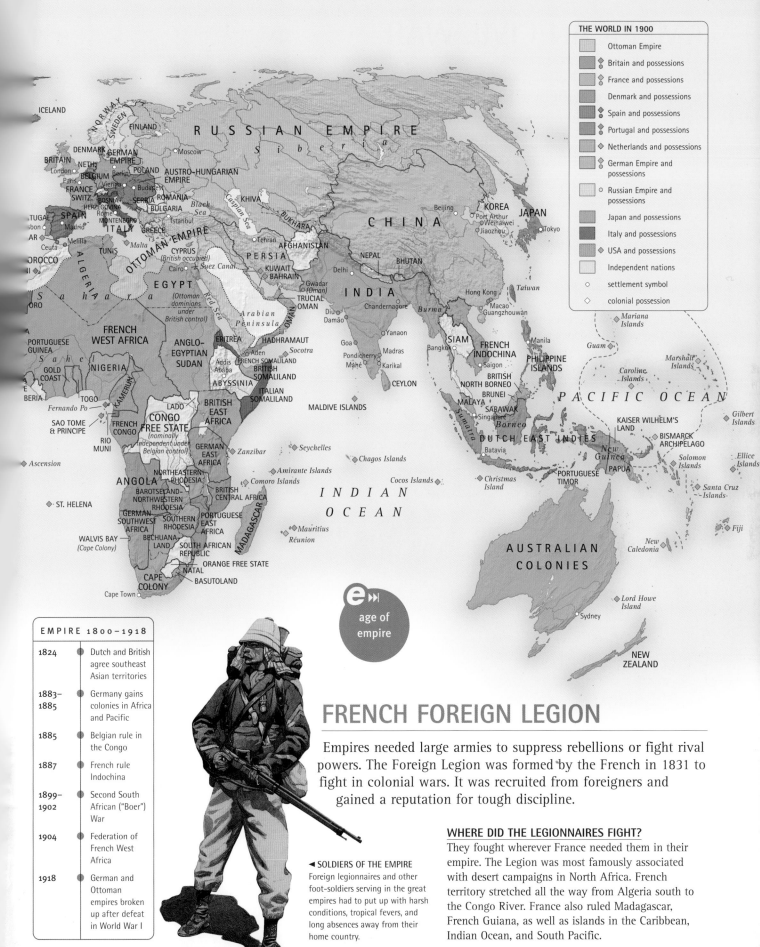

THE WORLD IN 1900

- Ottoman Empire
- Britain and possessions
- France and possessions
- Denmark and possessions
- Spain and possessions
- Portugal and possessions
- Netherlands and possessions
- German Empire and possessions
- Russian Empire and possessions
- Japan and possessions
- Italy and possessions
- USA and possessions
- Independent nations
- ○ settlement symbol
- ◇ colonial possession

e ▶▶ age of empire

EMPIRE 1800–1918	
1824	Dutch and British agree southeast Asian territories
1883–1885	Germany gains colonies in Africa and Pacific
1885	Belgian rule in the Congo
1887	French rule Indochina
1899–1902	Second South African ("Boer") War
1904	Federation of French West Africa
1918	German and Ottoman empires broken up after defeat in World War I

◀ SOLDIERS OF THE EMPIRE
Foreign legionnaires and other foot-soldiers serving in the great empires had to put up with harsh conditions, tropical fevers, and long absences away from their home country.

FRENCH FOREIGN LEGION

Empires needed large armies to suppress rebellions or fight rival powers. The Foreign Legion was formed by the French in 1831 to fight in colonial wars. It was recruited from foreigners and gained a reputation for tough discipline.

WHERE DID THE LEGIONNAIRES FIGHT?
They fought wherever France needed them in their empire. The Legion was most famously associated with desert campaigns in North Africa. French territory stretched all the way from Algeria south to the Congo River. France also ruled Madagascar, French Guiana, as well as islands in the Caribbean, Indian Ocean, and South Pacific.

FIND OUT MORE ▶▶ Medieval Africa 394–395 • Mughal India 407

AMERICAN CIVIL WAR

In 1860 and 1861 a group of southern states, known as the Confederacy, withdrew from the United States. A civil war began when the Confederates attacked a federal fort in Charleston, South Carolina. In 1865, the Union defeated the Confederacy in this fierce conflict.

▲ BATTLE OF THE IRONCLADS
Armour-plated ships known as "ironclads" exchange fire off Virginia in 1862. The Union's aim was to stop ships supplying the Confederacy.

WHY DID THE STATES FIGHT EACH OTHER?
The northern states were building an industrial economy. The agricultural southern states still relied on slave labour. They resented the increasing power of the north and feared that the federal government in Washington would impose reforms and end slavery.

HOW MANY PEOPLE DIED?
The USA was reunited at a terrible cost. The northern troops lost 359,000 soldiers, while the southerners lost 258,000. Civilians suffered from looting, and the devastation of railways, towns, and cotton plantations.

WHAT WAS THE UNDERGROUND RAILROAD?
This was a secret network of escape routes and hideouts for African-American slaves. Between 1786 and 1861, activists such as Harriet Tubman (c. 1820–1913) helped about 50,000 slaves escape to freedom in the northern states and Canada.

DID THE CIVIL WAR END SLAVERY IN THE USA?
Abraham Lincoln proclaimed an end to slavery in 1863 and it was finally abolished in the southern states after the war. African-Americans remained poor, and the southern states passed laws which prevented them from voting or gaining equal status despite constitutional amendments guaranteeing these rights.

ABRAHAM LINCOLN
1809–1865
Lincoln was elected President in 1860 and again in 1864. He supported strong federal government and opposed slavery. Having led the Union to victory in the Civil War, he was assassinated at a theatre in Washington, D.C., in 1865.

◄ UNDER FIRE
This howitzer (a short cannon) was the most common artillery piece used in the American Civil War.

GRANT VERSUS LEE ▼
In1864, the Union general Ulysses S Grant clashed with the Confederate general Robert E Lee in a bid to capture Spotsylvania Court House in northern Virginia. Casualties were heavy. Neither side won the battle.

American Civil War

FIND OUT MORE ▸▸ American Revolution 414 • Slave Trade 413

AUSTRALIA

The coasts of Australia were first mapped by Dutch explorers in the 17th century and by the British in the 18th. In 1788, the British founded a colony in New South Wales and went on to settle the rest of this vast land.

JAMES COOK
1728–1779
Captain Cook was a brilliant English navigator who explored the coasts of Australia and New Zealand. He landed at Botany Bay in New South Wales in 1778 and claimed the land for Britain. Cook was killed in Hawaii by natives of the islands.

WHY WERE CONVICTS SENT TO AUSTRALIA?
From 1788 until 1852 the British sent criminals to Australia for punishment. The new country was built with forced labour. Free settlers were soon arriving as well to seek their fortune – especially after gold was discovered in 1851.

WHAT HAPPENED TO THE ABORIGINES?
About two million Aborigines lived in Australia in 1788. By 1900 only 50,000 survived. Many died of diseases introduced by the settlers. Others were murdered or driven off their land. Some worked as police trackers, or as labourers on sheep stations.

WHEN DID AUSTRALIA BECOME A NATION?
The various colonies founded in Australia by the British were mostly granted self-rule in the 1850s. There was great rivalry between them, but they finally agreed to unite as states within a single federal Commonwealth in 1901.

Australian history

ABORIGINAL FISHERS ▶
Aborigine hunters and fishers could survive in the harshest environments, but they only just survived the European invasion and the long years of suffering that followed.

FIND OUT MORE ▶▶ Australia and New Zealand 274–275 • Exploration 400–401 • First Modern Humans 362–363

NEW ZEALAND

New Zealand is known to the Maoris as Aotearoa. Dutch and English navigators charted these islands and by the 19th century traders and whaling crews were landing there. The islands came under British rule in 1840.

New Zealand history

TREATY OF WAITANGI ▶
In 1840, the British signed a treaty with a gathering of Maori chiefs on North Island. It guaranteed Maori rights to the land, but these were ignored by the settlers.

WHEN DID NEW ZEALAND GAIN SELF-RULE?
Britain granted the colonists self-rule in 1852. The country prospered from sheep farming and from the discovery of gold in 1862. In 1893, New Zealand became the first country to give women the vote. In 1907, it became a Dominion, a fully independent nation within the British Empire.

WHAT BECAME OF THE MAORIS?
The Maoris had possessed firearms since the arrival of the first foreigners. After 1840, the settlers seized more and more land, so between 1845 and 1847 the Maoris rose up in revolt. A second war took place from 1860 to 1872. This won the Maoris representation in the New Zealand Parliament.

▲ MAORI TRADITION
The Maoris are descended from Polynesians who colonized Aotearoa about a thousand years before the arrival of the Europeans. They remain fiercely proud of their culture and its traditions.

FIND OUT MORE ▶▶ Australia and New Zealand 274–275 • Polynesia 396

WORLD WAR I

World War I (1914–1918) was the first war in history to be fought by many different nations around the world. About eight million men were killed, many in horrific ▸▸ TRENCH WARFARE, before the ▸▸ ARMISTICE in 1918.

Entente Powers and allies	Neutral Powers	Central Powers and allies	Greatest advance of Central Powers	Front lines November 1918

▲ WAR ACROSS THE REGIONS
Europe lay at the centre of the fighting. Troops came here from as far away as Africa, India, New Zealand, Australia, and Canada. The Western Front stretched from Belgium to Switzerland. The Eastern Front extended from the Baltic to the Black Sea. There was an Arab revolt against the Ottoman Empire in 1917 and Britain invaded most of the Middle East.

Guns fired from side turrets

▲ TANKS INTO BATTLE
Tanks were a British invention. They first appeared in 1916 and were used in battle at Cambrai, France, in 1917. Tanks were armour-plated. Their tracks could cross muddy trenches and crash through barbed wire.

WHY DID WAR BREAK OUT?
In the 20th century, European nations formed competing military alliances. War finally broke out in 1914 when a Serbian nationalist assassinated the heir to the throne of Austria. Austria went to war against Serbia, and many other countries joined in. On one side were the British, the French and Russian empires, Italy, and Japan (the Entente Powers). On the other side were the Germans, Austrians, Hungarians, Bulgarians, and Turks (the Central Powers).

WAR AND PEACE	
1914	Germany invades Belgium in order to attack France
1915	Gallipoli offensive in Turkey; Italy joins the Entente
1916	Naval battle off Jutland, Denmark
1917	USA enters the war on the side of the Entente; Russia leaves the war; Italy defeated by the Austrians; Arabs revolt against Turks
1918	Armistice ends the war

TRENCH WARFARE

In World War I, both sides dug long trenches as lines of defence, which stretched across Western Europe. These trenches filled up with stinking mud. Any order to go "over the top" and attack the enemy resulted in thousands of deaths.

WHERE WAS NO-MAN'S LAND?
The territory between the two front lines was called "no-man's land". It was a sea of mud, with broken stumps of trees and barbed wire entanglements. The area was raked by machine gun fire and pounded by heavy artillery, leaving craters big enough for soldiers to drown in.

DEATH IN GALLIPOLI ▶
The Gallipoli campaign between the Entente Powers and Turkey in 1915 included some of the worst trench fighting of the war. The campaign was a failure and cost the lives of many Australians and New Zealanders.

WHAT NEW WEAPONS WERE USED IN ACTION?

Various new technologies were available. In 1915, the German army used poison gas for the first time in warfare and it was soon in general use. The British were the first to introduce the battle tank. Submarines were now able to torpedo enemy shipping, forcing ships to travel across the ocean in convoys. Aircraft and airships were used to drop bombs, spy on enemy positions, and attack enemy pilots.

WHAT WAS TOTAL WAR?

This was war on a scale never experienced before. It was not just fought by professional soldiers. Most of the troops were civilian conscripts, called up to serve in the armed forces. Ordinary homes in cities such as London were bombed from the air. Even ocean liners carrying passengers from neutral countries came under attack. Entire national economies were geared towards the war effort.

▲ WOMEN GO TO WORK
A woman operates machinery at a munitions factory. In wartime, women had to take on work that only men had done before. Their proven abilities helped them to gain the vote after the war.

◄ "THE YANKS ARE COMING!"
On a poster, "Uncle Sam" calls on Americans to enlist in the army. Angered by German submarine activity, the USA joined the war in 1917. The arrival of fresh troops at this point in the war hastened the defeat of the Germans.

World War I

WILFRED OWEN
1893–1918
Many young men on both sides of the conflict, who had been idealists in 1914, became horrified by the war and its cruelty. One of them was the English war poet Wilfred Owen, killed just a week before the Armistice.

ARMISTICE

An armistice is a laying down of weapons. The guns of World War I finally fell silent at 11am on the 11th day of the 11th month of 1918.

DID PEACE FOLLOW WAR?

No, in Germany there was street fighting and starvation. In 1919, the terms of the peace were agreed at Versailles, in France. The settlement was harsh on Germany and this resulted in a sense of grievance which undermined any lasting peace.

▲ A LOST GENERATION
In war cemeteries across northern France, gravestones stretch as far as the eye can see. The war almost destroyed a whole generation. Of those who survived, many were left blind, disabled, or suffering from shock.

FIND OUT MORE ▸▸ Fascism 431 • World War II 432–433

REVOLUTIONARY RUSSIA

By the 1890s, many European nations were bringing in democratic reforms, but not Russia. Angry about social injustice, many Russians looked to socialism, anarchism, or ▶▶ COMMUNISM for an answer.

▲ TSAR NICHOLAS II AND HIS FAMILY
Nicholas II (1868–1918) came to the throne in 1895, but occupied himself with family life and failed to deal with Russia's growing problems. After the October Revolution of 1917, he and his family were imprisoned and then shot.

WHEN WAS BLOODY SUNDAY IN ST PETERSBURG?
In 1905, troops in St Petersburg gunned down workers who wished to present a petition to the tsar. This action resulted in strikes, mutinies, and uprisings all over Russia. As a result, a Duma, or parliament, was set up. However, the reforms it demanded were rejected by the tsar.

WHO OVERTHREW THE TSAR?
In March 1917, strikes, mutinies, and protests brought Russia to a standstill. Russian troops fighting in World War I deserted the Eastern Front. The tsar was forced from power and Russia became a republic. This became known as the February Revolution (as Russia followed a different calendar to Western countries).

WHEN WAS THE OCTOBER REVOLUTION?
The republican Duma failed to bring the chaos in Russia under control. A communist group known as the "Bolsheviks" rejected attempts at liberal reform. They appealed directly to workers to rise up in a communist revolution. The Bolsheviks seized power in "October" (that is, November) 1917.

▲ LENIN'S CALL
Vladimir Ilyich Lenin (1870–1924) returned from exile in 1917. He called for power to be handed over to Soviets (councils of revolutionary workers). After the October Revolution, he led the governing Communist Party.

COMMUNISM

Communists around the world were inspired by the writings of Karl Marx (1818–1883). Marx believed history was driven by economic forces and that a just and progressive society could only be created if the workers took control of the economic system.

WHEN WAS THE SOVIET UNION FOUNDED?
From 1918 to 1920 civil war raged through Russia as the communist Red Army fought opponents of the revolution ("the Whites"). The communists won and a Union of Soviet Socialist Republics ("Soviet Union") was founded in 1922. Only the Communist Party held power. Most industries came under state ownership and the economy was centrally controlled.

revolutionary Russia

◀ MAY DAY, 1920
A poster for International Workers' Day (or May Day) shows an idealized group of revolutionaries. At this time communist parties were being founded in many countries.

WHO WAS STALIN?
Lenin's successor was Joseph Stalin (1879–1953). His secret police murdered many of his opponents and millions were sent to forced labour camps. Stalin was criticized after his death, but the Soviet system failed to reform and collapsed in 1991.

REVOLUTIONARY CHINA

By the late 19th century, the Chinese Empire was growing weak and foreign nations were controlling its trade. In 1911 the last emperor, Puyi, was overthrown in a nationalist revolution. Many years of turmoil followed.

WHO CONTROLLED CHINA AFTER THE REVOLUTION?

Many forces fought to control China. First there were the nationalists, who founded a republic in 1912. Then there were the generals and regional warlords and, in 1921, the Chinese Communist Party. Finally, there was Japan, which gained Chinese territory in 1919.

CHINA 1912–1949	
1912	Chinese republic founded
1919	Japan gains Shandong
1931	Japan occupies Manchuria
1934–1935	The Long March
1937–1945	Japan invades China
1949	Communist victory

revolutionary China

◀ HARMONIOUS FIST SOCIETY
In 1900, this nationalist organization attacked foreigners living in China. Lurid reports were used to justify intervention by an international force, which suppressed the rebellion.

在毛澤東的勝利旗幟下前進

▲ MAO ZEDONG'S VICTORY
This poster dates from 1949, the year in which the People's Republic of China was founded. It shows the communist leader Mao Zedong in front of Beijing's Imperial Palace, with workers united together.

WHO WON THE STRUGGLE?

After 1925, Chiang Kai-shek became nationalist leader. Nationalists and communists became rivals but were forced into alliances as Japan overran China. Japan's defeat in 1945 was followed by civil war. By 1949, the communists had defeated the nationalists.

WHAT WAS "NEW CHINA"?

The nationalists fled to Taiwan and the communist leader Mao Zedong proclaimed a people's republic. Its successes in the 1950s included better education, literacy, and health. However, unrealistic agricultural and industrial reforms caused hardship, leading to political chaos during the ▶▶ CULTURAL REVOLUTION.

CULTURAL REVOLUTION

Economic failures caused dispute within the Chinese Communist Party. Fearing that the ideals of the revolution would be lost, Mao Zedong called for a "cultural revolution", a change in public attitudes.

WHO WERE THE RED GUARDS?

Students and young people took up Mao's ideas with fervour. They declared themselves "Red Guards", dedicated to never-ending revolution. They tore down temples, denounced their teachers, and rooted out "traitors". The suffering was immense. By 1967, the regular army was clashing with the Red Guards and Mao had little choice but to disband them in 1968.

DID CHINA REMAIN COMMUNIST?

When Mao died in 1976 there was a struggle for power. In the years that followed, China was still governed by the Communist Party, but it started to adopt some capitalist economic policies.

ALL TOGETHER NOW ▶
Chinese soldiers recite famous quotations of Mao Zedong. In the 1960s everything Mao did was publicly praised. There were pictures and statues of him everywhere. However, his political enemies were biding their time.

Red star represents communism

The Little Red Book of Mao's thoughts was brandished at mass rallies

FIND OUT MORE ▶▶ China's First Empire 378 • Imperial China 393

ASIAN CONFLICT

Asian conflict

The first half of the 20th century saw Britain, France, and the Netherlands being challenged by the peoples they ruled in south and southeast Asia. At the same time, Japan was trying to take the place of the Europeans and create its own Asian empire.

HOW DID GANDHI FIGHT FOR FREEDOM?

When Indian nationalists were demanding self-rule, one of the leading campaigners against the British was Mohandas K. Gandhi (1869–1948). Instead of calling for an uprising, Gandhi used non-violent methods of protest. He lived very simply and called for India to return to the traditional values of village life. He became known as Mahatma or "great soul". This man of peace was assassinated in 1948.

WHEN DID JAPAN BECOME POWERFUL?

After 1868, Japan turned itself into an industrial nation. It defeated Russia in 1904–1905 and annexed Korea in 1910. In 1919, it gained former German territories in Asia. During the 1930s, extreme nationalists and the military planned Japan's invasion of China. In the 1940s, during World War II, Japanese armies finally swept through southeast Asia.

ASIA 1920–1942	
1920–1922	Gandhi leads Indian National Congress Campaign
1926–1942	Nationalist agitation in Indochina
1940	Japan occupies French Indochina
1942	The Vietminh founded

PEACEFUL PROTEST ►
In 1930, Gandhi broke the law by marching to the sea to collect salt. Only the British were allowed to produce salt.

FIND OUT MORE ►► Age of Empire 422–423 • Revolutionary China 429

THE DEPRESSION

An economic depression is a period of falling prices, low production of goods, and high unemployment. The Great Depression of 1929–1934 caused hardship in the United States, in the countries of Europe, and in their overseas empires. Banks closed and firms went out of business.

WHAT WAS THE WALL STREET CRASH?

In 1929, US investors found that their stocks and shares had become worthless. All trading ceased on Wall Street, New York City's financial district, as the New York Stock Exchange crashed. Fortunes were lost overnight and factories laid off workers.

HOW WIDESPREAD WAS THE DEPRESSION?

The 1920s and 1930s were already desperate times in Australia and New Zealand, in Britain, and across Europe. When an Austrian bank collapsed, chaos spread to central Europe. Germany was struggling too, as it tried to recover from World War I and pay money to France as reparation for the war.

◄ QUEUING FOR SOUP
Hungry men line up for free soup at a public kitchen in New York City in 1931. By 1932 over 12 million Americans were out of work.

Depression

▲ MONEY FOR PLAY
German children use wads of banknotes as toy bricks. The German currency lost value so quickly that one loaf of bread could cost millions of marks.

FIND OUT MORE ►► Economy 302–303 • The State 308–309

FASCISM

In 1922 a political movement called fascism grew up in Italy. It took its name from the fasces, an axe emblem that symbolized state power in Ancient Rome. Fascists believed in the authority of the state. Extremely nationalistic, they opposed democracy and communism.

FASCIST DICTATOR ▶
Benito Mussolini (1883–1945) marched on Rome in 1922 and became Italian dictator in 1925.

WERE THERE FASCISTS IN OTHER COUNTRIES?

Fascism found supporters in many Western nations. It attracted people who were more worried about public order and unemployment than personal freedom. The National Socialist German Workers' Party was founded in 1920. The Falange, a fascist movement founded in 1933, took part in the ▶▶ **SPANISH CIVIL WAR**.

WHO WERE THE NAZIS?

Germany's National Socialists were known as Nazis. Their leader was Adolf Hitler. During the 1930s he provided work for the unemployed and built up Germany's forces illegally. Nazi thugs bullied, cheated, and murdered their way to power. They were extreme racists, consumed by hatred of the Jewish people.

ADOLF HITLER
1889–1945

Austrian-born Adolf Hitler served in a German regiment during World War I. Embittered by defeat, he organized the Nazis and their seizure of power in Germany. As dictator, Hitler persecuted Jews and crushed opposition. His invasions of neighbouring lands led to World War II.

▼ NUREMBERG, 1938
The Nazis staged huge political rallies, many of them in the city of Nuremberg. Here, soldiers march past carrying Nazi party banners bearing the words "Germany awake".

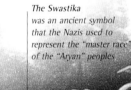

e ▶▶
fascism

The Swastika was an ancient symbol that the Nazis used to represent the "master race" of the "Aryan" peoples

SPANISH CIVIL WAR

Civil war raged in Spain from 1936 to 1939. An alliance led by General Franco overthrew the elected government of the Spanish Republic. Franco's supporters were Falangists, conservatives, monarchists, and Catholics. Fighting for the government were socialists, communists, and regionalists.

WHO JOINED THE WAR?

Franco was backed by fascist Italy and Nazi Germany. Government forces received help from the Soviet Union and were backed by anti-fascist volunteers from all over Europe and America. Many of these young idealists died fighting for Republican International Brigades. But the Republic fell, and Franco ruled Spain as dictator until his death in 1975.

▲ FASCIST SALUTES
Nazi salutes are given as Franco's troops take over the border town of Irún. German bombing of Spain outraged world opinion.

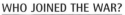

▲ "NO PASARÀN"
"They shall not pass!" was the rallying cry of the Republic as Franco advanced on Madrid. Both men and women fought to the bitter end, but Franco did pass. This tragic war left Spain bitter and divided. Each town still remembers its suffering.

FIND OUT MORE ▶▶ World War I 426–427 • World War II 432–433

WORLD WAR II

In 1939, Nazi Germany invaded its neighbouring countries, beginning a world war which left about 40 million people dead. Unlike World War I, this was high-speed warfare, or ▸▸ BLITZKRIEG. It ended with the discovery of the terrible truth about the Nazi ▸▸ HOLOCAUST and the unleashing of the ▸▸ ATOM BOMB.

World War II

▲ EUROPE AND NORTH AFRICA INVADED
This map shows the advances of the Axis countries in the early years of the war. German troops overran much of Europe and North Africa. In many of the lands they occupied, such as France, the USSR, Yugoslavia, and Greece, there was ongoing resistance from non-military fighters.

HOW DID THE WAR BEGIN?
The military power of Nazi Germany grew unchecked until its tanks invaded Poland. In 1939, Britain and France declared war against Hitler, but in 1940 he invaded the Netherlands, Belgium, France, Denmark, and Norway. Only a period of air warfare, the Battle of Britain, saved the United Kingdom from invasion.

Over 4,000 ships and landing craft took part in the operation

OPERATION OVERLORD ▶
The last phase of the war in Europe began on 6 June 1944 ("D-Day"). US, British, and Canadian troops landed by sea on the coast of Normandy, in occupied France.

▲ WAR IN THE PACIFIC
In 1941, Japan launched an unprovoked attack on Pearl Harbor, a US naval base in Hawaii. The USA, the world's most powerful nation, entered the war. The Pacific conflict with Japan lasted nearly four years.

WHY WAS THIS A WORLD WAR?
The Allies included British, Australians, New Zealanders, Canadians, and South Africans, as well as exiled French and Poles. They were joined in 1941 by two giants – the Soviet Union and the USA. The Axis alliance of Germany and Italy was extended to include Hungary, Romania, Bulgaria, and Japan.

WHEN DID THE TIDE TURN?
In 1942, the USA smashed Japanese naval power at the Battle of Midway. Allied victories in North Africa enabled an advance through Italy in 1943. In heavy fighting on Europe's Eastern Front, the Russians defeated the Germans at Stalingrad. By 1945, the Allies were invading Germany from east and west.

A WORLD AT WAR	
1939	Germany invades Poland; Britain and France declare war
1940	Germany invades most of western Europe; Italy enters war
1941	Germany invades Yugoslavia, Greece, Soviet Union; Japan attacks USA
1942	Japan invades southeast Asia and Pacific
1944	France liberated
1945	Allied victory

BLITZKRIEG

Blitzkrieg means "lightning war" in German. The term was first used in 1939 to describe the tactics of high-speed warfare which launched the Nazi invasion of Europe. It was made possible by new technology and weapons.

WINSTON CHURCHILL
1874–1965

Churchill had a long and controversial political career, which most people regarded as over in the years before the war. However, his outspoken opposition to Nazi Germany made him the ideal choice for Prime Minister in 1940. His determination, eloquence, and sense of humour made him a popular and successful leader.

WHAT WERE THE NEW WAYS OF WAGING WAR?
Blitzkrieg used fast tanks and aircraft to by-pass ground defences. Paratroops were dropped behind enemy lines. Civilians died in cities that were bombed. The British shortened blitzkrieg to "Blitz", to describe the massive bombing of their cities. The Allies also adopted blitzkrieg tactics and bombed German cities into rubble. This war also saw the development of radar for detecting enemy aircraft, as well as flying bombs, and rockets.

AIRBORNE TERROR ▶
The German Ju-87 (Stuka) bomber was used to attack shipping, tanks, or fortifications. This terrifying machine could dive at an angle of 80°. It was used in the Battle of Britain and on the Eastern Front.

HOLOCAUST

The Holocaust (meaning "sacrifice by burning") was an attempt to murder the entire Jewish people. German concentration camps had existed since the 1930s but this act of genocide was accelerated by Nazi leaders at Wannsee in 1942. About six million Jews died.

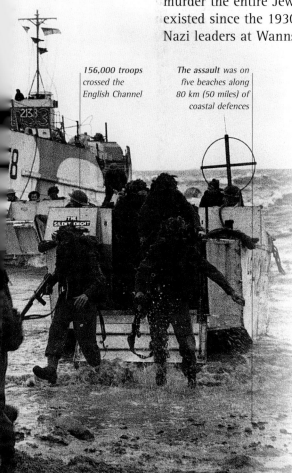

156,000 troops crossed the English Channel

The assault was on five beaches along 80 km (50 miles) of coastal defences

▲ DEATH CAMP
From 1940 to 1945, Auschwitz, in Poland, was the site of one of the worst death camps. Three to four million people, including Poles and Jews, were murdered there.

WHO DISCOVERED THE CONCENTRATION CAMPS?
In 1945, as Allied forces advanced, they found evidence of this monstrous crime. Jews from all over Europe had been rounded up, forced into cattle wagons on trains, and taken to prison camps, along with other peoples the Nazis despised, such as Roma. Some victims were forced to work as slave labour, others were killed immediately in gas chambers.

ATOM BOMB

Throughout the war the USA had secretly been developing the most destructive weapon ever known – the atom bomb. This produced energy by nuclear fission. In August 1945, the USA dropped two atom bombs on Japan. Japan surrendered.

WHY DID THE USA DROP THE BOMB?
The United States government wished to bring the war to a rapid end and prevent the loss of any more troops. Critics of the bomb believed that the extent of its power, and the resulting loss of so many civilian lives, was morally unacceptable.

THE MUSHROOM CLOUD ▶
Bombs were dropped on Hiroshima and Nagasaki. In Hiroshima, over 78,500 people died in one minute. Many victims died years later from the effects of radiation.

FIND OUT MORE ▶▶ Fascism 431 • Nuclear Energy 167 • World War I 426–427

INTERNATIONAL ORGANIZATIONS

Nations have always formed alliances. In the 20th century, many new international organizations were set up worldwide for economic and political reasons, defence and peacekeeping, health and welfare.

international organizations

WHY WAS THE UNITED NATIONS FOUNDED?
The League of Nations was founded in 1919 to keep the peace after World War I. But it failed to prevent World War II in 1939, so in 1945 the nations of the world set up a new organization, the United Nations (UN). Since then, the UN has encouraged international co-operation and worked to resolve conflict.

WHAT OTHER ALLIANCES WERE SET UP?
Some alliances have been political, such as the Arab League (1945) or the Organization of African Unity (1963). The European Economic Community (1958) grew from a small trading alliance into the European Union. Military alliances included the North Atlantic Treaty Organization (1949–) and the Warsaw Pact (1955–1991).

THE OLIVE BRANCH ▶
The United Nations flag shows the world surrounded by olive branches, a symbol of peace. The UN has sent peace-keeping forces around the world.

FIND OUT MORE ▶▶ World War I 426–427 • World War II 432–433

DECOLONIZATION

After 1945, European nations began to give up their colonies. In some places, power was handed back to local people peacefully. White South Africans refused to share power, creating a system of ▶▶ APARTHEID .

WHEN DID WINDS OF CHANGE BLOW?
In 1960, the British Prime Minister Harold Macmillan made a speech in South Africa, declaring that a "wind of change" was blowing through the African continent. He meant that the age of empires and colonies was coming to an end. Today only a few colonies or "overseas territories" still exist.

FRENCH ALGERIA ▶
From 1954 to 1962, the French fought nationalist rebels in Algeria. This war caused great bitterness among the Algerians and French who lived in the colony. Independence was finally granted in 1962.

APARTHEID

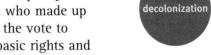

NELSON MANDELA
1918-

Nelson Mandela was a black lawyer who campaigned against apartheid. Imprisoned from 1964-1990, he became a symbol of resistance. After his release, he became South Africa's first black president.

Apartheid is a word from the Afrikaans language which means "staying apart". It was the South African government's policy of racial separation from 1948 to 1994. White people, who made up only 14 per cent of the population, refused to give the vote to black or Asian people. These peoples were denied basic rights and were not allowed to mix with the whites.

decolonization

WHAT WERE THE EFFECTS OF APARTHEID?
Black people were not permitted to live in areas reserved for whites. They were not even allowed to sit on the same benches. Many black people endured bad housing, poverty, and inadequate education. Black and white South Africans who protested against apartheid risked imprisonment or death.

WHEN DID APARTHEID END?
The end of apartheid came in 1994, when Nelson Mandela won South Africa's first democratic general election. This occasion marked the end of two centuries in which Europeans had attempted to rule the rest of the world. However, the newly independent nations of Africa still face many problems.

FIND OUT MORE ▶▶ Age of Empire 422–423

▲ PROTEST IN THE USA
Protestors against the Vietnam War march through Washington, D.C., in 1969. Many people in the Western nations believed this war to be unjust, and large public demonstrations took place around the world.

COLD WAR

After World War II, allies who had fought fascism together became rivals for world power. From 1945 to 1990, there was a period of tension called the Cold War. Capitalist countries, led by the USA, clashed with the communist countries of the Soviet Union and China.

CASTRO'S REVOLUTION ▶
Revolutionary Fidel Castro overthrew the Cuban dictator Fulgencio Batista in 1959 and made Cuba a communist state.

Cold War

WHAT WAS THE CUBAN MISSILE CRISIS?
Both sides in the Cold War were heavily armed with nuclear weapons. In 1962 the Soviet Union secretly stationed missiles in communist Cuba. The USA found out and demanded the missiles be removed. The Soviet Union gave in and the world narrowly avoided a nuclear war.

WHAT WAS THE IRON CURTAIN?
World War II had left communist governments in control of central and eastern Europe. They were opposed by the nations of western Europe and the United States. The two hostile sides, or "blocs", became isolated from each other. In a speech, British politician Winston Churchill said that it was as if an "iron curtain" had fallen across Europe.

WHAT WAS THE VIETNAM WAR?
In 1954, the French colonial army in Vietnam was defeated by communist rebels. The country was divided into North and South Vietnam, and the USA intervened to support an anti-communist government in the South. During the 1960s troops were sent to fight the communists. They failed to defeat them and Vietnam united under communist rule in 1975.

FIND OUT MORE ▶▶ Eastern Asia 268–269 • World War II 432–433

MIDDLE EAST

The Middle East saw much conflict during the last century. Its deserts contain the world's biggest oil fields, which have brought wealth to the area's rulers but also colonial interference and wars.

WHAT IS THE PALESTINE PROBLEM?
In 1948, the UN made part of Palestine the Jewish nation of Israel. Jewish people returned to their traditional homeland, but many displaced Palestinian Arabs became refugees. The struggle between Israelis and Palestinians for this land continues.

WHY HAS THERE BEEN FIGHTING IN IRAQ?
In 1979, Saddam Hussein became president of Iraq. Iraq invaded Iran and occupied oil-rich Kuwait, which was liberated by a US-led coalition in 1991. In 2003, the USA and Britain claimed Hussein remained an international threat and invaded Iraq. Hussein was overthrown but his supporters continued to fight the USA and its allies.

▼ THE SIX DAY WAR
This war in 1967 was the third of many fought between Israel and its Arab neighbours. Israel won, occupying large areas of Arab territory. The war left 300,000 Palestinians refugees.

Middle East

FIND OUT MORE ▶▶ International Organizations 434 • Nations 312 • War 313

HISTORY OF BRITAIN AND IRELAND

timeline

The history of the British Isles is the history of the four nations that live there: the English, Irish, Scottish, and Welsh. These nations have different languages and cultures, bringing great diversity to a relatively small region. The British islands originally formed around 8000 BC after the land bridge between England and France flooded. A succession of peoples travelled by boat to settle the islands in prehistoric times, but the recorded history of the British Isles begins with Julius Caesar's invasion in 55 BC.

55 BC Julius Caesar's first invasion of Britain; the Romans come to stay in AD 43

AD 60 Boudicca's rebellion against the Romans

c. 400–600 Christianity is brought by St Ninian to Scotland, St Patrick to Ireland, and St Augustine to England

c. 449 Anglo-Saxon settlement of Britain begins

787 First Viking raids on coasts. Vikings found Dublin in 841

802–839 Ecgberht (Wessex)

825 Ecgberht defeats Mercia; Wessex dominates in England

843–860 Kenneth MacAlpin (Scotland) unifies northern Scotland

844–78 Rhodri Mawr (Wales) attempts to unite much of Wales

871–899 Alfred the Great (Wessex) defeats the Vikings

946–955 Eadred (England) rules over a united England

1005–1034 Malcolm II (Scotland) unites Scotland

1005 Brian Boru (Ireland) recognized as "ard ri" (high king) of all Ireland

1014 Brian Boru is slain while defeating the Vikings at Clontarf

1016–1035 Canute (England) unites England with Denmark, Norway, and Sweden

1042–1066 Edward the Confessor (England)

1064 Harold, Edward's chief adviser, promises to support claim to the throne of William, Duke of Normandy

1066 Harold chosen as successor to Edward. William defeats Harold near Hastings

1066–1087 William I (England)

1071–1072 William I invades Scotland and compels Malcolm III to recognize him as his overlord

1086 Domesday Book completed

1124–1153 David I (Scotland)

1138 David I invades England but is defeated at Northallerton

---

WHAT IS THE UNITED KINGDOM?

The United Kingdom is properly known as the United Kingdom of Great Britain and Northern Ireland. Great Britain is made up of England, Scotland, and Wales. England and Wales were formally unified after 1536, though the English had dominated Wales for centuries. Scotland lost its parliament and joined England and Wales in 1707. These three countries were now governed by one monarch and through one Parliament. Ireland had been controlled by Britain since the 12th and 13th centuries, but it was not until the Act of Union of 1801 that a United Kingdom of Great Britain and Ireland was created. The southern part of Ireland became independent in 1922, while since 1997 Scotland has had a Parliament of its own, and Wales an Assembly.

1154–1189 Henry II (England)

1162 Henry II appoints Thomas à Becket archbishop of Canterbury (murdered in 1170)

1165–1214 William the Lion (Scotland)

1171 Henry II invades Ireland; Pope appoints him Lord of Ireland

1173 William the Lion invades England but is captured by Henry II

1189–1199 Richard I (England)

1189–1192 Richard I departs on Third Crusade

1194–1240 Llywelyn ap Iorwerth (the Great) (Wales)

1199–1216 John (England)

1205 Llywelyn ap Iorwerth marries Joan, daughter of John of England

1214–1249 Alexander II (Scotland)

1215 Barons force John to accept Magna Carta. The principle is established that monarchy should obey the rule of law

1216–1272 Henry III (England)

1217 Treaty between Scotland and England; peace for almost 20 years

1246–1282 Llywelyn ap Grufudd (the Last) (Wales)

1264 Barons defeat Henry III at Lewes

1265 Simon de Montfort summons first English Parliament

1267 Henry III recognizes Llwelyn ap Grufudd as Prince of Wales at the Treaty of Montgomery

1272–1307 Edward I (England)

1277 Edward I defeats Llywelyn ap Grufudd, who then rebels and is slain in 1282, after which Wales is formally taken over by England

1296 Edward I removes John Baliol from Scottish throne. Start of long Scottish alliance with France (the Auld Alliance). Scots rise against English rule and under William Wallace defeat the English at Stirling Bridge (1297)

1297 First representative Irish Parliament meets in Dublin

1298 Wallace defeated at Falkirk. Starts guerilla war

1305 Wallace captured and executed by Edward I

1306–1329 Robert I (Scotland)

1314 Robert I wins victory against English forces of Edward II at Bannockburn

1327–1377 Edward III (England)

1328 Robert I wins formal recognition of Scottish independence at the Treaty of Edinburgh

1337 100 Years War begins over French throne

1349 Black Death reaches England and kills half the population

1366 Statute of Kilkenny enforces writ of English law in Ireland

1377–1399 Richard II deposed by cousin Henry Plantagenet (1399)

1381 Peasants Revolt led by Wat Tyler; the Lord Mayor of London kills Wat Tyler at Smithfield

1399–1413 Henry IV (England)

1400 Owain Glyndwr opens campaign for Welsh independence after styling himself Prince of Wales. He makes a treaty with France and sets up a Welsh Parliament at Machynlleth. He goes into hiding after revolt is defeated in 1410

1403 Henry IV defeats rebel lords at Shrewsbury

1406–1437 James I (Scotland)

1413–1422 Henry V (England)

1415 Henry V defeats French at Agincourt

1422–1461 Henry VI (England)

1429 Joan of Arc begins to expel English from France

1437–1460 James II (Scotland)

1455 James II defeats Black Douglas family of nobles at Arkinholm

1455 Start of the Wars of the Roses between the Yorkists and Lancastrians over who is to rule England

1460–1488 James III (Scotland)

1461–1483 Edward IV (England) deposes Henry VI

1468–1469 Orkney and Shetland annexed by Scotland

1476 Caxton begins printing in England

1483–1485 Richard III (England)

1485 Richard III defeated at Bosworth by Henry Tudor

1485–1509 Henry VII (England)

1486 Henry VII marries Elizabeth, daughter of Edward IV, uniting York and Lancaster

1488–1513 James IV (Scotland)

1509–1547 Henry VIII (England)

1513 James IV is defeated and killed by the English at Flodden

1533 The Pope excommunicates Henry VIII after Henry forces the Archbishop of Canterbury to annul his marriage to Catherine of Aragon

1534 Henry VIII has himself made Supreme Head of the Church of England

1536–1539 Monasteries in England and Wales are dissolved

1536 Act of Union between England and Wales; Wales formally becomes part of England

1541 Irish Parliament declares Henry VIII king of Ireland

1542–1567 Mary, Queen of Scots (Scotland)

1549 *The English Book of Common Prayer* is published

1553–1558 Mary I (Mary Tudor) (England) returns England to Catholicism

1558–1603 Elizabeth I (England)

1559 Elizabeth I restores Protestantism

1560 Scottish Parliament introduces Protestantism

1567 Mary, Queen of Scots, flees to England after Protestant lords rebel against her plans to restore Catholicism

1567–1603 James VI

(Scotland). Mary's son, James, succeeds

1588 Spanish Armada defeated in English Channel

1603–1625 James VI of Scotland becomes James I of England and Ireland on Elizabeth's death. From now on the thrones of Scotland and England are united

1605 Catholic "Gunpowder Plot" to blow up Houses of Parliament is foiled

1625–1649 Charles I

1629–1640 Charles rules without parliament

1642–1649 Civil War. Parliamentarians defeat Royalists at Naseby in 1645

1649 Charles I is executed. England is ruled as a Commonwealth

1652 Cromwell quells rebellion in Ireland and conquers Scotland

1653–1658 Cromwell is Lord Protector of Britain and Ireland

1660–1685 Charles II, son of Charles I, restored to the throne

1665 The Great Plague

1666 The Great Fire of London sees much of the city of London destroyed

1685–1688 James II (James VII of Scotland)

1688 After James II suspends laws against Catholics, Protestants fear persecution, leading to the Glorious Revolution in which the Protestant William, Prince of Orange, replaces James as king

1689–1702 William III and Mary II (1689–1694)

1689 Bill of Rights limits the powers of the monarch

1689 William III of England invited to take over Scottish government from James VII. War breaks out between supporters of both

1689–1691 Campaign in Ireland between the forces of the exiled James II and William III

1690 Battle of the Boyne. William's army defeats James

1692 The Macdonald clan, slow to take the oath of allegiance to William, are massacred by the Campbell clan at Glencoe

1692 Catholics excluded from Irish Parliament

1701 Act of Settlement formalizes the succession to the throne so as to prevent further upheaval

1702–1714 Anne

1702 First daily newspaper, the *Courant*, published in London

1707 Act of Union between Scotland and England gives Scots seats at Westminster

1714–1727 George I

1721 Robert Walpole becomes the first British prime minister

1727–1760 George II

1733 John Kay invents the flying shuttle. A period of technological innovation known as the Industrial Revolution begins

1745–1746 Bonny Prince Charlie leads the last attempt to restore the Stuart dynasty in Britain

1756–1763 The Seven Years War between Britain and France. Britain wins North America and India. This lays the basis for the British Empire

1760–1820 George III

1775 The American Revolution starts. British forces are defeated by 1783

1776 James Watt produces the first commercial steam engine

1798 Rising of United Irishmen against Britain fails; some leaders are executed

1801 Act of Union between Britain and Ireland ends Irish Parliament and brings Irish seats at Westminster; Catholics are unable to stand for Parliament

1803–1815 Napoleonic War with Britain and other states. In 1815 Napoleon is defeated at Waterloo

1820–1830 George IV

1825 First railway starts between Stockton and Darlington

1829 Catholic Emancipation Act allows Catholics to stand for Parliament

1830–1837 William IV

1832 Great Reform Bill extends the vote to many in the middle class

1837–1901 Victoria

1838 Chartists petition Parliament, demanding more power for the poor and working people

1845–1847 The Great Famine. Over one million starve as potato blight hits Ireland

1854–1856 Crimean War

ENGLISH DYNASTIES	
1066–1154	Normans
1154–1399	Plantagenets
1399–1461	Lancastrians
1461–1485	Yorkists
1485–1603	Tudors
1603–1714	Stuarts
1714–1901	Hanoverians
1901–	Windsors

1858 Foundation of radical Irish nationalist Fenian movement in New York

1870 Irish Home Rule movement launched

1876 Queen Victoria becomes Empress of India

1895–1902 Boer War

1901–1910 Edward VII

1904 Britain and France sign Entente Cordiale; tensions with Germany mount

1910–1936 George V

1911 Parliament Act curbs power of House of Lords

1914–1918 World War I

1914 Home Rule bill passed,

but is suspended due to outbreak of World War I

1916 Easter Rising in Dublin against British government

1918 Women over the age of 30 are allowed to vote for the first time; the vote is extended to women aged 21 or over in 1928

1918 Majority of Irish seats won by republican candidates in post-war general election. Members found their own Parliament in Dublin

1919–1921 War of Independence in Ireland between British troops and Irish Republican Army

1920 Government of Ireland Act provides for parliaments and governments for southern and northern Ireland

1921 Anglo Irish Treaty leads to formation of Irish Free State 1922, and Irish Civil War 1922–1923

1936 Edward VIII abdicates. The BBC begins broadcasting its first regular television service from Alexandra Palace in London

1936–1952 George VI

1939–1945 World War II

1946 Welfare State introduced in the United Kingdom

1949 Republic of Ireland formally declared. Ireland leaves the Commonwealth

1952– Elizabeth II

1969 The "troubles" start in Northern Ireland

1972 Northern Ireland arliament suspended and direct rule introduced

1973 Britain and Ireland join European Union

1997 Referendums support creation of a Scottish Parliament and a Welsh Assembly

1997 Good Friday agreement sees new impetus to end the "troubles" in Northern Ireland

INDEX

A page number in **bold** refers to the main entry for that subject.

D

E

ACKNOWLEDGEMENTS

Dorling Kindersley would like to thank Jacqui Bailey, Kitty Blount, Laura Buller, Joe Elliot, Daniel Gilpin, Simon Holland, Jacky Jackson, Sarah Kovandzich, Esther Labi, Margaret Mulverhill, Margaret Parrish, and Nigel Ritchie for editorial assistance; Alyson Lacewing, and Lee Simmons for proof-reading; Sue Lightfoot for the index; Martin Copeland for picture research; Sheila Hanly, James Harrison, Clare Hibbert, Ian Probert, and Belinda Weber for link research.

Dorling Kindersley Ltd is not responsible and does not accept liability for the availability or content of any web site other than its own, or for any exposure to offensive, harmful, or inaccurate material that may appear on the Internet. Dorling Kindersley Ltd will have no liability for any damage or loss caused by viruses that may be downloaded as a result of looking at and browsing the web sites that it recommends. Dorling Kindersley downloadable images are the sole copyright of Dorling Kindersley Ltd, and may not be reproduced, stored, or transmitted in any form or by any means for any commercial or profit-related purpose without prior written permission of the copyright owner.

Picture Credits
The publisher would like to thank the following for their kind permission to reproduce their photographs:

Abbreviations key:
t-top, b-bottom, r-right, l-left, c-centre

1 AKG London: cl, cr. Corbis: Buddy Mays c. Getty Images: Helena Vallis cll. Science Photo Library: Steve Horrell crr. **2** Corbis: Christine Kolisch cr; Hal Beral crrr; Jim Winkley; Ecoscene cll. NASA: cl. Science Photo Library: crr; Dr. Arthur Tucker clll. **3** Genesis Space Photo Library: NASA, Lockhead Martin, IMAX crrr. Getty Images: Raphael Van Butsele cr. Science Photo Library: Art Wolfe cll; Hugh Turvey clll; Richard Wehr cl. **5** NASA: tc. Science Photo Library: Simon Fraser tl; Tek Image tr. **6** NASA: cl. Science Photo Library: c. **7** Getty Images: Raphael Van Bustele cb. **8–9** Science Photo Library: National Optical Astronomy Observatories. **10** DK Picture Library: ESA br. **10–11** NASA. Science Photo Library: Eckhard Slawik c. **11** Science Photo Library: John Sanford cr. Topham Picturepoint: HPI/British Library cl. **12** Science Photo Library: David Nunuk br; David Parker tr; Max-Planck-Institut Fur Radioastromie cl. **14** Science Photo Library: Mark Garlick cl. **15** Galaxy Picture Library: TRACE/Stanford-Lockheed Institute for Space Research cl. Science Photo Library: Dr Fred Espenak br; Mark Garlick c. Courtesy of SOHO/EIT Consortium. SOHO is a project of international cooperation between ESA and NASA: cr. **16** NASA: br, l. **16–17** NASA. **17** NASA: tr, c. **18** NASA: tl, c, bc, cal. Science Photo Library: NASA crb. **19** NASA: cl, c, bl. Science Photo Library: NASA br. **20** NASA: tr, cra, cl, bl. Science Photo Library: US Geological Survey br. **21** NASA: tl, cr, crb, cbr. Science Photo Library: Claus Lunau/Foci/Bonnier, Publications bc. **22** Anglo Australian Observatory: Royal Observatory, Edinburgh br. Corbis: Gianni Dagli Orti bc. Science Photo Library: Dr Seth Shostak cl; Jerry Lodriguss cb; NASA tc. SETI League photo, used by permission: tr. **23** Corbis: Charles O'Rear br. DK Picture Library: Natural History Museum bc, bcr. Science Photo Library: cl; Dr Fred Espenak cr; Lynette Cook tl. **24** NASA: cl, br. **24–25** Science Photo Library: Konstantinos Kifonidis. **25** NASA: tr. Science Photo Library: Max-Plank-Institut Und Physik and Astrphysik c; Mehau Kulyk br. **26** NASA: crb. Science Photo Library: Roger Harris cr; W. Couch & R. Ellis/NASA bl. **27** Anglo Australian Observatory: David Malin cra, cr, car. Galaxy Picture Library: Omar Lopez-Cruz & Ian Shelton/NOAO/AURA/NSF br. NASA: tr, c. Science Photo Library: Carlos Frenk, University of Durham bcr; Chris Butler clb. **28** ESA: cr. Science Photo Library: Starsem tr. **28–29** NASA: br. **29** NASA: tr, ca. Science Photo Library: br; David Ducros bl. **30** NASA: cr, bc, br, bcr, l. **31** DK Picture Library: Eurospace Center, Transinne, Belgium cl. NASA: br; c. Science Photo Library: tr. **32** Genesis Space Photo Library: NASA, Lockhead Martin, IMAX cra. NASA: tr, c, cr, bl. **33** NASA: tr, c, bl. Science Photo Library: NASA cl. **34–35** Corbis: James A. Sugar. **36** Mark Garlick tl. **36–37** Science Photo Library: ESA c **37** Corbis: Sally A. Morgan, Ecoscene br. Getty Images: Andre Gallant bl, bc, bcl, bcr. Science Photo Library: Mark Garlick cb. **38** Science Photo Library: David Ducros cl. **38–39** Science Photo Library: Jeremy Bishop. **39** Science Photo Library: tr, bl. **40–41** Corbis: Firefly Productions. **41** Getty Images: Helena Vallis br. **42** GeoScience Features Picture Library: bl. Getty Images: Randy Wells t. Science Photo Library: Tom Van Sant, Geosphere Project/Planetary Visions br. **43** Corbis: Lloyd Cluff bl. Rex Features: Sipa Press tr. **44** Corbis: Roger Ressmeyer cr. Hutchison Library: Robert Francis cra. US Geological Survey: D. A Swanson tr. **45** Corbis: Wildcountry c; Wolfgang Kaehler bl. **46–47** Getty Images: Tom Till c. **47** DK Picture Library: Natural History Museum tr. Getty Images/Photodisc Green: cr. Science Photo Library: Lawrence Lawry br. **48** Science Photo Library: Dr Jeremy Burgess c. **49** Science Photo Library: NASA br, t. **50** Corbis: Brownie Harris bc. Getty Images: Mike Surowiak tl. Science Photo Library: University of Dundee c. **51** Pa Photos: EPA European Press Agency br. Corbis: l. **52** Science Photo Library: Peter Ryan cl. **52–53** Getty Images: Marc Muench c. **53** Corbis: George D. Lepp tcr. Science Photo Library: Alan Sirulnikoff tl; Claude Nuridsany & Marie Perennou cl; George Post tr; Simon Fraser tcl. UCAR Communications: br. **54** Corbis: Rob Matheson c. NASA: bl. Science Photo Library: Larry Miller tl. **55** Corbis: Owaki-Kulla cr. Getty Images: John Lamb cl. Rex Features: Sipa Press b. Still Pictures: M & C Denis-Huot tr. **56** Corbis: Craig Tuttle cl. **56–57** National Geographic Image Collection: Volkmar Wentzel c. **57** Corbis: Paul A. Souders cr; Yann Arthus-Bertrand tl. Science Photo Library: NASA tr. Zefa: T. Allofs bc. **58** Bryan and Cherry Alexander Photography: John Hyde r. Corbis: Ralph A. Clevenger bl. **59** Corbis: Arthur Thevenart br; James Murdoch; Cordaiy Photo Library Ltd. bl. Getty Images: Arnulf Husmo cra; Art Wolfe crb; Steve Dunwell tr; Suzanne & Nick Geary c. **60** Getty Images: China Tourism Press tr; Harald Sund tl. **61** Alamy Images: Henryk Kaiser bc. Corbis: Philip James Corwin bl. Getty Images: Jamey Stillings br. Science Photo Library: John Mead c; US Department of Energy tl. **62** Science Photo Library: NASA t. Getty Images: Stuart Westmorland c; Terry Donnelly b. **63** Alamy Images: Brett Bauton tr; Geoffrey Morgan crb. Getty Images: Carlos Navajas cr; Frans Lemmens br. Science Photo Library: Science, Industry & Business Library/New York Public Library bl. **64** Corbis: Ted Spiegel tr. Getty Images: Andy Sacks cl. **64–65** Corbis: b. **65** Ecoscene: Robert Nichol cl. Getty Images: Ed Pritchard tr. Oxford Scientific Films: David M Dennis cr. **66** Corbis: David Stoecklein tr. Getty Images: Anthony Boccaccio cl. National Geographic Image Collection: Paul Chesley b. **67** Corbis: Macduff Everton cr; Mark L Stephenson tr. Zefa: Eugen bl. **68–69** Alamy Images: Steve Bloom. **70** National Geographic Image Collection: Joel Sartore bl. **70–71** Alamy Images: Steve Bloom c. **71** Corbis: James Noble bc. Science Photo Library: David Scharf br. **72** National Geographic Image Collection: Michael Nichols cr. Corbis: tl. Science Photo Library: Colin Cuthbert bl; Eye of Science bc. **73** DK Picture Library: M.I Walker cr. Science Photo Library: Dr Gopal Murti c; Dr Jeremy Burgess tr; M.I Walker bl. **74** Corbis: Bettmann bl. N.H.P.A.: Ant Photo Library br. **75** Corbis: NASA crb. DK Picture Library: Parc Zoologique de Paris cr. Science Photo Library: BSIP bc. **77** Corbis: Dean Conger bl, background; Jonathan Blair bl. The Natural History Museum, London: tr. **78–79** Eric Crichton Photos: background. **79** Science Photo Library: Chris Butler br. **80** Corbis: Ted Horowitz bc; Winifred Wisniewski, Frank Lane Picture Agency l. Nature Picture Library: Jeff Rotman tr. **82** Bruce Coleman Ltd.: r. National Geographic Image Collection: Paul A. Zahl bl. N.H.P.A.: T Kitchin & V Hurst c. **83** Corbis: Galen Rowell r; Hubert Stadler l. N.H.P.A.: Jany Sauvanet ca; John Shaw c, background. **84** Corbis: Peter Lillie; Gallo Images cl. Getty Images: Bernard Roussel c; Simeone Huber bc. N.H.P.A.: B & C Alexander br; Paal Hermansen cr. **85** DK Picture Library: AMNH cr. Science Photo Library: Dr Tony Brain br; Eye of Science tr; Library of Congress bl; Martin Dohrn cl. **86** Science Photo Library: David Scharf cr; John Durham br. **87** Oxford Scientific Films: Niall Benvie bl. Science Photo Library: Jan Hinsch tr. **88** Garden Picture Library: Frederic Didillon. **89** Science Photo Library: Dr Jeremy Burgess bcl, bcr; John Durham tr; Microfield Scientific Ltd. tl. **91** Getty Images: Peter Lilja ca. **92** N.H.P.A.: G. I Bernard c. **93** Science Photo Library: Darwin Dale tl; David McCarthy ca; Jonathan Watts bc. **94** Getty Images: Will & Deni McIntyre tl. **94–95** Getty Images: Christa Renee c. **95** Science Photo Library: Hermann Eisenbeiss tc, tr. **96** Getty Images: Andrew Mounter bl. Nature Picture Library: Peter Oxford cr. **96–97** Getty Images: James Balog c; Tim Davis cl. **97** Corbis: Hal Beral br. Getty Images: Art Wolfe crb. **98** Getty Images: Jeff Rotman cr; Joseph Van Os tr. Oxford Scientific Films: Chris Sharp bl. Visuals Unlimited Inc: cl. **99** Corbis: Joe McDonald cr. Getty Images: Photodisc Green/Santokh Kochar tr. N.H.P.A.: Stephen Dalton br. Science Photo Library: Eye of Science cl. **100** Getty Images: Digital Vision bl; Art Wolfe tl; Steve Hopkin br. N.H.P.A.: Stephen Krasemann tr. **101** N.H.P.A.: T Kitchin & V Hurst cr. Oxford Scientific Films: John Cheverton cl. **102** Alamy Images: Ali Kabas c-sponge. DK Picture Library: Natural History Museum crb. **103** Image Quest 3-D: Jim Greenfield br; Valdimar Butterworth cr. Science Photo Library: Gilbert S. Grant tl. **104** Tom Stack & Associates: br. **105** Alamy Images: SNAP tr. Oxford Scientific Films: cl. Science Photo Library: David Scharf cr; Eye of Science bc. **107** Wild Images: Tim Martin tr. **108** Oxford Scientific Films: Marty Cordano tl. Science Photo Library: Science Pictures Ltd. tr. **109** DK Picture Library: Natural History Museum cr. Nature Picture Library: Brandon Cole br. Oxford Scientific Films: tr. **110** Corbis: Naturfoto Honal l. Science Photo Library: Dr Tony Brain cr. **111** N.H.P.A.: Anthony Bannister br; John Shaw tr; Rod Planck ca. **112** Getty Images: Tobias Bernhard cl. **112–113** Getty Images: Jeff Hunter t. **113** Image Quest 3-D: Carlos Villoch tr; Peter Herring br. Nature Picture Library: Reijo Juurinen/Naturbild cr. **114** Corbis: Michael & Patricia Fogden bc. National Geographic Image Collection: George Gall l. **115** Corbis: Buddy Mays tr. N.H.P.A.: Ernie Jones cl. **116–117** Getty Images: Raphael Van Butsele c. **117** Getty Images: Douglas D. Seifert tr; Gallo Images cr. **118** Getty Images: Anup Shah bc; Steve Bloom c. Science Photo Library: Eye of Science cr. **119** Corbis: Tom Brakefield tr. FLPA – Images of nature: S & D & K Maslowski br. Science Photo Library: Manfred Kage tl. **120** Getty Images: Stuart Westmorland tl. N.H.P.A.: Stephen Krasemann cr. **121** Getty Images: Wayne R Bilenduke t. **122** Corbis: Darrell Gulin b. Nature Picture Library: Karl Amman tl. N.H.P.A.: Mark Bowler tr. **123** Auscape: Jean Paul Ferrero ca. DK Picture Library: Jerry Young bc. N.H.P.A.: Dave Watts tl, br. **124** The Natural History Museum, London: cr. Still Pictures: John Cancalosi tl; M & C Denis-Huot b. **125** Corbis: W. Perry Conway br. Getty Images: Nicholas Parfitt tr. Still Pictures: Michel Gunther cl. **126–127** Science Photo Library: D. Phillips. **128** Science Photo Library: Dr Gopal Murti cl. **128–129** Science Photo Library: Simon Fraser c. **129** Science Photo Library: Mehau Kulyk bc; Montreal Neuro. Institute/McGill, University/CNRI c; Scott Camazine br. **130** Science Photo Library: b; Mehau Kulyk cr. **131** DK Picture Library: EScience Photo Library/Denoyer-Geppert bc. Science Photo Library: t Andrew Syred cl; Simon Fraser br. **132** Biophoto Associates: bl, bc, br. **133** Science Photo Library: Andres Syred bl; Andrew Syred br; John Burbidge tr; Richard Wehr/Custom Medical Stock Photo c. **134** Science Photo Library: bl, r; John Bavosi tl. **135** Science Photo Library: cl. **136** Science Photo Library: BSIP VEM cl; CNRI bc, bcl. **137** Science Photo Library: Innerspace Imaging tr; John Bavosi br. **138** Science Photo Library: Alfred Pasieka bl; BSIP VEM bc; Mehau Kulyk tl. **138–139** Science Photo Library: Alfred Pasieka c. **139** Biophoto Associates: tr. Science Photo Library: Wellcome Department of Cognitive Neurology cb. **140** Science Photo Library: Mehau Kulyk bc. **140–141** Science Photo Library: Alfred Pasieka tc. **141** DK Picture Library: Denoyer Geppert Intl cr, br. Science Photo Library: Omikron bl. **142** Science Photo Library: Astrid & Hanns-Frieder Michler br; Omikron bl. **143** Science Photo Library: CNRI cb; Dr Tony Brain cr; George Bernard cl. **144** Science Photo Library: Eye of Science cl. **145** Science Photo Library: Professors P. Motta & F. Carpino/University "La Sapienza" Rome cr; Professors P. Motta & T. Naguro bc. **146** Science Photo Library: BSIP/Cavallini James crb; Prof. P. Motta/Dept. of Anatomy/University "La Sapienza", Rome bl. **146–147** Science Photo Library: Geoff Tompkinson t. **147** Science Photo Library: CNRI tr; GJLP br. **148** Robert Harding Picture Library: c. Science Photo Library: L.Willatt, East Anglian Regional Genetics, Service bl; Neil Bromhall t. **149** Science Photo Library: tr; Alfred Pasieka bl; BSIP VEM tl; Lauren Shear cr. **150** Corbis: Howard Davies tr. Getty Images: John Kelly l. **151** Science Photo Library: tr; CNRI cl; Simon Fraser br. **152–153** Getty Images: Dia Max. **154** National Geographic Image Collection: Brian Skerry tc. Panos Pictures: Heldur Netocny cb. **154–155** Science Photo Library: NASA bl; Tek Image c. **155** Getty Images: Jean Y Ruszniewski tcl. Image Source: tl. Science Photo Library: Bsip, Laurent tr; Richard Duncan br; Tek Image tcr. **156** CERN: br. Corbis: C.M.Leask/Eye Ubiquitous cla; Kennan Ward cra; Natalie Fobes cb; Ron Watts ca. Science Photo Library: Chris Butler tl. **157** US Department of Energy: tr. Science Photo Library: Philippe Plailly cla. **158** Science Photo Library: David Parker tr; Roger Harris bl; US Library of Congress cr. Geoffrey Wheeler: tl. **159** Corbis: Bettmann br. Science Photo Library: ArSciMed tr. **160** Science Photo Library: Erich Schrempp br; Julian Baum bl. **163** Corbis: Lester Lefkowitz tr; Peter Beck bl. The Art Archive: Royal Society/Eileen Tweedy cl. Rex Features: cr. **164** Alamy Images: Pictor International/ImageState bl. Corbis: James Noble tr. **165** Corbis: Duomo cl; Mark M. Lawrence br. Getty Images: Allsport Concepts/ Christine Kolisch cr. **166** Agence France Presse: cr. Getty Images: Chabruken bc; Terje Rakke l. **167** Corbis: Roger Ressmeyer bl. Hulton Archive/Getty Images: bc. Science Photo Library: Arthus Bertrand tr. **168** Rex Features: CNP cl. Science Photo Library: Dr. Arthur Tucker c. **169** Corbis: Christine Kolisch br; Mark L. Stephenson craa; cra, cr. Getty Images: Stuart Hunter cl. Science Photo Library: ESA tr. **170** Corbis: Gary W. Carter c; Jay Dickman l. Science Photo Library: Volker Steger tr. **171** DK Picture Library: Stephen Oliver cr. Getty Images: tr. Robert Harding Picture Library: cl. Science Photo Library: Pascal Goetgheluck br. **172** Corbis: Patrick Darby cr. Science Photo Library: Kip Peticolas l. **173** Corbis: David Butow tr. Science Photo Library: Tek Image br. **174** Corbis: Cees Van Leeuwen; Cordaiy Photo Library Ltd. l. Getty Images: Phil Degginger br. **175** Associated Press AP: bl. Science Photo Library: Lawrence Livermore National Laboratory tr. **176** Corbis: Joe McDonald tl; Martin Harvey; Gallo Images bl; Roger Tidman claa; clbb. Getty Images: Photodisc

Blue clb. N.H.P.A.: Kevin Schafer cla. **176–177** National Geographic Image Collection: Stephen G. St. John c. **177** Alamy Images: David Bishop/Phototake Inc br. Hulton Archive/Getty Images: ca. US Department of Defense tr. **178** PolaVisor, Copyright 2003 Winford Industries: cl. **178–179** Science Photo Library: Hugh Turvey c. **179** Science Photo Library: Alexander Tsiaras br. Getty Images: Ashok Charles clb. **180** Science Photo Library: Alfred Pasieka tr. **181** Science Photo Library: John Walsh tr; K.H Kjeldsen tc. **182** Science Photo Library: Alfred Pasieka cl; David Parker bc. **182–183** Science Photo Library: Kent Wood c. **183** NASA: tr. **184–185** Corbis: Louis K. Meisel Gallery.t. **185** National Grid Transco: br. Science Photo Library: Scott Camazine bl. **186** Ministry of Defence Picture Library: Crown Copyright/ MOD c. Science Photo Library: Alex Bartel l; Volker Steger/Sandia National Laboratory br. **187** Corbis: Grafton Marshall Smith br; Lester Lefkowitz cr; Norbert Schaefer tr.; cra. Science Photo Library: Colin Cuthbert crb; Copyright W. T Sullivan cl. **188** Science Photo Library: D. Roberts. **189** Corbis: Stephen Grohe c. Science Photo Library: David Parker tr; Rosenfeld Images Ltd. tl. **190** Getty Images: Photodisc Green/ TRBfoto clb; David Arky c. Zefa: Ausloser tl. **191** Associated Press AP: Elise Amendola cl; Loudcloud Inc cll. DK Picture Library: Science Museum bl. Getty Images: Roger Tully tl. Science Photo Library: Caida cr. **192** Corbis: Hulton-Deutsch Collection tc. Rex Features: Barry Greenwood bl. Science Photo Library: Roger Harris cl. **192–193** Courtesy of the BT Group plc 2003 c. **193** Alamy Images: Robert Harding Picture Library cra. Getty Images: Christian Lagereek crbb. Pa Photos: EPA crb; Martin Rickett cb. Science Photo Library: Mehau Kulyk tr. **194** Courtesy of Dyson: bl. Pa Photos: cl. **194–195** Science Photo Library: Peter Menzel c. **195** Science Photo Library: Peter Menzel c; Victor Habbick Visions tr, bl. **196–197** Getty Images: Digital Vision c. **197** Corbis: Fukuhara Inc br; Richard T. Nowitz c. Getty Images: Sandra Baker tr. **198** ImageState/Pictor: I. Porsche AG: r. **199** Alamy Images: Steve Allen tr. Corbis: Bettmann tl. Science Photo Library: G. Brad Lewis br. **200** Getty Images: Lineka tr. **200–201** ImageState/ Pictor: First Light b. **201** Corbis: Lester Lefkowitz cl; tr. Getty Images: Wayne Eastep bc. **202** Courtesy The Microflat Company: bl. Science Photo Library: Colin Cuthbert tl. **202–203** Arup: Colin Wade c. **203** Alamy Images: Andre Jenny tl; Doug Houghton tcr. Corbis: Grant Smith tcl; Massimo Mastrorillo tr; Sygma/Polak Matthew br; Tom Bean cr. **204** Corbis: Jeremy Horner ca. Getty Images: Chris Sattlberger bl; **204–205** Getty Images: Mark Segal c. **205** Corbis: Bettmann ca; Ted Horowitz cr. Getty Images: Jean Louis Batt bc. **206** Corbis: Lester Lefkowitz l. **206–207** Getty Images: Arnulf Husmo c. **207** Corbis: Mark Adams bc; Steve Chenn br. Science Photo Library: David Nunuk tc. 208 Corbis: Bettmann tr; Charles O'Rear bc; Layne Kennedy clb. Science Photo Library: bl; Andrew McClenaghan tl. **209** Science Photo Library: A. Barrington Brown cla; Dr Tim Evans r; James King-Holmes clb; Tek Image bc. **210** Science Photo Library: Darque, Jerrican bl; Simon Fraser ca. **210–211** Science Photo Library: Tek Image c. **211** Rex Features: Jeremy Sutton tr. Science Photo Library: Andrew Leonard br; Mauro Fermariello c. **212–213** Corbis. **214** Alamy Images: Gus tl. N.H.P.A.: Martin Wendler bl. **215** Corbis: Firefly Productions tr; James A. Sugar br; Tibor Bognar tl. **216** Corbis: Tim Page bl. Alamy Images: Steve Allen t. **217** Corbis: Vince Streano t. Popperfoto: Reuters br. **218** Pa Photos: Toby Melville t. Pictures Colour Library: bl. **219** Alamy Images: ImageState/Randa Bishop tr. Corbis: SETBOUN br. **220** Corbis: clb; David Batterbury; Eye Ubiquitous claa; Macduff Everton bl; Stephen Frink tl; Stocktrek c. Getty Images: Daryl Balfour cla; Digital Vision tr. Science Photo Library: Bernhard Edmaier clbb. **222** Corbis: Terry W. Eggers bl. Getty Images: Harald Sund cl. **223** Getty Images: Bob Thomas cr; Sandra Baker tr. **224** Bryan and Cherry Alexander Photography: cr, b. Corbis: Doug Wilson tr. **225** Getty Images: Eric Meola r; Ron Thomas cl. Pictures Colour Library: eStock tl. **226** Corbis: Bob Krist cl. Getty Images: B & M productions b. Oxford Scientific Films: Philippe Henry tr. **227** Corbis: Duomo cr. Getty Images: Bullaty-Lomeo tr; World Perspectives l. **228** Getty Images: Jack Dykinga bl. World Pictures: tr. **229** Getty Images: Chris Speedie l; Randy Wells cr. Robert Harding Picture Library: Photri tr. **230** Corbis: Joseph Sohm; ChromoSohm Inc ca. Getty Images: Brian Stablyk br; Photodisc Green bl. ImageState/Pictor: International Stock c. **230–231** Nature Picture Library: David Noton. **231** Masterfile UK: Bill Brooks br. Zefa: M. Fiala tr. **232** Corbis: Gavriel Jecan l. Getty Images: Andrea Pistolesi bc; Digital Vision cb. South American Pictures: Tony Morrison ca. **233** Corbis: John Madere cr; Stephanie Maze bc; Theo Allofs tr. Getty Images: Hans Strand br. **234** Corbis: Jeremy Horner cr.; l. **235** Alamy Images: Tropicalstock.net tl. Corbis: Michael Freeman br; Omar Bechara Baruque; Eye Ubiquitous cl; Roger Ressmeyer tr. **236** Corbis: Hubert Stadler ca; Michael Brennan bl. Lonely Planet Images: John Maier Jr br. **236–237** N.H.P.A.: Martin Wendler c. **237** Action Plus: Neil Tingle br. Corbis: Ricardo Azoury tr. Zefa: F. Damm cb. **238** Corbis: Yann Arthus-Bertrand c. Impact Photos: Visa Image br. Still Pictures: G Hind/UNEP bl. **239** Corbis: Lindsay Hebberd cr. Getty Images: Glen Allison tc. Pictures Colour Library: br. **240** Getty Images: John Chard cr. Robert Harding Picture Library: B Schuster br. Panos Pictures: Mark Henley bl. **241** Getty Images: Geoffrey Clifford br; Glen Allison clb. Lonely Planet Images: Craig Pershouse cr; Geert Cole tl. **242** Corbis: Yann Arthus-Bertrand cr. N.H.P.A.: Martin Harvey b. Panos Pictures: Betty Press cl. **243** Corbis: Sygma/Campbell William c. Getty Images: Guido Alberto Rossi br. Pictures Colour Library: t. **244** Corbis: Roger de la Harpe; Gallo Images tl. Empics Ltd.: Mike Egerton c. N.H.P.A.: Nick Garbutt bl. **244–245** Pictures Colour Library: b. **245** N.H.P.A.: Martin Harvey t. Pictures Colour Library: cl. Rex Features: Richard Young cr. **246** Getty Images: David Norton bl; Louis-Laurent Grandadam cl. Impact Photos: Ray Roberts tr. **247** Corbis: Elke Stolzenberg tr. Getty Images: John Downer br. **248** Corbis: Hans Strand cl. Getty Images: Rick England br. Lars Hallén: bl. Still Pictures: Dylan Garcia tr. **249** Corbis: Hans Strand tl; William Findlay tr. Still Pictures: J Vallespir/UNEP bl. World Pictures: br. **250** Corbis: Geray Sweeney bl; London Aerial Photo Library br; Sygma/Elder Neville tl. Getty Images: Jeremy Woodhouse cr. **251** Collections: Graham Burns cr; Paul Felix b. Getty Images: Stewart Bonney News Agency tl. Lonely Planet Images: Anne C. Dowie ca. **252** Action Plus: Franck Faugere/DPPI bl. Impact Photos: Gold Collection tr; Robin Laurance br. Pictures Colour Library: cl. **253** Corbis: Jose Fuste Raga/FMGB Guggenheim Bilbao Museoa. 2003 b; Roger Antrobus cl. Impact Photos: Gold Collection tr. **254** Getty Images: Suzanne & Nick Geary cr; Walter Bibikow b. Still Pictures: Magnus Andersson l. **255** Corbis: Ludovic Maisant clb. Getty Images: Anthony Cassidy cra; Hans Wolf b; Jorg Greuel tl. **256** Corbis: Michael Freeman cr. Getty Images: Robert Everts b. Lonely Planet Images: Paul David Hellander tl. **257** Corbis: Barry Lewis cl. Getty Images: Derek P. Redfearn cr; George Grigoriou t. Impact Photos: Peter Arkell bl. **258** Lonely Planet Images: Jonathan Smith tl. Panos Pictures: Clive Shirley cr. Rex Features: Tony Kyriacou br. Still Pictures: Bojan Brecelj bl. **259** Getty Images: Douglas Armand b. Art Directors & TRIP: V. Shuba tl. **260** Corbis: John Noble bl; Tom Brakefield tr. Katz/FSP: Van Cappellen/Rea br. Lonely Planet Images: Chris Mellor cl. **261** Corbis: Dallas and John Heaton tr. Getty Images: Andrea Pistolesi cb; Piecework Productions ca. **262** Hutchison Library: C. Nairn/GTV Disappearing World l; Trevor Page cr. Art Directors & TRIP: M. Lines br. **263** Alamy Images: Bryan and Cherry Alexander b. NASA: cl. Panos Pictures: Heidi Bradner tl. **264** Getty Images: David Hanson cr. Panos Pictures: Jon Spaull cl. Pictures Colour Library: b. **264–265** Corbis: Roger Wood tc. **265** Alamy Images: Ashfordplatt tr. Corbis: Peter Turnley clb. Pictures Colour Library: br. **266** Robert Harding Picture Library: T. Laird bl. Panos Pictures: Paul Smith tl; Penny Tweedie cr. **267** Alamy Images: Robert Harding Picture Library b. Corbis: Baldev/ Sygma tl; James Davis, Eye Ubiquitous cr. **268** Getty Images: Travel Pix tr. National Geographic Image Collection: David Edwards br. Pictures Colour Library: bl. **269** Alamy Images: Rex Butcher bl. Corbis: Bohemian Nomad Picturemakers br; Tibor Bognar t. **270** Corbis: Torleif Svensson tr. Robert Harding Picture Library: T. Hall br. Pictures Colour Library: bl. **271** Corbis: Macduff Everton r. Impact Photos: Alain Evrard bl. Pictures Colour Library: tl. **272** Alamy Images: Jon Arnold Images bl. **273** Corbis br. Getty Images: Kim Westerskov t. **274** N.H.P.A.: Gerard Lacz cl. Pictures Colour Library: tr, cr, b. **275** Corbis: Peter Beck bl. Getty Images: John Lamb br. N.H.P.A.: A. N.T tl. **276** Getty Images: Johnny Johnson bl. Robert Harding Picture Library: Photri tr. **277** N.H.P.A.: Paal Hermansen cr. **278–279** Corbis: Dallas and John Heaton. **280** Corbis: David Cumming; Eye Ubiquitous l. The Art Archive: National Museum Bucharest/Dagli Orti tr. **281** Werner Forman Archive: Schindler Collection, New York br. Popperfoto: tl. **282** Ancient Art and Architecture Collection: bcl, l; R. Sheridan bl. Bridgeman Art Library, London/New York: Egyptian National Museum, Cairo cb. Corbis: Randy Faris t; cr. The Art Archive: Musee du Louvre Paris/Dagli Orti c. **283** Corbis: Gunter Marx Photography bl; Yann Arthus-Bertrand tr. **284** Corbis: John Dakers; Eye Ubiquitous crb; Lindsay Hebberd tr. The Art Archive: Victoria and Albert Museum/Eileen Tweedy bl. **285** Alamy Images: Henry Westheim cl. Bridgeman Art Library, London/New York: Oriental Museum, Durham University bl. Corbis: Archivo Iconografico, S.A tr. **286** Bridgeman Art Library, London/New York: Ann & Bury Peerless/India Office Library, London bc. Corbis: Lindsay Hebberd tr, bl. DK Picture Library: Judith Miller & DK Picture Library – Sloans, USA cl. Rex Features: Geoff Dowen cr. **287** Corbis: David Reed tr. Getty Images: Photodisc Green/Michael Matisse bl. **288** Corbis: Andrea Jemolo tr. DK Picture Library: Glasgow Museum br. Sonia Halliday Photographs: l. **289** Alamy Images: Robert Harding World Imagery tr. Corbis: Adam Woolfitt tl; Geray Sweeney cr; Richard Bickel b. DK Picture Library: Powell Cotton Museum bl. **290** Bridgeman Art Library, London/New York: Giraudon/Musee Conde, Chantilly, France br. Panos Pictures: Karen Robinson cr; Marcus Rose cl. Rex Features: Sipa Press t. **291** Corbis: Blaine Harrington III t. Art Directors & TRIP: H. Rogers br. **292** Bridgeman Art Library, London/New York: Galleria dell' Accademia, Venice c. **292–293** Corbis: Alinari Archives b. **293** Getty Images: Michael John O'Neill cr. Ann & Bury Peerless: tl. **294** The Granger Collection, New York: tr. Rex Features: TDY cl. **294–295** Getty Images: Yann Layma b. **295** Corbis: Bettmann cr; Inge Yspeert cl. **296** Alamy Images: Joe Sohm cla, bl. Corbis: Peter Finger cr; Wendy Stone claa. Getty Images: Anthony Cassidy clb. Pa Photos: AFP Photo/Hector MATA tl. Rex Features: David Hartley clbb. **297** Alamy Images: Gianni Muratore bl; Wilmar Photography c. Corbis: Frank Leather; Eye Ubiquitous tr. Impact Photos: Javed A Jafferji br. **298** Kobal Collection: Warner Bros/DC Comics cl. Rex Features: Nils Jorgensen bl. **298–299** Corbis: Ron Watts c. **299** Advertising Archives: 'Coca-Cola' and 'Coke' are registered trade marks of the Coca-Cola Company and are reproduced with kind permission from the Coca-Cola Company br. Courtesy Freeplay Foundation: c. ImageState/Pictor: Coccon tr. **300** Corbis: James A. Sugar bl. Hutchison Library: Eric Lawrie cl. 300–301 Corbis: Bob Krist c. **301** Corbis: Jennie Woodcock; Reflections Photolibrary tr. Panos Pictures: Jeremy Horner cb. Popperfoto: br. **302** Robert Harding Picture Library: cl. **302–303** Rex Features: Sipa Press c. **303** Associated Press AP: Brian Branch-Price bc. Rex Features: Action Press tr. **304** Corbis: Sygma/Balaguer Alejandro br. Masterfile UK: Mark Tomalty bl. Popperfoto: Reuters tr. **305** Alamy Images: Rob Rayworth cr. Hulton Archive/Getty Images: Keystone bl. Science Photo Library: NASA tl. **306** Alamy Images: Gina Calvi cl. Pa Photos: EPA tr. Rex Features: Action Press (ACT) b. **307** Corbis: Peter Turnley tl; Roger Ressmeyer bl. Getty Images: AFP/Hotli Simanjuntak cr. Hulton Archive/Getty Images: Central Press cl. **308** Corbis: Richard Cummins cra. Getty Images: tr; China Tourism Press crb; Ken Ross br. Robert Harding Picture Library: E. Simanor l. **309** Corbis: Bettmann br. Popperfoto: cl. Science Photo Library: Astrid & Hans Frieder Michler tr. **310** Getty Images: V.C.L tr. Rex Features: Greg Mathieson b. **311** Corbis: Julie Dennis Brothers crb. Getty Images: bl. Pa Photos: tl. Rex Features: Sipa Press cra. **312** Corbis: Bettmann tr; Jay Syverson br. Magnum: Francesco Zizola cl. **313** Associated Press AP: Mark Richards, Pool cl. Corbis: Yogi, Inc c. Popperfoto: Reuters r. **314** Associated Press AP: Joe Marquette tl. Panos Pictures: Trygve Bolstad cr. Still Pictures: Harmut Schwarzbach bl. **315** Science Photo Library: NASA br. UN/DPI Photo: t. **316** Alamy Images: Karen Robinson/David Hoffman PhotoLibrary br. Popperfoto: Rick Wilking/Reuters l. **317** Panos Pictures: Piers Benatar cl. Popperfoto: Reuters/Haider Shah br; Reuters/Jerry Lampen cr. UN/DPI Photo: tr. **318–319** Photograph of Josette Bushell-Mingo as 'Rafiki' from the Original London Company of THE LION KING by Catherine Ashmore. **320** AKG London: Erich Lessing tr, cr. The Art Archive: Archaeological Museum Naples/Dagli Orti c; Archaeological Museum Naples/Dagli Orti tc; Palazzo Ducale Mantua/Dagli Orti br. Mark Roots Collection: Courtesy Michael Nelson Jagamara, from the collection of Mark Roots clb. **321** Bridgeman Art Library, London/New York: Mellon Coll., Nat. Gallery of Art, Washington DC tl, cl. The Art Archive: cb; National Gallery/Eileen Tweedy cr. Réunion Des Musées Nationaux Agence Photographique: Gerard Blot tc, c. **322** Corbis: Christie's Images tl. Topham Picturepoint: HIP/British Museum c. **323** © The British Museum: tr. Corbis: David Lees br. Hutchison Library: Carlos Freire cr. **324** Bridgeman Art Library, London/New York: Kunsthistorisches Museum, Vienna cl. Corbis: Bettmann c; Nathan Benn bl. Topham Picturepoint: UPP cr. Christo and Jeane-Claude: Surrounded Islands, Greater Miami, Florida 1980–83. © Christo, Photo: Wolfgang Volz: tr. **325** Bridgeman Art Library, London/New York: Stapleton Collection, UK tr. Magnum: Dennis Stock cl; Steve McCurry bl. Réunion Des Musées Nationaux Agence Photographique: Eugene Atget cr. **326** Alamy Images: Steve Allen cr. Courtesy Apple: c, background. © Christie's Images Ltd.: Charles Renni Mackintosh cl. The Art Archive: Villa la Pietra Florence/Dagli Orti tr. Kobal Collection: Paramount cll. Popperfoto: crr. Courtesy of the Trustees of the V&A Picture Library: ca. **327** Bridgeman Art Library, London/New York: Victoria & Albert Museum, London cbl. Cooper-Hewitt National Design Museum: Smithsonian Institution bcr. Corbis: Peter Harholdt br. DK Picture Library: British Museum tl; Cooper Hewitt cb; Judith Miller & DK Picture Library – Lyon & Turnball Ltd. ca; Judith Miller & DK Picture Library – Gideon Hatch bcl. Marimekko: designed by Maija Isola 1965 bl. Vitra Design Museum: George Nelson tr. **328** Corbis: Dallas and John Heaton cl; **328–329** Corbis: David Bell c. Getty Images: AFP br. **329** Associated Press AP: JAWOC tr. Corbis: Araldo de Luca crb; Dave Bartruff cra; Jim Winkley; Ecoscene c; Michael S. Yamashita br. **330** Lebrecht Collection: bc. Redferns: Elliott Landy cl.

cl. **330–331** Getty Images: Nick White c. **331** Corbis: Paul A. Souders tr. Lebrecht Collection: David Farrell crb. Redferns: David Redfern bc. **332** DK Picture Library: Johnny Van Derrick br. Lebrecht Collection: br. **333** Getty Images: Thinkstock cl. Rex Features: Brian Rasic (BRA) tr. **334** Apple Corps Ltd.: br. Corbis: Europa Press/G.G/Sygma cr. Lebrecht Collection: Rue des Archives/BCA r. Rex Features: SNAP (SYP) l. **335** Lebrecht Collection: Wladimir Polak tr. Redferns: Graham Salter b; Odile Noel tl. **336** ArenaPAL: Hilary Shedel bl. DK Picture Library: Stephen Oliver cr. **336–337** Sandro Vannini c. **337** Lebrecht Collection: Laurie Lewis b; Ron Hill cl. Linda Rich: tr. **338** Kobal Collection: MGM b. Redferns: Henrietta Butler t. **339** DK Picture Library: INAH cl. The Art Archive: Musee des Beaux Arts Dole/Dagli Orti bl; Victoria and Albert Museum/Eileen Tweedy tr. **340** Corbis: Philip Gould bl; Sygma br. Mary Evans Picture Library: tl. Kobal Collection: Joseph Shaftel Prods cr. **341** Mary Evans Picture Library: cr. Kobal Collection: 20th Century Fox/Tursi, Mario bc; Hammer cb; Selznick/MGM cbl. Moviestore Collection: 20th Century Fox cl. Reproduced by permission of Penguin Books Ltd.: tl. Topham Picturepoint: Heritage Image Partnership/British Library tl. **342** AKG London: bl. Bridgeman Art Library, London/New York: Leeds Museums and Galleries (City Art Gallery) UK tr. The Art Archive: British Library cl; Eileen Tweedy br. **343** Bridgeman Art Library, London/New York: Fitzwilliam Museum, University of Cambridge tr. The Art Archive: Lucien Biton Collection Paris cr. Mary Evans Picture Library: br. Pa Photos: Mok Yui Mok cl. **344** ArenaPAL: Colin Willoughby cl. Corbis: Michael S. Yamashita c. **345** ArenaPAL: Rowena Chowdry c. Photostage: Donald Cooper tr. Rex Features: Reg Wilson tl. **346** Kobal Collection: Damfx bl; Icon/ Pathe/Bailey, Alex br; Universal cl. Moviestore Collection: Columbia bc. **346–347** Kobal Collection: Lucas Film/20th Century Fox c. **347** Corbis: Sygma bc. DK Picture Library: OSCAR statuette is the registered trademark and copyrighted property of the Academy of Motion Picture Arts and Science car. Katz/FSP: PH Westenberger/Liaison cr. Kobal Collection: 20th Century Fox/Paramount tr; TOHO bl. Moviestore Collection: Eon Productions br. **348** AKG London: bl. Corbis: Bettmann tc; Hulton-Deutsch Collection br. Pa Photos: Stefan Rousseau cr. Popperfoto: Reuters crb. **349** Corbis: Barclay Graham/Sygma tr. Kobal Collection: Amblin/Universal cl; Dream Works/Allied Film Makers A. Ardmaan cr; Dreamworks LLC br. **350** Corbis: Michael Neveux br; cr. Courtesy of Oware Society: cb. Getty Images: Brand X Pictures tr. Rex Features: David Marsden cl. Courtesy Sony: tl. **351** Courtesy Apple: cll. Bang & Olufsen, AV Mediacenter 2003 cr; bl. Courtesy BlueroomStore.com: tr. Mary Evans Picture Library: tl. Moviestore Collection: Warner Brothers cl. Courtesy Nintendo: br. Pure Digital, a division of Imagination Technologies: c. Courtesy Sony: crr. **352** Action Plus: Glyn Kirk bl. Getty Images: Mark Thompson cl. **352–353** Sporting Pictures (UK) Ltd.: Huzilar c. **353** Associated Press AP: Bill Kostroun cr; Michael Conroy c. Corbis: Decamp Erik/Sygma br. Getty Images: David Rogers tr. **354** Bridgeman Art Library, London/New York: Marylebone Cricket Club, London, UK tl. Rex Features: Robin Hume bc. **354–355** Getty Images: Pascal Rondeau c. **355** Associated Press AP: Mark J. Terrill tr. Topham Picturepoint: **356** Alamy Images: Popperfoto tl. The Art Archive: National Archaeological Museum Athens/Dagli Orti br. IOC/Olympic Museum Collections: tr. **357** Corbis: Sygma/Ruszniewski J.Y cl; Sygma/Seguin Franck cr. Getty Images: Clive Brunskill tc; Mike Powell/Allsport br; Scott Barbour/Allsport c. **358–359** Corbis: Neil Beer. **360** AKG London: tl. The Art Archive: British Library bl; **360–361** The Art Archive: National Archaeological Museum Athens/Dagli Orti. **361** DK Picture Library: Mary Rose Trust tr. Werner Forman Archive: Ohio State Museum br. Silkeborg Museum, Denmark: tl. **362–363** AKG London: tr. **363** Bridgeman Art Library, London/New York: Lauros/ Giraudon r. DK Picture Library: British Museum c. **364** Ancient Art and Architecture Collection: Ronald Sheridan tr. Sonia Halliday Photographs: cl. **365** Ancient Art and Architecture

Collection: R. Sheridan tl. DK Picture Library: Arlette Mellaart br; Museum of London cr. **366** Corbis: Werner Forman bc. Robert Harding Picture Library: Robert Estall tr; Simon Harris c. **367** Ancient Art and Architecture Collection: tr. The Art Archive: Archaeological Museum Cagliari/ Dagli Orti cl; Genius of China Exhibition br; Musee Guimet Paris/Dagli Orti tl. **368** AKG London: Jean-Louis Nou br. **369** Ancient Art and Architecture Collection: cr. **370** Ancient Art and Architecture Collection: tl. DK Picture Library: British Museum bl. Werner Forman Archive: The Egyptian Museum, Cairo c. **370–371** Robert Harding Picture Library: George Rainbird Ltd. c. **371** DK Picture Library: British Museum br. Werner Forman Archive: Luxor Museum, Egypt r. Robert Harding Picture Library: Nigel Francis tc. **372** AKG London: Erich Lessing c. Ancient Art and Architecture Collection: tr, bc. Bridgeman Art Library, London/New York: Iraq Museum, Baghdad tl. **373** AKG London: Erich Lessing c, bc. The Art Archive: Musee du Louvre Paris/Dagli Orti tr. **374** AKG London: cr; Erich Lessing bl. Ancient Art and Architecture Collection: Ronald Sheridan background. DK Picture Library: British Museum tl. **374–375** The Art Archive: Dagli Orti c. **375** Ancient Art and Architecture Collection: tr. The Art Archive: Dagli Orti cr. **376** AKG London: National Archeological Museum cl; Rainer Hackenberg tl. DK Picture Library: British Museum bl. Sonia Halliday Photographs: br. **376–377** National Geographic Image Collection: Todd Gipstein c. **377** Ancient Art and Architecture Collection: tr. DK Picture Library: British Museum cr. The Art Archive: National Archaeological Museum Athens/Dagli Orti br. Sonia Halliday Photographs: tc. **378** Ancient Art and Architecture Collection: tr. Bridgeman Art Library, London/New York: Oriental Bronzes Ltd., London c. Corbis: Lee White br. DK Picture Library: British Museum cr. The Art Archive: Genius of China Exhibition l. **379** AKG London: Jean-Louis Nou tr, br. Bridgeman Art Library, London/New York: Museum of Archaeology, History of Culture, Vadodara, India bl. The Art Archive: bl. **380** Corbis: Michael S. Lewis br. DK Picture Library: American Museum of Natural History tl. The Art Archive: Archaeological Museum Lima/Dagli Orti tr. Werner Forman Archive: University Museum, Philadelphia tc. **381** AKG London: br. DK Picture Library: INAH tr. Corbis: tl. **382** AKG London: bl; Erich Lessing cl. The Art Archive: Galleria Borghese Rome/Dagli Orti br. **382–383** Robert Harding Picture Library: Adam Woolfitt b. **383** The Art Archive: Dagli Orti br. Sonia Halliday Photographs: Bibliotheque Nationale tc. **384** DK Picture Library: British Museum l. Sonia Halliday Photographs: tr. **385** The Art Archive: Biblioteca Nazionale Palermo/Dagli Orti tl; Dagli Orti tr. Sonia Halliday Photographs: br. **386** The Art Archive: British Library br; National Museum Damascus Syria/Dagli Orti cr. Sonia Halliday Photographs: cl. **386–387** The Art Archive: Dagli Orti c **387** The Art Archive: Dagli Orti br. Sonia Halliday Photographs: Bibliteque Nationale tc. **388** AKG London: br. Corbis: Richard Cummins tr. DK Picture Library: Danish National Museum cb; Statens Historika Museum, Stockholm tl; Viking Ship Museum, Norway bl. **389** AKG London: tr, bl, br. The Art Archive: Musee de la Tapisserie Bayeux cl. **390** Collections: Philip Craven bl. DK Picture Library: British Museum tl. **390–391** Ancient Art and Architecture Collection: b. **391** AKG London: Jean-Francois Amelot tl. DK Picture Library: British Museum br. Sonia Halliday Photographs: tr. **392** AKG London: tr, bl. The Art Archive: Victoria and Albert Museum/Eileen Tweedy tl. **393** AKG London: Erich Lessing br. The Art Archive: British Museum cr. Robert Harding Picture Library: T Waltham tl. **394** Werner Forman Archive: tl. Robert Harding Picture Library: J. Pate bl. **394–395** The Art Archive: Antenna Gallery Dakar Senegal/Dagli Orti c. **395** Werner Forman Archive: British Museum br. Robert Harding Picture Library: N. Wheeler tr. **396** Werner Forman Archive: Courtesy Entwistle Gallery, London bl. Robert Harding Picture Library: Geoff Renner r. **397** AKG London: Jean-Louis Nou c; Robert O'Dea tl. The Art Archive: Turkish and Islamic Art Museum Istanbul/Dagli Orti br. **398** AKG London: Turin Biblioteca Reale ca. Scala

Group S.p.A.: Palazzo Medici Riccardi, Firenze. **399** DK Picture Library: British Library cr. **400** Bridgeman Art Library, London/New York: Royal Geographical Society c. National Maritime Museum, London: b. **400–401** AKG London: c. **401** James Davis Travel Photography: br. DK Picture Library: British Museum tr, cra. Mary Evans Picture Library: cr. **402** AKG London: tl. Corbis: Galen Rowell cr. Scala Group S.p.A.: Biblioteca Nationale, Firenze. **404** AKG London: tr, c. Robert Harding Picture Library: P. Craven br. **405** AKG London: tr, c. The Art Archive: Bruning Museum Lambayeque Peru/Mireille Vautier br. **406** AKG London: tr. DK Picture Library: Wallace Collection bl. Mary Evans Picture Library: br. **407** AKG London: Victoria and Albert Museum tr. DK Picture Library: Wallace Collection c. Hulton Archive/Getty Images: Ernst Haas b. **408** DK Picture Library: Exeter Maritime Museum c. © Michael Holford: b. **409** Bridgeman Art Library, London/New York: Museum of the City of New York, USA b. Hulton Archive/Getty Images: Archive Photos cl. **410** AKG London: bcr. Corbis: Archivo Iconografico, S.A. tl; Gianni Dagli Orti bl. DK Picture Library: Establissement public du musée et du domaine national de Versailles c. The Art Archive: Christ's Hospital/Eileen Tweedy bcl; Russian Historical Museum Moscow/Dagli Orti br. Mary Evans Picture Library: bc. **411** Bridgeman Art Library, London/New York: Bibliotheque des Arts Decoratifs, Paris/Charmet bl; National Gallery, London r. DK Picture Library: Science Museum br. Hulton Archive/Getty Images: cl. **412** Bridgeman Art Library, London/New York: Collection of the Earl of Leicester, Holkham Hall, Norfolk cr; Royal Agricultural Society of England, Stoneleigh b. Rural History Centre, University of Reading: tr. **413** AKG London: tl, br. Corbis: Bettmann cl. DK Picture Library: Wilberforce House/Hull City Museums and Art Gallery t. **414** Bridgeman Art Library, London/New York: New York Historical Society br. The Art Archive: Musee du Chateau de Versailles/Dagli Orti t. **415** Bridgeman Art Library, London/New York: Bibliotheque Nationale, Paris br. DK Picture Library: Wallace Collection tr, tcr. Mary Evans Picture Library: c. **416** Bridgeman Art Library, London/New York: Charmet/Musee de la Ville de Paris, Musee Carnavalet, Paris tl; Peter Willi/Louvre, Paris br. **417** AKG London: tc. Bridgeman Art Library, London/New York: Phillips, Fine Art Auctioneers, New York, USA c. The Greenwich Workshop: 2003 Howard Terpning, Courtesy of The Greenwich Workshop, Inc b. **418** Bridgeman Art Library, London/New York: Bibliotheque des Arts Decoratifs, Paris clb. Corbis: Bettmann tr. Hulton Archive/Getty Images: Rischqitz bc. The Salvation Army International Heritage Centre: cla. Science & Society Picture Library: tl, bl. **418–419** Hulton Archive/Getty Images: c. **419** Corbis: Gianni Dagli Orti cr. Mary Evans Picture Library: br. **420** Bridgeman Art Library, London/New York: Private Collection tr. The Art Archive: Museo Bolivar Caracas/Dagli Orti bl. **421** Bridgeman Art Library, London/New York: Archives Larousse, Paris br; Giraudon/Laurose/Bibliotheque Nationale, Paris bl. Mary Evans Picture Library: tr. **422** AKG London: br. Hulton Archive/Getty Images: cl. **423** Mary Evans Picture Library: bc. **424** Corbis: Bettmann cr; Museum of the City of New York tr. DK Picture Library: Gettysburg National Military Park bl. Hulton Archive/Getty Images: MPI br. **425** Bridgeman Art Library, London/New York: Alexander Turnbull Library, Wellington, New Zealand br. Corbis: Anders Ryman bl; Dallas and John Heaton cr. DK Picture Library: Mitchell Library, State of New South Wales tl. **426** AKG London: cl. **426–427** AKG London: bc. **427** AKG London: tc. Corbis: Hulton-Deutsch Collection tr, cr; Michael St Maur Sheil bl. **428** AKG London: tr. Corbis: Bettmann tl. David King Collection: bl. **429** Bridgeman Art Library, London/New York: Private Collection cl. The Art Archive: William Sewell tr. Popperfoto: br. **430** AKG London: bl, br. Art Directors & TRIP: Dinodia tr. **431** Corbis: Swim Ink tr. Mary Evans Picture Library: tl. Hulton Archive/Getty Images: Fox Photos bl; Keystone br. Art Directors & TRIP: E Young c. **432** AKG London: cl. **432–433** The Art Archive: Imperial War Museum b. **433** AKG London: br. Corbis: Bettmann tl. The Art Archive:

Domenica del Corriere/Dagli Orti tr. Mary Evans Picture Library: cr. **434** AKG London: cr. Corbis: tr; David Turnley bl. **435** Corbis: Francoise de Mulder cr; Wally McNamee tl. Hulton Archive/Getty Images: Three Lions br.

Jacket: Front: Corbis: Bettmann fbl; Keren Su fbr; Sandro Vannini br. Science Photo Library: Peter Menzell, Dinamation br (dinosaur); NASA bl (astronaut); Alfred Pasieka bl. **Back:** Corbis: bc; Paul Hardy br (sphinx); Walter Hodges br; Lester Lefkowitz fbl; Renee Lynn fbr. Getty Images: Photodisc Green bl (wave); Stone bl. Science Photo Library: David Mack fbl. **Spine:** Corbis: Lester Lefkowitz. Science Photo Library: David Mack.

All other images © Dorling Kindersley.
For further information see: www.dkimages.com